# IRELAND'S ALLIES

## AMERICA AND THE 1916 EASTER RISING

### EDITED BY MIRIAM NYHAN GREY

*Published by*
UNIVERSITY COLLEGE DUBLIN PRESS
PREAS CHOLÁISTE OLLSCOILE BHAILE ÁTHA CLIATH
2016

First published 2016
by University College Dublin Press
UCD Humanities Institute, Room H103,
Belfield,
Dublin 4
www.ucdpress.ie

*ISBN 978-1-910820-13-1 hb*

Chapter 20, Thomas J. Rowland, 'The American Catholic press and the Easter Rising', originally appeared as 'The American Catholic press and the Easter rebellion', in *The Catholic Historical Review* 81:1 (January 1995): 67–83, and is reproduced by kind permission of the journal in this volume.

CIP data available from the British Library

Design by iota (www.iota-books.com)
Typeset in 12pt on 16pt Granjon with Norweister display titling
Printed in England on acid-free paper
by TJ International, Padstow.

*I ndíl chuimhne ar Lewis L. Glucksman (1925–2006) agus do mhuintir Chinn Eich.*

—

*'Tom operated successfully' – O'Sullivan*

# CONTENTS

# ACKNOWLEDGEMENTS

As I pen these lines, the sky is flooded with the illumination of the firework revelry that marks Independence Day in New York City. The staccato of firecrackers abruptly reminds me that for the Irish there is just no equivalent. Ireland's capacity to celebrate its independence is more complicated, highlighting the fact that comparisons present challenges for historians. In interpreting the past, the specific historical context is paramount, and when the topic pertains to a watershed moment, historians must be even more careful invigilators of the specific historical context. Still, in general terms, Ireland's Easter Rising of 1916 has commonalities with the American break from British dominion celebrated on the fourth day of July in the United States.

The United States, and New York specifically, has long served as a nerve centre for Irish nationalism but this is not the only reason for this volume's focus. More practically, New York University's Glucksman Ireland House provided the wellspring for the initiative. The idea for this collection evolved out of conversations begun in spring 2014 about New York's role in the Rising and how Glucksman Ireland House NYU could contribute to dialogue on the role of New York a century ago. Much gratitude is due to the committee that emerged out of those early conversations, graciously chaired by Sophie Sweetman McConnell, and with the input of Marion R. Casey, Terry Golway, Sean P. Kelly, J. J. (Joe) Lee, Judith McGuire, Cormac K. H. O'Malley, Peter Quinn and myself.

Glucksman Ireland House has been part of New York University since 1993. Much of what we do – our academic programmes, research initiatives, preservation efforts, and public events – is the result of the generous support of Loretta Brennan

Glucksman (and the late Lewis L. Glucksman) and a dedicated Board of Advisors led by Judith McGuire. Kathy Gilfillan sits on our board, and we would like to especially thank her for her support of this volume specifically. Without all of this collaboration, our vision for Irish Studies could not be realised, and this publication is no exception.

Over a 15-month period starting in September 2015, Glucksman Ireland House NYU marked the centenary of the Easter Rising through programming that informed the political and cultural milieu of contemporary Irish America. We are memorialising much of our intellectual commemoration through the pages of this book and through the dynamic exchange of ideas on which the research was based. The contributors to this volume, many of whom delivered papers or keynotes at our April 2016 symposium 'Independent Spirit: America and the Easter Rising', have made the experience so pleasurable and we have been humbled by their generosity of time and spirit. *Go raibh míle maith agaibh go léir.*

From an editorial and personal point of view, I would like to express special thanks to Joe Lee and Marion Casey. Their unstinting support and help on this project were critical. I have learned so much from both of these fine scholars in my decade at Glucksman Ireland House NYU. Joe's approach to scholarship provides endless rich insights and vibrant conversation in our little home at the foot of Fifth Avenue. Marion's encyclopaedic knowledge of Irish America is a touchstone for anyone who grapples with the complexity of the Irish experience in the United States. I would also like to salute other colleagues for their good counsel and words of encouragement during these recent busy months, especially Linda Dowling Almeida, Pádraig Ó Cearúill, Kelly Sullivan, Thomas Truxes, John Waters and Nicholas M. Wolf. Francis M. Carroll was also incredibly generous with editorial advice for which I am most grateful.

Our symposium, primarily organised so proficiently by Marion Casey, provided Irish New York with an opportunity to engage with the scholarship in the pages of this book. The events of those few days were successful due to the assistance of many: Maura Anand, Linda Dowling Almeida, Danny McDonald and the staff of the Pier A Harbour House, Lisa Dwan, Dave and Colin Farrell, Ellis Garey, John P. Harrington, Alec Henson, James Higgins, Tim Meagher, Tim Mitchell, Patrick Mullins, Antoin Ó Dubhthaigh, Rachel Thimke, and The Glee Club of the Friendly Sons of St Patrick in the City of New York.

Glucksman Ireland House NYU gratefully acknowledges grants from NYU's Global Research Initiatives (Office of the Provost), NYU's Global Network University, and the endorsement of our team of deans including Georgina Dopico, Anna Harvey,

G. Gabrielle Starr, Thomas J. Carew and formerly Joy Connolly. We would also like to recognise the support of Ireland's Department of Foreign Affairs and Trade, specifically through New York's Consul General of Ireland, Barbara Jones. We are indebted to the members of the United Irish Counties Association of New York Inc. Centenary Committee; most especially John J. Garvey, Geraldine O'Reilly Johnson, Mary McMullan, Mae O'Driscoll, Gerry O'Shea and John T. Ridge. I am personally very grateful for the friendships of Joe Long, Rev. Patrick Moloney, Joe McManus, Mae O'Driscoll, John Ridge, and Ken Tierney with whom I have learned so much about Irish America in the past few years.

The practical assistance provided by our American copy editor, Nicholas Mirra, and our Irish indexer, Jane Rogers, and our support staff was unsurpassable and is appreciatively accredited to Amber Celedonio, Cassandra Coste, Anne Solari Dunn, Eli Elliot, Ellis Garey, Caroline Heafey, Alec Henson, Reah Rajmanjal, Shannon Rider, and Nancy Wu. Special thanks are due to Rachel Thimke who helped with this manuscript from its early days. I would also like to acknowledge Patricia Byrne, Brian Crowley, Michael E. Chapman, Lisa Dolan, Michael Foight (Villanova), Máire Kennedy, Georgette Keane (American Irish Historical Society), Shane MacDonald, Stephen MacEoin, and Eithne Massey for assistance with images. Of course, thanks are also due to the University College Dublin Press, its peer reviewers, and especially Noelle Moran and Damien Lynam for their assistance in seeing this project through to fruition with professionalism.

Six of the chapters in this volume were authored or co-authored by candidates or alumni of our Master of Arts in Irish and Irish-American Studies. As scholars, it gives us immense pleasure to see ground-breaking new scholarship evolving out of this important and unique programme. Thank you for providing us with the opportunity to mentor you and to shape your journeys through the intricate map of Ireland's foot-print on our intellectual world. My own scholarly expedition was shaped years ago by Denis McSweeney and E. Arfon Rees, and while neither of them has yet read this book, their munificent mentorship implicitly echoes in how I have fostered relationships with my students.

I have been blessed to have always had supportive family around me. Loving thanks are due to Con, Noreen, Clare, and Emma Nyhan who have provided caring sustenance from Ireland, San Francisco, and Florence. In more recent years, I have also had the good fortune of the unstinting backing of my (long suffering!) husband, Eon Grey, and the joy that personifies our little Irish-Jamaican New Yorker, Aodhán Nyhan Grey. I owe you all so much and am always appreciative. *Míle buíochas*.

One contributor to this volume has called the Easter Rising a 'transatlantic enterprise' and indeed it was. Not entirely dissimilarly, this book has emerged from a type of transoceanic cooperation of an intellectual variety. It truly was a team effort. Thank you one and all.

*Miriam Nyhan Grey*
*New York, 4 July 2016*

# ABBREVIATIONS

## ORGANISATIONS, NAMES, PLACES, AND TITLES

| | |
|---|---|
| AFL | American Federation of Labor |
| AOH | Ancient Order of Hibernians |
| ATS | American Truth Society |
| CU | Congressional Union |
| DAN | Deutsch-Amerikanischer Nationalbund |
| DMP | Dublin Metropolitan Police |
| FOIF | Friends of Irish Freedom |
| GAA | Gaelic Athletic Association |
| GIS | German Information Service |
| GPO | General Post Office, Dublin |
| GSNY | Gaelic Society of New York |
| INFA | Irish Nationalist Federation of America |
| IOO | Independent Orange Order |
| IPL | Irish Progressive League |
| IPP | Irish Parliamentary Party |
| IRB | Irish Republican Brotherhood |
| ITGWU | Irish Transport and General Workers' Union |
| IWFL | Irish Women's Franchise League |
| IWW | Industrial Workers of the World |
| MP | Member of Parliament |
| NAACP | National Association for the Advancement of Colored People |

| NAWSA | National American Woman Suffrage Association |
| NWP | National Women's Party |
| RIC | Royal Irish Constabulary |
| TD | Teachta Dála |
| UILA | United Irish League of America |
| UNIA | Universal Negro Improvement Association |
| WSPU | Women's Social and Political Union |

## SOURCES, ARCHIVES, AND LIBRARIES

| AANY | Archives of the Archdiocese of New York |
| ACUA | American Catholic History Research Centre and University Archives |
| AIA | Archives of Irish America |
| AIHS | American Irish Historical Society |
| ASCAP | American Society of Composers, Authors and Publishers |
| BMH | Bureau of Military History |
| CBS | Crime Branch Special |
| CO | Colonial Office Papers |
| ENA | English National Archives |
| IPUMS | Integrated Public Use Microdata Series |
| MCIHP | Maloney Collection of Irish Historical Papers |
| MSPC | Military Service Pension Collection |
| NAI | National Archives of Ireland |
| NARA | National Archives and Records Administration |
| NAUK | National Archives of the United Kingdom |
| NLI | National Library of Ireland |
| NMI | National Museum of Ireland |
| NYPL | New York Public Library |
| NYSZ | *New-Yorker Staats-Zeitung* |
| OFLA | O'Fiaich Library and Archive |
| PRO | Public Record Office, London |
| RGASPI | Russian State Archive for Social and Political History |

# CONTRIBUTORS

MAURA ANAND holds an MA in Irish and Irish-American Studies from New York University and a BA in Irish and English and a Higher Diploma in Education from University College Dublin (UCD). Her MA thesis examines Padraig Pearse's visit to the United States in 1914 and is excerpted for her single-authored chapter in this volume. She has a keen interest in the transatlantic figures that dominated Irish-American nationalism in the early decades of the twentieth century.

ÚNA NÍ BHROIMÉIL lectures in American History at Mary Immaculate College, University of Limerick, Ireland. She is a graduate of NUI Galway, and earned her Ph.D. at Lehigh University, Pennsylvania. She is the author of *Building Irish Identity in America, 1870–1915: The Gaelic Revival* (2003) and has published articles on the Irish-American press, the formation of female Catholic teachers, and using visual methods in historical research. She is currently writing a book on John Quinn, the Irish-American lawyer and patron of the arts.

DAVID BRUNDAGE is professor of History at the University of California, Santa Cruz. He has published widely in the fields of American immigration and Irish diaspora history, including a chapter in the landmark volume, *The New York Irish* (1996), edited by Ronald Bayor and Timothy Meagher. His book, *Irish Nationalists in America: The Politics of Exile, 1798–1998*, was published in 2016, and his essay, 'Remembering 1916 in America: the Easter Rising's many faces, 1919–1962', appeared in the collection, *Remembering 1916: The Easter Rising, the Somme, and the Politics of Memory* (2016), edited by Richard Grayson and Fearghal McGarry.

JUDITH E. CAMPBELL holds a D. Litt. in Irish and Irish-American Studies from Drew University. She is a retired business executive and a trustee of Drew University, where she is the current chair for the Centre for Religion, Culture, and Conflict Advisory Board, an organisation devoted to the study of global peace. Her research is concentrated on the life of Mary Jane O'Donovan Rossa and her husband, Jeremiah. Currently preparing her doctoral thesis for publication, she is the author of 'Reflections of a Fenian widow', in *History Ireland*, July 2015.

FRANCIS M. CARROLL is professor emeritus at St John's College, University of Manitoba, where his specialty was Irish history and the history of American foreign relations. Carroll is a graduate of Trinity College Dublin, the University of Minnesota, and Carleton College. He has held visiting fellowships and professorships at Columbia University Law School, University College Dublin, University of London, St Thomas University, and Boston College. He has published 11 books and numerous articles.

MARION R. CASEY is clinical assistant professor of Irish Studies on the faculty of New York University's Glucksman Ireland House NYU, where she is also director of Undergraduate Studies. In addition to many journal articles, book chapters, and public history exhibitions, she is the co-editor with J. J. Lee of *Making the Irish American: History and Heritage of the Irish in the United States* (2006). She is a graduate of University College Dublin, where she studied Irish America under David N. Doyle, and earned her Ph.D. in American History from New York University under the direction of David M. Reimers.

MICHAEL DOORLEY is an associate lecturer in History and International Relations with the Open University in Ireland. He is the author of *Irish American Diaspora Nationalism: The Friends of Irish Freedom, 1916–1935* (2005). He has published several articles on the Irish experience in the United States. These include 'Irish Catholics and French Creoles: ethnic struggles within the Catholic church in New Orleans, 1835–1920', in *The Catholic Historical Review* and 'Judge Daniel Cohalan: a nationalist crusader against British influence in American life', in *New Hibernia Review*. His essay 'The friends of Irish freedom' appeared in *The Atlas of the Irish Revolution* (2016). He is currently working on a biography of Daniel Cohalan.

PATRICIA KEEFE DURSO is an assistant professor of English at Fairleigh Dickinson University. She holds a Ph.D. in American Literature from George Washington

University. Her publications include articles on contemporary Irish-American writers Maureen Howard and Mary Gordon, and Irish writer Sebastian Barry. Her essays have appeared in collections such as *Too Smart to Be Sentimental: Contemporary Irish-American Women Writers* (2008), *Multiethnic Literature and the Canon Debates* (2006), *Anglophone Literatures/English Literatures* (2002), and various journals. She is currently researching representations of the Virgin Mary in contemporary Irish and Irish-American literature.

KATE FEIGHERY is currently the archivist at the Archives of the Archdiocese of New York, where she has worked since 2012. She received her undergraduate degree from Ursinus College in 2006, an MA in Irish and Irish-American Studies from New York University in 2010, and an Advanced Certificate in Archiving, also from New York University, in 2012. She is a certified archivist, and serves on the board of the Association of Catholic Diocesan Archivists and as a consultant for the New York Irish History Roundtable.

TERRY GOLWAY is a senior editor at Politico New York. He was director of the Kean University Centre for History, Politics and Policy, was a member of the *New York Times* editorial board, and was city editor of the *New York Observer*. He holds a Ph.D. in US History from Rutgers University. He is the author of more than a dozen books, many of them on Irish-American history. A revised edition of his biography of John Devoy, *Irish Rebel: John Devoy and America' s Fight for Ireland's Freedom*, was published by Irish Academic Press in 2015.

MIRIAM NYHAN GREY is associate director of Glucksman Ireland House NYU, where she is also director of Graduate Studies for the MA in Irish and Irish-American Studies programme. She earned her Ph.D. in History and Civilisation from the European University Institute, after having undertaken an MPhil at University College Cork (NUI). With an interest in the intersections of migration, race, and ethnicity, she focuses primarily on migrant experiences in comparative settings. She hosts the Glucksman Ireland House NYU Radio Hour and has recorded oral histories as part of her research in Ireland, England, and the United States. Her book, *'Are You Still Below?': The Ford Marina Plant, Cork, 1917–1984* (2007) provides an illuminating history of Ireland's only Ford factory. She is currently preparing a book manuscript on postwar Irish migration.

ANDREW S. HICKS holds an MA in Irish and Irish-American Studies from New York University and a BA from Colby College. After a decade working in international education and cultural exchange, he dedicated two years to archival research focused on Joseph McGarrity and Art O'Murnaghan. Interested in the confluence of cultural revival, diaspora nationalism, and migration, his co-authored chapter in this volume is excerpted from the research for his MA thesis. He now lives in Hong Kong.

MARY C. KELLY is professor of History at Franklin Pierce University, New Hampshire, where she teaches Modern American and Irish History. She graduated from NUI Galway with a Modern Irish History MA and from Syracuse University with a Ph.D. in Modern US History. Her scholarship on the Irish-American historical experience includes *The Shamrock and the Lily: The New York Irish and the Creation of a Transatlantic Identity, 1845–1921* (2005), and *Ireland's Great Famine in Irish American History: Enshrining a Fateful Memory* (2014). She is currently researching Irish-American political culture in the 1916 era.

J. J. LEE is director of Glucksman Ireland House NYU where he is also Glucksman professor of Irish Studies and a professor of History. Professor Lee came to New York University in 2002 from University College Cork, where he chaired the History Department and served for periods as dean of Arts and as vice president. Educated at University College Dublin, the Institute for European History in Mainz, Germany, and Peterhouse, Cambridge, he has also been a fellow of Peterhouse. He has held visiting fellow/professor appointments in Britain, continental Europe, and the United States and is the author of numerous books and articles.

GERARD MACATASNEY holds a BA and MA from the University of Ulster and a Ph.D. from the University of Liverpool. He has written a number of books and articles on the Great Famine/An Gorta Mór including *This Dreadful Visitation: The Famine in Lurgan/Portadown* (1997); *The Hidden Famine: Poverty, Hunger and Sectarianism in Belfast* (with Christine Kinealy) (2000) and *The Dead Buried by the Dying: The Great Famine in Leitrim* (2014). He is author of *Seán Mac Diarmada: The Mind of the Revolution* and *Tom Clarke: Life, Liberty, Revolution* (2012). Currently, MacAtasney is researching a study of the Great Famine/An Gorta Mór in Ulster.

LUCY MCDIARMID is Marie Frazee-Baldassarre professor of English at Montclair State University and past president of the American Conference for Irish Studies. The recipient of fellowships from the Guggenheim Foundation, the Cullman Centre for Scholars and Writers at the New York Public Library, and the National Endowment for the Humanities, she is the author or editor of seven books. Her most recent monographs include *At Home in the Revolution: What Women Said and Did in 1916* (2015), *Poets and the Peacock Dinner: The Literary History of a Meal* (2014) and *The Irish Art of Controversy* (2005).

EMMET O'CONNOR completed a BA at University College, Galway in 1977, an MA in Galway in 1979 and a Ph.D. at St John's College, Cambridge in 1984. Since 1985 he has lectured in the School of History in Ulster University. Between 1983 and 2001, he co-edited *Saothar*, and is an honorary president of the Irish Labour History Society. He has published widely on labour history, including *Syndicalism in Ireland, 1917–23* (1988); *Reds and the Green: Ireland, Russia, and the Communist Internationals, 1919–43* (2004); *A Labour History of Ireland, 1824–2000* (2011); and *Big Jim Larkin: Hero or Wrecker?* (2015). At present he is working on a study of the Irish in the Spanish Civil War.

JOHN T. RIDGE, a native of Brooklyn and an alumnus of St Francis College, is a founding member, past officer and current president of the New York Irish History Roundtable, established in 1984. He has published frequently in *New York Irish History* in addition to an essay in *The New York Irish* (1996). He is also the co-author with Lynn Bushnell of *Celebrating 250 Years of the New York City St Patrick's Day Parade* (2011). In 2012 he donated a large collection of rare materials to NYU's Archives of Irish America, including records from the Ancient Order of Hibernians and the Friends of Irish Freedom.

THOMAS J. ROWLAND is the author of *In the Shadows of Grant and Sherman: George B. McClellan and Civil War History* (1999), and three interpretive presidential biographies of Franklin B. Pierce (2011), Millard Fillmore (2013), and Ulysses S. Grant (2015). He has published articles on Irish-American and Catholic history in the *Journal of American Ethnic History*, *Éire-Ireland*, and the *Catholic Historical Review*. He earned a Ph.D. in History from The George Washington University and holds an MA in Theology from the Washington Theological Union. He has been a senior lecturer in History at the University of Wisconsin-Oshkosh since 1998.

ROBERT SCHMUHL is the inaugural Walter H. Annenberg-Edmund P. Joyce chair in American Studies and Journalism at the University of Notre Dame, where he is also the founding Director of the John W. Gallivan Program in Journalism, Ethics and Democracy. He is the author or editor of over a dozen books, including *Statecraft and Stagecraft: American Political Life in the Age of Personality* (1990, 1992, and 2016) and *Wounded Titans: American Presidents and the Perils of Power* (1996). His collection of essays, *In So Many Words: Arguments and Adventures*, was published in 2006, with a new, expanded edition, *In So Many More Words*, appearing in 2010. His book, *Ireland's Exiled Children: America and the Easter Rising*, was published by Oxford University Press in 2016.

ED SHEVLIN holds an MA in Irish and Irish-American Studies from New York University and a BA in Historical Studies from SUNY Empire State College. In 2015 he was named an NYU Gallatin Global Human Rights Fellow and spent a summer interning in Belfast at the Pat Finucane Centre. In 2011 and 2013 he received Fulbright grants for the Gaeltacht Summer Language Study programme. His chapter in this volume on John A. Kilgallon originated as a graduate seminar paper in autumn 2015 and was further revised in collaboration with Marion R. Casey.

PATRICK M. SWEENEY holds an MA in Irish and Irish-American Studies from New York University. Before moving to New York, he studied History at the University of South Carolina with a focus on Environmental, New South, and Reconstruction-era American History. Patrick currently works at the National 9/11 Memorial and Museum's Education Department where he is endeavouring to further explore the Irish-American experience through the study of memory and memorialisation. His chapter in this volume is excerpted from the research for his MA thesis.

R. BRYAN WILLITS holds an MA in Irish and Irish-American Studies from New York University. He is a native of West Michigan where he studied European, Irish, and German History at Grand Rapids Community College and Aquinas College. Willits has also lived and studied in Ireland and Germany, attended Eberhard Karls Universität Tübingen, and later worked as a teacher in the Baden-Württemberg region. Willits currently works at the National 9/11 Memorial and Museum and is a regular contributor to *Irish America* magazine. His chapter in this volume is excerpted from the research for his MA thesis.

DAPHNE DYER WOLF is a Ph.D. candidate in the History and Culture programme at Drew University. Her research focuses on the intersection of nineteenth-century

Irish land issues and popular culture. After working over 20 years at the *The Star-Ledger*, Newark, New Jersey, she received an MA in Irish and Irish-American Studies from New York University in 2011. In 2013, she was a co-curator with Marion R. Casey of a travelling exhibit, 'Labor and Dignity: James Connolly in America', sponsored by the Irish Department of Foreign Affairs and Glucksman Ireland House NYU. A contributor to *Irish America* magazine, she has also published essays in the *Australasian Journal of Irish Studies* and *The American Journal of Irish Studies*. In 2014–15, she taught United States History at Northern State Prison in Newark, New Jersey, as part of the NJ-Step programme.

NICHOLAS M. WOLF is a research data management librarian at New York University and an affiliate faculty of Glucksman Ireland House NYU. He has published on the history of the Irish language – most recently the double-prize-winning book *An Irish-Speaking Island: State, Religion, Community, and the Linguistic Landscape in Ireland, 1770–1870* (2014) – and on the cultural history of Ireland through essays and articles in the *Irish Times*, *Éire-Ireland*, *New Hibernia Review*, the *Journal of British Studies*, and the *Australasian Journal of Irish Studies*. He is an assistant editor at *Éire-Ireland*.

# LIST OF ILLUSTRATIONS

Cover: Image adapted from a postcard *c.* 1910. In the United States, in the half century before the 1916 Easter Rising, Ireland was often represented by a green flag with a golden harp. It was frequently entwined with the Stars and Stripes to symbolise the dual loyalties of the Irish in America. Moloney Collection, Archives of Irish America, New York University, used with permission.

Front page of *The Clan-Na-Gael Journal*, 21 November 1914, featuring a story on 'Big Jim' Larkin as a speaker at an event marking the forty-seventh anniversary of the Manchester Martyrs. Joseph McGarrity Collection, Digital Library@Villanova University, used with permission. ..................... 149

Photograph of Daniel F. Cohalan. American-born but with close-ties to Co. Cork, Cohalan was a strong supporter of Irish cultural nationalism and a close associate of John Devoy. He was central to the founding of the Friends of Irish Freedom in March 1916. Library of Congress LC-USZ62-67890, used with permission. ..................... 150

Photograph of composer-conductor Victor Herbert disembarking in New York from the SS *Imperator* on 25 June 1914 after his fateful trip to England. Library of Congress LC-USZ62-116285, used with permission. ..................... 164

Image of Victor Herbert's manuscript score for 'Soldiers of Erin' (1916). Victor Herbert Collection, Music Division, Library of Congress 44.00.01, used with permission. ..................... 183

Front page of *The Fatherland*, 8 March 1916. Before the United States entered the war, the possibility of German aid for Ireland was more than a pipedream for Irish nationalists. This syncretistic and iconic cover art suggests how Irish society, economy, and landscape might be transformed by such a partnership. Joseph McGarrity Collection, Digital Library@Villanova University, used with permission. ..................... 184

Photograph of John Quinn at the Sleepy Hollow Club taken by an unknown photographer in Westchester, New York, *c.* 1915. Aline and Eero Saarinen Papers, Archives of American Art, Smithsonian Institution, used with permission. ..................... 200

Photograph taken at a reception hosted by William Bourke Cockran at his Long Island, New York home. Bourke Cockran (far right) crossed party lines in 1912 to support the Progressive candidates for president of the United States, Theodore Roosevelt, and governor of New York, Oscar Straus (centre). Also pictured are, left to right, Anne Ide Bourke Cockran, Sarah Lavanburg Straus, and Eleanor Butler Roosevelt. Library of Congress LC-B2- 2480-15, used with permission. ..................... 214

Portrait of author and diplomat, Sir John Randolph Leslie (3rd Baronet). Known as Shane Leslie, he provides an illustrative example of an Anglo-Irish nationalist with strong American ties. Leslie was a prominent figure in New York in the 1916 era

# FOREWORD

How should historians approach the Easter Rising of 1916? Obviously, it is a seminal event that has to be engaged with and addressed. The problem – which is not exactly an original observation – is hindsight. We know what came afterwards and we often just assume this is what happened, this is what we have to explain about that spring week in Ireland. But to see the Rising through the eyes of the decision makers who did not know what was coming next and who might have done things differently in a number of unanticipated situations, if they actually knew what the consequences would be, for me that's always the test as a historian. The first question to ask is not 'what do I know about this, what do I think about this?' It is 'why do I think what I think about this?'

When you look at the chronology, for example, the Irish Republican Brotherhood in Ireland (IRB) and Clan na Gael in the United States decide in September 1914, one month into the First World War, that they are going to have a rising before its end. Nobody knew how long the war was going to last but there was a widespread view that it might be over by Christmas. If you are planning on having a rising that will happen before the end of 1914 – they either had extraordinary predictive capacity or this is virtually a rhetorical statement – then you have an awful lot of work to do very quickly. Once one begins looking closely at what is actually happening on the ground, as distinct from the way things can be romanticised retroactively, cooperation and coordination become key for maximum effect.

What exactly was going through the minds of the main organisers, on both sides of the Atlantic, between September 1914 and the actual Rising in April 1916? Support for the Irish Parliamentary Party and John Redmond had dominated diaspora politics in the United States for 20 or more years until vacillation and weakness in Redmond's response to the arming of the Ulster Volunteers in the spring of 1914 gave Irish

Americans pause. The hardened Fenian leader of Clan na Gael, John Devoy, emerges from the margins of Irish-American nationalism to become, in a sense, the spider at the centre of a different transatlantic web. More research is required to establish the extent to which the substantial funding that increasingly flowed towards the Irish Volunteers, and especially the IRB, in fact derived from a transfer in direction from the earlier sources of supply for Redmond or came instead from tapping new pockets. Whichever it may turn out to have been, it seems clear that without these American funds no rising on the scale originally envisaged could even have been contemplated.

Redmond and Devoy were thus simultaneously pursuing two diametrically opposed strategies to achieve their objectives: Home Rule for Redmond and a republic for Devoy, Redmond through diplomacy, Devoy through rebellion. Neither could have anticipated the reaction to Redmond's speech at Woodenbridge on 20 September 1914, in which he urged Irish support for the British war effort. There was a sea change in Irish-American opinion and Redmond rapidly lost support in the United States. You then enter the crucial period before the Rising. A group of individuals for whom New York City was a psychological, intellectual, and pragmatic space come together and shape the course of Irish history. This volume pushes us to rethink what happened in the run-up to 1916 by positioning ourselves in their world, in Irish America, and from a perspective about which there have been easy assumptions made for far too long.

The rapport established between Devoy and German diplomatic representatives in New York facilitated Roger Casement's attempts to procure arms from Germany as well as recruits from among Irish prisoners of war in Germany. Now, if you position yourself in that room in Liberty Hall on Easter Sunday when news of the capture of the *Aud* and the loss of the expected guns arrives, what do you do? Basically the plans you have been working on with Ireland's 'exiled children in America' for the best part of a year have collapsed, there is no chance of victory in a military sense, and you know that you are likely to be arrested in a couple of days. The Easter Monday Rising, therefore, is not the Easter Sunday Rising postponed by one day. It is simply a different rising. We need to spend a lot more time thinking about what happens in that very short 24 hours as they adjusted to the devastating news that the expected German guns and ammunition had been captured. Irish-American assistance is side lined in that space and the men in Dublin are on their own.

The reason Padraig Pearse is where he is and becomes iconic in terms of the Rising is because the plan for it was different from the one they actually found themselves substituting for it, on the hop, if you will. The Proclamation of the Republic he reads was largely completed six days before Easter Monday and is a reflection of the original

Sunday plans and ambitions for success. I suspect Pearse did not fire a shot in the General Post Office, that he spent much of his time composing highly propagandistic messages meant to last. Where this really matters, it seems to me, is in the decision to surrender. If we put ourselves back into the position of someone trying to make that decision at that time, how do we reconstruct their thought processes under that sort of immense pressure? In addition to saving lives, it is also quite possible that Pearse's decision was based on a calculation that the Monday Rising in effect had been a public relations exercise, a critical gesture, from the very beginning.

And, indeed, the world's eyes were on it, especially in New York. The impact on the media there in an American presidential election year, during the First World War, is very different from that in Ireland where there is virtually universal condemnation. Pearse as well as Connolly and Clarke had seen first-hand how journalism and public opinion were integrated in the United States. From this perspective, Irish America's role in the Rising is far more complicated than financing the purchase of the precious weapons that never arrived. It was in a key position to take Pearse's gesture and translate it into a media sensation to raise awareness and lobby for recognition of Irish independence on the international stage. The Easter Rising had such an impact on Irish America that it was able to sustain its commitment to the republican cause in Ireland even when the United States allied with Britain in the war effort the following year. From then until the end of the treaty negotiations at Versailles, there was a truly impressive blend of ideological commitment and practical realpolitik demonstrated by Irish Americans that otherwise might have been more difficult to achieve and sustain.

Historiographically, this volume extends the timeline of Irish America's role in the Rising and significantly expands our understanding of relationships between key players in the United States and Ireland whose commitment to Irish independence, however it was to be achieved, was unwavering. I am immensely proud that the new research represented by this important publication has been inspired and nurtured by Glucksman Ireland House, the Centre for Irish and Irish-American Studies at New York University.

*J. J. Lee*
*New York, July 2016*

# INTRODUCTION

## *Miriam Nyhan Grey*

*As regards Ireland, Irish America paused.*
Shane Leslie, 1917[1]

*No New York. No Easter Rising.*
J. J. Lee, 2015[2]

As 1916 dawned a coterie of activists were engaged in a project that sheds intriguing light on the pulse of Irish New Yorkers at the time. This initiative involved the founding of a weekly journal aimed at Irish-American readers and driven by a particular editorial line; that promulgated by the Irish Parliamentary Party in the form of Home Rule for an Ireland within the British Empire. On the American side the project was supported by the IPP's sister organisation in the United States, the United Irish League of America (UILA). The very first issue of the publication, aptly named *Ireland*, boldly proclaimed its objectives by describing itself as a 'periodical devoted to the interests of Ireland, to encouraging interest in Irish art, industries, music, literature and history, and more especially to supporting the IPP in restoring and preserving self-government in Ireland'.[3] In case readers were left with any doubt as to its political leanings, the editorial opened with a full-page 'New Year's greeting from Mr. Redmond':

> There are apparently a few men in America calling themselves Home Rulers, who desire, if they can, to prevent Ireland deciding for herself on this momentous issue

[support of Britain in the war in Europe], and who are engaged in the effort to with-hold from their countrymen in America the real facts of the case, and to mislead and to confuse them in their judgment. I am well aware that the overwhelming majority of our countrymen in America are prepared to let Ireland decide for herself, as true Home Rulers should, that they too, sympathize with the struggle which the Allies are making for the principles of liberty and for the maintenance of small nationalities in Europe.[4]

In getting to the core objective of *Ireland* he asserted:

It is essential, however, that the truth, not only about the progress of the war, but about the situation in Ireland, should be made known widely in America: and your journal will fulfill a most valuable and patriotic duty if it reflects in its columns what is really happening here at home on the soil of Ireland.[5]

The rationale and motivations behind *Ireland* are interesting to ponder.[6] At a time of high anxiety for Home Rulers committed to asserting Irish support of the British cause in the war in Europe, it is noteworthy that energy and resources were being channelled into a new Irish-American periodical. The establishment of *Ireland* exemplifies an important milestone in how Redmond connected with Irish America. It highlights his capacity to try and rally those who were still loyal to him, particularly in the key hub of Irishness that constituted New York in 1916. But the appearance of *Ireland* cannot be seen as anything other than a defensive move. The project bears the hallmarks of someone scrambling to adjust to a new reality in which the odds are increasingly unfavourable. It demonstrates the tactics of a leader sensing that he is in very real trouble in, and with, Irish America. It shows his awareness of a loss of support, not only for himself personally, but increasingly for Home Rule, the goal that had so energised Irish Americans for decades. It implied that the alternative orthodoxy in relation to Ireland's sovereignty, a complete break from Britain as espoused histori-cally by Clan na Gael[7] in the United States, was firmly in the ascent. Not only this, but the decline in UILA support had more pragmatic implications, aspects of which are explored in this volume. The UILA had been a major financial component of the IPP in Ireland (perhaps to the tune of $500,000) in the decade and a half prior.[8] A loss of American support would, and did, have significant financial implications for a political party long accustomed to a steady transatlantic stream of American dollars. In sum, *Ireland* shows that Irish America mattered.

The fledgling journal lasted just 15 months and by most barometers was a failure. But a crude assessment of its practical role as a medium misses the point. *Ireland*'s importance lies in the fact that it provides tangible evidence of the shift in Irish America that had been in gestation since 1912 and fomented from 1914, providing insights on Irish New York in the early months of 1916 before things changed dramatically with news of the Easter Rising in Dublin and the heavy-handed British response to it. Understanding how something like this could emerge in Irish America at that precise moment allows us to see how Irish politicians, even those at the highest echelons of power, courted the sizable Irish-American constituency. It demonstrates that those who promoted Home Rule for Ireland felt they urgently needed a voice in the United States, particularly in light of the defection of the *Irish World*, historically Home Rule's most vocal champion. Mostly, *Ireland* reminds us that Irish America counted as much to republican nationalists (who aspired to a complete separation from Britain) as it did to Home Rulers (who were content to have a degree of self-government for an Ireland within the British Empire). And one of the reasons Irish America carried so much clout was the sheer weight of demography: emigration had 'created an Irish diaspora which became an integral part of the historical development of their native land'.[9]

The nucleus of that diaspora was the largest Irish city in North America, New York. Honing in on New York helps us to define the 'broad context of Irish American history'[10] especially inasmuch as it represents the major cosmopolitan centre for the development of Irish identity and ethno-politics in the United States. As Ronald H. Bayor and Timothy J. Meagher observed: 'The New York Irish have always stood for Irish American communities writ large: not just a political machine but Tammany Hall; not just a cathedral but St. Patrick's; not just a St. Patrick's Day parade but a march up Fifth Avenue by thousands upon thousands.'[11]

Indeed, New York was a very Irish city in 1916, with a metropolitan area that surpassed Dublin and Belfast. Of the 4.7 million New Yorkers in 1910, the population of those actually born in Ireland was 252,672[12] but that count did not include children of Irish immigrants, of which there were many.[13] A conservative estimate would posit that no less than 350,000 New Yorkers (probably significantly more) were either Irish-born or of Irish parentage in 1916. Moreover, the large-scale and sustained migration of the nineteenth century meant that many thousands of New Yorkers were second, third or fourth generation Irish by the turn of the twentieth century; as late as 1890 some 399,348 (26.8 percent) of Manhattan Caucasians had Irish immigrant mothers.[14]

But demographics were only one element of how New York could be described as the American epicentre of Irish nationalism in the period under scrutiny, 'the main locus of activities for constitutional home rulers and separatist revolutionaries',[15] 'the seedbed' of 1916.[16] The background and reactions of Irish New York to the events of 1916 reveal a constellation of ethno-political (encompassing both political and ethnic factors) patterns and an infrastructure not without complexity (an observation that holds as much weight today as it did in 1916). The focus also demands a discrete chronology to allow for changes in sentiment brought about by American entry into the First World War on 6 April 1917, which introduced 'a new set of difficulties for Irish American republicans'.[17] The guide needs to carefully identify the features of the Irish New York community in the lead-up to the 1916 Easter Rising, especially in how they related to one another through the medium of newspapers, community leaders, ethno-political organisations as well as the institutions of the Catholic church. That is precisely what this volume does. To put it simply, this volume traces the interfaces of an ethnic community and in doing so creates a new context for understanding the connection between the United States and the Easter Rising.

The attentive scholar asks questions that are not always easy to answer. Those questions relate to how ethnicity transfers across generations, which is important. If we concede that New York was very Irish city in 1916, we must ask what exactly that means. The profiles in this collection would indicate that at least at the level of those most visible in the Irish ethno-political community, almost all were born in Ireland (Devoy, McGarrity, Bourke Cockran, O'Donovan Rossa, Kelly, Farley) or else the offspring of someone born there (Herbert, Cohalan, Quinn). In many ways, it is easy to accept how the Irish-born could be stimulated on matters related to the sovereignty of the homeland. Unpacking the ways in which those who were born and raised outside Ireland asserted their interest in Ireland is vastly more complex and is especially thought-provoking during critical moments when the question of loyalty to the United States was also in a spotlight. It was a tumultuous time for ethnic groups in the United States. In May 1914, the US president, Woodrow Wilson, famously remarked that 'some Americans need hyphens in their names because only some of them have come over'[18] and while this volume is concerned less with the high-level politics and diplomacy of a significant era in world history, certain structural considerations are necessary. The way in which international events were capable of shaping the politics of ethnicity, as they did in the period under scrutiny, is highly relevant as Mona Harrington has pointed out:

The problem took modern shape at the outset of World War I in 1914, when the United States faced the question of whether or not to join England and France in fighting Germany. In debating the interest of the United States in relation to Europe, Americans had to consider what interests they held in common as Americans, what activities, rights, profits, hopes were important enough to the whole society to be worth the lives of young men. This meant that Americans had to confront as well the interests that divided them, particularly the differing interests of the many immigrant groups … Whatever the choice the United States made – even the choice of neutrality

– inevitably would raise strong feelings among those of its people whose homeland might be jeopardized by its policy.[19]

The specifics of geography are worth noting here also, especially in how they allow us to see linkages between migration and nationalism. Scholars of the Irish diaspora have not fully grappled with the possibility that migration can be seen as an engine of anticolonialism or of ideological change.[20] With that in mind we need to develop robust profiles of the key players and elements on the ethno-political landscape in order to test whether being an immigrant, or the child of an immigrant, significantly shaped how they engaged with Ireland's sovereignty. Michael Goebel's study makes an interesting point with regard to Paris but the same questions can and should be applied to the great immigrant hub of New York: 'The metropolis disproportionately drew the entrepreneurial and the politicized in the first place, who were more likely to leave behind an imprint in the long run. And the exile experience then promoted the conversion of little-known activists into statesmen and famous intellectuals even further.'[21] In ways, this probes how New York functioned as a vantage point that clarified the contours of an empire by fostering the example of how a republic could thrive after a British colonial experiment. We can easily draw on evidence to suggest that the American setting, in concert with notions of political independence and the immigrant experience, decisively shaped expressions of Irish nationalism. Certainly the goings-on *c.* 1916 did not mark a new departure, as the distinguished scholar of Irish America Timothy Meagher reminds us:

> Nationalism – the commitment to restore some political autonomy to the old country – was an essential part of Irish American life almost from the birth of the American republic. From the United Irish Exiles in the 1790s and early 1800s to the Repeal movement in the early 1840s to the Fenians of the 1860s, the Land Leaguers and Home Rulers in the 1880s to the Friends of Irish Freedom and members of the American Association for the Recognition of the Irish … and … Clan na Gael … Irish Americans have invested considerable resources of time and money into freeing the old country.[22]

These matters also raise the spectre of representativeness. When one refers to Irish New York or to a community, what do those terms mean? To what extent are we, as historians, accurately representing the impulses of Irish New Yorkers of over a century ago? As we know, it presents a 'real historical challenge to reconstruct reactions in light of the information actually available to the public at the time'.[23] How much weight should we place, for example, on a national membership of Clan na Gael of 40,000 in 1910? Moreover, what exactly did membership of any ethno-political organisation mean? In this regard, we must proceed cautiously. Of course, not all Irish New

Yorkers read an 'Irish' newspaper, nor did they participate in socio-ethnic or ethno-political organisations, or give large (or even small) sums of money to nationalist projects. But this did not mean that 'they lacked nationalist sympathies or were indifferent to Ireland'.[24] And we must acknowledge that organising in the ethnic community often depended on the presence and abilities of a small number of key individuals.

Nevertheless, when we collate the various strands, as expressed in gatherings, fundraising, praying, reportage, and organising, we cannot say that Irish New York was at all uninterested in Ireland and the developments occurring there. But we do need to be balanced in our interpretations and remember that for many Irish New Yorkers the practical demands (earning a living, establishing a home, educating their children, sending monies back to family members in Ireland) pushed more overt gestures of ethno-political engagement down the priority list. It is also worth considering that often an organisation had a huge influence 'beyond its numbers'.[25] Of a 1907 Boston gathering of the UILA, one observer noted: 'Their organization fitted easily into the corner of a small tap-room. But what a figure they cut on paper!'[26] Robert Schmuhl reminds us that most Irish Americans 'were less inclined to make a definite commitment to any organization with an avowed agenda, but saw merit in a greater degree of freedom for Ireland',[27] although clearly in moments of crisis the general patterns could be spurred to change significantly, as many chapters in this volume accentuate. It is also clear that certain elements of American society fostered activism in immigrant groups: 'the voluntaristic ethos of the society – its free choice, free movement, free assembly, and free expression of belief – has made it possible for people to express and act on their feelings for the ancestral country.'[28]

If we return to *Ireland* we may glean insights into some of the tensions that were being brought to the surface by the IPP's wartime policy and the American reverberations of that position. In attempting to put Irish America in her place, an *Ireland* writer, possibly the publication's president, John G. Coyle, observed: 'No doubt, the emotional crisis produced by the war was one to stir many pulses. But it is one thing to feel one's pulses stirred here in North America, quite another to shoulder the responsibility for action whose consequences Ireland must bear.'[29] The thrust of the argument, reiterated over and over, is that certain members of the diaspora were out of touch with Ireland. These remarks place the tension in a transnational setting, in that events in Europe involving 'principles of liberty' and the 'maintenance of small nationalities' were impacting upon Ireland but were being unduly influenced by certain American elements. He continues, naturally showing no hint of what was on the horizon in Dublin during Easter Week:

The country is settling down to the enjoyment of what has been won by years of struggle … There has been a very natural tendency … for people to lose touch with affairs in Ireland. The interest remains, but there are a lesser and lesser number who keep their thoughts in close association with that of the men who daily face actual conditions in Ireland, and who are doing the day-to-day work arising out of her problems and necessities.[30]

The journalist does all but actually name the person who bears the main brunt of his ire, but only the least uninformed readers would not have identified John Devoy – the personification of the republican nationalist tradition – as the target as the editorial progressed: 'Thus it happens – thus it has happened – that when a situation fraught with new difficulty arises, we are apt, all of us, to look at it through our own spectacles. This man still thinks of Ireland as he thought of it in 1867 and takes his course accordingly.'[31] Further using Devoy as an example, he gets to the heart of an issue that strikes a chord with diasporic communities today: the correlation between the length of time away from the homeland and the ability (or lack thereof) to have an accurate sense of life there:

In the main, it is only the man who is recently arrived from Ireland whose mind is filled with the problems of to-day. There are men, thirty years and more out of Ireland, who when they go back to the scenes of their youth are amazed at the changes that have taken place. But how many thousands never go back, and so never get their views corrected. And yet the people who live there go on living in the new conditions that the others know little about. They do their work, they discuss their affairs, they meet and decide upon policies and modes of action, they choose their leaders, and they work with those leaders.[32]

For those involved in *Ireland*, the problem was clearly with those who had not had the 'correction' of at least returning home to see how life there had improved. Even from its inception the commentary reveals the crux of the issue in this period: the increasing strain between the UILA camp and those who leaned towards Clan na Gael in articulating Irish sovereignty. J. J. Lee's observations are worth reiterating as they get to the core of the struggle of Irish nationalism in the period: 'Redmond and Devoy were pursuing two diametrically opposed strategies to achieve their objectives, Home Rule for Redmond and a Republic for Devoy, Redmond through diplomacy, Devoy through rebellion.'[33] While the UILA outlook dominated in Irish New York, as it did for the decade and a half from 1901 on, Devoy would have to wait patiently, and that he did. By 1914 he could come 'out of the wilderness after obscure but consistent years' as Shane Leslie observed at the time.[34]

Setting the tone for this volume, Devoy's thoughtful biographer, Terry Golway, charts the evolution of the leading figure of the republican nationalist tradition in the United States. No survey of the ethno-politics of Irish New York in the lead-up to 1916 would be complete without an early examination of this Kildare-born New Yorker and by extension of his main opposition in the period, exemplified in the form of the UILA. Providing an insightful counterpoint to Devoy, Francis M. Carroll outlines the history of the UILA and in so doing draws our attention to an issue that is fascinating for present-day historians to explore. The outlook for the Home Rule nationalist tradition up until early 1914 seemed promising; the only competing claim for nationalist impulses, the republican nationalist one, was utterly marginal. But change things did, especially from spring 1914 onward.

In fact, the pages of *Ireland* through the early months of 1916 provide rich examples of the themes and impulses outlined in the chapters on Devoy and the UILA. The first hint of what lay ahead appeared in the 19 February issue with an innocuous report raising 'no particular objection' to an upcoming Irish Race Convention to which 500 Irishmen had indicated support. The sentiment of the gathering was largely dismissed, presented as having 'its roots in bitterness, remembered or transmitted'.[35] The reporting of the convention concluded with a rather pragmatic, arguably arrogant, view of the mandate of the organisers:

> It isn't pleasant for England. It is part of the price she pays, every now and again, in some corner of the world, for acting the tyrant in Ireland. Tyranny is always repaid in hatred, and no man can with authority command another to remove from his bosom the hatreds engendered of old wrongs. If five hundred gentlemen propose to ventilate their feeling there is no denying them. What may with some propriety be questioned is their right to speak in the name of Ireland. Their ability to set a course for Ireland, which Ireland must follow, is, of course, out of the question altogether.[36]

But, by the 4 March issue, the publishers were clearly more rattled by the impending gathering. The reportage showed signs of concern and a degree of urgency. The first page of the issue was devoted to a long report, openly attributed to John G. Coyle, entitled 'No Irish Race Conference is needed'. Another long report outlined the opposition of Irish-American organisations to the initiative. Coyle reminded American readers of their duty:

> The Irish in America, realizing that this great war puts all Americans in a position where great care and caution are required to avoid breaches of neutrality, and to prevent undue influences of any foreign powers affecting the course of the Administration,

deplore any attempts, either by pro-Germans or pro-Allies, to hamper the progress or mar the peace and security of America.[37]

In strongly worded resolutions the Irish-American societies were provided with a platform, through column inches in *Ireland*, to assert their representativeness of the Irish-American populace and the fact that they were 'unsubsidized by any foreign power'. The first resolution was devoted to asserting 'American neutrality as to *all* the contestants in the European war'.[38] The next resolution returned to a familiar trope that appears over and over on the pages of *Ireland* in these early months:

> That the Irish in America believe that the Irish in Ireland are better judges of their rights, their policies and their duties than any number of praiseworthy and well-meaning men of their race in America, or any number of professional Irishmen in America, or any number of the descendants of exiled Irishmen in America, whose only idea on the Irish question is the legacy of hate inherited from the days of oppression and who are ignorant of, or shut their minds to, the happy change that has come over the Green Island since the rule of democracy has been substituted for that of feudalism.[39]

The question of who is speaking for Ireland and who has the right to speak for Ireland is a recurrent theme and it is particularly noteworthy here as it comes up later in the 1910s and early 1920s and dominates the historiography.

What these observers did not know, or if they did know chose to ignore, is that certain Irish New Yorkers were in fact intimately connected with the views of some in Ireland. Gerard MacAtasney's chapter provides the background to how Thomas J. Clarke found himself in New York establishing not inconsequential connections with Devoy in the decades prior to 1916. By outlining Clarke's American sojourns we get a sense of how important the United States was logistically and inspirationally, not only when Clarke lived there but more decisively once he returned to Ireland in 1907. It has been observed that Clarke was one of the men most responsible for the Rising, the other being Seán Mac Diarmada.[40] Yet it is difficult to imagine how a rebellion could have taken place in Ireland without the input of Devoy. As Golway shows, Devoy was the key link between the Irish Republican Brotherhood (IRB) and the German government, the main propagandist for the IRB's American allies, and a critical source of funds for the Rising. The personal relationship that bound Clarke and Devoy, in a tie of transnational loyalty, is vital background and has been under-studied.

Of course, the United States had long provided a haven for Irish activists, so Clarke was no anomaly in that regard. David Brundage's 2016 monograph on Irish diaspora nationalism provides an indispensable chronology and analysis of the waves of Irish nationalists who made the United States, and often more specifically New York, home.[41] The late scholar of Irish America Dennis J. Clark privileged the United States as 'the premier democratic republic of the modern world', serving for generations as 'a model and an ideal for the nationalist'.[42] Clark also explained, of American Irish relations: 'If patriots were harried from the Irish shores, there was always hope that they could regroup and carry on their writing, teaching and agitating from the shelter of the United States. Things were never so bad with the Irish nationalist that he could not draw some hope from the American quarter.'[43]

And as the twentieth century began little had changed in that regard as the chapters on the American visits of Padraig Pearse, Sir Roger Casement, James Connolly, and 'Big Jim' Larkin show. To date, many scholars have paid but cursory attention to the significance of Pearse's American visit, but Maura Anand's meditation causes us to rethink just how impactful this actually was. When Pearse arrived in New York in February 1914 his primary goal was fundraising. By the time he returned to Ireland some three months later his focus had expanded considerably. Anand lingers on what one scholar has described as 'the most formative three months of his life.'[44] In this context it is worth noting that five of the seven signatories of the Proclamation of the Provisional Government of the Irish Republic spent time in the United States. In fact, the chapters in this book are littered with examples of transatlantic exchange and connection in the forms of letters, remittances, trips, cables, bonds of kinship and friendships.[45] The Pearse example prompts us to (re)consider the role of an American visit in shaping Irish nationalists and requires us to recognise a period in the United States almost as a rite of passage for Irish nationalists of all hues.

Lucy McDiarmid contemplates the professional and personal implications of another 1914 visitor to New York,[46] Sir Roger Casement. McDiarmid adds a fascinating segment, showing that New York's role 'in Casement's fate was significant'.[47] Through his itinerary we are brought swiftly into the web of intrigue linking Dublin, New York, and Berlin in those critical months of 1914 that had reverberations right into Easter Week 1916. We learn about how New York decisively shaped his personal life, revealing 'methodologies of concealment and discovery'.[48]

The particulars of Casement's movements in the United States prompt us to reflect on the American-based activists who provided critical support to Irish nationalism in the lead-up to 1916. During his visit Casement was closely connected to Joseph McGarrity, another Ulster man like Clarke and Casement himself, with whom he got on famously. Born and raised in Co. Tyrone, McGarrity represents Irish nationalist engagement in his adopted city of Philadelphia. But more importantly, McGarrity provides the best example of the next generation of activists that was coming forth under Devoy's tutelage. Maura Anand, Andrew S. Hicks, and R. Bryan Willits's novel examination of the McGarrity houseguests of 1914 further validates the need for historians of diaspora nationalism to pay more attention to McGarrity, both in the specific sense and also as a rich example of an 'ethno-political entrepreneur'.[49] Despite his Philadelphia address, McGarrity was a central character in the New York scene.

Turning back to New York and to a female perspective, Dr Gertrude B. Kelly allows us to discreetly interrogate the shifting associational landscape of 1914 that led her to founding Cumann na mBan in December 1914. By building on themes exposed in the McGarrity chapter, my own chapter highlights, through the example of Dr Kelly, the need to look closely at 1914 in order to grasp the Irish-American backdrop to 1916. This pioneering physician provides an excellent example of the advancement from Home Rule to republican nationalism, and in this she is much more representative of the thrust of Irish America than others surveyed in this volume. Lingering on the examples of Irish nationalist women, Judith E. Campbell pulls Mary Jane O'Donovan Rossa out from the shadow of her iconic husband. Mary Jane's story of strength, passion, and politics is almost as colourful as that of Jeremiah. The ways in which she used her own status and that of Jeremiah to draw attention to Ireland make for compelling reading and should inspire more long overdue scholarship on women in the Irish diaspora.

The notion of the United States as a haven for Irish nationalists is revisited in the chapter on 'Big Jim' Larkin. A confident biographer of the labour leader, Emmet O'Connor outlines how Larkin sought global recognition by crossing the Atlantic.[50] His engagement with German America and anti-war agitation allow us to widen our focus for the coordinates of Irish America. O'Connor emphasises the fact that, until the Rising, the 1913 Dublin lockout had been the biggest event in recent Irish history as far as the American media was concerned, reminding us how integral labour issues were to Irish nationalism. But Larkin is an illustrative example in another way. He, like the subject of the following chapter on Justice Daniel F. Cohalan, was not born in Ireland (Larkin was a Liverpudlian by birth). For scholars of ethnicity, nationalists born outside the homeland provide more bountiful rewards than the native-born. It has already been suggested that it is easy to see why those born and raised in Ireland could be roused about the fate of their place of birth; much more complex is the way in which those born in the diaspora became stimulated about Ireland's fate. Cohalan offers one of the best examples of an American-born activist who was a major player in nationalist circles, not least through Clan na Gael, in the period under scrutiny.

Michael Doorley assuredly elucidates Cohalan's devotion to cultural and republican nationalism and his role in the establishment of the Friends of Irish Freedom (FOIF). The FOIF emerged out of the convention that had drawn so much criticism in the pages of *Ireland* in February and early March 1916. For the UILA, the evolution of this organisation presented a threat to the course to Home Rule. The journal had snidely projected a turnout of 500 at the event and must have been unnerved by the headcount of 2,000.[51] Blatantly undermining the motives and rationale of the new body, an *Ireland* editorial presented historic examples of how earlier rebellions, especially when England was elsewhere preoccupied, had resulted in catastrophic failure:

> But of Emmet, and of Fitzgerald, and of Young Ireland in '48, it can be said that desperate ills went far to justify the desperate remedy. In the state of Ireland today, there is not only no such reason to spur gallant souls to action, there is on the contrary very good reason why the beneficiaries make the conservation of those national gains the prime and constant object of their patient, calculating cool headed solicitude.[52]

Bringing New York back into focus, the report concluded:

> If the advice of the New York convention were taken, the action of even a few young men in Ireland might easily result in soul searching horrors, and in setting Ireland back a century. And for reward there would be only the amused contempt of the patient, calculating Germans who would be the sole possible beneficiaries in that welter of ruin.[53]

*Ireland*'s reference to 'calculating Germans' overlooked those like Victor Herbert, the musical celebrity and the inaugural president of the FOIF. His intertwined Irish, German, British, and American connections widen our scope to locate the transatlantic spheres in which many actors moved, reminding us that the global is inscribed in the local, and vice versa. Marion R. Casey's chapter perceptively explores the roots of Herbert's sense of nationalism and furnishes us with a deeper appreciation of his engagement with ethno-politics. Casey is the first scholar to interrogate the composer in this way, charting his political evolution through a robust interpretation of how his ethnic influences were made manifest in his music.

R. Bryan Willits's chapter demonstrates how, in many ways, Herbert was just one 'strand in a complex tapestry'.[54] Willits has done a great service to scholars by deploying the German-American press to translate, quite literally, exactly what was reported about Ireland and how, more generally, German-Irish relations evolved. His chapter makes requisite reading on how inter-ethnic cooperation drew on pre-existing and well-established relations between the two largest ethnic groups in the United States.

Of course, Irish-American views of Germany were not monolithic as the subject of the next chapter abundantly demonstrates this. John Quinn, lawyer and patron of the arts, had been deeply invested literally and metaphorically in Irish cultural nationalism, but by 1916 his commitment had waned considerably. Úna Ní Bhroiméil reveals the extent to which Quinn complicates generalisations about Irish America and allows us to appreciate the multifaceted nature of how Americans related to Ireland in concert with views of Britain and Germany. Primarily drawing from Quinn's letters, Ní Bhroiméil provides us with insights on 'a community and a social world that was taken for granted by the correspondents and that allows us to interpret intimate and complex networks of influence'.[55]

Another man of the law, like Cohalan and Quinn, Sligo-born US congressman William Bourke Cockran was a world-famous orator who influenced American and global politics at the highest level for many decades. Like many of his social and political standing, he had been a committed Home Ruler and was a personal friend and avid supporter of Redmond. But by 1916 Bourke Cockran was prepared to call for American intervention to secure Irish independence by drawing on the example of Cuba. Patrick M. Sweeney innovatively uses examples of Bourke Cockran's speeches to convey his role in shaping public and political opinion on Ireland in the United States. Bourke Cockran also had personal links to the periodical *Ireland* through his close friend and brother-in-law, Shane Leslie, an Irish-born convert to Catholicism and Home Rule advocate, who was associate editor of the new venture (and a cousin of Winston Churchill).

Mary C. Kelly's exploration of some of the taxonomies and anomalies demarcating Protestants and Catholics within the Irish-American political culture of 1916 provides food for thought in the next chapter. Kelly's survey prompts consideration of how lines of Irishness were actually drawn and how religion contributed to how Irish Americans were roused by matters of nationalism. Some of the prominent Irish New Yorkers of the period had links to Ireland that were not defined by links to Roman Catholicism: Bourke Cockran and Herbert both had Protestant mothers, Shane Leslie and Dr Thomas Addis Emmet (a prominent New York physician, grandson and namesake of the famous exiled United Irishman and grandnephew of Robert Emmet) were Catholic converts; Dr Gertrude B. Kelly may also have been of mixed religious heritage.[56] Non-Catholic activism would be most explicitly demonstrated a few years later with the founding of the Protestant Friends of Ireland in New York in 1919.

No scrutiny of the backdrop to the Rising on the American end is complete without an appreciation of just how much of an impact cultural nationalism had in the United States. It can be reasonably contended that engagement with Ireland through the cultural prism groomed many of the leading activists for the more purely political impulses that became more visible, and ever more mainstream, from 1914 onward. Addressing the nexus of culture and politics, Nicholas M. Wolf describes the prevalence of the Irish language in New York and maps out some of the organisations dedicated to the preservation and revival of the language. His analysis stirs necessary contemplation of how a linguistic movement in the United States grappled with Ireland's national question and in doing so adds yet another layer to the associational culture of Irish New York.

A pioneering educator, especially through the medium of Irish, one of the goals of Pearse's 1914 visit to the United States was to publicise and fundraise for his educational experiment at St Enda's. During his time in New York, he inspired a 23-year-old American named John A. Kilgallon to leave his Queens home and travel to Ireland to study. Kilgallon would end up in combat in Dublin in 1916 and subsequently interned in Frongoch before being deported back to the United States. Marion R. Casey and Ed Shevlin use newly available sources to reveal Kilgallon's life both before and after his formative experiences in Ireland. The Kilgallon story reminds us of the Rising's ability to shape the lives of New Yorkers and provokes interesting subjective consideration of ethnicity. Kilgallon also perfectly embodies the long tradition of dual loyalty in American diaspora nationalism that inspired combat duty for two countries. In some ways, Kilgallon's example points to another aspect of the New York Irish community of the period, the class cleavage that generally delineated Home Rule nationalists from their republican counterparts. It is not unfair to assert that the UILA generally attracted support from 'upper and middle-class Irish Americans'.[57] While the Kilgallons cannot be seen to be struggling hand-to-mouth immigrants (nor should we assume that they were die-hard Irish republican nationalists), they were not of the professional class or socio-economic standing of many of those profiled in this volume.

John T. Ridge, in charting county associations, sheds light on the complexity of identity for thousands of Irish New Yorkers. His musings are essential in helping us appreciate how an individual could simultaneously see himself as a Corkman, an Irishman, an American and a Brooklynite, all in one breath. Probing the substrata of how immigrants self-identified, beneath the level of national identity, is significant. In achieving his goal, Ridge draws on a source and theme that are central to the research for this volume, that of newspapers. Notwithstanding the obvious limitations that newspaper sources can present historians, the power of media and public opinion is a leitmotif that overhangs this entire volume, manifesting itself in almost every chapter in some guise. Implicitly, Ridge's chapter also reminds us again that IPP's direct infiltration of the journalistic space of Irish America, through *Ireland*, was a very instructive development.

In fact, up until *Ireland*'s arrival on the scene in early 1916, the variety of opinion on Irish nationalism had been reflected in four nationally circulated weekly publications emanating from Irish New York.[58] The *Irish World*, the *Irish Advocate*, the *Irish American*, and *The Gaelic American* collectively mirrored prevailing thought in the community. The *Irish Advocate*, founded in 1893, generally supported Home Rule and the UILA. In fact, John G. Coyle, who as has been noted was president of *Ireland*, was a regular contributor to the *Advocate* and was visible in its columns due to his activities in the UILA. The *Irish World*, founded in 1870 and at one time the largest weekly newspaper of any kind in the United States, abandoned Redmond in the autumn of 1914, as is contextualised in this volume.[59] The *Irish American* was a venture of Clareman Anthony J. Brogan, which ran until 1914 when he sold out to embark on an expedition to Germany.[60] From its founding in 1903, *The Gaelic American* was the organ of Clan na Gael and specifically of its founder and publisher, John Devoy, and described as the 'voice of anti-League views'.[61] Of course, alongside the ethnic newspapers lay a dense network of Catholic newspapers with an Irish veneer. One scholar maintains that 'nearly every city in the north and middle-west had an Irish-Catholic newspaper; perhaps 500,000 families subscribed to these at the close of the nineteenth century.'[62]

Indeed, the Roman Catholic church played a significant role in Irish-American life and so it is natural to assume that the events of 1916 would echo in religious spheres. The stance taken by the Irish-born Cardinal John Farley reflects the outlook of the New York hierarchy to matters pertaining to Ireland in this tumultuous period. Kate Feighery's stimulating chapter draws on the example of the Irish Relief Fund and by exposing an inherent disconnect between the church and its Irish-American flock. Farley was willing to support relief for Ireland but would in no way support the rebellion, desperate to assert the Americanness of the Catholic church. Feighery's examination calls our attention to the need for scholarship on the members of the American clergy who were unwilling to toe the party line and were visible in republican nationalist circles across the United States. Continuing with the journalistic theme, Thomas J. Rowland surveys the American Catholic press to illustrate the attempts to balance American neutrality with an interest in Irish self-government. On many levels, Rowland's chapter complements that of Feighery's by lingering on the role of the church and its potential scope to shape opinions and responses on Ireland.

New York reacted vocally to news of the Rising. A colour poster portraying James Connolly's execution (commissioned to publicise the October 1916 fundraising bazaar at New York's Madison Square Garden) is used by Daphne Dyer Wolf to re-cast the memory of the agitator who, in life, had been little known and often ignored by Irish America. Wolf's thoughtful treatise, reflecting on the period Connolly spent living in New York, prompts consideration of what may be the first visual depiction of Connolly's death. Robert Schmuhl, drawing from the research for his indispensable biographically driven study on the American role in the Rising, adds a pithy survey of reactions as reported by the American press, in an environment where the First Amendment offered freedoms unavailable in Britain or Ireland (especially for the sentiments espoused by organs like *The Gaelic American*).[63] Here Schmuhl expounds the significant, if overlooked, role of the media in shaping non-Irish-American opinions during this critical time for both the United States and Ireland. His chapter serves to reiterate that the Rising, and its aftermath, prompted a reconceptualisation of Ireland by Americans and Irish Americans.

The penultimate chapter of the volume by Patricia Keefe Durso looks at the interconnections between the Irish and the Irish-American suffrage movements in the period encompassing the Rising. Using the *Irish Citizen* and *The Suffragist*, Durso uncovers robust examples of how the suffrage movements on either side of the Atlantic 'intersected and helped to shape and support each other'.[64] The last chapter of the volume places the aftershocks and inspirations of Ireland's Rising in another fascinating comparative context by looking to other groups and their nationalist impulses. David Brundage draws on his deep engagement with diaspora nationalism to connect the Irish example to anticolonial movements of India and pan-Africanism based in New York. He provides a compelling analysis of how the Rising provided 'an extremely potent example of the ability of a handful of militants to challenge a great empire; of a revolutionary dynamic that could sweep aside compromises and halfway measures (such as Home Rule) almost overnight; and of the deeply inspiring willingness of dedicated rebels to sacrifice their own lives for the sake of a larger cause'.[65]

It would be 6 May before any significant reporting of the Rising appeared in the pages of *Ireland* and, by that time, many of the leaders had already been executed. The front page, carrying a curt statement from Redmond, left readers in no doubt as to who in the United States should shoulder the blame:

> The misguided, insane young men who have taken part in this movement in Ireland have risked, and some of them lost, their lives. But what am I to say of those men who sent them into this insane and anti-patriotic movement while they have remained in the safe remoteness of American cities?[66]

An extract from a paranoid cable to *Ireland* from Redmond continued along the same vein inside the issue:

> The whole thing has been organized by those in Ireland and in America who have always been open and irreconcilable enemies of Home Rule and of the Irish Party. Though the hand of Germany was in the whole thing, it was not so much sympathy for Germany as hatred of Home Rule and of us which was at the bottom of the movement. It was even more an attempt to hit us than to hit England.[67]

However, by the very next issue, on 13 May, the editorial viewpoint had drastically changed and the accusatory sentiment was now suddenly directed at England. The impact of the change in public sentiment in light of the full details of the trials and executions is palpable. The issue's front page carried a poem entitled 'England, Was It Well Done?'. The poet, a Mary Josephine Murray, was not shy in her criticism, even alluding to the diasporic nature of the Irish experience:

> Could you not, thinking of how we came
> In hundreds when need was dire,
> Temper your justice with mercy,
> Not add to the smouldering fire?[68]

The betrayal felt by those who had remained loyal to Redmond's call to support Britain in the war in Europe (of which there had been many in the United States) was laid bare in the longest stanza:

> We who have rallied to aid your side
> In spite of the bitter years
> Of sorrow and wrong; who are sharing now
> Your burdens, your grief, your fears—
> We mourn, alas, with a heartfelt woe
> The madness of what they planned—
> But why not be generous, England?
> Think of the troops we've manned.[69]

Editorial commentary inside the issue observed that the events had 'developed exactly as was forecast in details by Mr. John Devoy in New York' in March at a public meeting. The writer continued:

> History will have to tell us, sometime, why what was clear to Mr. Devoy in New York was not clear to the authorities in Dublin Castle, and why they were unable to

adopt any other course than the one they were publiclly [*sic*] warned would bring on the rebellion.[70]

Shane Leslie observed of the events of Dublin's Easter Week 1916 that Irish America 'paused'.[71] His use of the term is instructive. The pause was the culmination of responses to events in Ireland over a four-year period (including the formation of the Ulster and Irish Volunteers, the spectre of partition, the Larne and Howth gun-running, Bachelors Walk and Redmond's sentiments at Woodenbridge). But, the pause to which Leslie referred was the Rising and the executions that 'forced Irish Americans (and Americans in general) to think about Ireland and its future new ways'.[72] Recalling events, Leslie remarked: 'During the week of the Dublin revolt, when news was coming in uncertain scraps, the voice of Irish America was lifted not unlike the chorus of a Greek tragedy, given over to apprehension, memories, and query, while some fordestined [*sic*] crime is occurring within.' Expanding on Irish-American reactions, he remembered:

> It was possible to know Irishmen in the streets of New York by their expression. Sorrow, anxiety, exaltation, and a tangle of atavistic feelings were struggling in their features … They were roused on a sensitive point and an outburst of lyrical anger swept through the continent from New York to the Golden Gate.[73]

Irish New York as a Greek chorus is a useful analogy. The chapters of this volume provide an array of voices that help us understand what it meant to be interested in Ireland from the vantage point of New York *c.* 1916.

POSTSCRIPT

*Ireland* ceased publication on 7 April 1917 one day after the United States entered the war in Europe in support of the Allies.[74] A new chapter of Irish-American nationalism had begun.

# POBLACHT NA H EIREANN.

## THE PROVISIONAL GOVERNMENT
### OF THE
# IRISH REPUBLIC
## TO THE PEOPLE OF IRELAND.

IRISHMEN AND IRISHWOMEN : In the name of God and of the dead generations from which she receives her old tradition of nationhood, Ireland, through us, summons her children to her flag and-strikes for her freedom.

Having organised and trained her manhood through her secret revolutionary organisation, the Irish Republican Brotherhood, and through her open military organisations, the Irish Volunteers and the Irish Citizen Army, having patiently perfected her discipline, having resolutely waited for the right moment to reveal itself, she now seizes that moment, and, supported by her exiled children in America and by gallant allies in Europe, but relying in the first on her own strength, she strikes in full confidence of victory.

We declare the right of the people of Ireland to the ownership of Ireland, and to the unfettered control of Irish destinies, to be sovereign and indefeasible. The long usurpation of that right by a foreign people and government has not extinguished the right, nor can it ever be extinguished except by the destruction of the Irish people. In every generation the Irish people have asserted their right to national freedom and sovereignty ; six times during the past three hundred years they have asserted it in arms. Standing on that fundamental right and again asserting it in arms in the face of the world, we hereby proclaim the Irish Republic as a Sovereign Independent State, and we pledge our lives and the lives of our comrades-in-arms to the cause of its freedom, of its welfare; and of its exaltation among the nations.

The Irish Republic is entitled to, and hereby claims, the allegiance of every Irishman and Irishwoman. The Republic guarantees religious and civil liberty, equal rights and equal opportunities to all its citizens, and declares its resolve to pursue the happiness and prosperity of the whole nation and of all its parts, cherishing all the children of the nation equally, and oblivious of the differences carefully fostered by an alien government, which have divided a minority from the majority in the past.

Until our arms have brought the opportune moment for the establishment of a permanent National Government, representative of the whole people of Ireland and elected by the suffrages of all her men and women, the Provisional Government, hereby constituted, will administer the civil and military affairs of the Republic in trust for the people.

We place the cause of the Irish Republic under the protection of the Most High God, Whose blessing we invoke upon our arms, and we pray that no one who serves that cause will dishonour it by cowardice, inhumanity, or rapine. In this supreme hour the Irish nation must, by its valour and discipline and by the readiness of its children to sacrifice themselves for the common good, prove itself worthy of the august destiny to which it is called.

Signed on Behalf of the Provisional Government,

THOMAS J. CLARKE,

SEAN Mac DIARMADA,    THOMAS MacDONAGH,
P. H. PEARSE,    EAMONN CEANNT,
JAMES CONNOLLY.    JOSEPH PLUNKETT

# CHAPTER ONE

# JOHN DEVOY AND THE EASTER RISING

## *Terry Golway*

On an early February day in 1916, an ageing Irish immigrant trudged across Park Row near New York's City Hall in the company of a much younger Irishman, a ship's steward. They found a table in Haan's restaurant, a gathering place of journalists and politicians. There, the younger man handed the older man, John Devoy, an envelope containing a secret message from the Irish Republican Brotherhood (IRB) in Dublin.[1] It was written in a code Devoy did not recognise at first, but when he realised that this was no ordinary message, he returned to his office, shut the door, and painstakingly decoded it.

'We have decided to begin action on Easter Sunday,' the message read. 'We must have your arms and munitions in Limerick between Good Friday and Easter Sunday. We expect German help immediately after beginning action.'[2]

It could be said without exaggeration that John Devoy had been preparing himself for this moment since his formative years in Famine-ravaged Ireland. On that winter's day in 1916, Devoy was 73 years old, hard of hearing, and half-blind. Since arriving in New York in 1871 he had worked ceaselessly to extend the struggle for Irish freedom to the shores of the United States. He was a leading figure in the secretive American arm of the Irish revolutionary movement, Clan na Gael, but he also moved freely in mainstream politics.[3] His was an often lonely struggle, and at times a dangerous one as well, for Devoy was unafraid to make enemies, and he possessed a vocabulary of invective and slander that few could match. For a short time during a particularly turbulent period of his life, he carried a pistol to defend himself just in case words failed.[4]

In 1916, John Devoy was the key link between the IRB and the German government, the main propagandist for the IRB's allies in the United States, and a critical source of funds for the Easter Rising.[5] He had met personally with Padraig Pearse and Joseph Plunkett during their visits to New York. As editor of *The Gaelic American* in New York, Devoy employed an assistant named Thomas J. Clarke for several years before Clarke returned to Ireland to attend to other business. Devoy met James Connolly briefly during Connolly's American years, and he provided Sir Roger Casement with speaking engagements and introductions to German diplomats in New York, and helped arrange for Casement's fateful trip to Germany in 1914.[6]

Any exploration of the Rising as a transatlantic enterprise, as it so clearly was, must take into account the role that New York played as a source of funds and support, and as the site of negotiations between the rebels in Dublin and the German government. And any account of New York's role requires an examination of the formidable and perhaps irreplaceable presence of John Devoy, the man Pearse referred to as the 'greatest of the Fenians'.[7]

For a man who inspired such high praise, John Devoy has been lost to history on both sides of the Atlantic. It could be said that Jeremiah O'Donovan Rossa has been accorded a more prominent place in the Rising's narrative, for that tortured, unrepentant Fenian managed to die at a fortuitous time in the run-up to Easter Week. But it was Devoy who sent Rossa's body back to Ireland, leading to the memorable funeral and graveside oration that have such an indelible place in the Rising's history.

He devoted nearly all of his waking hours to marshalling American public opinion on behalf of Ireland and Irish America. He was ruthless and unforgiving, and he rarely missed an opportunity to question the motives and character of those who disagreed with him. His newspaper assailed his onetime friend Rossa, and he publicly blamed another onetime friend, Michael Davitt, for the murder of a Clan na Gael ally, Dr Patrick Cronin, in Chicago in the late 1880s.[8] Without excusing his ability to lose friends and alienate people, it can be said of Devoy that his passion for Ireland left room for neither diplomacy nor, at times, discretion. And it was passion that kept him awake at night, kept him at his lonely desk to the day he died, and kept him going when others would have surrendered.

In the United States, Devoy found a place in the frantic world of New York journalism. A friend of his from childhood, James J. O'Kelly, a onetime Fenian himself, was a drama critic at the *New York Herald*, one of the city's best-known newspapers. Devoy became one of several Fenian exiles on the *Herald*'s staff, joining not just O'Kelly but Jerome Collins, the paper's meteorologist and the founder of Clan na Gael, and Joseph I. C. Clarke, a reporter and playwright.[9]

Journalism became Devoy's platform, the source of his power as an advocate, a disciplinarian, and even as an educator. After several years at the *Herald*, culminating in his appointment as the paper's foreign editor, Devoy founded two newspapers, the *Irish Nation* (published from 1881 to 1885) and *The Gaelic American*, founded in 1903, which he ran until his death in 1928.[10]

With Irish America attaining political influence a generation after the Famine, Devoy recognised that mobilising that power on Ireland's behalf would require more than rhetoric and half-baked conspiracies destined for failure. It would require public agitation, mass organisation, and attainable goals. And so, on Sunday, 25 October 1878, six years after arriving in New York, the *New York Herald* – Devoy's employer – featured a prominent news story on page one bearing the headline, 'An Irish new departure'.[11] The article announced that Irish-American nationalists had sent a telegram to Charles Stewart Parnell, leader of the Irish Parliamentary Party, offering to cooperate with him if he agreed to several conditions, including support for 'self-government' in Ireland, an intentionally vague phrase.[12]

Historians have long debated the significance and even the very existence of the New Departure, at least from an Irish perspective. In the United States, however, it was very real, indeed, for it allowed Devoy to mobilise Irish America around two issues, one very specific (land reform) and one purposely ambiguous (Irish self-government). And it gave Devoy an opportunity to work with Michael Davitt and others in the creation of a mass political movement, the American Land League, on Ireland's behalf.[13]

The American Land League, founded in 1880 as an adjunct of the Land League in Ireland, raised money on behalf of Parnell's campaign against landlordism, recruited mainstream Irish-American politicians, clerics, and labour leaders, inspired non-Irish political activists like Henry George and James Redpath, and identified an issue – the need for land reform – that was easily understood and thought to be attainable. 'The Land League,' writes American historian Eric Foner, 'was the first nationalist organization to unite the Irish-American community.'[14]

The American Land League had more than 1,500 branches across the country. The money it raised in its first two years ($500,000 in 1882 currency[15]), the support it offered Parnell, Davitt and their colleagues during the Land War, and the publicity it generated on behalf of Ireland's plight led Parnell himself to declare, during a rally in Madison Square Garden, that Irish Americans were 'virtually the arbiters of this Irish question'.[16]

Such practical successes established Devoy as the voice of Irish-American nationalism, and created a working alliance between Clan na Gael in the United States and the IRB in Ireland. All of these factors would be critical three decades later, when the Easter rebels were planning their revolution and counting on aid, financial and otherwise, from the United States. That help, however, might never have been possible had Devoy given up the cause in the 1890s, when Clan na Gael split into two warring factions.[17] A dispute over leadership, tactics, and goals led to the Cronin murder, referenced above, and prompted Devoy to carry a firearm in case he crossed paths with his rival for Clan dominance, Alexander Sullivan of Chicago.

The last decade of the nineteenth century and first decade of the twentieth were Devoy's wilderness years, a time when so much of what he had hoped for and worked for seemed lost. If he had any cause to re-read a long-ago letter from John Boyle O'Reilly advising him to stay away from Irish politics and to go into business, he might well have smiled, bitterly, in recognition of its wisdom. But he did not, in fact, give up. Quite the opposite. In a display of his extraordinary willpower and determination, he set about the daunting task of reuniting Clan na Gael, re-establishing himself as the voice of Irish nationalism in America, and reviving an Irish sense of identity among the children and grandchildren of immigrants.[18] Without his work in the 1890s and the early 1900s, the American network on which the Easter rebels depended might not have existed.

It was a lonely and thankless task. He described a particularly frustrating journey to Albany and Troy in upstate New York, where he tried unsuccessfully to bring disillusioned comrades back into the movement. He was told he was wasting his time. One former activist told him he would never 'touch Irish affairs again'.[19] He was invited to meetings where only a handful of people showed up to hear him. And on one cold, snowy night in Albany, after yet another disappointing round of recruiting, he was attacked by a pack of dogs. He escaped with only minor injuries, but only because police officers were nearby and heard the commotion.[20]

And yet, by the turn of the twentieth century, Devoy had single-handedly doubled membership in his wing of Clan na Gael, from about 4,000 in 1894 to nearly 10,000 six years later.[21] The organisation that seemed doomed to irrelevance reunited in 1900, with Devoy named as the organisation's secretary, a job that paid $100 a month. Not long thereafter, Devoy hired a new personal assistant for $15 a week – Tom Clarke, living in New York after spending 15 years in prison for his role in the dynamite campaign in the 1880s.[22]

Devoy and Clarke founded *The Gaelic American* newspaper in 1903 to serve as the voice of the transatlantic Irish republican movement in the United States.[23] And it was through *The Gaelic American* that Devoy not only stirred up recruiting for Clan na Gael, but began to define the Irish cause in terms that the American-born Irish, those with fading attachment to Ireland beyond gauzy abstraction, might understand.

The front page of *The Gaelic American* regularly featured news of British threats not only to Ireland but to the United States as well, especially its traditional policy of avoiding entangling alliances with European powers. Through his journalism and his own political activity, he campaigned against an arbitration treaty between Britain and the United States that came before the senate in 1911, saying it would lead to an outright military partnership between the two countries. 'We love America more than we hate England,' Devoy explained during a rally in New York. Among those who heard Devoy's speech was a German diplomat named George Von Skal – who would later become a key intermediary between Devoy and the German government.[24]

In the same spirit, he also campaigned against efforts to create Anglo-American harmony during centennial commemorations of the War of 1812, and he assailed Andrew Carnegie's Peace Society as a front for those who wished to drag the United States into an alliance with Britain and to transform Americans into West Britons. Devoy even attacked a movement among the city's elites to replace the 'Star-Spangled Banner' (which was not yet the official US national anthem) with 'My Country 'Tis of Thee' in New York's public schools. Devoy reminded his Irish-American audience that the music for 'My Country 'Tis of Thee' was the same as the British national anthem. No coincidence there, he wrote. 'The amount of English money spent in organized efforts to Anglicise the American people must be enormous,' he wrote.[25]

As a European war grew inevitable, Devoy's anti-British crusades invariably put him in closer contact with Von Skal and his colleagues in the German consulate. The tacit alliance between the Irish and Germans in New York was made formal when Devoy aligned Clan na Gael with a group called the Friends of Peace, which advocated continued American neutrality as Europe drifted towards war.[26] Devoy believed the combined political clout of the nation's Irish and German communities was essential to counter the activities of those he called 'Anglomaniacs' who occupied high places in American politics, journalism, and society itself. They would be eager to see the United States enter the war on Britain's side, an outcome that, among other things, would make Irish-American support for would-be rebels in Dublin not just difficult, but treasonous. American neutrality also allowed for the German diplomatic presence in the United States to become critical for the rebels' plans. As the armies of Europe prepared to turn the Continent into a slaughterhouse, England's difficulties became Ireland's opportunities thanks in part to the organisational and diplomatic ground-work John Devoy had put into place during his long years of agitation before the war.

The guns of August had only just opened fire when Devoy met with his new partner, Von Skal, and the German ambassador to the United States to discuss matters of mutual interest.[27] Devoy informed the ambassador, a suave, English-speaking count named Johann Heinrich von Bernstorff, that Ireland would rise in rebellion at some point during the war. The Irish wished to create a formal alliance with Berlin, Devoy explained, and would request German assistance when the time came.[28] They did not want money – Irish Americans would provide that. They wanted arms, ammunition, and German officers.[29]

The ambassador agreed to convey Devoy's message to Berlin, and soon the IRB and Berlin were communicating with each other through Devoy in New York, setting in motion the conspiracy that led to the ill-fated arms shipment from Germany aboard the steamship *Aud*. As Devoy became a familiar figure in the German consulate on Wall Street in lower Manhattan in the months before the Rising, he quietly began withdrawing thousands of dollars from a secret account in the Corn Exchange Bank, which had a branch steps away from his newspaper office on William Street in down-town New York. In late 1915, he sent more than $100,000 to Dublin in increments of 5,000 and 10,000.[30] Couriers who brought messages to him from Dublin returned with the cash.

But perhaps the most valuable commodity that Devoy sent to Ireland in 1915 was not cash, but a corpse. Jeremiah O'Donovan Rossa died on Staten Island on 29 June.[31] He and Devoy had met in prison in the late 1860s, they had travelled together to New York in 1871, and they became bitter enemies in the 1880s when Devoy supported Parnell while Rossa supported the dynamite campaign. In the end, though, they recon-ciled, and when Rossa died, Devoy sent his body home to Ireland for a funeral that Pearse made famous. At Glasnevin, Rossa was eulogised as the embodiment of the unrepentant Fenian, as well he was. But he shared with Devoy another trait: in the end, he was an Irish man who had lived in the United States nearly half his life and was a symbol of the hidden narrative embedded in the story of the Rising, the role of the exile.

Devoy hoped to follow Rossa's path across the Atlantic, although he had a desti-nation other than Glasnevin in mind. He planned to join the rebellion, despite his age, his poor hearing, his terrible eyesight, and his other maladies, insomnia included. When he told Rossa's widow Mary Jane that he had made arrangements, she implored him to remain in the United States.[32] Nothing, of course, came of the plan, but its very existence speaks to the man's fierce determination. Instead, Devoy remained at home and continued to serve as the IRB's intermediary with the Germans. He informed them of the timeline for the Rising, and passed along the rebels' request for an arms shipment to arrive between 20 April and Easter Sunday.

Privately, Devoy worried about the seemingly sudden decision to rise. He later wrote that he and his allies in Clan na Gael thought their Dublin colleagues would wait 'until the war situation [in Europe] became more favorable'.[33] But the decision was made, and Devoy brushed aside any lingering doubts. It was a point of dogma with him that the IRB made decisions for Ireland, and Clan na Gael made decisions about the Irish in America.[34] It was this very point that would lead to his clash with Éamon de Valera over the role of Irish America in 1920.

Devoy's dispatches to Berlin in March and early April focused on details for the planned arms shipment, including codes to be used between the ship and the rebels. The IRB's military council included a code to be used if a German submarine made its way to Dublin Bay in conjunction with the Rising, a request that, Devoy wrote, 'indicated a misconception of the naval conditions under which the German submarines operated' in the North Atlantic.[35] A submarine, of course, never appeared and never was going to appear; Devoy wrote off the request as unrealistic.

But even Devoy's usual hard-headed judgement seems to have gone missing during the weeks leading to the Rising. He sent a long memo to Berlin analysing the number and quality of British troops and local constabulary in Ireland. Of the 40,000 troops stationed in Ireland, he wrote, 30,000 were poorly trained with 'few competent officers, no trained non-commissioned officers, little artillery, and few machine guns'.[36] Opposing this force were 40,000 Irish Volunteers, he wrote, and when action began, some 50,000 National Volunteers under the control of John Redmond would join the fray. The new Irish front would require the British to withdraw 500,000 troops from the Continent.

This was, to put it mildly, wishful thinking. There were about 12,000 Irish Volunteers, not 40,000. It is impossible to know what the German general staff would have made of this report, if anyone in authority actually saw it. That it came from one of the most unromantic of Irish rebels shows that even hard-headed John Devoy was not immune to dreaming.

In early April, virtually on the eve of the Rising, Devoy was served with a subpoena ordering him to testify about the activities of pro-German groups in the United States.[37] (There was no such investigation of pro-British groups.) If the intent was to intimidate Devoy, it failed, but not long after he testified, American agents raided the German consulate in New York and scooped up documents that included Devoy's correspondence with Berlin.

Devoy's work was not restricted to shadowy conspiracy and backroom meetings as Easter approached. He also organised a new public organisation called the Friends of Irish Freedom (FOIF), which brought together mainstream figures like Congressman William Bourke Cockran, the oratorical inspiration of Winston Churchill, composer Victor Herbert, and others who are examined in this volume.[38] The FOIF held a two-day convention six weeks before the Rising to demand that 'Ireland may be cut off from England and restored to her rightful place among the nations of the earth'.[39] But only a handful of the 500 Irish Americans who attached themselves to the FOIF knew that this demand was about to be articulated in something other than words.

Devoy could do little more than wait and prepare to defend the rebels in print as Easter Week neared. He may have suspected that the Rising would end in futility, because on 14 April, with the Rising just over a week away, Philomena Plunkett, sister of Joseph Plunkett, arrived in his office with a new message from the IRB: the arms shipment was not to land any earlier than Easter Sunday.[40] But it was too late to alert the *Aud*'s crew of the change in plans. Years later, Devoy would write that the confusion over the arms shipment, which he had done so much to arrange, 'was responsible for turning what would have been the most formidable insurrection in Irish history ... into one which was ... and foredoomed to military defeat'.[41] The *Aud* arrived off the Kerry coast on Holy Thursday, waited nearly a day for a signal from the shore, and then was spotted and captured. Twenty thousand rifles, machine guns, and ammunition never made their way into the rebels' hands.

It is hard to imagine what Devoy might have been thinking as he followed the events of Easter Week in his newsroom in lower Manhattan. After it was over, he wrote, 'The men of Dublin have redeemed the honor of Ireland and restored the lost prestige of the Irish race. They have brought back the soul of Ireland and made a new epoch in Irish history.' Fine words they were, but Devoy surely must have been profoundly disappointed. He had devoted years for this moment, and it had ended as so many other rebellions had ended.[42]

He led a rally of support for the rebels in the Cohan Theatre on 30 April, a day after the surrender in Dublin, during which he allowed a glimpse into his private bitterness. He raged at his colleagues in the New York press for their coverage of the Rising. They were, he said, 'unnaturalized Englishmen'.[43] For Devoy, there was no greater insult, aside from those not fit for print. Devoy saw New York's immigrants, most especially the Irish, as keepers of the American democratic spirit, while their social betters sought to create in New York an aristocratic society modelled on Victorian Britain. Whether or not Devoy was wrong or simply paranoid is another issue. What is clear is that he saw himself and the larger Irish-American community as a bulwark against British influence in American politics, culture, and education.

After the Rising, he would continue his agitations even as his health problems, particularly his hearing, worsened. He lived for another dozen years after 1916, returning to Ireland in 1924 as a guest of the Free State he supported, reuniting with a long-lost love from his days as a youthful organiser in the Fenian movement, and returning yet again, this time in a coffin, in 1928.

Upon his death, *The Times* of London said that he had been 'the most bitter and persistent, as well as the most dangerous, enemy of this country which Ireland has produced since Wolfe Tone'.[44]

John Devoy would have been delighted.

# CHAPTER TWO

# THE COLLAPSE OF HOME RULE AND THE UNITED IRISH LEAGUE OF AMERICA, 1910–18

## THE CENTRE DID NOT HOLD

## *Francis M. Carroll*

John Devoy's stance is crucial in understanding Irish America's view of Ireland's geopolitical status as the twentieth century dawned. But it behoves us to remember that Clan na Gael's outlook was that of the minority for protracted periods. Much more representative, certainly up until 1914 in the United States, was the objective as espoused by Home Rule most prominently demonstrated by the United Irish League of America (UILA).[1] As mentioned in the introduction to this volume, Home Rule did not satisfy the aspirations of Devoy and his associates, but it did prove attractive to the majority of Irish Americans in the decade and a half prior to 1916. And Home Rule was not a new concept to those of Irish descent who made the United States home. Charles Stewart Parnell had brought Ireland and his Irish-American supporters to a fever pitch at the prospect of Home Rule in the 1880s and early 1890s, only to be defeated by the divorce scandal, the split in the Irish Parliamentary Party, and the rejection of Home Rule by the House of Lords.

Almost a decade later the Irish Party was reunified in 1900 under John Redmond and by 1910 and 1912 a new dawn seemed to appear with the promise of Home Rule, once again warmly supported by the Irish communities in Ireland and the United States. Of course we know that Redmond and Home Rule were hated by elements at both ends of the Irish political spectrum – unionists at one end and republican nationalists at the other – although both of these groups appeared to be extremist minorities. The mass of Irish people at home and abroad, the hierarchy of the church, much of the establishment, a majority in the House of Commons, all seemed to support Redmond and Home Rule. By 1914 the Home Rule Bill was finally passed and on the statute books and Redmond was for all practical purposes the premier-designate, although no one could have expected the cataclysmic effect of the war in Europe.

The Irish Parliamentary Party was reunited in 1900 after almost a decade of rancour and ineffectiveness following the Parnell split. Redmond was elected leader to bring the factions back together. Although the leader of the Parnellites, he had not alienated the major figures in the other factions of the old party and thus he was a suitable person to lead a reunited party. The reunification of the party was supplemented by affiliation with the United Irish League. The League had been created in 1898 by William O'Brien to agitate for land reform in Co. Mayo and the west of Ireland. Upon assuming leadership of the party, Redmond became chairman of the League in 1900. The United Irish League became the political machine and the fundraising body for the party in Ireland, as the Land League had been under Parnell.[2]

John Redmond, Patrick McHugh, and Thomas O'Donnell travelled to the United States in the autumn of 1901 promoting a new organisation, the UILA, and raising money. A gathering of some 15,000 people in Chicago was the most spectacular of several meetings in New York, Baltimore, and Washington, DC, to get the UILA started. After earlier consultations with Redmond, over 150 representatives met in New York in December 1901 to formally found the UILA. John F. Finerty, editor of the *Chicago Citizen*, was elected president, Patrick Egan vice president, John O'Callaghan secretary, and Thomas B. Fitzpatrick treasurer. Michael J. Ryan, a successful lawyer and city solicitor of Philadelphia, succeeded to the presidency in 1906; and when O'Callaghan died in 1913 he was replaced by Michael J. Jordan of Boston. William Redmond, John Dillon, and Edward Blake were able to tour the United States from February to June of 1902, promoting membership in the new body and raising about $100,000[3] for the party.[4] Redmond saw to it that the UILA was led by moderate constitutionalists and would not fall into the hands of the republican nationalist groups in the United States – Clan na Gael. He also insured that the organisation took its lead from Ireland on policy matters. The *Irish World*, edited by Patrick Ford in New York, threw its support behind Redmond and the League, giving the Home Rule movement a powerful voice within the Irish-American community. This was a promising beginning for the relationship between the UILA and the Irish Parliamentary Party.[5]

The creation of the UILA provided Redmond and the party with significant financial resources to support Irish MPs without independent means and to fight three general elections. But that support needed constant wooing. Between 1901 and 1910 Redmond and various leaders of the party travelled to the United States and Canada nine times and were able to raise several hundred thousand dollars. In response to the crucial January 1910 election, Michael J. Ryan assured Redmond that 'you can safely count on a fairly generous remittance from this side'.[6] Redmond made a tour of the United States in the autumn of 1910 to prepare for the anticipated second election and, together with T. P. O'Connor who toured Canada, raised over $100,000. Joseph P. Finnan concludes that the party raised much of its revenue in Ireland, but these figures indicate how vital the UILA was in helping to finance the Irish Parliamentary Party. This money also made Redmond vulnerable to the unionist accusation that he was the 'Dollar Dictator', subsidised from a foreign country to change the British constitution.[7]

The middle years of the first decade of the twentieth century saw the fortunes of Home Rule and its political arm go up and down. The Liberals were returned to office in 1906 and were not keen to pursue the Home Rule legacy of Gladstone. However, the constitutional crises of 1909 to 1911, with the Liberals becoming dependent on the Irish Parliamentary Party after the December election and the subsequent removal of the House of Lords veto, ensured that the Liberal government would be able to pass a Home Rule measure into law within two years. All of the parliamentary pieces were now in place for the successful realisation of Irish aspirations for self-government through the legislative process. The prospects of the Irish Parliamentary Party and Home Rule soared. American public figures were not slow to recognise this. President William Howard Taft travelled to Chicago to speak at the Irish Fellowship Club on St Patrick's Day 1910, and Patrick Egan, vice president of the League, made arrangements for Redmond to host former US president Theodore Roosevelt for lunch at the House of Commons in June.[8]

Prime Minister H. H. Asquith introduced the Home Rule Bill on 11 April 1912. Leaders of the Irish community in New York responded immediately, cabling Redmond: 'Hearty congratulations to you and [the] Irish Party on marvelous success, and to Irish people on splendid prospect afforded by Home Rule Bill,' signed by Senator James A. O'Gorman, Congressman William Bourke Cockran, Mayor William J. Gaynor, Judge Morgan J. O'Brien, Judge Martin J. Keogh, John D. Crimmins, John Quinn, and eight others. Bourke Cockran wrote separately, 'At this moment when we all feel that the destinies of the race are in your hands, every one of us is confident that no safer custody could be found for them.'[9] Newspapers, the *Irish World*, as well as the *New York Times*, regarded the introduction of the bill as the beginning of the fulfilment of the Home Rule promise.[10] Judge Keogh commented later after reading Redmond's speeches in parliament, 'I cannot help writing to congratulate you on your statesmanship, dignity, temperance and eloquence.' Keogh told Redmond, 'You have achieved more than I believed it possible to be done in the lifetime of an Irish Leader in our day, and more than all, you have race at home and abroad solidly, sincerely and almost unanimously with you.'[11]

The Home Rule Bill passed its third reading on 17 January before going to the House of Lords where it was defeated on 30 January 1913. The bill then started a second and third series of readings in the Commons and rejections in the Lords, finally passing on 25 May 1914, now ready for royal assent. In the interval, of course, resistance in Ulster to the idea that unionist portions of the province might be brought under an Irish government based in Dublin grew by dramatic proportions, including the recruitment of the Ulster Volunteers. The Ulster unionist leaders were supported by the Tory leadership in England and by elements of the British army to an extent that bordered on open rebellion. Redmond seemed confident that the threat of Ulster unionist defiance could be overcome by compromise, guarantees, and assurances. Others drew different conclusions from Ulster's example and in late 1913 the Irish Volunteers were formed in Dublin, creating thereby two paramilitary organisations in Ireland.[12] By the spring of 1914 Redmond was pressured to concede the possibility of several counties in Ulster opting out of a Home Rule government, which was especially worrying to Irish Americans.

As is demonstrated in the chapters in this volume on William Bourke Cockran and Dr Gertrude B. Kelly, it is possible to see in the spring of 1914 the first cracks in what had been the accepted understanding of an all-Ireland Home Rule government. Such an astute political participant as Congressman Bourke Cockran, who just two years before had been extravagant in his praise of Redmond, was dismayed that the leader had allowed the idea of the exclusion of parts of Ulster to become part of the negotiation process. 'Irishmen here have been shocked beyond expression to learn that partition of the Island has become not merely a proposal that might be considered, but a proposal that has actually been accepted,' he concluded, indifferent to the pressures to which Redmond had been subjected. But in a telling moment, 25 March 1914, sounding more like a spokesman for Clan na Gael, he added, 'If a revolt were started in Ireland, I think the Irish in America would support it to a man.'[13] Somewhat similarly,

John Quinn, who also had signed the cable of congratulations to Redmond on the introduction of the Home Rule Bill in 1912, complained in 1914, 'I regard English politics and even Irish politics, outside of those few Protestants of the North, as simply beneath contempt, weak, flabby, cowardly.' Quinn's biographer B. L. Reid says Quinn had concluded that Redmond and his surrogates were 'arch criminals' who should have stopped the Ulster obstruction and seen to the implementation of Home Rule.[14] Quinn resolved by the summer of 1914 that the Home Rule Bill was inoperable with the north defiant and that the only hope was 'the arming of the National Volunteers'.[15]

The spring and summer of 1914 brought further complications. The Irish Volunteers had grown to such a scale that Redmond could not claim to speak for the country without some voice in this nationalist paramilitary counterpart to the Ulster Volunteers. Among the ramifications of this move was the degree to which in the southern Irish context it linked the respectable constitutional movement to the threat of using more revolutionary methods. However much this move was bitterly opposed by Clan na Gael in the United States, it was warmly supported by the UILA, which now began raising funds to support the Irish Volunteers. Thus the summer of 1914 saw the irony of both the UILA and the Clan raising money for the Irish Volunteers stateside.[16] The second complication was the Buckingham Palace Conference in which the exclusion of counties in Ulster was again a matter of consideration, now perhaps entrenched, although by 24 July no agreement could be reached about any territorial limits or time limits. Then on 26 July guns were delivered to the Irish Volunteers at Howth, the counterpart to the Larne gun-running in the north in April. The efforts of the authorities to intervene led to the confrontation between crowds of people and British troops in Dublin, with the result that the troops fired on the crowd, killing three people and wounding many. In the context of rising tensions in Ireland, these events were seen by many as the beginning of civil war in the country.[17] Irish America watched with a sense of unease.

An even greater complication emerged in early August of 1914 with the onset of major conflict in Europe. Britain declared war on 4 August but in the debates in parliament the day before, Redmond famously assured the House that the government could withdraw troops from Ireland and that the country would be defended by its armed volunteers from the south and the north.[18] This revealed that Redmond's notion of Ireland, even if self-governing, as an integral part of Britain and the British Empire, was quite distant from independent Ireland in the minds of many of his supporters in the United States. Redmond's urging of Irishmen to enlist in support of the war on 20 September at Woodenbridge, immediately following the king's assent of the Home

Rule Bill and its suspension until the end of the war, was regarded by many as open betrayal. For Ireland to march in step with Britain was too much, especially for Irish Americans. On the other hand, Home Rule was now passed into law, on the statute books and completed, albeit postponed until the end of the war.

The Gaelic American had always fought Redmond and condemned Home Rule as a travesty, but the Irish World had been the strongest supporter of Redmond, Home Rule, and the UILA. Nevertheless, the paper, edited by Robert Ford since the death of his father, Patrick, in 1913, had been distressed at the thought of the exclusion of parts of Ulster and became increasingly hostile about the prospect of Irish participation in the war. 'The accursed Union ended', the Irish World wrote, and it ran an editorial exclaiming that 'Home Rule is come at last.' The paper said that to his credit, Redmond had extracted Home Rule from a reluctant parliament. However, the paper challenged his support for the war. 'Mr. Redmond invited young Irishmen to accept the King's shilling, shoulder a musket and go to the Continent to fight and die in England's service. In doing so he exceeds his powers. He never received a commission from the Irish people to act as a recruiting sergeant for the British Army.'[19] The Irish World vigorously attacked Redmond's speech at Woodenbridge, saying among other things that Irish Americans had sent money to the Irish Volunteers to prepare them to defend Ireland. 'Any other use of those dollars would be a breach of faith.' The paper also printed letters from numerous readers protesting Redmond's encouragement of Irish support for the war effort.[20] Patrick Egan, vice president of the UILA, who had served as the business manager of the Irish World, resigned in protest. Others complained that the paper was taking an anti-British position 'for purely selfish reasons'. The Irish World, once the leading newspaper in the United States supporting Redmond, had become an embittered critic. The defection of the Fords left the Irish leader and his outlook without the voice of a major newspaper in the United States.[21]

The UILA was also troubled by Redmond's efforts to make Ireland part of the British war effort. Redmond wrote to Michael J. Ryan, the president of the UILA, on 17 September on the eve of the Home Rule Bill receiving royal assent, and attempted to explain his decision to support the war and encourage Volunteer enlistments for the purpose of practical military training, noting also that the Irish people 'unquestion-ingly'[22] supported the war. Ryan replied coolly that he appreciated that Redmond had acted 'with the hope of advancing Ireland's interests', but that 'all my sympathies are with Germany, and I believe that nine-tenths of the Americans of Irish blood think as I do.'[23] More importantly, Ryan concluded that in the circumstances of the war no funds could be raised for the Irish Parliamentary Party. 'Home Rule has been placed on the Statute Book, and the work of the League in America can end in honor,' he wrote, indicating clearly that everything was now changed. Speaking for T. B. Fitzpatrick, the treasurer, he concluded, 'Our suggestion would be that you authorize its [the League's] termination here.'[24] This proposal triggered a serious split in the UILA executive. Patrick Egan, vice president, wrote to Redmond that for the sake of the organisation Ryan should be replaced by Dr John G. Coyle, who was a dynamic force in the New York Municipal Council of the League. Egan felt that the UILA had much more work to do, particularly in the context of the war.[25] Leading figures in the Chicago Irish-American community attempted to draft a letter for Redmond showing support among the American Irish notables, but it proved so difficult to get enough prominent people to sign the letter that it was never sent.[26] In order to avoid a confrontation, Ryan cancelled the scheduled meeting of the UILA national convention in December, although the New York Municipal Council held a large conference rather in defiance.[27] Had the war ended by Christmas, as some optimists had predicted, these growing fissures might have been papered over, but of course the war continued unabated. The practical effect of Ryan's decisions was the termination of public activity by the UILA.

A new crisis that emerged early in 1915 was the decision of T. B. Fitzpatrick and Ryan to close the national office of the UILA in Boston. The postponement of the UILA annual national conference had been something of a shock, but Michael J. Jordan assured Redmond that 'our organization will be preserved here until such time as you consider there is no longer any need for it.'[28] However, less than two months later, Jordan wrote to Redmond on 25 February 1915 that Fitzpatrick and Ryan had decided to close the national office in Boston because there was not enough business during the waiting period imposed by the war to justify the expense of about $1,500 a year. Jordan thought this would be a disaster. 'The closing of the office means the death of the organization,' he concluded, adding that it would also be seen as a triumph for Clan na Gael and the now hostile *Irish World*.[29] Patrick Egan supported Jordan, arguing that closing the office would be a 'severe blow to Mr. Redmond and his party at home, as well as to the vast majority of our earnest patriotic fellow Irishmen in this country'.[30] After an acrimonious exchange of correspondence between members of the executive committee, the New York Municipal Council agreed by 12 March to pay the expenses of the office until July.[31] A partial solution to the office problems was worked out whereby the UILA would share office space and staff with the Catholic Federation of the Archdiocese of Boston. However, this did not really compensate for the fact that the UILA was now completely inactive. Money problems began to plague the UILA and, as Alan J. Ward has shown, by 1915 Redmond had to subsidise the League.[32]

The scaling back of UILA activities with the onset of the war and the loss of support by the *Irish World* left the Home Rule movement in the shadow of the activities of Clan na Gael and the pro-German forces in the United States that rapidly captured public attention. As we learn from R. Bryan Willits's chapter in this volume, Irish-German events were frequently held promoting the idea that Germany victorious in the war would be in a position to see that Ireland obtained far greater independence than anything Home Rule offered.[33] Many of the UILA leaders recognised that the organisation had to find a new media source to counter this repeated message. As early as October, Patrick Egan had offered to provide Irish material to the mainstream press in the United States and later to start a new paper, and in December Michael Jordan mentioned to Redmond that the *Sacred Heart Review* in Boston could be acquired.[34] There was even a discussion of a newspaper financed by the British press baron Lord Northcliffe.[35] In 1915 Redmond sent Alderman Daniel Boyle, MP from Co. Mayo, to the United States to talk with UILA leaders and assess Irish-American attitudes. In October Redmond asked Boyle to look into starting a newspaper. He urged that 'you ask our leading supporters to produce a moderate sum of money which would be required to start an Irish American weekly paper, produced in a high class style, to give the true facts, week by week, with reference to the war, and more particularly, with reference to events and opinions in Ireland.' Redmond was confident there would be a large audience for a quality paper with an Irish perspective.[36] Boyle was able to raise the money and on 8 January 1916 the new journal *Ireland*, described in some detail in Miriam Nyhan Grey's introduction to this volume, was published out of offices on West 40th Street in New York. Dr John G. Coyle was president, and Stephen McFarland treasurer; the editor was Joseph C. Walsh and the associate editor Shane Leslie. Leslie was well connected in the United States and was able to obtain contributions from such distinguished figures as Cardinal James Gibbons, Archbishop John Ireland, and Monsignor Sigourney Fay. Leslie wrote to Redmond, 'If we can touch the bishops, lawyers, judges, doctors and professional men we can exert the influence you desire.'[37] Unfortunately, the paper, pitched towards this professional middle-class readership, did not find the large audience that Redmond had anticipated. The journal certainly did not compete with the *Irish World* or *The Gaelic American* within the Irish community. By late 1916 Michael Jordan complained to Redmond that 'for all practical purposes this paper is useless.'[38] Redmond and the UILA never found an effective newspaper to reach the Irish-American community after the defection of the *Irish World*.

The Rising was as much a surprise and a shock to the leaders of the UILA as it was to Redmond and the Irish Parliamentary Party and the immediate reaction of UILA leaders was that the Rising was a betrayal. Patrick Egan, Dr John G. Coyle, Stephen McFarland, and John J. O'Connell led a large public meeting in New York on 28 April. A resolution was passed stating 'That this meeting express its unqualified sorrow and amazement at the unpardonable wrong now being perpetrated against the whole people of Ireland by the present insane insurrection,' and they blamed the Rising on 'unreasoning enthusiasts' and German 'intrigue'.[39] The Boston UILA, led by Michael J. Jordan, T. B. Fitzpatrick, and Dr Henry V. McLaughlin, sent Redmond assurances of their loyalty and confidence in his leadership. The Boston Irish 'Ardently supports you and the party,' their cable read.[40] In Chicago William Dillon, the brother of the Irish deputy leader John Dillon, thought the Rising would not have much lasting effect, while the president of the Irish Fellowship Club, P. T. Barry, argued that the Irish people were loyal Home Rulers who supported the war and that the insurrection was not 'Irish' at all.[41] What effect these denunciations of the Rising might have had on the sentiments of the Irish-American community at large is impossible to say.

The executions of the leaders of the Rising, however, brought rapid protests in the United States. Stephen McFarland cabled Redmond on 4 May, 'Irish in America contrasting execution of Dublin leaders with treatment of Ulster and South Africa [and] are revolted by this sign of reversion to savage repression.'[42] Michael J. Ryan communicated from Philadelphia, 'the executions have alienated every American friend and caused a resurgence of ancient enmities. Your life work destroyed by English brutality,' and he concluded ominously, 'Opinion widespread that [the] promise of Home Rule was [a] mockery.'[43] Shane Leslie told Redmond that 'the rising only called out sympathy for you', but that the executions sent 'a wave of fury sweeping through Irish America'.[44] The effect in the United States of the executions in Dublin was to draw moderates, the UILA Home Rulers, together with the revolutionary advocates, Clan na Gael and the Friends of Irish Freedom, in public protests. And just as it did in Ireland, the image of the Irish Parliamentary Party and efficacy of Home Rule were diminished and gradually disregarded. The failure of Lloyd George and the British government to work out an agreement to implement Home Rule in the summer of 1916 further eroded confidence that it would ever come to pass. Even the British embassy staff noticed the decline of the moderates. J. Joyce Broderick reported to the Foreign Office in January 1917, 'The United Irish League of America has practically passed out of existence.'[45] As Shane Leslie concluded with considerable insight, 'I think I may say that until you are in charge of a provisional government, Irish America will prove intractable to all except German agents.'[46]

American entry into the war on 6 April 1917 altered the situation once again. The public linkage of Irish and German groups and pro-German activity was stopped and public hostility towards the Allies was no longer tolerated. The proposition of resolving the Irish question in order to build closer Anglo-American relations to facilitate winning the war had a fresh appeal. President Woodrow Wilson certainly made it known to the British government that an Irish settlement would ease domestic resistance to the war within the Irish-American community.[47] Shane Leslie saw a fresh opportunity even before war was declared. He wrote Redmond on 15 March, 'The moderates certainly have a game to play if the pieces on the board can be reached.'[48] To some extent, the Irish Convention was the British response, a constitutional convention bringing together most of the Irish stakeholders. If successful, this would be one of the biggest pieces. Another piece was the UILA itself. There had not been a national meeting since 1913, but Michael J. Ryan convened an executive committee meeting in Washington, DC, on 3 May. Redmond wrote to the committee that Ireland was at a critical point. Sinn Féin had revived after the Rising and seemed to have lots of money from the United States. Redmond feared that a general election was likely to be called, and although he thought 'we have the overwhelming mass of people with us,' the Irish Party would need funds to fight Sinn Féin. If successful at the polls, he said, 'The battle for Home Rule is practically won, as now all parties in England are anxious for a settlement, and a settlement on broad, generous terms.'[49] Michael J. Jordan reported to Redmond that the meeting drew executive committee members from all over the country and was a great success. Harmony prevailed and it was agreed, 'the organization was determined to continue the fight [for Home Rule] to the end.' Jordan noted that the feeling around Washington was that Home Rule needed to be settled in order to get on with the war and he learned on good authority that President Wilson 'is straining every nerve to see that the Home Rule Bill goes into effect'.[50] Leslie wrote a similar letter describing the meeting and the atmosphere in Washington. He thought there had been a real revival of hope and that feelings towards Redmond himself had improved. However, the League returned to the inactivity that had characterised the organisation since 1914. Leslie also warned that the Irish-American community was at a very delicate place: 'In their present temper it would be extremely dangerous to disappoint even our moderate friends in their hope.'[51] It was another shrewd insight and a quiet alarm bell.

During the summer of 1917 the Allied powers sent mission after mission to Washington to try to construct an integrated relationship with the United States in the midst of a war, now two and a half years on. A group of distinguished Irish

Americans led by John Quinn met with A. J. Balfour, then British foreign secretary, on 4 May and discussed the Irish situation, although UILA leaders were not among them. They emphasised that the Irish Parliamentary Party had 'lost its influence here because of the repeated postponements and evasions of the Home Rule question', and they stressed that extending Home Rule to Ireland would strengthen the war effort.[52] Redmond, now engrossed in the Irish Convention, was also anxious about the financial position of his party after no funds had been raised in the United States since 1914. In May he had appealed to the national executive committee of the UILA, but he was also told that an Irish mission to the United States could revive support for Home Rule and also raise money for the Irish Party. In June 1917 T. P. O'Connor, the old Irish Party stalwart, and Richard Hazleton, a younger MP from Co. Louth, arrived to begin a tour of the United States. Things started well with a meeting at the White House with President Wilson and other meetings were arranged with American political leaders, prominent Irish Americans, and members of the Catholic hierarchy. However, it proved impossible to arrange large public meetings. The hostility of the rank and file Irish Americans was too great. O'Connor recalled, 'I wasn't two minutes in the hotel before I found, through the Irish servants, that I was living in an atmosphere of violent anti-British hatred which was extended to me.' Even the memorial service for William Redmond, John Redmond's younger brother and an Irish Party MP, killed in battle at the front, was interrupted by 'Sinn Féin' hecklers.[53] O'Connor confessed in a letter to John Dillon that the UILA had disintegrated. 'There is no organization,' he wrote, 'probably it has ceased to exist.'[54]

O'Connor and Hazleton may have raised as much as $73,500,[55] but they had travelled extensively along the East Coast and the upper Midwest for about a year soliciting funds, increasingly from among O'Connor's non-Irish friends. As for the implementation of Home Rule, a very solemn Cardinal Gibbons told O'Connor that 'since Ireland has not received, in this crisis of the English Government [the war and US support], the Home Rule which she has been contending for, she has practically no hope in the future.'[56] Hazleton reported to Redmond that efforts to enlist support from Irish Americans and to raise money were not going well. The 'Sinn Féiners' were simply putting Irish matters aside until they could openly support a republic after the war, while the moderate Irish Americans were now focused on 'Americanism' and winning the war. Writing privately to Shane Leslie in late 1917 he was more pessimistic. If the Irish Convention agreed on a settlement everything would work out, but if 'the Convention fails, there is no longer any room for our party here or in Ireland'. It all depends, Hazleton concluded, on whether Britain 'is willing to deliver the goods'.[57] Leslie became increasingly pessimistic also. He had run into the intransigent hostility of the Irish-American communities while trying to arrange public meetings for O'Connor and Hazleton, and had to accept his failed weekly journal, *Ireland*; he concluded by 1917 that 'it is too late to retrieve the Irish Party.'[58]

The end of this story in 1918 is well known. John Redmond died, the Irish Convention failed to agree on an acceptable constitution for Ireland, the British government attempted to impose conscription on Ireland, bringing the Irish Parliamentary Party members home from Westminster and linking them with the resurgent Sinn Féin party. The First World War ended in November and in the general election of December 1918, the Irish Parliamentary Party was virtually swept from the field, with Sinn Féin winning 73 seats and reducing the once dominant Irish Party to six. In the United States it is clear the UILA was moribund by the end of 1917.[59] It is interesting to speculate about what might have happened if the Home Rule Bill had been put into operation – in 1914 or 1916 or 1917 or even 1919. Would the very modest form of self-government encompassed in the Home Rule Bill have satisfied the mass of the Irish people? Would the earth-shaking transformations brought about by the world war – the collapse of empires and the emergence of new states – have drawn the Irish people to demand greater sovereignty? Certainly the failure to put the Home Rule Bill into operation served as a standing rebuke to Redmond, the Irish Parliamentary Party, and the United Irish League, and discredited the whole mode of trying to work within the British constitutional system. The world war also gave currency to the ideas of 'self-determination' and 'the rights of small nations', as they were being worked out in Central Europe at that very time.

Certainly by 1919 the failure of the constitutional system seemed to offer no credible alternative to defiance, rebellion, and complete independence.[60] And certainly in the United States, earlier than in Ireland itself, can be seen the anxiety, the disillusionment, the defection that led to the collapse of support for the Home Rule movement. As with the 'widening gyre' of Yeats's 'Second Coming', for the Irish Parliamentary Party and the UILA, things fell apart. The centre did not hold.

## "Help the Men in the Gap."

Address of

# Hon. Michael J. Ryan,

### Philadelphia.

With the Compliments of the

## United Irish League of America

*John O'Callaghan*
SEC'Y.

ROOM 32, GLOBE BUILDING
BOSTON.

In the

Grand Opera House, Brooklyn, N. Y.

March 4, 1906.

# CHAPTER THREE

# TOM CLARKE'S NEW YORK
## A REFUGE (1880) AND A HOME (1899–1907)

### *Gerard MacAtasney*

New York was clearly a critical location for Irish nationalism in the early twentieth century, second only to Dublin. It is a place that can be seen as an incubator for individuals, organisations and modes of communication that had the potential to reach audiences as close as Queens and as far as Queensland. New York shaped key figures who would play not insignificant roles in the events of 1916 and the preceding years. One of these was a man called Thomas J. Clarke who spent two periods of his life there. Insights into Clarke's American connections are important in underscoring how transatlantic links were forged and maintained over time and how these crucial points of contact could shape events in Ireland. In 1880 Clarke arrived as a young man with fellow members of the Irish Republican Brotherhood (IRB) in order to evade arrest in Ireland. After spending almost 16 years in prison he returned in 1899 in an attempt to find employment. Both of these experiences were to have a significant impact and the connections he made in the United States would shape his own destiny in significant ways.

Thomas James Clarke was born on 11 March 1857, the eldest child of four born to James and Mary Clarke (née Palmer). His place of birth has been questioned in recent scholarship and it has been contended that he was born out of wedlock in Co. Tipperary.[1] But at least one source indicates that Clarke himself believed he was of the diaspora in that he was born in an 'English garrison town' and later his son would list the Isle of

Wight as his father's place of birth.[2] A mixed marriage, James was a Protestant from Co. Leitrim, while Mary Palmer was from Co. Tipperary. As a teenager James had joined the British army and went on to serve in the Crimean War (1853–6).[3]

In April 1859 James was drafted to South Africa, where the Clarkes lived for more than five years, until they returned to Ireland in 1865.[4] On their return, the Clarkes eventually ended up in residence in Dungannon near to St Patrick's Catholic Church.[5] Tom attended the local St Patrick's National School and became a monitor (assistant teacher) until the school closed in 1880 as a consequence of a declining roll.[6] In school he evinced a great interest in Irish history in spite of the fact that his father tried to discourage him by maintaining that Ireland could never become independent due to the power of the British Empire.[7] His interest was further stirred by the arrival of John Daly of Limerick, a veteran of the 1867 Fenian Rising. Daly had led an unsuccessful attack on a police barracks in Kilmallock, Co. Limerick, and in the aftermath had been forced to flee, first to England and then to the United States. He returned to Ireland in 1869 and eventually worked as a full-time organiser for the IRB.[8] It was in this role that Daly addressed a meeting at which Clarke was present in 1878. It seems that this event proved pivotal in influencing individuals such as Clarke and local men Billy Kelly and Louis McMullen in believing that insurrection was the only viable means of achieving Irish independence.[9] Meeting John Daly would have a profound impact on Clarke's life politically and personally.

Both Clarke and his closest friend, Kelly, were also members of a local dramatic club and in 1880 they travelled with an excursion organised by the club to Dublin. While there they were introduced to Michael Davitt by John Daly and according to Kelly part of their discussion centred on the possibility of organising an IRB circle in Dungannon. A short time afterwards the circle was formed in the town and Tom Clarke was appointed as the centre, in charge of 23 men.[10] Daly again visited Dungannon to address the members, focusing on 'the intensive organization of the IRB with the object of taking military action against the RIC – the drilling, training and arming of the members of our organization for that objective'.[11]

Like most towns in the north of Ireland Dungannon suffered from sectarian animosity and on 15 August 1880, it was the scene of a 'dreadful and fatal conflict between the authorities and the people'.[12] Known as Lady Day, on this occasion parade participants were attacked by a crowd of Protestants. A riot ensued in which stones were thrown at the police, who read the Riot Act and opened fire on the crowd with live ammunition. One man died and a further 27 were injured, including Billy Kelly's brother, Patrick. Only one casualty was reported on the side of the police.[13]

What was not recorded in the press, however, was that on the night following the riots the IRB, including Clarke and Kelly, ambushed 11 RIC men. Kelly recalled how 'we opened fire on the police and they escaped into a public house. Reinforcements of police arrived on the scene and we had to retreat.'[14] A couple of weeks later, on 29 August, with the authorities continuing to search for them, Clarke, Kelly, and a few others left Dungannon and boarded a ship for the United States. Clarke's decision probably had more to do with these recent events rather than his recent unemployed status. Prior to leaving, the group obtained a transfer from the Dungannon circle of the IRB to Camp No. 1 in New York.[15]

The party arrived in New York in October 1880 and immediately made its way to the house of Tyrone Clan na Gael member Patrick O'Connor. Shortly after admission to that organisation Clarke was appointed as its recording secretary and found employment in a shoe shop and in the spring of the following year both Clarke and Kelly went to work in the Mansion House Hotel in Brooklyn, Kelly as a boiler man and Clarke as a night porter.[16] That summer they joined the Napper Tandy Club run by Dr Thomas Gallagher. According to Kelly, 'the purpose of this club was the instruction of its members in the use of explosives.'[17] Soon after joining Kelly had to move to Garden City, New York where his employer had opened a new hotel, but he maintained contact with Clarke who told him 'of the continuation of his lessons on explosives under Gallagher'.[18] Part of these lessons included trips to Staten Island to experiment on rocks with nitroglycerine. In effect these experiments were the prelude to a Clan na Gael bombing campaign in England and by his participation Tom ensured his life would change irrevocably.

Early in 1883, Clarke seemed destined for a successful career in the hotel industry as he was due to take up a new post as manager of the Brighton Beach Hotel. This represented a significant improvement in fortunes from his previous employment as a night porter, but the plans of the Clan leaders were put into action soon afterwards and he never attained the position. In March, Timothy O'Riordan, secretary of Clan na Gael's Camp No. 1, ordered him to prepare for a highly secret mission.[19] Under instructions from O'Riordan, Clarke travelled to Liverpool under the assumed identity of Henry Hammond Wilson, purporting to be an Englishman who was simply returning home.[20]

In England Clarke worked mainly alongside Thomas Gallagher and Alfred Whitehead in the procurement and manufacture of explosives. He rented a room on the third floor at 17 Nelson Square, Blackfriars Road, London, on Saturday, 31 March 1883, informing his landlady that he was staying there as he was studying 'for the medical' and had a tutor at Charing Cross.[21] However, the police had been closely following the movements of the men and on 5 April Clarke, together with Gallagher, was arrested at his lodgings. Although he had no incriminating documents in his possession, his portmanteau was found to contain an India-rubber stocking full of a liquid stated to be a dangerous explosive.[22]

Clarke, still maintaining the pseudonym Henry Hammond Wilson, appeared at the Central Criminal Court, Old Bailey, London, on 28 May 1883, with his co-accused. The men were charged with levying war, conspiring to 'destroy and damage by nitro-glycerine and other explosive substances', and conspiracy to murder, and were tried under the Treason-Felony Act of 1848. All the prisoners pleaded 'not guilty'. Clarke's defence was that he had not actually committed any such acts as those alleged, that commission of no such overt acts was proven against him, and that intention to commit a crime did not in itself constitute a crime.[23]

The main prosecution witness was a former member of Clan na Gael, Joseph William Lynch, who on being arrested had turned state's evidence. Before the trial ended both Whitehead and William Ansburgh made statements of innocence to the jury but Clarke simply remarked that he would let his case 'go to the jury as it stands'.[24] The jury, after deliberating for slightly more than one hour, acquitted Ansburgh and Bernard Gallagher but found Thomas Gallager, Whitehead, John Curtin, and Wilson 'guilty'. The judge then sentenced these four men to penal servitude for life.[25]

After enduring 15 years of physical and mental torture in the English prison system, Clarke was released in September 1898 and soon returned to Ireland.[26] He spent some time recuperating with his mother and sister in Dublin and then travelled to Dungannon with James Egan and John Daly, where they were met by a deputation from the local Amnesty Association. An address of welcome was read by a member of the Irish National Foresters offering Clarke congratulations on his 'survival and deliverance from a living tomb after undergoing nearly 16 years' imprisonment for a crime of which we still believe and know you were not guilty'.[27] Some months later, in March 1899, Clarke travelled to Limerick and was bestowed with the Freedom of the City at the behest of the city's mayor, John Daly.[28]

What Clarke needed most critically was employment and in May 1899 the Amnesty Association sent an application in his name for the vacant post of clerk of the Rathdown Poor Law Union. The Amnesty Association saw part of its remit to secure jobs for former political prisoners. They maintained that Clarke was 'not a dynamitard' based on the fact that he had been tried under the Treason-Felony statute and was therefore 'de jure a Political Prisoner'. In addition, they argued that he had been sentenced as a result of 'perjured evidence.'[29] Indeed Clarke's candidature was supported by a wide variety of colleagues and public representatives. Cordier Marmion, a Dungannon-based justice of the peace, recommended him 'with confidence' while John Redmond, MP, in stating that he had had 'many opportunities' to judge his 'character and abilities' during the 'distressing period' of his imprisonment, revealed how he subsequently formed for Clarke 'feelings of the greatest respect and goodwill'. Another parliamentarian, John Dillon, told Clarke he would make a 'thoroughly competent official' and expressed the hope that 'it will be recognized by any Irish Board controlled by Nationalists that your claim to their consideration is stronger than any other who is likely to come before them.'[30] These testimonials proved to be in vain as the post was subsequently allocated to another candidate.

With little prospect of a job in Ireland Clarke wrote to Devoy in New York to ask him to organise a lecture tour. In this he was hoping to emulate the success of John Daly who on his release had travelled across the Atlantic. Due to the efforts of Devoy, Daly enjoyed a lucrative lecture tour during which he had outlined his experiences in prison, furnishing him with enough money to start a bakery business in Limerick.[31] Clarke hoped for a similar response from the American side but he was to be grievously disappointed as Devoy refused to help him. While Clarke was deflated by the news, Daly was incensed, remarking, 'It's about as cold-blooded an epistle as ever I read, but keep it to yourself for the present. All I can, or will say now Tom, is never say die. We lived through a bloody sight worse than the cold indifference of Mr Devoy and his friends.'[32]

From a modern perspective it is difficult to understand why Devoy should have refused a man who had just served almost half his life behind prison bars. The presumption is that Clarke would have been lauded by Fenians throughout the world and had all his financial needs met but it is important to examine the refusal in context. Almost from the time of his incarceration Daly had been a cause célèbre in Irish political circles and had a pedigree that included involvement in the last rebellion in the country in 1867. Further to this he had been arrested in 1876 after a Home Rule meeting in support of Isaac Butt.[33] In 1895, while still in prison and running as a Parnellite candidate, he was elected unopposed as MP for Limerick. When members of the Irish Parliamentary Party complained in the British House of Commons of maltreatment of Irish prisoners, they invariably focused on the case of Daly.[34] Hence, when he was released he was regarded as a hero by those in Fenian circles.

By contrast, Tom Clarke was just one of 21 Irish prisoners who languished in Chatham and Portland prisons in the 1880s and 1890s. Demands for his release did not become significant until the mid-1890s when most of the other prisoners had secured freedom. He had entered prison as a relatively young man and would have been regarded by those in the IRB and Clan na Gael as just another 'foot soldier'. In other words, Tom Clarke meant much less to Devoy than did John Daly and while the latter may have vouched for him, this seems to have made little impact on the old Fenian. Nonetheless, while he faced difficulty in trying to obtain a job, another aspect of his life was bringing him much happiness. In Louis Le Roux's rather hagiographical account (1936) he states that 'even before she met him, Kathleen Daly [John's niece] … had regarded Tom with romantic admiration.'[35] The reality was revealed by Kathleen in her memoirs some years later when she remembered how, initially, 'I was keenly disappointed. His appearance gave no indication of the kingly, heroic qualities which Uncle John had told us about; there was none of the conquering hero which I had visioned. He was emaciated and stooped from the long imprisonment and hardship.'[36]

During his stay in Daly's home, when he was being awarded the Freedom of Limerick, she acknowledged that 'his appearance receded into the background and the man Uncle John had portrayed was revealed.'[37] Several times each year the Dalys rented a holiday lodge in Kilkee, Co. Clare and in the summer of 1899 Clarke spent a month with the family. It was during this period that Kathleen and he became romantically involved and got engaged.[38] The match did not meet with the approval of her family, mainly due to the fact that he remained unemployed. Thus, as he had also done in 1880, he made the decision to emigrate to the United States. The hope was that once he obtained steady employment, Kathleen would follow. Acquaintances noted that Clarke was so disenchanted with his life at this point that he seriously contemplated going to fight with the Boers during the Anglo-Boer war in South Africa.[39] Yet, he determined instead to attempt to carve out a new life for himself in the United States and so in early October 1899 he sailed across the Atlantic with his sister Maria. Before he left, Kathleen was depressed, telling him 'I hate to think of you going to the United States, it seems so far away.'[40]

On arrival in New York Tom and Maria rented an apartment on 109 West 94th Street and he soon secured employment as a pattern-maker in the Cameron Pump Works on East 23rd Street at a wage of $15 a week. In the evenings he worked as a night clerk at the Clan na Gael headquarters for a further $15 a week.[41] To enable him to be closer to his work they soon moved to 363 West 36th Street, an apartment which he described as 'more compact and homelike'.[42] During his employment at the pump works he harboured hopes that in the future he would be able to establish his own business. He was very aware of various factions amongst the Irish organisations in the city. In relation to establishing a business he commented that 'this scheme will take a couple of months to work up and I see I have to calculate upon a certain amount of hostility on the quiet from "<u>Friends</u>" who are not satisfied unless I become a "party man" and allow myself to be made a tool of by such "friends".'[43]

Nonetheless, Clarke immersed himself in the activities of various Irish groups. In February 1900 the Tyrone Ladies Association of New York presented him with a life-sized bust of himself as he appeared prior to imprisonment.[44] He became an officer in the Tyrone Men's Association which then appointed him as a delegate to the New York United Irish Societies' Committee.[45] He also attended social events organised by the Irish Volunteers and the Brooklyn branch of Clan na Gael, informing Kathleen,

> I attend meetings in various parts of New York and Brooklyn almost every night and address those present. It rouses the greatest enthusiasm amongst the great majority of them and this is being felt by the folks who are blocking the way to anything being done that would be accepted by me – for some folks here would like to see me stranded so that they could step in and assist me on conditions of owning my soul and making a tool of me – but they'll never succeed in that.[46]

Eventually, after a delay of seven months, Kathleen travelled to New York in July 1901 where she was met by Tom. Together at last, they were immediately married on 16 July in St Augustine's Catholic Church, on Franklin Avenue between 168th and 169th Streets in the Morrisania section of the Bronx. A witness to the marriage ceremony was Major John MacBride who had been in the United States since the prior February on a speaking tour with Maude Gonne.[47] The Clarkes settled in at 175 Russell Street, Greenpoint, Brooklyn, and Tom was elected president of the local Clan na Gael club where he heavily promoted Irish music, language, and dancing.[48] Kathleen later recalled his efforts:

> He published a journal under the auspices of the Celtic Club called *The Clansman*, and it was a real propagandist Irish-Ireland publication. One article he wrote for it that I remember was on the Irish language, in which he said that a free Ireland without its language was inconceivable, and that the Gaelic League was doing invaluable work for Ireland in reviving the language, and deserved the support of every Irish man and woman.[49]

For the 1905 issue Clarke asked John Daly to write a special piece for the journal. 'When the time comes for the men at home to strike,' Daly concluded his essay on the current state of Ireland, 'they will not be found wanting in fidelity to the old cause, and I hope the Irish beyond the seas will lend them no small assistance.'[50] The remark was prophetic given the support of the Irish in the United States in the ensuing years.

Clarke was an eager participant in the activities of the Brooklyn Gaelic Society where, as a member of the lectures committee, he helped arrange talks for members on a variety of topics relevant to Irish culture. On the rare occasions during which he was able to relax he liked to go camping and fishing with fellow Clan na Gael member and future editor of *The Gaelic American,* James Reidy, at City Island on Pelham Bay.[51] In 1902 Kathleen gave birth to their first son, Daly, named after her uncle John.[52] A short time later Tom lost his job at the Cameron Pump Works and was reduced to his earnings of $15 a week with the Clan. To supplement this meager income Kathleen, aided by her family in Limerick, bought an ice cream and sweet shop in Greenpoint while Tom applied to become a road sweeper with the New York City Cleansing Department, but was refused.[53] His main duties at Clan headquarters were to act as private secretary to Devoy and it appears that, despite the latter's previously unhelpful attitude, he had developed a good relationship with the veteran IRB man. Devoy, as Terry Golway's chapter in this volume has suggested, was a notoriously prickly individual but his respect for Clarke was reflected in the fact that he asked him to oversee the establishment of a journal that would represent the voice of the IRB. Given his financial difficulties this was a major opportunity and in September 1903 *The Gaelic American* was launched with Devoy as editor and Tom as his assistant.[54]

Clarke's immersion in Clan activities is highlighted by his membership of its military wing, the Irish Volunteers, and on 1 January 1906, he was appointed to the rank of regimental adjutant in the Second Infantry.[55] His respect for previous generations who had risen in arms against British rule in Ireland was reflected in a couple of his own initiatives. For example, in seeking to revitalise an inactive IRB veterans' association in New York, he instigated a search for the graves of Fenians in the city. When approximately 40 previously forgotten and neglected sites had been located he ensured they were looked after by the veterans. Thus, on the annual Decoration Day, they laid wreaths on each grave.[56] Another commemoration introduced by Clarke was the yearly pilgrimage to the grave of Matilda Tone (wife of Wolfe Tone) at Brooklyn's Green-Wood Cemetery, held as close as possible to the pilgrimage in Ireland to the grave of her husband at Bodenstown.[57]

From 1903 onwards the Clarkes lived at 1551 Fulton Street, Brooklyn, but it appears that around this period Kathleen began to suffer regular bouts of ill-health and soon their young son was diagnosed with diphtheria, necessitating a six-week period of quarantine for mother and child. In August 1905, after the near-death of Daly, Kathleen and her young son travelled to spend a few months with her family in Limerick.[58] While his wife and child were recuperating in Ireland Clarke received the news that he had become an American citizen.[59] But within a few months of returning to the United States Kathleen's health again faltered and she was advised by a doctor to permanently move to the country. In the spring of the following year the Clarkes bought a small market garden farm in Manorville, Long Island, about 70 miles east of New York City. This purchase was only made possible by the support of the Daly family in Limerick and with the move Tom was forced to resign his position at *The Gaelic American*.[60] In her memoirs Kathleen commented how she 'loved the land and growing things and the joy of being together all the time'.[61]

And yet Kathleen claimed that shortly afterwards 'Tom was hinting that he would like to go back to Ireland and get things moving.'[62] Despite her initial opposition she eventually relented and the family decided to return home. This explanation seems plausible enough given that Clarke may have been influenced by his experience of a young breed of Irish republicanism while in New York. In 1905 the Dungannon Clubs of Belfast had been established by Denis McCullough and the Lisburn Quaker, Bulmer Hobson. This group sought to articulate an argument in favour of the total separation of Ireland and Britain and eschewed any notion of participation in parliamentary politics. The activities of this nascent republican grouping were covered in great detail by *The Gaelic American* through the reports of their Irish correspondent, Patrick McCartan, from Carrickmore in Co. Tyrone. McCartan was on very friendly terms with leading Clan na Gael members such as fellow Carrickmore man Joseph McGarrity, who in turn was close to Devoy. Indeed, *The Gaelic American* emerges as a vital source for early twentieth-century republicanism as the activities of the Dungannon Clubs, the National Council, and others were largely ignored by the domestic Irish press. For example, it was *The Gaelic American* that first printed a speech by Seán Mac Diarmada given in Newry in 1907.[63]

These developments made an impact on Clan leaders, so much so that in 1907 Bulmer Hobson undertook a lecture tour of the United States organised by Clarke. Over a number of weeks Hobson spoke to huge gatherings in various American cities.[64] Hobson was an accomplished speaker and Clarke could not have failed to have been impressed by him. For Clarke and others, Hobson was representative of a new, vibrant Fenianism and there is no doubt that this experience made an impact on him.

The Clarkes returned to Ireland in November 1907. Their return was noted by the British authorities who reported the arrival of Thomas J. Clarke, 'ex-convict and dynamiter'.[65] The family stayed in Limerick for a few weeks but within days Tom had travelled to Dublin to meet with leading republicans such as P. T. Daly, Major MacBride, Fred Allen, Jack O'Hanlon, and James Egan.[66] The haste with which

Clarke sought out fellow republicans would appear to support the contention that he returned to Ireland for political reasons. And yet he had not ruled out the possibility of returning to the United States, writing to James Reidy in December:

> I have made up my mind to stay on this side if I can possibly do so; in any case I would not think of returning till middle of summer as Katty tells me there will be a visit from the stork in March – so there you are – there's what living the simple life – 'close to nature' – brings on a fellow.[67]

Many years after these events, Kathleen attempted to portray the family's return as one motivated solely by political considerations, in order to elevate the post-Rising status of her husband. She was adamant until the day she died that her husband, and not Padraig Pearse, would have been president of any future republic, maintaining that Pearse was 'very ambitious and as vain as a peacock'.[68] Portraying a situation in which she reluctantly returned home in order to allow Tom to focus on work for a rebellion would only have assisted in enhancing such a belief.

The reality was somewhat different, however, and it is likely that two key factors must have heavily influenced the decision to return to Ireland. As has been noted, Kathleen Clarke regularly suffered from ill-health but she was also very close to her family and this may well have played a part in any decision. But the major factor was the family's inability to attain a sustainable livelihood in the United States. Although Kathleen claimed to have loved her life on the farm, there is little doubt that for someone like Clarke, with no experience of rural life and suffering from a heart condition, it would have proven difficult to make a viable commercial undertaking on the land. Although nothing was directly said about the latter Kathleen gave a glimpse of a possible financial motive when writing to Tom about his efforts to find a suitable site for a shop in Dublin, asking, 'Have you told her [Hannah] anything about our reason for coming home, how we are fixed at present or anything concerning us other than the fact that you wish to get into business?'[69]

Strong evidence of financial difficulty was revealed in another letter from Kathleen when she enquired, 'did you ever write to Jones about the Long Island lots … It always strikes me as queer how we were talked out of them and our money.'[70] Indeed, Clarke himself lamented that they had arrived home with 'a load of debt that has to be cleared off'.[71] Long after returning home Clarke was engaged in regular correspondence with both John Daly and James Reidy about the American properties. Although the maintenance of them had been entrusted to Reidy who ensured that they were let, Clarke was keen to sell both in order to ensure that John Daly obtained something for his outlay. In April 1909 he enquired of Reidy whether it would be possible to sell either property and commented that 'if so by all means go ahead – using your own judgement whether to do so by direct advertising or through a real estate agent'.[72] A challenge was that Clarke had purchased both farms at the height of a property boom and with the market now in the doldrums there was little to do but hope they could be rented until economic conditions improved. Two years later Clarke revealed to John Daly Reidy's belief that 'it was a mistake buying so far away from the city' and pointed out that Reidy had made a substantial profit on properties bought in the suburbs of Brooklyn 'while Maple farm and Calverton would be doing well if they'd bring their own and expense'.[73]

In later years Kathleen confided to family members that they had indeed been forced to return due to lack of money. While in the United States they had been financially supported by the Daly family. Although the money was always believed to have come from John Daly, it was his niece Madge who ran a very successful bakery business in Limerick and it was this money that enabled her sister Kathleen to purchase the sweet shop in New York. Similarly, the farms on Long Island were bought by the Dalys and while initially registered in the name of Tom Clarke, they were almost immediately transferred to that of John Daly.[74] Madge Daly had offered to set up her sister and brother-in-law in business if they returned to Ireland. While his business occupied much of his time Clarke made sure to involve himself in political affairs; the advice and experience he could impart proved invaluable to the rising generation he had first witnessed in New York.

After living for eight years in the United States it is likely that Tom Clarke departed for home with mixed emotions. New York was the city that had offered him a livelihood when Ireland would not and it was there that he was married and had started a family. Yet, despite his best efforts and those of his in-laws, he continued to struggle financially throughout his time there. In addition, his young wife did not appear to adapt to the American climate and regularly suffered bouts of illness. Aside from these personal issues the main problem he encountered was the division amongst the various republican groupings in the United States and the apparent lack of sincerity amongst them. This was highlighted in his comments to John Daly when he remarked:

> Jack old man I won't trust myself to tell you how I feel for the way you have helped me in this matter. God knows there does be a great lump rise in my throat when I compare your *friendship* with the thing that goes by that name among mostly all of my acquaintances in the United States.[75]

The fact that this comment was made only months before he returned to Ireland demonstrates that Clarke's experience did not improve throughout his time in the United States. What appears to have particularly perturbed him was the fact that while much was being said, little was being done. In one letter he complained:

> Things here are *not* satisfactory – by no means. I am sick of a good deal of what I see. The demoralization has taken place here as on your side. Here we are 'getting ready' – making preparations, when we should be acting. But where's the good. A fellow can do nothing but keep on churning his wrath.[76]

This latter observation reinforced the impression that Clarke was a man of action. It was written just over a year after he had emerged from almost 16 years of harsh imprisonment and been snubbed by Devoy. Yet he remained wedded to the republican philosophy of revolutionary violence as the only means of removing British rule from Ireland. In January 1909 he had been home for slightly more than a year and his experience of Irish republicans was in marked contrast to that of their American counterparts. In a letter to James Reidy he rejoiced that

> There is a splendid set of young fellows – earnest, able and energetic – around Dublin, with whom it is a pleasure to work, fellows who believe in *doing* things, not in gabbing about them only. I'm in great heart with this young, *thinking* generation. They are men; they'll give a good account of themselves.[77]

These 'young fellows' included Bulmer Hobson, Denis McCullough, Pat McCartan, and of course his protégé, Seán Mac Diarmada. Their words and actions made the reports he had edited for *The Gaelic American* come alive while at the same time Clarke's return gave this group a figurehead around which to rally. His continued importance in IRB and Clan circles was emphasised by the arrival in Ireland in October 1910 of James Reidy, James Mark Sullivan, and John J. Teevans, all of whom were described by the authorities as 'well-known members' of Clan na Gael. This party stayed with John Daly in Limerick and their visit may well have been in connection with the launch of a new IRB-backed newspaper – *Irish Freedom* – that same month.[78] Having worked with Devoy on *The Gaelic American* Clarke would have been very aware of the necessity of such a journal to propagate the republican message.

The summer of 1911 saw further visits by prominent American Clan members. McGarrity spent six weeks in July and August honeymooning and visiting, amongst others, John Daly, Bulmer Hobson, John MacBride, Seán Mac Diarmada, and Clarke.[79] During this visit McGarrity was so impressed by what he saw of Countess Markievicz and the boys of the Fianna that he offered to underwrite the rental of the hall in which they drilled. A gesture of this nature was emblematic of McGarrity,[80] who is profiled later in this volume. His close friendship with fellow-Carrickmore man Pat McCartan, allied to his financial support, had proved crucial to the initial success of the Dungannon Clubs. Although the authorities kept a close watch on him they were unable to ascertain the precise purpose of his trip; the Dublin Metropolitan Police could only surmise that he had 'some secret mission and was combining business with pleasure'.[81] Significantly, they had no doubt that 'the reports of appointments of IRB officials in certain Ulster counties synchronize with the visit of McGarrity.'[82]

Some weeks later, in September and October, similar journeys were undertaken by leading Irish Americans Judge Daniel Cohalan (an increasingly influential figure in the Clan and confidant to Devoy, as Michael Doorley's chapter in this volume will outline) and Reverend Denis O'Sullivan, the latter 'believed to be on a mission for the Clan na Gael of some importance'.[83] In addition, a hurling team representing the United States played matches in Cork, Limerick, Thurles, and Waterford. This in itself was a reflection of the success of the policy adopted some years earlier by the IRB of infiltrating all cultural and sporting organisations – in this case the Gaelic Athletic Association (GAA). Some of these individuals had been to Ireland before and it is evident that Clarke's presence in the country was the catalyst for their making the effort to cross the Atlantic. Thus, while Clarke may have left the United States, the Americans did not leave him since they believed that he was central to any future revolutionary activities. For his part, Clarke realised the importance of his American comrades and throughout the critical period in the lead-up to 1916 he communicated regularly with them. This correspondence included news about the latest happenings in Ireland as well as his feelings about what was unfolding. For example, he told Devoy in June 1913:

> There will probably be a general election before the Home Rule Bill is placed on the Statute Book. Even suppose it passes, a general election must in the ordinary course take place soon after. If by any chance, and it is not unlikely, a Unionist Government comes into power they'll suspend its [Home Rule] operation. This is not so much my own opinion as that of most of the well-informed folk here with whom I am in contact.[84]

Informing him of the recent pilgrimage to Wolfe Tone's grave at Bodenstown, where the attendance numbered more than 5,000, he commented, 'I'm feeling ten years younger since Sunday. At last we see tangible results from the patient, plodding work of sowing the seed. The tide is running strongly in our direction. *We have the rising generation*.'[85] This sense of optimism was replicated in a subsequent letter to McGarrity a couple of weeks after the formation of the Irish Volunteers in November 1913:

Joe, it is worth living in Ireland these times – there is an awakening – the slow, silent, plodding and the open preaching is at last showing results, things are in full swing on the up grade – and we are breathing air that compels one to fling up his head and stand more erect … from the national point of view it is brighter than it has been in many a long year – certainly as far back as my memory goes.

Hundreds of young fellows who could not be interested in the National Movement, even on the milk and water side, are in these volunteers and are saying things which proves that the right spot has been touched in them by the volunteering. Wait till they get their fist clutching the steel barrel of a business rifle and then Irish instincts and Irish manhood can be relied upon … 'tis good to be in Ireland these times.[86]

Regular communication with Devoy was maintained throughout 1914 with Clarke addressing him as his 'uncle' in an attempt to confuse the authorities. On 14 May he reiterated the emotions inspired by the formation of the Volunteers:

And the change that has come over the young men of the country who are volunteering! Erect, Heads up in the air, the glint in the eye, and then the talent and ability that had been latent and is now being discovered! Young fellows who had been regarded as something like wastrels now changed to energetic soldiers and absorbed in the work, and taking pride that at last they feel they can do something for their country that will count. Tis good to be alive in Ireland these times.[87]

Of course the new movement was soon beset by competing interests both from within and without. Just before the split occasioned by John Redmond's assertion that they fight for Britain in the war in Europe, Clarke, rather optimistically as it transpired, attempted to reassure Devoy:

You have sized up the situation here correctly. The program that Redmond is working upon is just what you have mapped out, but he will fail and will be smashed. Day by day the situation has improved since the Provisional Committee's betrayal. That Betrayal was almost entirely due to Hobson and Mac Neill.

We are standing in the ranks of the Volunteers to a man – a splendid spirit. The cities and towns are quite safe and some whole counties and a great many country sections. This I know from first-hand information. Take it for granted *Redmond cannot control this movement.* Even now in spite of the decision of the Provisional Committee he no more controls the cities and towns than a man in Timbuctoo.[88]

When a couple of weeks later Volunteers successfully landed the arms at Howth, Clarke wasted no time in immediately sending a special cable to *The Gaelic American* stating, 'The authorities outwitted. Two thousand rifles landed at Howth yesterday. Slight skirmish returning to Dublin. Lost twenty rifles. Otherwise all well.'[89] Clan na Gael members throughout the United States were kept informed in great detail of the events in Ireland by the one man they knew they could trust implicitly. In later years Denis McCullough maintained that:

> Tom Clarke's reputation enabled the younger men, Seán Mac Diarmada, Bulmer Hobson, Diarmuid Lynch, P. S. O'Hegarty, etc, to move forward with his backing in organising, preaching and teaching the value and necessity of a physical force movement. It protected them from the usual charges of youthful over-enthusiasm and of insincerity. I say with every confidence that Tom Clarke's person and Seán Mac Diarmada's energy and organizing ability were the principal factors in creating and guiding events to make the Rising possible.[90]

For these younger men, Clarke's return to Ireland from a bastion of republican and Fenian ideals ensured the presence of what one historian has called 'the apostolic link with an earlier generation of Fenians'.[91] It is clear that the link between the Irish-based leaders, like Tom Clarke, with the American-based Clan na Gael is critical in understanding the planning of the Rising. Without spending eight years in New York and maintaining strong transatlantic relationships on his return to Ireland Clarke would not have sustained the respect and trust of figures such as Devoy and McGarrity. Their financial clout, political acumen and relative freedom of expression meant that they were vital cogs in the machine that produced the Rising. Central to every aspect of the organising and execution of it all was an American citizen, Thomas James Clarke.

# CHAPTER FOUR

# THE BOLD FENIAN WIFE
## MARY JANE O'DONOVAN ROSSA

*Judith E. Campbell*

The struggle for Irish independence was waged on both sides of the Atlantic Ocean in the nineteenth and early twentieth centuries. There were a number of people whose deeds regarding Ireland earned them celebrity status in the United States. Some of these patriots used their celebrity to continue the battle for the minds, hearts, and wallets of the growing population of Irish Americans. One of the foremost of these icons was Jeremiah O'Donovan Rossa, who became a transatlantic celebrity both honoured and ridiculed by the Irish, the British, and the American populations – sometimes all at once. His life reflected all that was destructive about the British and Irish relationship as well as all that was possible with the involvement of the diaspora in the United States. He is perhaps best known for his glorious funeral in 1915 that galvanised the strength and commitment of the Irish rebels preparing for what they hoped would be the final rebellion. Standing at the head of the mourners was his wife of more than 50 years, Mary Jane O'Donovan Rossa. Her story is one of courage, fortitude, passion and politics, as compelling as her husband's.

Mary Jane Irwin was born in Clonakilty, Co. Cork, in 1845.[1] The daughter of a Young Irelander and convent school educated, she was married at 19; prison widow at 20; mother at 21; and celebrated poet, lecturer, and fund-raiser in the United States at 23.[2] She understood how to use her own and her husband's celebrity to bring the quest for Irish freedom to audiences in the United States and was a key to keeping the Fenian flame alive before the 1916 rebellion. Her poetry and readings brought together both cultural and political nationalism at a time when unity of purpose was most important.

Rossa and Mary Jane created this celebrity by the power of the pen, public speaking, and the ingenious use of the growing strength of the press. Mary Jane was more than a partner in Rossa's life; she was the architect and the protector of his celebrity. The decision she made to bury Rossa at Glasnevin Cemetery was, she believed, 'the lesson of his life and would constantly appeal to the hearts of thousands of his loving countrymen and women prolonging after death his powers to circumvent and worry the English government in Ireland'.[3] She recognised the power of public events and dreamed Rossa's last act would honour his passion for a free Ireland.

Rossa was a well-known public figure during his lifetime. He had written one of the definitive prison diaries, *A Prison Life*, published in 1874 after being serialised in *The Irishman* in Dublin.[4] He also published the memoirs of his early years as a Fenian, *Rossa's Recollections*, in 1898, again serialised, this time in his own newspaper the *United Irishman*.[5] His experiences were widely reported by the press when he was elected to parliament while in prison in 1869, and again shortly after arriving in exile to the United States, when he ran for election against Boss Tweed in New York City in 1871.[6] However, he was best known for his life-long commitment to the violent overthrow of British control in Ireland.

Mary Jane became a celebrity in the United States during Rossa's time in prison. Americans already knew her as a founder in Ireland of the Ladies' Committee (called the Fenian Sisterhood in America) in 1865.[7] This group was known as the fund-raising arm of the Fenians but, according to John Devoy, they were, perhaps more importantly, 'the keepers of important secrets, traveling from point to point bearing important messages, and were the chief agents in keeping the organization alive in Ireland from ... early 1866 until the rising on March 5, 1867.'[8] Mary Jane resigned from the Ladies' Committee when she developed concerns about the distribution of funds that had been raised in the United States and soon after left for New York.[9] In 1867–8, she travelled throughout the United States giving lectures, reading poetry, and acting as a catalyst for keeping Rossa's imprisonment and the cause of Irish freedom in the minds and hearts of the people. Her events were a great propaganda success for the Fenian cause. Importantly, she also did very well financially, which was her major goal in going to the States, as evidenced by a notice stating she earned $1,125 from two readings in Chicago.[10] She was given more than money at some events; she received bracelets, necklaces, and even a gold nugget from some of her audiences.[11] She became a cherished celebrity as she worked her way across the continent, first north to Hartford, Providence, Brookline, Boston, Portland, Rochester, Montreal, and Quebec; and then west to Cleveland, Dayton, Chicago, Detroit, Peoria, Toronto, Louisville, Leavenworth, and Omaha; and south to Savannah, Atlanta, Augusta, New Orleans, Mobile, Memphis, and St Louis, stopping in many others towns along the way.[12] Her travel schedule was gruelling, as she appeared more than once in some of the cities. She kept a scrapbook of her reviews, which were invariably glowing, like the one from the *Argus* in Albany, New York, 10 October 1868:

> Mrs. Rossa is a genuine Irish lady, talented and cultivated, and one in whom every daughter of Ireland should enlist her interest … being deprived of her husband's support, Mrs. Rossa has sustained herself and her children by her literary labors. For this, if no other reason, she deserves to be encouraged and patronized; but aside from all this, she is endowed with intellect, beauty and accomplishments, qualifications that should induce the America public … those who love Ireland will admire Mrs. O'Donovan Rossa; and those who never saw Ireland, cannot fail to appreciate her beauty and highly cultivated talents.[13]

The American Fenian Brotherhood was in turmoil in 1868. John O'Mahony, the original organiser of Fenianism was criticised for inaction when no rebellion had been planned for in 1865. At that time, many Irish-American men had just been released from serving in the Civil War and were ready to fight the British. They believed this battle could be waged on their side of the Atlantic as well. O'Mahony helped to lead these impatient warriors in an ineffectual foray into Canada at Campobello Island in 1866. They believed Canada was Britain's vulnerable underbelly. But it failed miserably. William Randall Roberts, who led a subset of the organisation, proceeded to usurp power from O'Mahony and attempted to lead yet another foray into Canada in 1867, but no raid took place.[14] It left the organisation in shambles. It was not an auspicious time for the Fenians on either side of the Atlantic, and Mary Jane worked hard keeping good relationships with all the factions. Her letters to her father at the time include conversations about the plan to 'keep the good men of both sides as your friends'.[15] As Devoy later said: 'The Fenian organisation was hopelessly split during these years but both sections, bitterly hostile to each other, could meet in peace and harmony at her readings and remember for the moment that they had a common cause to serve.'[16] Roberts became very helpful to Mary Jane during her first year in New York. It was a time of particular financial difficulty for her, and she stayed in his family home on Bloomingdale Road in Manhattan. He also advised her to publish the poems she had been writing and sell them throughout the Irish-American community. He brought together some other wealthy Irish Americans who underwrote the $800 cost of publishing *Irish Lyrical Poems*.[17] The first advertisement for the book appeared in November 1867 and the book itself published in the winter of 1868. Selling at $1.25 a copy, it gave Mary Jane hope of some success.[18] She sent copies to all of the New York papers asking for a notice of sale to appear. George C. Halpine, the editor of the *New York Citizen* (also known by his fictional character, Miles O'Reilly), took great interest in Mary Jane and her work. He introduced her to Horace Greeley, the well-known writer, politician, and editor of the *New York Tribune*. Halpine and Greeley convinced Mary Jane that she should pursue a role as a professional public reader.[19] With their encouragement Mary Jane arranged to be tutored by the then famous Joseph E. Frobisher, who held classes in elocution at the College of the City of New York and the Cooper Union Free Academy.[20] A year later, Frobisher would describe her as the 'martyr poetess' who read and captivated her audiences. He was not surprised at her success for she had 'everything in [her] favor – health, strength, ambition, and youth and beauty'.[21] Her first professional reading, to a standing-room-only crowd, was held at the Cooper Institute on 16 June 1868. The description of the event appeared in newspapers well beyond New York City. *The Sun* called it a 'rich intellectual treat, a feast of the season, a flow of poetry and eloquence'. The article described Mary Jane's voice as 'full, clear, and somewhat nerved with a patriotic fervor; her accentuation is distinct, with a slight touch of that sweet Munster brogue which adds a peculiar grace to her readings … she is one of nature's gifted daughters, and will assuredly make her mark as a reader of poetry'.[22] Horace Greeley introduced Mary Jane to the audience and she read one of Miles O'Reilly's poems called 'The Green Flag'. O'Reilly himself did a reading, as did Professor Frobisher, and sitting on the platform showing her support was social reformer and feminist Susan B. Anthony.[23] Mary Jane had joined the world of achieving women.

Her goal to be friendly with all the various factions of the Irish Americans had been very insightful. It helped not only Mary Jane but also the organisations with their own fundraising and recruiting. Mary Jane attracted larger audiences and the organisations held meetings alongside her events. All the factions wanted to claim her as their own. She was so popular that during the national Irish Republican Convention held in Chicago in 1869 to support the political party of President Grant, one of the delegates proposed universal suffrage as a platform plank, with Mary Jane the example to justify why women should have the vote.[24] During a time when the common perception argued that Irish-American organisations were populated by the rabble of society and took advantage of the low-income populace by stealing their money for a desperate cause, those in 'respectable' positions attended Mary Jane's events. The 'Prison Widow', as she called herself, appealed not only to the factions within Fenianism but also to diverse social strata.[25] All of these audiences were met with 'a handsome lady of about five and twenty, with flashing black eyes and majestic figure, robed in black and green velvet', who had a lasting impact when she 'stood up, and, stretching her right hand aloft, declared in a rich contralto voice, that "Ireland shall be free!"'[26]

Later, when Rossa was released from jail and exiled to the United States, Mary Jane was seen as one of the catalysts of his release, along with the Amnesty movement in Ireland, Rossa's own efforts to publicise his mistreatment in prison, and Prime Minister Gladstone's continued struggle against his cabinet to find a way to calm Irish tensions. Much of the American press, however, gave the credit to Mary Jane. An article in the *Cleveland Daily Leader* called 'A wife worth having' was typical:

> Instead of folding her hands and waiting for charity to seek her … she began a course of readings throughout the states … The people everywhere received her warmly, as a heroic woman in misfortune is always received, and the funds she gathered were at once devoted to securing her husband's pardon and to the education of her children. Though pecuniarily successful, she could not buy her husband out of prison, but she did better, she created a public sentiment which not even British law could withstand.[27]

Five Fenians were released together on 7 January 1871: Rossa, Devoy, Henry Shaw Mulleda, John McClure, and Charles Underwood O'Connell. They were exiled from Ireland: 20 years for Rossa and John McClure, five years for Devoy, and four years for Charles O'Connell and Henry Mulleda.[28] They arrived in New York instant celebrities. When in the United States alone, Mary Jane was a frequent topic of press coverage; now, on the arrival of the *Cuba*, she was barely mentioned. If she was upset by the juxtaposition, there is no evidence of it in her writings. She was still the true Victorian woman who thought her role was in the background until reality forced her into the limelight.[29] In those first months she did appear at speaking events alongside her husband, occasionally reading a poem – particularly when the audience demanded her appearance.[30] Large crowds met the exiles. One of the first major events soon after their arrival was a parade reportedly attended by as many as 300,000 people in New York City. All the fanfare culminated in a trip to Washington and an event with the president: Mary Jane's second visit to Grant in three months.[31] The couple then took advantage of their welcome and went on tour to the West, earning enough to come back to New York to find a home.

But their life in New York was difficult. Between 1871 and 1877 Mary Jane had five more children. The first three, Kate, Frank, and Maurice, all died in infancy, while the next two, Sheela and Eileen, survived.[32] Also during those years, four of Rossa's five sons from his previous marriages had come to the United States; only Florence Stephens stayed in Ireland with his Buckley grandparents. Denis went to Chicago to work, Con was apprenticed as a machinist in Jersey City, and John graduated from New York University Law School in 1877.[33] John's graduation was a highlight that year, but sadness returned when another son from Rossa's first marriage, Jeremiah, died from consumption at the family home in Brooklyn on 23 December 1877, at the age of 20.[34]

Rossa's business career was also troubled and scattered, first as a salesman for Hibernia Insurance and then as a travel agent for Williams & Guion Black Star Lines.[35] Soon he tried wine and liquor sales, and later leased the Northern Hotel at Cortlandt and West Streets near South Ferry.[36] When the Northern Hotel did not succeed, he took over a hotel at 182 Chatham Street on Chatham Square on the Lower East Side.[37] The renamed O'Donovan Rossa hotel became the hub of Irish-American activity and the home of many other Irishmen such as Devoy, who lived at the hotel and was treated as a family member. When times were good the Rossas shared their good fortune not just with Devoy but with Mary Jane's sisters Amelia and Isabel Irwin, who joined the staff there as well.[38]

Notwithstanding his business shortcomings, Rossa became Irish America's celebrity. He gave speeches throughout the country and became the face of Irish nationalism as the founder of the 'Skirmishing Fund' and the 'Dynamite School'.[39] He wrote for multiple newspapers and gave frequent speeches making inflammatory statements consistently supporting rebellion in Ireland. He frequently said some outlandish things in Patrick Ford's *Irish World*, like answering the question 'what quantity of dynamite would be necessary to blow up the English garrison?'[40] But as the rest of the United States was outraged by his call to violence, Irish Americans loved him. Irish-American organisations, however, were never sure they could manage this very forthright voice. Even his close friend Devoy began to despair of Rossa's very public approach to what Devoy believed should be secret endeavours and publicly criticised him.[41]

Despite his boisterous behaviour, his personality was one of outer calm and he possessed a deeply religious attitude. Mary Jane and Rossa's Catholic faith remained a cornerstone to their life even though the church continued to censure their politics. Rossa was considered a good and loyal friend who met his neighbours with a smile and a nice word. For all his talk of violence, he was a man who never raised his voice in anger or used bad language to his children.[42] His relationship with his wife was one of love and devotion.[43] His family understood that his body and spirit were badly damaged by his years in prison, and his fervour for Irish freedom was the singular motivator in his life. Throughout these difficult years, Mary Jane was the solid base for the family. As Devoy would later say:

> During all the vicissitudes of his checkered life … his wife was his loyal companion and his best adviser, often restraining his more impetuous nature, but aiding and assisting him always and softening where she could the asperities of controversies and keeping for him a home that was ever pleasant and attractive. She preserved for him a circle of friends outside the controversies and clashes of Irish politics and was the center of a social circle of her own.[44]

But in addition to their celebrity the couple also lived with ridicule and stress. In late 1877 Rossa lost yet another business, the hotel on Chatham Square.[45] On a lecture tour in Toronto the following March he was injured in an anti-Irish riot and spent time in hospital.[46] He had a major falling-out with Devoy, who took over the Skirmishing Fund and claimed Rossa was mishandling donations. Devoy wrote that Rossa was drinking heavily and disclosing secret plans.[47] Rossa vehemently refuted the charges but the situation was so financially precarious that Mary Jane made arrangements to take her three children back to Ireland in August 1878. Interestingly, Michael Davitt accompanied Rossa to the pier to see Mary Jane and the children off. Davitt was making his first visit to the United States and just beginning his relationship with Devoy, which would later culminate in what Rossa despised as Devoy's 'New Departure'.[48] Mary Jane returned to New York in November 1878 while the children stayed in Clonakilty for nearly a year.[49] While she was gone, Rossa treated his health problem by a short stay in Madison, New Jersey, with his friend Father McCartie.[50] Recognising the family's distress, some Irish-American groups undertook fundraising efforts, but Mary Jane and Rossa soon returned to the lecture circuit and further crisis was averted. Shortly after the children returned from Ireland, Mary Jane gave birth to another child, Amelia, who lived only five months.[51] Rossa publicly continued to promote skirmishing despite the fact that Clan na Gael controlled both the fund and most of the bombings. However, since Rossa was personally identified with the bombings both he and Mary Jane were targeted, each survived assassination attempts. Mary Jane was shot at but not hurt while attending a speaking event in Montreal in 1881.[52] Later, an Englishwoman named Lucille Yseult Dudley shot Rossa outside his Chambers Street, New York City, offices on 2 February 1885.[53] Rossa survived the attack but the ensuing arrest and trial of Mrs Dudley were a great sensation in Ireland and London as well as the United States. Rossa claimed Dudley was an agent of the British government and was angry when she was ruled insane and sent to an asylum.[54]

In the 1880s the Rossas lived for a short while in Philadelphia and then moved to Brooklyn, where Mary Jane had six more children.[55] Isabel, Jeremiah, Mary Jane, and Margaret Mary thrived, but neither of the last two, Alexander Aeneas and Joseph Ivor, born in 1889 and 1891, survived more than a few months.[56] Tragedy struck again when James Maxwell, their beloved firstborn, died in 1893, 18 months after he was injured while serving as an engineer on board the *Seward*, a US Revenue Service ship.[57] This death was nearly more than Mary Jane could bear. When Rossa's exile from Ireland, after 20 years in the United States ended, Mary Jane, who had six children aged seven to 15 at home, did not feel she could leave when Rossa made his first trip back to Ireland in 1894.[58] Rossa travelled around the country but was disappointed that he found no opportunity to make arrangements for a permanent return. He did run as a candidate for city marshal while in Dublin but lost the election by a very wide margin.[59] Undaunted, his speeches were as vitriolic as ever, and while in London he was expelled from the House of Commons for shouting out during a session that the assassination attempt on his life had been ordered by the British government.[60]

While Rossa was gone for three months in 1894 and six months in 1895, Mary Jane not only kept the family financially afloat by writing and editing the *United Irishman* and doing an occasional lecture, but also moved to a house on Staten Island.[61] This was an improvement over their last home in Brooklyn and closer to the cemetery where James Maxwell and her other children were buried. The newspaper subscriptions and donations from the Irish-American community sustained them, as both Rossas had few speaking engagements that created only sporadic additional income after 1895. For Mary Jane these included speaking at the annual Emmet commemoration in New York City, reciting in Irish a James Clarence Mangan poem at Cooper Union, and doing a selection of readings with Maud Gonne at the Manhattan Academy of Music in 1900.[62] She also became active in the suffrage movement in 1896, distributing petitions for signatures. Always thinking of how to manage a message, Mary Jane wrote a letter to Mariana Wright Chapman, a great leader in the movement, suggesting better ways for the promulgation of information to reach supporters who did not read newspapers.[63]

Rossa always intended to go back to Ireland. After a short trip in 1904 to dedicate a memorial in Skibbereen he let supporters in Ireland know he was interested in making a permanent move, and in 1905, when his family's financial situation was most difficult, was offered a position on the Cork County Council.[64] He was overjoyed, but Mary Jane was anxious about leaving her children behind in the United States. The two youngest girls, Mary Jane (Jennie) and Margaret (Daisy), sailed with them in 1905 and stayed for a few months, but they returned to their lives and jobs in New York. Mary Jane and

Rossa lived at 9 Chapel Street, Cork, in a donated house.[65] Mary Jane's unhappiness led to real illness. A letter to her daughter written on Ash Wednesday 1906 is filled with homesick concern for her children. Her closing lines read: 'Oh how I wish I could be home! Lord, have pity and shorten my misery.'[66] Her terrible headaches became debilitating and she had trouble recovering from a difficult case of pneumonia she suffered that winter. They sent for their daughter Isabel, a nurse, who arrived in April 1906.[67] Shortly after her arrival Rossa agreed to return to the States, leaving behind everything he had hoped for. In a book written many years later, their daughter Daisy commented: 'It was Poppa's biggest sacrifice.'[68]

Mary Jane and Rossa continued to publish the *United Irishman* together on their return, with Mary Jane doing more and more of the writing. Rossa managed to get a political appointment job in the Brooklyn Clerk's office as a rapid transit inspector in late 1906, but when civil service exams were later required, he no longer qualified.[69] After 1907, any other paid employment was elusive. For a time, three of the Rossa girls lived at home working and helping with support, but the family had only the money from dwindling subscriptions to the newspaper. Rossa did occasional speaking engagements and continued to be the firebrand against British rule. The Irish-American community never deserted their hero, and, like many, Dr Thomas Addis Emmet sent regular donations.[70]

Rossa's body never really recovered from his prison years, his assassination attempt, and his frantic pace of travel and speaking. After 1909, he aged and weakened to become an invalid. Mary Jane became his full-time nurse and sole editor of the newspaper, which she finally shut down in 1910.[71] In 1912, when the *United Irishman* was defunct, Mary Jane asked Devoy to acknowledge some donations Rossa had received in *The Gaelic American* and took the opportunity to tell Devoy he 'once was like a brother and has still a place in our hearts. Though [that place was still] unclaimed'.[72] She lamented the lost friendship having succumbed to a fiercely fought public battle more than 30 years before. She expanded on this thought in a letter two months later when she brokered a peace between them, telling Devoy: 'I think if you could come and talk of your earlier labors again, before those differences of opinion crept in, it would do him [Rossa] a world of good. He has a simple loving heart and you were very dear to it long ago. Bury the between times and be again the younger brother.' Rossa himself wrote a note to Devoy, which she enclosed.[73] Mary Jane also had another motive: she needed Devoy's help in marketing copies of Rossa's books, as her own sales network was shrinking after she closed the paper.[74] Devoy came to visit Rossa and realising how difficult were their circumstances arranged for donation petitions in his paper, *The Gaelic American*. These additional donations were needed to support the family and to enable Rossa's hospitalisation.[75]

After the reconciliation Mary Jane and Devoy were in constant contact and in November 1913 news from Ireland made Mary Jane rejoice in what she called 'something tangible shaping itself on the national horizon … the return of the Irish People to the old doctrine of physical force'. But this made her sad as well: 'I could sit and cry for him, poor old faithful banner bearer, poor old wolfhound of the cause, fading away slowly in mental decline while the mutterings of the longed for storm had beat on deaf ears.'[76] Devoy became a frequent visitor to Rossa and a good friend to Mary Jane for the rest of her life.

Rossa's last two years were spent at St Vincent's Hospital, Staten Island, where he died on 29 June 1915.[77] Thousands turned out for his funeral, walking from his home on Richmond Terrace to mass at St Peter's Church. His body was then kept at St Peter's Cemetery until the sailing to Ireland. As Mary Jane wrote later in *The Gaelic American*, she had promised Rossa he would be buried in Ireland, and years before his death they told the County Cork Association that he would have a public funeral and be buried with his family in Skibbereen.[78] Rossa had been a committee man on the Terence Bellew MacManus funeral in Dublin in 1861 and knew well the effect of a public funeral.[79] However, Mary Jane decided more could be gained with a public funeral in Dublin rather than Cork, particularly with the help of Tom Clarke and Devoy. The day after Rossa died, Mary Jane wrote to Clarke thanking him for his assistance in their 'mission' and enclosing a check for $20 to have him purchase a plot in Glasnevin Cemetery.[80] After she returned from Dublin, Mary Jane wrote a series of articles of her reflections on the Dublin funeral for *The Gaelic American*: describing her good friend Clarke ceremonially closing the lid on the casket at her request; sitting in a carriage at the head of Parliament Street near where the *Irish People* offices had been, as the procession to Glasnevin began; and sitting spellbound while Padraig Pearse spoke his 'heart striking' oration.[81] When she was leaving Liverpool to sail home she wrote to Clarke, 'I leave Rossa to rest in his native sod convinced that Ireland was never so close to the fruition of his dreams as at this moment, and inspired with an ardent desire to help with heart and soul always and everywhere, that cause of freedom in the service of which O'Donovan Rossa lived and died.'[82]

Mary Jane was impressed with all the new breed of republicans she met in Dublin but especially the women: her guide, Kathleen Clarke; the women of Cumman na mBan she met at a meeting she attended; but most of all Countess Markievicz. Her poetic description in *The Gaelic American* is remarkably visual:

Then there is that picturesque and versatile lady … tall and fair, young and golden haired, with bright blue eyes of soldier keenness, and wild rose complexion, dashing and boyish, recklessly brave, yet appealingly feminine, an Irish girl of the 'ascendancy' as she explained herself, married to a Polish count … a writer, speaker, an insatiable seeker for knowledge … she is very good tempered, which is lucky, as she is also said to be a capital shot.[83]

On returning home, Eileen O'Donovan Rossa finally married John McGowan after many years of courtship, leaving her mother alone at home.[84] Mary Jane's financial situation became desperate. In a letter to her daughter Daisy she laments that she was unable to sell the house and could not spend the winter there as it was in such disrepair and she could not afford to fix it. She moved in to the New York City apartment of her daughters Jennie and Isabel. Far away from all her books and with no means to write her autobiography as she had wished, she despaired: 'the fear at eventual poverty and dependence check completely any inclination to present productivity I might have – I always felt that I earned my living – If I were younger and could undertake a lecture or reading tour to clear expenses, I would do as I always have done.'[85] But she could not this time.

Mary Jane knew the planned rebellion was coming soon, particularly after Eileen received a letter from Captain Craven, who spent time with them in Dublin, telling her they were awaiting imminent word in Ireland.[86] Mary Jane wrote to Devoy on 6 April 1916, about the impending activities: 'these seem to be the dead days, before the storm, when no sound is in the air,' and reminded him, 'it should make no difference who was arrested for relays of substitutes were appointed to fill their places, and if all else failed the women were coached to continue the work.'[87] So she was undoubtedly pleased when she heard of the start on Easter Monday. However, she was horrified when she read of the news of the executions in the 4 May *New York Times* and wrote a letter to Daisy: 'They were the bravest and noblest and simplest of true patriots – they knew they were facing death but they had no premonition that they would be shot without ministrations of their Church or human burial.' She describes the 'savage British law who – turned machine guns on the people as well'.[88]

Mary Jane immediately became more politically active and spoke at major rallies held in New York, donating the flag that had draped Rossa's coffin to be used at a gathering of 4,000 people in Carnegie Hall to commemorate the executions.[89] In another letter she called the flag 'a treasured personal gift from Tom Clarke, Pearse and MacDonagh – the Irish Volunteers, the symbol of their hope and aspirations before enfolding Rossa's body as the most significant sign of their love for and faith in him'.[90] In the last months of her life she was still thinking of the Irish people and her love for them. In a letter three weeks before her death, asking Daisy to attend an Irish event, she says:

> Bella and Jane [her other daughters] are not like Papa, they have little interest in or appreciation of genuine Irish people who as victims of English oppression seem uncouth and unpolished to a newer more prosperous generation here. The Irish people have souls and brains and great overflowing hearts susceptible of the highest cultivation – and where they lack it – is the fault of the despotism that has been stamping on them for centuries. It is a miracle that they have preserved the human virtues under a systematic course of misgovernment and persecution unprecedented in the world's History.[91]

In July 1916 Mary Jane was still speaking at large gatherings of Irish Americans and writing poetry to honour the soldiers of the rebellion. After a 'Women's Mass Meeting' on 10 July, she read a new poem called 'The Heroine of the Irish Rebellion of 1916'. She wrote to Devoy the next day and was anxious for him to publish it.[92] He published it the next week.[93] When she died suddenly of heart failure on 17 August 1916, the poem about the Countess, a poem about Padraig Pearse, and a lengthy lyric poem about Rossa were found in her desk and lovingly saved by her daughter, Sheela O'Donovan Rossa MacIntyre, and her husband, John.[94] Devoy was so struck by her sudden death that he wrote a long, beautiful obituary lamenting that Mary Jane 'was never at any time in her valuable life more useful to the Irish cause'.[95] If, as is said, the Fenians were the pilot light of Irish nationalism leading up to the 1916 rebellion, there is no doubt that Mary Jane and Rossa were transatlantic keepers of that flame.

# CHAPTER FIVE

# DR GERTRUDE B. KELLY AND THE FOUNDING OF NEW YORK'S CUMANN NA MBAN

## Miriam Nyhan Grey

*Oh my brothers! let no blind feelings of revenge against the state and its tools lead you to play into its hands by attempting to meet force with force … Remember that the employment of force leads to the redevelopment of the military spirit, which is totally opposed to the spirit that must exist in the people before anything that we wish for can be brought about.*
Dr Gertrude B. Kelly, 1886[1]

*Briseann an dúchas trí shúile an chait.*
Irish proverb[2]

If Mary Jane O'Donovan Rossa can be seen to represent one example of an Irish New Yorker with a deep passion for Ireland, she cannot be held up as the archetype. No less than today, there were many ways to be impassioned about Ireland from the American vantage point, most particularly during a period in which the status of women was in flux. As is often the case for the spouse of a famous person, Mary Jane has heretofore been remembered mostly in relation to her famous husband, Jeremiah. While Dr Gertrude B. Kelly eschewed the general convention of her generation by remaining unmarried,[3] her status did not limit her activism; in many ways it enabled and enhanced it.

Like O'Donovan Rossa, Kelly leveraged personal relations, a professional profile, and sensitivity to history to highlight Ireland's struggle for self-determination. While Mary Jane was hailed as the wife (and oftentimes voice) of the renowned Fenian, Dr Kelly's standing derived from her remarkable professional stature. Dr Kelly's narrative provides a useful follow-on from that of Mary Jane as their goals were comparable but they had simultaneously differing and compatible ways of trying to achieve them. Kelly also represents a younger generation of nationalist but perhaps more notably her progression from constitutional to republican nationalism is much more representative of Irish America more generally. In this way, Kelly illuminates the backdrop to New York and the 1916 Easter Rising in a very important way.

As late as summer 1914, Dr Kelly had publicly and emphatically located herself with the Irish Parliamentary Party camp in the associational landscape of Irish New York.[4] But by December 1914 she was pivotal in founding the first New York branch of Cumann na mBan (Irishwomen's Council) to raise funds and sympathy for the Irish Volunteers in Ireland.[5] So, where did her deep interest in Ireland stem from? What were the circumstances under which she abandoned the United Irish Women of New York, and the goal of constitutional nationalism, for a more immoderate stance? Admittedly, her founding Cumann na mBan is a crude barometer of her changed outlook of how Ireland's self-determination could be achieved, but her action in this reminds us that American responses to 1916 can only be understood by starting with 1914. Arguably, 1916 did no more than ignite an issue that had been percolating for two years for Irish Americans.

Gertrude was born Brigid Kelly on 10 February 1862, in Carrick-on-Suir, Co. Tipperary, in the Diocese of Waterford and Lismore, quite possibly in the Carrick-on-Suir workhouse where her father was the schoolmaster.[6] She came to the United States in 1873 at the age of 11.[7] It seems she was destined to have activist leanings: her teacher mother, Kate (Catherine) Forrest Kelly, had been involved in the Irish labour movement and the Ladies Land League and was associated with Fanny Parnell.[8] Her father, Jermiah, also a teacher, was an advocate of educational equality.[9] Apparently, Jermiah was dismissed from a teaching position in the Carrick-on-Suir Union due to his Fenian leanings and he departed for the United States in 1868.[10] There he would become the founding president of the Land League of New Jersey and was closely connected to Patrick Ford's *Irish World* newspaper.[11] Gertrude, who went by the name Bride with intimates, was one of at least 11 children born to Jermiah and Kate that they raised in New Jersey.[12] She showed promise from a young age, one source claiming that at age 15 she was principal of the public school at Bull's Ferry, New Jersey; this may be exaggerated but she was reported as a teacher in the 1880 census.[13] Judging by her professional and activist trajectory, it can be deduced that she was strongly influenced by her home environment. If Ford's *Irish World* was prominent in the Kelly home, which it seems it was, it is noteworthy that Ford, at least until 1886, 'advocated a variety of late nineteenth-century radical causes' and that he 'supported women's rights, African-American rights, and temperance, and he railed against British and American imperialism'.[14] In 1873, the year Gertrude herself arrived in the United States and the start of a great economic depression, Ford became a strong supporter of labour and industrial movements.[15] Thus, she came of age in a home in which these matters were of great consequence, the daughter of a man who would assert that 'the social war is not an Irish question only – it appeals to a common humanity.'[16]

In 1884, Gertrude graduated from the Women's Medical College of the New York Infirmary. This training hospital was one of the few institutions in the country offering instruction to women doctors and was pioneered by the famous Blackwell sisters who were critical in the advancement of women in medicine.[17] After a period interning, Dr Kelly took charge of the surgical clinic of the New York Infirmary and in time would be promoted to demonstrator of anatomy, secretary of the College Faculty, and eventually to professor of surgery.[18] She clearly excelled in a field in which women were a relatively new phenomenon and were required to break glass ceilings in both the practice and training of women physicians.[19] From 1887 until 1917 Dr Kelly would run and become well known for her surgical clinic at the hospital's dispensary at 321 East 15th Street.[20] At her professional height, she was recognised as a pioneer in the field of major abdominal surgery and was one of the first women medical specialists in the United States.[21]

Understanding her formative years and influences help us to contextualise the activist we pick up in 1914 and provokes a central, if somewhat rhetorical, question. How did Dr Kelly's early life in Ireland and in urban New York and New Jersey shape her as a female advocate for those less privileged than she?[22] Dr Kelly's personal history is replete with examples of how her worldview had been honed with both Irish and American influences, long before an almost chance meeting led to the formation of Cumann na mBan in New York.

In the late 1880s Dr Kelly (along with her brother, John Forrest Kelly) had been a regular contributor to the individualist anarchist periodical *Liberty*, which offered a unique perspective on labour and women.[23] The only scholar who has done significant research on Kelly contends that her writing in *Liberty* was likely rooted in her knowledge of the social and political challenges of Ireland and also in how she related these issues to an American setting. Her introduction to individualist philosophy was facilitated through the columns of 'Honorius' in the *Irish World*.[24] She believed that the differing histories of the United States and Ireland did not demand 'differing economic and political analysis'.[25] The timing of her arrival in the United States must be noted in the context of an era when land reform 'became a watchword of Irish attitudes to grievances in both Ireland and the USA'.[26] It was in this setting, and through the influence of Ford's *Irish World*, that Dr Kelly became a proponent of the economic principles of Henry George, author of *Progress and Poverty* and *The Irish Land Question*.[27] In summary, the intersections of nationalism and land and labour reform (with large servings of feminism and suffragism thrown in) were well germinated in Kelly by 1914.

In organising her rally of Irish women at Carnegie Hall in March, Dr Kelly was highlighting a moment of high anxiety for her and other Irish New Yorkers. They were protesting intimations of Ulster's partial exclusion from the Home Rule Bill.[28] Dr Kelly was no different to many others, including political moderates like William Bourke Cockran and John Quinn, who saw this development as a 'calamitous concession rather than a wise compromise'.[29] She clearly wished to highlight the evolving political situation in Ireland from the female viewpoint, something she would repeat in founding Cumann na mBan. The packed crowd, actually comprised of both sexes, reflected the great and good of Irish New York and of parts of Ireland's diaspora, as far as Australia and London and as close as Canada.[30] Speeches alternated with music and poetry, all of which were delivered and performed by women. The meeting was, however, slated as also being 'supported' by a who's who of influential individuals and organisations, including Dr Kelly's brother, John, lawyer and philanthropist John Quinn, jurist Daniel F. Cohalan, a justice of the Supreme Court of New York, a New York City commissioner, a colonel of the 69th Regiment, *Irish World* journalist Robert Ford, wife of the mayor of New York, Mrs John Puroy Mitchell, the mayor of Jersey City; and a delegation from the Scottish Home Rule Society. A number of men were present on the platform, including some clergy and Dr Kelly's friend and fellow physician, Dr Thomas Addis Emmet.[31] Interesting as this is, for the purposes of this chapter it is the description of Dr Kelly that is the most insightful and emblematic of much of her activity:

> One of the least conspicuous figures in the gathering, yet the one who was the very spirit of the meeting, was Dr. Gertrude B. Kelly, the originator of the great rally. Putting forth all her energies, leading and encouraging others yet avoiding publicity

herself, she it was who brought the idea to success, When called upon for a speech, she modestly demurred, saying, merely: 'Ladies and gentlemen, I have no voice to fill this big hall, so, in the name of my mother, I thank you one and all.'[32]

The question is, what kind of cultured and socially connected woman could command this impressive audience and high-level support, while simultaneously appearing to be rather introverted personally? Why was her agenda to promote the topic as a women's initiative so paramount? This event provides a rich example of how Dr Kelly could utterly commit herself and others to engagement with an issue. Yet she resisted the limelight for herself and when pressed to speak she invoked the spirit of perhaps her first, and most important, female role model, that of her mother. The resolutions passed that day questioned the authority of the power holders in Ireland and clearly asserted the agency of Irish women as wives, mothers, and sisters.[33] Ireland's nationhood was presented as an ethical issue that transcended politics. The resolution's conclusion cannot be read as being anything less than a direct challenge to John Redmond and is particularly remarkable given the Kelly family's supposed support of him. One biographical account maintains that Dr Kelly's brother, John, to whom Dr Kelly was exceptionally close,[34] had sponsored Redmond's 1910 trip to the United States.[35] At the very least, Dr Kelly was known as being 'prominent in UIL affairs' and as such her public challenge to the leadership back home is striking and marked the beginning of the end of her support for constitutional nationalism as advocated by leaders like Redmond.[36]

By early July 1914, Dr Kelly was willing to publicly express confidence in the IPP's abilities but was fiercely opposed to the 'geographical mutilation of Ireland'.[37] A resolution stating her opposition to this was carried and cabled (on her instruction) to Dublin's *Freeman's Journal* as well as to the main Irish leaders including T. P. O'Connor, Edward Carson, and Redmond.[38] She provocatively offered '$100 worth of bullets for the friends of Queen Mary who may try to defeat the cause of political liberty … this gathering has unlimited confidence in the determination of the leaders … to stand unflinchingly, and if necessary, go down fighting, for the absolute conservation of every foot of Ireland's soil'.[39] The idea of going 'down fighting' was becoming more probable and acceptable to Dr Kelly and marks a departure from her earlier discourse on labour issues[40] and Ireland. Attitudinal shifts were occurring amongst the Irish in the United States as support for the newly formed Irish Volunteers became more and more visible. Presumably Dr Kelly would have known, for example, about the large gathering on 1 June 1914, at the Tuxedo Hall in New York City aimed at corralling support for the Irish Volunteers in the United States.[41] Before long,

Dr Kelly would herself demonstrate a female-led commitment to the cause of the Irish Volunteers in New York. As matters accelerated appreciably in the summer and early autumn of 1914 in Europe, Irish America closely watched the response to the Howth gun-running on Dublin's Bachelor's Walk[42] and the outbreak of war. Clan na Gael's Joseph McGarrity later reflected on the tense months: 'Every news item from Dublin, Belfast or London ... was eagerly read by both the organized and unorganized Irish in America.'[43] As we saw in the chapter on the United Irish League of America, Redmond's Woodenbridge speech was a breaking point for a huge segment of Irish America. Dr Kelly was no exception. Her evolution as a republican nationalist had been in the making since the prior March. Soon after Woodenbridge, Kelly took to the columns of *The Gaelic American* to state her exasperated viewpoint. Her remarks reflect the contemporary pulse of many in the Irish-New York community:

> We were asked to give of our store to help put weapons into the hands of our youth to protect our own four green fields, and we responded gladly to the call. From mine and field, and workshop and laboratory and counting house came the response, loud and increasing day by day. The light in the eyes of the young as they trooped into the meeting rooms here in New York was good and glorious to see. Suddenly our hearts are cold, our faces blanched, our souls depressed, our meeting rooms empty, our receipts almost nothing, our young men apathetic.[44]

Giving a female voice to things, Dr Kelly reflected:

> We women have hesitated to give our adherence to the physical force party, not that we did not sympathise to the utmost with its aims, but that in our capacity as consvervators [*sic*] of the race we hoped to call a halt to the immolation of Irish youth. If Irish youth must be sacrificed – for God's sake let it be sacrificed in Ireland for Ireland, not in foreign soil for our ancient enemy.[45]

Redmond's call for Irishmen to fight in the British army had incensed her. She wrote a telling letter to William Bourke Cockran conveying her despair at developments. As is typical of her penchant to match words with deeds, she wondered what could be done: 'Is there anything we can here do to help matters? Dr. [Thomas Addis] Emmet writes "my heart is broken for Ireland and the Irish people".'[46] By December, Dr Kelly had found a way.

The establishment of the Irish Volunteers in Ireland in October 1913 had been followed by a female response some six months later. The first branch of Cumann na mBan came together in Dublin on 5 April 1914,[47] and its goals were stated as:

1. To advance the cause of Irish Liberty.
2. To organise Irishwomen in the furtherance of this object.
3. To assist in arming and equipping a body of Irishmen for the defence of Ireland.
4. To form a fund for these purposes to be called the 'Defence of Ireland Fund.'[48]

A couple of months later a member of this new organisation, Sydney Gifford, arrived in New York.[49] Gifford was a journalist who wrote under the pen-name 'John Brennan'. She was intent on publicising and fundraising for the Irish Volunteers in Ireland and had an aspiration to start American branches of Cumann na mBan.[50] As the months of 1914 progressed, Gifford was disappointed not to have easily connected with like-minded nationalist New York women but an encounter with Dr Kelly at a Gaelic League lecture would change this.[51] Rallying women to the Irish cause was already a clear objective of the medic and her encounter with Gifford was a happy meeting of minds. Perhaps Dr Kelly was tired of always being in a gender minority, as was so often the case in her profession as well as her Irish activities.[52] Her call for a preliminary meeting of women interested in the 'Protection of Irish Nationality' was set for Monday, 14 December 1914, at the Hotel McAlpin on 34th Street in New York City. Writer and educator Mary Colum, fresh off the boat from founding Cumann na mBan in Dublin,[53] was there and, along with Gifford, presented their 'claims of their society in [for] recognition in America'.[54]

Dr Kelly ensured that the first meeting of New York's Cumann na mBan would generate a 'high pitch of enthusiasm'[55] and according to the *Washington Post* a crowd of 200 turned out for it.[56] Some of the speakers from her March rally spoke again, and some new voices were heard. She chaired the meeting and asked an elder mentor, Mrs Margaret Moore, to speak first.[57] Moore gave 'a spirited address' in which she 'recalled the services which the women of Ireland rendered to the Land League and declared that as the women came to the rescue then they would come to the rescue now'.[58] Most of Moore's speech focused on objecting to conscription for the British army in Ireland.[59] The strong German-Irish alliance was put on display by having Celtic scholar Kuno Meyer address the gathering. He claimed that a German victory would mean an 'Irish victory also' and when he mentioned meeting Roger Casement in Berlin there was 'much applause'.[60] The speaking concluded with the voices of three newly arrived Irish sojourners: Mary and Padraic Colum and Sydney Gifford. They outlined the objectives and (albeit short) history of the Irish Volunteers and of Cumann na mBan. Resolutions, pledging support of the former and establishing the latter, were 'unanimously adopted'.[61] Dr Kelly also used the platform of this gathering to express her outlook on her homeland:

Ireland … will when this war is over take her place among the independent nations of the world. And we are going to start in now and raise funds with which to buy guns for the patriots of Ireland. Conscription will soon begin, and the Irish in Ireland will be forced to go to war for England. But if we get guns for them they'll be able to decide what they'll do for themselves.[62]

It is unsurprising to note that Dr Kelly's Cumann na mBan was not an exact replication of the Irish body. As one scholar explains:

it differed from the parent group in Ireland in that it did not see itself as a female aid society to a men's organization (the Irish Volunteers). The Irish Women's Council followed Kelly's sense of professional purpose as a female physician; it kept separate from male authority and it maintained Kelly's position that women must take advantage of their unique powers to protect the 'race.'[63]

One historian maintains that the evolution of New York's Cumann na mBan exemplified an impetus for activism that 'combined philanthropic and patriotic interests and a yearning for participation within long-standing male spheres'.[64] From this vantage point we can only speculate as to the psychological impact that the treatment of the Ladies Land League by the male leaders had on the young Kelly. As such, there is real continuity in her having Moore at the first meeting of Cumann na mBan. Clearly Dr Kelly was challenging the status quo as it had existed for Irish nationalist women from the early 1880s, and in this she provides a clear example of the 'ideological legacy' of the earlier movement.[65] The long-term impact of the dissolution of the Ladies Land League, relevant in the context of Dr Kelly's personal history and intimate exposure to the League by her parents is notable:

The subsequent playing down of the women's actual role was a calculated effort to discourage the next generation of women from believing that it might be possible for them to assume the mantle of the Ladies Land League. For the next 20 years, no group of women activists emerged … The legacy of the Ladies' Land League was the bitter realisation that if women wanted to be politically active, they had either to form their own organisation or accept subordinate status. [66]

At this juncture, it is worth reiterating that Dr Kelly's engagement with political matters was only one part of her engagement with her sense of Irishness and dedication to her place of birth. As it had done for many of the Irish in the United States, the Gaelic revival had inspired a deep interest in cultural nationalism and she was prominent in activities like the Gaelic League, the Gaelic Society, and the Pageant Movement.[67]

More broadly, it is instructive to place the associational culture of Irish New York in a wider temporal and transnational context, especially as the backdrop to 1916. In the early years of the twentieth century we see clear examples of the establishment of organisations that had evolved out of those in the homeland. The Gaelic League[68] is an early example but this pattern would continue and the emergence of Cumann na mBan in an American context exemplifies that. There are two points that are particularly salient here. First, the new organisations were often adapted slightly to fit the American setting; Dr Kelly's lack of deference to male authority either in Ireland or in New York is a case in point. Second, the impetus for the American organisations typically evolved out of at least one Irish individual coming to the United States and establishing the organisation by tapping into long-established Irish-American networks. Sydney Gifford and Mary Colum must have been considerably buoyed in their mission to establish Cumann na mBan in New York by connecting with an activist as well known and respected as Dr Kelly. Through this method, Ireland was plugging into pre-existing social and political capital and networks, which was key to the success of fledgling organisations. The formation of 'The Fianna League of America'[69] provides another illustration of this pattern. Early in 1914 a senior Fianna na hÉireann officer, Michael Lonergan, arrived in New York from Ireland.[70] Soon thereafter, having been inspired by the encouraging response he saw to a newsreel of the annual Bodenstown pilgrimage in a New York movie theatre, Lonergan established an honorary Fianna na hÉireann organisation with the support of prominent Irish Americans.[71]

In John Devoy's recollections some stimulating points on the associational cleavages of Irish New York surface that pertain to both Gertude and her brother John Forrest Kelly. It is very possible that the old Fenian saw Gertrude in the same vein as he did her brother, who Devoy described as 'a very clever man, absolutely sincere. He was a convert from Parliamentarianism but retained all his prejudices towards the Clan-na-Gael, and a strong personal antagonism against some of us.'[72] Devoy essentially commended activism even if it had been in the misguided direction of Redmond in the past; he was emphatic in pointing out that 'while events had proved' him to be right that Home Rule was inadequate for Ireland, he did not have 'an inveterate prejudice against all men who had taken Redmond's side'.[73] He saw it that any such accusations 'had no foundation in fact. We gladly welcomed the co-operation of numerous men who stood by Redmond until he attempted to induce the Irish Volunteers to enlist in England's army, because we knew them to be sincere and able to render effective help to the cause'.[74] Devoy continued by completely dismissing the actions of one individual as he 'had never [even] been prominent in the United Irish League or in any other Irish movement, and had no standing among Irish-Americans'.[75] This insight allows for speculation as to how he might have seen Gertrude and her shift from being a committed United Irish Leaguer to leading an initiative like Cumann na mBan. Overall, Devoy's view of women and of female activism requires further examination.[76]

No doubt, the old Fenian was conscious of the many Irish Americans who took scant interest in Ireland and did little or nothing in terms of organising, communicating, or fundraising. So he could respect those like Dr Kelly (and her brother) who had at least done something for the cause and this helps us in considering how he might have viewed her. All this helps explain the relative prominence of Dr Kelly's activities in the columns of *The Gaelic American* and her reference to his 'friendly columns'.[77] No doubt Devoy was also aware of the Kelly family's connection to the Fords of the *Irish World*, with whom Devoy was by this time in 'perfect accord'[78] following Robert Ford's break with Redmond after Woodenbridge.[79] On some level, Devoy must have approved of what Dr Kelly was doing as his reach and influence on the community was not insignificant, especially in circles in which Dr Kelly felt increasingly comfortable.[80]

For nationalist Irish women in New York who had been in the minority in aspiring to more than Home Rule, bringing someone like Dr Kelly into the fold was welcome and meaningful. Diarist Rose McDermott[81] published a statement

> testifying to the willingness of women to take their rightful place in the independence effort. She remarked on how happy she was to hear Dr. Gertrude Kelly articulate such a strong feminist-nationalist reaction against what she considered the lame rhetoric of the Irish Parliamentary Party, and drew attention to the Party's support for the inclusion of able Irishmen into Britain's World War recruitment plan.[82]

However, a 1915 communication from Mary Jane O'Donovan Rossa to Devoy would suggest that not all nationalist women in New York were completely on board with the new organisation. Mary Jane wrote Devoy questioning his decision to give the film reel of her husband's funeral to the Cumann. Given our knowledge of Dr Kelly and her vision it is difficult not to interpret Mary Jane's commentary as being somewhat pointed in Dr Kelly's direction:

> Pardon me for getting so stirred up about it, but while I have a great respect for women's work in general, I have not seen in societies that there may be a good deal of obstruction to the good intended caused by the unavoidable membership of a few contrary or foolish or self-important people, unscrupulous enough to override their fellows. And while women's societies can be a great auxiliary help to the plans of

men, I don't believe in giving unlimited licence or permitting them a chance to go into competition with men in men's work. I believe in votes for women, of course. Every woman does these days, and I have always done so for every individual woman, no matter how silly or perverse, can think to the point where her affections or interests are concerned. But I am old-fashioned enough still to cling to the notion that men are the lords of creation and women at their best when kindly cooperating in all that reason and conscience approve, and under guidance, with modesty, not self-asserting ... If they are social or church or charity societies, they are sufficiently competent to manage their own concerns independently of men. But patriotic- ! I would give the men despotism over them and ban whoever murmured ... I'm very glad I have not yet joined the Women's Committee, and I won't ever if they are not dominated by the Clan na Gael and animated by the sole desire of aiding and abetting, not rivaling them ... I see now about the women quarrelling. Well, no matter how good workers they may be, if you have not them under discipline to you they will be as much a distraction and worriment as a help. Don't be asking them to oblige you by doing this or that, but take the reins in your hand and lay down the law for them. Do that to-morrow evening and if they are mutinous, believe me you may be glad they disband.[83]

Offering insights on the complexity and generational layering of Irish New York, Mary Jane drew a clear line in the sand regarding the loyalty of Irish nationalist women. In the postscript of the same letter she proclaimed: 'I am a Clan na Gael Auxiliary woman absolutely and only commend the Cumann na mBan in Ireland; and here if it is affiliated to and under command of the right body of men.'[84] O'Donovan Rossa and Dr Kelly, although both committed to an independent Ireland, differed considerably on how women's organisations should relate to their male counterparts, and indeed to Ireland, as the source of authority. Locating Dr Kelly in the context of the evolving status of women, most explicitly mapped on the trajectory of the suffragette movement, is central here. She had known of the challenges facing women, simply for being women, for her entire career.[85] Early on, she had differentiated herself from other feminists as she believed that there is 'properly speaking, no *woman question*, as apart from question of human right and human liberty'.[86] According to one obituary, Kelly was 'intensely a suffragist'.[87] In this sense, it was little wonder that Kelly was a key player in the formation of Cumann na mBan as its evolution came at just the right time in terms of her focus on Ireland and on the rights of women. Patricia Keefe Durso's chapter in this volume does more to excavate the suffragist ties that bound Irish and Irish-American activists in this period.

Unfortunately, Dr Kelly's personal papers have not survived[88] and even if they had, it is unlikely we would know the depths of her knowledge as 1916 loomed. Given her alleged closeness to her brother John it is very possible that she was aware of his purported involvement in a German-American plot that entailed sending the Irish-American newspaper proprietor Anthony J. Brogan to meet with Casement in Germany in early 1915.[89] Her standing in the community and her range of contacts make it probable that she also knew that something was percolating while the British were preoccupied with the war. In October 1915 she was reported as asserting:

> it would not be surprising 'to hear that arms have already been purchased and stored in New York, in expecting that a way be found of landing them in Ireland' and it was also asserted that 'if conscription is ordered an uprising will follow in Ireland,' and that '100,000 Irishmen are ready in New York to go back if needed and if they could get there to join such a movement.'[90]

The chasm that had become increasingly evident in Irish organisations – as they grappled with a new landscape on how best to help Ireland – took a toll on Dr Kelly in early 1916. Following the New York Gaelic Society's failure to send delegates and to support the statement of principles of the Irish Race Convention in March, she resigned from the organisation.[91] She had categorically and publicly stated her commitment to the ideals espoused by the convention in acting as a signatory of the announcement.[92] Not all the members of the Gaelic Society were ready to accept that republican nationalism was rapidly overtaking constitutional nationalism as the dominant orthodoxy of Irish America. But Kelly had never shied away from standing behind her principles. Her 1916 resignation from the Gaelic Society was no different from her departure from the periodical *Liberty* decades earlier when she openly disagreed with its influential editor, Benjamin Tucker.[93]

Available evidence makes it difficult to track Kelly as much as we would like in 1916 but it is clear that Irish New York responded immediately to news of the Rising and Kelly continued to be a prominent personality in this dynamic landscape of fundraising and activism. Cumann na mBan, then meeting twice a month, held a major meeting on 19 May 1916, and collecting for the Volunteers was clearly a priority.[94] Unsurprisingly, we see her name crop up on the Irish Relief Fund Committee.[95] But one of her most overt reactions was to do what she did best: to help found an organisation, and in the autumn of 1917 the Irish Progressive League was born. The next chapter in Dr Kelly's activist compulsion had begun.[96] American entry into the war in Europe and the years of upheaval in Ireland saw her involved in a dock strike, protests, petitions, picketing, organising, and an arrest.[97] All this was simultaneous with her dedication to social welfare: she practiced medicine into her late sixties.[98]

Dr Kelly was the ultimate broker both within and outside the Irish community of New York and beyond. Among many others, she had met Padraig Pearse during his 1914 American sojourn and Francis Sheehy Skeffington while on his 1915 visit to New York.[99] When lawyer and activist Jeremiah A. O'Leary was on trial on conspiracy charges she took to the stand in his defence.[100] Exiled republican Liam Mellows was doubtless happy to have her in a New York courtroom when he was charged with having forged seaman's papers.[101] A Hindu group wanted to make contact with the Irish movement, so labour pioneer Elizabeth Gurley Flynn put it in touch with Dr Kelly and it ended up marching in the St Patrick's Day Parade.[102] Upon birth-control advocate and open lesbian Dr Marie Equi's[103] incarceration for violating the Espionage Act, Kelly used the platform of the State Convention of Women Doctors to highlight her case.[104] Nor did she delay in alerting the lord mayor of Dublin about her shock at the 'inhuman and uncivilized treatment' of republican Ernie O'Malley in 1922.[105] When petitioners were needed to assist in freeing labour leader Big Jim Larkin from Sing Sing Prison, she was among them.[106] She delivered the children of her friends and fellow activists, like those of Peter and Helen Golden.[107] W. E. Du Bois was on the guest list for her 1929 testimonial dinner at which a massive crowd of 800 gathered to celebrate her remarkable life.[108] Active in a plethora of causes, across a range of groups, and over many decades, if there was one common thread it was her support for what her friend, labour lawyer Frank P. Walsh, described as the 'down and out'.[109] A link to Ireland was often, although not exclusively, another common thread for her. She acted as a go-to person for many who traversed the Atlantic during a momentous period in Irish history.

This chapter has used Dr Kelly as an example of the multidimensional engagements, changing circumstances, transnational networks, and evolving worldviews of Irish New Yorkers in the years culminating in 1916. By examining a discrete temporal and activist slice of her life it can be seen that she engaged with the status of Ireland in simultaneously dynamic, atypical, and exemplary ways. Her involvement in Cumann na mBan is yet another demonstration of how she was a member of 'every Irish society on record'.[110] Her focus and interest in Ireland was significant and unwavering throughout her life and it evolved out of a particular family background and exposure to both Irish and American politics and engagement with civic society. Nor was her passion for Irish causes diluted or delimiting in terms of her capacity to organise around non-Irish issues. In this way, this chapter picks out just one, albeit very central, strand in her diverse range of interests and activities over a busy life-time on a range of social, cultural, and political issues. Dr Kelly's activities related to Ireland, especially in the six or seven years after the Rising, warrant discrete study as they fall outside the temporal focus of the current volume and are especially active years for her.

To many New Yorkers, both Irish and non-Irish, of 100 years ago, the name Dr Gertrude B. Kelly would have been very familiar, and yet today she is forgotten despite the thousands of lives this 'many sided woman'[111] touched in her long professional and activist career as physician, feminist, social activist, and Irish nationalist. At the opening of the Dr Gertrude B. Kelly Playground on West 17th Street in New York City in 1936, Mayor Fiorello La Guardia placed 'Dr. Kelly and Jacob E. Riis foremost among those in city welfare work'.[112] Even more ironic and relevant to the scope of this chapter – and given her passion for the status for the land of her birth – Kelly seems to warrant only passing mentions in Irish historiography despite the fact that it was once observed that there was 'not an Irish worker, or lecturer, dramatist or actor, painter or poet' to whom she did not extend a 'welcome and a helpful hand'.[113] She reminds us 'that women did a lot more for the Irish cause than take up guns in 1916' or help 'ferry messages and tend the wounded' by underscoring how they 'played a full and equal role in the shaping of Ireland, at least as strongly abroad as in Ireland itself',[114] albeit a role that has heretofore been woefully under-studied.

Kelly exemplifies the profile of an Irish New Yorker who had robust transatlantic networks of contact and knowledge which allowed her to interface very effectively between the United States and Ireland.[115] Individuals like Dr Kelly were crucial in this period and had a function that has been heretofore overlooked from this vantage point. Most of those who played roles similar to hers were Irish-born and this intimacy with Ireland is meaningful,[116] but so was their connection with and understanding of the United States. Brokers like Dr Kelly knew Ireland and understood the Irish but could interpret and fashion that knowledge and social capital in the American setting. From this vantage point we must remember that Dr Kelly was herself an immigrant first and foremost.[117]

Dr Kelly was 'rooted in the Irish American community' but also challenged some of its most 'essential orthodoxies'.[118] Here was a woman who was 'impeccably Irish', who was a socialist, a self-proclaimed 'pagan'.[119] Her friend Hanna Sheehy Skeffington probably put it best when she observed that Kelly was 'a champion of the Negro, a warm admirer of the colored people, a friend of India, a militant suffragist, but, above all, a friend of Ireland'.[120] From an American perspective Dr Kelly is noteworthy as she demonstrates the legacy of the radical, social-reform bloc of Irish America and as a counterpoint to the more prominent and more conservative profile of the Irish in the United States. The latter is often erroneously used as a catch all term to describe the entire group, but we should not assume that the Irish in the United States (particularly its women), no more than any other ethnic or racial group, were at any point in time monolithically anything.[121]

*For their generosity in reading drafts of this chapter I would like to express thanks to Linda Dowling Almeida, Maura Anand, Marion R. Casey, Ellis Garey, J. J. Lee, Emma Nyhan, and R. Bryan Willits.*

# CHAPTER SIX

# CASEMENT, NEW YORK, AND THE EASTER RISING

## *Lucy McDiarmid*

*For it is not every day that even an Irishman commits High Treason –
especially one who has been in the service of the sovereign he discards and not
without honour and some fame in that service.*
Roger Casement, Berlin, 7 November 1914[1]

*I am a hotel citizen, a hotel patriot.*
Joseph Roth, *The Hotel Years*[2]

'I *must* get a house of my own, of some sort, and settle down,' Roger Casement wrote
his cousin Gertrude Bannister in May 1914, after he had retired from the consular
division of the British Foreign Service. But he was never to have a house of his own;
Casement was a perpetual traveller and visitor, moving about the globe on ships and
trains and a famous submarine. His life was lived in the transience and semi-privacy of
hotels and other people's houses and then, finally, the RIC barracks at Tralee, Brixton
Prison, the Tower of London, Pentonville Prison, and Glasnevin.

Casement went to New York in July 1914 to raise funds for arming the Volunteers.
He spent three months there (18 July–15 October 1914) before leaving for Germany.
His letters from New York show a life as peripatetic, in miniature, as his years in the

Consular Service; he changed hotels several times and stayed with at least three different friends. He wrote his friend Dick Morten on the stationery of the Prince George Hotel with the address crossed out and the Philadelphia address of Joseph McGarrity, an Irish-American businessman, written in.[3] Casement had no fixed residence, and 'If I die, or anything happens to me,' he wrote, Gee (Gertrude Bannister) should get in touch with McGarrity or with John Quinn, the New York lawyer and art collector.[4] At various times during his sojourn in New York, Casement was the guest of Judge Daniel F. Cohalan (in Manhattan) as well as of Quinn and McGarrity; he stayed at the Belmont Hotel in Manhattan and the St George Hotel in Brooklyn Heights.[5]

Casement's main contact in New York was John Devoy and it was with the support of Devoy, McGarrity, and Cohalan, the 'Revolutionary Directory', that Casement's plans for the German expedition evolved. New York's role in Casement's fate was significant: it offered him the means to transform his political and personal ambitions. With the funds available from Clan na Gael and the reluctant support of its leaders, Casement was able to change the scope and the scale of his mission outside Ireland. The scope of his mission changed from fundraising for the Irish Volunteers, so they could afford guns and ammunition, to a much larger goal, three kinds of help from Germany: a promise of endorsement for an independent Ireland, a supply of weapons, and authority to create an Irish brigade from soldiers in the British army taken as German prisoners of war. The scale changed from negotiation with Irish-American members of Clan na Gael to negotiation with a department of state, the German Foreign Office. In his final weeks in New York, Casement was engaging in even higher politics, producing a 'formal address' to Kaiser Wilhelm.

And it was on the streets of New York that Casement encountered an old friend, the man who became something like a romantic partner, albeit a dishonest and unfaithful one. The decision to have the young Norwegian sailor Eivind Adler Christensen accompany him to Germany as 'manservant' and translator dramatically altered Casement's private life: it gave him the close friend he had long wished for. His 'Lines written in Very Great Dejection at Genoa …' in 1900 had expressed that need in poetry ('No human hand to steal to mine / No loving Eye to answering shine'), but they had also expressed bewilderment at his own sexuality:

> I sought by love alone to go
> Where God had writ an awful no: –
> Pride gave a guilty God to Hell –
> I have no pride – by Love I fell.

Love took me by the heart at birth
And wrought from out its common Earth,
With soul at his own skill aghast
A furnace my own breath should blast.

Why this was done I cannot tell:
The mystery lives inscrutable –
I only know I pay the cost –
With heart, and soul and honour lost ...[6]

The word 'gay' had not yet come into use as the accepted term for 'homosexual', and although the word 'homosexual' was at this time beginning to appear in print, Casement never used it. Nor did he ever mention the Wilde trial (1895); his own discursive practices treat homosexual behaviours as sin, as crime, or as pathology.[7] Although he never gives a name to the particular issue that inspired this poem, it is clearly an attempt to talk about 'love'. What its author longs for is a loving relationship and not a series of short-term sexual contacts, brought about by the 'furnace' of lust. Having been born ('Love took me by the heart at birth') and created differently from the norm in the way of love, he lives in self-condemnation, 'With heart, and soul and honour lost ...' The chance meeting with Christensen on Broadway in July gave Casement the opportunity, in his secret, risky trip to Germany, to travel openly with a male lover.

The authorising group to which Casement owed his legitimacy also changed. When he left Ireland in July, Casement was a member of the Provisional Committee of the Volunteers. As he was en route to New York, Eoin MacNeill, chairman of that committee, wrote a letter designating Casement 'the accredited representative of the arms subcommittee'.[8] When he left New York in October, and while he was in Germany, his expenses were paid by Clan na Gael, but he had no official title; moreover, both Devoy and Cohalan harboured doubts about Casement's competence. 'In effect,' writes Casement's biographer Jeffrey Dudgeon, Casement 'became the first Irish ambassador sent into Europe since Wolfe Tone arrived in Paris in 1796.'[9] However, there was as yet no Irish state; and neither the Volunteers nor the Irish Republican Brotherhood had sanctioned the mission. Towards the end of his stay in Germany, Casement felt isolated from both sets of handlers. As he wrote to Count von Wedel in the German Foreign Office, by March 1916 it was 'eleven months since I had direct communication from Ireland and over three months since I had received any news from America'.[10] By then, Casement was representing neither the Clan nor the Volunteers. Devoy's letter of 16 February 1916 to Count Bernstorff, the German ambassador to the United States, implied that the Clan wanted to keep Casement away from Ireland: 'In case an expedition [German military support of Ireland] should be sent to Ireland, we wish him [Casement] to remain in Germany as Ireland's accredited Representative until such time as the Provisional Government may decide otherwise. John Devoy, Secretary of the Irish Revolutionary Directory.'[11] The phrase 'Ireland's accredited Representative' was respectfully worded, but the duration of 'until such time as the Provisional Government may decide otherwise' was obviously indefinite.

Before he left Ireland for New York, Casement's work for the Volunteers entailed practical help for its Provisional Committee, on which he served. The background to Casement's stay in New York began in a hotel room in Dublin. On Monday 15 June 1914, Casement was lying sick in bed in Buswells, his hotel of choice in Dublin. He was feeling 'seedy' and yet, wrote Maurice Moore, 'his mental energy continued unabated.'[12] The members of the Provisional Committee of the Volunteers gathered around his bed to discuss John Redmond's ultimatum. Redmond had published a letter in the *Irish Times* threatening that if the committee did not accept his proposal to add to their number 25 members selected by himself, he would create another organisation 'quite independent of the Dublin Provisional Committee' of Volunteers and loyal to the IPP.[13]

At 10 a.m. Casement's friends on the Provisional Committee, Moore and Bulmer Hobson, arrived in his room, and they decided the appropriate response to Redmond was resignation. 'While they were with me,' Casement writes, 'Tom Clarke and Sean MacDermott came to urge me to fight Redmond, and I refused.'[14] The next day, Hobson went again to Buswells and persuaded Casement that they should 'accept, under compulsion, R's demand – and go on with our work of trying to get rifles and arming only such corps as we trusted.'[15] When the committee voted, the majority – reluctantly – voted to allow the Redmond men in, but, as Hobson writes, 'the Redmondite control proved completely illusory. The work was carried on by the officers and people who had started the movement. Except that the wrangling in the Provisional Committee was a waste of time and a nuisance, it had hardly any effect on the development of the movement.'[16]

For Clarke, who had been a close friend of Hobson's, 'the rift was very bitter, and Tom would not forgive him or trust him again.'[17] Clarke also disallowed MacNeill from giving the oration at the imminent Wolfe Tone commemoration, as had previously been planned. [18] One more such response had implications for Casement in New York: Devoy – an IRB man like Clarke and Mac Diarmada – fired Hobson from his position on *The Gaelic American*. He had been the Dublin correspondent, but Devoy was angry at what he saw as the 'surrender' to Redmond. [19]

Both sides of the Redmond issue took care to present their views about the vote to the Clan. Tom Clarke sent Patrick McCartan, a member of the Supreme Council of the IRB, to the States to explain their position to McGarrity and Devoy. Hobson, not yet having received Devoy's letter about his newspaper column, wrote introducing Casement as a 'friend', and Casement wrote Devoy introducing himself. Casement arrived before McCartan, and the first week of his visit was taken up with establishing his legitimacy as a representative of the Volunteers. In this endeavour he was helped by his personal charisma and by circumstances. After his first meeting with Devoy in New York on 20 July, Casement wrote a response to Devoy's attack on Hobson. He defended Hobson's integrity, explained the thinking behind the 'surrender', and emphasised the importance of arming the Volunteers. [20] Devoy showed the letter to the other members of the Revolutionary Directory, and 'while they were not convinced by it that yielding control of the Volunteers to John Redmond was justifiable,' Devoy wrote, they were 'impressed by the downright sincerity of the man, and it was decided to utilize his services in collecting funds for the purchase of arms'. [21] Whatever they thought of his vote approving Redmond's demand, that is, his 'downright sincerity' would be useful in inspiring audiences to give money.

The delivery of the guns for the Volunteers at Howth on Sunday, 26 July at noon also raised Casement's standing in the opinion of Irish Americans. [22] As McCartan wrote, by the time of his arrival 'Casement had established himself in the confidence of the Clan na Gael because the Howth gun-running had taken place … and Casement had told them all about this before it actually happened, the preparations for it and the arrangements.' [23] Casement had been the liaison between the Provisional Committee of the Volunteers and the London committee – Alice Stopford Green, Molly Childers, and others – who supplied funds for the guns and ammunition. It was Mary Spring Rice who had the idea that guns bought in Germany could be transported to Ireland in a 'fishing smack'. The brilliant skippering that delivered the guns to Volunteers at Howth at precisely the arranged time, when the bells were ringing noon, was done by Erskine Childers. In the event, the boat used was the yacht *Asgard*, given to Molly and Erskine Childers as a wedding present by her parents. [24]

The success of the gun-running was clearly due to the collective effort of all involved: the various people who helped make the plans, contributed money, bought the guns, sailed on the yacht, and coordinated the Volunteers who met the *Asgard* on its arrival and arranged their distribution. Casement was one part of this operation, but because the Clan first heard of this venture from him, 'they accepted the fact that he was largely, if not entirely, responsible for this event.'[25] McCartan wrote two accounts of the evening when the good news reached Philadelphia, where Casement was staying with McGarrity. In his witness statement for the Bureau of Military History, McCartan gently mocks their excited anticipation:

> Joe McGarrity told me afterwards that he and Casement had gone walking out that Sunday night of the Howth gun-running, expecting some news of it at any moment. He said they stood gazing anxiously eastwards as if, by the very intensity of their gaze, they could see over the distance what was happening in Ireland. It was a stupid but natural kind of thing to do.[26]

In another account, McCartan left a vivid image of the actual moment when Casement heard the news at McGarrity's house; they must have gone inside after their glances eastward. 'When they received the glad news that the Asgard had safely landed its cargo at Howth, Casement, who was playing in the drawing-room with the eldest McGarrity child, Mary Joseph, in his excitement threw the child up in the air with a cry of delight.'[27] 'Consequently,' McCartan remarks, 'Casement was in high favour with the whole of them when I arrived and he needed no credentials from me or anyone else at that stage.'[28]

At the 'first receipt of the news,' Casement wrote William Bourke Cockran, 'two companies of Irish Volunteers here in Philadelphia put up ... 3000 dollars.'[29] The news of the guns' delivery was immediately followed by bad news, the murder of three innocent civilians and wounding of many others at Bachelor's Walk by soldiers from the King's Own Scottish Borderers attempting to disarm the Volunteers carrying the guns from Howth.[30] The arrival of the guns marked a major turning point in Casement's relationship to Clan na Gael, as did the violent attack on unarmed citizens. There could not be two opinions about this disaster, and their shared outrage drew Casement closer to Devoy. They were photographed together as they left a protest meeting in Philadelphia organised by McGarrity for Sunday 2 August. The protest 'took the form of a monster funeral procession for the Bachelor's Walk victims. Three hearses with empty coffins led line of march ... A packed house heard Casement denounce the killings. A collection netted over $2,000 to buy more arms for the Volunteers.'[31] Casement also spoke with similar persuasive power at many other places, such as the meeting of the Ancient Order of Hibernians in Norfolk, Virginia, on 24 July, and at Irish-American gatherings in

Chicago, Baltimore, and Buffalo.[32] John Quinn, not as radical as the members of the Clan na Gael, gave $250, a generous amount for 1914. The weeks of speaking and fundraising were the pleasantest and most successful times of Casement's stay in New York.

On 1 August, Germany declared war on Russia; on 3 August, Germany declared war on France and invaded Belgium. On 4 August, England declared war on Germany, and the United States declared its neutrality.

These international events determined Casement's actions for the rest of his life. He had only two more years to live: he was hanged on 3 August 1916. At this point the scope and scale of Casement's mission in New York changed: it became more ambitious, more daring, and riskier. For the rest of his time in New York, Casement's preoccupation was Germany: how to get there and how to persuade the Germans to support Ireland. The drama of another hotel room episode offers a view of Casement's life at this time. His friends Mary and Padraic Colum, newly arrived in New York from Ireland, observed the small theatrical moments in the life of a person deeply involved in covert revolutionary activity.

Casement, Mary Colum writes, 'was staying in a hotel in Brooklyn, and he invited us to tea there the next day'.

> We were sitting in his room; I had poured the tea, and we were talking and munching bread and butter, when Casement with a warning glance said to me in the elementary Irish which was all he or I knew, '*Foscail an dorus* [Open the door].' I rose and swung the door open. There stood outside, silently, a waiter. 'What do you want?' Casement asked. 'I came to see if you needed more hot water,' and the man moved down the corridor slightly confused. 'See, I'm being watched,' Casement said.[33]

Colum was sceptical of what she presumed was Casement's paranoia, but several days later, as they were indulging in the American habit of eating ice cream in a drugstore, she

> saw him start slightly, and, following his glance, noticed the same waiter in everyday clothes standing near us at the counter. 'Ah, George,' said Casement, 'buying stamps, I suppose?' 'Who would have you spied on?' she asked him; 'The British Embassy,' he said, and there was an undertone of hysteria in his voice … 'They are watching all Irish nationalists in America on account of the war.'[34]

That 'undertone of hysteria' was noted by others. John Butler Yeats, who met Casement in August while he was staying in Quinn's apartment, thought he sounded like 'a very nice girl who is just hysterical enough to be charming and interesting among strangers and a trial to his friends'.[35] Quinn himself thought Casement 'seriously ill' and had a doctor examine him. The doctor remarked that Casement would not take his advice.[36] Quinn and J. B. Yeats both complained that Casement kept muttering, 'Poor Kaiser'. To the American journalist Poultney Bigelow (who disagreed with this point of view entirely), Casement wrote, 'I pray day & night, "God save Germany!"'[37] To Alice Stopford Green he wrote, 'Poor Germany!'[38]

From the August declarations of war up to 15 October, the day Casement boarded the *Oskar II* for Norway, whence he would go by train to Germany, Casement appeared to think of nothing besides 'poor Germany'. There is little in his letters about the Volunteers except the amount of money he had previously collected ('$6,000 or $7,000 the last three weeks,' he wrote Stopford Green on 15 August) and the difficulty of collecting it now: 'Had it not been for the war I could have got $50,000 easily for the Volunteers.'[39] His political writings published at this time gave both geopolitical grounding to his views and statistics about Irishmen fighting for England, so the case he made for a German alliance with Irish revolutionaries was put rationally. Everyone who saw him in New York, however, noted his emotional intensity, and his letters were full of phrases like 'This war is a crime and a calamity and no man can see the end of it. I may never see the end of it' and 'I am well in health but sad at heart.'[40] On 1 September, his fiftieth birthday, he wrote Gertrude Bannister, 'I will say nothing of this war. You know my fixed convictions. It has come, however, like a thief in the night, and I fear may wreck everything good in Europe.' The most positive assessment of Casement came from former president Theodore Roosevelt, who (after their meeting on 9 August) wrote that he found him 'charming'.[41] Casement, however, 'always regarded [Roosevelt] as a fraud'.[42]

Casement's German interests were not new; they had been evolving over a number of years. After his 1912 tour of Germany with his friend Dick Morten, Casement was using Germany to make the kind of anti-British statements he made regularly in 1914: 'They are magnificent organizers,' he told Ernest Hambloch; 'You English have nothing to compare with what they do. They are a fine race.'[43] His ideas for an Irish brigade composed of Irish prisoners of war taken by the Germans may have been inspired by a lunch with John MacBride in May 1913, during which they discussed the Boer War. After it, he wrote Alice Stopford Green that 'the story of the Irish brigade "was a fine fight and should be told".'[44] Later in 1913 he worked, with no success, 'to make Queenstown a port of call for [the] Hamburg-Amerika line' after the Cunard line decided to omit Cork from its route.[45] Bulmer Hobson mentions even earlier interests in an Ireland-Germany alliance:

As early as 1910 [Casement] and I had much discussion about the coming war, and how such a situation should be met by the people in the National movement. As a result of these discussions I wrote some articles in 1912 called When Germany fights England, what will Ireland do? They were published in 'Irish Freedom.' In 1913, at my request, Casement wrote a lengthy memorandum on the position of Ireland in the event of a war between England and Germany. I got the manuscript, in his own handwriting, and Pádraig Ó Riain typed it in my office and we destroyed the original. In the beginning of 1914 I took this document to New York and, with the help of Devoy, had it given to Count Von Bernstorff, the German Ambassador in Washington.[46]

As early as 9 August Franz von Papen, military attaché to Ambassador Johann Heinrich von Bernstorff, referred (inaccurately) to Casement as the 'leader of all Irish associations in America' when he wrote to the Foreign Office in Germany. Casement, he said, had 'contacted' him 'for the purpose of cooperation with Germany'.[47]

Casement was doing more than praying for Germany and muttering sadly about the Kaiser; he was closely involved in the communications between Clan na Gael and representatives of Germany. Although the exact date has not been ascertained, records show that Casement was introduced by Devoy to von Papen and also to George von Skal, a German-American journalist and author.[48] It is not clear if he was present at the first meeting, which took place on 24 August at the German Club in Manhattan.[49] According to Devoy's account,

> The point was stressed that a rebellion in Ireland would necessarily divert a large part of the British army from the fighting front on the Continent and that therefore it would be to Germany's interest to help Ireland in her fight for freedom.
>
> Count Bernstorff listened attentively and with evident sympathy, asked many questions, so as to be sure he fully understood our position, and he promised to send our application to Berlin.[50]

It was the next day, however, that 'a statement of Ireland's case', probably drafted by Casement was sent to the German Foreign Office, and an address to the Kaiser, written by Casement, was signed by the Revolutionary Directory. In the first of these documents, Casement, in terms consistent with those mentioned at the meeting, suggested three kinds of aid that Irish nationalists might request from Germany: arms; a brigade to be composed of Irish prisoners of war; and 'a statement of positive intent towards Ireland'.[51] The address to the Kaiser was written in lofty, flattering language: 'We feel that the German people are in truth fighting for German civilization at its best and certainly in all its less selfish forms.' On a more practical level, it pointed out that England's 'unchallengeable mastery of the seas' was due to its 'possession of Ireland'.[52]

The letter ended with a flourish, saying that the signatories 'pray' that 'Your Majesty may have power, wisdom and strength of purpose to impose a lasting peace upon the seas by effecting the independence of Ireland and securing its recognition as a fixed condition of the terms of final settlement between the great maritime Powers'.[53] It may have been the reverential and quasi-religious language that led Devoy to note that although he and the other members of the Directory signed the address, 'we of the Clan would have worded some portions of it differently.'[54]

Casement spent much of August and September writing and publishing. His various articles on the subject then closest to his heart, pieces written over the previous three years, were published in New York and Philadelphia as a pamphlet titled *Ireland, Germany, and the Freedom of the Seas* and later in Berlin as *The Crime against Europe: A Possible Outcome of the War of 1914*.[55] On 5 October the *Irish Independent* printed a letter by Casement arguing against Irish enlistment in the British army. Statistics showed, he wrote, that 'There are already far more Irishmen in the British army, in proportion to the population of the two countries, than there are Britons, properly speaking, i.e., inhabitants of the island of "Great Britain".' Yet Ireland was declining economically, losing 'acres of … tillage', and (in words that anticipated de Valeran imagery) 'hearths sending up smoke from the happy family gatherings'. Under these circumstances, then, Ireland had no reason to support Britain in 'continental warfare'. The letter ended, as Casement's polemical writings generally did, with a resounding flourish. 'Let Irishmen and boys,' he urged, 'stay in Ireland. Their duty is clear – before God and before man. We, as a people, have no quarrel with the German people. Germany has never wronged Ireland, and we owe her more than one debt of gratitude.'[56] The *Independent* responded 'editorially', wondering why 'a gentleman … who gave his services for reward to the Empire' should not care 'what may happen to the Empire now'.[57]

At some unrecorded date, probably in early August, Casement determined to go to Germany himself to urge the German Foreign Office to grant the Clan's requests and to organise an Irish brigade. '[I]t is not every day that even an Irishman commits High Treason,' he wrote on 7 November in his 'German diary', and by publishing his letter in the *Independent* he had already made his treasonous inclinations clear to the world.[58] He was not happy about going; 'I am very wretched and despondent,' he wrote his friend Dick Morten; 'I feel old and broken-hearted.'[59] He knew the trip was fateful: as he wrote Gee on 2 December, '*I gave up everything* when I crossed the sea to get here.'[60]

No one else was enthusiastic about Casement's proposed journey. John Quinn wrote T. W. Rolleston in Dublin, 'I knew he was going to Germany. I tried to persuade him against it.'[61] In his *Recollections*, Devoy says, 'When he first broached the project, I discouraged him for several reasons. While I recognized his intimate knowledge of foreign affairs, I had doubts of his temperamental fitness to deal with the Germans in the conditions then existing.'[62] Devoy also thought that with Casement's 'tall figure, striking features and very dark hair' he would be detected by British officers who would be bound to board the ship (as indeed they did). McGarrity recorded that after a final meeting with Casement at Judge Cohalan's, the Judge 'beckoned me into the parlour and asked me: "Have you absolute confidence in this man?" I answered, "I will trust him with my life. You've had nothing like him since Tone."'[63]

The reaction of the IRB, as described by Patrick McCartan, was more nonchalant. Its members did not trust Casement because of his vote in June acquiescing to Redmond's demand, nor did they much care what happened to him; his close friendships on the Provisional Committee of the Volunteers were not with Clarke, Mac Diarmada, and the other IRB members. McCartan wrote that he had 'a document from Casement about the formation of the Brigade in Germany' and, when he returned to Ireland,

> I gave it to Tom Clarke and it was he read it to a meeting of the Supreme Council. After having read it, he said to them, 'Now you have all heard this and you understand what is in it, so we will destroy it' – and he put a match to it on the spot. I had made no copy of it and there was now nothing of this historic document except the memory of it.
>
> The reaction of the meeting at the Supreme Council to this proposition was that they had approved of his going to Germany and, if he thought he could do some good in this project, well, let him fire away and perhaps some good might come out of it [.] [A]t any rate, he was doing this on his own and they could not stop him anyhow; it would be good if it worked out and, if it did not work, there would be no harm done.[64]

Or, as Devoy puts it, the Supreme Council approved the Clan's decision 'reluctantly'.[65]

In his *Recollections*, Devoy records a visit to Casement in Brooklyn, no doubt at the same hotel where Mary and Padraic Colum had been shown the spy behind the closed door. 'Casement was very frugal in his expenditures,' Devoy writes; 'Even so, on one occasion when we visited him at the St. George Hotel, a very quiet place on [*sic*] Brooklyn Heights, we realized that his personal funds must have been low, and gave him $1,000.'[66] Devoy does not say what precisely made him realise that Casement's funds were 'low'; was there something about the 'very quiet' hotel that struck Devoy as not entirely appropriate for someone like Casement? Whatever it was about the setting, it provoked a generous handout.

Devoy obviously was not aware that the St George was known for its 'willingness to accommodate gay men on a short- or long-term basis', as Yale Professor George Chauncey has written.[67] A *New York Times* article cites the observation of Michael Korie that in the years after the First World War, in 'early gay society', the St George was 'rumored to be predominantly gay'.[68] An anonymous blogger refers to it as 'famous (even infamous) as both a cruising spot, a hookup spot (where two men could rent a room together without any fuss), and a home for many gay men (who lived in the hotel long-term)'.[69] Having been in New York on two earlier occasions, in 1890 and 1912, Casement was evidently familiar with its gay spaces and deliberately sought them out. On the 1914 visit, his first night in New York was spent at the Belmont Hotel, located at Park Avenue between 41st and 42nd Streets, and therefore convenient to the central 42nd Street axis that then as now was known as an area for gay hustlers and gay bars.[70] Walking west on 42nd Street, he would first have reached Times Square, long a centre of gay life in the form of hotels, bars, nightclubs, and theatres.[71]

This is the entry describing Casement's first evening in New York in 1914, written in what is called his 'German diary' because he wrote it in Berlin, attempting to record his recent experiences in the States:

> Strolling down Broadway in the thought of perhaps locating old points of view, like Pond's and the Hotel he lived in in 1890, a young Norwegian sailor spoke to me – and him I befriended – and told him to see me next morning. I mention him and the chance meeting because he is destined to figure largely in the end of this story. His name was Eivind Adler Christensen, 24 years old, of Moss, Norway. He had run away from his father's house, after getting a severe beating for playing truant at school and had stowed away on an English collier ... When he met me he was out of work, starving almost, & homeless. He was grateful for my help and I saw him once or twice in New York where, with the help I gave him, he got work.[72]

This is not a 'black' (explicitly sexual) diary, but the account above is clearly a censored description of a walk and an encounter with sexual implications. As later events made clear, Casement was not simply 'strolling'; he was cruising.

'Pond' was James B. Pond, whose famous lecture bureau had managed tours of American celebrities such as Mark Twain and Vachel Lindsay, and Irish celebrities such as Lady Gregory and W. B. Yeats. Casement had accompanied Herbert Ward on a 'Pond's Celebrity' tour in 1890.[73] The 'hotel' from which Pond operated his business was Everett House, a 'first-rate hotel on Union Square'.[74] And Union Square at this time, according to a 1910 example cited by George Chauncey, was 'one of the city's best-known cruising areas'.[75] Scholarship such as Chauncey's *Gay New York: Gender, Urban Culture, and the Making of the Gay Male World, 1890–1940* makes it possible to decode this paragraph of the 'German diary'. The map of his walk Casement gives us in this non-'black' diary reveals, in Chauncey's words, 'the visibility of the gay world to gay men as well as its invisibility to the dominant culture'.[76] As the locations mentioned indicate, and as Casement's subsequent move to the St George Hotel confirms, Casement knew and was at home in New York's 'cruising areas', those 'old points of view', as he calls them.

What Casement does not say, but what Dudgeon has established, is that the 'Norwegian sailor' he purports to have met for the first time ('him I befriended') was not a new friend but an old one. Casement and Eivind Adler Christensen had met in Montevideo, Uruguay, probably in 1908.[77] They met in a lavatory; later Casement 'visited [Christensen] in [his] rooms', and Casement gave him jewellery 'and money to the value of $900'.[78] As Dudgeon explains, Christensen was bisexual, married but willing to service gay men for money. He was also a con man and criminal; when Casement met him in 1914 on Broadway, Christensen had a wife and a child, but while in Germany with Casement, he married a second woman. His subsequent life was a tangle of petty crimes and dishonesties.

And so as well as enabling Casement to transform the scope and scale of his mission, New York also enabled Casement to transform, however unfortunately, the nature of his romantic life, making cruising unnecessary because he was travelling and briefly living with a seemingly steady boyfriend. The official reason for Christensen's presence on the journey was his fluency in German; the unofficial reason must have been the personal relationship.[79] As Dudgeon points out, 'Up to this point' – before Casement left New York for Germany – 'he was able to divorce his private life from his official and public life.'[80] The late twentieth-century metaphor of 'the closet' offers a clear conceptual line dividing the two separate compartments of Casement's life, the sexual and the 'official', 'public' life. Christensen had been Casement's sexual partner and was privy to the hidden part of Casement's life, a life involving practices then considered 'abnormal', 'perverse', and criminal. Dudgeon writes that Christensen opened the closet that Casement was in, but in a way it was Casement who created a passage between the closet and the world outside it by determining to take Christensen with him to Germany.[81] To introduce into his public life as an operative supported by the Clan na Gael someone from his hidden private life, even someone presented as a 'servant' who could speak German and who therefore served an official purpose, was to expose that hidden life to the world, to diplomats, to hotel employees, and to everyone in Norway and Germany with whom the unreliable Christensen gossiped, drank, and kept company.

And that 'public' life, once Casement consorted with German diplomats in New York and with the German Foreign Office in Berlin, was now treasonous and thus hugely risky itself. At the most vulnerable period of his career, Casement introduced into his subversive political activities an intimate friend who could jeopardise his mission, his reputation, and his life. When, then, upon their arrival in Christiania, Norway, Christensen went to the British legation and spoke to officials there, betraying Casement in the hope of earning a large sum, he exposed all Casement's transgressive activities: he told Secretary Francis Lindley, the lower official he was able to see, that Casement was part of an 'Irish-American-German conspiracy' and that 'his relations with this Englishman were of an improper nature'.[82] The information given by Christensen was the 'earliest mention on official records of Casement's sexual preference'.[83] Casement never entirely understood Christensen's betrayal; instead he believed, as Christensen told him, that the Legation had sought his services in capturing Casement. But as Séamas Ó Síocháin writes, 'Christensen, it seems likely, was playing a double game, seeing possible advantages for himself, especially financial gain, on both fronts.'[84]

In his *Recollections*, Devoy claims to have been suspicious of Christensen from the start, mostly, it seems, because of Casement's poor judgment. At the final meeting of the Clan leaders with Casement on 10 October at Judge Cohalan's apartment, Devoy missed the important information about Christensen's provenance:

> During our discussion, owing to my deafness, I missed one very important statement. That was Casement's announcement that he had decided to take with him as a servant or companion a Norwegian sailor named Christensen whose acquaintance he had recently made, but of whose character and antecedents he knew absolutely nothing, and of whom he had never heard before. Those present at the consultation, after questioning Casement, accepted his judgment and were convinced that Christensen's knowledge of English and German and his Norwegian nationality would be a great help to Casement, who did not know German. I heard enough of the talk to understand that he proposed to take a Norwegian along, but missed the fact that the acquaintance between the two was only of a few weeks' duration. Had I understood that, I would have objected strongly to Christensen's going as Sir Roger's companion. The thorough knowledge of the man's character, which I later acquired through a visit of some weeks he had made in New York while Casement was in Germany, made me deeply regret that he had been thus allowed to become a participant in our activities.[85]

It was, of course, only Christensen's alleged provenance that he missed hearing about, for Casement had known his 'companion' for longer than a few weeks. The real truth would have been even less acceptable to the Revolutionary Directory.

As a high-treasonous gay man, Casement was in at least two closets and required a lot of hiding. In the famous photograph with Devoy, taken on 2 August after the protest rally in Philadelphia, his head is turned away from the photographer. He may have been anticipating his trip to Germany and thus may have wished not to have a photograph on record, or he may have been hiding his official, 'professional' identity from a potentially blackmailing lover.[86] He had an unusually large number of names in 1914. In a letter to McGarrity Casement signed himself 'Your fond sister Mary', and in another the signature was 'Bridget'.[87] Just before he left New York for Germany, Casement changed hotels, registering in the new one as 'R. Smythe'.[88] (He also made fake reservations at the LaSalle Hotel in Chicago.) To help Casement sail undiscovered, the Clan gave him the passport of Clan member James Landy: Casement was schooled in Landy's background ('Your mother's name was Joyce') and washed his face with buttermilk, which had the alleged ability to lighten the complexion.[89] In Berlin, Casement registered in his hotel as 'Mr. Hammond'.[90] Discovered in McKenna's fort in Curraghane by RIC Constable Bernard Reilly, Casement identified himself as 'Richard Morten'.[91]

Casement also changed nationalities. When the *Oskar II* was intercepted by the British ship HMS *Hibernia* and its passengers searched, Casement (according to the story Christensen told Devoy) responded in outrage to the British naval officers. He

> assumed an air of indignation and a good imitation of an American accent, and said in a loud voice, with an oath which I never heard him use: 'This is an outrage. Can't an American gentleman travel on a transatlantic steamer without being treated as a thief by these damned Englishmen?' The young officers seemed taken aback by the unexpected outburst and withdrew without making a search.[92]

To Constable Reilly, Casement said, 'I am an Englishman.' A life between accents, nationalities, allegiances, and genders, hybrid and subversive, was given local habitation in these aliases. No wonder fellow travellers on the *Oskar II* assumed he was a spy.[93]

In the short term, the major transformations enabled by Casement's stay in New York were successful in fulfilling his ambitions: the city supplied him with the money and personal fulfilment that a major metropolis can offer in abundance. His connections there and the funds at their disposal enabled him to travel to Germany and to stay there, engaging for much of the time with German government officials. Those same funds, collected by Clan na Gael, also covered the expenses of keeping Adler Christensen as a servant. But in the long term, his desires, political and personal, were frustrated entirely. The Irish Brigade was small and its members, for the most part, not interested in fighting for Ireland; nor did Casement want them to risk their lives for a venture he thought bound to fail. As Dudgeon writes, Casement 'did everything, short of informing the English enemy, to undo the rising'.[94] The ship carrying arms, the *Aud*, had to scuttle itself when it was detected by the British as it sat in Tralee Bay. And having landed in Ireland, on Banna Strand, Casement was unable to get to Dublin and stop the Rising. From the military point of view, Casement's German adventure and his return to Ireland complicated an already complicated situation.

Christensen's duplicity had effects on British intelligence before the Rising and on the rumours circulated about Casement at the time of his trial and his appeal. And of course it has also had an effect in the long term, the opening up of Casement's sexuality as a subject for discussion, debate, and research over the course of the last century. Two handwriting experts have declared the disputed diaries authentic, and the combined weight of their judgments, a number of Casement's undisputed poems, his residence at the St George Hotel in Brooklyn, and numerous other details make his sexual preference unambiguous.

Apart from the funds raised for the Volunteers in July, then, Casement's American trip did not supply useful aid for those who were planning the Rising. Yet in this brief segment of his life, as in all the rest of it, social history is enriched by attention to the complicated life of this idealistic man. The many records and accounts generated during the time Casement spent in the United States show us the ways information about covert activities is circulated or kept from circulation: the secret conversations, the deafness, the pseudonyms, the gossip, the diaries, the invisible gay life, the gun-runnings, the deceptions, and the betrayals. Casement's American trip reveals the methodologies of concealment and discovery.

Casement had 32 hours in Ireland, the first of which was happy, as he wrote in a passage that has become famous:

> When I landed in Ireland that morning (about 3 am) swamped and swimming ashore on an unknown strand, I was happy for the first time for over a year. Although I knew that this fate waited on me, I was for one brief spell happy and smiling once more. I cannot tell you what I felt. The sand hills were full of skylarks rising in the dawn, the first I had heard in years – the first sound I heard through the surf was

their song as I waded through the breakers and they kept rising all the time up to the old rath at Currahane where I stayed and sent the others on and all round were primroses and wild violets and the singing of the skylarks in the air and I was back in Ireland again.[95]

'He was lying away below high water mark,' wrote Monteith, 'the sea lapping his body from head to foot, the bigger waves splashing all over him. His eyes were closed'.[96] The landing on Banna Strand afforded Casement the only moments of peace and stability he had enjoyed since leaving Ireland for New York almost two years earlier.

*For help with various aspects of the research for this essay, I would like to thank Marion R. Casey, Jeffrey Dudgeon, Madeleine Humphreys, Frank Miata, Miriam Nyhan Grey, Margaret O'Callahan, Fionnuala Walsh, and R. Bryan Willits.*

# CHAPTER SEVEN

# THE MAN IN PHILADELPHIA
## JOSEPH McGARRITY AND 1914

## Maura Anand, Andrew S. Hicks, & R. Bryan Willits

*He took keen delight … in teaching her little prayers in Irish.*
McGarrity describing Padraig Pearse playing with his young daughter in 1914[1]

*God Bless Sir Roger and send him safe to his journeys end,*
*and save him from all his enemies.*
Nightly prayer said by McGarrity's young daughter *c.* 1914[2]

On 21 February 1914, two visitors from Ireland, Padraig Pearse and Bulmer Hobson, convened a meeting with John Devoy in the offices of *The Gaelic American* on William Street. Hobson presented Devoy with a document outlining the potential role of Irish America in the event of Britain and Germany going to war. The author of the document, as Hobson reported it, was Sir Roger Casement. As the meeting was finishing, the senior Clan na Gael man, Joseph McGarrity, walked in and was handed the 'able document', having disembarked the 2 p.m. train from Philadelphia.[3] An historic chain of events was gently put in motion with this low-key gathering.

During the months of 1914, McGarrity would welcome not only Pearse and Hobson, but also Casement to his Philadelphia home at 5412 Springfield Avenue, for short but noteworthy visits.[4] This chapter locates McGarrity as a significant yet under-studied figure in the plans that culminated in the Rising by examining him through the prism of his houseguests of the spring, summer, and autumn of 1914. Using this temporal focus underscores aspects of McGarrity's profile as it had evolved by this crucial period and contextualises his function in the preparations for the Rising. McGarrity played a key role in the funding, logistics, and aspirations of the republican nationalist vision of the events of 1916 in the United States. He acted as a communications portal, regularly corresponding with a variety of individuals who shaped the Irish strategy, especially his older ally and mentor in New York, John Devoy.[5]

There were those like Devoy, Mary Jane O'Donovan Rossa, and Dr Gertrude B. Kelly who had by the outbreak of the First World War lived for decades in the United States. But the older guard looked to a younger generation of activist who would take an interest in Ireland's right to self-determination. A prime example of the new crop of Irish republicans is provided by Joseph McGarrity, an Irish immigrant who had made Philadelphia, not New York, home. Cognisant of the fact that McGarrity's role in 1916 warrants reassessment in light of newly available sources, this chapter hones in on a discrete chronology to unpack the transatlantic and American networks at play in the run-up to the Rising. Despite being from Philadelphia, McGarrity became central to the scene in New York and Ireland, and it would be an omission not to include him in a collection of this scope.

Given the longevity and centrality of his role in transatlantic Irish nationalism, it is remarkable that more has not been written about McGarrity. Only two significant studies have been undertaken, although he was ubiquitous on the landscape of Irish-American republicanism for the early decades of the twentieth century. F. X. Martin, perhaps when compiling *Leaders and Men of the Easter Rising: Dublin 1916*,[6] noticed a lacuna in the historiography and encouraged Marie Veronica Tarpey to research McGarrity and Clan na Gael.[7] For scholars interested in the man from Carrickmore, it is to two published works written over four decades ago that one must refer: Marie Veronica Tarpey's *The Role of Joseph McGarrity in the Struggle for Irish Independence* and Sean Cronin's *The McGarrity Papers: Revelations of the Irish Revolutionary Movement in Ireland and America, 1900–1940*.[8] A helpful (unpublished) chronology of his life is also provided in *The McGarrity Chronicles* by Helene Anne Spicer.[9] McGarrity has earned entries in reference works such as the *Dictionary of Irish Biography* and the *Encyclopedia of the Irish in America*,[10] but in general it is fair to say that he is a figure who deserves more scholarly attention. This chapter contributes to our understanding of McGarrity in a novel way by focusing on a specific year of the 47 he devoted doggedly to the cause of Ireland.[11] Overall, the centrality of McGarrity is key to understanding the American role in the Easter 1916 Rising.

By 1914 Joseph McGarrity had been in the United States for 22 years. Tarpey provides a worthy overview of his early biography and draws extensively from a personal history that McGarrity himself dictated to his daughter in 1939, just one year before his death.[12] Born on a farm in Creggandeveskey, Carrickmore, Co. Tyrone, on 28 March 1874, McGarrity's childhood bears the hallmark of life in rural Ireland during a period of activity related to agrarian reform, Home Rule, and Fenianism.[13] In 1892, not yet 18, McGarrity decided to migrate to the United States, following in the footsteps of his siblings.[14] The story of his leaving Ireland (by stealing away without warning), crossing the Atlantic (in the company of a small group of Native Americans who spoke no English), and getting to Philadelphia without any money (where he meets his sister for the first time) makes for riveting reading and is a rich source for scholars of late nineteenth-century Irish immigration.[15] Even the account of his journey to the United States suggests that as a young man McGarrity was very likeable and found it easy to bring people along with him, a trait which bleeds into his activism on Ireland in no small way. Within two decades of his arrival, he was an American citizen, married, with a growing family.[16] Crucially, he was also a successful businessman (a wholesale distributor of liquor)[17] and from September 1912 was a member of the national seven-man executive of Clan na Gael (having joined the Clan in 1893 and being elected district officer for Philadelphia in 1904).[18] In the weeks before March 1914, the McGarritys welcomed a writer and educator into their home. His name was Padraig Pearse.

McGarrity was not unused to visitors from Ireland. When Bulmer Hobson, arguably one of the most powerful people in the republican movement and at the apex of his IRB career, helped to arrange Pearse's trip for the financially compromised St Enda's school, he personally attested to the hospitality of McGarrity.[19] Hobson enjoyed a successful speaking tour in the United States for a two-month period starting February 1907 and had spent time in Philadelphia.[20] As we saw in the previous chapter, in the intervening years Hobson was regularly in communication with Devoy and McGarrity and it is thus unsurprising that he sought the support and sanction of them for the dedicated schoolmaster.[21] After all, in 1910 McGarrity had offered the family farm in Carrickmore to Hobson in an effort to help with his friend's financial precariousness.[22] More generally, between 1907 and 1914, it is clear that McGarrity was regularly called on to provide patronage to his Irish-based counterparts. It is almost certain that McGarrity would have met with Hobson, along with so many others of his Irish-based contacts, during his 1911 honeymoon in Ireland.[23]

The timing and significance of Hobson's 1914 visit to the United States, where he was reunited with McGarrity, are worth pondering and really demand more in-depth and dedicated examination. Correspondence suggests that Hobson had toyed with the idea of travelling with Pearse to the United States but an October 1913 letter to Devoy seems to suggest that he changed his mind: 'This I am not inclined to do, and in any case I would not consent unless I knew that my going over on such a mission had your approval.'[24] The language used in addressing Devoy sheds light on an interesting dynamic between the two and accentuates the esteem with which the older campaigner was held. Hobson's tone is all the more worthy of note as he was not known for his deference to others[25] and his remarks also demonstrate just how dependent the movement was on Irish America:

> Of course I know the difficulty you are constantly in from the number of demands made on the Irish-Americans from this country, and I am often ashamed of the way in which we are always begging for help from America. But in such case as this we cannot help it. The people who have the money here won't give it, and we have either to ask our friends in America or see things wiped out which are of great value or importance to the movement.[26]

But matters reached new levels of urgency in the late months of 1913 when the newly formed Irish Volunteers needed weapons. This would become more challenging when, within ten days of its founding, a ban on the legal importation of arms or ammunition without a permit had been put in place.[27] Hobson's decision to travel was also precipitated by the changing political scene as partition and a war between Britain and Germany became increasingly possible and a need to take action appeared more and more imperative for nationalists. Although penned some two decades later, McGarrity's reflections on the topics discussed in his home one late March 1914 night are insightful:

> They [Pearse and Hobson] both talked of the war between England and Germany as though it was an accomplished fact. Roger Casement's articles forecasting the war had gripped Hobson, who seemed quite positive that England was about to fight her last great war, in which the Empire would be smashed, and in which Ireland either with her own resources, or with the aid of Germany, would *break the connection with* England and re-establish her independence.[28]

With this in mind, we should not underestimate the importance of the decision that had been taken to send Hobson to the United States on 12 February 1914,[29] ostensibly to secure the cooperation of Devoy and McGarrity in a plan that would deeply influence

Irish history. Within days, two leading Gaelic League organisers, Diarmuid Lynch and Thomas Ashe, also left for the United States on a fundraising mission.[30]

Pearse's time with McGarrity did much to cement a firm and fast friendship between two men who were deeply committed cultural nationalists, as we see in Maura Anand's chapter on Pearse in this volume. They had much in common: their age profiles, their similar political interests, as well as a passion for reading and writing poetry. Pearse even presented a book of his poems to his friend as a leave-taking gift.[31] McGarrity was energetic, enthusiastic, and relatively young at 40, in contrast to Devoy who was in his seventies by that time. McGarrity appeared to be assuming an increasingly prominent role in Clan business, even serving as Devoy's ears on important matters as the older Fenian was progressively suffering hearing loss.[32] Later it was McGarrity, and not Devoy, who was credited with being 'the principal agent in organizing his [Pearse's] American tour'.[33]

Hobson and Pearse had separate itineraries and immediate objectives on their respective tours, but 23 March would find them sharing the podium as guest speakers at a fundraising event in Philadelphia. Both of them stayed with McGarrity and his family, who later remembered this as 'one of the treasured memories of my life to recall the scene in my home, 5412 Springfield Avenue, Philadelphia, with Pearse and Bulmer Hobson present'.[34] It is easy to imagine the ritual of the three men sitting in the McGarrity kitchen late into the night, drinking tea and talking animatedly about the Irish cause and the prospect of war.[35] Surely the Curragh Mutiny, when British army officers said they would resign their commissions if ordered to Ulster to suppress unionist opposition to Home Rule, which had happened only a few days prior, would also have featured as a topic of discussion.[36] McGarrity recalled:

> These hours seemed to fly with unusual swiftness! The prospect of Ireland once again standing to arms in defence of her ancient right, the plans for help from a great power, the general awakening that was taking place all over the country; such topics made us forget our immediate surroundings and think only of the prospect of the fight![37]

Despite the desperately serious nature of the topics of the discussion, the visit of Pearse, and presumably that of Hobson, bore the hallmarks of ordinary houseguests who were being welcomed into a typical family home. Pearse clearly enjoyed the interaction with his hosts during his visit and the memory of Pearse playing with his daughter stayed vividly with McGarrity:

> Sometimes he would take our little girl on his knee and hum an old song or a lullaby. His favourites were 'Gallon Gay' and 'Jack Smith, filly fine, Can you shoe this horse

o'mine.' Often, too, he would get the child to repeat the hymn – 'Daily, daily, sing to Mary' – and when she would lisp *Contempation* instead of *Contemplation*, he would laugh heartily and make her repeat the verse again.[38]

During the visit Pearse fell ill, extending his stay with the McGarritys, who looked after him until he was fit enough to travel back to New York to fulfil his upcoming fundraising events. In an April letter Pearse wrote:

> I want to thank you all for your kindness to me while in Philadelphia as if it were not enough to inflict myself on you I inflicted my illness on you. I will long remember your great kindness and especially your own generosity and thoughtfulness exhibited in such countless ways little and big.[39]

To increase Pearse's opportunity to raise more funds for St Enda's, McGarrity assisted him in extending his tour by arranging some additional speaking engagements. As Pearse's main focus of support in Philadelphia, McGarrity coordinated the work of others in the surrounding area such as Fr Coghlan of Pennsylvania, who was a life-long proponent of Ireland's self-government.[40] Pearse returned to Philadelphia for a second engagement on 26 April where he attended a banquet with Devoy,[41] and it is obvious that he greatly appreciated McGarrity's efforts to secure lecturing opportunities to benefit St Enda's saying, 'I cannot say how I appreciate your goodness in undertaking this second fixture for me. You and Philadelphia are great.'[42] McGarrity did a lot for Pearse, demonstrating not only the esteem in which he held the younger man and his mission, but also highlighting traits that contributed to McGarrity's success as an activist. He wrote letters;[43] made appointments; drove him around in one of his swanky cars (which Pearse admired so much);[44] and did things like facilitating Pearse's meeting with Professor Weygandt of the University of Pennsylvania, who was deeply interested in the work of St Enda's.[45]

Hobson's 1914 visit was a lower-key affair than his visit of 1907 during which he had introduced the Sinn Féin movement to the United States and gained fame as a skilled speaker.[46] His 1914 sojourn saw him act as courier of the document written by Casement, and he took advantage of his time in the United States to speak about conditions in Ireland.[47] The earlier adulation he received on his first trip, when he was lauded by McGarrity, may have been diminished and eclipsed by the presence of Pearse, who by this time was apparently the better speaker and a favourite of the crowds. Hobson departed the United States on 24 April 1914, the very night arms landed for the Ulster Volunteers in Larne and the Irish political landscape was significantly altered.

Pearse's trip extended for a couple of weeks after that of Hobson and it is clear that the schoolmaster had been particularly taken by his time with McGarrity: 'Once more I want to thank you for all your work for me, and your own great generosity alike in giving in hospitality and in time. I shall always think of you as the personification of generosity and of Philadelphia as its home.' He continued, 'Remember me to Mrs. McGarrity and to all in your home' and he closed with an invitation to McGarrity to come to Ireland that summer.[48] After his departure, the McGarrity home would not be without a houseguest for long; another major historical figure in the years culminating in 1916 arrived on their doorstep. Not dissimilar to the experiences of Pearse and Hobson who recently had been welcomed to 5412 Springfield Avenue, the new guest would develop a close friendship and political alliance with McGarrity. That man was Roger Casement.

As Lucy McDiarmid has outlined in her chapter in this volume, when Casement travelled to the United States in the summer of 1914, his primary function was to represent the Irish Volunteers, acting on behalf of his long-time friend and fellow Volunteers co-founder, Bulmer Hobson.[49] Casement had to first earn, at the very least, a modicum of Devoy's respect and he did so with the following description from Hobson of Devoy ('the old man') and McGarrity ringing in his ears:

> I would suggest that you keep in closest touch with the old man when you arrive. He and the chairman of the committee [McGarrity] are safe guides – the two best men in the country … There will be plenty who will want to 'capture' you because your name might help them politically, but our two friends will always give you the true facts of any such attempts. They know the country and conditions and you will meet many who will promise much and do very little.[50]

He was following a well-trodden path beaten by previous Irish nationalists who had come to the United States to raise money and support for their cause, and carried on from New York to McGarrity's residence in Philadelphia where he landed in mid-July 1914.[51]

His visit to McGarrity was a pragmatic one since McGarrity was president of the Irish National Volunteer Fund Committee of America, whose object was to 'aid the people of Ireland to organize, arm and equip a permanent national army of defense for the protection of their rights and liberties and to maintain the Territorial Integrity [sic] of Ireland'.[52] Even before the funding of the Irish Volunteers had been formalised, McGarrity had already raised money to buy arms and had received instructions from Eoin MacNeill on what was most needed for the cause.[53] Just as McGarrity welcomed Casement, the Howth plan was in motion with significant input from both men.[54]

Whether McGarrity knew Casement personally at this juncture is not certain, but he was most likely aware of Casement's human rights campaigns and career as British consul, and had more recently been acquainted with Casement's analysis of the increased tension between Britain and Germany from which Casement and Hobson believed Ireland could ultimately benefit.[55] We can reasonably speculate that Casement came up in conversations between McGarrity and Hobson, given the nature of their personal relations. By the time Casement arrived at McGarrity's Philadelphia residence, the task at hand for both men was the acquisition of money and arms for the Irish Volunteers. McGarrity obliged by providing Casement with $4,000 soon after his arrival.[56]

They were also in each other's company at McGarrity's home throughout the anxious hours leading up to the anticipated landing of the arms. In a telling recollection, Casement described the scene on that nervous night, underscoring McGarrity's impressive skills of organisation and public relations:

> The threatening situation in Europe following the cowardly murder of the Austrian Arch Duke Ferdinand and his Consort, and the ultimatum to Serbia gave me cause for some anxiety. At other times I should have been even more anxious but the fears for the landing of the guns at Howth swallowed up all other fears for the time. I had told only John Devoy and Joe McGarrity of the scheme planned before I left Ireland. It was timed for the forenoon of Sunday 26 July. That Sunday I spent at McGarrity's in great anxiety and on tenterhooks. It was a very hot day. At 7 p.m. Joe and I walked down the fields in front of his house until full twilight fell and darkness came. We lay on the grass and talked of Ireland – and often, watch in hand, said, 'now it is midnight in Dublin – now 1 a.m. – soon something must come over the cables.' About 9 p.m. one of the subeditors of a Philadelphia paper I need not name rang up Joe over the phone and told him a news message had just come in that instant saying that a landing of rifles for the Irish Volunteers had been effected near Dublin that day, that the British troops had been called out to disarm the Volunteers and had fired on them killing several persons and securing the rifles. Joe flew down to the Hibernia Club. Later on a message came from him to his wife to tell me that the guns had not been captured by the troops but retained by the Volunteers.
>
> We hardly slept that night. Joe returned about 2 a.m. (on the Monday morning) and told me he had already taken the steps necessary to have a great protest meeting for the following Sunday, 2nd August, in one of the big Theaters of the City and had announced me as the Chief Speaker!
>
> … So whether I liked it or not I was now in it up to my neck. I would have wished to keep quiet, but from every national point of view it was necessary this meeting should be held and if held that it should lack no support I could give it. So I reluctantly agreed to a step already taken in my name.

… From this on to Sunday 2nd August, McGarrity was busy and more than busy in the arrangements for the Sunday meeting. I was a passive agent in his strong hands. He did everything …[57]

The dedication that Casement and McGarrity shared in funding and arming the Volunteers surely played a role in bringing the two men together. But from their cooperation in these rallies and fundraisers and their clandestine machinations with representatives of the German government in the United States, a strong relationship developed between the two that is clearly evident and is not lost on Casement's biographers.[58] The hospitality that McGarrity and his family provided meant something special to Casement and appears to have gone beyond their shared ideals and revolutionary activities. He wrote to Mary Hynes, McGarrity's mother-in-law – shortly after having spent time at the McGarrity home in late July – intimating what it had meant to him:

I want to thank you all – first Mrs. McGarrity and yourself for your welcome to your home and for all your unfailing kindness to me while I was there … You were all so kind and nice to me that I felt I was in Ireland – that means I was at home. This is not to bid you goodbye at all, because I shall surely see you again; but just to say how much I felt your great kindness of heart and goodwill.[59]

But the affection flowed in both directions. Several days before his departure for Germany, Casement was with the McGarrity family for the last time. McGarrity's notes evoke a scene that is a curious admixture of friends, family, sentimentality, and the business of secret revolutionary activity. He recalled that it was 'a touching scene Sir Rs parting (he showed considerable emotion)', and Casement implored his friends to care for 'Ja Ja' (Casement's nickname for Meave, McGarrity's daughter), Mary Joseph (McGarrity's son), and to take Patricia, the family dog, out every day. McGarrity recalled 'shaking his hand saying God take care of you, Sir Rs reply was Oh no, God Save Ireland, I replied and You'.[60]

In his three-month stay in the United States Casement left such an impression on McGarrity and the other members of his family that this undercurrent of intimacy continued to flow from the pages of letters and memos that concerned 'Blackbird'– the pet name given to Casement by McGarrity due to his striking, swarthy features. Just days after his departure, concerned about the mission as much as the man, McGarrity recorded his reaction to the 'great news' that a British cruiser, *Hawke*, had been sunk by a German submarine. 'At least that Hawke will not [capture?] our blackbird,' he recalled thinking upon hearing the news; 'God guard my blackbird wherever he be.'[61]

This final thought echoed the prayer said by his daughter 'Ja Ja', whose nightly recitations for Casement are provided as the epigraph of this chapter.

This affection for Casement was also noted by Kuno Meyer, who, just after Casement's departure for Germany, played a key role in promoting Casement, his mission, and the ties between Germany and Ireland while on a speaking tour of the United States. While in Philadelphia, Meyer actually stayed in the very bed where Casement slept while at 5412 Springfield Avenue, and told Casement that McGarrity's children continued to pray for him each night.[62] Casement had instructed Meyer to visit McGarrity along with several others, but referred to McGarrity with a special warmth and called him a trusted friend for whom he felt the affection of a brother.[63] Meyer was particularly fond of McGarrity too, and wrote to Casement after his arrival to tell him that he was very pleased with all his friends, especially 'him of Philadelphia'.[64]

Meyer and McGarrity remained in constant contact as Casement's situation in Germany developed, and it has been suggested that both may have even played a role together not just in Irish revolutionary affairs during the First World War, but also in aiding an Indian nationalist conspiracy that involved many of the same German agents of intrigue stationed in the United States, including Franz von Papen who was instrumental in sending Casement to Germany.[65] McGarrity may have been chosen for this project by von Papen as a result of a message from Casement that put McGarrity at the top of the American list of individuals who could identify those suitable for sabotage.[66] In any event, one hardly needs to read between the lines of the letters that passed between McGarrity, Casement, and Meyer to find not just the crucial details involving their underground activities, but also a real sense of camaraderie and concern that suggests more than a relationship based solely on mutual geopolitical interests and intrigue.

Although McGarrity and Casement were only intermittently in each other's company while they frenetically travelled and worked to promote, fundraise, and organise, their trust and dedication to the other remained strong well after Casement left the McGarritys' Philadelphia home and landed overseas. McGarrity tended to Casement's requests when he could and sent his friend, Father John Thomas Nicholson of Philadelphia, to Germany to help Casement in his task of forming the Irish Brigade.[67] McGarrity even corresponded personally with Irish prisoners of war in Germany, and told one:

> you will meet a Father Nicholson in the camps he is Irelands [sic] true friend. You will also meet a tall man with a beard named Sir Roger Casement. he is also a true friend of

Ireland he is to form an Irish brigade and I hope you will join it atonce every Irishman here is praying for Germany to win and if she does she will free Ireland.[68]

Casement's time in the McGarrity home was multidimensional and productive, and it was there that he wrote and published several articles.[69] It was around this time too that Dr Patrick McCartan travelled to the United States ostensibly to explain to his old friend McGarrity, and others, about the exact nature of the battle to control the Volunteers.[70] McGarrity and McCartan were old close friends who had both grown up in Carrickmore and had shared in the experience of living in Philadelphia until McCartan returned to Ireland in 1905.[71] The day after his 1914 arrival in Philadelphia, McCartan and McGarrity were bound for New York to meet with Casement and Devoy, and it was there that McCartan was provided 'with a sense of Clan ambitions for a major armed showing in the context of the coming war between Britain and Germany'.[72] It was also from McGarrity's home that McCartan secured from Casement a document about the formation of the Irish Brigade in Germany, which he brought back to Ireland and was later read at the IRB Supreme Council.[73] These connections provide intriguing examples of how McGarrity and his family home were conduits of so many critical interactions in this period.

Overall, it is certain that McGarrity was constantly in touch with Ireland and with some of the most influential figures in the nationalist movement, including Tom Clarke,[74] Hobson, Casement, Seán Mac Diarmada,[75] McCartan, MacNeill, and Pearse, among others. But crucially he was also a leading figure in the network of Irish activists across the United States and in that way he provided a vital interface between Irish and Irish-American nationalism, just as his older ally Devoy had done for decades. McGarrity is the most prominent example of neglected republican nationalists in places beyond New York; John T. Keating in Chicago[76] who died in 1915 is another good example but there were others whom historians have generally overlooked. The friendships and interrelations of these individuals require examination, especially as they were not static, responding to changes in the political environment that were being shaped by local, national, and international realms. Hobson's fate provides a case in point: when he returned to Ireland in May 1914 he met with 'political turmoil'[77] and a course of events which would quickly see him diminish in significance.[78] When Pearse set off for the United States on 8 February,[79] on a long-planned tour that was mainly a mission to save his educational initiative, Hobson had bigger concerns and was a more influential figure. Within months, Pearse was on the ascent almost in tandem with Hobson's declining power. McGarrity weathered this change in personnel perfectly and took up with Pearse almost where Hobson left off. As F. X. Martin observed, personalities 'have always counted for much in the course of Irish history'.[80] In the period under scrutiny, McGarrity is the epitome of personality.

Of course, McGarrity's communications and relations with his 1914 houseguests neither began nor ended in 1914. Nor, as we have seen, was the scope of McGarrity's activity limited to Hobson, Pearse, and Casement. In March of 1914 McGarrity tested his strength and powers of organisation with a large gathering in Philadelphia 'whose purpose was to protest English contentions about the use of the Panama Canal'.[81] Much of his energy in 1914 was also devoted to securing the release of the Fenian Luke Dillon from a Canadian prison after which Dillon became McGarrity's right-hand man in Philadelphia.[82] Increasingly, a stint in Philadelphia and connecting with McGarrity was a rite of passage for many Irish activists. Within days of his arrival in the United States, labour leader Jim Larkin was slated to speak at a large Manchester Martyrs gathering in the City of Brotherly Love.[83] It is difficult to imagine that McGarrity was not behind the important public relations opportunity provided in having a purported descendent of a Manchester Martyr, embodied in Larkin, on the podium for the Irish of Philadelphia.[84]

There are so many aspects of McGarrity's endeavours that warrant further examination. This chapter has unpacked a specific theme and chronological focus but McGarrity was active on matters relating to Ireland for all of his adult life. His role as an activist who influenced the Irish-based republican nationalists and led Irish-American involvement is under-examined, as is the way in which he was able to rally the Irish of Philadelphia. He was clearly well connected and successful with powerful and wealthy Irish Americans.[85] But historian Dennis Clark has drawn attention to how McGarrity relied on a network dependent on individuals like Mike McGinn to mobilise for the nationalist cause by devising situations where no one could avoid the obligation of contributing:

> At one point, he [McGinn] demanded that saloonkeepers contribute cash to the cause from every third round of drinks. At factories where there was heavy Irish employment, he had men stationed on payday to collect on the spot. He had people patrol the entrances to savings banks to importune thrifty old ladies who were making deposits to forgo savings in favor of contributions to the Irish war chest.[86]

It is easy to lose sight of the fact that McGarrity balanced all this activity alongside a growing family[87] and his business interests, and it is worth noting that McGarrity was aware that his activities were not going unnoticed in certain quarters. An August 1914 entry in his personal notebook makes mention of a letter sent to another Clan member by the British secret service, promising rewards in return for spying on meetings of the

Irish Volunteers Fund Committee.[88] It is difficult to imagine how he handled it all and a communication from his Chicago-based, Cork-born ally, John T. Keating, would suggest that the pressure under which McGarrity was placing himself was not without impact. In December 1914, Keating wrote to Devoy, 'heard nothing from Joe McG recently. I hope he is feeling OK. I was afraid of [for] him when I last saw him. He was fatigued, nervous & run down & his smoking was excessive.'[89] We do not know how Kathryn McGarrity felt about her home being almost a halfway house for all these impassioned men. Perhaps she saw it as a way for her immigrant husband to remain connected to home. Nonetheless, the myriad of demands on McGarrity seemingly took a toll on his personal life and is sensitively captured by Tarpey:

> Mrs. McGarrity was to learn only too soon that her husband was more truly married to the Irish Republican dream. That Joseph McGarrity loved Kathryn there is no doubt. That he loved Cathleen Ní Houlihan first and fiercely there is no doubt either. But this other woman would take Joe away from his wife time and time again.[90]

It is important to remember just how committed McGarrity was to a non-sectarian vision of his home province. This is a trait that would define his engagement with Ireland for life. There is no stronger way to convey his vision than to use his own words. Penned in 1914, the poem was presumably his response to an environment in which the partition of Ireland was seeping into the discourse. Through his lines in 'To My Orange Countrymen' we get an insight into an optimistic vision of alliances that could not, nor ever would, materialise. The events of the decade to follow would lead McGarrity to strenuously protest partition, in both words and deeds, until his dying day. His poetic lines make particularly poignant reading:

> Shall we stand up and spar and fight
> As to which creed is wrong or right?
> While foreign knaves with guilty hand
> Still draw the life-blood from our land.
> No, for our land there is no hope
> If you for King, and I for Pope
> Shall fritter precious time away
> Disputing what the band shall play.
> So now, in spite of James or Bill,
> Let you and I a bumper fill
> Our hearts for one great purpose join,
> Forgetting Limerick and the Boyne.

And with a stripe of lily white
The orange and the green unite,
And side by side upon the plain,
We'll rend the despots galling chain.
Ah! That has been the tyrant's dread,
That orange and green, instead of red
Should float above a gallant band
Whom Saxon might, could not withstand.
Our country free they long have taught
To you, would be with danger fraught
They taught you that the Pope of Rome,
Would rule the land from Peter's dome.
What if upon the Sabbath day
We kneel at different shrines to pray?
There's but one God for you and me
There's but one land we'll die to free.
Wolfe Tone and Emmet gave their blood,
McCracken, with Lord Edward stood,
And Orr the scaffold did ascend,
All died their country to defend.
Shall we forget those heroes slain,
And still as bigot slaves remain,
To make a foreign horde secure,
In wringing taxes from the poor?
Swear by the blood that Emmet shed,
Swear by the heroes that are dead,
That we shall hence united be
In spite of Saxon plot or plea.
Oh! may God speed the coming day
When I can grasp your hand and say,
'Farewell to feud you fought with me,
We'r well repaid our land is free.'[91]

In many ways, 1914 can be seen as the anchor of McGarrity's deep-seated commitment to Irish self-government. In 1915 he prevented British attempts to infiltrate Clan na Gael.[92] In 1916 he was central in organising the Friends of Irish Freedom and in staging the Rising from the American side. Later he led protests in Philadelphia and New York following the suppression of the rebellion and the executions.[93] By 1920 alone his commitment to Ireland and Irish America would express itself in founding a newspaper; running for congress; organising the 1919 Irish Race Convention; and raising $1,000,000 for the Irish Victory Fund.[94] McGarrity's dedication to a united Ireland would remain with him until death and lead to his breaking with some of his closest allies like John Devoy (in 1920) and Éamon de Valera (in 1936).[95] As a key American-based organiser in the run-up to the Rising, it is abundantly clear that his role in its planning and financing cries out for re-examination in light of sources made available more recently. There is no doubt that contextualising him from the vantage point of 1914 allows us to gain a more nuanced understanding of the preparations for 1916, the *modus operandi* of a major figure, and the scholarship yet to be undertaken on the American dimension of Irish nationalism.

*The authors wish to sincerely thank Miriam Nyhan Grey for her exhaustive help in researching and writing this chapter. Much gratitude and credit is due to her vision of how to approach this complex historical figure. We are also appreciative of the readings of the chapter undertaken by Francis M. Carroll, Marion R. Casey, Michael Doorley, Terry Golway, and J. J. Lee.*

# CHAPTER EIGHT

# 'ST. ENDA'S IS NOW ONLY PART OF A BIGGER THING …'[1]

## PADRAIG PEARSE'S AMERICAN INTERLUDE

## *Maura Anand*

Two years before the Easter Rising, almost to the day, a young man enjoying the sights of New York had a silhouette portrait done at the top of the Woolworth Building, then the tallest building in the world.[2] In the course of that excursion, an interesting silhouette of Padraig Pearse was captured; few are aware that it was fashioned in New York during Pearse's visit of 17 February to 7 May 1914.[3] When he embarked on his one and only visit to the United States in an effort to raise funds for his school, St Enda's, he could probably be best described as a cultural nationalist. His interest in education, particularly through the medium of the Irish language, had been his main focus, and he was known primarily for his activities in the Gaelic League, and as a writer and educator. On his return to Ireland some three months later, his focus had expanded, as the epigraph of this chapter suggests. It is clear that Pearse's interest in the destiny of Ireland was evolving, particularly from 1913 onwards.[4] Some conclude that it was while on this lecture tour in the United States that Pearse completed 'his conversion to extreme republicanism'.[5] In keeping with the approach taken by Lucy McDiarmid on Casement's three-month American sojourn, this chapter places Pearse's historic visit to the United States under the spotlight.

Pearse first came to public notice as a young man with a vision for the overhaul and improvement of education for Ireland's youth, most particularly with an emphasis on child-centred education and on the preparation of the character of young boys for future manhood.[6] He founded St Enda's in 1908, but if he had any revolution in mind at that time it was a revolution in education. He had visited Wales and Belgium observing their educational systems, principally with a view to their treatment of bilingualism,[7] and was similarly impressed by the American public school model that prepared children for responsible citizenship through free education for all social classes.[8]

Many leading families in the Irish-Ireland movement entrusted their children to Pearse's new model school.[9] With Thomas MacDonagh[10] as Pearse's assistant, the school seemed to flourish and its popularity gained momentum. Not only did Pearse's brother, mother, and sister have a part to play in the school by taking on various administrative and teaching roles but others, like Padraic Colum, Douglas Hyde, and William Butler Yeats, were among St Enda's friends and supporters.[11] By all accounts the new school had 'captured the imagination of the wider nationalist population in a particularly overwhelming fashion'.[12] Even as late as 1915, when the first flush of enthusiasm for it had somewhat abated, Maud Gonne praised St Enda's, mentioning it in a letter to John Quinn. 'I don't know what I would give to be able to live in Ireland and have my boy educated at Pearse's school,' she wrote.[13] It must have been encouraging, and perhaps later influential, to Pearse to see that St Enda's could have a transatlantic appeal: a 1910 letter indicates that the influential Irish-American jurist Martin J. Keogh was interested in sending his two sons to St Enda's.[14] Pearse clearly was thinking about travelling to the United States at the time: another letter indicates that he was hoping to go 'to America in a year or two on a lecturing tour on behalf of the School'.[15]

St Enda's had encountered financial difficulties as a result of a move from its original premises at Cullenswood to the larger and costlier mansion known as the Hermitage.[16] In addition, Pearse had opened a sister school for girls, St Ita's, in 1910, but it was never to achieve the success of St Enda's. When it closed in 1912, he was left with a mountain of debt.[17] This placed Pearse under severe financial strain, with problems staving off creditors: even with the support of the loyal and dedicated teaching staff, he was keenly aware that the school's finances had reached crisis point.[18] His visit to the United States in 1914 was planned with a view to placing its finances on a more secure footing.[19]

Ruth Dudley Edwards contends that Pearse was determined not to disclose to the pupils that he was on an American fundraising tour and that it should be stressed that he would return in a few weeks.[20] However one pupil, Rónán Ceannt, sent a shamrock to New York to him for St Patrick's Day,[21] and towards the end of March Pearse wrote a letter to the boys, to be read out upon their return to school after Easter in mid-April. In it, he stated he would be home soon and advised them to work hard, even promising them a day off in celebration of his return.[22] Perhaps the pupils were not privy to the real purpose of the tour, but at least some were aware that Pearse was in the United States lecturing and that he was extending his stay.

Pearse was deeply committed to Gaelic culture and the furtherance of the Irish cultural identity. He had been the editor of the Gaelic League publication, *An Claidheamh Soluis*,[23] and as a teacher of the Irish language a primary focus was in the restoration of Irish as the spoken language in Ireland. After St Enda's move to the Hermitage, it is evident that he became increasingly inspired by Robert Emmet.[24] His interest soon spread to include Theobald Wolfe Tone, but at this time he would still have been considered a moderate within the Wolfe Tone Club, where he occasionally attended lectures and meetings.[25] In time he became a more proficient public speaker, particularly gaining recognition for orations on Emmet and Tone.[26] In 1912 he founded the organisation Cumann na Saoirse, an Irish-speaking political society, and an associated newspaper, *An Barr Buadh*.[27]

Just as Pearse was seriously contemplating an American sojourn, his political philosophy underwent a significant transformation. Historian J. J. Lee unpacks some of the aspects of Pearse's worldview most effectively:

> While he had by 1913 begun contemplating the possibility of rebellion, he was still struggling to reconcile his gradualist approach of 1912 with his perception of the growing improbability of home rule. The contradictory impulses can be gleaned from his behaviour throughout the year when he continued to retain hope of home rule while moving, should it founder, to contemplate the alternative of rebellion.[28]

By November 1913, Pearse felt that the Gaelic League was a 'spent force', stating the 'vital work to be done in the new Ireland will be done not so much by the Gaelic League itself as by men and movements that have sprung from the Gaelic League or have received from the Gaelic League a new baptism and a new life of grace'.[29] Despite evidence to suggest that he saw the Irish Volunteers and IRB organiser Bulmer Hobson as being extremist as late as the summer of 1913,[30] Pearse himself sought admission into the organisation in December.[31] Is it possible that his eagerness to join the IRB at that juncture was linked to ideas of enhancing and broadening his American networking base? Even if this is a reach, the timing of his induction into the brotherhood is interesting in relation to his overseas trip. Here again Lee locates the Pearse of the period:

In 1913 however, as he strove to convince the IRB leaders of the genuineness of his revolutionary aspirations, he embarked on a publication campaign which could at times strike strident notes. A classic example was *The Coming Revolution* in November 1913, in which he announced the shift from cultural to political in his priorities, now disingenuously presenting his Gaelic League years as having been intended from the beginning as merely an apprenticeship for the political struggle. In order to dispel the image of him as a 'harmless' cultural nationalist, he virtually set about reinventing himself in a manner likely to appeal to the 'hard men' of the IRB.[32]

So how, if at all, did his American tour fit into this? One might assume that Clan na Gael[33] support of Pearse visiting the United States was the natural order of things. However, evidence suggests that he initially approached the wealthy Irish-American patron John Quinn for assistance in setting up a tour. As we see in Úna Ní Bhroiméil's chapter in this volume, Quinn had been a key player in Douglas Hyde's successful 1905–6 American tour,[34] but he now refused to assist Pearse.[35] In order to get help in crossing the Atlantic, Pearse had to use other means through contacts much less politically moderate than Quinn.

Hobson had written to John Devoy in July 1913 advising him of Pearse's intent to make a trip, assuring the older campaigner that Pearse was 'all right and in line with us here and is a regular contributor to "Freedom"; the work he is doing is really of national importance,' adding in a postscript that Tom Clarke and Seán Mac Diarmada were in agreement with his evaluation.[36] In the absence of a reply from New York, Hobson sent a follow-up letter in October, again seeking approval from Devoy before solidifying any firm plans.[37] In this letter Hobson referred to a meeting between Pearse and the prominent Irish-American jurist, Daniel F. Cohalan, which had taken place a month earlier. Cohalan promised to help Pearse upon his arrival in the United States.[38] Hobson also received a positive response from the other key Clan na Gael figure, Joseph McGarrity,[39] who would feature prominently as an influence on Pearse, as we have seen.[40] There is a sense of deference towards Devoy in the tone of Hobson's letters to him and the older man clearly had veto power in matters of importance as it is evident in their communications that Hobson was regularly 'awaiting instructions' from the old Fenian.[41]

Once plans were firmly put in place for Pearse's visit, *The Gaelic American* newspaper elevated him as a coming attraction in advance of his arrival by publishing his Volunteer speeches and giving him a wealth of publicity.[42] McGarrity was already touting Pearse as a dynamic Irish nationalist in an effort to whet the appetite of the crowds before he ever set foot on American soil.[43] Pearse appears to have been well aware of the necessity to get 'boomed' in the Irish-American papers prior to his tour and curated suitable material for that specific purpose.[44] He left from Queenstown (Cobh) on 8 February 1914, on the SS *Campania*, arriving in New York on 17 February,[45] after a harrowing journey due to adverse weather conditions.[46]

Fundraising in the United States for Irish causes and charities was nothing new.[47] The pages of *The Gaelic American* are replete with examples of collections for Ireland in 1914 alone and Americans were not unused to being asked to help Ireland. Clearly the consistency and frequency of the appeals for financial help could become tiresome, as is illustrated in the following doggerel written by John Quinn later that year upon receipt of yet another appeal for monetary aid, this time from Pearse:

> Damn, damn, damn the Gaelic Leaguers,
> Damn the Parliamentarians too,
> Damn, Damn, Damn the Clan-na-Gaelers
> Damn all the Irish missions through and through,
> I am sick and tired of their stories
> Of all their hard luck tales and plaints;
> I think that they have become a race of spongers,
> And have long since ceased to be the land of saints.
>
> ...
>
> Redmond is senile,
> Carson's heroics a bore,
> The Volunteers are flabby
> The Parliamentary Party a whore.
>
> ...
>
> And thank God and the saints that we here
> In benighted U.S.A. will be free
> From their damned appeals by night and by day.[48]

Pearse's visit coincided with that of Diarmuid Lynch and Thomas Ashe who also arrived in February on a lengthy and extensive fundraising tour on the Gaelic League's behalf.[49] Simultaneously, collecting was under way on behalf of the ailing Jeremiah O'Donovan Rossa, with acknowledgements for donations to that fund published weekly in *The Gaelic American*.[50] Devoy was also assisting the Irish Volunteers, as an April 1914 letter from The O'Rahilly attests.[51] Nevertheless, Pearse's visit was seen as significant enough to warrant advance publicity in *The Gaelic American*. He also received a modicum of publicity from the more moderate *Irish World*, where his work and fundraising efforts as headmaster of St Enda's had due mention.[52] Some of his objectives are clearly outlined in an appeal run in a March edition of *The Gaelic American*:

> I believe that in appealing on behalf of St. Enda's I am appealing on behalf of the most important thing in Ireland. Our work is radical: it strikes at the root of anglicisation. Infinitely the most vital duty of the hour at home is to train the young in an Irish way for the service of Ireland. It is to this we have set our hands. The work of St. Enda's, be it remembered, is not confined to its own sixty pupils, but, through the influence it has already had on the spirit and curricula of the other schools and colleges, extends to every boy and girl in Ireland. It is the literal truth to say that the whole experiment of Irishising education must stand or fall with St. Enda's.[53]

Although Irish Americans still supported Home Rule and John Redmond at the time of Pearse's visit, significant shifts were beginning to take place that make his timing of note. On 9 March, less than three weeks after the start of his tour, the Home Rule Bill was given a second reading offering the compromise of the partial exclusion of Ulster for a period of six years.[54] This development was seen as a calamity by many moderates in New York who were shocked at the idea of the 'dismemberment' of Ireland.[55] We can only speculate as to how Pearse and his American hosts were responding to the shifting reality, particularly as 1914 progressed, that their view of Irish nationalism might actually overtake the existing orthodoxy of Home Rule and support of John Redmond. McGarrity's comments on this period shed further light on how Pearse's mission to publicise St Enda's was eclipsed by bigger developments in Europe:

> I did not grasp at the time the real importance of St. Enda's. The uppermost thought in my mind was the growth and equipment of the Volunteers. Every news item from Dublin, Belfast or London concerning the arming of the Ulster Volunteers was eagerly read by both the organized and unorganized Irish in America.[56]

Pearse's itinerary generally consisted of a series of lectures and speaking engagements in and around New York, Massachusetts (Springfield), Pennsylvania (Philadelphia), Rhode Island (Providence), and Delaware (Wilmington). It appears that his early speeches in the United States may have focused more on literary and educational subjects, but over time the emphasis is reputed to have shifted. It is suggested that he became sensitive towards the level of interest audiences had in the Irish Volunteers, and that therefore, early in the tour, he began to rely more heavily on his Volunteer connection for material, relegating his appeal for St Enda's to the closing part of his speeches.[57] As matters became more pressing with regard to Ulster, this seems logical.

He clearly saw his presence in the United States as an opportunity to give 'a view of Irish affairs which will have the advantage of being new to them, with the additional advantage of it being true' and his observations on American understanding (or lack thereof) are instructive:

> Since I have landed in this country I have not seen in any American newspaper a reference to Ireland that was even approximately accurate in its facts. Personalities the most diverse are confounded; antagonistic movements are spoken of as if they were identical; phases of the same movement are made to appear mutually destructive; men are represented as holding the exact views they exist to combat.[58]

He continues by giving specific examples of how he sees the American media misrepresenting or misinterpreting Ireland:

> You identify the national movement with the Home Rule episode; you regard the newly formed Volunteers as a force designed to help the British Government to suppress Sir Edward Carson; you speak of the dramatic movement as if it were embodied in the Abbey Theatre; you imagine that the literary revival in Ireland is expressing itself in English. We, on our side, have doubtless many mistaken notions as to American life and politics, but I do not think we make such blunders as these.[59]

This interview sheds light on the confusion about printed news from Ireland and is also interesting evidence of the power of first-person viewpoints at this time. The next part of the commentary proves particularly interesting and prophetic in light of what we know comes next and it is worth noting that this excerpt was italicised in the *Irish American Weekly*:

> If Home Rule comes, a Separatist Party will at once make its appearance in the Irish House of Commons backed by a strong armed movement outside; if Home Rule does not come, the whole nation will automatically swing back to the policy and methods of the Fenians. In either event, the year 1914 will mark, not the beginning of a peace with England, but the beginning of a new and stirring chapter in the Irish struggle for independence.[60]

Had Pearse already sensed the changing nature of Irish-American associational allegiances when he made the concluding comments? 'I write from the standpoint of a Separatist, but I believe that the majority of those who call themselves Home Rulers will accept my view of the situation.'[61]

In terms of his itinerary, his calendar was easily filled with scheduled appearances at various Irish-American societies and clubs, and based on the evidence which has survived, he probably spoke at upwards of 20 events.[62] The Long Island Clan na Gael staged a major Emmet commemorative event in Brooklyn on 1 March, to a rousing crowd of 2,500 who turned out in blizzard conditions.[63] He raised the roof with his Emmet speech and told the eager and receptive audience that 'before this generation has passed the Volunteers will draw the sword of Ireland'.[64] Around that time he became concerned that his appeal for St Enda's was taking time to gain momentum and, in a letter to McGarrity, reflected that the task of attracting donations to St Enda's was a daunting one.[65] Naturally, it was easier to get attention and rouse Irish-American audiences on the matter of arming or organising the Irish Volunteers that spring rather than on a more abstract and long-term investment in an educational institution like St Enda's. One could argue that the geopolitical developments in Ireland overtook Pearse's ability to privilege his initial American agenda: his school.

Nevertheless, McGarrity did his best to help and made sure that Pearse's upcoming events were well advertised in *The Gaelic American*.[66] A week later he again spoke at an Emmet commemoration event, this time a concert, with Bulmer Hobson sharing the platform.[67] According to Hobson's later reflection, this trip to the United States was aimed at ascertaining German interest in the 'national movement in Ireland' and that Pearse knew nothing of that agenda.[68] Nevertheless, with Hobson by his side, Pearse's speech was even more incendiary, as the following excerpt referencing England illustrates: 'We pursue her like a sleuth-hound; we lie in wait for her and come upon her like a thief in the night; and some day we will overwhelm her with the wrath of God.'[69] Speeches on Emmet were ideal conduits for bringing the subject matters of nationalism, political aspirations, and republican ideals to the fore.[70]

Pearse was invited to attend the Irish Volunteers Ball held at the Terrace Garden on 58th Street in New York City, on St Patrick's Day, to speak about the growth of the Irish Volunteers.[71] Another noteworthy event on his agenda was in Philadelphia on 23 March, where he made a speech that was later described as a 'masterpiece' by McGarrity.[72] Decades afterwards McGarrity fondly recalled the nights he spent with Pearse and Hobson in the kitchen of his own home in Philadelphia, where they spent hours upon returning from such meetings drinking tea and talking about Ireland's destiny:

> These hours seemed to fly with unusual swiftness! The prospect of Ireland once again standing to arms in defence of her ancient right, the plans for help from a great power, the general awakening that was taking place all over the country; such topics made us forget our immediate surroundings and think only of the prospects of the fight.[73]

Pearse and McGarrity, both poets and only five years apart in age, cemented a warm friendship.[74]

Pearse spent the Easter holiday and the following week in New York City and during that time was invited to address the Mayomen's Association.[75] In between engagements he managed to contact a distant relative of his mother, who contributed generously to the St Enda's school fund.[76] The St Enda's Field Day event at Celtic Park in Long Island City in mid-April was probably the most ambitious single event of his American itinerary. It was a day-long event with Irish ballads, the Irish War Piper's Band, hornpipe and reel contests, football, and a hurling match, all culminating in an evening of Irish and American dancing to McIntyre's First Regiment Irish Volunteers' Band. The programme for the event pointed out to attendees that the new 'Volunteer Army' had 'corps in twenty-six of her thirty-two counties. After all the centuries Ireland's military spirit remains as robust as when she achieved her greatest victory in arms. Therein lies Ireland's hope.'[77] The Field Day was attended by 2,500 supporters. An incident was sparked when some Redmondites heckled Pearse and he had to be assisted by members of the New York Irish Volunteers.[78] As is demonstrated in John T. Ridge's chapter in this volume on the associational culture of Irish New York, many of the area's Irish associations were slow to abandon Home Rule. At the Field Day Pearse encountered the resistance to moving away from constitutional nationalism first-hand.

He had several other speaking engagements in Philadelphia and New York,[79] and on 6 May, his last night in the United States, he received an enthusiastic welcome when he was introduced by poet and activist Peter Golden to crowds at the Harlem Gaelic Society.[80] Initially, he had planned to return to Ireland by 21 March, but he decided to extend his stay until 7 May apparently at the invitation of Clan na Gael.[81] In addition, Pearse wrote to his mother of his intention to return to the United States for a further tour from October 1914 until the spring of 1915.[82] He returned to St Enda's only a month before the end of the school year. Clearly the pupils of St Enda's had missed their popular headmaster, because they gave him a rousing welcome upon his arrival back on 15 May.[83] The extension of his time abroad is important as it clearly indicates an acceleration of the shift in his priorities and that Pearse found the United States ideologically, logistically, and financially worthwhile.

By the time of his departure the fund for St Enda's yielded almost $3,300 but it is likely that the trip netted Pearse around $4,000[84] once all the donations were received and tallied.[85] By means of comparison and as a demonstration of the scale of support for Home Rule we should recall, as Francis Carroll explained in his chapter, that the Irish Parliamentary visit to the United States managed to net $100,000.[86] Further donations trickled in after Pearse's return home, *The Gaelic American* continuing to accept donations on his behalf.[87] Fundraising events for St Enda's continued even after his departure, details of which can be found in the Celtic Park Field Day programme.[88] He received donations from far afield, for example, from the 'Patriot Priest', Father Michael Hannan of Butte, Montana,[89] and he also received monies from Salt Lake City, Utah.[90] McGarrity sent a personal gift of £700 in gold[91] to Pearse in July to be used for the school and would continue to provide monetary support afterwards.[92]

While he was still in the United States, and in addition to soliciting donations, Pearse contemplated other methods of securing the future of St Enda's.[93] He advertised opportunities for American boys to enrol at the school and was successful in gaining three American pupils, John Kilgallon[94] of Far Rockaway and William Collins of New York, who both arrived at the school in September 1914,[95] and Eugene Cronin of Brooklyn, who actually accompanied him on the ship back to Ireland.[96] Pearse was aware that very few families might be willing to send a boy 3,000 miles away from home for a secondary education and was realistic that the idea held limited appeal.[97] He also considered leasing the Hermitage to Americans as a summer residence, a suggestion put forward by his mother, but soon realised the futility of that idea as he knew the building would not be luxurious enough for wealthy Americans, based upon the high living standard he had himself observed and witnessed while in the United States.[98] Other American fundraising strategies for St Enda's were considered during his visit, including naming classrooms after donors and mounting acknowledgement plaques in the school.[99]

Although Pearse moved primarily in Clan na Gael circles while in the United States, his status as a cultural nationalist, writer, and educator allowed him to also reach out to other Americans. One such prominent figure was John Quinn, who came to admire Pearse's work. Although his initial communication with Pearse was cool, he did invite him to his home, afterwards recalling poignantly:

> I remember his sitting near a window in my drawing room and looking out into Central Park, covered with snow, about twelve o'clock at night, and talking about his hopes and dreams for Ireland; and I remember well, and often think of it as I look at that chair and out of that window, his saying, quite simply, 'I would be glad to die for Ireland ... any time.'[100]

Although their political views differed significantly at times, such was Quinn's interest in Pearse that he appealed to the politically moderate William Bourke Cockran to support St Enda's, with a promise he would match Bourke Cockran's contribution.[101] During the course of his time in New York, Pearse also met with Dr Thomas Addis

Emmet, Robert Emmet's esteemed grandnephew, which must have been particularly meaningful.[102]

Historians differ on the cause and timing of the switch in ideology that thrust Pearse into militancy. Joost Augusteijn has reservations that there was any noticeable shift towards revolutionary methods while on the American trip, whereas Ruth Dudley Edwards, Elaine Sisson and Seán Farrell Moran place greater importance on the time spent in the United States as the catalyst.[103] J. J. Lee credits the American trip as a factor but cites events at home as the ultimate cause of Pearse's change in approach.[104] Rather than attributing the major shift in Pearse's purpose in life from pedagogue to patriot to a particular identifiable single event on the visit to the United States, it was probably a confluence of contributing factors. Timing and events in Ireland and beyond certainly played a part. Remember that while he was sightseeing in New York and engrossed in his mission to save St Enda's from financial ruin and publicise the Irish Volunteers, arms were landing in Larne for the Ulster Volunteers.

On a more personal level, Pearse had the opportunity to take a hiatus from the day-to-day running of St Enda's, freeing him from the minutiae of the daily routine, which of course provided him the pause and luxury to envision a larger focus. The American tour allowed him to meet with influential, like-minded individuals, and have the opportunity for discourse about the future of Ireland in a republic where opinions could be expressed largely without fear of reprisal. He had the close-knit network of Clan na Gael at his disposal and the advantage of publicity in *The Gaelic American*. He had the unique opportunity to make speeches and lecture repeatedly on the same subject matter, giving him a fluency of oratory that increased his dynamism and perfected his delivery. The alleged adulation of the crowds surely appealed to his ego.

He developed friendships, especially with Joseph McGarrity, which influenced and determined the course of the remainder of his life. He spent time in the company of impressive men of note, like Judge Cohalan, who had fulfilled his earlier promise to Pearse by using considerable influence to get additional donations for St Enda's.[105] He spent time in the company of dedicated separatists, becoming accustomed to his newly acquired and more deliberate stance on Ireland's destiny. His heightened confidence prepared him for a potential future leadership role. As one scholar has noted, in the United States he 'met, in men like Devoy and McGarrity, revolutionaries beside whom the militarism and fanaticism of his Dublin colleagues paled into milksop petulance'.[106] Finally, it must be noted that, just as American readers were following the developments that ultimately led to war in Europe in the summer of 1914, Pearse found himself in a setting in which other examples of diaspora nationalism might have offered him some new perspectives.

'After he came back from U.S.A nothing was too extreme for him.'[107] In Ireland he quickly gained attention as a radical and was somewhat ostracised by some.[108] Several pupils left St Enda's when their parents became apprehensive of Pearse's political views. In a letter to McGarrity in September 1914, he reported, 'We have fewer boys than last year. My political opinions are looked upon as too extreme and dangerous and parents are nervous.'[109] In March 1915, Pearse wrote to Desmond Ryan's father advising him, 'Yes, we are having a struggle, but other interests distract my attention from St. Enda's and then it does not seem so bad.'[110] Pearse was clearly already on a certain path and even his beloved St Enda's took a back seat to his larger vision for Ireland. In August 1915, he was chosen by Tom Clarke to deliver the oration at the graveside of O'Donovan Rossa.[111] If Pearse did meet the ailing Fenian while he was on his American sojourn, no evidence of such a meeting has yet come to light. But it seems that Mary Jane O'Donovan Rossa, in April 1914, did discuss the plan to bring the old Fenian home for burial when the inevitable occurred.[112] We can only speculate, but perhaps Mary Jane heard the young, energetic Pearse deliver a fiery speech and suggested him as a possible orator. In any case, as of May 1914, Pearse too could claim a place in the pantheon of Irish Fenians who had breathed the republican American air and was, by definition, now part of a 'bigger thing'.

How Pearse's American trip relates to the evolution of his political philosophy is worth pondering. For example, what is the correlation, if any, between his more hard-line stance and his induction into the IRB immediately prior to his coming to the United States? Or, if John Quinn had agreed to help Pearse when he initially sought assistance, would the Pearse that emerged in 1914 have been different, given the circles he would have moved in with well-known Irish-American moderates? As historians, we are always challenged to attempt to convey the significance of historical events without imposing the weight of what we know happens next. With the evolution of partition as an issue and the arming of the Ulster Volunteers, Pearse was provided with a bird's eye view of Irish-American reactions. Did this experience leave a lasting mark? That is difficult to definitively argue but one can point to Pearse's sojourn in the United States as coming at a significant time in the evolution of his segue from pedagogue to patriot and, as such, warrants due consideration, forcing us to ask other questions. If war had not erupted, would Pearse have returned to the United States, as he indicated he would? How might he have expanded his political ideas and contacts across the Atlantic? What kind of relationship would he have built with Irish America? While the United States played a huge role in his own destiny, Pearse never returned to New York or to McGarrity's home in Philadelphia or to the top of the Woolworth Building. His destiny was in Dublin in 1916.

*I would like to express thanks to Brian Crowley for his generous assistance in researching this topic. I am also grateful for feedback on this chapter provided by Marion R. Casey and J. J. Lee. The mentorship provided by Miriam Nyhan Grey has been crucial not only to this chapter but also during my journey through the Masters of Arts in Irish and Irish-American Studies at Glucksman Ireland House NYU.* Go raibh míle maith agat.

# CHAPTER NINE

# 'BIG JIM' LARKIN, THE UNITED STATES AND THE EASTER RISING

## *Emmet O'Connor*

*I have nothing to say on the Irish question.*
New York Times, 30 April 1916

A product of the Irish diaspora, James 'Big Jim' Larkin is the greatest hero of the Irish working class; the man who led 'the risen people' against the Dublin employers in the 1913 lockout, and a trade unionist pure and simple, with a unifying message of solidarity.[1] At least, that is how the Irish trade union movement has chosen to remember him, and would like to preserve him. In the process, it has tried to forget his controversial career after 1913 that contributed to chronic internecine friction in the movement and ignore his nationalism, which laid the basis of intermittent confrontation between Irish and British-based trade unions, confining the labour association with republicanism to James Connolly. In reality, Larkin's views on the national question were exactly the same as Connolly's, and before his departure to the United States in 1914 Larkin was by far the more influential. Connolly enjoyed a transatlantic reputation as a polemicist on the far left, but he lacked Larkin's ability to move the masses. Tall, well-built, and a powerful, natural orator, with a fertile mind and volcanic energy, Larkin was one of the great labour champions in an age of greats.

Where Connolly had the advantage was that he could write on politics, concisely and consistently, had a balanced personality, and a mature commitment to the cause. Larkin, on the other hand, became a victim of his personality. A man of great strengths of character as well as great weaknesses, success from 1911 had encouraged him to develop a personality cult. Defeat in 1913 and 1914 turned his egotism to egomania, and left him prey to his most serious faults: insecurity, pettiness, and jealousy. In Ireland, Larkin's nationalism arose from a strategic response to the problems of the labour movement. In the United States, he grew self-indulgent, and his worst features came to the fore in his response to 1916's Easter Week.

Born in Liverpool in 1874, Larkin was raised in an Irish enclave near the south docks, and imbibed the Fenianism of his family.[2] Such was his identification with Ireland that he would insist he had been born in the maternal family homestead in south Down. In 1907, he arrived in Ireland as an agent of the Liverpool-based National Union of Dock Labourers. Since the Great Famine, Irish trade unions had been retreating into the British labour movement, as the economy and population declined. Initially Larkin rebuffed overtures to form an Irish union, saying it would be wrong to divide workers on national lines. But his experience of Irish industrial relations, exacerbated by mounting friction with the union executive over his militancy and insubordination, brought him to the conclusion that British unions would never commit sufficient resources to tackle the anti-union outlook of Irish employers. In 1909 he launched the Irish Transport and General Workers' Union (ITGWU). The preamble to the rules confirmed that the union would be not Irish merely, but nationalist as well: 'Are we going to continue the policy of grafting ourselves on the English Trades Union movement, losing our identity as a nation in the great world of organised labour? We say emphatically, No. Ireland has politically reached her manhood [sic].'[3] It marked the start of a project that led to the rebirth of an Irish labour movement. Influenced by syndicalism and American revolutionary industrial unionism, Larkin hoped to unite all Irish workers in 'one big union'. And now that nationalism was water to the mill, he endorsed Irish-Irelandism with the sentimental blarney of the exile. 'To Irishise everything from Dunleary to Ceann Leime is our object … Our metropolis is Dublin – bad as it is,' declared his paper, the *Irish Worker*.[4]

Irish labour historiography has usually treated labour and nationalism as dichoto-mous.[5] But with Larkin, as with Connolly, the two were integral. Separatism was central to ITGWU strategy, and of tactical benefit. Republican nationalists were notably more sympathetic to strikers than constitutional nationalists in the strike wave between 1911 and 1913, and the difference became more pronounced after August 1913, when the

Dublin Employers' Federation locked out over 20,000 workers to smash the ITGWU and its syndicalist ideas.[6] In January 1914, Larkin admitted defeat and advised his members to get their jobs back as best they could. The ITGWU emerged from the lockout more aggressively nationalist. Up to 1916 it would criticise republicans not only for not being socialist, but for not being republican. Larkin initiated the shift in emphasis: he lost his appetite for union work after the lockout and took a keener interest in politics. In March 1914, with Seán O'Casey, he turned the Citizen Army, formed during the lockout as a picket militia, into a pocket army, with a republican constitution. In June, after a section of the IRB dissented from John Redmond's demand that the Irish Volunteers come under his control, Larkin led the Citizen Army to join republicans at the annual Wolfe Tone commemoration and formed a friendship with Tom Clarke.[7]

Two factors in particular intensified Larkin's nationalism. One was the Liberal government's suggestion that the Home Rule crisis might be defused through partition. As an 'Ulsterman', Larkin was incensed, and responded with a manifesto that was more nationalist than socialist:

> Fellow workers,
>     To us of the Irish working class the division of Ireland into two parts is unthinkable. To us as Irish men the cutting off of that province or any part thereof which gave to our country such men as Shane O'Neill, Hugh Roe O'Donnell, Aodh Rua O'Neill, McCracken, Orr, Francis Davis, 'The Belfast Man,' and the host of northern men who battled for freedom, and which from a labour as well as a national point of view is of such importance, is an act of pure suicide and should not be persisted in. We claim Ulster in its entirety, her sons are our brothers, and we are opposed to any attempt to divide us.[8]

The outbreak of world war in August acted as a second catalyst in driving Larkin into a deeper Fenianism. Even before the simmering crisis in the Balkans had bubbled over, the *Irish Worker* called on 'every man who believed in Ireland as a nation to act now. England's need, our opportunity. The men are ready. The guns must be got, and at once.' A few were 'got', smuggled from Liverpool by Larkin's boyhood friend, Fred Bower.[9] Throughout August and September Larkin made it very clear that he favoured a rising and deplored the pro-war policy of 'Judas' Redmond.

Quite possibly, Larkin's febrile response was affected by stress. The lockout brought him international renown but left him exhausted and aggravated his personality problems. Big Bill Haywood, co-founder of the Industrial Workers of the World (IWW), had suggested a speaking tour of the United States when the pair met at a rally in Manchester in November 1913. In December it looked alluring to one who always found defeat difficult to face. Over the coming months Larkin enquired about lecturing with contacts in New Zealand, South Africa, New York, and Butte, Montana, where many Irish had gone to mine the 'copper mountain'.[10] By September, he had become so awkward to work with that his colleagues were happy to let him go. On 23 October 1914, shadowed by two detectives, he boarded the Liverpool boat at Kingstown, Dublin with two suitcases and a black trunk.[11] Connolly took over as commandant of the Citizen Army, editor of the *Irish Worker*, and acting general secretary of the ITGWU.

Why Larkin left seemed of no consequence to his comrades. Little credence was given to his statement in the *Irish Worker* that he was going to raise funds for his cash-strapped union. Some, including friends like O'Casey, thought he wished to evade impending trouble over ITGWU insurance money misspent on the 1913 struggle. The common assumption, actually expressed in an illuminated address from the Dublin trades council, was that he needed to recuperate and would be back before too long.[12] It was an indication of how secretive Larkin could be. He had long wanted to move on, tired of failure and running a crippled union. He needed action and success. Haywood believed the United States to be the start of a world tour. Larkin kept his options open by remaining titular general secretary of the ITGWU and leaving his Liverpudlian wife, Elizabeth, and their four children in Dublin. Another explanation was held by the Dublin Metropolitan Police (DMP), who reckoned that he was already receiving money from the Germans through Clan na Gael and that his 'real object' in the States was to 'advance German interests'.[13] Whether this was true would become very important in 1923.

After a short stopover in Liverpool, Larkin landed in New York on 2 November. He made his home in Greenwich Village, where he would live again during his two later periods in the city, in 1918–19 and in 1923. He first presented his credentials to the Socialist Party of America, and then called the offices of *The Gaelic American* with a note from Clarke asking John Devoy to 'do what he could for him'.[14] Larkin intended to make a living out of speeches on labour topics and opposition to the world war, and would have preferred to work with the socialists, but Devoy was quicker to help him with speaking engagements, some featuring stage armies of German Uhlans and Irish Volunteers. Another offer of assistance came from Captain Karl Boy-Ed, the German naval attaché, who said he would pay $200 per week for propaganda and sabotage. Larkin replied that he was already engaged in organising strikes that would disrupt war-related industries. When Boy-Ed persisted, Larkin explained that he did not want a German victory, favouring a military 'deadlock' leading to workers' revolts in the belligerent countries, and would not take money from the Germans or collude in sabotage on humanitarian grounds.[15] As early as January 1915, Larkin had come to the attention of the French ambassador, Jules Jusserand, who reported to Paris that Kuno Meyer, the famous German Celticist, was making 'every effort to stir up German sympathies in Irish circles', and had 'publicly fraternised with the semi-anarchist politician Jim Larkin who is well known here'.[16]

By now Larkin was running into trouble. The socialists were hostile to the German connection. Compounding the problem, the press sensationalised his meetings, giving prominence to his denunciation of Britain and support for Germany, highlighting heckling and disruption, claiming that he had called for bomb throwing, and referring to him as an 'IWW agitator'.[17] His association with the IWW alienated the right wing of the Socialist Party. In fact, he long declined to join any left wing group in the United States to avoid cramping his style. It was simply that his initial contacts were mainly with old friends of Connolly.

Superficially, Larkin began drifting away from Clan na Gael. Devoy said the New York socialists had turned him against Clan, and that Clan activists were alienated by Larkin's attacks on them.[18] However, it may be that the Germans wanted a more clandestine relationship. The British claimed to have intercepted a message from the Foreign Office in Berlin to their Washington embassy on 28 January advising Devoy: 'Support of Larkin entails loss of sympathy in many quarters of Ireland.'[19] A minute from the Irish Chief Secretary's Office to the DMP on 3 March noted: 'Larkin has dropped his German Uhlan and Irish Volunteer shaking hands & is at present an ineffectual socialist speaker.' There was no objection to a proposal from the Commissioner of Dominion Police in Canada to discontinue reporting on Larkin's speeches. The DMP's main concern was to secure evidence of treason, which it now had in plenty, and to have advance warning should Larkin try to return to Ireland. The DMP maintained its own informants in New York for some months, but its interest in Larkin faded until a renewed alarm in 1917.[20] In reality, Larkin was developing more secretive contacts with the Germans and Clan na Gael.[21] When in New York he continued his almost daily visits to Devoy in the offices of *The Gaelic American*.[22] But he was still determined to be his own man and a free agent.

In mid-July 1915, Larkin began a lecture tour of the Pacific states in San Francisco. Concentrating on three themes – the war, industrial unionism, and Ireland – he brought them together in a way that was open to misinterpretation:

> In this war was the workingmen are being used by both sides as tools. I believe the
> Allies are absolutely in the wrong, and personally I object to the British government at

all times. England has been the bully of the world, and her outcry against the German campaign in Belgium is humbug. England has always interfered with the development of small nationalities. For every crime the Germans have committed in Belgium, England has committed one hundred in Ireland.[23]

'We are not pro-German,' he insisted, 'as has been often said. We are pro-human–for all mankind instead of for a limited nationalism that must always breed wars.'[24]

The Germans continued to cultivate Larkin. He and Devoy were chez Judge Daniel F. Cohalan the night Kuno Meyer brought Roger Casement's first message from Germany.[25] On returning to New York in April 1915, Larkin was informed of 'antagonisms' between the German authorities and Casement that were hampering Casement's efforts to raise a liberation army from Irish prisoners of war. Thinking that one from a working-class background might do better, the Germans proposed that Larkin go to Germany via Spain, but 'for various reasons' the enterprise failed. Larkin suggested that Robert Monteith go in his stead. Monteith had served in the British army and was employed for many years as a foreman in the ordnance depot at Island Bridge Barracks, Dublin. He joined the Socialist Party of Ireland in 1911 and was dismissed from his job on security grounds in November 1914. He then worked as a drill instructor with the Irish Volunteers in Limerick, and went to the United States in August 1915. He was duly seconded by Clarke and arrived in Berlin in October.[26]

The public lectures did not solve Larkin's financial problems, and in September 1915 he reverted to his old trade, and became an organiser for the Western Federation of Miners. For him, this was a regression. If the dream of a world tour had crumbled, he wanted to agitate, not organise. He left the job after three weeks when the Germans offered him more lucrative work. In the early summer he had initiated a deeper collusion, and requested Devoy to act as a conduit for proposals to the Germans and the receipt of money from them. In the autumn, he was invited to travel from Montana to Washington, DC to meet the German diplomat, Count Georg Muenster zu Derneberg. Again, he was pressed to supervise sabotage on the waterfront, and again, he insisted, he refused.[27] As an example of the kind of work he was willing to do, he cited the disruption of arms production through strikes in the Remington Arms companies in Bridgeport, Connecticut.[28] A strike for shorter hours per day had hit the Remington companies in July and led Remington and three other munitions companies to concede the eight-hour day. Larkin was based in New York at the time, and the press attributed the unrest to German agents.[29] Devoy claimed that an arrangement was made for the Germans to bankroll agitation of that kind. For political or legal reasons, he must have suspected he was under surveillance and Larkin demanded that the monies be transmitted through Devoy, who agreed with reluctance, feeling he was being used. The total amount received is unknown. Devoy recalled a request for the substantial figure of $10,000 to $12,000 being readily accepted, but not the period involved. Thanks to the Germans, Larkin spent two years doing what he liked best: speaking, writing, editing, publishing, and travelling, ranging from coast to coast and south of the border. He made Chicago his base and persuaded Elizabeth to join him with the two youngest children.[30]

Keeping an eye on Dublin, Larkin worried about Connolly's intentions. He called repeatedly for action in Ireland. In early September, Kuno Meyer found him reassuring on preparations for the Rising.[31] But he did not want Connolly grabbing the glory. Both his brother, Pete, a fellow transatlantic agitator, and Francis Sheehy Skeffington, who was prominent in a variety of radical causes in Dublin, carried home messages for Connolly to 'pull out of it', and in late 1915 or early 1916 Larkin cabled him 'not to move'.[32]

The Easter Rising came as a bombshell. At once, Larkin grasped that he had been upstaged on a grand scale. The lockout, the biggest event in recent Irish history as far as the American press was concerned, had been overtaken. Adding salt to the wound, the American papers invariably connected him with events in Dublin, explaining the Rising as another revolt by the 1913 militants, and introducing Connolly and Constance Markievicz – the exotic Polish countess – as his former lieutenants. Some papers had him on the barricades in Dublin, others would note he was safely remote from the shooting.[33] For several days he remained incommunicado. When the press finally managed to reach him at home on the telephone on 29 April, the day Padraig Pearse and Connolly surrendered, his only comment was, 'I have nothing to say on the Irish question.' Efforts to pursue the point were 'unavailing'.[34] His close friend Jack Carney later defended the silence on the ground that speaking out would have landed others in jail.[35] It was a lame excuse. The Rising and Connolly's posthumous stature never ceased to rankle Larkin. In private he frequently traduced his old underling, saying he had destroyed the revolutionary force created in 1913 and that Connolly should never have gotten mixed up with 'the poets'.[36]

It was a different matter in public. Once the worst of the shock had passed, Larkin offered public lectures on the Easter Rising and its personalities, and organised a commemoration in Cohan's Grand Opera House, Chicago, on 21 May. His nerves were badly unsettled. When Dr K. A. Zurawski of the Polish Federation condemned the English for murder in 'true Russian style', 'a dapper young man' in the fifth row, Matthew Thomas Newman, protested: 'I have lived in Ireland and my mother came from a long line of Ireland's best. But such ballyrot makes me ill. I say why do you try to put over such ridiculous drivel?' Running from the stage, Larkin seized Newman fiercely, and threw him out of the theatre. During his address, he grabbed one of three rifles stacked on the stage and brandished it aloft.[37]

In July Larkin was back in Butte to hail 'a working class rising to keep Irish boys out of the British army'. He went on to lambast patriots who 'knew nothing about Ireland … did nothing but talk a lot of sob stuff about Ireland in order to keep you Irish workingmen divided among yourselves …You lose your class … while listening to these mercenary phrase mongers talk … about Irish freedom.' When the editor of the *Butte Independent*, unofficial organ of the Butte Irish associations, rose to protest, Larkin rounded on him savagely.[38] That same month, in an obsequious, self-serving article in *The Masses*, he presented himself and Connolly as partners in building the ITGWU and the Citizen Army and jointly drafting the 'declaration' of the insurgents. To impress readers of the leading monthly of the American revolutionary left, he claimed that the aim of the 'declaration' was 'a co-operative commonwealth … based on industrial democracy'. Justifying his absence from the action, he suggested that the Rising was premature and forced on the rebels by the threat of conscription. 'Though fate', he added, 'has denied some of us the opportunity of striking a blow for human freedom, we live in hopes that we, too, will be given the opportunity.'[39]

In June Larkin had been joined by Carney, who stayed with him and Elizabeth in Chicago. Carney was like a pocket version of Big Jim, impassioned, eloquent, egotistical, cavalier with facts, fractious, and ferociously loyal to his role model. He claimed to have served the ITGWU in Dublin during the 1913 lockout, and, more doubtfully, to have worked on the *Titanic* and fought in the Easter Rising. In the same month as the Rising he landed in New York on the *Snowden* from Glasgow. Carney's arrival allowed Larkin to realise his ambition to publish a paper, and together they produced the *Irish Worker*.[40] The masthead claimed to incorporate Connolly's papers, the *Harp* and the *Workers' Republic*, and the *Irish Worker* advertised its association with Easter Week.[41]

Meanwhile, Larkin was living dangerously. In February 1916 the German military attaché in New York, Wolf von Igel, brought him to a sabotage plant at Hoboken for a demonstration of how chemical explosives were manufactured. On 18 April von Igel was arrested at the German consulate as he awaited Larkin's arrival.[42] In July, Larkin's presence coincided with two of the most notorious acts of German sabotage. The Bureau of Investigation knew he was in San Francisco to meet the German consul before the Preparedness Day Parade bomb on 22 July, in which ten people were killed, and was visited daily by Tom Mooney, who was sentenced to death for his part in the plot.[43]

Larkin then travelled to New York to see Devoy, and was walking on Broadway at 2 a.m. on 30 July when he heard the massive munitions explosion on Black Tom Island.[44]

With the United States' entry into the war in April 1917, Larkin's situation became steadily more uncomfortable. In early 1917 the British embassy told the US State Department that he was active in a Chicago-based conspiracy to 'obstruct the manu-facture of war materials'.[45] Coincidentally or not, the Bureau of Investigation began to track him from February 1917. The *Irish Worker* was suppressed and when Larkin continued to denounce the war he was arrested repeatedly. In June, the Espionage Act extended repression to all forms of anti-war activity. Larkin's final secret mission took him to Mexico City in September as a courier for his German handlers at the behest of Clan na Gael. Tired of his refusals to become a saboteur, the Germans broke with him, and had him robbed and left penniless.[46] He then returned to the left, moving to New York, where he was central to efforts to turn the Socialist Party of America into a communist party. The project would lead to his imprisonment following the Red Scare of 1919. Released on a free pardon in January 1923, he was deported at the instigation of J. Edgar Hoover in April.

Easter Week carried a sting in the tail for Larkin. On his return to Dublin on 30 April 1923, the ITGWU's immediate concern was how to integrate its dictatorial general secretary into a proposed five-man collective leadership. Matters came to a head on 30 May, when Larkin summoned William O'Brien, the union's de facto leader since 1917, to his office. We can only speculate on Larkin's timing. Certainly, he had seen enough to know that much had changed, and was not the man to sit patiently and perfect a campaign to take back 'his' union. The recriminations about how the union was run in his absence drifted to the American mission. Once again, Larkin insisted on what he had been saying for weeks, that he had not gone to the United States to raise funds but had been sent by Connolly, Pearse, and Clarke to assist the national cause. In the climate of the time it seemed not just bumptious but irreverent to be calling on three dead heroes of Easter Week as apologists for his absence from the independence struggle. Kathleen Clarke had already written to the press asking for evidence, and she was backed in the controversy by Lillie Connolly and Devoy. In July *The Gaelic American* would publish a front-page attack, reprinting letters from Mrs Clarke, Mrs Connolly, and O'Brien all refuting Larkin's claims.[47] Larkin made no reply. It was not his style to explain. At their meeting on 30 May O'Brien suggested they put the case to a jury appointed by the Irish Labour Party and Trade Union Congress. It may have been the tipping point. Next day, Larkin called a meeting of the ITGWU's No. 1 branch, where he denounced O'Brien.[48] It was the beginning of a disastrous split, not just in the ITGWU, but in the Dublin labour movement, that would linger into the 1950s.

When Larkin contemplated an autobiography in the 1940s, Carney suggested he omit the American years.[49] They had tarnished his reputation with both separatists and socialists. But he believed that he had worked hard for both causes. He had indeed, and a man more in control of his emotions and with a more subtle mind would have managed to get credit for it. What Larkin had was honest passion, and it was his passionate commitment to Irish freedom that led him to insist on his place in the national struggle. At a personal level, he relished his time in New York and loved the bohemian atmosphere and kindred spirits he found in Greenwich Village. Back in Ireland, and struggling with endless adversity, there was nothing he liked better than to reminisce about his freewheeling American expedition, and talk of its gangsters and banksters, its prisons and its race problems, and, especially, its boxers and revolutionaries.[50] Now that Larkin's impact in the United States is being uncovered, it is worth looking too at American influences on Larkin.

# The Clan-Na-Gael Journal

L. XXVIII. | PHILADELPHIA, NOVEMBER 21, 1914. | ONE DOLLAR PER YEAR

# 7th Anniversary Celebration of the Martyrdom of Allen, Larkin and O'Brien

## ACADEMY OF MUSIC, TUESDAY EVENING, NOVEMBER 24th, 1914

## REDMOND DRIVEN FROM VOLUNTEERS

### Provisional Committee Takes Decisive Action Against Him.

### NO LONGER CREDITED

### His Program at Variance With Principles and Aims of Real Irish Patriots.

As an attempt was being made to identify the Volunteers with the recruiting meeting in Dublin, the following statement was issued recently:

Headquarters Irish Volunteers,
4 Kildare street,
September 24, 1914.

To the Irish Volunteers—Ten months ago a Provisional Committee commenced the Irish Volunteer movement with the sole purpose of securing and defending the rights and liberties of the Irish people. The movement on these lines, though thwarted and opposed for a time, obtained the support of the Irish nation. When the Volunteer movement had become the main factor in the national question, Mr. Redmond decided to acknowledge it and to endeavor to bring it under his control.

Three months ago he put forward the claim to send twenty-five nominees to the Provisional Committee of the Irish Volunteers. He threatened, if the claim was not conceded, to proceed with the dismemberment of the Irish Volunteer organization.

It is clear that this proposal to throw the country into turmoil and to destroy the chances of a Home Rule measure in the near future must have been forced upon Mr. Redmond. Already, ignoring the Irish Volunteers as a factor in the national position, Mr. Redmond had consented to a dismemberment of Ireland, which could be made permanent by the same agencies that forced him to accept it as temporary. He was now prepared to risk another disruption and the wreck of the cause intrusted to him.

The Provisional Committee, while recognizing that the responsibility in that case would be altogether Mr. Redmond's, decided to risk the lesser evil and to admit his nominees to sit and act on the committee. The committee made no representations as to the persons to be nominated, and when the nominations were received the committee raised no question as to how far Mr. Redmond had fulfilled his public undertaking to nominate "representative men from different parts of the country." Mr. Redmond's nominees were admitted purely and simply as his nominees, and without co-option.

Mr. Redmond, addressing a body of Irish Volunteers on last Sunday, has now announced for the Irish Volunteers a policy and program fundamentally at variance with their own published and accepted aims and pledges, but with which his nominees are, of course, identified. He has declared it to be the duty of the Irish Volunteers to take foreign service under a government which is not Irish. He has made this announcement without consulting the Provisional Committee, the Volunteers themselves, or the people of Ireland, to whose service alone they are devoted.

Having thus disregarded the Irish Volunteers and their solemn engagements, Mr. Redmond is no longer entitled, through his nominees, to any place in the administration and guidance of the Irish Volunteer organization. Those who by virtue of Mr. Redmond's nomination have heretofore been admitted to act on the Provisional Committee, accordingly cease henceforth to belong to that body, and from this date until the holding of an Irish Volunteer Convention the Provisional Committee consists of those only whom it comprised before the admission of Mr. Redmond's nominees.

At the next meeting of the Provisional Committee we shall propose—

1—To call a Convention of Irish Volunteers for Wednesday, November 25, 1914, the anniversary of the inaugural meeting of the Irish Volunteers in Dublin.

2—To reaffirm, without qualification, the manifesto proposed and adopted at the inaugural meeting.

3—To oppose any diminution of the measures of Irish self-government which now exist as a statute on paper and which would not now have reached that stage but for the Irish Volunteers.

4—To repudiate any undertaking, by whomsoever given, to consent to the legislative dismemberment of Ireland; and to protest against the attitude of the present government, who under the pretense that "Ulster cannot be coerced," avow themselves prepared to coerce the Nationalists of Ulster.

5—To declare that Ireland cannot, with honor or safety, take part in foreign quarrels otherwise than through the free action of a national government of her own; and to repudiate the claim of any man to offer up the blood and lives of the sons of Irishmen and Irishwomen to the service of the British Empire, while no national government which could speak and act for the people of Ireland is allowed to exist.

6—To demand that the present system of governing Ireland through Dublin Castle and the British military power, a system responsible for the recent outrages in Dublin, be abolished without delay and that a national government be forthwith established in its place.

The signatories to this statement are the great majority of the members of the Provisional Committee of the Irish Volunteers, apart from the nominees of Mr. Redmond, who are no longer members of the committee. We regret that the absence of Sir Roger Casement in America prevents him from being a signatory with us.—(Signed) Eoin MacNeill, chairman Provisional Committee; Ua Rathghaille, treasurer do; Thomas MacDonagh, Joseph Plunket, Piaras Beaslai, Michael J. Judge, Peter Paul Macken, ex-Ald.; Sean MacGiobuin, P. H. Pearse, Padraic O'Riain, Bulmer Hobson, Eamonn Martin, Conchubhair O'Colbaird, Eamonn Ceannt, Sean Mac Diarmada, Seamus O'Conchubhair, Leon Ua Cogan, Peter White, Liam Mellows, Colm O'Lochlainn.

**DON'T FORGET**

**Celebration of Allen, Larkin and O'Brien, Academy of Music, Tuesday evening, November 24. Tickets on sale at Irish-American Club, 726 Spruce street, or at Academy on night of entertainment.**

The messages of congratulations cabled to John Redmond by the United Irish League, the Hibernians and others for the past ten years would make rather unpleasant reading in view of the new role now being filled by "the chosen leader of the Irish race at home and abroad," that of a recruiting sergeant for John Bull.

**JIM LARKIN**

**The Great Irish Labor Leader and Grand Nephew of the Manchester Martyr, Michael Larkin, Who Has Come All the Way From Dublin to Address the Meeting in Honor of His Kinsman**

## RIDDER SEES LOSS OF COLONIES

Is not the picture which England presents to the world today a sad one? A handful of Englishmen, big-waisted, big-pursed, swaggering before four-fifths of the earth as the proprietor of the rest, and all this without the ability to put an army in the field as large as Montenegro's! She has gathered her allies from far and near, her colonials from the ends of the earth, and what has it availed her against Germany and Austria? Strip her of India, of Australia and South Africa, of Ireland and finally of Canada, which clings to her only because of its proximity to the United States, and what have you? And the stripping process is not so far from its inception.

The revolt in South Africa is but one of the symptoms which mark the rapid advance of decay. The protest of Ireland has not culminated as yet in insurrection, but it is no less unmistakable.

Is it unthinkable that those distant parts of the Empire which are reserved by England to fight her battles for her will see in all this a picture of what English support and protection is worth? Will they not possibly ask themselves if in a similar hour of need they would fare better than Belgium fared? What support could Australia, for example, expect as against Japan, when Belgium, close at hand, and to London a much more vital defence of Bow Bells, is sent to her grave with so little ado? And when they have thought these thoughts and answered them as they only can be answered, will not the decomposition of the Empire on which the sun never sets, though at times it must blush to shine, have set in?"

## THE SPEAKERS

The speakers of the evening will include Dr. C. J. Hexamer, of Philadelphia, president of the German-American Alliance of the United States, and one of the most popular German-Americans in this city. Dr. Hexamer has always worked in sympathy with the Irish people of this city. He has championed the cause of the Boers and other victims of England's greed.

From New York will come one of the ablest German-American orators in the United States, Henry Weismann, Esq., a life-long friend of Ireland and the Irish people. By his co-operation and many acts of kindness he has endeared himself to our people. At a meeting recently held at Terrace Garden, New York, he brought the audience of 5000 Irish and Germans to their feet with rousing cheers when he declared that the German Eagle would ere long float over Westminster and that an independent Ireland would be one of the results of a German triumph over the allies. It is to be hoped that the Irish people of Philadelphia will give these German friends of Ireland a genuine Irish welcome.

**DON'T FORGET**

**Celebration of Allen, Larkin and O'Brien, Academy of Music, Tuesday evening, November 24. Tickets on sale at Irish-American Club, 726 Spruce street, or at Academy on night of entertainment.**

## SIR ROGER CASEMENT WARNS AGAINST LURE OF SAXON SHILLING

### Home Rule Bill at Present Is Trick to Secure Enlistments.

### FACTS AND FIGURES

### Investigation Shows That German Nation Is Not Enemy of Ireland.

The following statement was issued by Sir Roger Casement to the Irish papers. The "Irish Independent" mutilated the document, suppressing whole paragraphs, and publishing it as if it had been written in the form it appeared:

"I observe that while the Home Rule Bill has been 'put on the Statute Book,' it is expressly debarred operation for one year, 'or the duration of the war.' In announcing the course decided on by the government, the Marquess of Crewe, the Liberal leader in the House of Lords, ventured the opinion 'that the placing of the bill on the Statute Book would induce Irishmen to rush to enlist for the war.' Instead, then, of terming this promissory note (payable only after death) a 'better government of Ireland bill,' would it not be truer to describe it as a 'Bill for the Better Enlistment of Irishmen in the British army?' There are already far more Irishmen in the British army, in proportion to the population of the two countries, than there are Britons, properly speaking, i.e., inhabitants of the island of Great Britain. The British regular army numbered about 240,000 men at the beginning of this year. Of these, the War Office returns showed that slightly over 30,000 were Irishmen. The population of Ireland was some 4,350,000 persons; the population of Great Britain slightly under 42,000,000. It will be seen that Ireland contributed to the army about 1 in 145 of her population; Great Britain something like 1 in 200. Moreover, the disproportion of Irishmen actually serving in the British army is much greater than these figures reveal.

"It is admitted in the War Office returns that many essentially 'English' regiments are in reality composed mainly of Irishmen from the great manufacturing districts of Great Britain. Thus 80 per cent. of the 'South Lancashire Regiment' consists of Irishmen. The late Duke of Cambridge, when Commander-in-Chief of the British army, said, in unveiling a memorial at Reading to the Berkshire Regiment, that it should rightly be called the 'Corkshire Regiment,' as so many of its men came from the South of Ireland and its Colonel bore 'so singular an English name as MacCarthy O'Leary!'

"Possibly one reason Lord Crewe is so anxious that the promissory note on Irish Home Rule should induce Irishmen to 'rush to enlist' is to be found in the great disparity of sexes revealed by the census returns of Great Britain. From the 1911 census, it appears there were 1,322,536 more females in Great Britain than men, while in Ireland the excess of females over males was only 8346. While these figures may explain the force of the suffrage movement in England and

(Continued on Second Page)

## Proceeds to Be Given to the German and Austrian Red Cross Fund

# CHAPTER TEN

# JUDGE COHALAN AND AMERICAN INVOLVEMENT IN THE EASTER RISING

## *Michael Doorley*

*The Rising in Ireland is the greatest and most effective blow that has even
been struck at England.*
Daniel Cohalan, *New York Times*, 1 May 1916

*From an early boyhood I have been taught to believe that the only country
whose enmity, the only country whose hostility, the only country whose wiles
America need fear at all was the country, from which Washington and the
revolutionary heroes delivered it.*
Daniel Cohalan, speech at Irish Race Convention, 4 March 1916.
Cited in *The Gaelic American*, 11 March 1916

If Liverpool-born Big Jim Larkin demonstrates how one individual born in the Irish diaspora could articulate a vision of Ireland's destiny, then New York-born judge Daniel F. Cohalan provides an illustrative American example. It is easy to see how the Irish-born could become exercised on matters to do with Irish self-determination. More complex, and in ways more interesting, are the impulses of those who were born outside of Ireland and yet dedicated themselves to it in no small way. Judge Daniel Florence Cohalan is best remembered today for his famous dispute with Éamon de

Valera that traumatised the Irish-American nationalist movement in the United States in the 1920s. Yet Cohalan was a significant player in the Irish-American nationalist world in New York prior to the 1916 Easter Rising. Even the de Valera-owned *Irish Press* noted after his death in 1946 that 'Cohalan was a sincere friend of Ireland's cause' and the help that he gave to the independence movement in the United States in the early years was of the greatest value.[1]

This chapter will examine Cohalan's contribution to the Rising from four different perspectives. First, it looks at his contribution to Clan na Gael, the American-based Irish nationalist organisation that played such a key role in instigating the Rising. This includes an examination of Cohalan's role in setting up and promoting *The Gaelic American* newspaper that represented the voice of the Clan on Irish, American, and international affairs. Second, it examines his active role in cultural nationalist activities in the United States. Some of the leading figures of Irish cultural nationalism on both sides of the Atlantic who were later active in the Rising itself approached Cohalan in search of funds and support and were always assured of a warm welcome. Third, it discusses Cohalan's role in the actual Rising and in particular his role in facilitating Roger Casement's visit to Germany. Finally, and most importantly, this chapter examines Cohalan's key role in the establishment of the Friends of Irish Freedom (FOIF), which was launched just six weeks prior to the Rising. Cohalan used the FOIF to exploit the Irish-American emotional response to the Rising and to campaign against American participation in the First World War.

At first glance, Judge Daniel Cohalan appears an unlikely Irish rebel. He was born in Middletown in upstate New York in 1865. Both his parents, Timothy Cohalan and Ellen O'Leary, came from Co. Cork and had arrived in the United States as children.[2] Daniel had a privileged American upbringing. After graduating from Manhattan College, he entered the legal profession and like many aspiring Irish-American lawyers became active in the Democratic Party organisation in New York City, Tammany Hall. Tammany boss Charles Francis Murphy spotted Cohalan's talents and in 1906 he became 'Grand Sachem', or associate leader of Tammany. Cohalan's close association with Murphy led to his appointment to the State Supreme Court bench in 1911.[3] Throughout his life Cohalan took an active interest in American affairs and corresponded with leading political figures of the day. These included Senators William Borah and James Reed, Bainbridge Colby who later became secretary of state in the Wilson administration, and labour lawyer and activist Frank P. Walsh.[4]

The reasons for Cohalan's immersion in radical Irish nationalism can be partly attributed to his family heritage. In 1848, Daniel's father Timothy, then a boy aged 12, left Ireland as the Great Irish Famine raged.[5] Timothy became an active member of Clan na Gael soon after its foundation in 1867.[6] The Clan, under the leadership of John Devoy, became a formidable advocate of Irish revolutionary nationalism in the United States. It also helped to maintain the Irish Republican Brotherhood (IRB) in Ireland. As Devoy pointed out in his memoirs, the revolutionary movement in Ireland 'was maintained almost entirely by moral and material support from the Clan na Gael'.[7]

Cohalan identified with the revolutionary tradition in Irish nationalism and appears to have inherited his father's hatred of the workings of the British Empire. He joined the Clan soon after his graduation from Manhattan College in 1885. Although Cohalan would later become a New York supreme court judge, and therefore was duty-bound to implement the law of the United States, he, like many of his Irish-American judicial colleagues, did not believe that Irish revolutionary activities were unlawful. In his speeches and writings, he continually justified armed insurrection against the British Empire in the cause of freedom for oppressed peoples. Indeed, some of his earliest speeches were directed against British oppression of the Boers in South Africa. In 1900, at a Clan rally in New York City's Hoffman House, Cohalan expressed a hope that 'the two struggling republics of South Africa should be victorious in their magnificent fight for continued existence'.[8]

Cohalan also linked his support for Irish nationalism to his own deeply felt American patriotism. In a biographical sketch on Cohalan that appeared in the Ancient Order of Hibernians (AOH) publication, the *National Hibernian Digest*, in 1948, John J. Sheahan headed his piece with the title: 'Daniel F. Cohalan, defender of American principles and an ardent lover of Ireland'.[9] Cohalan was especially critical of the increasing ties between Britain and the United States that were forming in the early twentieth century.[10] He felt that such an alliance would be a threat to American interests and would restrict the growth of democracy among oppressed peoples within the British Empire.[11] As he later explained in a pamphlet entitled *Democracy or Imperialism, Which?*: 'If imperialism grows, it grows at the expense of freedom. If democracy grows, it grows at the expense of imperialism.'[12]

Throughout his life, Cohalan remained very attached to Ireland and West Cork in particular. In 1899, he married a Cork woman, Hanna O'Leary, who was a niece of Monsignor John O'Leary of Clonakilty, and a cousin of his mother's family.[13] In 1909 the couple purchased a house in Glandore, Co. Cork, not far from the townland where his grandfather and father were born.[14]

Glandore House proved to be the ideal summer home for the Cohalan family until the 1930s. This sometimes drew satirical comments from the New York press.

Forrest Davis, writing for the *New York Herald Tribune*, in 1931 referred to Cohalan as the 'Yankee Squire of Glandore', given his frequent 'pilgrimages' to the 'old land'.[15] Cohalan appears to have also used his frequent visits to Ireland for the benefit of the IRB. An Irish police 'Crime Branch Special' report for August 1906 pointed to him as a likely dispenser of Clan funds to the IRB: 'The Irish Republican Brotherhood has been showing increased activity during August. The Clan na Gael delegate D. F. Cohalan was in Ireland for the greater part of the month and it is highly probable that funds for organizing purposes have been received through him.'[16]

Meanwhile, in the United States, Cohalan was district officer for the Clan in the New York area and presided over the Clan's biennial conventions as chairman from 1902 to 1910.[17] Tom Clarke, who joined the New York Clan after a long prison sentence in Britain, and who later featured prominently in the Rising, commented on Cohalan's organising talents in relation to Clan meetings. In a letter to a member of the IRB in Ireland, Major John MacBride, Clarke wrote: 'Things are now humming in the District – Not a jar [out of place] and physical and physical force alone is the word that gets stronger day by day. Cohalan is doing magnificent work – he won't stand for any nonsense.'[18] Devoy also valued Cohalan's links with the corporate world. During a period when Cohalan was ill in 1913, John Devoy wrote to Joseph McGarrity, the influential Clan leader in Philadelphia, about the absence of wealthy men at a Clan reunion. Devoy lamented that 'none of the rich men were there and we will have to get after them. Cohalan's sickness was a bad blow to us as he was going to tackle a lot of the moneyed men'.[19]

In his biographical sketch of Cohalan for the *National Hibernian Digest*, John Sheahan also commented on Cohalan's reputation as a public speaker and his commitment to the Clan: 'Cohalan spent his nights attending and speaking at Irish meetings in the New York metropolitan area – sometimes he spoke at three or four [Clan] meetings in one night – and by his eloquence, tireless energy and example brought many new and influential members into the various clubs.'[20]

Cohalan's organisational talents within the Clan became well known. Although not a member of its executive, Cohalan exercised considerable influence on its policies, especially through his close association with Devoy. According to a later account by a member of the Clan executive, James Reidy, the Clan executive consulted Cohalan 'when important decisions had to be made'.[21] The strong-willed Devoy knew his own mind but he was nevertheless willing to take advice from Cohalan, especially on American and international issues.[22]

Devoy's willingness to heed Cohalan's advice is especially evident in the establishment of *The Gaelic American* newspaper in 1903. In a later account of the reasons for the establishment of the paper, Devoy argued that the Clan needed 'a defender in the press, and a public voice to enunciate its principles'.[23] Devoy decided that the paper should be run as a publishing company, in which outsiders held stock. Cohalan, with his legal background, played a key role in this decision. In the company's articles of incorporation, Cohalan is listed as president of the board of directors of the Gaelic American Publishing Company and his name also appears on the share certificates.[24]

Devoy also claimed that he had wanted to call the new newspaper the *Irish Nation*, the title of an earlier Clan newspaper that had failed for financial reasons in the 1880s. However, Devoy admitted to having been overruled by Cohalan who favoured the title *The Gaelic American*. Cohalan felt that this title better reflected the growing popularity of the Gaelic revival then taking place in Ireland and in the United States itself. This movement represented a growing interest in the Irish language and ancient games such as hurling and Gaelic football. A circular promoting *The Gaelic American* stressed that the paper would give special attention 'to the Gaelic revival, which is the surest sign of the resurgence of the old race and the old spirit of Ireland'.[25] Indeed, the inclusion of the word 'Gaelic' in the title of the newspaper in ancient Celtic script clearly indicates sympathy with the aims of this revival.

The fact that the usually obstinate Devoy backed down to Cohalan on the proposed title of *The Gaelic American* is an indication of Devoy's respect for Cohalan's counsel and Cohalan's role in establishing the Gaelic American Publishing Company.[26] Meanwhile, Devoy served as editor, and Tom Clarke served for a time as assistant editor before his return to Ireland in 1907 to help revitalise the IRB, as we learned in Gerard MacAtasney's chapter in this volume.[27] Clarke, given his close relationship with Devoy, subsequently became an important linkman in relations between the Clan and the IRB. According to the *Irish Press*, Cohalan met with Clarke in Glandore in the summer of 1914 to obtain a full report on the political situation in Ireland.[28]

Cohalan's interest in the Irish cultural revival contrasted starkly with that of the aged Devoy who was somewhat sceptical of the value of the Gaelic League. In what could be considered a mild reprimand, Devoy complained to Cohalan in November 1911 that 'The time of our men is constantly taken up with raising money for the League [Gaelic League], to the neglect of our own work.'[29] However, Cohalan's frequent visits to Ireland provided him with insights into the Irish cultural awakening, and his influential role in *The Gaelic American* newspaper ensured that such cultural activities received proper coverage. The newspaper both championed Irish cultural events in its columns and endorsed fundraising efforts on behalf of the Gaelic League. While these objectives were not political, many cultural nationalists later became involved in revolutionary nationalism. Corkman Diarmuid Lynch, who worked closely with Cohalan in organising Gaelic League activities in New York, later took part in the Rising and was subsequently deported to the United States after his release from prison in 1918.[30]

Reflecting his commitment, Cohalan entertained visiting Irish cultural nationalists in his large house on 23 East 94th Street in New York City's wealthy Upper East Side. These included Douglas Hyde, leader of the Gaelic League, and Padraig Pearse, later proclaimed president of the Irish Republic during the 1916 Rising.[31] According to Forrest Davis, a reporter for the *New York Herald Tribune*, Cohalan, like an eighteenth-century squire, held court in both New York and Glandore:

> Here and abroad, he keeps a sort of salon where piety, wit and learning make the best of it together. His board here seats fourteen. You may find there George Russell, 'AE,' some of the Irish players, Jim Reed, a stray Jesuit metaphysician; Denny Lynch, biographer of Tweed, and Bainbridge Colby, all at one sitting.[32]

Cohalan shared his passion for assisting Irish cultural activities with another prominent Irish-American lawyer and patron of the arts, John Quinn.[33] As will be explored in a later chapter in this volume, Cohalan became chairman of the finance committee for the Gaelic League Fund in the United States and with the help of Quinn organised Douglas Hyde's successful American tour in 1906.[34] We have seen in Maura Anand's chapter in this volume how in 1914 Pearse also conducted a lecture tour of the United States to aid his struggling Irish-language school, St Enda's. Pearse had also turned to Cohalan for support. Cohalan's papers contain an appreciative letter from Pearse thanking him 'for his generous subscriptions' to St Enda's college, and for his 'unceasing and successful efforts to put me in touch with other good friends'.[35]

Cohalan, adhering to the revolutionary tradition of the Clan, believed that Home Rule, achieved by constitutional means, was not the answer to Ireland's legitimate claims to nationhood. In a 1903 speech at a Clan na Gael gathering at the Hoffman House in New York City, Cohalan stated 'that Ireland was sure to be free of England, and it would be by arms in the way that the United States had won its freedom'.[36] Drawing on his knowledge of international relations, he believed that if a foreign power defeated the British Empire in an international conflict, then the freedom of Ireland could be secured. In the same speech, Cohalan declared that

> Ireland's true interests will therefore be best served by a steady resolute and progressive policy of organisation among her own people the world over and the cultivation of alliance with England's enemies with a view to the eventual reconstruction and

re-establishment of an Irish nation – the founding of a true Republic – on the ruins of the British Empire.[37]

Cohalan put forward such views at Clan meetings around the country. At one such meeting in 1905, in Providence, Rhode Island, local Clan member John Gannon wrote to Devoy complimenting Cohalan on a speech that pointed to weaknesses within the British Empire: 'Dan [Cohalan] made a very able and clear address on England's position showing the small hold she had on some parts of her dominions and the discontent in other parts her standing as a military power, each part of which he defined in a masterful manner.'[38]

Cohalan worked closely with Devoy and McGarrity in facilitating Casement's mission to Germany following the outbreak of war in Europe. McGarrity's papers indicate that a meeting took place in Cohalan's house on 5 October where the three Clan leaders decided that $3,000 would be given to Casement.[39] They also agreed that an interview with the German ambassador to the United States, Count von Bernstorff, should be arranged. Cohalan's papers in the National Library of Ireland (NLI) also contain a letter from Casement to Cohalan, dated Thursday 8 October 1914. This indicates that Casement used the offices of *The Gaelic American* to coordinate meetings with Clan and German diplomatic representatives in New York. In his note, Casement suggests a meeting in Cohalan's house at 7 p.m. on the following day, Friday, before meeting in the German club at 9 p.m.

My Dear Judge
I write to suggest that we meet at your house tomorrow Friday at say 7. That would give us time for an exchange of views before reaching the club at 9.00. You can phone to the *Gaelic American* office if this does not suit otherwise I shall call on you at 7.00 Friday.[40]

McGarrity's notes indicate that this meeting actually took place on 10 October, though keeping to the same venue and schedule suggested by Casement.[41] McGarrity, Cohalan, Casement, and Devoy met in Cohalan's house from 7 p.m. to 8.15 p.m. The four men then made their way down to the German Club for the 9 p.m. meeting with von Bernstorff and other German officials. These included Dr Bernhard Dernburg, whom the *New York Times* later described as the Kaiser's 'personal agent in this country'.[42] Count Bernstorff approved Casement's mission and 'wrote a letter of recommendation for Casement to the German Imperial Chancellor, Theobald von Bethmann Hollweg'.[43] McGarrity has also left us an account of a final meeting with Casement at Cohalan's house on 14 October before Casement left for Germany.[44] In Germany, while Casement's mission to recruit an Irish brigade among captured Irish prisoners of war failed, his attempt to secure a German declaration in favour of Irish independence succeeded. The undersecretary of state for the Foreign Office, Arthur Zimmermann, published a declaration that if 'the fortunes of war should lead German troops to the shores of Ireland, they would land there not as a force of invaders ... but as armed forces of a befriended government'.[45] In a letter from Germany to Cohalan in November 1914, Casement indicated his pleasure at the German declaration. Knowing Cohalan's animosity towards the British Empire, he indicated his hope that this declaration would actually encourage oppressed peoples to challenge the British Empire.

> I forgot to say the first declaration (to appear next month) will be officially commn [communicated?] to all the German embassies and delegations throughout the world for issue there and also to the press here from the foreign office. It will also be specifically sent to Turkey, Egypt and India if possible.[46]

Redmond's support for the British war effort led to radicalisation of Irish-American nationalist opinion. Devoy recognised that the time was now ripe to launch a more open Irish-American nationalist organisation that would appeal to Irish Americans dissatisfied with Redmond. At a meeting of the Clan executive on 11 December 1915, Devoy recorded the decision to hold a preliminary meeting, to which leading Irish-American figures such as Robert Ford, the editor of the *Irish World*, would be invited. It was envisaged that this preliminary meeting would organise the holding of a large Irish Race Convention, which would in turn launch the proposed open organisation. Cohalan appears to have been instrumental in organising this preliminary meeting and the later convention. According to Devoy's minutes of the meeting:

> The conclusion reached was that a recommendation be made to the DO's [District Officers] ... that we approve of the calling of a conference under the conditions named by D.F.C [Daniel Florence Cohalan]. Namely, that a small private conference be held on Sat Dec 18 to lay down the lines of action to be submitted to it, the organizations and individuals to be invited and the time and place of the meeting [Convention].[47]

The massive Irish Race Convention, held in New York on 4 March 1916, attracted 2,300 delegates from across the United States. *The Gaelic American*, in its extensive coverage of the convention, proudly declared that: 'Everything moved like clockwork and not a cog slipped.'[48] Cohalan, a New York State Supreme Court judge, with political and legal contacts across the US, proved the ideal candidate to both organise the convention and lead the new organisation. His presence and influence within the Tammany system, undoubtedly led to a large legal presence at the convention. Devoy later noted in his memoirs that 'At no previous Irish convention was there even one [State] Supreme Court Judge; there were five at this, besides several other judges of lesser rank, and a large number of lawyers.'[49]

Several members of the judiciary present made rousing anti-British and anti-Redmond speeches. Judge John Goff, a colleague of Cohalan on the State Supreme Court bench declared to applause that 'I want to see the power of England broken on land and sea. It is treason to our race to hope for or help in an English victory.' He also stated that he refused to believe that hostility to England which had been 'maintained for centuries in the face of famine and persecution' had suddenly given way to 'zealous loyalty for an empty formula labeled home rule'.[50]

Referring to the war in Europe, Cohalan took a strong pro-neutrality stance and warned of the dangers of an Anglo-American alliance to American interests. He argued that this ran contrary to the democratic intentions of the founding fathers of the United States whose determination to remain free of Britain represented true Americanism: 'From an early boyhood I have been taught to believe that the only country whose enmity, the only country whose hostility, the only country whose wiles America need fear at all was the country, from which [George] Washington and the revolutionary heroes delivered it.'[51]

Out of this Irish Race Convention the Friends of Irish Freedom (FOIF) was born. Victor Herbert, the renowned Irish-American composer, was named as FOIF president. However, real power rested with the 17-man executive of which 15 were Clan members. Daniel Cohalan remained the dominant figure on this executive and was the acknowledged leader of the FOIF. [52]

The new movement dedicated itself to bring about the 'national independence of Ireland' but, as can be seen from the speeches at the convention, it had other more American objectives. In their correspondence about the need for a new organisation, Cohalan and Devoy perceived that British influence in the United States was increasing and was bent on dragging the United States into the European war on the Allied side. Such a development would be more likely to ensure a German defeat and thus ruin the chances of an independent Ireland emerging out of the ruins of the British Empire.[53]

Cohalan's fears about British attempts to enlist American support had some foundation. Early in the war, the British navy cut the cables carrying German communications to the United States. The British government also established a war propaganda bureau known as Wellington House to 'inform and influence public opinion abroad'. The bureau supplied a list of 13,000 influential Americans and 500 American newspapers with regular news of the war.[54] Commenting on the founding of the FOIF, *The Gaelic American* declared that 'the pro-British movement is now confronted by an organized Irish race throughout the land.'[55]

In February 1915, the military council of the IRB informed Devoy that they intended to stage a rebellion during the following Easter.[56] In response, the Revolutionary Directory of the Clan forwarded funds to the Irish Volunteers. McGarrity, in a later memorandum on the Rising, writes: 'The R.D. [Revolutionary Directory] met on March 10th at 23 East 94th at New York, Lynch [Diarmuid Lynch] who was in the United States was returning to Ireland and we sent by him £2300 pounds to the Volunteers.'[57] This address was Cohalan's home and suggests that Cohalan was fully involved in Clan preparations for the Rising. German historian Reinhard Doerries, who has drawn on German archives for his work, *Prelude to the Rising*, has also identified Cohalan's name in a number of communications between Casement and the Clan. One undated message from Casement to Cohalan (probably November 1914) reads: 'Here everything favorable. Authorities helping warmly.'[58]

When the American secret service raided von Igel's office just days before the Rising, one document seized indicated that Cohalan had been in touch with German authorities requesting their support for the rebellion. The captured cable read:

> The Irish revolt can only succeed if assisted by Germany; otherwise England will be able to crush it, although after a severe struggle. Assistance required. There would be an air raid on England and a naval attack timed to coincide with the Rising; followed by a landing of troops and munitions and also of some officers, perhaps from an airship. It might then be possible to close the Irish harbors against England, set up bases for submarines and cut off food exports to England. A successful Rising may decide the war.[59]

At the time of the raid, newspapers were not informed of the substance of the documents seized, though they were informed that a raid had taken place. However, in September 1917, when the United States itself had joined the war as Britain's ally, the American government released this document to the press.[60] Cohalan then denied the veracity of this message claiming that its release was an attempt to discredit him. Certainly, the timing of the document's release, 18 months after the raid, and when the United States was at war with Germany, appears an obvious attempt to silence Cohalan. Yet the presence of Cohalan's message in the German archives would indicate that it was actually sent by von Igel, thus challenging Cohalan's public claim that this document was a British forgery.[61] Given Cohalan's leadership role in the Clan, and his previous contacts with the German government, it therefore seems very likely that Cohalan made this appeal.

Cohalan's message to Germany was, in any event, largely a restatement of the earlier request from the IRB for 'a few superior officers' and arms to be sent to Ireland to coincide with the revolt. Other Clan communications with Germany, indicate that McGarrity made similar appeals. In one such message, McGarrity pleaded with Casement to put pressure on the Germans to get a small force of German troops to Ireland:

> Can nothing be done to get a small force with a quantity of arms to Ireland? A small force with a quantity of arms would I believe get such support as would enable them to if not free Ireland at least to keep the field until peace would be declared which with Germany the victor would or should mean Ireland independent.[62]

Despite these appeals from McGarrity and Cohalan, the Germans, fearing the strength of the British navy, refused to send troops. As fate would have it the weapons dispatched by Germany to Ireland were intercepted and the course of history was changed.[63] After much confusion, the Rising did go ahead though on Easter Monday and according to McGarrity's later memorandum a message was sent from a rebel sympathiser in Valentia Island coastguard station to New York on Saturday night 22 April, which read, 'Tom successfully operated on today.' This was a prearranged signal from the IRB to the Clan to indicate that the Rising was going ahead. It is not clear who in New York first received this message, but McGarrity indicated that he received this message by telephone from 'D.F.C.', a term used in Clan correspondence to indicate Daniel Florence Cohalan.[64]

The failure of the German arms shipment enabled British forces to suppress the Rising much more easily than they might otherwise have done, but only after much heavy fighting in Dublin. Nevertheless, the FOIF sought to exploit the propaganda value of the failed rebellion to the utmost degree. In a speech in Pittsfield, Massachusetts, on 30 April, Cohalan declared that 'The Rising in Ireland is the greatest and most effective blow that has ever been struck at England.' He argued that news of the Rising 'will spread all over the British Empire with Gallipoli and Kut-el-Amara, win the Indians, hearten the Egyptians and show Japan upon what a weak reed she leans'.[65] The British ambassador to the United States, Sir Cecil Spring Rice, in a report to the London Foreign Office, expressed alarm at the extent of Irish-American 'excitement' especially following the British execution of rebel leaders. In May 1916 he quoted Cohalan as saying in a New York speech that 'If the arms going to Ireland had ever gotten there, the mere sample of warfare which was shown by the handful of revolutionaries would have been a real revolution.'[66]

While the FOIF attracted large numbers to such anti-British demonstrations, membership was still low. According to FOIF records, the organisation listed only

2,891 members in 1917, of whom 1,495 were based in New York.[67] This relatively low membership was partly due to an oppressive atmosphere that discouraged any displays of 'hyphenism'. Even before American entry into the war, President Woodrow Wilson, in a speech to congress in October 1915, questioned the loyalty of so-called hyphenated Americans and declared that '[they] ... have poured the poison of disloyalty into our national life.'[68]

Yet despite its small size, the FOIF gave the impression that it was bigger than it actually was. It organised receptions and speaking tours by so-called emissaries from Ireland. These included Liam Mellows, who had taken part in the Easter Rising, and Hanna Sheehy Skeffington, the widow of Dublin pacifist and journalist Francis Sheehy Skeffington, murdered by a British officer during the Rising itself. The FOIF also played a prominent role in fundraising for the 'relief of suffering in Ireland' and by mid-July the fund amounted to $100,000. It also sent appeals and petitions on behalf of Irish prisoners to congress.[69]

Besides publicising Irish events in the United States, the FOIF, in alliance with German-American groups, also engaged in a campaign to preserve American neutrality. On 4 February 1917, at a New York public meeting of the FOIF, Cohalan declared that if the United States fought on the side of the Allies, it 'would be fighting for the combined subjection of Ireland, India and Egypt to English rule'.[70] However, in the face of deteriorating relations between the United States and Germany, and the German resumption of unrestricted submarine warfare, Cohalan's campaign failed. On 6 April 1917, the United States declared war on Germany.

After the United States' entry into the war, the FOIF adopted a low public profile with many branches closing for the duration of the conflict. Irish Americans had always prided themselves on their loyal support of the United States in times of war and Cohalan believed that attacks on Britain could be construed by a pro-Allied media as disloyalty to the United States. In an interview with the Catholic newspaper the *Brooklyn Tablet*, Cohalan argued that Irish Americans would always be 'present in defense of the flag and support of American institutions'.[71] This FOIF inactivity caused some resentment among visiting Irish nationalists such as Liam Mellows. At the second Irish Race Convention in January 1918, Liam Mellows told shocked delegates that 'The state of affairs at home is so desperate that you people are acting like a lot of curs if you do not speak out.'[72] Joseph McGarrity also wanted a more active policy by the FOIF. However, despite this simmering discontent, Cohalan's views prevailed. Once the war had ended, the FOIF adopted a much more vocal approach and attempted to link Irish national demands to President Wilson's policy of self-determination for small nations. Against the background of the Irish 'war of Independence, it went on to achieve its greatest strength and by 1920 membership numbered 275,000 members'.[73]

Cohalan's devotion to Irish nationalism and to anti-imperialism was unapologetic and sincere, but it can only be fully understood in the context of his innate sense of patriotism towards the United States. This impulse infused his outlook on Ireland with an American and international flavour that was sometimes misinterpreted by nationalists in Ireland. Nevertheless, Cohalan, in the words of Tom Clarke, did 'magnificent work' in helping to organise the Clan in the years before the Rising. His energies ranged from the causes of Irish cultural nationalism to more risky projects like assisting Casement in getting from New York to Germany. He did much to ensure the successful emergence of the FOIF at a difficult time in Irish-American history by harnessing the momentum of significant numbers of Irish-born and American-born Irish nationalists, especially in New York. Through Cohalan we are provided with a rich example of Irish-American activism in the early decades of the twentieth century. While historians continue to debate his tempestuous relationship with de Valera in 1919 and 1920, the verdict on Cohalan's decisive contribution to the American dimension of the Easter Rising is unambiguous.

# CHAPTER ELEVEN

# VICTOR HERBERT, NATIONALISM, AND MUSICAL EXPRESSION

## *Marion R. Casey*

*Mr. Herbert was having the time of his life. Much of the man's passionate devotion to Ireland, much of his hatred of England was written into the score of 'Eileen'; he conducted with all the ardor of a rebel.*
Unidentified newspaper critic, March 1917[1]

*Sit in a darkened room and leave your mind free from prejudice while you listen to a voice chanting an ancient Irish Banshee song. Give your imagination fair berth and see if it isn't the wail of a cantor in [a] synagogue – wonderfully beautiful music – or a song of the Far East, a Grecian folk song, the shriek of the American Indian in a war dance, a snatch of Gregorian music, or even some of the Chinese music that one hears a bit of in Frisco. It's all the same.*
Victor Herbert, undated interview[2]

When Victor Herbert was named president of the Friends of Irish Freedom in March 1916, few could have predicted that the bon vivant composer of favourite American operettas would emerge as the spokesperson for Irish independence in the weeks before the Easter Rising in Ireland.

None of the criteria commonly used by historians to explain American support for Irish nationalism – as a defensive reaction to discrimination, as a radical critique of American capitalism, or revenge for the Famine – fit Victor Herbert who, at age 57, was arguably at the pinnacle of his career.[3] He had composed music and conducted for band, orchestra, and stage to great critical acclaim. That success, both artistic and financial, ensured Herbert a place in elite social circles in New York and Pennsylvania that included wealthy patrons of the arts and theatre as well as connoisseurs of good food and drink. On the other hand, he frequently socialised in his shirt-sleeves with the multi-ethnic musicians under his command who adored him not least because he was generous to a fault, fluent in several languages, and able to switch between them effortlessly.[4]

In other words, a tight ethnic subculture did not circumscribe Victor Herbert. As events dramatically unfolded throughout 1916, his sense of patriotism took an interesting turn that was reflected in the music he composed. This chapter explores the nature of Herbert's relationship with Irish America in the early twentieth century in light of his career as a composer and the three significant articulations of musical nationalism he wrote during that fateful year for Ireland: the pioneering motion picture soundtrack for *The Fall of a Nation*, the romantic Irish opera *Eileen*, and the anthem 'Soldiers of Erin'.

Victor Herbert was born in 1859. His mother was Fanny Lover, the daughter of the artist and author Samuel Lover. It is through this maternal line that Herbert traced his Irish ancestry during his lifetime, leading to assumptions that he was born in Dublin and that his paternal line was Irish too. His most recent biographer, for example, mistakenly identifies him as one of the Herberts of Currans and Cahernane in Killarney, cousins of the Herberts of Muckross House.[5] However, earlier accounts of Herbert's origins are much vaguer on his father, said to have died in 1861. Edward Waters concluded, 'If Fanny ever told her son anything more, he never disclosed it to his children or to his closest friends.'[6] She was the overwhelming influence on Herbert's earliest years; he rejoiced 'that the memories of my earliest childhood are inseparable from the Irish melodies sung over my cradle by my mother'.[7] Fanny Lover had learned this repertoire from her father and young Victor spent 1862–6 being raised in Samuel Lover's home in Sevenoaks, southeast of London in Kent. The impact on the child was profound and life-long, emerging in full force in 1916, as will become evident.[8]

When her son was seven years old, Fanny Lover married a German doctor. For the next 20 years, until his emigration to the United States in 1886, Victor Herbert's entire formation as man and musician was in Germany, especially Stuttgart. In fin-de-siècle New York City, he segued seamlessly into a cultural scene that was heavily German at the time and was to be equally important to him. He duly applied for American citizenship in 1893 and was naturalised in 1902 while conductor of the Pittsburgh Symphony Orchestra.[9]

With a sense of ethnicity that was more complex than most, Herbert's choice to identify himself as an Irishman and to involve himself in Irish nationalism has perplexed all of his biographers. They conclude that his ties with Ireland were tenuous at best and thus essentially an emotional indulgence.[10] They focus instead on the astonishing versatility that produced a body of work for cello, violin, piano, band, and orchestra, in addition to operas and operettas that made Victor Herbert a household name across the United States.[11] His rigorous schedule of conducting engagements, such as important guest appearances with the New York Philharmonic in 1904, 1905, and 1906 and a regular summer residency in Philadelphia's Willow Grove Park made him a musical celebrity.[12] From 1909, phonograph recordings extended the wide reach of his music and artistic sensibilities in professional and domestic spheres.[13] In late 1913, he was one of the original founders of the American Society of Composers, Authors and Publishers (ASCAP) and he carefully shepherded its early efforts to protect artistic copyright.[14] For all of these reasons, Victor Herbert is frequently hailed as the foremost American composer of his day, a claim that conveniently sidesteps his self-identification. But at a time when American music, conductors, and musicians were struggling to be recognised as equal to their European counterparts, Herbert's Irish roots and his German training mattered far less than his adoption by the American public.[15]

Nevertheless, from his earliest days in the United States, Herbert was exploring his Irish heritage through music. He composed *Irish Rhapsody for Grand Orchestra*, a symphony that referenced Thomas Moore's *Melodies*, for the Gaelic Society of New York and conducted the premiere at its Feis Ceoil agus Seanachus at the Lenox Lyceum in 1892. Herbert based his understanding of what constituted 'Irish' music 'on the non-chromatic style in which the Irish bards composed for their harps'. Later in life he reflected on his facility with this idiom, 'As a composer I have analyzed the traditional airs in an effort to understand as well as to enjoy [Irish] music. Apparently I have succeeded, for I have been obliged to disclaim the use or adaptation of any existing folk songs or dances.'[16] The *Irish Rhapsody* proved so popular that, according to one of Herbert's biographers, 'to its own detriment … it was played to death [and] … killed itself as an independent concert number.'[17] Many subsequent film scores, including for John Ford's 1952 classic *The Quiet Man*, are simply imitations of the *Irish Rhapsody*, which is why it sounds so familiar to modern ears but, in 1892, it inaugurated the revival of American interest in Ireland's ancient music via the classical concert stage personified in Victor Herbert himself.

The Gaelic Society and Herbert continued their relationship for many years there-after. At its thirty-second annual song festival in April 1911, he conducted the orchestral premiere of the Irish-language version of the 'Star-Spangled Banner'.[18] The next year, its members presented him with a citation elaborately decorated with reproductions from the *Book of Kells*. 'While in musical and operatic accomplishment you are the hope and pride of this mighty new land of our adoption,' it read in part, 'you are also an honor to the Old Land with its musical traditions represented by the harp on its flag.'[19] Herbert was pleased. When the society earmarked the proceeds from their 1912 Feis Ceoil for the Gaelic League in Ireland, Herbert arranged for the big draw to be an appearance by the popular soprano Alice Nielsen.[20] The following year, Idelle Patterson was the Gaelic League soloist at Carnegie Hall on Easter Sunday evening when Herbert conducted a 75-piece orchestra in a 'program of Irish music, ancient and modern'.[21] Such Irish concerts during this period built upon familiar compositions by Moore, Lover, Wallace, Balfe, and Villiers Stanford but increasingly introduced audiences to lyrical works in Gaelic set to music, like Donnchadh Ruadh Mac Conmara ('Ban-Chnoic Éireann, Oigh'), as well as Irish compositions for orchestra by Swan Hennessy ('Petite Suite Irlandaise'), Augusta Holmès ('Noël d'Irlande'), and Herbert himself.[22]

As in most endeavours Victor Herbert undertook in his very busy life, he threw himself wholeheartedly into Irish circles. Many of the patrons of the 1913 Gaelic Society concert were members of New York City's cultural and professional elite who also knew Herbert from the Friendly Sons of St Patrick, which he became a member of in 1908, and the American Irish Historical Society (AIHS), which he joined in 1911.[23] Both organisations had overlapping networks of relationships among such cosmopolitan men as Congressman William Bourke Cockran, Dr Thomas Addis Emmet, and the state Supreme Court judges Morgan J. O'Brien, Martin J. Keogh, and Victor J. Dowling. All, like Herbert, were active in multiple spheres of influence and their names and patronage carried weight in politics, society, and the arts. Such relationships casually exposed Herbert to constitutional and republican opinions on nationalism then current among educated Irish-American professionals. They became more intimate when, for example, he worked with Joseph I. C. Clarke to set the poem 'New Ireland' for men's voices a cappella. Clarke, who retired in 1913 as chief of publicity for Standard Oil, was president of the AIHS and an active member of Clan na Gael.[24]

By the time Herbert became president of the Friendly Sons in 1915, his Irish politics were clearer. At the one hundred and thirty-first annual dinner of the society that year, one of the guests of honour was Mayor John Purroy Mitchel, grandson of the Young Irelander John Mitchel. Herbert replied to Mitchel's speech in no uncertain terms:

I am sure you all love the roseate outlook for autonomy that our worthy Mayor has painted to you. I do hope that this Legislature at Albany if they do pass a Home Rule Bill for New York City will pass a better one than the English Parliament passed for our country. No matter what people will tell you about the Irish Home Rule Bill, and even if it be His Honor, the Mayor, I beg to disagree with him. The Irish Home Rule Bill is a check without a date.[25]

The Gaelic American made this front-page news, observing that 'there was very general applause when Mr. Herbert characterized the Home Rule Bill as a fake.'[26]

Subsequent events indicate that members of the Friendly Sons who were also in the Clan like Clarke and Judge Daniel F. Cohalan had the ear of the famous composer.[27] Six weeks before the Easter Rising, Herbert opened the first Irish Race Convention at the Hotel Astor in New York. Twenty-three hundred representatives from all across the country assembled for two days to advocate for strict enforcement of neutrality laws to prevent the United States becoming involved in the world war.[28] The appeal of the convention for Herbert, whose biographers all disclaim his ability as a politician, lay in the argument that freedom for Ireland, a European island not a British one, would enable her 'to take her place again among the nations of the world'. This was expanded upon in one of the resolutions passed on 5 March:

> May we hope that Ireland will emerge from this situation proud and free … to resume her old work, with her old language and her old methods, for liberty and education, and humanity; and to demonstrate again to an admiring world that there is need of, and room for the small nations, to the end that each may work out its destiny according to its gifts, and each may in its own way make its various contributions to civilization and progress. Therefore we hail with great satisfaction the reawakened spirit of Nationality which has appeared in so many forms in Ireland.[29]

The convention created a new national lobbying organisation, the Friends of Irish Freedom (FOIF), which included among its several objectives 'the revival of the language, literature, music and culture of the Gaels'.[30] Herbert's emergence as president of the FOIF was therefore in keeping with his previous work on behalf of the Gaelic League. However, Judge John W. Goff, a 68-year-old Wexford native with deep connections to the revolutionary principles espoused by the Clan, was put forward first.[31] When he demurred in favour of Victor Herbert, it may have been strategic given the Clan executive's advance knowledge of plans for the Rising, but there is no evidence to conclude that Herbert was merely a convenient shield for the Clan, nor that he was aware of the secret life of men like Judge Cohalan.[32] The FOIF presidency was never inevitable, even though Herbert was simultaneously president of the Friendly Sons, a vice chairman of the Irish Race Convention, and a Protestant, all clearly a propaganda advantage.[33] One biographer suspects that the 'eloquent and fiery essay' on the Irish situation published under Herbert's name in the *New York Sun* on 26 March was written by Cohalan.[34] 'In spite of the sophistry of Carson and the ráiméis of Redmond', it reads,

> the Irish at home and abroad, with their old instinct as a fighting race, recognize and feel that England is being beaten in this present war. They have no sympathy or pity for the country which has ever tyrannized over the weak and truckled to the strong. Ireland to-day, Mr. Redmond to the contrary, is not with England, and every day is preparing more and more to look out for herself.[35]

Despite the national name recognition that made such a political statement newsworthy, the public's perception of Herbert's actual nationality was confused. In announcing the first FOIF meeting in Massachusetts on 19 April, the *Boston Globe* devoted a whole column to this. 'Put a spiked helmet on the president of the Friends of Irish Freedom,' it declared, 'and he would pass for the subject of the Kaiser.'[36] Herbert's protestations to the contrary made for good press.

In trying to understand this seemingly sudden transformation of Victor Herbert from musician to politician it is helpful to think about the other ways in which he was making headline news during 1916. In January, ASCAP lost its appeal in a copyright infringement case with Shanley's, a high-end New York restaurant owned and operated by a large extended family from Co. Leitrim that offered cabaret entertainment during dinner. Herbert immediately appealed again, this time all the way to the US Supreme Court. The case was ongoing throughout the year and is indicative of his ability to multi-task as well as the tenaciousness of his commitment to causes he believed were just.[37]

On 24 April, as the rebels occupied the GPO in Dublin, Herbert was conducting the Boston opening of his operetta *The Princess Pat*. With a lightweight plot that revolved around the former Patrice O'Connor who marries foreign royalty, its popularity with the public and critics led to a national tour in 1916.[38] One of the hits Herbert composed for the princess's soprano voice was 'Two Laughing Irish Eyes'. At a time when the market was already saturated with derivative Tin Pan Alley tunes with titles like that, the only reason for Herbert to write such a song was to translate what was fast becoming cliché into a more 'respectable' musical form, opera.[39] 'Two Laughing Irish Eyes' was recorded for the Victor label in December 1915 and was in thousands of American living rooms during 1916, bridging the gap between high- and low-brow Irish musical tastes.[40]

Even more central to Herbert's understanding of ethnic identification and musical expression was his work during the first six months of 1916. All during the Irish Race Convention and the first weeks as the head of the FOIF, but especially during the tensions of Easter Week and its aftermath, Herbert was writing a commissioned score for the film *The Fall of a Nation*. This was a sequel to D. W. Griffith's landmark 1915 silent film *The Birth of a Nation*, produced and directed by the author of both books, Thomas Dixon. The challenge for Herbert – one that he relished – was to compose the first 'original symphonic score for a full-length feature film' so that the music audiences heard actually related to the dramatic images on the screen, timed with precision to each scene. It would be 'Grand Opera Cinema', another elevation of a popular art form.[41]

The project developed long distance from late 1915, with Herbert dependent upon verbal descriptions to create 'a thousand separate compositions' for the scenes.[42] 'Believe me when I tell you,' Dixon wrote from Los Angeles,

> that our battle scene will make the *Birth of a Nation* look like thirty cents compared to a million dollars … We give you a picture of those great guns lit with the glare of hell at night belching flame 12 feet high with 60 gunners swarming around them like so many demons. The caption is: THROUGH THE NIGHT THE GREAT GUNS ROARED THE DEATH KNELL OF A NATION.

Herbert replied on 4 December, 'Your 42 Centimeter gun [16.5 inches wide] episode will be hard to depict musically – but I will promise you to let loose my wildest imagination on the subject.'[43]

Not only was Dixon difficult to work with, he was no Griffith. The plot of *The Fall of a Nation* depicted the invasion of an unprepared United States by 'The Imperial Federation of Europe' and it was not long before Herbert detected the not too subtle implication that this was Germany even though Dixon had repeatedly promised the invaders would be from an imaginary country.[44] By February 1916, Herbert was exasperated with last minute changes, improbable suggestions, and trying to block the recurring German references. He protested, 'To offend hundreds of thousands of our best citizens that way would be a great mistake … I studied in Germany and although an Irishman have a soft spot for that country and its people.'[45] In another letter, he told Dixon, 'I will not be a party to the violation of our President's proclamation of neutrality.'[46]

When the film opened in New York on 6 June 1916, critics praised Herbert's music but lambasted Dixon's picture.[47] By then, the British had executed 15 of the Irish rebel leaders for treason in wartime, including seeking military aid for Ireland from Germany. There is no doubt that increasing calls for American involvement in the First World War as well as isolationist versus preparedness rhetoric, combined with the rapid events in Ireland and calls for self-determination for small nations, made work on *The Fall of a Nation* delicate for Herbert, especially given the nationalist language in the long list of resolutions passed at the Irish Race Convention and his assumption of a leadership role in the FOIF. Even though he dutifully promoted the film in May, distancing himself from Dixon was rather easier than avoiding the escalation of anti-German prejudice in the music world.[48]

Ten days before the film's premiere, on 27 May, Herbert and his orchestra shared the Carnegie Hall stage with Johanna Gadski, Otto Goritz, and Fritz Kreisler in an Irish Relief Fund concert that realised more than $10,000. The *New-Yorker Staats-Zeitung* promoted this event by encouraging German support for 'the bereaved of the Irish freedom-martyrs' and promised that 'the cooperation of such great artists … guarantees a rare pleasure.'[49] Gadski, famous as a Wagnerian soprano at the Metropolitan Opera, was married to Hans Tauscher, a German munitions dealer, who had been arrested on 30 March and was awaiting trial on espionage charges.[50] She sang the popular nineteenth-century Irish standard 'Kathleen Mavourneen' for this concert, which took place on the very same day that an editorial in *Musical America* responded to protests against her forthcoming appearance at Yale for an open-air performance of *Die Walküre*. The journal suggested that 'those whose outraged patriotism outruns their artistic appreciation can best serve all ends by staying away from Mme. Gadski's performances.'[51] While the Irish in her Carnegie Hall audience gave her an ovation 'such as no singer ever received in the Metropolitan Opera House', in some quarters this was seen as further proof that Herbert was 'German to the backbone and … active in German propaganda'.[52] In fact, programming Mme Gadski when her name was headline news for remarks she made in defence of her husband was not only an honourable thing for Victor Herbert to do for a colleague, but risky for both of them in an increasingly hostile climate.[53]

Awareness of such sentiments may have pushed Herbert in a new direction for, by August 1916 when Sir Roger Casement became the sixteenth Irish execution for consorting with the Germans, the press had already leaked word of a new Victor Herbert opera, his first on an Irish theme.[54] The link between Herbert and his grandfather, the well-known composer and novelist Samuel Lover, rarely went unremarked, particularly in the Irish-American press. The five years of Herbert's youth in Lover's household were integral to his identification as an Irishman but he had only ever expressed this connection through stand-alone pieces like the *Irish Rhapsody*. As the acknowledged master of the light opera genre of his day, Herbert was certainly overdue for drawing upon his grandfather's work for inspiration. On the other hand, the proliferation of Irish melodramas that had enjoyed recent success on the New York stage and screen was no less a challenge for Herbert than *The Fall of a Nation*, which makes *Eileen* worth contextualising.

Even before 1916, the consensus among connoisseurs was that Victor Herbert had 'elevated the standard of light music [and] established artistic operetta over inane musical comedies'.[55] The latter had proven especially lucrative when the plays were star vehicles for popular Irish tenors that were set in Ireland and contained songs that generated sheet music sales, especially in the heyday of New York's Tin Pan Alley between 1903 and 1919.[56] Chauncey Olcott, with his sweet voice and 'ingratiating acting' style, had 'a large and loyal audience' among Irish Americans. He also composed songs, several of which have had a very long afterlife and remain familiar today, like 'My Wild Irish Rose' (1899), 'Mother Machree' (1911), and 'When Irish Eyes Are Smiling' (1912).[57] Success bred imitation and, by 1916, the market was flooded with Irish melodramatic material for stage and piano.

Olcott was a contemporary of Victor Herbert and, like him, was the son of an Irish woman. Both men represent the two strands of Irish musical expression – one commercial, the other art – that were simultaneously being balanced in American popular culture in 1916.[58] Audiences inclined towards Olcott preferred sanitised nostalgia about Killarney and Tipperary, Irish eyes, and dear old mothers. Under these circumstances, any appeal to memory that turned a blind eye to reality in contemporary Ireland and overlooked painful episodes in its history was potentially lucrative. In contrast, Herbert's audiences were the product of 50 years of occupational and educational mobility. His Irish America was actively cultivating respectability on a number of fronts including 'race pride'.[59] A positive image rather than profit was their motivation. While Olcott veered into the realm of the stage Irishman they hated, Herbert's companions in the Friendly Sons, the AIHS, and the FOIF were in many ways exploring Ireland's musical heritage as a form of nationalism. 'In Victor Herbert,' Joseph I. C. Clarke predicted, 'I see a man who may yet do something great in this way for his race and ours.'[60]

Herbert's decision to write an Irish opera in 1916 must be considered with both these forms of expression in mind. His world – for all that it was concert halls, orchestral and choral music – also overlapped with Tin Pan Alley through his music publisher, M. Witmark & Sons. One of the company librettists was Rida Johnson Young with whom Herbert worked on his popular and commercially successful 1910 production *Naughty Marietta*. Young spent the next four years working with Olcott and the composer Ernest R. Ball on Irish melodramas set in late eighteenth-century

Ireland – *Barry of Ballymore* (1911), *Macushla* (1912), *Isle O'Dreams* (1913) and *Shameen Dhu* (1914) – all of which produced songs for the piano in the parlour.[61]

It is therefore no surprise that Henry Blossom, the author Herbert worked with in 1916 on *Eileen*, relied on a plot that would have been very familiar to theatre audiences and critics when he set the action 'on the West Coast of Ireland during the 1798 Rebellion'. There, the republican hero Captain Barry O'Day slips into Ireland from France 'to lay the ground for expected French assistance'. A series of mistaken identities combined with love for Eileen Mulvaney, the Anglo-Irish heroine, saves the day with 'a general amnesty to all rebels'.[62] In damning it as an 'awkward and diluted shillalah drama', the *Times* review of its New York premiere in May 1917 perceptively concluded that Blossom

> doubtless gathered his material and atmosphere by reading for quite half an hour in some public library … as far as it betrays any knowledge or feeling for Irish custom, Irish spirit, and Irish lore, it might have been written by a young man from Wyoming whose sole impressions of the Emerald Isle were derived from two visits to a theatre where Andrew Mack was playing and one conversation with a man who had once (long ago) seen a play by Dion Boucicault.[63]

Weak librettos were perennially cited in criticisms of Victor Herbert operettas, five of which Blossom was responsible for before *Eileen*. In one generalised assessment, 'he was thwarted by the taste of the day, by the exigencies of his circumstances, by his very fertility, which made compliance and compromise all the easier.'[64] Is this why Herbert agreed to write music (which the critics praised) for such a clichéd Irish vehicle (which they condemned)?[65] Remember, *Eileen* was composed in the immediate aftermath of the Rising, when Ireland had once again looked to the Continent for assistance in gaining liberty from Great Britain and had been bitterly disappointed. Amnesty for *Eileen*'s rebels, if only on the New York stage in 1917, was only too easily contrasted with the 16 executions the previous year when seen through Irish-American eyes. Some of *Eileen*'s songs, too, are clearly attempts to rise above Tin Pan Alley, but at the same time they are reminiscent of it; Herbert reinterpreted 'My Little Irish Rose', the tenor Fiske O'Hara's song from the 1908 musical *Dion O'Dare*, and reimagined 'Too-Ra-Loo-Ra-Loo-Ral', Chauncey Olcott's number one hit from 1913, as a French pavane instead of a lullaby. Sheet music sales of 'Thine Alone', *Eileen*'s famous love song, soared and the opera 'reached the musically untrained and taught them to appreciate the difference between music of the day and music of all time'.[66]

*Eileen* was also the first Herbert orchestration for a traditional Irish instrument, incorporating uilleann pipes into the opening of Act III. Francis X. Hennessy, whom

Herbert most likely knew from Irish concert circles, was cast to play them.[67] Similar agency can be seen in the casting of the heroine. 'Grace Breen (whoever she is) is Eileen,' the *Brooklyn Eagle* reviewer wondered before commenting, 'She has a carefully cultivated voice, but no stage presence and no acting ability.'[68] This is most unusual for a composer known for tailoring his work to the strengths of his sopranos, thereby making the careers of Alice Nielsen, Fritzi Scheff, and Emma Trentini. Grace was a 'very pretty' Italian-trained singer who made her New York debut in 1913 and was known for her rendition of Irish songs. She was also the daughter of Joseph I. C. Clarke's old friend from their Fenian days, New York City police magistrate Matthew P. Breen, a native of Co. Clare.[69] Just a few months after the opening, Grace Breen married Clarke's son, William, on the eve of his deployment to France, after which she retired from her brief but historic stage career as Eileen Mulvaney.[70] Recognising the importance of such interlocking networks in Irish New York was *The Gaelic American*'s review: 'The entire cast is splendidly chosen, Miss Grace Breen in particular winning her way to the hearts of the audience' – which was full of the 'most prominent Irish people in the city' on opening night.[71]

Herbert intended this light opera to also be a paean to his beloved grandfather who had toured the United States in 1846–7 with *Irish Evenings* that featured humorous songs of his own composition set to old Irish melodies. As late as 1916, 'The Low-Backed Car', 'The Bowld Sojer Boy', 'Molly Bawn', and 'The Four-Leafed Shamrock' were still popular with Irish-American audiences. Lover converted his romantic ballad about a 1798 rebel, Rory O'More, into a novel with the subtitle *A National Romance* that was so popular it was adapted for the stage in 1836 and made the transatlantic reputation of the actor Tyrone Power.[72] The longevity of *Rory O'More* in the United States – a new edition of the novel was published in 1903 – was certainly a motivating factor behind its selection by the American film company, Kalem, for one of the historical dramas it shot on location around Killarney in 1911.[73] While Herbert could have claimed a patriotic heritage as his inspiration – Samuel Lover was six years old in 1803, a witness to British reprisals in Dublin in the wake of Emmet's rebellion[74] – *Eileen* is set in the same time period as *Rory O'More* precisely because it was a known frame of reference for explaining Irish nationalism to American audiences.

For the New York Irish more specifically, the rebellions of 1798 and 1803 had been annually referenced in commemorations from at least the 1870s.[75] By 1916 Robert Emmet eclipsed Wolfe Tone as the focus because of work completed at the turn of the twentieth century: Joseph I. C. Clarke's drama *Robert Emmet: A Tragedy of Irish History* (1888), the actor Brandon Tynan's critically acclaimed interpretation *Robert*

*Emmet: The Days of 1803* (1903), Dr Thomas Addis Emmet's *Memoir of Thomas Addis and Robert Emmet* and Kalem's film *Bold Emmet: Ireland's Martyr* (both 1915). Emmet was also elevated at Clan na Gael-sponsored gatherings in New York to mark his birthday, which attracted high profile Gaelic revivalists from Ireland like W. B. Yeats in 1904 and Padraig Pearse in 1914, who addressed thousands. This connection was so entrenched by 1916 that the Irish Race Convention was intentionally scheduled to open on 4 March.[76]

At the time of the Irish Relief Fund Bazaar at Madison Square Garden in October, as Herbert asked 'all present to rise in memory of the "Irish Martyrs of 1916"', he was still writing *Eileen* and referring to the work-in-progress as *Hearts of Erin*.[77] It was under that latter name that it opened in Cleveland, Ohio on New Year's Day 1917 as part of a pre-Broadway tour.[78] On 17 January, now in Boston, Massachusetts, it became *Eileen* with the newspapers reporting that *Barry O'Day* had been considered too.[79] Three nights later, at a private dinner given by Mayor James Michael Curley, Herbert said, 'In writing *Eileen* I wrote from my heart, not from the consideration of my pocketbook. If I had written from my pocketbook … it would have been a failure. I think I have made a success of my attempt to express to the people of this country the true sentiments of the Irish people in Ireland.'[80]

Herbert's biographers suggest that the origin of the title change was a calculated management decision over concern that the public might think *Hearts of Erin* was a drama instead of an opera.[81] But Herbert broke during the summer of 1916 with his first producer over a contract demand that would have given the composer control of such changes and in a December 1916 interview he implied that 'if he could have chosen any title more Irish than *Hearts of Erin*, the chances are he would have taken it.'[82] That chance came during their month in Boston, when Herbert and Blossom were able to make extensive cuts to the score and the libretto.[83] Despite an unverified claim that the Clan na Gael leader Judge Daniel F. Cohalan's 16-year-old daughter, Aileen, was the inspiration, it is almost certain that Herbert selected the name with something else in mind.[84]

*Eileen* owes its title to Herbert's youth in Germany where the most popular 'Irländisches Volkslied' was identical to the old Irish air 'Eibhlin a Ruin'. Its original Gaelic lyrics had been translated into English during the nineteenth century by Gerald Griffin and Thomas Davis[85] but it was as 'Robin Adair', with lyrics by John Braham, that the air was most widely known. As the latter it was adapted into German by Wilhelm Gerhard in 1826 as 'Treu Und Herzinniglich' and became part of a genre of music associated with nation building and patriotism that was perceived as more valuable than folk songs of the peasantry.[86] Consequently, it was a standard in the repertoire for male choirs and became representative of modernity and the middle class in German cities.[87] It remained in print in Germany for the rest of the century and was part of the mandatory 'Volkslieder' curriculum students learned to sing in school.[88] If Herbert – who was famous for his musical recall – did not learn it in his Stuttgart classroom as a boy, he would certainly have encountered the air as Thomas Moore's 'Erin, the Tear and the Smile in Thine Eyes' at home from his mother, who was 'very musical, a fine pianist and very much her father's daughter'.[89] Ten years after emigrating, Herbert programmed and conducted 'Eileen Aroon' for Irish Day at the 1896 St Louis Exposition; it was an equally popular recital piece with 'Robin Adair' in pre-war United States, so much so that Kalem suggested the air as an appropriate accompaniment to the first reel of its 1911 film *The Colleen Bawn*.[90]

In other words, changing the title more closely associated it with a nationalist song tradition about Ireland that was current in both English and German on both sides of the Atlantic, and was being revived in Irish by the Gaelic League. It also directly placed *Eileen* in relation to contemporary movements to encourage national operas in Ireland and the United States[91] while simultaneously providing an opportunity to write the waltz 'Eileen, Alannah Asthore', completed on 9 December 1916, as an operatic counterweight to all the Eileens, Colleens, and Kathleens then populating Tin Pan Alley.[92] In Cleveland, Boston and New York, Victor Herbert conducted the premieres of *Eileen* with a broad smile on his face and made remarks from the stage, all variations on the theme that with this operetta he had achieved a life-long ambition. 'I have spent the best part of my life in the United States,' he said to the audience at the Shubert Theatre on 19 March 1917. 'I have been a citizen for many years. I think I am today a good American. But I was born in Dublin and all my forefathers were Irish.[93] It has been the dream of my life to write an Irish opera, one that would add to the glory of its traditions. Now that dream has been realized. You must know how I feel. This is the happiest day of my life.'[94] He directed all the profits of *Eileen*'s post-New York national tour to the Irish Relief Fund.[95]

Victor Herbert's biographers neatly situate *Eileen* as the culmination of a flirtation with Irish nationalism. However, perhaps 'Soldiers of Erin' is better evidence of Herbert the nationalist as well as his most enduring musical contribution to modern Ireland.

At Irish events in the United States before the Easter Rising, various songs were used to balance the 'Star-Spangled Banner' on concert programmes including Michael Joseph McCann's 'O'Donnell Abú', Thomas Davis's 'A Nation Once Again', and T. S. Sullivan's 'God Save Ireland', all of which were nineteenth-century nationalist favourites. Herbert had tried his hand at an American national anthem, 'Columbia', in 1898 and at an Irish one as early as 1907 when, he arranged 'God Save Ireland' to an air from George Petrie's collection of ancient Irish music for the Gaelic Society of New York.[96] Two years later Herbert wrote an arrangement of the 1798 air 'The Boys of Wexford' for lyrics composed by his fellow Friendly Son, Judge John Jerome Rooney. Thereafter, 'Old Ireland Shall Be Free' appeared regularly on programmes as the anthem, including at the Irish Race Convention in March 1916 where Herbert led the Glee Club of the Friendly Sons in an a cappella version for male voices. Its third verse and chorus are worth quoting:

> Wolf Tone has shown us what to do,
> And Emmet is not dead;
> Each Irish heart was leal and true
> When Dan O'Connell lead;
> Our Parnell's mound is holy ground,
> And holier yet shall be,
> When full confessed from East to West,
> Old Ireland shall be free.
>
> Chorus:
> Old Ireland shall be free, we swear.
> Old Ireland shall be free!
> In deathless troth we pledge our oath,
> Old Ireland shall be free![97]

This same desire in Irish America for appropriate musical expressions of their nationalism in the first decades of the twentieth century inspired the Irish tenor John McCormack to record 'A Nation Once Again' in 1906 and Victor Herbert to write a new setting for 'O'Donnell Abú' in 1915.[98]

His 'stirring finale' to *Eileen* in 1916 – 'When Ireland Stands among the Nations of the World'– had a sheet music and recording afterlife that was promptly imitated.[99] This was because it was an anthem that conveyed a powerful political message during the First World War and was one of the main reasons *Musical America* called *Eileen* 'a bit of propaganda'. It was completely in keeping with Herbert's role as president of the FOIF.[100] One would be hard-pressed to find Ireland's proclamation of independence and self-determination for small nations in Henry Blossom's usual vocabulary, but not in Herbert's:

> I can hear, in fancy, now, her children singing!
> I can see her well-beloved flag unfurled!
> And with heart and soul I pray,
> God may speed the blessed day
> When Ireland stands among the nations of the world![101]

*Musical America* related a story about Herbert's pleasure when told that 'his opera would do more for the cause than a princely gift of money' before commenting: 'Indeed, when one listens to Mr. Herbert's music (as to John McCormack's singing), how could one deny the Irish anything?'[102]

It is not known exactly when Herbert decided to write the new anthem 'Soldiers of Erin, The Rallying Song of the Irish Volunteers' but it seems to have been in concert with his work on *Eileen*. Its germination began in the New York living room of Mollie Monteith, wife of Captain Robert Monteith who was then on the run in Ireland, during the autumn of 1916. 'It was a cheerful room and well visited,' her daughter Florence recalled:

> Father Robert O'Reilly from the West of Ireland was now stationed at St. Gabriel's on East 36th Street. He always brought his violin when he came to call on the Monteiths. He wanted to learn the 'Soldier's Song.' It had not been set to sheet music yet, so [I] played it by ear on the old piano, and Davie [her brother] sang the words. Father played it over and over for a few weeks until he got it perfect. Later, he contacted the great composer Victor Herbert about setting it on paper for printing. One afternoon Davie met Father by appointment and they went to the studio. Victor Herbert listened to the violin and voice and worked on the arrangement. When it was printed they put it into the hands of Mrs. Slattery of the Irish Industries Depot, Lexington Avenue, New York.[103]

For all practical purposes, 'Soldiers of Erin' appeared simultaneously with Cathal MacDubhghaill's arrangement of 'A Soldier's Song' published in Dublin in December 1916.[104] Both use the same melody and English words of the Peadar Kearney and Patrick Heeney composition that was sung in the GPO during the Easter Rising and in the internment camps afterwards. Only their first lines vary ever so slightly: 'I'll sing you a song, a soldier's song' (United States) rather than 'We'll sing a song, a soldier's song' (Ireland). Just how Fr O'Reilly connected with Victor Herbert is unknown, but the result was a score for orchestra as well as the piano version that Mrs Slattery published for the benefit of the Gaelic League. The priest claimed copyright for editing the latter and it was duly filed in the United States on 14 January 1917.[105]

As early as 2 March it was on the West Coast, as part of the Emmet programme of the Knights of the Red Branch in San Francisco; by May it was being sung at a rally in Hibernian Hall, Seattle.[106] A 50-piece orchestra under Herbert's baton played 'Soldiers of Erin' at a special Carnegie Hall programme to mark the first anniversary of the Rising. *The Gaelic American* reported that

> Mr. Herbert … created an atmosphere of patriotism and a feeling of kinship and association with all those who died for Ireland that it was impossible to resist. He thrilled and inspired the entire proceedings in a really magnificent way.[107]

The mainstream papers, in contrast, focused only on the speeches made that evening rather than the music; the *Times* mentioned that Herbert conducted 'The Star-Spangled Banner' while the *Tribune* reported 'a programme of Irish music was given' without ever mentioning Herbert.[108] *The Gaelic American* detected bias and complained that 'Soldiers of Erin' would be more widely known if Woolworth's had not refused to carry it in its stores.[109] But by the time Éamon de Valera arrived in 1919, the song had in fact been sung as the Irish national anthem all across the country for a full two years. While Victor Herbert did not live long enough to see this song officially adopted by the Irish government in 1926, it was certainly his version as performed widely in the United States and recorded for the Emerson label in 1919 that gave it so much traction.[110] He modestly called it his 'small contribution to the cause of Ireland'.[111]

In the spring of 1914, the Friendly Sons of St Patrick had unveiled a monument to US naval commodore John Barry in Washington, DC on 16 May, followed by a concert of Irish music with the group's Glee Club that Victor Herbert had started the previous year.[112] It was an occasion that melded Irish and American patriotism in a manner appealing to his sensibilities and yet he was not there. A brush with death while in London in April meant Herbert could not return to the United States until 26 June 1914, fate thereby placing him in a ringside seat as the Home Rule crisis in Ireland escalated.

Arriving in London on 13 April, Victor Herbert took his wife and daughter on a nostalgic tour of the places where Samuel Lover had lived and that he had not seen since he was a child. On 18 April, the London correspondent for the *New York Times* tracked Herbert down and filed a special report that described him as 'an ardent Home Ruler and keenly interested in the Ulster imbroglio'. A direct quote from the composer was sent to New York:

I would like to meet this man Carson. I am in the pink of condition, and fit for a fight. If I do not get a commission to write a new opera while I am here I guess I will enlist, and not with the Ulster volunteers either.[113]

Coming two years before the Rising, as well as before he became politically active in the Irish groups he was associated with in New York, the way Herbert frames this is like a palimpsest of Irish-American nationalism at the moment Home Rule was degrading. We do not know what Herbert read or to whom he spoke while recuperating in Brighton following a serious appendectomy on 25 April but the Larne gun-running and the passage of the third Home Rule Bill in the British House of Commons were major news stories for the remainder of his stay in England. If we extrapolate from his sentiments as expressed on 18 April, he must have keenly followed events in Ireland because he certainly stepped up his commitment to Irish nationalism after his return to the United States, as we have seen. In its review of *Eileen*, the *New York Times* could not resist a dig at Herbert for this commitment: 'all through the first act one kept expecting a German U-Boat to poke its periscope through the shamrock sea. And then one at last realized … that there were no Germans in the plot a'tall, a'tall.' The *Tribune* twisted that another way: 'Hist! It must have been a German propagandist who placed red-coats in the play at these critical times.'[114]

Herbert was not a neophyte when it came to nationalism. The music world in the United States was no less political than Irish America; it was just expressed differently there. Critics and composers rather than politicians and revivalists argued about how best to represent a nation's pride and feeling in an art form.[115] The large body of classical music at the end of the nineteenth century that was associated with Germany, France, and Italy was intimidating but there were some willing to take the chance.[116] In a 1907 interview Herbert remarked: 'Just as soon as the opportunity arrives when the American composer can with dignity find a market in this country for an opera he might write I will be among the first to present my claims.'[117] That opportunity came in 1909 when Herbert agreed to write a grand opera in English. From then until the premiere of *Natoma* in February 1911, the music world debated the definition of American opera and generated great anticipation for a story set in 1820 in southern California, using American Indian musical themes and characters. There was so much hype that Herbert was referred to 'as a symbol of patriotism and democratic life' by the Philadelphia *Record*, which went on to claim 'he was to American music what Emerson and Whitman were to American literature.'[118] Naturally, neither Herbert nor *Natoma* could meet such high expectations. But, if we consider that while Herbert was composing *Natoma*, he was also writing for the Gaelic Society of New York and the Friendly Sons of St Patrick, we can see how he was exploring varieties of nationalism through musical expression. Irish music was far more familiar to Herbert than that of Native Americans but the impulse was the same. It is in this context that we can best understand *Eileen* – a 'light opera of grand opera impressiveness',[119] on an Irish nationalist theme with Irish national music that at the same time, by being sung in English, was another Herbert contribution to the evolution of American cultural nationalism.

In February 1917 Herbert led a delegation of the Friends of Irish Freedom to the White House to plead for American neutrality.[120] But after the United States entered the war in April, he wrote 'Can't You Hear Your Country Calling?'(1917) even as many of his colleagues in the music world like Mme Gadski became targets in an hysterical purge of German culture. 'It struck him as utter nonsense, this refusal to understand the enemy. Burning books, outlawing languages, proscribing music – these were not the way to enlightenment, or to winning a war,' Claire Purdy wrote of Herbert in 1944 but, as Neil Gould asked in 2008, 'What was the Irish advocate, the cultural German, the loyal American to do?'[121] He continued to programme Beethoven and Wagner whenever possible despite their being banned by most symphony orchestras into 1918.[122] With his only son serving with the American forces at the Marne and the Argonne, Herbert composed the patriotic ode 'Call to Freedom' (1918) and promoted the sale of Liberty Bonds.[123] His Irish friends who had been on the Barry statue committee in 1914 presented one of Robert Emmet to President Wilson on 28 June 1917 for the main rotunda of the Smithsonian's Museum of Natural History with an inscription that read in part, 'I wished to procure for my country the guarantee which Washington procured for America.'[124] In a sense, the personal and professional risks Victor Herbert took on behalf of Irish freedom in 1916 were towards the same end, with musical notes for his epitaph.

'Soldiers of Erin'
Piccolo.
2 Flutes.
2 Oboes.
Clarinets in
Bass Clarinet.
Bassoons.
Contra Bassoon.
Horns.
(Trumpets.)
Trombones.
Tuba.
Tympani.
Drums.
Triangle.
Tambourine. Castanets, etc.
Piano or Harp.
Violin I.
Violin II.
Viola.
'Cello.
Bass.
Orchestra Score No 7 "The Crest"

PRICE 5 CENTS

# THE
# Fatherland
(TITLE REG. U.S. PAT. OFF.)

## A Weekly

Vol. IV

MARCH 8th, 1916

No. 5

*Drawn by Thomas Fogarty for the frontispiece of James K. McGuire's book:*

## WHAT GERMANY COULD DO FOR IRELAND

# A BRITISH SPY WRITES TO SIR EDWARD GREY

# CHAPTER TWELVE

# THE STEREOPTICON
## GERMAN AND IRISH PROPAGANDA OF DEED
## AND WORD AND THE 1916 EASTER RISING

## R. Bryan Willits

*The Irish and the Germans, for the first time in my knowledge, seem to have
joined their several lunacies in one common attack against England and
incidentally against the Administration for being too friendly to England.*
Secretary of state John Hay to Henry White, March 1900

*In case of trouble, there are half a million trained Germans in America who
will join the Irish and start a revolution.*
State secretary for Foreign Affairs Arthur Zimmerman, 1916

The subject of the last chapter, renowned American composer Victor Herbert, provides
a rich example of the possible intersections of Ireland, Britain, and Germany in an
American setting. But Herbert personified just one strand in a complex tapestry of
ethno-political alliances that defined ethnic New York in the lead-up to the Easter
Rising. Such alliances were made evident as German-Irish collaboration formed the
backstory to the narrative that emerged on 25 April 1916, when the disturbances
in Ireland made front-page news across the United States. While some newspapers
printed the tenebrous details of violent episodes outside Maryborough (Portlaoise),
and others made reference to a mysterious cyphered telegram from Ireland that

announced the outbreak of revolution, it was the arrest of Sir Roger Casement and the sinking of the *Aud* that recurrently appeared in the limelight amongst the headlines of a multitude of American newspapers.[1] Casement's arrest and the events that followed also received ample attention in the German-language press in the United States with coverage that immediately emerged in support of Casement and the Rising. This did not, however, mark the inauguration of a bond between German and Irish Americans, but reflected an existing connection between the two diasporas that manifested before and during the First World War through fraternisation, political agitation, and widespread propagandistic efforts in both the German and Irish ethnic press. It was within this already existing context of mutual support that representatives of the German government in the United States worked with Clan na Gael to organise and promote Casement's mission to Germany. It is therefore unsurprising to note that once the Rising commenced, these same individuals then turned the organs tied to the German Information Service (GIS) in the United States towards promoting the Irish rebellion.

The *New-Yorker Staats-Zeitung* (*NYSZ*), the largest and most important German-language daily in the United States, took the lead in explaining the meaning of Casement's arrest and the Rising to its German-speaking readers.[2] Much of the coverage of Casement's arrest in the mainstream American press was verbatim in tone and covered Casement's past career as British consul, Sir Arthur Conan Doyle's claims that Casement had gone mad, and the famous Findlay affair.[3] But the manner in which the *NYSZ* described the Findlay affair clearly placed Casement as the protagonist by accentuating the way he revealed to the world the 'murderous politics of the British' and how they sought 'through criminal means' to catch him. German officials on both sides of the Atlantic overestimated Casement's position as the 'leader of all Irish associations in America'. But, as was also noted in Lucy McDiarmid's chapter in this volume, by the end of Casement's tenure in Germany, he had lost faith in the German commitment to help Ireland, and had likewise fallen out of favour with the Germans.[4] Nonetheless, his promoters at the *NYSZ* continued to present an image of Casement that stressed his fame, his Irish identity, and the primacy of his role in the struggle for Irish freedom. Thereafter, the *NYSZ*'s detailed reportage of the Easter Rising and its after effects continuously occupied the front pages for an entire month with only a few exceptions where coverage was bumped to inside pages.[5]

The *NYSZ*'s view of Casement and the Rising was no aberration. The foundations for an entente between the German and Irish diasporas in the United States went back at least to the second Anglo-Boer War, when German and Irish organisations like the Deutsch-Amerikanischer Nationalbund (DAN)[6], the Ancient Order of Hibernians, and Clan na Gael rallied in support of the Boers and protested what they saw as British cupidity and rapine in southern Africa.[7] Relations between influential individuals and organisations in both of these communities continued to evolve as they supported the Boers both financially and militarily while also criticising the United States government for not supporting the besieged Boers as they had supported the Cubans in their war against Spain.[8] The Anglo-Boer War gave Irish and German Americans a sense of an impending alliance between the United States and Britain even at the turn of the century, and while many saw Britain as the common enemy of their respective countries of origin, they argued against an Anglo-American alliance not only as Irishmen or Germans, but as Americans who held that any foreign alliance, and especially one with Britain, would have deleterious effects on the United States.

Cooperation between German and Irish Americans later came to a head in the pre-First World War years as these same groups militated against the 1911 Taft Arbitration Treaties between Britain and the United States, which they believed created this illegitimate, de facto alliance.[9] George von Skal, a German journalist with ties to the German embassy and the *NYSZ*, went on to be conspicuously vocal in this campaign against the treaties and appeared alongside John Devoy at mass protests where they functioned as keynote speakers and representatives of their ethnic communities.[10] The relationship that developed between Devoy and von Skal not only served them in their efforts to stymie the arbitration treaty, but also endured for years thereafter, ultimately keeping the principal Irish revolutionary leader in the United States in contact with the officials of the German imperial government.[11]

As naval disputes between Germany and Britain reached fever pitch and war seemed increasingly likely, Devoy's most recent plans for his long-held revolutionary agenda entered their nascent stages and became further enmeshed with the possibilities of German support.[12] This became especially important at the advent of the First World War, when the Clan's dedication to revolutionary nationalism gained purchase with other Irish nationalists who defected from the ranks of Home Rule supporting organisations like the United Irish League of America.[13] The revolutionary, physical-force option for Irish independence now seemed increasingly realisable, especially with the support of Irish America's established German allies, whose fatherland happened to be the chief rival of the British Empire.

Meanwhile, other organisations constituted of Irish and German Americans emerged from the pre-war context including the American Truth Society (ATS), established under the leadership of Jeremiah A. O'Leary, an Irish-American lawyer who, on top of being a vehemently anti-British Irish nationalist, took a markedly pro-German stance on the war.[14] O'Leary took an active interest in Irish politics in the first decade of the twentieth century, and established the first Sinn Féin Society in America.[15] He also joined the Clan, and was highly regarded by the leadership as an able orator who 'had done more in a practical way to open the eyes of the American public' to the 'evil forces working in the interest of England'.[16]

The combination of Irish, German, and American elements surrounding O'Leary epitomised the cooperative nature of much of the Irish and German-American population. In one characteristic example, on the occasion of the one hundred and thirty-eighth anniversary of Robert Emmet's birth, the Clan organised an event in Philadelphia with O'Leary as the main speaker. The programme began with the orchestra playing Irish, German, and American airs, and after O'Leary's oration and a showing of the footage of O'Donovan Rossa's funeral, the audience joined together to sing 'The Star-Spangled Banner', 'Wacht Am Rhein', and the old Fenian classic, 'God Save Ireland'.[17] O'Leary also denounced aspects of the American establishment that favoured the British. In one famous instance, he directly attacked President Wilson's Anglo-centric inclinations, and was repaid in kind with a widely publicised telegram from Wilson that accused O'Leary and his ilk of being disloyal Americans and stated that he 'would feel deeply mortified to have you or anybody like you vote for me'.[18] Wilson's response was not just pointed at Irish nationalists, since O'Leary also enjoyed the support of the German-American community, who made up 80 percent of the ATS's membership during the war.[19] The myriad of steadfast ties between these groups evinced in the ranks of the ATS and at Clan commemorations showed that Irish collusion with the Germans in the Rising was not a singular event, but rather, emerged from a context where cross-communal cooperation had long served both the German and Irish-American communities in their protestations against Britain and American involvement in the war.

When the perennial assumptions of these German and Irish Americans came to fruition as the First World War commenced, von Bernstorff, the German ambassador to the United States, saw to it that the GIS was reorganised in an attempt to ensure that sufficient propaganda found its way into the hands of American citizens.[20] A new office was set up in New York City in 1914 at 1123 Broadway, initially under the management of a number of individuals closely connected to von Bernstorff.[21] It became standard practice for individuals both officially and unofficially tied to the German embassy to work in a number of capacities for the GIS, which the embassy ultimately financed and directed along with those in its pockets.[22] Amongst the most notable was George Sylvester Viereck, who figured prominently in the GIS's schemes as editor of the obdurately pro-German weekly *The Fatherland*, whose headquarters were at 1123 Broadway as well.[23]

The means by which the GIS sought to influence American opinion involved a broad range of activities and methods for transmitting information. Despite British efforts to cut the cables of services that provided America with news unfavourable to the Allied cause, the German government was still able to use a wireless service that sent dispatches directly from Nauen, Germany, to receiving stations in Sayville, Long Island, and Tuckerton, New Jersey.[24] They also employed sympathetic correspondents in the United States and in Germany, while the GIS created and distributed films, pamphlets, and books friendly to their cause. They bought the *New York Daily Mail* and made overtures to buy other papers that would support their official line. They arranged lecture circuits for pro-German intellectuals; financially supported and organised pacifist and pro-neutrality organisations; disseminated pro-German materials through the DAN and the ATS; underwrote pro-German publications like *The Fatherland*, *Vital Issue*, *The International*, *Fair Play*, and the *NYSZ*; and through these various channels supplied some 500–800 newspapers across the country with information.[25]

The GIS also targeted specific ethnic groups in the United States. Along with the Jewish and German population, they directed a significant amount of attention towards the Irish. At 42 West 42nd Street in New York City, the agents of the GIS maintained a separate Irish Press and News Service, which was managed by James K. McGuire, a leading member of the Clan and a onetime mayor of Syracuse, New York.[26] McGuire also served as a director of the ATS and as chairman of the executive committee of the Friends of Irish Freedom.[27] He owned multiple newspapers and publishing companies; was on the advisory board of a newspaper that the GIS attempted to form; used his influence to facilitate arms shipments to the Germans; and was even involved in procuring the necessary kit needed to smuggle Casement out of the country when he embarked on his mission to Berlin.[28] As the head of the Irish Press and News Service, McGuire was paid by the GIS to send copious articles favourable to the German and Irish cause to roughly 20 newspapers at least two or three times a week.[29]

McGuire was also a propagandist in his own right and authored two books that advanced the virtues of German aid in securing Irish independence. The first of these, *The King, the Kaiser, and Irish Freedom*, published in 1915, reminded readers of Casement's recent success in Germany and made the claim that Americans had 'learned to love the Germans as the best friends of Irish freedom in America'.[30] *The Fatherland* carried regular advertisements for his books, while his second book, *What Could Germany Do for Ireland?*, appeared in 1916 with its frontispiece even making its way onto the cover of *The Fatherland*'s 18 March 1916 issue.[31] While readers of *The Fatherland* may not have known that McGuire and Viereck were both on the GIS payroll, articles in *The Fatherland* lionising McGuire along with copious promotion of his books emerge in hindsight as part of a broad scheme to promote the agenda of the German government and their Irish allies through avenues intertwined with the GIS.

In addition to supporting Viereck's *Fatherland*, von Bernstorff also managed to secure the necessary funding to keep the *NYSZ* afloat throughout the war years. The paper's circulation increased steadily until the Americans joined the war, more than trebling its circulation of about 45,000 in 1910 to 138,029 in 1916.[32] Despite this, the *NYSZ* was continually in debt, and began receiving subsidies in the autumn of 1914 through a German government sponsored investor who was able to maintain a controlling interest in the paper to ensure the editorial perspective remained pro-German.[33] The other 500-plus German-language papers across the country were generally left to their own devices, but the prominence of the *NYSZ* as the largest German-language daily in the United States made its continued control under its owner and editor, Herman Ridder, so important to von Bernstorff that he told Berlin, 'Its collapse would be most disadvantageous to our interests.'[34] If the *NYSZ* was an exceptional case in terms of official involvement, it was seen as a crucial one since it had been held for decades as an important institution in the German-American community, and could now be used as a privately owned American paper that would continue to further Berlin's agenda.[35]

Ridder and his likeminded sons, Victor and Bernard, also consorted on a regular basis with prominent members of the Irish nationalist community. On 24 June 1915, the Friends of Peace called a meeting to protest against the United States' involvement in the war and to inveigh against the exportation of arms and ammunition to belligerents. In typical fashion, the meeting was organised under the auspices of a number of German and Irish groups including the DAN, Clan na Gael, and the ATS.[36] Among the main speakers were Devoy, von Skal, and Bernard Ridder, who had by this time succeeded his father as editor of the *NYSZ*.[37] It was but one prominent case amongst many where the leaders of the Clan and those in league with the German embassy and their propaganda mission demonstrated together, drawing large crowds consisting mostly of those of German and Irish extraction. Such demonstrations were earnest attempts to keep the United States out of the war, but the motivation of the participants was surely primed by the belief that United States' entry in the war would certainly mean American aid for Britain.

It was also common to find within the pages of the pro-German press promotions for charities, events, organisations, and publications where the leaders in the Irish nationalist and German communities were again in league. In one such example, full-page advertisements for the first Irish Race Convention along with articles appealing to their Irish readers appeared in *The Fatherland*, urging readers to attend a conference that would seek to examine the relationship between Ireland, Irish America, and Britain.[38] Similarly, advertisements for the ATS abound in these publications, and O'Leary's portrait even appeared on the cover of the 13 November 1915 issue of *The Fatherland*, with the caption, 'The Champion of Real Americanism'. These newspapers implored readers to join the ATS and to attend lectures delivered by O'Leary; in one instance the net proceeds generated at the event were divided between the German Red Cross and the Irish Volunteer Fund.[39] Where advertisements and endorsements for the *NYSZ* appeared in *The Fatherland*, as did reprinted letters expressing support for *The Fatherland* from the Ridders, so too came advertisements for Devoy's *The Gaelic American* and letters from Irishmen urging their families to read both *The Gaelic American* and *The Fatherland*.[40] While such letters might have been of dubious origin, their publication still demonstrated that one of the most outspoken organs for the German cause repeatedly devoted significant page space to procuring Irish support not only for their own newspaper and the *NYSZ*, but also for the *The Gaelic American*.

The readers of the *NYSZ* would not have found anything out of place when the column 'The War Situation Day to Day', though normally written by Bernard Ridder, was instead penned by Jeremiah O'Leary on 27 April 1916 as part of the paper's ongoing defence of Casement and the Rising. These were not the words of an unfamiliar Irish voice, but rather, the rhetoric of a man with whom readers of any GIS supported newspaper would have already been quite familiar. In O'Leary's editorial, Casement's cause became the cause of Theobald Wolfe Tone and Robert Emmet, but also of America and its founding fathers while the Rising was likened to the Boston Tea Party. 'It has been asserted that Germany has aided Ireland,' wrote O'Leary,

> Let us hope so. Germany owes it to Ireland to do so, just as France owed it to the United States … Some New York newspapers have called Sir Roger Casement a 'renegade' and 'traitor'. From the British standpoint our own Washington was a traitor, but from the American standpoint he was a patriot. Casement's crime is love of country. Casement's ideals are American ideals. Casement's example was the American Revolution. We cannot condemn him without condemning ourselves … If Sir Roger Casement is insane, George Washington had the same disease. The disease might be well styled 'dementia Americana' or 'dementia libertatis'. It is a disease that spells disaster to tyranny. God Save Ireland.'[41]

The use of Casement's name in front-page headlines also suggests that the *NYSZ* editors assumed that their readers were already familiar with Casement and would have taken an interest in the recent developments of his career. Aside from the publicity he gained in his human rights campaigns in Africa and South America, Casement had also been publicly seeking German aid for Irish independence through his writings since at least 1911. From this point forward, his essays positing the virtues of a German and Irish alliance were published throughout Ireland, Germany, and the United States.[42] While his essay 'Ireland, Germany and the next war' was published in Ireland under the nom de plume Shan Van Vocht in the July 1913 issue of *Irish Review*, Casement's stance became especially evident in 1914 when all pretences were dropped and he published a collection of his essays under his own name. This collection was redacted while Casement was in New York in order to make a special appeal to American readers, and appeared under various titles like *The Crime against Ireland and How the War May Right It*, and, *Ireland, Germany, and Freedom of the Seas: To Free the Seas, Free Ireland*.[43] The Celtic Press, a publishing company in Philadelphia with ties to Joseph McGarrity, also published Casement's essays in the early months of 1915 under the title *The Crime against Europe: A Possible Outcome of the War of 1914*, which was promoted in publications connected to the GIS.[44] Ultimately, this body of work showed that Casement's allegiance to Ireland and his hope for German aid gained attention in Germany and Ireland well before the war, and by late 1914 had garnered the support of sympathetic publishers in the United States.[45]

While in the United States, Casement also called for action beyond words when, in the preface to *The Crime against Ireland*, he declared, 'The rest of the writer's task must be essayed not with the author's pen, but with the rifle of the Irish Volunteer. As a contribution to the cause of Irish freedom this presentment of the case for Germany, friend of Ireland and foe of England, is now published.'[46] As established in other chapters in this volume, Casement had already helped put rifles from Germany into the hands of Irish Volunteers by aiding in the famous Howth gun-running, while his quest to get German support for Irish independence was to reach new heights in the United States shortly after publishing the aforementioned collection of essays.[47] Meanwhile, Casement's publishing activities in the United States were virtually tailor-made to fit the plans of the GIS and their Irish propaganda branch as his works aimed to argue for the bonds of Germany and Ireland while appealing to an American audience.

Although Casement came to the United States with the intention of raising funds and to secure much needed officers for the Irish Volunteers, while in New York he met Devoy and through him, found his way into the inner circle of the German embassy.[48]

According to Devoy's account, it was sometime before 21 August 1914, that Devoy and several others from the Clan first met with von Bernstorff and other high-ranking officials from the embassy to discuss what would eventually become a key aspect of Casement's mission to Germany, namely, procuring German weapons and officers for a rebellion in Ireland.[49] Devoy recalled von Bernstorff listening 'attentively and with evident sympathy' to the Clan's proposals. He also claimed that it was only after this meeting that the Clan's communications with Germany were 'conducted chiefly through Captain von Papen', the German military attaché. But by the time the Clan had met with von Bernstorff, Casement and von Papen had already discussed all the elements of Casement's mission that would eventually be supported by the Clan.[50] On 9 August, von Papen sent a message to the German Foreign Office stating that Casement was 'ready to land arms for fifty thousand in Ireland with own means', that he believed 'the movement' could only be successful if the Germans declared 'that after victory it would favor liberation', and that there was 'special success hoped for with the Irish regiments'.[51]

In less than a month, Casement went from a fundraiser for the Volunteers to a confidant of the German embassy and of the Clan na Gael Revolutionary Directory. Meanwhile, his stentorian declarations demanding an alliance between Ireland and Germany were followed on 17 September by an open letter to the Irish people imploring them not to fight with the British in a war that was not theirs, claiming that Ireland had no quarrel with the Germans.[52] On 31 October 1914, Casement landed in Berlin, and within a matter of weeks got the declaration he sought when he convinced the Germans to formally declare their intent to liberate Ireland in the event of an invasion.[53] This was arguably the last of Casement's successful dealings with the Germans, however, but it would not have seemed as such if one relied solely on the propagandised reports of his activities in Germany that continued to emerge in the United States.

Casement also found support for his mission to Germany in the famous German scholar Kuno Meyer, who previously helped Casement publish and circulate his articles in Ireland and in Germany.[54] Meyer worked closely with both Clan na Gael and the GIS while in the United States, undertaking in late 1914 a lecture circuit promoting both Casement and the Kaiser's efforts in the war.[55] At the Clan commemoration of the Manchester Martyrs on Sunday, 6 December, at the Brooklyn Academy of Music, he delivered a panegyric on Casement that lauded his endeavours to create an alliance between the German government and the Irish; celebrated the creation of an Irish regiment from the Irish prisoners of war in Germany; and reassured his audience that he and his countrymen all believed an invasion of both England and Ireland was inevitable.[56] Though his activities in America were not always looked upon with favour, Meyer's speeches and public appearances were closely watched and received a considerable amount of attention in the press, thereby furthering the propaganda value of Casement's mission.[57]

Publications associated with the GIS also reprinted Meyer's speeches along with commentary supporting his celebrations of Casement and his pro-German stance on the war. This was done with speeches like that delivered at Terrace Garden 17 December 1914, in which Meyer derided Sir Arthur Conan Doyle's claims of Casement's insanity. He also sarcastically told the audience that when he had dined with Casement in Berlin a few weeks before, 'he was so hopeful, had such a good appetite and seemed altogether so sane in body and mind that this news has come as a great shock to me.'[58] Likewise, once word of Casement's arrest appeared in the *NYSZ*, they did not depict him as a lunatic traitor to the British cause thought by many to be mad as some of the English-language papers had, but rather, continuously referred to Casement with a degree of deference by often adding variations on the theme 'the famous Irish patriot' as a prefix to his name.[59]

Although some papers failed on 25 April to make any mention of the Rising in Dublin or disturbances anywhere else in Ireland aside from those related to Casement and the *Aud*, further news of the Rising did emerge in the American press that day as Robert Schmuhl's chapter in this volume will so pointedly show. Along with the *NYSZ*, a number of newspapers mentioned reports of a cyphered, private dispatch and rumours in the financial district that exclaimed the 'outbreak of revolution in Ireland'.[60] While cagey about the details, these papers hinted that the rumours originated with Devoy, yet some remained sceptical since ciphered messages were in fact regulated by the British throughout the war.[61] Nevertheless, it appears that such a message, reading 'Tom [Clarke] successfully operated on today' did go through to New York where it was allegedly received at Devoy's residence.[62] Through the efforts of the brothers Tim and Eugene Ring – who were privy to the plans of the Rising and who also exercised a great deal of control on the daily operations of the cable station off the Co. Kerry coast on Valentia Island – a message was sent from Valentia to New York just before the Easter Rising broke out.[63] How exactly the message leaked to the American press is difficult to say, but the result was such that some American newspapers were quick to speculate on the possibilities of full-fledged revolution in an integral part of the British Empire.[64]

As news of the Rising continued to make its way onto the pages of the *NYSZ*, coverage of the insurrection was located within the context of the First World War, and was accompanied by a focus on developments in the United States involving Devoy and the Clan while the 'Tory' press in the United States continued to be attacked in Ridder's editorials.[65] A special timeline under the headline 'England's black April' was printed on 30 April, detailing the losses throughout the British Empire, at the top of which was a section under the heading: 'Revolution in Ireland'.[66] Editorials written by Devoy for *The Gaelic American* were also reproduced in the *NYSZ*, thereby providing a broader platform amongst the readers of the German press for Devoy's claims that Irish America's funding and arming of the Irish insurrectionists were no more a breach of American neutrality than American involvement in Cuba, or the aid given to the Allies by J. P. Morgan and American munitions factories.[67]

The *NYSZ* conveyed a more certain grasp on the details of the Rising as it progressed, and claimed that there seemed 'to be no doubt, that the uprising in Ireland was planned in a meticulous way for Easter Sunday', and that the 'advance against the English coast by German Naval Forces and the "Zeppelin" raids were also a part of the large scale plan'.[68] Whether or not the original intention was to attack England on 24 April in order to assist the Irish remains however unresolved, as there are many inconsistencies in the historical record concerning the dates, plans, movements, and recollections of those involved in this aspect of the Rising.[69] Whatever the plans of the German navy might have been, the *NYSZ* concluded that these events were in fact intrinsically linked, as would British intelligence likewise conclude in a White Paper published in 1921 that investigated the Rising. Moreover, depending on the reader's allegiance when it was reported, the news of such multifaceted German military assistance would have worked to the benefit of those seeking to demonstrate that the worst case scenario had materialised, but also would have bolstered the hopes of those who wanted to see a favourable situation for the Irish revolutionaries.[70]

As Easter Week came to a close and the insurrection in Ireland was quelled, the *NYSZ* continued to persist in calling on German Americans to give money and support to a Red Cross committee under the auspices of the Dublin Club of New York. A short article that appeared on 4 May ordered: 'Germans to the fore! Aid for Ireland – remember the widows and orphans of the Irish patriots! Hearts Open! Hands Open! Irish patriots died in the streets of Dublin for their fatherland, for freedom.'[71] Though the Rising was over, the cross-community associational culture of the Irish and German Americans continued to persist.

When the executions came, no about-face or change of tone like those found in many of the mainstream English-language papers was required of the papers driven by the GIS since they had supported the Rising and denounced the British as murderers all along. Events and charities for the benefit of the families of the 'Irish martyrs' continued to be advertised in the *NYSZ*. In one example, alongside an article containing an Irish American's vitriolic reactions to the executions, the *NYSZ* advertised a concert at Carnegie Hall where proceeds went to an Irish relief fund headed by Cardinal John Farley, which is further explored in the chapter by Kate Feighery in this volume. In specifically calling on German-speaking America, the paper demanded:

> No German and no Austrian and Hungarian should be absent when it is necessary to provide victims of British tyranny with urgently needed aid! One hardly needs to be reminded, that the Irish have always stood with the Germans shoulder to shoulder at all times and on all questions which have become pressing as a consequence of the war.[72]

Casement's arrest was the first certain news of the Rising that Americans read, but by 3 August, his execution came as the last of the British reprisals. In Viereck's editorials, Casement also became the first and the last in the sense of a Johannine apocalyptic, when his execution was likened to 'another nail driven into the bleeding hands and feet of Ireland by her British executioners. Ireland's cup of sorrow is filled to the brim,' Viereck wrote, 'but salvation is apt to follow crucifixion.' Viereck also reminded his readers that this was also about the United States, because, England's justice is like American neutrality. It has two faces. It dooms to death Irish patriots, but it bestows Cabinet appointments on Irish rascals. Yet a place on the gallows is more honorable than a place in the Asquith Cabinet. The company of the hangman is preferable to Viscount Grey's ... England's action against Casement was not justice' he concluded, 'but Murder.'[73]

Meanwhile, Kuno Meyer returned to Germany with T. St John Gaffney, the recalled Irish-born American consul general at Munich, and founded the German-Irish society in Berlin, which operated out of the same premises used by the Official German Press Bureau, and focused on furthering the aims of revolutionary Irish nationalists.[74] Further overtures for additional military support were made between the Germans and the Irish in their ongoing war against Britain, though nothing militarily significant materialised after Casement's mission ended in failure.[75] In their fight to keep the United States out of the war, the efforts of the GIS were also for naught, but the lingering effects of paranoia focused on German agents operating in Ireland that haunted the British secret service may in the end have had the most enduring effect in the aftermath of the Rising. The GHQ of MI5 in Dublin later lamented that after German collusion with the Irish Republican Brotherhood (IRB) culminated in the Rising, MI5 put most of their efforts into finding German spies in Ireland until the end of the war, where they should have been focusing on the reorganisation of Irish nationalists under the IRB, who eventually carried on with the revolutionary agenda.[76]

While there is a good deal of research examining Casement's impact after his execution, the historiography focusing on Casement lacks a thorough examination of his legacy in the eyes of the Germans. In the foreword of the 1953 edition of Robert Monteith's account of his experiences with Casement and the Irish Brigade, von Papen claimed that it was 'an honor for a German to be asked to write the foreword to a book devoted to the recounting of the struggle of the Irish people for their freedom'. He considered it one of 'the most unforgettable impressions of [his] political life' to have come into contact with Casement and to 'have contributed to the far-reaching resolution' which encouraged Casement to set out for Germany. Such words came from a man whose post-Easter 1916 political life involved serving as chancellor of Germany in 1932, and then vice chancellor under Adolf Hitler for 18 months.[77]

When he wrote his memoir, Karl Spindler, captain of the *Aud*, knew that Casement was intent on getting to Ireland to call off the Rising. Had the British not intercepted the *Aud*, Casement's plans might have spoiled Spindler's mission and German designs on having a foothold inside the British naval blockade just as well. Nonetheless, Spindler too wrote of Casement as a gallant hero many years after his death.[78] But Spindler and von Papen were both directly involved with Irish events and therefore had a vested interest in retroactively portraying the *Aud* gun-running as an intrepid affair, while Casement had in fact become an ineffectual nuisance in the eyes of many who dealt with him in Zossen and Berlin.[79] The impact that the Rising had on those Germans involved may yet be worth further examination, but it must be remembered that Irish republican revolutionary intrigues were just one of several plots supported by the Germans during the war, as is evinced by Emmett O'Conner's chapter on James Larkin in this volume. In consideration of this, not to mention the fact that Germany would undergo a most turbulent metamorphosis in the decades that followed, it remains doubtful that the gestalt of the Casement mission and the Easter Rising has left any sort of enduring legacy in German minds or historiography.

Spindler himself later became the object of celebration in the United States when he travelled across the country in 1931 on a lecture circuit directed by the Clan and their supporters.[80] His exploits were widely celebrated from coast to coast by Irish nationalists who decorated him with medals and awards, while the lectures were timed to coincide with the 15-year anniversary commemorations of the Rising. Events like these belie the notion that Irish and German Americans jettisoned their connections after their failures in the First World War, as Irish leaders following Spindler's lectures continued to espouse the need for further cooperation between the Germans and Irish in the United States.[81] Yet there is much evidence to support the notion that the role the United States played in ensuring Germany's defeat in the First World War created a context in which German Americans became more reluctant to celebrate their support for their fatherland or even their heritage, while it has often been similarly suggested that Irish republicans downplayed the extent to which they courted German support. Even with the questionable historical exactitude of memoir and commemoration in mind, the fact that Captain Raimund Weisbach – the man who fired the missiles that sunk the *Lusitania* and later captained the submarine that brought Casement from Germany to Ireland before the Rising – took part in the fiftieth anniversary commemorations of the Easter Rising as an official guest of the Irish government, stands as a reminder that the German and Irish alliance was still commemorated if not celebrated later in Ireland too.[82]

The German and Irish connection in the Rising came after over a decade and a half of cooperation between a significant portion of the German and Irish diasporas in the United States. In this time, the actions of Irish and German organisations repeatedly caught the attention of the American establishment, and especially those whose international allegiances tended towards the Anglo-centric. The political and martial potential for this alliance became particularly poignant as the inevitability of war between Germany and Britain became increasingly apparent. On the side of those who supported Britain and the Allies, fear of an Irish and German cabal increased while those on the side of the Clan, the German embassy, and other organisations which drew on the nationalist sentiments of the Irish and German population, continued to call for the cooperation of these diasporas and their homelands to help Ireland achieve independence.

The diaspora nationalism of Irish and German America co-mingled and coalesced in the United States as Ireland flirted with rebellion and Germany with global, imperial war. Not only did this cooperation manifest itself in the ranks of the nationalist organisations that asserted themselves in American politics even before the First World War, but it then reified in the combined propaganda efforts of Clan members, the servants of the German imperial agenda, and their allies once the war finally began to rage. In the final hour, the suspicions of those who opposed the Clan and accused the Germans in America of supporting saboteurs were ultimately vindicated. But at the same time the accusations made by individuals like Viereck, the Ridders, O'Leary, and Devoy that the United States was far from a neutral player even before it officially took part in the war seemed equally justified as well. The propaganda of the GIS that emerged from this context was not aimed then at disproving the intentions of the Germans and Irish to collude in affecting revolution in Ireland, but attempted rather to show that such action was in fact inspired by the ideals of the American system and by the men and women who were the heirs to its revolution. Notwithstanding the military failures of Easter 1916, and while the leaders of this Irish and German nexus also failed to prevent American entry into the war as they propagandistically combined Americanism, German imperialism, and Irish nationalism in a manner reminiscent of an image spuriously superimposed by a stereopticon, their connections were not illusory, and though ultimately tragic, should not be seen as a farce, nor disregarded.

# CHAPTER THIRTEEN

# AN AMERICAN OPINION
## JOHN QUINN AND THE EASTER RISING

*Úna Ní Bhroiméil*

*Someone said 'The dead writers are remote from us because we know so much
more than they did.' Precisely, and they are that which we know.*
T. S. Eliot

'The Man from New York,' as John Quinn was known by those whose work he patronised
and whose cultural activities he assisted financially, was actually a Midwesterner from
Fostoria, Ohio. Born of Irish immigrant parents, he arrived in New York by a circuitous
route through the University of Michigan, Washington, DC, Georgetown, and Harvard.
Choosing New York to begin work as a corporate lawyer in 1895, he became a committed
New Yorker, and a fervent believer in the advantages the East Coast city gave to him
and to everyone else.[1] Quinn was well known in New York professional circles as a
lawyer and as a patron of the arts – particularly of literature and of modern art. Once
actively invested in Democratic Party politics, by 1916 he was no longer involved with
the Democratic Party and he did not participate in Irish-American politics at the local,
state, or federal level. A wealthy man, he nonetheless worked extremely hard for the
money he earned, and he was constantly anxious about financial security.

Much of what is known about Quinn is because of the archive of letters his family
donated to the New York Public Library, which were curated according to his will by
his close friend and companion at the time of his death, Jeanne Robert Foster.[2] He saw

himself in a particular light and wanted a certain version of himself portrayed to the world – a man of letters, cultured and urbane, and a friend of Ireland. Although this portrayal could put a particular slant on the way we perceive Quinn and his attitudes, his letters comprise a significant body of writing at a particular point in time.[3] Liz Stanley suggests that letters always represent the moment of their production and that the 'present tense' of a letter persists long after the time of writing has passed.[4] Quinn's letters then are a germane and interesting source for examining his mind set and contextualising his outlook in the years leading up to 1916 and to the Easter Rising at its point of occurrence. The letters are a crucial means of getting into the lives and minds of Quinn and of his correspondents as well as recapturing the actual voice of Quinn from his own time and era, as it has not been, as Roy Foster points out, 'misted by hindsight'.[5] Quinn's letters crisscrossed the Atlantic to friends in Ireland, England, and France, and went to various cities within the United States, preserving relationships and bonds across distance and time. But the collection also contains letters to people he met regularly in New York and so we get an insight into a community and a social world that was taken for granted by the correspondents and that allows us to interpret intimate and complex networks of influence.[6]

Although an Irish American, Quinn was not a member of any Irish society in New York. His first trip to Ireland was in 1902 when he went to buy paintings from Jack and John B. Yeats and met all the Yeats family as well as George Russell (AE), Douglas Hyde, George Moore, T. W. Rolleston, Edward Martyn, and Lady Gregory, most of whom he communicated with all his life.[7] On the basis of congenial friendships made and an embracing of the Irish cultural revival, Quinn organised two significant lecture tours or missions to the United States – those of W. B. Yeats in 1903 and of Douglas Hyde in 1905–6, both of which were tremendously successful both financially and for creating an awareness of Irish culture in the United States.[8] While Quinn was justly proud of these achievements, they gained for him a reputation for wealth and for helping Irish causes that he later came to bitterly regret. The Irish in Ireland saw Quinn as representative of 'wealthy' Irish Americans who might be induced to subscribe to their ventures and to influence other wealthy Irish Americans to support them also.[9] As was demonstrated in the earlier chapter on Pearse, Quinn had become the go-to person in New York for the Irish and this irritated him intensely. Writing to Gordon Craig in 1915, he explained his frustration:

> Years ago I helped my friend W. B. Yeats in his first lecture tour in this country. That was a great pleasure. But I have paid for it since because about every Irish man or Irishwoman that believes he or she has capacity or qualifications for a lecturer has

thought that I was a sort of lecture bureau and has made himself or herself an infernal nuisance to me. This extends to lecturers, writers, poets, priests, patriots, actors, artists, philanthropists, politicians, liberators, soldiers, rebels, parliamentarians, nuns, school teachers, college presidents, hospitals, and St. Patrick only knows what if St Patrick is paying any attention to Irish affairs these days.[10]

Quinn was not averse however to supporting Irish causes. In fact he usually gave some money towards projects in which he had no interest because friends asked him to.[11] But he objected to his precious time being taken up with presumptuous 'beggars' who believed him to be made of money and time. He explained his resentment in a letter to Judge Martin J. Keogh in November 1912 after a request from his friend to subscribe towards the Irish Christian Brothers' school in New York:

> I am willing to go a long way towards helping Irishmen who come out here and are willing to help themselves and who don't ask for money. The members of the Abbey Theatre company who came out here last year were also an exception to the hoary procession (I would not object to putting this in simplified spelling) from Ireland asking for financial assistance for this that and the other reason.[12]

Quinn's fondness for the Abbey Theatre was coloured by his personal relationship with Lady Gregory but also by the reception the company had received in New York and in Philadelphia when they had first performed Synge's *Playboy of the Western World* in 1911.[13] It caused a life-long falling-out between Quinn and John Devoy and an antagonism towards those whom Quinn called 'Pathriots'.[14] Decrying the uncultured and base way in which the company was threatened by fruit throwers and obscenity shouters and what Quinn termed the 'rioters and defamers of Irish women' purporting to be 'true' Irish Americans, he condemned them as uncultured and uneducated rednecks.[15] He also despised what he regarded as their sentimentalism and their maudlin, romantic notion of the past:

> Too many 'patriots' are given to boasting and Synge satirized boasting; they want to sing of 'Ninety-Eight' and 'Killarney' and Synge gave them a slice of life, brutal or cruel in its satire if you please, but I prefer his art to the 'jingles' of the patriots because it is alive and vital and the 'jingles' have lost their vitality long ago.[16]

But Quinn did have an Irish circle in New York.[17] His response to the anger of Devoy's Irish Americans at the *Playboy* reveals his class and position in the city. The Irishmen with whom he associated were predominantly lawyers or judges like Martin J. Keogh, James Byrne, Charles Burlingham, Lawrence Godkin, Victor J. Dowling, Daniel F. Cohalan, and William Bourke Cockran. Their common profession bound them together in the city and their friendship with Quinn had periods of intensity and others of casualness.[18] They met at the courts, at the bar association, at clubs such as the Coffee House and the Manhattan Club, and they lunched and dined together. Quinn regularly exchanged books with these men and with their wives and kept up conversations about concerts, literature, and art in letters back and forth. They also discussed Irish affairs, the European war, and American politics. One of the things that may have bound them together more closely as Irishmen in New York was a perceived prejudice against them in the city at the bar and in the legal profession. Quinn alludes to this in a letter to James Byrne's wife, Helen, in March 1911:

> Anyone who says there is no prejudice against the Irish in certain professional and business circles in this town simply does not know the fact. The reasons for this prejudice may be this or that. Everything but a miracle has a reason or a cause. I am not explaining the cause. I am merely stating the fact.[19]

These men, many of whom travelled to Ireland on visits and on holidays, saw themselves as Irish. They were predominantly Catholic.[20] They did not need to engage with the robust ethnic or local political associational culture to mark their ethnicity. These were the Irish that Quinn described to Russell as being the 'self-respecting and courageous Irish here' who were disgusted by the constant appeals for help for Ireland's cause.[21] They were what Quinn called the 'thoughtful Irish', the middle-class professional Irish, working in the heart of New York.[22] They provided a circle of like-minded people bonded together by a shared cultural mentalité, by geographical location and by social class.[23] It is with this circle that Quinn discussed events in Ireland and in Europe in the years leading to 1916.

Quinn could be classed as a political 'moderate' in that he was a supporter of Home Rule and not of the 'radicals'.[24] But his attitude to Redmond and Carson belie this to some extent. In a letter to Keogh in 1911 Quinn was already wary of the prospects for Home Rule for Ireland even though he was in favour of it if it could be achieved:

> Whatever one may feel about Redmond, he is the man at the head of things and it seems to me there is no use in weakening him in any way just now. But I fear that the Liberals will cheat him and play him as they have done in the past. The Liberal Government is one of the strongest cabinets that has existed in any government in the last fifty years.[25]

However in 1912, when the Home Rule Bill was finally on the statute books, Quinn joined in a cable to Redmond congratulating him on his success. While he justified the inclusion of his name in the congratulatory telegram to Redmond in a letter to Russell by saying that he had joined in the sentiment because, first, it would irk Devoy, and second, because as Ireland's 'cause' was now almost within reach, there would now be an end to requests for 'help' from America, Quinn could not quite hide his own pragmatic view of the situation:

> I felt the time had come to make a trial of something; that it was a compromise, but that a defective plan if worked upon with good intentions will oftentimes work out better than a perfect plan with bad intentions or entered upon in a bad humor ... I have felt that if Ireland asked later on for more Home Rule, even though the present grant was inadequate, England would be very glad to go on making concession after concession.[26]

It has been noticed in earlier chapters in this volume that the *Irish World* supported Redmond up to the September day in 1914 that Redmond called for the Irish Volunteers to enlist in the British army, but Quinn did not rate Redmond as a politician or as a man even before that fateful proclamation.[27] After a dinner with Bourke Cockran in May 1914 where they discussed the 'Irish situation', Quinn wrote again to Keogh:

> outside of Carson, who has demonstrated that he is really a very great leader and a wonderful tactician, there is not a first-class political mind in the whole of Ireland; and in saying this I include not only O'Brien but Healy and Dillon and Redmond and the whole caboodle. Three years ago was the time for Redmond to have demanded that the Government stop the drilling and arming in Ulster.

In this vein, he continued:

> Three years ago was the time when a statesman would have acted. Nobody but a damned fool would think that the Ulster Volunteers intended to invade the rest of Ireland. They have no expectation of capturing Dublin Castle or of raping the nuns in Wexford or of storming a Limerick ham factory. They are quite content to have won their bluff which is to be excluded.[28]

Quinn, who did not rate those he termed the 'so-called National Volunteers' or their 'maudlin vaporings' either, however, blamed Redmond and the British government for the debacle:

> Think what Parnell would have done in Redmond's place. Parnell would have met force with force ... the English government showed cowardice in the face of the avowed treason of a section of the English Army led by Tory officers, younger sons and place hunters; and secondly that Redmond and his gang sold out and betrayed the Irish cause and consented to the dismemberment of Ireland. Redmond ought to be hanged in effigy in every town and county of Ireland. He ought to be mobbed in the streets of London by Irishmen. If the Irish had as much spunk as the militant English suffragettes, they would prevent this betrayal.[29]

Quinn's opinion that force should have been used against the Ulster Volunteers reveals a concept of Ireland that was clearly based on the island as a territorial unit. Quinn was very supportive of the use of force in facing down the Ulster Volunteers and in resisting the exclusion of Ulster from the Home Rule settlement. He consistently accused Carson of treason and likened his actions to those of the Confederacy in the American Civil War:

> I do not advocate bloodshed, but I would give them their fill if they are crying for it. If, for example, the Ulster fanatics attacked the Customhouse or the law courts or the post office, I predict that it will have the same effect as the rebels in the South firing on Fort Sumter.[30]

Writing to Ernest Boyd at the British consular service in Baltimore in August 1914, Quinn reiterated this view:

> The war is awful; the conditions in Europe are hellish. As for Ireland – the only hope in my judgment is the arming of the National Volunteers. The Home Rule question is not settled and is only is abeyance. They will never get their rights until they are armed.[31]

On this, all shades of Irish-American opinion were ideologically united. Irish America was not a monolith. There was no 'typical' Irish American although some stereotypical images might suggest otherwise. What is fairest to say is that Irish Americans rarely presented a united front. This opposition to the exclusion of Ulster and to the partition of the island was one such occasion. Moderate Home Rule supporters were shocked at the acquiescence of the Irish Parliamentary Party and gatherings took place in New York to protest against the 'dismemberment of the island'. The three New York attorneys, William Bourke Cockran, Morgan J. O'Brien, and Quinn, all stepped forward publicly to donate to the huge fundraiser for the Irish Volunteers held in Philadelphia in June 1914 where Roger Casement was famously photographed with Devoy.[32] This fervent belief in resisting the exclusion of any part of Ireland from Home Rule by force if necessary was one that Quinn held doggedly until it happened.[33] In this, at least, he was in ideological agreement with Devoy.

But the outbreak of war in 1914, as Quinn stated in his own words, 'changed everything'. It fired his imagination and ire at one and the same time.[34] His visceral dislike of Germany (and of Germans and German culture more generally), which he castigated at every opportunity in his letters fused with his antagonism towards Devoy and those whom he termed the pro-German Irish.[35] Even though he had previously been politically involved with the Democratic Party, Quinn decried Wilson's neutral stance and described him as weak and indecisive.[36] He was supportive of the Allied cause from the beginning of the war and became ever more committed, especially to France, as the war dragged on.[37] On many occasions, Quinn stated that he would join the war effort if he did not have a business to run and responsibilities to his own firm.[38] Initially he was friendly with Kuno Meyer when he was in the United States on a lecture tour in 1914. In a letter to Meyer in December, Quinn listed those Irish Americans who were his friends and colleagues in New York, such as James Byrne, Daniel F. Cohalan, and Victor Dowling, who were interested in receiving invitations or tickets to his lectures.[39] While he had received a letter from Maurice Leon, a French attorney working in New York, who warned Quinn that Meyer was an agent of 'German propaganda' who brought over artifacts such as dumdum bullets and was trying to sway Irish Americans by stating that Germany's opponents were barbarians, Quinn nonetheless corresponded with Meyer until August 1916, considering him a 'man of urbanity and of the world'.[40] This was also Quinn's attitude to Casement to whom Quinn gave money as well as accommodation and time.[41] Writing to James Byrne in October 1914 he described Casement, who had stayed with him for a month, as 'perfectly delightful, chivalrous, high souled and a spirit of fire' but also tried to 'impress upon him that the place to play Irish politics is in Ireland or in Great Britain and not here'.[42]

Quinn was at once right and wrong in this statement and in this belief. While the centre stage for Irish politics was of course in Ireland and in Britain, the key to future success lay in *which* Irish side the Irish Americans chose to support with money and with arms – the National Volunteers who were now following Redmond into war or the smaller Irish Volunteers who broke with Redmond and who under Eoin MacNeill sought to break with Britain. Casement also looked to win the American Irish away from Redmond and towards armed insurrection. Quinn's aloofness from the day-to-day affairs of Irish-American politics and agendas as well as his disdain for the begging nature of Irish missions to the United States led him to overlook the significance of the American Irish to Irish politics in a very real way, believing that most Irish Americans thought as he did.[43]

It may appear here as if Quinn's views were deeply inconsistent. He was at the intersection of a series of circles. His friends were sometimes friends with his enemies and these intimate enmities at times meant that his views on people in particular were unpredictable. It is evident from his letters that he placed great store in how he person-ally felt about people, his relationships with them, and theirs with him. This can be seen clearly in his reaction to the sinking of the *Lusitania* in 1915, and the drowning of his friend and Lady Gregory's nephew, Hugh Lane. Quinn encapsulated in a letter to Charles Shannon what he felt:

Poor Sir Hugh Lane. He was here two weeks and I saw a great deal of him … We discussed casually the possibility of the Germans trying to sink the *Lusitania*. My feeling was that they would not be such demons as to commit such a massacre but that, at any rate, if they did sink the *Lusitania* they would only do it after warning and after giving the passengers sufficient time to take to the boats … It was the most cowardly thing that was done in the history of the world and the most brutal.[44]

Thus, for Quinn, not only did the *Lusitania* harden his attitude towards Germany and the war as it did for many Americans, but the war was made intensely personal. The settling of scores became for him a particular objective. This took many facets – one was his unwavering support for France that saw him deliver the Lafayette Day address in Union Square in September 1917 and be awarded the Legion of Honour by the French government in 1919.[45] But another was deep antagonism towards anyone or any movement that supported or courted Germany.[46] This included Irish revolutionaries in the United States and would become even more apparent in the aftermath of the Rising in 1916.

Quinn had no sense whatsoever that the Easter Rising would occur at all or when it did. His immediate reaction was to describe it as a fiasco and as lunacy and he wrote to Joseph Conrad that he was disgusted and depressed by it. He went on to explain and contextualise his opinion of it:

Of all the idiotic asses that ever were these Sinn Feiners are the worst. Before the breaking out of the war I was in favor of nationalist Ireland arming itself. The war changed everything. Now the asses will be deprived of their arms. If they had kept their organization and gradually increased their stock of arms and drilled, after the war they would have been in a position to take up their claims to a fuller measure of Home Rule with some show of force.

On how England could respond, he remarked:

It would be more difficult for England to put down a rebellion started because Ireland was divided or because she didn't get real Home Rule in spite of repeated promises, in the peace following the war, than it is now. The thing could not have succeeded. From a military point of view it was complete and utter lunacy. It all goes back to the essential falsity of Irish life; listening to the big speeches, the worship of Robert Emmet, the refusal to face facts, preferring talk to acts and expecting miracles to happen.[47]

Some of what Quinn said was justified, especially in a military context. But his outrage and indignation at what he perceived to be a wasted opportunity for calm heads and calculated tactics point to his lack of engagement with the realities of Irish political life, save as an interested but detached onlooker. For all his condemnation of the Irish preferring talk to acts, it was the action of albeit a minority of the Volunteers that caused him to react so vehemently. His general impression of the Irish, honed over the previous decade, came together with his attitude to the 'patriots' in the United States who had also in a practical way funded the arming of the Volunteers, and none of it spoke to his 'thoughtful' notions of statesmanlike persuasion. His annoyance with the lack of success of the rebellion is clear also. In a letter to James Huneker, he included the American Irish in his wrath:

> Robert Emmet's fiasco and his sophomoric slush set back the real improvement in Irish conditions for a quarter of a century, at least till Catholic emancipation in the early thirties. The next great Irish hero, Thomas Davis and his Sinn Feiners, by their flash in the pan of '48, set it back again for forty years. Parnell realized that cutting cow's tails off and shooting landlords might be right up to a certain point, but they never could get self-government that way and he stopped it.

Departing from the historical examples, he then shifted to his outlook on how things stood:

> Just as Redmond was about to get something, a half loaf is better than no bread, along come these asses. If England is wise she will not count this against the real Ireland for these idiots do not represent Ireland. I know what I have been talking about. I know Connolly. I know Pearse. I have had him at my place here. I know Professor MacNeill. I know Casement well. And I know young Plunkett. He was over here last autumn. The Declaration of Independence signed by these five asses, not O'Neill [*sic*] shows that they had Robert Emmet in mind and every one of them probably had a speech from the dock up his sleeve. It's a damn shame that the pathriots over here who took precious good care not to risk their skins could not be shown up.[48]

Of course Quinn did not 'know' these men, aside from Casement, any more than he knew conditions on the ground in Ireland.[49] He linked them in his mind's eye with the 'patriots' whom he so loathed in New York and his emotional antipathy to their actions and to their lack of achievement when there was a larger, and to him a more important, war going on, infuriated him. Even though he was in communication with many of those who were pivotal in Dublin, he had no sense of the urgency that was at the heart of the Rising.[50] According to Reid, his biographer, Quinn spoke and wrote about the Rising in 'several voices' and his reaction to it was 'complex, if not simply confused'.[51] But although Quinn certainly spoke fondly of Pearse and defended Casement literally to the death, he never wavered in his opinion that the Rising was madness.[52] In January 1917 he wrote to Hyde lamenting the fact that the Gaelic League had been captured by such 'extremists' and that the 'fools' and 'misguided leaders' of the Rising did not have his sympathy as did men like Hyde and MacNeill.[53] He

claimed to speak for the 'thoughtful' Irish in America and now he also stated unequiv-
ocally that the Volunteers did not represent the 'real Ireland'. But after April–May
1916, what was the 'real' Ireland?

By the time that Quinn wrote to most of his correspondents about the Rising, the
British had executed the leaders and this mitigated his criticism somewhat and focused
his attention on the actions of the British and the mistake they had made rather than
on the folly of the insurrection.[54] Writing to Lady Gregory in June 1916, describing
Pearse, MacDonagh, and Plunkett as 'children' and as young men who knew 'nothing
of international affairs or of life itself', he stated that 'up to the time that they were shot,
I was perfectly prepared to say openly that it was a mad, rash, ill-advised, stupid act.'[55]
But following on the 'colossal blunder' that the English made in shooting the leaders,
the manner in which they had been shot in groups every few days, and in particular the
shooting of the wounded Connolly, the impact and impression on the United States had
been so enormous that it was one that Quinn, the prolific letter writer, found 'impossible to give you by letter'.[56] Apart from his own disillusionment, which is evident in this
letter, Quinn revealed that he had no choice but to keep silent on his own view of the
Rising as the condemnation of the executions was so powerful in the American press:
'England threw away the greatest chance she has had since the war began to favorably
influence public opinion in this country. Personally it is a great grief to me. It has closed
my mouth against saying that the uprising was rash, mad and foolish.'[57] In a letter to
his friend and fellow attorney in New York, Charles Burlingham, Quinn remarked on
how his silence was being interpreted in Irish circles in New York. Reaffirming that he
considered the Rising 'futile and absurd', he wrote that it had become impossible for
him to speak or write anything 'without giving my opinion of England's act, from an
English point of view, and so I preferred to say nothing. My silence has been criticized
by a great many Irish here, but that doesn't worry me.'[58]

Caught between his support for the Allies and the general revulsion of the United
States against the executions, Quinn's opinion of the Rising did not change but his
public response to it did.[59] His self-imposed silence, though uncharacteristic, did not
last long as he took up the fight to have Casement's execution for treason commuted.

How can all that has been said about Quinn's attitude to the Rising and to
Germany be reconciled with his untiring defence of Casement? Reid maintains that
it was 'the Irishman, the sentimentalist, the pragmatic politician, the guilty idealist
and the conscience-stricken friend' who spoke when Quinn tried to save Casement.[60]
Quinn was loyal to a fault to his friends even when he disagreed with them and he
certainly liked Casement and abhorred the tactics that were being used to discredit

him personally and to question his loyalty to Ireland.[61] In a memorandum to the British Foreign Office, Quinn urged the British to reconsider as the previous executions had strengthened the 'irreconcilables' in the United States:

> It has given new life to the extremist Irish agitation in this country … I speak with knowledge here when I say that the irreconcilables want him executed. They are preparing for it … it will be the greatest disappointment to the radicals here if he is not executed. They are doing nothing for him … Leniency to Casement now, the commuting of his sentence after his trial to imprisonment for life and his release after the war under amnesty would go far to encourage the feeling in the minds of thoughtful and sympathetic Americans that after all the execution of these fifteen men was brought about in a moment of panic and that Great Britain had got her sober second thought and that her dealing with Casement represented the real Great Britain.[62]

Quinn's efforts to save Casement represented at once his version of Britain, which he termed the 'real' version, as he had with Ireland, and his efforts to win back the baton of influence for the 'thoughtful' Irish Americans who could liaise on a level with the United States State Department and with the British Foreign Office in a language of magnanimity they could all understand. For Casement, his efforts were in vain and he was executed. Even though many of his friends congratulated him on his essay on Casement in the *New York Times Sunday Magazine* in August where Quinn stated that he was proud to have been his friend, Germany was again cited by Quinn as the ultimate betrayer and in letters to Cecil Spring-Rice in Washington he stated that he was attacked by the Germans and by the pro-German Irish for his stance.[63] On restoring influence to the pro-Ally Irish he had also failed and he recognised that. This had been his worry since the executions and in a letter to Maud Gonne in July he outlined the nature of the response to 1916 and of his consequent marginalisation:

> I attended a memorial meeting at Carnegie Hall and helped to organize it and to get prominent speakers. But I stipulated that the Germans should be kept away. That was agreed to. It was broken in three respects by Cohalan and Devoy: first they had a ridiculous judge here called Gavegan who had taken a prominent part in the so-called race convention that was held here this spring, preside though I had expressly stipulated that he should not.

Unleashing his anti-German sentiment he continued:

> Secondly, they had Victor Herbert, who although his mother was Irish is German to the backbone and who has been active in German propaganda, call the meeting to order which I had expressly stipulated against. And thirdly before I got there the band had played and the audience had sung the 'Wacht Am Rhine.' That was before

Bourke Cockran and I got to the platform. If they had sung or played that while I was there I should have walked off the platform.[64]

He believed sincerely that there was no chance that the United States could now enter the war on the Allied side as the British had lost so much credibility in America.

However, all was to change again in April 1917. When America did enter the war on the Allied side in April, Quinn felt once more that things were finally as they should be. He became very involved in Irish affairs – he promoted Home Rule, wrote an introduction to George Russell's and Horace Plunkett's addresses to the Home Rule Convention, published and distributed it, advocated for the amnesty of the political prisoners, especially MacNeill, led a delegation to Balfour when he visited Washington, DC, and met with T. P. O'Connor at Theodore Roosevelt's request.[65] His generosity was called upon for Ireland as always – he took a $100 box for a John McCormack concert in May 1917 with proceeds to be divided equally between the Irish Relief Fund and the Duc de Richelieu's tuberculosis fund.[66] But his focus was primarily on the war and on his friends' sons who were fighting in it.[67] He admitted in a letter to Russell that he was only interested in Ireland as a part of the British Empire, that his interest in Irish affairs was tangential and that he wanted Home Rule to be resolved for Ireland so that the country could release the soldiers locked away from the front and supply recruits to defeat Germany.[68] Quinn was clearly more interested in the United States winning the war than he was in settling the Irish question. He never visited Ireland again and made France his primary focus for the rest of his life.

Quinn was a very principled man. He regarded himself as a nationalist.[69] But the concept of an Irish republic was not one he believed in. In a letter to James Byrne in June 1917 he stated: 'The irreconcilables are impossible. They still think that Ireland ought to be an independent republic. The attempt to make the cause of Ireland and that of Belgium, Serbia and Poland identical, seems to me to be an absurdity.'[70] Quinn would have been happy with a non-partitioned Ireland and with colonial Home Rule within the British Empire. While he called himself a nationalist, the reality was that he viewed culture and urbanity and cosmopolitanism as beyond the bounds of the narrow hatred for England that he saw as the version of nationalism espoused by Irish revolutionaries in the United States. He believed strongly that they did not represent him or indeed the great body of American Irish opinion.[71]

Quinn's resistance to and abhorrence of Anglophobia made him despise those who were committed Anglophobes. His embrace of English 'taste' and literature has led to the assumption that he was an Anglophile.[72] But the old binaries of Anglophobe and Anglophile are of limited use in assessing Quinn. To suggest that Quinn was simply an

Anglophile is to fall into the trap of looking at him through Devoy's eyes. To Devoy, there was no nuance, no ambiguity, no grey. His Anglophobia was sincere and, for him, well founded. Quinn's antipathy towards Germany was stronger than his desire for Ireland. Everything in his view needed to be subsumed in favour of the war effort. In this, he was and remained steadfast and this is clear from his letters and from his actions. His attitude to Ireland was filtered through this lens. Yet being an Irish American appeared to make him feel compromised in some way. This is possibly why he felt more comfortable in committing himself wholeheartedly and publicly to France.

Quinn was a supremely self-conscious member of the middle-class, professional intelligentsia in New York. He interacted with middle-class intellectuals in Ireland, many of whom formed part of the 'Revolutionary Generation'.[73] He saw himself as part of an urbane and cultured network that transcended the narrow confines of nationalism. His disdain for Chicago and even the University of California at Berkeley because of what he saw as their provincialism and lack of culture suggests an enthusiastic embrace of urban cosmopolitanism that revolved around the nexus of cultural capitals such as New York, Paris, London, and, at times, Dublin.[74] This is clear also in his access to Washington political and diplomatic circles. While his easy access, especially to British diplomats and dignitaries, was ridiculed by Devoy, Quinn's role may have been less as an Anglophile and more as a man who knew his way around Washington, DC. Having worked there as a young man, and especially after his successful campaign to remove the duty on imported original works of art in 1913, he clearly believed he knew the players and fancied himself as one.[75]

There were many Irish-American reactions to 1916. Quinn's was one borne of long attachment to and affection for the Irish, and also of intense irritation and antagonism towards the Irish. He found and clung to like-minded people. But not all his compatriots were like-minded. He was, as an American, detached and distracted by war. He believed that his was the right reaction and that he knew the way forward. As a lawyer, a fine orator, and persuader used to argument and reasoned debate, he believed that logic and persuasion could bring out the real and true nature of any particular situation. He also recognised the battles he could not win. When his was not the course adopted, he let it go.

*The author gratefully acknowledges the award of a sabbatical semester by Mary Immaculate College, Limerick to conduct research on John Quinn at the New York Public Library (NYPL), and Tal Nadan of the Manuscripts and Archives Division of the NYPL for assistance with sources.*

# CHAPTER FOURTEEN

# 'BURSTS OF IMPASSIONED ELOQUENCE'
## WILLIAM BOURKE COCKRAN, AMERICAN INTERVENTION, AND THE EASTER RISING

## Patrick M. Sweeney

*Their steps never faltered … on their way to another world. They knelt down, muttering a prayer, the firing party…was drawn up in order, the command to make ready was almost whispered, the commanding officer of the volunteers turning his head aside to hide his emotion. Then came another short command to take aim, immediately followed by the fatal word… 'FIRE!'*[1]

News of these executions reached New York quickly. From ward to ward, and on every street corner, newsboys and criers read off the day's ominous headlines one by one.

Arrest and Trial of the Offenders
An Armed Populace Clamor for Their Blood
Intense Excitement in the Mob-Ruled City.[2]

New Yorkers of every stripe eagerly opened the papers that morning to get what one *New York Times* article described as a 'Detailed Account of the Recent Troubles'.[3] An *Irish Times* editorial described the events as 'cruel and unjustifiable', and one of its New York correspondents even wrote, 'Nothing here has caused greater excitement than the execution – murder we call it … by a Government which will not last long in that Country.'[4] In London, *The Times* itself even characterised the events as an outright 'massacre'.[5] According to the latest reports arriving in New York, many still in that beleaguered and historic capital city were 'in fear and trembling', half-expecting widespread and indiscriminate retaliations against the local populace in response to the action of these few so-called 'rebels'.[6] It looked as if civil law had all at once been completely supplanted by the law of military occupation. To many American readers, it seemed that all of the prisoners had surrendered themselves up willingly – but to no avail. The sentence of death by firing squad had been made. 'Not a sound was heard', the *New York Times* reported; 'the young men thus cruelly sentenced to meet an early and sudden death marching firmly forward' accompanied by priests from the prison.[7] Readers in the United States would have observed even from the earliest reports that sympathy for the rebels had been less than widespread before the executions began. Evidently, popular opinion and support at the outset had been mixed at best.

As the prisoners met with their Catholic priests and wrote their final letters, one witness recalled that 'many a spectator's heart bled' while still others condemned those imprisoned outright, believing their actions futile and foolish, or at the very least, idealistic and ill-timed. 'Death to the traitors!' cried one member of the crowd outside that now infamous prison.[8] But as the shots rang out and news of the executions spread across the city and country, the gauge of public opinion began to shift. One witness remarked, 'Thousands I may say, who hitherto were either neutral or even sided with' the occupying force 'have now become their bitter enemies. Many families are in mourning. A general feeling of disgust pervades the community.'[9]

Americans reeled at the news of the executions and at the speed with which the situation seemed to have spiralled out of control. Many Americans were directly invested in the emerging nationalism of what would one day become a neighbouring, small island republic. Many more, fresh from the Civil War, were keenly aware of the notions of self-determination and self-governance that were at the heart of both this conflict and of their own evolving ideas of American identity and status. But should the United States intervene? True, that island had played an oft-historic role in the United States' own growth and maturation. And admittedly, that small country had long been ruled by an elite minority who viewed themselves not only as socially privileged but even ethnically superior. But to go to war with a major European power in support of another's independence struck many as extreme. Was it the United States' business, her duty, to meddle in the nationalistic aspirations of others?

It would take another 27 years, but the answer to those questions was, decidedly, 'yes'. In support of Cuban independence, congress officially affirmed 'An act declaring that war exists between the United States of America and the Kingdom of Spain' on 25 April 1898 – almost 30 years after eight medical students had been executed in Havana by Spanish troops.[10] Young, idealistic – perhaps even 'foolish' – those eight students (aged 16–21) had allegedly defaced the grave of a Spanish folk hero and were subsequently arrested, condemned, stood before the wall, shot, and thrown into paupers' graves four at a time.[11] It was one spark amongst many others that had recently stoked the fires of an already budding surge for independence in Cuba, this time capturing attention worldwide. That movement eventually drew in a United States that was wrestling with its own notions of imperialistic duty and expansion. It also became the legal and moral basis for many who would soon call upon the United States to take up arms again – this time in the twentieth century and in the cause of Irish independence.

Throughout the final decades of the nineteenth century, the United States' intervention into Cuba's independence struggle dominated both dinner tables and political forums across the country. Those articles from December of 1871, bringing the first accounts of the executed Cuban students, had a lasting impression on many Americans and brought many more face to face with the concept of intervention for the first time. When the United States went to war with Spain in 1898, congress asked for 50,000 volunteers – they received more than twice that number.[12] Americans had indeed endorsed intervention and, to some extent, their own status as a major Atlantic power. For one young man in particular, having immigrated to New York City from Ireland only three months before the tragic events in Havana, the United States' sluggish yet ultimately firm response to the Cuban executions of 1871 was the seed of much of his diplomatic and political worldview.

Growing up steeped in the lore of Irish nationalism, William Bourke Cockran proved an unfailing and outspoken champion of Irish independence all his life. As a United States congressman and world-renowned orator and legal mind, Bourke Cockran would bring the cause of Irish independence to the forefront of global political dialogue.[13] The parallels between the Cuban executions and those of the leaders of Ireland's Easter rebellion are unmistakable. They too were arrested, condemned, stood (mostly) before the wall, and shot. Their cause, their deaths, and the near seismic shift in the populist opinion of their countrymen at home and abroad following the executions, in the mind of Bourke Cockran, warranted strong American action without delay. For him, the precedent for American intervention had been established 45 years earlier on the streets of Havana, and he was determined to remind not just Irish America but the entire Atlantic world that the United States had the means and mandate to intervene on the side of independence once more. Irish and American nationalism, and determining the United States' role in bringing about an independent Ireland, were Bourke Cockran's life-long passions.[14] They were both causes that reached fever pitch in the spring of 1916.

As will be discussed, Bourke Cockran was able to bring the full weight of his Irish patriotism to bear on the world stage as a seven-term New York congressman. His reputation as a firmly entrenched power broker at the highest levels of American politics enabled him to influence events on both sides of the Atlantic, and his commitment to the notion of an independent and sovereign Ireland informed his every position.[15] Around the United States and across a Europe mired in its First World War, Bourke Cockran railed at 'English barbarity' when the balance of world power teetered on the abyss.[16] As the United States debated whether or not to enter into the expanding global conflict, he supported neutrality but also Britain's moral cause in the Great War, writing as late as 1915 that 'the English people are fighting the battle of civilization.'[17] But, after news of the Easter Rising and subsequent executions reached the United States, the once-pacifist Bourke Cockran publicly condemned the British government despite the delicate diplomatic climate.[18] From that point forward, he was consistent in one message over all: that in the cause of Irish independence, 'America is where Ireland can be helped.'[19]

A complete study of Bourke Cockran's outspoken support of Irish nationalism does not begin or end with his response to the Easter Rising. His frequent contact with key figures in the Irish nationalist movement spanned decades; he was also one of 'a mere handful of wealthy and responsible Irish Americans' funding the Irish Parliamentary Party before 1916.[20] However, by analysing some of Bourke Cockran's earliest and most widely covered public speeches delivered immediately after the executions in Ireland, one can begin to understand not only the logic and inspiration of his positions but also their far-reaching and enduring impact.

Bourke Cockran's goal was immediate intervention by the United States in response to the executions of the leaders of Ireland's Easter Rising. He endeavoured to marshal American public and political support behind the notion of intervention by linking the history of Cuban independence with that of Ireland. More importantly, he strove to remind Americans that the United States had boldly entered into a war inspired by outrages, amongst others, like the execution of eight Cuban medical students in Havana. It must be said that the parallel between Cuba and Ireland, their nationalist movements, as well as the United States' role in their independence, was not a connection made by Bourke Cockran exclusively. 'Don't you think,' wrote William T. Stead, the English journalist and Home Rule advocate to John Redmond in 1901, 'it might be worthwhile suggesting, if you have not already done it, that the time may come when the American government may find in Ireland as effective a means for intervention as she had found in Cuba?'[21] However, Bourke Cockran's respected profile in the United States undoubtedly lent to that idea an additional degree of weight and credibility. So too would his consistency.

In 1896, at a speech given by Bourke Cockran on the twenty-fifth anniversary of the Cuban executions, he gave a rousing call for American intervention in Cuba. It was reported that at one point during his speech 'the applause was terrible … Men and women, too, stood up in their seats and shouted, waving hats and handkerchiefs'.[22] The public speeches referenced later in this brief analysis, from May and June of 1916 in particular, demonstrate the emotional evolution and logical development of Bourke Cockran's reaction to the Rising as well as the rapid maturation of his unwavering call for American intervention in Ireland. Bourke Cockran's unique brand of transatlantic Irish-American politics is a necessary component of any discussion of the United States' response to Easter 1916. That discussion would, in turn, be incomplete without reference to Bourke Cockran's own development from immigrant to American.

William Bourke Cockran was born at Carrowkeel, Co. Sligo, on 28 February 1854 to a middle-class Catholic farming family of some note in the local community.[23] Local Sligo historian Padraic Feehily claims that William Bourke Cockran, known as Bourke Cockran to most, was sent from Sligo town at the age of nine to France to pursue a religious education at the behest of his newly widowed mother. Already a well-spoken boy, he was her third son, and she envisioned for him a career in the priesthood.[24] His mother, Harriet White Cockran, converted to Catholicism from her Protestant faith upon her marriage to Martin Cockran, despite the earnest objections of her family.[25]

Feehily describes Bourke Cockran's return to Ireland in 1868 at age 14 from his studies at the Marist Brothers College near the French city of Lille, to a Cockran family now in some degree of financial straits.[26] However, it was reported that in France, at the Institut des Petits Frères de Marie, Bourke Cockran had performed remarkably well academically, repeatedly recognised by the faculty as having natural gifts of memory and public speech – skills that one teacher remarked placed him at the top of the class 'with no second near him'.[27] Bourke Cockran was soon enrolled in St Jarlath's College in Tuam, Co. Galway, where he became immersed in the native Irish language.[28] Three years after his return to Sligo, fluent now in French, Latin as well as English and (to a limited extent) Irish, 17-year-old Bourke Cockran immigrated to a New York City dominated by Irish-American political and social upheaval.[29] Deciding to invest himself completely into this new environment, he would not return to Ireland again until 1875, and then only briefly, to report on the O'Connell Centenary in Dublin for the *New York Herald*.[30]

In his first year in the United States, Bourke Cockran found employment briefly as a porter, then as a clerk for a local department store, although there is some debate as to whether the latter is accurate.[31] What is clear is that within his first month in the United States, Bourke Cockran left New York for a brisk trip to Washington, DC, and managed to observe a congressional debate first-hand from the public gallery.[32] He returned to New York more determined than ever to harness his budding and undeniable talent for public oration. Soon he found employment as a teacher, and later as principal of St Teresa's Academy, a Catholic girls' school in Tuckahoe, New York. For the next four years, Bourke Cockran would hone his public speaking, linguistic, and debating skills as a teacher by day while studying earnestly for a legal career by night.[33] In August of 1876, Bourke Cockran was awarded his Certificate of Naturalisation as an official American citizen.[34] Shortly after his naturalisation, Bourke Cockran was admitted to the bar as an attorney in the state of New York and spent two years in Mount Vernon practicing law before returning to New York City in 1878.[35]

The political career of William Bourke Cockran, one that spanned nearly 40 years and propelled him into the elite spheres on both sides of the Atlantic, began in 1881. Not yet 30 years old, Bourke Cockran's natural propensity for brilliant oration quickly earned him an invitation to serve as the spokesman for the Irving Hall Democracy, a faction opposed to Tammany Hall at the Democratic State Convention in 1881.[36] It was as a Tammany delegate, at the Democratic National Convention in Chicago in 1884, that Bourke Cockran first gained national attention. Still representing the New York minority within the Democratic Party, Bourke Cockran delivered an extraordinary speech opposing the nomination of Grover Cleveland, despite Cleveland's overwhelming support from other Democratic delegates.[37]

Within two years, Bourke Cockran was elected to the House of Representatives as a Democrat from New York's 12th District.[38] In 1887, by age 33, Congressman Bourke Cockran had taken his seat in the forum that he had viewed as an observer less than two decades before. An editorial from the *Evening World* covering those congressmen newly arrived in Washington singled Bourke Cockran out, citing his 'remarkable gifts as a speaker and political leader' and 'his rare intellectual equipment' and described him as 'a natural orator of extraordinary power' whose 'influence will be felt'.[39] He went on to serve seven more terms as congressman from various districts around New York.[40]

The years between 1912 and 1920 have been described by one historian as a period of 'comparative political inactivity'[41] for Bourke Cockran – and it is this characterisation that this analysis of his 1916 speeches regarding the Rising challenges. Hardly 'politically inactive', he was in fact fully engaged with the key political issues of the time, both within the United States and abroad, speaking publicly at rallies and gatherings on both sides of the Atlantic.[42] In his public and private life, Bourke Cockran's 'Irishness' was worn on his sleeve; his Irish birth and self-made status gave him a unique political and philosophical insight that was widely recognised. His biographer, Robert McElroy, suggests 'that he was not born an American made him analyze the more critically the meaning of his new allegiance, and see more clearly, perhaps, than he could have seen as a native-born American.'[43] He lived and worked at the epicentre of Irish-American nationalism, New York City, and his public speeches attest to his role as one of the most active, vocal, and effective American politicians on the subject of Irish independence.[44] From May to June of 1916, Bourke Cockran began to formulate his position, based on what he viewed to be the legal and historical precedent of the United States' intercession into Cuba 18 years earlier.

Bourke Cockran had played a prominent role in many Irish Home Rule gatherings and fundraising events held in and around New York and had long supported the Irish Parliamentary Party's policy of peaceful, constitutional means.[45] His relationship with John Redmond in particular could be described as that of a trusted political advisor (and reliable financier) to the Irish Party leader. In 1903 Redmond tried to woo Bourke Cockran from the US congress: 'In the name of the Irish Party, I invite him to join our ranks and give us the aid of his unparalleled experience and matchless eloquence in what we believe are the last stages of the struggle for Irish rights in the British Parliament.'[46] Although he declined, evidence suggests that Redmond used Bourke Cockran as an Irish-American sounding board for years, especially on Home Rule.[47] Bourke Cockran's reluctant split with the party of Redmond only came after Woodenbridge, and his final hopes for any peaceful transition to Irish independence vanished with the news of the executions of Rising leaders, several of whom he had known both personally and professionally.[48] That was a point of no return for him and for many.[49] Some Irish-American organisations even came out openly in favour of war with Britain on the side of Germany.[50] Shane Leslie, Bourke Cockran's close friend, brother-in-law, and fellow Home Rule supporter, wrote,

> It was possible to know Irishmen in the streets of New York by their expression. The effect of the Rising was one thing. The effect of the executions was another ... They were roused on a sensitive point and an outburst of lyrical anger swept through the continent from New York to the Golden Gate.[51]

At the crest of that wave of 'lyrical anger' was the voice of William Bourke Cockran.

On 14 May 1916, Bourke Cockran addressed nearly 3,500 persons at a Carnegie Hall rally, all eager to hear their own outrage put into words as only Bourke Cockran could deliver them.[52]

Ladies and gentlemen … Words certainly are unnecessary to show the barbarity of this massacre. On that, judgment of the globe, even in England herself. Nor is it necessary to say one word to vindicate the quality of these last fifteen martyrs whose blood has been shed, and the soil of Ireland, sanctified to freedom, shall soon become its theatre.[53]

This was Bourke Cockran's first public reaction to these events. After his opening statement, his response and proposed action became more structured and refined as he made the case for American intervention. He waded immediately and unflinchingly into 1916 myth-building. To Bourke Cockran, as soon as the rifle bullets were fired, these men were seated among a pantheon of tragic Irish heroes from bygone centuries.

Their high excellence is confessed even by their butchers … It has been said here that these men were equal to the best men who constitute the highest type of citizenship in other countries. But this description fails to do them justice. They were not only equal to the best that could be found in any other country, they were far superior to any that could be found in any other part of the world … It is not because amongst these fifteen were included poets of unquestioned genius, writers of unusual brilliancy, scholars of the highest attainments, orators of enormous power … I say not in all the experience of the world of mankind, not in the well-known martyrology of Ireland herself, not among the lines recorded in the annals of patriotism throughout the world could there be found any one generation, much less in one country, fifteen men equal in talents, equal in virtue, equal in self-abnegation, of lives so absolutely spotless, of purposes so pure, of ideals so lofty, as these men who have been butchered by the authority that declared their butchery essential to its own existence.[54]

It is difficult to read these words, as it must have been to hear them, without acknowledging them as a most passionate and highly political eulogy. They are the words of an American and an Irishman – but also of a lawyer and a politician well versed in cultivating public opinion. Bourke Cockran was aware of a need to identify himself as one possessing the credibility and historical acumen required to make such claims:

Friends, I have spent some time studying the history of mankind. I have followed with some degree of painstaking labor the development of political institutions in all ages … I say now without any fear of contradiction that never before in the whole range of recorded experience has a political system dared to affront the judgement of the world with the statement that it must kill, slaughter, destroy the best of human life in order to preserve its own existence.[55]

His claim of an academic familiarity with social history rings true. Well able to transport his audiences for hours to flashpoints of democratic progress as far back as the Magna Carta and ancient Greece, in this spring 1916 oration Bourke Cockran gave to his

Carnegie Hall audience a lesson in Anglo-Irish history ranging from the Norman invasion to the Statutes of Kilkenny, Richard II, Elizabeth I, Cromwell's conquest, and more.

Bourke Cockran also attempted to appeal to the jury of public opinion by using his own personal transformation as representative of the shift that the American public must surely undergo after learning of the Irish executions. From this point forward, the situation is altered, and there can be no going back.

> Now, my friends, I am here to make a confession. For thirty years I was one among many Irishmen who believed, and who frequently expressed in perfect belief that it was the part of wisdom of Irishmen to forget – at least to forgive and try to forget – the dreary history of wrongs and oppression extending over seven centuries, in the hope that in the better day which we believe to be dawning, these two nations might be able to unite in productive cooperation for the benefit of both. And now behold the consequences of this. The fowlest murders ever committed on Irish soil by the government which has made Irish history a blot upon the fame of mankind are fresh before our eyes. The noblest Irishmen that ever lived are dead – dead by the bullets of a soldier, shot like dogs for asserting the immortal truths of justice and attempting to discharge the inexorable duty of patriotism.[56]

This is language at once poetic and incendiary; the case was being made. Time after time, Bourke Cockran ascribes a common bond to all of his listeners. He is not speaking to Americans, or to Irishmen, or even to the British government alone. His audience spanned the Atlantic world and he knew it.[57] Two weeks later in Chicago, Bourke Cockran was slated to speak at another rally to call again for American intervention in Ireland even as the Chicago police received mailed threats of violence from those unsympathetic to the Irish nationalist cause:

> CHIEF HEALY:
> Take steps to stop this Irish meeting. If you fail the lives of 100s will die. This is final!
> LOYAL SONS OF BRITAIN[58]

When Bourke Cockran's speeches on flashpoint global events like the Easter Rising were published, they were widely read,[59] not least because his personal life had given him notoriety too. His romantic affair with Jennie Churchill was the subject of much gossip. She was the mother of Winston Churchill, who later named Bourke Cockran as his most profound influence in public oration (and to some degree, political policy).[60] She was also the widow of Lord Randolph Churchill, who had penned the slogan 'Ulster is Right, Ulster will Fight' in opposition of Irish Home Rule only ten years before. Bourke Cockran was not phased, although it is probable the irony could not have escaped him.[61]

Bourke Cockran asked that Carnegie Hall audience on 14 May, 'What must WE do now?' and again called for collective citizenship. 'Ladies and gentlemen, the question now arises: What is the future? What duty does this tragedy impose on us? What does it impose on civilized nations every-where and especially this nation holding as it does the primacy of civilization?'[62] He unapologetically assumed the United States' burgeoning exceptionalism as a conceded fact and, still one year away from American entry into the First World War, positioned President Wilson and the cause of Irish independence within the larger theatre of current global conflict. The events of Havana in 1871 never escaped the mind of Bourke Cockran, and with a running start, steeped again in a long history of Irish victimhood, he made the case.

> While the government discharges its essential function, no other government has any right to interfere with its administration or to question it … The government of England from the very day it was established in Ireland was avowedly intended to exterminate the Irish people. When it was found impossible to exterminate them then it was deliberately attempted to degrade them by confiscating their property, by excluding them from industry, by refusal of access to the fountains of education and by deliberately pandering to every base impulse of human nature … ruthlessly condemning to death the best of the population as these fifteen [who] have just been slaughtered … Instead of progress we have ruin. Instead of patriots … we have martyrs … occupying newly made graves in the ground … one Wolfe Tone expiring by his own hand rather than suffer strangulation at the hands of the English hangman, we have fifteen men … butchered by the government which ought to have protected them.[63]

Primed with candid imagery, the Carnegie Hall audience next heard perhaps the most clearly articulated call to arms in Ireland's defence ever uttered by an American politician.

> Ladies and gentlemen, I have not told you this merely to awaken the harrowing memories but to ask what now?
>
> Voice [presumably shouted from audience] Down with England!
>
> No, ladies and gentlemen, let me say to my friends, not even now do I want to say down with any nation or with anybody. I say still, Up with Ireland. I am here to say only Up with Ireland.[64]

But more than an emotional plea was needed. Bourke Cockran needed a legal precedent, and he had one. As his speech came to an end, he reminded the audience that the United States' intervention on behalf of Cuban independence had been a success, something he had said as early as 1896.[65]

It was at a meeting in commemoration of their massacre in Chickering Hall 20 years ago that I had the privilege of making the first speech in this country urging intervention on behalf of the Cubans. That speech was derided at the time as incendiary and unneutral but in two years intervention was an accomplished fact.[66]

Less than six weeks after this address, Bourke Cockran was on the stump again, now with an objective more clearly defined, one that could be delivered with legal logic and precision. On 25 June, in Boston's Symphony Hall, to a crowd of 2,500, the call for American intervention for Irish independence was first articulated without reservations.[67]

This meeting is wholly pro-American. It is in its membership, its spirit and its purpose ... Its immediate object is to express the horror awakened ... by the massacres of unarmed men in Dublin ... Among the agencies of civilization this government [United States] is properly counted the most formidable and the most beneficent. We are here to ask its aid in ending the political system which brings discredit on all civilization. We are invoking the principle which was pursued eighteen years ago when on a neighboring island this republic intervened to end atrocities unspeakable.[68]

While the political career of Bourke Cockran was marked by periods outside of official public service, his work as a prominent attorney remained consistent throughout his adult life. Before 'invoking the principle' of intervention to those gathered in Boston, he first delivered what could be described as the opening remarks of his case. Careful to identify the assembly as 'pro-American', his location of legal precedence and his use of historical evidence are clear indications of how Bourke Cockran's legal mind blended geopolitics with courtroom experience.

Now for one reason which impels the United States to intervene in Cuba, there are a thousand reason[s] impelling it to intervene in Ireland. The conditions are analogous in every respect but one. The outrages which this government felt called upon to end in Cuba lasted for ten years. The outrages which we now denounce ... have existed unbrokenly in Ireland ... not for ten years nor for ten times ten years, but for ten times ten times ten years![69]

With Bourke Cockran as the prosecution, the American people as the jury, and the British government on trial, there was no doubt as to the charges being brought to bear. Still, it would be inaccurate to characterise Bourke Cockran's position as unilaterally anti-English. As late as 1916, his political philosophy and positions allowed him condemn the British government's presence in Ireland while remaining diplomatically neutral on British authority in other realms.

We are not here to complain of English authority, or to assail English authority in England ... nor in Canada nor in Australia, nor in South Africa, where it is supported by the judgement and affection of the populace. But we demand that it end in Ireland where for 900 years it has been a fountain of bloodshed, of oppression, of wrong, of injury, of destruction.[70]

The United States' entry into the war as an ally of Great Britain, dashed the hopes of Bourke Cockran and many Irish Americans for intervention in Ireland.[71] And while Bourke Cockran's scores of public speeches, interviews, and private correspondence favoured an intervention policy that never materialised, there is no doubt that those calls helped to frame, indeed to amplify and even further validate, that call as it was echoed by many Irish Americans. The British government weighed more heavily the protests and concerns voiced by American elected representatives like Bourke Cockran than those of the general public.[72] While Bourke Cockran moved across the country mobilising support for direct American intervention, reminding any who heard his words that the United States had intervened before in Cuba and that not to do so now for Ireland would surely be a 'blot upon our government',[73] the American president and senate were conducting an enquiry. Senate Resolution 196 was submitted to the US Foreign Relations Committee on 2 June 1916, in regard to the 'Revolution in Ireland', 'requesting that inquiry be made as to the safety of American citizens in Ireland, and what steps, if any, may be necessary and proper for protecting their lives and property'.[74] The secretary of state brought this matter directly to President Wilson, who responded with a letter read before the senate on 13 June that directed them to find a solution 'consistent with the recognized law of nations'.[75]

Bourke Cockran kept up his insistence that the United States broker peace and independence for Ireland, by one means or another, for the rest of his life. Back in congress by 1921, the last term served before his death, Bourke Cockran introduced House Resolution 150 on 15 July 1921. He asked that the United States support his

earnest hope that the negotiations now proceeding between representatives of the English government and of the Irish people may result in a complete reconciliation of both nations on conditions that will make justice and freedom the birthright of everyone dwelling in either country.[76]

In an obituary published after his death in March 1923 it was said of Bourke Cockran that 'his chief enthusiasm centered on three great themes: the Irish Race, the Roman Catholic Religion, and the Ideals of Liberty.'[77] His application of legal and diplomatic principles, geopolitical history, a natural gift for oration, and indeed his very own immigrant experience, all allowed Bourke Cockran, in the spring and summer of 1916, to consistently remind the Atlantic world of the immense potential of the United States in the cause of Irish independence by recalling the vivid memory of the United States' liberation of Cuba.

# CHAPTER FIFTEEN

# THE HAND OF FRIENDSHIP
## PROTESTANTS, IRISH AMERICANS, AND 1916-ERA NATIONALISM

## *Mary C. Kelly*

*Both in religion and politics the Irish need the visible symbol.*
Lady Wilde, 'The American Irish'[1]

*His nation made his name their battle cry, his sorrow their sorrow his glory their glory.*
Shane Leslie, 'Robert Emmet, failure and hero'[2]

Following the 1916 Rising, Constance Markievicz wrote to a friend from her prison cell: 'Don't count on my getting out for ever so long, unless a real fuss is made (home and America). I don't see why they should let me go.'[3] The Countess's resignation is unsurprising, but equally predictable is her citation of American support. Her fluency with half a century of separatist rhetoric crisscrossing the Atlantic by ship and cable left her well placed to invoke American assistance. In tandem with her Protestant compatriots Robert Erskine Childers, Alice Milligan, Bulmer Hobson, Roger Casement, and others, she displayed keen patriotic fervour.[4] Meanwhile, in the United States, the bewhiskered countenances of Jeremiah A. O'Leary, John Devoy, and Joseph McGarrity embodied an Irish-American nationalist continuum inherited from Fenian, Clan na Gael, and United Irish League campaigns and reconfigured in 1916 in the Friends of Irish Freedom. The predominantly Catholic memberships of these organisations reflected traditional nationalist affiliations and identifications within the larger ethnic communities but, as in Ireland, Protestant support for the struggle for independence also materialised.

What follows explores some of the taxonomies and anomalies demarcating Protestants and Catholics within the Irish-American political culture of 1916. For too long scholars have largely ignored Protestant-sourced radical activism and nationalist support, including factors of denominational affiliation and associated class-based, socio-economic, geographic and cultural signifiers, and doctrinal distinction. For example, we know surprisingly little about Protestant nationalists who spent the early portion of their lives cloistered in Irish ascendancy privilege, and who subsequently abandoned this identity or converted to Catholicism. They defy easy classification. Further, despite a lengthy record of acknowledgment of the marginalisation, at best, of Irish Protestant immigrants within the American ethnic narrative, we still lack an established knowledge-base on their American urban settlement.[5] Recent research has shed new light on their presence in the larger communities, but this scholarship underscores the obscurity of Irish Protestant activist organisations compared with much more populous Catholic examples. Historians of the Irish-American historical experience should also seek evidence of Protestant influence and support within these spheres, despite the elusive quality of those currents. That said, as this short appraisal argues, whether couched within fraternal orders or operating as rogue elements or isolated cabals and representing no small challenge for historians interested in moving beyond comfort zones of numerical significance and organisational affiliation, this collective merits due attention within the 1916 framework and within the broader Irish-American historical record.

The Irish Protestant denomination most commonly referenced in accounts of the Irish in America is the Presbyterian Scotch Irish, or Ulster Scots,[6] distinguishable from Anglicans and members of other traditions such as Methodism by public fidelities to crown and parliament.[7] Unlike Colonial-era Scotch-Irish settlers, Anglicans tended to avoid explicit ethno-religious expression[8] outside the convivial quarters of fraternal groups.[9] Coded as acceptably WASPish,[10] Anglicans, Methodists, and provincial (non-Ulster) Presbyterians made up roughly ten percent of Irish immigrants in the 1700s[11] and produced public figures of the order of New York Colonial governor William Cosby, attorney general Joseph Murray, and merchants Anthony Duane and his son, James Duane. Contemporary credos shielded Irish Protestants from association with Famine floodtides, and sustained them on pathways of unobtrusive assimilation.

Lisburn tycoon Alexander T. Stewart (1803–76) promoted philanthropic rather than nationalist associations, but American-born Dr Thomas Addis Emmet (1828–1919), grandnephew of 1803 revolutionary Robert Emmet,[12] openly committed to the cause of Ireland's independence. In 1903 Emmet quoted barrister and MP Isaac Butt in a manner more reflective of Wolfe Tone than Clan na Gael-style separatism: 'Let it [Ireland] be governed for the good of the whole people. Let us abandon the policy of maintaining any English interest, or any Protestant interest, or any class interest, or any interest but that of the Irish people.'[13] But in 1911, the Virginia native cast Presbyterian Orange Order members as bêtes noires for both Catholics and (Anglican or Methodist) Protestants:

> I deem it as a great injustice to class the majority of the people termed Protestants with the Orangemen. Those familiar with the past history of Ireland know that the greater portion of her leaders have not been Catholics, and many of the truest and best friends to the interests of the country at large have not been identified with that faith. The only enemies to Ireland's future peace and prosperity are the Orangemen, whose sole purpose in existence is to breed discord under the cloak of religion; with these the mass of the Protestants of Ireland have no more in common than have the Catholics.[14]

In distancing himself from the Orange identity and from memories of 1870s New York street riots pitting Orange paraders against Catholic protesters, Emmet referenced a host of transplanted Irish divides.[15] By 1916, Protestant ethnic heritage endured within the Friendly Brothers of St Patrick, Friendly Sons of St Patrick, the Charitable Irish Society,[16] Hibernian Provident Society, Scotch-Irish Society, Ulster-Irish Society, Loyal Orange Institution, and others.[17] In contrast to the pro-independence collectives, reminders of the Protestant contribution to the nationalist heritage proliferated. Popularly venerated as transcendent martyrs rather than as unsuccessful revolutionary leaders, Theobald Wolfe Tone, Robert Emmet, and the Young Irelanders organisation of the 1840s occupied a distinct niche within the ethnic culture. Lady Wilde's (Speranza) 1877 work, *The American Irish*, referenced the 'splendid eloquence' of 'the great orators Grattan, Plunkett, Bushe',[18] for example, while revolutionary protagonist John Mitchel promoted an incendiary discourse within the evolving nationalist narrative. Framing the Famine as an act of English perfidy, Mitchel's imprimatur as a transgressive Protestant separatist imbued Irish-American activism with a quality few contemporary Catholics could emulate – an important consideration and a prime example of the largely unexamined role of acceptable Protestant influence within a nationalist narrative popularly characterised by a Catholic identity.[19] A 1915 *Gaelic American* reminiscence of Mitchel's observation of an Irish Papal Brigade in Paris in

1860 reminded readers of this distinction: 'They fell upon him and embraced him. An Irish Protestant, who would act that way towards men who had fought for the Temporal Power of the Pope must surely have had strong sympathy with the Irish race, as well as with the Irish Cause.'[20] As Mitchel's name settled alongside those forebears whose militancy transcended their denominational affiliation, his name was regularly invoked: 'I appeal to you from the dear old homeland,' an Ulster writer advocated in 1914, under the heading: 'Belfast man from Armagh appeals to the Irish in America to stand by the principles of Tone, Emmet and Mitchel.'[21] Public remembrances of Tone and Napper Tandy had long proven popular, but escalated in association with the prospect of rebellion prior to 1916, for example, 'Patrick Pearse's eulogy of Theobald Wolfe Tone' in *The Gaelic American*.[22] A primary personification of the modern nationalist tradition in Ireland in the wake of his ill-fated Dublin rebellion in 1803, Robert Emmet garnered the lion's share of tributes within the Irish community across the Atlantic. His association with the collectives that produced the Fenian Brotherhood in the 1850s[23] elevated his memory as a nationalist martyr and paved the way for events such as the 'Great Emmet Night in Brooklyn' in March 1914, which marked the one hundred and thirty-sixth anniversary of his birth and offered a compelling premonition of the Rising. Over 2,000 people braved a blizzard to hear Governor Martin H. Glynn welcome *Irish Freedom* editor and 'sturdy Northern nationalist' Bulmer Hobson and 'P. H. Pearse'.[24] Could the audience discern the relatively obscure Pearse's potential to join Tone and Emmet in the nationalist pantheon from his assessment of the situation in 1914?

> But England, we are told, offers us terms. She holds out to us the hand of friendship. She gives us a Parliament with an Executive responsible to it. Within two years the Home Rule Senate meets in College Green and King George comes to Dublin to declare its sessions open. In anticipation of that happy event our leaders have proffered England our loyalty. Mr. Redmond accepts Home Rule as a 'final settlement between the two nations' … Would Wolfe Tone have accepted it as a final settlement? Would Robert Emmet have accepted it as a final solution? Either we are heirs to their principles or we are not. If we are, we can accept no settlement as final which does not '*break the connection with England, the never-failing source of all our political evils*'; [*sic*] if we are not, how dare we go on an annual pilgrimage to Bodenstown, how dare we gather here or anywhere to commemorate the faith and sacrifice of Emmet?[25]

Clan na Gael in Philadelphia also hosted an Emmet celebration the same week, including a dramatic rendering by Division 63 of the Ancient Order of Hibernians.[26] Even Emmet's brother-in-law, barrister Robert Holmes, who had served as counsel in

Ireland for John Mitchel in 1848, earned a citation for his patriotism and a comparison with 1798 revolutionary Napper Tandy.[27] Safely historicised Protestant revolutionaries also permeated the Friends of Irish Freedom's founding in 1916, with at least three Boston branches named for Emmet and Roger Casement.[28] Swiftly enshrined as a new-minted hero upon his arrest and execution, Casement had earned recognition in the ethnic community by 1915, with *The Gaelic American* noting that

> Being himself an Antrim Protestant, he was able to secure the help of the most influential business men of Belfast in arousing the country … This was good, practical work for the business interests of Ireland, fraught with hope of a union of all creeds, classes and political parties for the good of their common country.[29]

This culture of commendation for Protestant nationalists incorporated some of the obvious incongruities referenced earlier here. Both before and after the Famine watershed, Ireland's radicals sought the overthrow of the Anglo-Irish controlled land system, the endowment of Catholic-based education and governance systems, and the revival of Gaelic-sourced language and traditions. These aspirations endured on the credence that the ascendancy would only relinquish power when forced to, and they underscore the challenges faced by Protestant revolutionaries in a political culture dominated by such conflicting interests. Predominantly Catholic Irish-American campaigners, meanwhile, supported the nationalist cause while contending with transplanted versions of the same struggles. Could these Catholic Irish Clan or FOIF members exorcise the legacy of landlordism and coffin-ship trauma in partnership with members of a caste they held responsible for these calamities? How could Protestants in New York or Boston or Chicago preserve an ethnic identity fraught with negative association for Catholic activists *and* support armed insurgency against British authority? And all this within a political culture subject to fluctuating political currents across the Atlantic? These issues remained, but endowed Protestant voices occasionally infiltrated Irish-American nationalist channels in the late nineteenth and early twentieth centuries.[30] The precise degree of their influence is difficult to measure, and its transatlantic foundations constitute an important consideration, but they commanded attention in press and lecture circuits for articulating perspectives normally considered divergent, and even heretical, on both sides of the religious divide. Speranza observed in 1877: 'The Irish live on dreams and prayer. Religion and country are the two words round which their lives revolve.'[31] Lady Wilde cited the Catholic foundation of ethnic nationalism and the discordancy evoked by the prospect of Catholic-Protestant alliance, a perspective articulated from a different standpoint in 1914 in an *Irish American Weekly* article entitled 'Why I am a nationalist'.

Proclaiming that his Irishness trumped his denominational affiliation, 'a young Ulster Protestant youth' claimed that his faith should not bar him 'from being filled with the burning patriotism for which noble men, both Protestant and Catholic, sacrificed their lives'. Citing the linguistic and literary heritage rendering Ireland distinct, he quoted Protestant 'men with lofty purposes, who scorned bigotry and intolerance and who believed that every man born within the shores of Ireland, no matter how or in what way he worshipped God, had a right to call himself an Irishman'.[32]

In Ireland in the same year, as the threat of a third Home Rule Bill pushed half a million Ulster unionists into opposition to Home Rule and mobilised the militant Ulster Volunteer Force,[33] Arthur Griffith, James Connolly, Irish Volunteers, IRB members, and a coterie of like-minded Protestants organised for rebellion. Protestants amounted to roughly 20 percent of Ireland's population in 1916 and, as Dorothy Macardle noted, 'still held the position of ascendancy and, in fact, composed the country's governing class'.[34] The minority of Anglicans who defied their patrimony to offer moral or financial support to the cause included Gaelic revivalist Dr Douglas Hyde (later first Free State president) and, to a lesser extent, Anglican cooperative agriculturalist Horace Plunkett among their number – anomalies in a movement dedicated to the overthrow of the ascendancy caste.[35] As a correspondent in the *Church of Ireland Gazette* noted in 1911, with some license:

> Men of good will, Roman and Protestant alike, have been striving … to make her happy and self-reliant. The face of the country has changed, not because of the work of the Nationalist Party – far from it – but owing to the efforts of non-political Irishmen like Horace Plunkett and to the conciliatory legislation which George Wyndham, William O'Brien and others helped to carry through in 1903, whereby half the land in Ireland, within the past few years, has passed peacefully from landlord to tenant … Belfast and Cork are coming ultimately together for the first time since the Plantation of Ulster.[36]

Ironically, the Independent Orange Order (IOO) (1903) founder and imperial grand master of Ireland also dramatically changed course towards Irish self-determination, in stark contrast to his Orange unionist comrades and their pro-British platform. Journalist Robert Lindsay Crawford had established the *Irish Protestant* journal in Dublin in 1903 to counter anti-Catholic unionist propaganda and rebut David Patrick (D. P.) Moran's 'Irish-Ireland' campaign in *The Leader*. By 1906, he was ejected from the *Irish Protestant* (which folded in 1915), the IOO, and the Ulster Liberal Association's paper, the *Ulster Guardian*, thanks to his nationalist sympathies.[37] His struggle to surmount his identity crisis prompted reflections on the situation from campaigner-historian Alice Stopford Green, herself a daughter of a Co. Meath arch-deacon.[38] Commending Crawford for his nationalist exertions, she observed:

> I am more and more persuaded that until Ireland has some form of self-government there should be no public discussions between Irish Protestant and Irish Catholic, because such a discussion now means an appeal to the English Nonconformists and that is no court of appeal for lovers of Ireland. For the present all are united in one cause alone, to try and get some decent government in the country. When that is done we can fight out our religious matters between ourselves, and the lay Catholic will become more important than he now is.[39]

Green's aspirations eventually materialised, but Crawford moved to Canada and then to the United States where he personified the transatlantic character of Protestant Irish nationalist support, particularly in his role as president of the Protestant Friends of Ireland organisation by 1919.[40] Dublin's *Church of Ireland Gazette* sidestepped these complexities after the Rising, however, remarking: 'the religious element did not enter in any way into this unfortunate rebellion. We heard no whisper of old sectarian feuds. It was no case of Roman Catholics *versus* [sic] Protestants.'[41] But a week later, the same organ quoted the archbishop of Dublin in declaring that: 'This is a greater quarrel than any between Roman Catholic and Protestant, Unionist and Nationalist. It is the long impending quarrel between the forces of authority and the forces of anarchy.'[42]

For Irish Americans, any attempts to formally integrate Catholic and Protestant nationalists involved a similar tangle of loyalties and typecasts. The Ancient Order of Hibernians accepted only Catholic members. Neither the Irish National Federation nor Irish National Alliance actively pursued this goal. Since 1903, the United Irish League had supported the Irish Parliamentary Party and Parnell's constitutionalist successor, John Redmond, but stopped short of promoting a Catholic-Protestant alliance. The *New York Times* in 1911 reported 'leader of the Independent Nationalists' and Cork MP William O'Brien greeting 'our faithful kindred in America' with the statement: 'All sections of the Nationalist Party are ready for co-operation in testing to the uttermost Mr. Asquith's home rule pledges.' However, he continued, it was not in Ireland's best interest to try to unravel the intricacies of English politics. He concluded: 'by involving Ireland in British party quarrels, we shall be making it impossible to carry home rule against the solid Unionist opposition and an Irish Protestant minority driven at bay', and referenced the 'better spirit which is now beginning to show itself in the unionist Party and among our Protestant countrymen'.[43] Despite this, Redmond's 1912 visit to America 'to appeal to his American compatriots for "moral and material support" for the Home Rule bill' prompted the *Times* comment:

The bitterness that is only too sure to ensue is already shown. It springs from the resistance to the bill of the North-of-Ireland men, who are Unionists and Protestants ... If the leaders of the Irish Nationalists and the Irish Unionists could have been shut up together on bread and water until they could agree on rational home rule for Ireland, with a pledge that such an agreement should be embodied in law, we believe that it could have been reached. But the effort to force Home Rule on the North of Ireland is bound to be full of grave risks.[44]

Could Irish Americans reading these reports distinguish supportive Protestants from professed enemies of nationalist ideologies? A practical response would focus on the depth of support and degree of commitment to the cause proffered by the former element. As tensions escalated in 1914, such distinctions were increasingly thrown into relief. In July, the Irish Volunteer Fund Committee in New York sent an ominous message signed by Joseph McGarrity and other members to Redmond affirming the need to fundraise for arms accumulation and the necessity of securing a united Ireland from the Home Rule Bill:

We would approve any concession to Ulster Protestants which would allay their distrust of an Irish National Government, and would join them in resistance if their liberties or interests were attacked. But dismemberment of Ireland on religious lines will prolong and intensify sectarian strife, hurt Ulster equally with the rest of Ireland, and bring shame and humiliation to the race throughout the world. It is in your power to prevent that. If you fail to do so, you will be held responsible for the resulting evil, and for Mr. Ryan's effort, made in your name, to prevent united action of the race in America in Ireland's hour of sorest need.[45]

The same men gathered at the Irish Race Convention in New York to launch the Friends of Irish Freedom in March 1916, 'to encourage and assist any movement that will tend to bring about the national independence of Ireland'.[46] Citing Protestant heroes throughout the proceedings, grandees Victor Herbert (born to Protestant parents), Dr Thomas Addis Emmet, and Meath-born Monsignor Henry A. Brann[47] nominally presided, while McGarrity, Daniel F. Cohalan, John T. Ryan, and Jeremiah A. O'Leary made up its nerve centre.[48] 'From the scaffold in Thomas Street, Dublin, one hundred and thirteen years ago ... Robert Emmet proclaimed his faith in Irish Nationhood. If the principle for which he died was right then, it cannot be wrong now,' intoned Vice President Justice John W. Goff at the ceremonies.[49]

Against the backdrop of the Rising's outbreak in Dublin a month later, front-page headlines in New York proclaiming 'Ireland still true to Emmet's principles' and 'Counsellor Jeremiah O'Leary of New York pays tribute to the memory of Emmet and extols his principles'[50] gave way to extensive and adulatory coverage of Countess Markievicz's role and sentencing and the August execution of Roger Casement.[51] Equally predictably, the Orange Order asserted ringing opposition to 1916, the FOIF, and the idea of American government involvement in Ireland's situation.[52] The *Church of Ireland Gazette* pondered the complexities of the Irish-American situation:

> What guarantee is there that an Irish 'settlement' based on the exclusion of Ulster would placate Irish-American opinion? That opinion, so far as it is dangerous, is the opinion of extremists – of men who stand for 'Ireland a nation' in the same extreme expression of that doctrine as the men who proclaimed a Sovereign Irish Republic on Easter Monday. Will these men be placated by this 'settlement'?[53]

Even as the decades pass, the mystique of 1916 endures and its contradictions continue to fascinate. As we have seen in this cursory consideration, Protestant support for radical activism and the Easter Rising should not be viewed in monolithic or standardised terms, particularly given that such support represented both an anomaly within the ethnic nationalist narrative and a logical manifestation within its course. A much stronger sense of the extent of the Protestant Irish presence within nationalist circles and even the scale of their urban establishment in America is needed before judgments on their political and cultural influence can be made but, from the present standpoint, we can at least argue that acceptance of committed Protestant supporters in nationalist collectives and within the broader ethnic culture reveal crucial parallels between the Irish-American and Irish branches of the movement. That distinctions between pro-independence and loyalist Protestants and veneration of Protestant contributors to the modern nationalist chronicle featured in both contexts represent correlations that also merit further attention as the legacy of 1916 continues to be explored, both for their influence in the transatlantic framework of the 1916 Rising and within the ethnic culture as a whole.

THE
STAR SPANGLED
BANNER
IN
IRISH.

TRANSLATED BY REV. EUGENE O'GROWNEY.

# CHAPTER SIXTEEN

# THE IRISH-LANGUAGE COMMUNITY IN NEW YORK ON THE EVE OF THE EASTER RISING

## Nicholas M. Wolf

*O abair an léir duit, le fáinne an lae,*
*an bhratach bhí 'n air áirde le tuitim na h-oidhche?*
*Tríd an chath bhí riabha 's na réalta geal-ghlé,*
*ag á luasgadh go h-uasal, 's ag misniughadh ár g-croidhthe.*
'An Bhratach Gheal-Réaltach' ('The Star-Spangled Banner'),
translated by Eoghan Ó Gramhnaigh, 1898[1]

For residents of the United States who spoke Irish, pressed for its revival, or sought to link it to a broader programme of Irish national renewal, the decade preceding the Easter Rising was marked by the usual pressures of reconciling a unique Irishness based on language with volatile international politics and by the shifting features of the domestic Irish-American community. As with the Irish-American community in general, the members of the American Irish-language community – particularly those, both American- and Irish-born, who actively defended the language through membership in Gaelic societies – had to situate their use of a distinctive (and increasingly politicised) linguistic marker against a rising tension within British and Irish politics over the constitutional status of Ireland and demands for a unified American response to gathering world conflict. This was certainly the case in New York City, a place populated by more Irish-born residents whose first language had been Irish than any other location in the United States, and the city most densely served with revivalist organisations.

Artifacts of this period such as the Irish translation of 'The Star-Spangled Banner', issued as a songbook by the newspaper *An Gaodhal* in 1900, illustrate this complexity. 'An Bhratach Gheal-Réaltach' was completed by the language activist and priest Eoghan Ó Gramhnaigh, who had come to the United States at the end of his life to stave off tuberculosis. His body following his death in 1899 served as a point of contact between American and Irish language-revival movements by way of an elaborate 1903 repatriation involving processions and requiem masses on both sides of the Atlantic.[2] Arranged by Martán J. Ó h-Éidhneacháin (M. J. Henehan), a member of the Irish Language Society of Providence, Rhode Island, 'An Bhratach Gheal-Réaltach' was performed at many of the concerts and social gatherings of the various Gaelic societies active in the United States, and was an especially favoured closing piece to the music festivals put on by the New York Gaelic Society throughout the early twentieth century.[3]

By appropriating a distinct marker of American loyalty and translating it to Irish, the Irish-language community in the United States could reconcile a growing sense of linguistic identity with their patriotic aims at a time when the question of Irish-American sympathies with Germany sparked intense scrutiny. On a more subtle level, the lyrics of 'The Star-Spangled Banner' and its historical context as a defiant statement against British aggression – boosted by Ó Gramhnaigh's use of the words *sluagh borb Sacsan* (uncivilised, violent English forces) to translate 'foes' in the second verse – reminded listeners of the potential for a shared American and Irish view of past British aggression that could usefully be deployed to highlight perceived parallel injustices in British treatment of Irish national aspirations in the years leading up to 1916.[4]

Many details about the extent of the Irish-language community in the United States remain unknown, although well-executed sketches have been conducted since the late 1970s, including a rich look at the language in New York by Kenneth Nilsen.[5] Since these studies have devoted greater attention to the years before 1900, it is especially interesting to consider the unique features of the Irish language in New York in the early twentieth century given the maturity of the Irish-American community at that time. Although historians have documented the presence of Irish speakers in

North America since at least the seventeenth century, the mid-nineteenth-century wave of immigration clearly established a global Irish-language diaspora unprecedented in the history of that language. The mixing of a Famine-era generation of native Irish speakers, a subsequent Connacht-dominated wave of immigration in the 1870s and 1880s, and a newly arrived cohort of immigrants at the turn of the century who had been raised in an atmosphere of vigorous cultural nationalism in Ireland led to a distinct historical moment for the American Irish-language community between 1900 and 1916. As will be demonstrated here, that community was well-established economically – or at least poised to attain that security – even as it likely retained a distinctive identity based in part on the language. It was also eager to shape ongoing discourses about the place of Irish in modern society, even as the wider trajectory of language revivalism (and beyond that, political nationalism) in turn moulded Irish-American advocacy in ways that could be divisive and controversial. This was especially true for the language community in New York at two moments: the reaction to the outbreak of war and the controversies surrounding the response to mobilisation by constitutional and republican nationalists in Ireland in 1914, and at the time of the 1916 Rising itself. Tracing developments in these unsettled decades helps refine scholarly knowledge of the global Irish-language community in its diverse local manifestations for a time period known to be tumultuous, but not yet understood on its own – in this case, New York – terms.

Nearly 290,000, or 21 percent, of the 1.36 million Irish-born residents of the United States surveyed in the 1910 federal census claimed Irish as their mother tongue.[6] The 1910 count was the first in which enumerators asked foreign-born respondents to give their mother tongue as well as their country of birth. This new question supplemented a previous yes-or-no query, put to all respondents and not just the foreign-born, about the individual's ability to speak English. Although the new question about mother tongue was asked only of the foreign-born (meaning the census did not measure American-born speakers of languages other than English – even if they were bilingual), and although it revealed information about the respondent's first language and not his or her proficiency or continued use of the language at the time of the census, this question for the first time made it possible to understand the linguistic backgrounds of first-generation immigrants. Thus, at the very least, more than a quarter-million Irish-born Americans who were still alive in 1910 had been raised with Irish as a mother tongue and would have had varying degrees of proficiency depending on their time in the United States and opportunities (or inclinations) to use it with fellow native speakers in their community.

In fact, this figure of 21 percent may slightly understate the proportion of native Irish speakers in the foreign-born population. As Table 1 reveals, the 1920 census, which phrased the question of mother tongue in the same way, showed a higher proportion of claimants of Irish as a mother tongue among the same immigrant cohorts, with closer to 28 percent of the 1.02 million surviving foreign-born Irish in that year recorded as having Irish as a native language. Comparing the features of decennial arrival cohorts for each decade between 1830 and 1909 across the two censuses indicates that this was a result of a higher proportion of Irish-language claimants returned in 1920 across all cohorts, not an influx of recent arrivals between 1910 and 1920. Given that death rates were highly unlikely to be different between English-language and Irish-language mother-tongue claimants, this means that enumerators in 1920 had either been more diligent in marking responses to this question, or respondents were more willing to acknowledge Irish as a mother tongue — or perhaps both. In any case, it is not unreasonable to suggest that closer to one-quarter or more of the Irish-born in the United States on the eve of the Rising had been raised with Irish as a first language, and that even for those in this category who no longer actively used it, it was a familiar aspect of their identity for which they likely still retained a passive comprehension.

*Table 1: Proportion of Irish-born claiming Irish as mother tongue,*
*United States, by decade of arrival*

| Decade of Immigration | Percent Claiming Irish, 1910 | Total Claiming Irish, 1910 | Percent Claiming Irish, 1920 | Total Claiming Irish, 1920 |
|---|---|---|---|---|
| 1830–9 | 20.9 | 903 | 40.1 | 204 |
| 1840–9 | 25.1 | 8,922 | 33.4 | 4,175 |
| 1850–9 | 27.4 | 31,708 | 34.8 | 12,526 |
| 1860–9 | 25.2 | 42,913 | 27.0 | 20,162 |
| 1870–9 | 21.9 | 35,998 | 32.6 | 34,478 |
| 1880–9 | 21.4 | 75,203 | 27.5 | 68,594 |
| 1890–9 | 19.8 | 52,042 | 25.2 | 51,815 |
| 1900–9 | 16.6 | 42,116 | 27.2 | 58,096 |
| Total 1830–1909 | 21.4 | 289,905 | 27.8 | 250,050 |

Although the proportion of Irish-born immigrants whose mother tongue was Irish varied slightly over the decades, the linguistic characteristics of arrivals were remarkably stable in the course of more than half a century. Many of the slight differences over time match what would be expected given the historical record. The 1850s, when Famine-driven emigration brought a strong shift to the west and especially the south of Ireland as sources for arrivals, resulted in an American Irish-born generational cohort in which more than one-third had Irish as a mother tongue. This was followed by another uptick in proportional Irish claimants in the 1870s and 1880s that was almost certainly driven by Connacht Irish speakers fleeing the near-famine conditions of a later potato blight starting in the late 1870s. Focusing on the mother tongue of Irish-born by decennial age cohort, however, shows a strong consistency across age groups, with those born in the middle of the nineteenth century about as likely to have had Irish as a mother tongue as those born in the 1870s or 1890s. A similar conclusion arises from a comparison of age at immigration, calculated by subtracting an individual's age from the census year to find their birth year, then subtracting that result from the year of immigration and binning the results to account for the inaccuracies in reported ages common in historical censuses. For 1910, for example, the census indicates that an individual who arrived aged 20 to 29 was just as likely to claim Irish as a mother tongue as somebody who arrived in their 60s. It is striking, in other words, how steady the proportion of Irish-mother-tongue claimants remained over the 80 years preceding the First World War.

*Table 2: Proportion of Irish-born claiming Irish as mother tongue, by birth-year cohort, United States, 1910*

| Birth Year | Percent Claiming Irish, 1910 |
|---|---|
| 1901–10 | 18.2 |
| 1891–1900 | 11.6 |
| 1881–90 | 17.0 |
| 1871–80 | 19.7 |
| 1861–70 | 20.6 |
| 1851–60 | 21.3 |
| 1841–50 | 25.3 |
| 1831–40 | 28.1 |
| 1821–30 | 25.9 |
| 1819–20 | 22.9 |

*Table 3: Proportion of Irish-born claiming Irish as mother tongue, by age at time of arrival, United States, 1910*

| Age at Arrival Cohort | Percent Claiming Irish, 1910 |
|---|---|
| 0–9 years old | 21.7 |
| 10–19 years old | 20.6 |
| 20–9 years old | 21.0 |
| 30–9 years old | 23.9 |
| 40–9 years old | 24.7 |
| 50–9 years old | 27.1 |
| 60–9 years old | 21.4 |
| 70–9 years old | 29.1 |
| 80–9 years old | 20.2 |

Broadly similar findings can be made for the Irish-born of New York City, defined here as consisting of residents of the five New York counties of Kings, Queens, Richmond, Westchester, and New York (i.e., Manhattan and for the purposes of this analysis, the Bronx), and the four New Jersey counties of Bergen, Essex, Hudson, and Union.[7] It can be safely stated that at least 40,000 out of more than 300,000 Irish-born residents of these counties (as returned in 1910) had been raised with Irish as a mother tongue, or between 12 and 20 percent of this population. This means that while the Irish-born of New York City and surrounding areas were slightly more likely to have had English as a mother tongue than elsewhere in the country, this concentration of 40,000 individuals was the single largest population of Irish-language claimants in the United States. Trends in terms of arrival cohorts evident in the country as a whole also held true for New York, if not more so, with those arriving in the 1850s and again in the 1870s and 1880s exhibiting a greater tendency to have had Irish as a mother tongue (Table 4). Examining the spatial distribution of this community by county shows that although the largest single concentration of Irish claimants in terms of gross numbers lived in Manhattan and the Bronx, in keeping with general trends for long-term members of an Irish-American population that had matured and found financial stability in the city, the suburbs and boroughs of the city located in Westchester County, Staten Island, and New Jersey featured a higher proportion of Irish-language claimants among their foreign-born than the inner city (Table 5, Figure 1).

*Table 4: Proportion of Irish-born claiming Irish as mother tongue, New York City and surrounding counties, by decade of arrival*

| Decade of Immigration | Percent Claiming Irish, 1910 | Total Claiming Irish, 1910 | Percent Claiming Irish, 1920 | Total Claiming Irish, 1920 |
|---|---|---|---|---|
| 1830–9 | 25.1 | 101 | 100.0 | 102 |
| 1840–9 | 6.6 | 300 | 16.4 | 201 |
| 1850–9 | 12.9 | 1,806 | 36.9 | 1,414 |
| 1860–9 | 12.0 | 3,607 | 17.8 | 2,337 |
| 1870–9 | 12.5 | 4,016 | 24.1 | 4,788 |
| 1880–9 | 13.1 | 10,833 | 21.8 | 13,010 |
| 1890–9 | 12.6 | 9,427 | 17.3 | 9,466 |
| 1900–9 | 11.6 | 8,929 | 20.6 | 13,882 |
| Total 1830–1909 | 12.3 | 39,019 | 20.6 | 45,200 |

*Table 5: Proportion of Irish-born claiming Irish as mother tongue, New York City and surrounding counties, by county of residency*

| | County | Percent Claiming Irish, 1910 | Total Claiming Irish, 1910 | Percent Claiming Irish, 1920 | Total Claiming Irish, 1920 |
|---|---|---|---|---|---|
| New Jersey | Bergen | 15.5 | 700 | 36.0 | 969 |
| | Essex | 12.9 | 2,408 | 23.9 | 3,887 |
| | Hudson | 24.5 | 7,826 | 37.3 | 7,763 |
| | Union | 39.1 | 1,804 | 9.0 | 590 |
| New York | Kings | 9.6 | 6,825 | 14.0 | 7,266 |
| | New York (including Bronx) | 8.5 | 13,332 | 19.7 | 26,312 |
| | Queens | 21.4 | 1,803 | 20.2 | 2,070 |
| | Richmond | 17.2 | 605 | 27.0 | 1,090 |
| | Westchester | 23.3 | 3,918 | 28.7 | 3,676 |

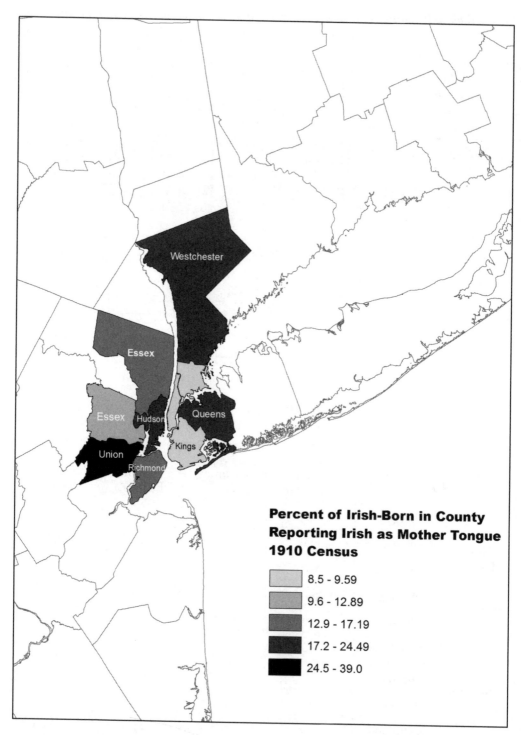

*Figure 1: Proportion of Irish-Born claiming Irish as mother tongue, New York and surrounding counties, 1910*

Put another way, given that approximately two-thirds of all Irish-language claimants enumerated in 1910 or 1920 had arrived prior to 1890, these individuals were well represented within the established Irish-American community that was more and more likely to reside outside Manhattan. These earlier cohorts were also unlike representatives of the new arrivals who hailed from an increasingly Anglicised Ireland – only 15 percent of the Irish population were returned as having Irish in 1901– who tended to settle (at least initially) in Manhattan. Thus, between 34 and 44 percent of all Irish-born claiming Irish as a mother tongue were found in Manhattan and the Bronx, but those whose mother tongue had been English were found in higher numbers there too, so that pockets of higher proportioned Irish-first communities existed in the surrounding suburbs.

Undoubtedly this was a diverse population, particularly in terms of class, but some generalisations about a 'representative' New York Irish American whose first language had been Irish can be assembled from these data. Relying on the 1910 returns for occupation, and keeping in mind the roughness by which occupations can be assigned to a social class and the way in which women's work was predominantly unidentified given the census recording scheme, the Irish-born community was characterised first and foremost by its lower-middle-class status (defined here as skilled and semi-skilled, artisanal, domestic, and clerical positions done outside of factories or without mass-production techniques), and to a lesser degree by labouring-, working-, professional-, and middle-class occupations.[8] Approximately 60 percent of those claiming Irish as a mother tongue were in this lower-middle-class group, but so too were 59 percent of those who claimed English as a mother tongue. Among working-class Irish-born individuals, 28 percent of those claiming Irish as a mother tongue, along with 24 percent of those whose mother tongue had been English, fell into this category. Among the middle-class occupations, 12 percent of Irish-language claimants were assigned to this category, as were 17 percent of English-language claimants. Thus, while both language communities were equally represented by lower-middle-class work, those with English as a mother tongue were slightly better represented by middle-class occupations and less represented by working-class positions, although not to such an extent that it would be accurate to speak of a serious class difference in the two language communities.

The typical profile for a resident of greater New York whose mother tongue was Irish in the second decade of the twentieth century was therefore generally that of someone working in a lower-middle-class position whose occupation ranged from semi-skilled to highly skilled, increasingly that of someone who had arrived between the 1880s and early 1900s (given the attrition of early arrival cohorts as a result of old age), and someone who made their residence in either the city core or the nearby suburbs. Ironically, given that the proportion of Irish-born New Yorkers whose mother tongue was Irish was as high as 20 percent, a person plucked at random from the Irish-born population in New York in 1910 or 1920 would have been more likely to have been a native speaker than somebody selected from Ireland. On the other hand, unlike the individual selected from Ireland, the New York Irish American had fewer opportunities to interact with a broadly active Irish-language community on a scale akin to the *gaeltachtaí* of Ireland, and might not in fact have used the language on a daily basis, especially outside of the home.

The majority of Irish Americans, whatever their opinion about the Irish language and its relationship to Irish identity, the politics of national independence, or their status as an ethnic community, did not participate in any of the various organisations active in sponsoring classes in Irish or raising money for revival movements in Ireland. Membership in societies dedicated explicitly to the language across the entire country would have numbered only in the thousands, and even if the increasing support from American societies such as the county associations or the United Irish League for Irish classes and Irish-language revival is taken into account, the evidence strongly indicates that regular attendance at core business and instructional meetings was irregular.[9] A modern Irish course taught at Columbia College by Michael A. O'Byrne, for example, struggled throughout 1914 and 1915 to build enrolment beyond eight students, and there is an indication that many of the city's language society members made a habit of doubling up their weekly class attendance at the various classes offered by the city's myriad Gaelic organisations in order to sustain demand for all of them.[10]

But even if the Gaelic societies and Irish classes were only one means by which Irish Americans negotiated their relationship to the language, the organisations offered by far the most visible advertisement of the existence of the Irish language in an American context. Those societies had in some cases reached their third or fourth decade of existence by 1916 and could rightly claim a highly respected status in the community even as the twentieth century brought a new phase in their development. New York City by the outbreak of war was home to the Brooklyn Philo-Celtic Society (1874), New York Society for the Preservation of the Irish Language (1878), New York Philo-Celtic Society (1878), New York Gaelic Society (1878), Harlem Gaelic Society (1899), Greenpoint Gaelic Society/League (1899), Brooklyn Gaelic Society (c. 1902), and a host of smaller societies whose historical background is less clear, including the Irish Gaelic Society, Jamaica Gaelic Society, Yonkers Philo-Celtic Society, Red Branch

Gaelic League, and St Brendan Gaelic Society.[11] The classes offered by these organisations were increasingly supplemented by those offered by county associations, ladies' auxiliaries, and other Irish groups inspired by the growing popularity of the Gaelic League in Ireland.

While the various Gaelic societies were independent and even competitive over their work – the creation of the Harlem Gaelic Society in 1899, for instance, was portrayed initially by the New York Gaelic Society as an attempt to undermine its own resources – a number of ties bound them together.[12] Since 1898, with the founding of the Gaelic League of America, an annual meeting assembled delegates from most major societies across the country with the goal of furthering the aims of the American societies with regard to defending Irish cultural identity and language heritage and, where possible, providing support to the Gaelic League in Ireland. Given the strength of these societies in the Northeast, especially Boston, New York, and Philadelphia, East Coast metropolitan areas were especially well represented in the League by way of its sub-branches, including the Gaelic League of New York. The other common thread linking the New York societies was the handful of patrons who often provided support to numerous organisations, binding together the Gaelic organisations at a higher level and building connections to the broader Irish-American associational landscape. These patrons included well-known individuals such as Cardinal John Farley, William Bourke Cockran, Thomas Addis Emmet, Daniel F. Cohalan, Gertrude B. Kelly, Denis A. Spellissy, and Victor Herbert. Beyond this top layer of noted figures, many of the higher officers and instructors of these societies, including Major Edward T. McCrystal, Diarmuid Lynch, Michael A. O'Byrne, William J. Balfe, Frank Hynes, John Byrnes, and Liam O'Dowd, served terms as officers in more than one society, or split their time between service to a local society and the state Gaelic League. As Úna Ní Bhroiméil has highlighted, these societies lacked a cohesiveness that might lend itself to a unified relationship to the Gaelic League of Ireland and especially to its fundraising needs, but in terms of their own internal goals for the advancement of the Irish language in New York, their interrelatedness was closer than it might at first appear.[13]

The Gaelic societies had always maintained their own unique view of the desired place of the Irish language in the United States. It was of course recognised that the language would not become a daily community language in the United States, and therefore the aims of these societies would always differ from that of the Gaelic League in Ireland.[14] This did not mean that the use of Irish would be confined to classes and musical performances hosted by language societies, as was evident by the positive responses given to locals who pressed for the public use of Irish, as in the case of the decision by Rev. John T. McNicholas to offer the rosary in Irish during Lent in March 1916 at the Church of St Catherine of Sienna on 69th Street.[15] But unlike their Gaelic League counterparts in Ireland, who were perpetually grappling (often problematically) with the relationship between the restoration of the language and the culture of the rural *gaeltachtaí* where Irish remained in widespread use, American proponents necessarily took a different line on the future of the language in the city. The question of supporting Irish was first and foremost for the members of these societies a matter of restoring a perceived degradation of Irish culture, whether in Ireland where it was evident in the reduced fortunes of the language, or in the United States where support for the language was a way to assert middle-class respectability and a global status for the Irish no different from that of Germans, Italians, or Russians.[16] Many of these revivalists, like their first-generation Irish-mother-tongue compatriots, were also members of a cohort born in Ireland in the last quarter of the nineteenth century – the 'nationally minded' generation of middle-class Home Rulers identified by historian Senia Pašeta who had been exposed in intermediate education and university life to a general Celticism, a distinct Irish nationality, and a sense of an inevitably independent Ireland that their education had trained them to lead. This generation, with their particular outlook on how to express their nationality in the United States, would remain Redmond supporters in the twentieth century, drift towards republican nationalism, or be supplanted by a younger cohort.[17]

As a result, the activities of the Gaelic societies in New York in their twentieth-century manifestations often took on a conservative tone in retrospect, particularly when one considers the contrasting energetic explorations by Irish revivalists of what a Gaelic and *gaeltacht*-based cultural life might look like in Ireland. It is striking, for example, to contrast the feverish debates over grammar and eager accounting of Irish-language manuscripts of the initial Gaelic columns prevalent in Irish-American newspapers of the nineteenth century with the staid annual Thomas Moore celebrations in Central Park and the operatic Carnegie Hall concerts typical of the twentieth-century New York societies. For instance, the enthusiasm and rigour of Mícheál Ó Lócháin –founder of the Brooklyn Philo-Celtic Society and the first modern publication (*An Gaodhal*) to feature extensive Irish-language content – in building a network of classes and pressing for the use of Irish in New York were not matched by subsequent iterations of this movement following his death in 1899.[18]

This assessment has its limitations, however. If, as scholars have emphasised, the language revival community in the United States was concerned first and foremost with the defence of pride in Irish culture and history in an American context, then a closer look at some of these activities demonstrates notable achievements on the part of the Gaelic societies. Gaelic societies' patrons and members had, for example, brought visibility to the Irish language at the highest political levels of American politics, most notably through the meeting between Douglas Hyde, president of the Gaelic League, and Theodore Roosevelt in 1905 that had been arranged by the New York lawyer John Quinn as part of Hyde's fundraising tour.[19] In 1912, the Gaelic League of New York could confidently invite Roosevelt and his successor, William Taft, to a dinner in honour of Pádraig Ó Dálaigh, general secretary of the Gaelic League.[20] And while the classes and activities of the Gaelic societies necessarily operated in isolation from the Irish-speaking heartlands of Ireland, and while many members were not by any means fluent speakers, instructors were almost always Irish-born native speakers who exhibited long-term dedication to their evening teaching activities.

Even the extensive musical programmes, with their focus on formal European musical styles, were not as far removed from an Irish-language context than they first appeared. In keeping with a general push to place Irish cultural forms on the same plane as other European (especially German and Italian) art forms, renowned Irish singers and composers like Helen O'Donnell, Thomas Egan, John McCormack, and Victor Herbert were trumpeted in concert announcements, often alongside upcoming performances of works by Wagner, Verdi, and Puccini.[21] Neither the Irish language nor its more prevalent rural cultural context in Ireland was excluded from these productions, however. Operatic performances were often supplemented by demonstrations of eight- and four-hand reels and jigs, harp and violin pieces, and other types of entertainment that contemporaries would have interpreted on one level as comparable to the ethnographic rediscovery of rural music also reflective of European interest of the time. More importantly, formal music in Irish was influenced by efforts on both sides of the Atlantic to inject the Irish language into the art form, notable in the New York Society for the Preservation of the Irish Language's production of Paul Mac Swiney's idyll 'An Bárd agus an Fó' in New York in 1884; Annie Patterson's Irish-language compositions; Thomas O'Brien Butler's full opera, *Muirgheis*, which debuted in Ireland in 1903 and was slated for a New York premiere that was disrupted when Butler was killed on the torpedoed *Lusitania*; and Robert O'Dwyer's *Eithne* (1909), the first full opera to feature an Irish-language libretto.[22] The New York societies were explicit in their intention to deploy Irish-composed, and preferably Irish-language, librettos to compete directly with other national musical forms. As one headline in the New York *Sun* noted of the New York Gaelic Society's plans for hosting original Irish opera in January 1914: 'Sons of Erin hope for grand opera in Irish'.[23]

The Gaelic League in Ireland had long been explicitly apolitical in its work, an approach that was evidently emulated by the Gaelic societies in the United States. The League and its American allies were often at pains to remind the warring pro-Redmond and republican nationalist camps of the 1910s that the Irish revivalists included unionists, nationalists, Protestants, Catholics, Irish Parliamentary Party supporters, and Sinn Féin enthusiasts. 'The Gaelic League is nonpolitical and nonsectarian, yet many Irishmen in the United States seem to think that the Gaelic League is opposed to Redmond and his party,' protested Father M. Collins in a letter published in the *Irish American Weekly* in May 1912.[24] The constitution of the New York Gaelic Society had explicitly excluded the expression of political stances at its meetings.[25] But just as such a position became increasingly untenable in Ireland as a new generation of Gaelic League members pressured Hyde to move the organisation to a more radical nationalist position, in the United States Gaelic Society members found themselves increasingly buffeted by warring conservative and republican nationalist camps even as the language itself was becoming more politicised when its revival was championed by a larger swath of the nationalist community.[26] The American language revivalists had always seen the fortunes of Irish as inseparable from machinations of British policy in Ireland. But by 1916 the wider nationalist community was also eager to track news of any conflict over speaking Irish as a sign of nationalist resistance, as when the Oxford language professor Claude Chavasse was fined early that year for insisting on speaking Irish to the Ballingeary police, prompting John Devoy's *Gaelic American* to proclaim that it was now a 'crime to speak Irish'. Linking the episode to the wartime context, the newspaper noted that this was indicative of how Britain treated small nations, and in a letter to the editor on the matter, it was pointed out that Chavasse had been sentenced under the Defence of the Realm Act.[27] Although not as overtly, the activities of individuals like Kuno Meyer, the German Celtic scholar who embarked on a series of lectures and newspaper editorials in support of Germany in the early years of the war, served to further forge connections between Irish revivalists and advanced nationalism, if not outright support for Germany.[28]

This was the atmosphere faced by members of the Irish revivalist community in New York when war arrived in 1914. The untenable nature of remaining apolitical in the face of these currents, or even of preventing a drift among members towards the anti-Redmond camp, can be illustrated through the experience of the New York Gaelic Society in reaction to events at the New York State Gaelic League meeting of December 1914, and again at the famous Irish Race Convention on 4–5 March 1916 that led to the founding of the Friends of Irish Freedom on the eve of the Easter Rising.

As has been elucidated in a number of chapters in this volume, by the fall of 1914, following Redmond's decision to commit the Volunteers to service in the war and a growing unease with the delayed implementation of Home Rule, a noticeable shift away from the Parliamentary Party and towards some type of advanced nationalist position had taken hold among a sizeable portion of the Irish-American community.[29] Supporting Germany, or at least questioning the neutrality of the United States in its relationship with Britain, became the new marker of the radical wing of this republican nationalism that pitted Irish-American loyalty to the United States against their opposition to British wartime policy in Ireland. When a delegate at the state League meeting of December 1914 claimed that President Wilson was 'brought up with British gold', it prompted the New York Gaelic Society representatives to leave the hall. One of those delegates, Anne E. McAuliffe, an American-born schoolteacher, vice president of the Women's Teachers' Association of New York, and vice president of the Gaelic Society, chose to resign from the League entirely in response to the event. Attempts by Michael O'Byrne to retain her as a part of a bulwark against the passage of radical motions by the League membership ultimately failed.[30]

A more serious breach occurred more than a year later in response to the Irish Race Convention organised by members of Clan na Gael and held at the Hotel Astor. The Irish language had not been on the agenda or demands of either the convention planners or its opposition, although a number of noted revival societies, members and patrons, including Herbert, Spellissy, O'Byrne, Cohalan, and Kelly, were signatories to the convention announcement.[31] On receiving an invitation to attend, the New York Gaelic Society initially appointed four delegates, President John McKee, McAuliffe, the financial secretary and language instructor Michael Clynes, and a general member, Patrick Devlin. McKee and McAuliffe balked, however, at the requirement that attendees support the convention's statement of principles in order to attend, seeing it as a violation of the society's apolitical stance. In the end no official delegates were sent.[32] This decision, and no doubt the disjuncture between members and the leaderships of McKee and McAuliffe that prompted it, led to further internal conflict. By early April 1916 Kelly had resigned, followed by Spellissy and Cohalan. Defiantly, member John Kelly 'moved that their resignations be accepted on the ground that the Gaelic movement came first and that they were not to dictate to us how to run the society'.[33]

Initial news of the Rising did not produce any thaw in this standoff, and at the subsequent meeting of 7 May 1916 – held in the middle of the week of the execution of the rebel leaders – Kelly and Clynes went further by securing a controversial motion on a 12-to-10 vote to end the membership of the Gaelic Society in the state League. There were, however, signs that the tide was already moving in a different direction. The Irish language had been visible at the meeting convened on 30 April by the United Irish Societies and Clan na Gael at the Cohan Theatre. Father James O'Mahony recited the 1798 rebel poem 'An Spailpín Fánach' in Irish before reading out the gathering's resolutions advocating American opposition to British aggression and a unified push for Irish independence.[34] The case of Diarmuid Lynch, initially sentenced to death for his role in the Rising, also exposed a powerful link between certain corners of the American language revival movement and republican nationalism. Lynch, who had been a president of the New York Philo-Celtic Society and the Gaelic League of New York, was instrumental in building a financial bridge between Clan na Gael and the Irish Volunteers in 1914 while on a fundraising tour for the Irish Gaelic League. His reputation as a fierce advocate of the language during his time in the United States, combined with the highly visible inquiry by the US congress into his death sentence and the subsequent reversal of his court-martial thanks to pressure by the consul in Dublin, made it all the more difficult to view American language revival members in an entirely apolitical light.[35]

At the 7 May meeting McAuliffe and Clynes offered to stand down as officers to stop the spate of resignations, and after the full impact of the executions had taken effect, Devlin wrote to McKee on 17 May pleading with him to convene an extraordinary meeting of the society to reconsider the motion of withdrawal from the League. By the time of that meeting on 24 May, the executive committee of the state League had passed its own resolution expressing condemnation of the executions, and the motions to be considered by the society had expanded to include an expression of sympathy for the 'Irish martyrs' and a denunciation of 'the British Government for their ruthless treatment of the Irish heroes'.[36] The 24 May meeting itself was highly contentious, and while in the end the motion to leave the state League was withdrawn and the resolution sympathising with the executed leaders passed, the extended and heated denunciations of the Redmondites by one faction prompted a crowd of parliamentary party supporters to leave. McAuliffe herself resigned from the society, ending her affiliation permanently. Embarking on this new willingness to engage in political discussion, the society went on to pass a resolution on 9 August 1916 condemning the execution of Roger Casement.[37]

As was the case with a number of Irish-American organisations, similar to what John T. Ridge underscores in his chapter in this volume, the Easter Rising brought to members of the Irish-language community in New York an end to the possibility of apolitical response to the national question and a radicalisation of the nationalism of many members who had previously been staunchly in favour of a Home Rule solution in Ireland. The apparent uptick in those professing Irish as a mother tongue in the 1920 census, as had been the case in the 1901 and 1911 Irish censuses taken in a post-Gaelic League landscape, may very well have been a result of the growing connection between advocacy of the language and support for republican nationalism. Numerically speaking, this linguistic community remained robust in the first two decades of the twentieth century, albeit relatively invisible given their English-speaking environment. Nevertheless, the language was clearly inseparable from the larger Irish-American experience, and would continue to be so for as long as immigration from Irish-speaking regions in Ireland continued.

*The author wishes to thank Ellis Garey, Miriam Nyhan Grey, John T. Ridge, and Vicky Steeves for their assistance with this research. Thanks are particularly due to Marion R. Casey for her guidance in completing this chapter and for her work in bringing to scholars' attention the records of the Gaelic Society of New York, now held at the Archives of Irish America, New York University.*

We fought the same foe & for the same reason

PEARSE          WASHINGTON

A. Gaehle

Fighting the Same Foe for the Same Reason
(From the Fatherland, New York.)

# CHAPTER SEVENTEEN

# THE IRISH COUNTY ASSOCIATIONS IN NEW YORK AND THE EASTER RISING

## John T. Ridge

No city was as closely connected to Ireland as was New York in 1916 even though separated by 3,000 miles. The city's large Irish community (immigrant as well as intergenerational) with its vibrant political, cultural, and social organisations, plus a constant transit of people to and from the homeland, kept New York close to the centre of events. In 1916, when Dublin rose in rebellion, the reactions of New York's Irish were varied and, for many organisations, tentative at first.

The aftermath of the Easter Rising, as has been demonstrated in previous chapters in this volume, ensured that the New York Irish turned away from Irish parliamentarianism towards fervent republicanism, aligning with those who sought a solution to the Irish question by force of arms. Only about six days away by ship and constantly receiving news by cable from Ireland, New York entered into a phase of history where it was decisive in Ireland's political future.[1] The variety of opinions on Irish nationalism was best reflected in three weekly newspapers published in New York as the First World War began: The *Irish World*, the *Irish Advocate*, and *The Gaelic American*.[2] But how these newspapers covered the activities of the New York Irish community differed widely.

Every issue of the *Irish Advocate* had detailed reporting on the doings of a hundred or more Irish societies, evidence of the city's robust associational culture. The *Advocate* had none of the pretensions of being a national newspaper for the American Irish like the *Irish World*, whose social coverage was briefer and much more sporadic. *The Gaelic American* was by far the poorest chronicler, except for those societies with sentiments like those of Clan na Gael or Cumann na mBan. Even then, coverage was usually directly linked with paid advertising with the result that only about a half dozen or so of the Irish county associations regularly committed themselves to advertise their events in its pages. So clearly was *The Gaelic American* known to be opposed to Redmond, the Irish Parliamentary Party, and the United Irish League of America (UILA) that any advertisement placed in this newspaper by one of the New York Irish societies was virtually an endorsement of its editorial outlook.

Of all the Irish associations in New York in the prelude to the Rising, those based on county of origin had the closest connections to home.[3] They were composed mainly, and sometimes entirely, of immigrants from Ireland's 32 counties. Although the earliest of these date back to the late 1840s, it was probably not until the 1890s that all of them were extant in New York at one time. They were primarily social organisations that brought friends and relatives from home together for 'reunions' as a way to keep in touch with one another. Because Ireland contributed unevenly to the size of the emigration pool, the strength of county associations varied widely and some parts of Ireland, consequently, produced county associations in New York which were relatively inactive or dormant for long periods of time. The larger counties, or those with a lot of immigrants living in New York, had no problem maintaining a prosperous society from year to year, with some counting close to a thousand members on their roll. Large or small, they all tried to keep in touch with developments in Ireland.[4]

For many members who were single immigrant men, living in rooms or boarding houses in Manhattan, it was easy to attend county meetings and social events. In other nearby parts of the city like Brooklyn and the Bronx, the national fraternal organisation the Ancient Order of Hibernians (AOH) was more dominant. The AOH, whose membership was most often geographically based on the local Roman Catholic parish, was about equally divided between supporters of the moderate Irish Parliamentary Party and the more republican Clan na Gael sympathisers. In the years before 1916, these two competing nationalist visions for Ireland fought a never-ending struggle for control over the AOH and the United Irish Societies, a powerful umbrella organisation. Unlike the AOH, county constituent sentiment in the United Irish Societies was still strongly in favour of the UILA and John Redmond.

It should be noted that county societies in New York were often male-only organisations for long periods of time. But this did not mean that women did not participate.

Ladies auxiliaries were common across the landscape of county organisations and over time the gender barrier was dropped by most.[5] Interestingly, the smaller counties often pioneered combining of the sexes; perhaps driven by necessity when the population to draw from was smaller than that of the larger counties. The female organisations supported the male equivalents but they also ran their own fundraising and social events until they were folded into the main organisations.

There had always been close ties between various county organisations in New York and the UILA especially in the glory days when it appeared that Home Rule would actually come to pass in Ireland. Many county societies sent two permanent delegates to all the UILA meetings in New York as part of its Municipal Council, whose officers and leaders were also active with the counties, for example, Patrick J. Brennan, manager of Kilkenny's football team, and Dr Joseph P. Brennan, president of Westmeath County Society.[6] These delegates became so attached to the UILA that they began to operate as virtual political commissars in the Irish county ranks. Additionally, in order to solidify county support, some of the branches of the UILA were named after specific localities, such as Armagh, Aughawillan (Leitrim), Ballinamuck (Longford), and Waterford.[7]

The UILA had the difficult task in the months between the outbreak of war in Europe and the Rising of convincing Irish Americans that the Home Rule cause was not lost and that Ireland had not been betrayed by Britain. The rivalry and conflict between the leaders of the UILA and the revolutionaries led by John Devoy grew increasingly bitter. Devoy attacked the UILA in every issue of *The Gaelic American*, pointing out the Irish Parliamentary Party's loyal support for British war efforts in lieu of the increasingly ephemeral prospect of Irish self-rule.[8] This battle for influence spilled into the ranks of almost all the individual county societies, where republicanism was usually, at least until 1914, the minority opinion.

The UILA and its allies within some of the Irish county organisations had certain advantages over the republicans. The Irish Parliamentary Party represented the home constituencies of most of the Irish in New York with the exception of those areas where unionists prevailed. As has been illuminated in earlier chapters in this volume, Irish politicians regularly visited New York to raise money for the Irish Parliamentary Party and socialised with their former neighbours and supporters at venues like Carnegie Hall. Irish-American businessmen and politicians more often aligned themselves with the increasingly successful Redmondite cause than with the idealism of the republicans whose efforts had suffered one failure after another for more than 100 years.

Redmond in particular was treated like royalty by most of the Irish county societies during his several visits to New York. In October 1910 when he arrived with what the

Irish-American press referred to as his 'Irish Envoys' the *Irish Advocate* reported on the mass meeting held in Carnegie Hall:

> Practically every Irish organization was represented. The Ancient Order of Hibernians sent a large delegation. The Irish Counties Athletic Union occupied boxes and reserved seats. The Board of Erin [a faction of the AOH that was strongly pro-Redmond] was also largely represented. The two associations of Corkmen in the city occupied boxes in the first tier and the Louth Men's Society had two boxes assigned to them. The Armagh Men's Association, the Clare men and the Kerry men were also very prominent in the audience.[9]

Two years later in 1912, another major UILA rally was held in New York at their headquarters on Madison Avenue. It was the largest gathering of delegates from the affiliated Irish organisations ever held and included many representatives of the county societies. The prospect of limited government for Ireland had by this time won over even some of the most die-hard nationalists. Even Jeremiah O'Donovan Rossa seemingly converted to the moderate side of nationalism and joined the UILA in 1904.[10] A measure of freedom was at last at hand and the 1912 UILA gathering seemed to represent the defeat of republicans in New York once and for all:

> In the audience were many old Fenians and Land League men, who have grown grey in the service of Ireland, and who were as enthusiastic as the youngest recruits who were present. The object of the meeting was to ratify the action of the Irish National Convention, in accepting on behalf of the people of Ireland, the Home Rule bill introduced by Premier Asquith in the House of Commons.[11]

Here it is interesting to note that the hit of the 1914 New York St Patrick's Day parade was a banner carried by the Cavan Men's P. & B. Association that read 'From Ulster, but Home Rulers'.[12] No doubt, the Cavan banner was inspired by the increasing discourse surrounding Ulster and Home Rule as the spring months of 1914 progressed. However, when Britain postponed the implementation of the Home Rule legislation, it is clear that the fortunes of the UILA began to fade rapidly in New York and reverberated in the county associations.[13]

At the best of times almost all 32 Irish counties had functioning organisations in New York bearing their names. 1916 was not, however, the best of times. Immigration from Ireland, from the perspective of the New York Irish engaged in promoting social, cultural, and political activities, had declined precipitously over the previous half-dozen years. The outbreak of war in 1914 reduced the flow of Irish immigration to a mere trickle.[14] As bad as it was for Ireland, new immigrants were the lifeblood of Irish activities and it was not long before this dip in numbers had consequences for the active organisations. Membership for the counties in Leinster and parts of Ulster declined, yet before the Tipperary Men's National Social and Benevolent Society went defunct, it landed arms for the Nenagh Volunteers on the Galway coast, and Carlow New Yorkers, though small in numbers, authorised $200 for the Carlow Volunteers in 1914.[15] During the course of 1916 counties Antrim, Carlow, Derry, Down, Laois (Kings County), Meath, and Wicklow had organisations that were inactive or just barely able to run an occasional social gathering and they expressed no opinion on the Rising that ever made it into the newspapers.

A few more societies, although fairly active hosting social events, seem to have deliberately held themselves back from becoming involved in the events of 1916. Any mention of just how their members felt about the rebellion is absent. In lieu of any evidence to the contrary, these societies, about a dozen in number, remained neutral in the eyes of the public. A dozen other counties took a clear position in sympathy with the rebels, if not in actual resolution but with action to support the victims of the insurrection. A few more deplored, on simple humanitarian grounds, the suffering in the old country but took no additional position. A number of Irish counties let their action rather than words speak for them. These counties participated in various events to raise money for the Irish Relief Fund. Galway not only donated the proceeds of its annual games to the cause, but both the football and hurling teams performed in several benefit games throughout the summer and autumn of 1916. Other teams donating their services included Kilkenny, Cavan, Cork, Kildare, and Waterford. While resolutions in outright condemnation of the Rising could be found in statements made by the UILA leaders in New York, the few county societies with strong links to the UILA – like Armagh, Mayo, and Westmeath – were more circumspect, merely reaffirming an attachment to Redmond and his cause.[16]

Just how a county organisation reacted to the Rising often depended on which individuals were its key players. The Kerrymen's Patriotic and Benevolent Association, for example, responded very quickly to the news of the rebellion, meeting on Sunday 29 April, in a special session where they voted the considerable sum of $1,000 'to the revolutionary movement in Ireland'.[17] This was in keeping with their actions of almost two years earlier, in August 1914, when Sir Roger Casement garnered $500 directly for the Irish Volunteers; a few days afterwards, he appeared as an invited speaker at the Kerry Men's Festival and Picnic. The fact that the money was handed to Casement personally was a firm political statement that the republican faction of the Irish Volunteers would get the money and not the Redmond wing.[18] In 1914, the president of the Kerry Men was Eugene O'Sullivan, a committed nationalist, who was also president of the Celtic Club of Clan na Gael for two terms.[19] The Kerry society was, in fact, a hot bed of militancy in the period:

> They succeeded in having the 'standing orders' of their organization 'suspended' in order to place one thousand dollars in the 'Rising' fund. All other matters pertaining to the Society seemed to have been sunk in the feverish activity centered on this work of preparing Ireland for the fight.[20]

It was a former player on the All-Ireland Championship Kerry football team, Dan McCarthy, who led the motion on the floor of the New York Kerry Men's meeting to provide that $1,000. McCarthy's father was an old Fenian who had been involved in arming the Irish Republican Brotherhood and suffered arrest in Land League days. 'Help them', shouted Dan, 'and in return I will handle your games at Celtic Park and make a success of them. I will also wear the Kerry sweater that day to show that my heart is in the right place.'[21] Shortly after the Rising, 55 Kerrymen set up the St Brendan's branch of the Friends of Irish Freedom.[22]

The Co. Tyrone Association was similarly committed to the 1916 Rising and very emotionally so because one of its former leading members, Tom Clarke, was one of the chief architects of the rebellion. As Gerard MacAtasney has thoroughly outlined in his chapter in this volume, Clarke had lived in New York for many years before returning to Dublin to commit himself fully to his life's work of breaking the British connection with Ireland.[23] In New York he had been well known personally by many Tyrone Men, especially those who were also members of the Irish-language and cultural group, the Philo-Celtic Society. In June 1916, the following resolution was passed:

> That as men and women of Tyrone we naturally feel a sense of conscious pride that the patriot and martyr Thomas Clarke, being nurtured and reared in the shadows of the castle of the O'Neill at Dungannon, and an officer of our Association, conducted himself with gallantry and intrepidity while leading his men in battle and later when confronting his cold-blooded murderers in a manner worthy of the noblest traditions of Tyrone; That we deplore the loss of Clarke, Pearse, McDonough, Plunkett, Connolly, McDermott, Ceannt and their brave comrades who were murdered with all the savagery characteristic of English Imperialism and That we direct this resolution be indelibly inscribed on the records of the Association, and a copy hereof be forwarded to the President of the United States, the British Imperialist Government and the Provisional Government of the Republic of Ireland.[24]

Some of the most dedicated activists in the months and years to follow would be the members of the Tyrone Ladies who were the principal workers at the fundraising efforts to help the republican cause in Ireland.[25]

A previous connection to republican nationalism was an important factor in determining whether a county came out in support of the Rising. The Claremen's organisation had fought a long battle against landlordism and for tenant rights from the time of its founding to just before the outbreak of the First World War with a committee that specifically addressed land issues only. Its most influential members were veterans of the land war in Clare, and its treasurer, John Clune, was known as 'the first Fenian in Clare'. Consequently, its donation of $600 to the Irish Relief Fund was second only to Kerry in the days after Easter Week.[26]

The Co. Limerick Men not only had close ties to the Limerick patriots Edward Daly, Cornelius Colbert, and Seán Heuston, who were executed after the rebellion, but one of its active members was James Reidy, Devoy's assistant editor at *The Gaelic American*.[27] Limerick passed a hard-hitting resolution at a meeting on 7 May 1916:

> Whereas, this splendid race, after many unsuccessful attempts to establish an independent Irish nation, at last in this historic year 1916, saw the goal of their hopes in sight, struck the blow for independence by successful revolution, and established the Irish Republic: Therefore, Be it Resolved, that the Limerick Men's B. and S. Association, in meeting assembled, heartily endorse the Irish revolution.[28]

As part of its resolution Limerick recalled Patrick Sarsfield and the defence of Limerick in 1690–1, historical nationalist imagery that was also referenced in the resolution of the Co. Kildare Men's Association when they called to mind the hangings that took place in that county after the failure of the 1798 Rising. Kildare offered assistance 'morally and financially to the loved ones left behind of the men who gave their lives as a willing sacrifice in a good cause'.[29]

Despite having organised a big 'Leitrim Home Rule Festival' in May 1916, the thrust of the Leitrim Men's response was aimed at the 'British government's murder of the Irish insurrectionary war prisoners', while at the same time pledging that their 'monster demonstration and public meeting' on 30 May 1916, at the Central Opera House on East 67th Street 'will not be used as a criticism of the policies of a section of the Irish people previous to the murder of the Irish insurrectionists'.[30] Copies of the resolutions passed by those assembled were forwarded to Redmond and the British ambassador to the United States, Cecil Spring-Rice. The demonstration itself, however, was clearly an endorsement of the revolution and prominently featured Mary Jane

O'Donovan Rossa. After decades of support for the efforts of the Irish Parliamentary Party and Redmond, led by honorary Leitrim member Captain Stephen McFarland, the Leitrim Men experienced a change of attitude as a result of the executions in the wake of the Rising:

> Amid the wave of resentment, detestation and horror against the British Government's murder of the Irish insurrectionists which has swept like a tidal wave over not only the United States, but the entire civilized world, no body of men are more pronounced in their attitude than the Leitrim men of New York, many of whom, as individuals, were inclined, despite her perfidious record, to believe that England was awakening to the progress of civilization and that her hypocritical cant about the rights of small nations had some semblance of sincerity.[31]

Neighbouring Co. Sligo responded in a similar manner to Leitrim. The Sligo Men donated all the proceeds of its annual athletic games to the cause of Irish Relief, sparked by the actions of the British government in the wake of the Rising:

> The unfortunate and tragic events which have recently occurred in Ireland have brought about with other consequences a condition of unspeakable want and distress. The punishment which England so mercilessly by execution, imprisonment or deportation to hundreds if not thousands of fathers, husbands and sons has fallen with extreme severity on countless women and children, and many of the aged in unhappy Erin.[32]

Outrage over British reprisals prompted the Co. Monaghan Men to pass the following:

> Resolved, That we, the members of the County Monaghan Men's S. and B. Association, in meeting assembled, express our sincere sympathy with the Irish revolutionists who lost their lives in the uprising in Dublin and with the wives and families, and that we bitterly condemn England for her barbarous treatment of their leaders whom she so ruthlessly shot to death after their unconditional surrender.[33]

The absence of comment from other county societies explicitly endorsing the Rising may not have been a political decision at all, but a move to enable their individual fundraising efforts to be as broad in appeal as possible. This was certainly the case with the Dublin Club. All its statements emphasised a charitable motivation to take care of approximately 2,000 families who had been rendered homeless by the fighting in Dublin:

> We citizens of the United States, natives of the Irish capital, familiar with the conditions that normally prevail in our native city, learning of the distress that now exists there and eager to alleviate by every means in our power the hardships of our kindred at home appeal to the generous men and women of our race, irrespective of political

or religious belief, to come to the rescue of the homeless women and children of our native city now that a crisis confronts them.[34]

The Dublin Club had a history with republican nationalism that dated back to 1914 when Stephen Holland, a prominent member of the Dublin branch of the Irish Volunteers, arrived in the city and quickly helped to influence the Club to donate $250 for the purchase of arms. In a succession of public rallies, a strident nationalist tone was always set by the Dublin Club in their choice of speakers such as the writer Seamus MacManus, Peter Golden, the poet and later founder of the Irish Progressive League (IPL), and Eleanor Rogers Cox, a witness to the rebellion whose collected works advocating an Irish Republic were published in New York in 1916. At a time when support for the Irish rebels was about to largely evaporate as the United States' entry into the First World War became imminent, the Dublin Club was the only county group to celebrate the first anniversary of the Rising with a St Patrick's Day commemoration 'in memory of the heroes of Easter Week'.[35]

Co. Louth, although the smallest county geographically in Ireland, was particularly vocal in expressing support for the revolution in Ireland through its recently reorganised Co. Louth Men's Association. Spurred on by the reprisals of the British military, a formal resolution reflected the intense feeling of many in the New York Irish community:

> That whereas the return of England to her bloodthirsty policy of forcing her unwelcome and uninvited rule on our native land has been dearly demonstrated by the recent cold-blooded murder of fifteen of her patriots and the sentencing of many others to long terms in English dungeons, who, acting under the noble impulse of love for their native land dared to assert the independence which is justly theirs, and drive the despised and hated Saxon from our shores.[36]

At least two Co. Louth-born New Yorkers, Frank Coburn and Jim Finn, returned to Dundalk shortly before the Rising to take part in the activities. Both were members of the Louth football team in New York and Coburn was also a Clan na Gael member. Both left the Knights of Hibernia Hall in Dundalk on Easter Sunday to make their way to Dublin with the Irish American Alliance, an armed wing of the AOH in Ireland.[37] Coburn and Finn escaped capture by the British and, after a period on the run, made passage to New York.[38]

Often more than one society vied for the leadership of fellow immigrants. There were several reasons for this, most often because the established organisation had grown old and tired and inactive, or sometimes it related to regionalism within the county as when big cities competed with rural areas (Co. Dublin Association vs. Dublin Club). The Sons of South Armagh, as the name implies represented the southern portion of the county, even though the Co. Armagh Society still existed. While the latter continued to support the policies of John Redmond, the Sons of South Armagh took on a decidedly republican tone. It denounced British rule in Ireland and supported the Irish Relief Fund with donations and an athletic field day in order that 'the money go to alleviate the sufferings of the patriotic survivors of the Irish rebellion'.[39]

For the majority of Irish county organisations, statements regarding the Rising were either non-committal or they were unsuccessful in finding their way into print. Apparently, no official statement was ever published on the 1916 events by the associations representing Cavan, Derry, Donegal, Down, Galway, Kilkenny, Laois (Queens County), Longford, Mayo, Roscommon, Tipperary, Waterford, Westmeath, Wexford, or Wicklow; assuming there were in fact organisations representing each of these counties at this moment in history. However, there were some notable actions. Roscommon sent its former president, Thomas Rock, a supporter of Padraig Pearse's St Enda's school as well as a Clan na Gael member, as its official delegate to the Irish Race Convention in March 1916.[40] In September Westmeath's Dr Brennan told the *Freeman's Journal* that he had 'unwavering confidence in John Redmond'.[41] When asked to comment by the *Irish Advocate*, Martin Sheridan, the famous athlete and an honorary member of the Mayo Men, said,

> Tis not the first time that England did this. She murdered members of my own imme-
> diate family. P.W. Nally was done to death by that cursed government. The King of
> England will be looking for a job shining shoes before this war is over. I have lost
> some of my dearest friends over that hated Empire of criminals. Poor McDonough
> and Pearse were my friends, and Major John McBride was also an old friend of mine.[42]

Ireland's largest county, Cork, was split in 1916 into two factions over support for a proposed athletic ground in Yonkers, but the division also produced a fierce compe-tition for a couple of years as to just which faction could endear itself to Redmond and the Irish Parliamentary Party. While the older society, the Cork Men's Patriotic and Benevolent Society, under its president and longtime UILA officer John P. Hayes, clung to the hope that Redmond would be able to deliver on Home Rule for Ireland, it voiced 'condemnation of the English Government's cowardly, inhuman and unmerciful action in putting to death our fellow Irishmen in Dublin, who so manfully, honorably, and heroically died for the means by which they believed the freedom of Ireland, their native land, could be won'.[43]

The breakaway faction, the Corkmen's Mutual Aid Society, which disbanded a year later in 1917, issued a strong resolution condemning the Rising:

> We further deplore, as Irish men by birth or descent, the action of a small faction of our brethren in Dublin during the past week, which did not have the sympathy or support of the overwhelming majority of the people of Ireland, and their sympathizers throughout the world, as citizens of this great republic, lovers of liberty and freedom the world over, we pledge our undivided support to John E. Redmond and the real leaders of the overwhelming majority of the Irish people in Ireland, and we extend to them our heartfelt sympathy and cooperation in the future as in past as against feudalism and intolerance.[44]

The strongest support for the rebellion came from a half-dozen or so counties, Kerry, Limerick, Clare, Leitrim, Sligo, Dublin, Louth, and Tyrone, all of which issued resolutions that placed them firmly in support of that cause. Strong support also came from several more counties, Armagh, Galway, Kildare, Offaly (Kings County), and Monaghan in fundraising efforts, but no specific statement or resolution backing the rebellion has been found. A number of county athletic teams also played at fundraising efforts for Irish relief including Kilkenny, Cork, Cavan, Offaly (Kings County), and Waterford.

We know from the records of Ireland's Bureau of Military History that at least 24 men from New York City and Yonkers took part in the Easter Rising, some of whom had gone back to Ireland specifically to join in the rebellion. In 1951, the *Irish Advocate* identified six survivors of Easter Week still living in the city and participating in commemoration events,[45] which had been held annually in New York with the support of the Irish county organisations.

The events leading up to the Easter Rising and its aftermath were played out in the ranks of the individual county organisations of New York. While some of them immediately supported the rebellion, others were slow or reluctant to desert the Irish Parliamentary Party cause that they had so long followed. The minutes and other records of these societies have unfortunately been lost for most; but, through accounts in the New York Irish weeklies, the activities and attitudes of almost all of the 32 counties can be determined to some extent. What is evident is that the reactions and opinions expressed by the individual county societies shed fascinating insights into the complexities of the Irish-born immigrants of New York *c.* 1916.

# HOW THE IRISH PRESS IS GAGGED.

## [CONFIDENTIAL.]

*The Editor*

You are requested to give careful consideration to the following before publication :—

1. Resolutions and speeches of Corporations, County and Urban Councils, and Boards of Guardians.

2. Letters from soldiers connected with the late rising in Dublin.

3. Extracts from American newspapers, or private letters sent you from individuals received from America.

4. Criticisms in the form of letters from individuals on the late rising in Dublin, of a violent nature.

5. Letters sent you from men arrested in Dublin in connection with the late rising now in detention.

6. Indiscretions made by other papers either in Foreign or Home Press should not be published.

No objection will be taken to any publication of above provided the language is moderate; doubtful matter should be submitted before printing.

*Decies,*

Lieut.-Colonel,
Press Censor.

Headquarters,
   Irish Command,
     Dublin,
      June 5th, 1916.

# CHAPTER EIGHTEEN

# BIFOCALISM OF US PRESS COVERAGE
## THE EASTER RISING AND IRISH AMERICA

## *Robert Schmuhl*

On Tuesday 25 April 1916, the *Washington Post* published two front-page stories that added out-of-the-blue and arched-eyebrow intrigue to its coverage of the war in Europe. The more prominent one (placed at the top of the page) carried this headline about the arrest of Roger Casement:

Capture Sir Roger in Irish Filibuster

The other, though shorter, displayed bolder typeface for its four-word heading:

Revolt On in Ireland

This article combined two separate dispatches, one with a London dateline and the other filed from New York on 24 April, that fateful Easter Monday: 'Reports of a serious revolutionary outbreak in Ireland reached New York today and caused excitement in Irish circles here,' the *Post* began its account, noting later that 'it was rumored that sympathizers in this country are lending aid to the Irish revolutionists.' The next two paragraphs put on the record – and from day one – some of the difficulties journalists faced in covering the Rising and what followed:

Two apparently innocent cablegrams, but which were really cipher messages, brought first news of the rebellion. News of their receipt leaked out despite efforts to keep the matter secret. The movement, according to reports, has met with considerable success.

In Irish circles it was stated that the same censorship which has kept secret for three days the news of the capture of Sir Roger has now clamped the lid on all aisles of escape for news from Ireland.[1]

Like the *Post*, the *Chicago Tribune* on 25 April took note of what was being discussed in New York the day before, but the newspaper hedged with its headline:

## Revolt in Dublin, Rumor

The three paragraphs that followed – on page two, with the streamer atop page one proclaiming in 72-point type: 'FOIL GERMAN-IRISH PLOT' – constituted a report of uncon-firmed conversations along with warnings of possible inaccuracies in the brief item:

A rumor circulated around town [New York] today that the Irish in Dublin had revolted and seized Dublin castle. The story had it that the revolt had quickly spread over a considerable section of the country and that the British authorities had been overwhelmed.

While a great many prominent Irishmen in town had heard this report, it was impossible to discover how it had started or on what authority it rested.

One version was to the effect that the news had first come to the publisher of an Irish periodical in a code message from the other side. This did not seem probable, however, as code messages are not permitted by the British censors.[2]

Despite the qualifications and cautionary phrases, the article provided a local angle to events across the Atlantic Ocean and raised the possibility that 'the publisher of an Irish periodical' in New York, presumably John Devoy, was the first recipient of the news.[3]

In the dispatches originating from New York the day the Rising began, someone a century later can readily identify the seeds of what might be termed 'the bifocalism' that characterised American press coverage of what newspapers termed the 'revolt', 'rebellion', 'insurrection', 'rising', 'filibuster', 'uprising', or 'outbreak' in Ireland. Metaphorically similar to spectacles for mature scholars, this journalistic bifocalism took account of events occurring off in the distance thousands of miles away as well as the reactions (and reverberations) closer to home within Irish America. The dual foreign and domestic approach meant that news about all that was happening in Ireland (interestingly, often encapsulated in columns published under the standing head 'European war summary') combined with reporting about organisational, indi-vidual, financial, and political responses involving the 'exiled children' living in the United States. The trick for print journalism at the time was to try to keep the evolving stories – afar and nearby – in focus simultaneously.

The *Washington Post* and the *Chicago Tribune* mentioned censorship in their initial reports. With the restrictions on reporting, details explaining the actual events in Dublin were, by and large, filtered through governmental censors and arrived in the United States from London sources. Several newspapers, including the *New York Times*, published this striking paragraph in a dispatch originating in London, which appeared on 28 April, the fifth day of the Rising: 'Dublin is further from London today than Peking is from New York, so far as communication for the general public is concerned. No Irish newspapers have reached here since the rising, and passenger traffic has been for the most part suspended. The only information comes through official channels.'[4] At the time, of course, neither censorship nor 'official channels' affected how the press in this country treated reactions within the opinion-rich and firm-minded Irish-American communities. Viewpoints of every green or orange hue received ventilation in the nearly 2,500 daily newspapers circulating in 1916.[5] (Today there are about 1,300.)[6]

Given the chaos of combat and censorial control, Roger Casement received the preponderance of early coverage. An internationally known figure, he had embarked on a mysterious mission from Germany to Ireland that was riddled with questions. Indeed, on April 26, the *New York Times* and the *Washington Post* quoted the 'Directors of the United Irish-American Societies' that Casement 'did what [George] Washington and the American patriots did, and now, by no strange coincidence, their foe is his foe'.[7]

From the early days of the Rising until the executions ended, journalists in the United States kept using American history, especially the revolutionary and founding periods, for contextual points of comparison. By evoking the Battle of Lexington and other events readers of whatever ethnic background saw what was happening in Ireland – in Mark Twain's (attributed) rhyme scheme of history – as similar to the United States' fight for independence. As days passed, Padraig Pearse replaced Casement as Ireland's Washington, with Sir Roger then becoming a twentieth-century Benjamin Franklin – or, in the estimation of some, equivalent to the radical abolitionist John Brown. In some journalistic quarters, John Redmond could not escape resemblance to the traitorous Benedict Arnold. Fifty years after the Rising, Conor Cruise O'Brien titled his often-quoted essay 'The embers of Easter'.[8] For Americans in 1916, rather than noticing flickers of embers, they heard echoes of their own past wafting across the Atlantic.

Parallels from history constituted just one – and, frankly, a relatively minor – facet to the American coverage. Major articles provided interviews with Irish Americans or visitors from Ireland, accounts of meetings or rallies (most in sympathy with the rebels), reports of possible American involvement in the Rising, and editorial commentary on the merits (or drawbacks) of the rebellion from American points of view. For the nearly three weeks encompassing the Rising and the executions in Dublin, the domestic dimensions not only complemented but also contextualised the reportage originating in Ireland or Great Britain. Extensive in both scope and volume, the coverage took advantage of the First Amendment to express criticism of British actions or the rebel cause and to advocate some kind of resolution of the Irish question. However, this working of a free press worried Whitehall and its representatives over in Ireland. Indeed, shortly after a press censor's office was established in Dublin in early June 1916, a directive was sent to all newspapers in Ireland that included a warning 'to give careful consideration' to any reprinting of 'Extracts from American newspapers, or private letters sent you from individuals received from America'.[9] Somehow Devoy acquired a copy of the official directive and published it in a special box in *The Gaelic American* on 8 July 1916, along with an editorial comment as the headline: 'How the Irish press is gagged'.[10]

Several sound journalistic reasons kept the local angle of the Irish insurrection on the news agenda of the American press during the spring and summer of 1916. First, a considerable percentage of Irish Americans resided in cities where large, metropolitan newspapers circulated. The 'exiled children' of the Proclamation were curious, and many wanted to participate, however they could, in the post-Rising activities within their own urban communities. Second, from the first day forward, Devoy's involvement became a part of the story, particularly in New York, which was this naturalised US citizen's residence and base of operation. Third, the possibility that the upheaval in Dublin and its aftermath might metastasize and become a serious internal threat to the British Empire, as it engaged in the First World War, was a global concern of interest to the public at large, not just the American Irish who had relatives and friends in the middle of the crossfire overseas. In summary, consequential international events were taking place, which had domestic connections and implications that deserved diligent pursuit by a press protected by the Constitution's Bill of Rights.

On Saturday 29 April, Pearse surrendered. That day – and as one indicator of the story's magnitude in the United States – the *New York Times* devoted 18 articles of varying lengths and types to the Rising. Astonishingly, eight of those 18 landed on page one, with two concentrating on specific American angles. One raised the possibility of the US government taking legal action against Devoy for violating neutrality laws, while the other offered a closely observed account of the rivalry between Irish Americans favouring the rebels and those supporting Home Rule. Headlined 'One Clancy quells an Irish uprising', the article opened by focusing on opponents of the

United Irish League of America, the sponsors of the meeting. Noting that 'twenty-five Irishmen and perhaps as many Germans' showed up to take the side of Casement and Germany, the ruckus provoked police intervention:

> As for the disturbers, every one of whom when approached refused to give his name, their bravery was of the vocal and not physical kind, a fact that was quickly proved when the whole crowd was dispersed by one determined young policeman, Charles J. Clancy, of the East Fifty-first Street Station. Clancy is a type of Irishman described at the meeting as 'imported, but not hyphenated.'[11]

Like most news stories at the time, there was no by-line, but in this case the point of view of the writer is unquestionably on display. The phrase 'One Clancy' engages in Irish-American stereotyping; however, the 'little Irish policeman with the cold gray eyes' merits approval rather than the more customary put-down. He becomes a hero for maintaining order among American Irish of differing opinions about the Rising.

The next day, with headlines announcing 'Dublin rebellion is near collapse' (*Boston Globe*) and '"President's" surrender reported' (the *Washington Post*), the traditionally more comprehensive Sunday editions published quickly assigned and completed features, providing background for understanding and evaluating the Rising. For example, the lead story in the *New York Times Sunday Magazine* considers 'Ireland's sudden revolt', and it presents lengthy quotations of 'prominent Irish-Americans' that both applaud and denounce the previous week's activities across the Atlantic.

Thorough in scope, the handling privileges neither approach. At one point Jeremiah A. O'Leary, president of the American Truth Society, notes, 'I would rank this fight at Dublin with the Boston Tea Party and the battle of Lexington. But don't forget how far that shot at Lexington was heard.' Besides his historical comparison, there is a certain prescience in O'Leary's opinion about the future: 'If the sequel to the fighting at Dublin is wholesale hanging and shooting of Irishmen by English officials there is no doubt of the outcome. Under such circumstances, a war of revolution is a foregone conclusion.'[12] In another section the Home Rule viewpoint of the Irish Parliamentary Party receives full consideration, with Joseph C. Walsh, a supporter of Redmond, commenting:

> What one cannot help thinking, however, is that it can be only a matter of days before those who have entered upon these rash and unthinking courses will realize their folly. Those, including some people on this continent who ought to know better, who are guilty of having encouraged them, will soon be shown to be powerless to shield them. Those who have defied Mr. Redmond's counsels will before long be demanding Mr. Redmond's intercession.[13]

What is remarkable to any observer decades later is that such a complete story appears in the magazine section of a newspaper just one week after news of the Rising first broke.

The same day that 'Ireland's sudden revolt' appeared, other American newspapers carried their own lengthy Sunday features about the situation, reflecting the journalistic judgment that a big story with US resonance was unfolding overseas. The *Washington Post* explained 'How England deals with high treason', using Casement's case as the news hook. The final sentence even makes a prediction, one of many that would subsequently prove wrong:

> The fact that there has been no case of any one having been put to death for high treason since that time [1820], that is to say, for close upon 100 years, may be taken as an assurance that Sir Roger Casement's life will be spared, and that the British government will withhold from him the crown of political martyrdom, by treating him as what he is, namely, a poor lunatic.[14]

Padraic Colum, the Irish-born poet and writer, also contributed an essay to the *Post* that Sunday about 'the fundamental conflict between Irish nationalism and British imperialism'[15] – and he was quoted extensively in the *Sunday Magazine* of the *Times*. The *Boston Globe* published two articles for background and context. One, written on 15 April, had just arrived in the mail, and it described the pre-Rising mood with this opening sentence: 'There is an ugly feeling in Dublin.'[16] The other story is a flattering feature, 'Sir Roger Casement's astounding career', that concluded (like the article in the *Post*) with the opinion that he would not receive capital punishment. 'It is not believed that he will be executed,' the anonymous writer noted. 'Certainly if the Nationalist party members can prevent his becoming a martyr they will do so, for they realize that it would confuse the minds of many people who do not know the story of Irish politics and Home Rule.'[17]

Amid such grave, life-or-death reports about the Rising, others took a different angle. The *Times* in its comprehensive coverage of 30 April even devoted space on page two to a vignette of reaction with a Tarrytown, NY, dateline. The opening paragraph is a model of specificity – and unintended humour of the darkish variety:

> John Dalton, a 200-pound Irish porter employed by Allen Lehman, who has leased Mrs. Charles J. Gould's estate here, went crazy today from brooding over the Irish rebellion and news which he had received from relatives in that island which led him to believe they might be endangered. The Lehman family were all away from the house at the time and the servants fled from the place in terror when Dalton took off all his clothes, put on a black domino mask, and turned on all the gas in the house.[18]

Despite this absorbing tale of human interest, if not local colour, the announcement of surrender by the rebels did not reduce journalistic interest in the Rising. In fact, with the fighting over, the news focus shifted to explaining in detail what had happened and how Irish Americans were reacting to the events of Easter Week. On 1 May, exactly a week after Pearse read the proclamation establishing the Provisional Government of the Irish Republic, many American newspapers published the complete text to acquaint US readers with the stated justifications for the rebellion.

A series of hastily arranged public meetings (in New York, Philadelphia, Newark, Pittsfield, Massachusetts, and elsewhere) took place that Sunday and received coverage on Monday 1 May. Several thousand people attended the gathering in New York, and according to one account, 'not half those who wanted to attend were permitted to enter.' The *Los Angeles Times*, in an 'exclusive dispatch' from its New York bureau, stressed 'the Yankee Doodleness of the occasion' and observed that Judge John Jerome Rooney 'made a speech that would make the laziest flag in town flutter'.[19] The report on page one of the *New York Times* quoted at length every speaker, including Devoy, who avoided any mention of his principal nemesis, Woodrow Wilson, or the president's administration but 'denounced the newspapers of New York which have favored the cause of the Allies'. One measure of the comprehensiveness of the story is its lead, which makes little effort to be selective:

> The George M. Cohan Theatre was crowded to the doors last night with Irishmen, Irish women, and Germans, who had gathered there in the name of the United Irish Societies of America to voice their approval of the present uprising in Ireland, to sing the songs of Germany as well as of Ireland, to denounce John Redmond as a traitor, to cheer a reference to the sinking of the 'munition ship Lusitania,' to pass a resolution urging the recognition of the belligerency of Ireland and the linking of the Emerald Isle to the Teutonic powers as a military ally, and to compare Sir Roger Casement to George Washington.[20]

Nearby on the *Times* front page, Redmond had his say in an article that printed a cable the Irish nationalist leader sent to Walsh, his American friend and editor of the magazine *Ireland*. Redmond pointed the finger of blame for the 'whole disgraceful plot' at 'irreconcilable enemies of Home Rule' from both Ireland and the United States. In a judgment of dubious merit, Redmond went so far as to claim: 'Though the hand of Germany was in the whole thing, it was not so much sympathy for Germany as hatred of Home Rule and of us which was at the bottom of the movement. It was even more an attempt to hit us than to hit England.'[21]

With all the stories about meetings within Irish-American communities and statements directed to those communities, a newspaper reader looking back on events might conclude that the Rising and the reporting about it were having an impact on public opinion in the United States. The 'exiled children' became concerned about bellicose activities that seemed related to the First World War, and the journalism of that time tried to keep the people informed about those activities and their complexities. Some newspapers, notably the *New York Times*, were unwavering in their editorial opposition to the rebel cause. Others took a more restrained, less combative approach. For example, on 2 May, the day before the first executions, the *Washington Post* and the *Chicago Tribune* published editorials critical of the revolt that also included warnings about seeking vengeful retribution.

Arguing that the rebellion was 'poorly organized and poorly executed' and that it 'relied upon Sir Roger Casement, a harebrained if not insane agitator', the *Post* projected into the future with specific advice for Britain about responding to the revolt:

> The uprising, abortive as it proved to be, is nevertheless a reminder that the Irish question remains to be settled. Ireland must have a greater measure of home rule. If the British government has not entirely lost its balance, it will not make fierce reprisals in Ireland, but will deal tolerantly even with the ringleaders of the insurrection … History is too full of instances of brutal and excessive measures by England in dealing with Ireland, and it ought to serve as a warning against such a policy now.[22]

The *Tribune* pronounced the 'romantic futility' of the Rising but took a tack similar to the *Post* to conclude its editorial: 'There is a hint that this now subdued Irish rebellion will not be followed by many executions to give a new set of memories to the Irish. It would be a wise England that saw the Irish revolt compassionately.'[23]

Despite such expressions of caution, firing squads assembled at Kilmainham Gaol on five days between 3 May and 12 May. This period is crucial in pinpointing the crystallisation of public opinion in Irish America opposing British policies and practices in Ireland. On 4 May, for instance, the *New York Times* interviewed a cross section of the American Irish – disparate figures favouring Home Rule to republican-minded nationalists. The main headline above the article put in sizable type a recurring word and theme of the subsequent coverage:

Call Executed Men Martyrs to Cause[24]

Other newspapers had reporters collect reactions to the first executions, providing local angles to this international story with its domestic repercussions and reverberations. As more coverage of what was happening became available, responses became louder and more pointedly anti-British. By analysing the coverage sequentially, one can track the shift in public thinking: from inchoate confusion to cogent recognition. In a matter of days, Americans concluded that the rebel cause deserved at least a hearing and that Britain had definitely gone too far in reacting to the uprising.

Just as the Rising coverage of Sunday 30 April, amplified the daily news reportage with extended features and commentary, this approach repeated itself a week later – on Sunday 7 May. In the *New York Times Sunday Magazine*, Joyce Kilmer developed a particular angle that other writers and historians would subsequently mine. The title of Kilmer's article was 'Poets marched in the van of Irish revolt', and Kilmer (himself a well-known poet) mentions the executions of Padraig Pearse and Thomas MacDonagh, which took place on Wednesday, just four days earlier. Colum, only in the United States since 1914, was Kilmer's main source in sketching out the centrality of literary figures to the rebellion, and there are many examples of their work to illustrate their talents.[25]

Moreover, the *Washington Post* published what has become known in the news business as 'a tick-tock' – a comprehensive and chronological account of events that allows the public to see the sequence and sweep of related activities. In this instance, the article began on 24 April with 'a dash by members of the Sinn Féin into the general post office' and concluded on 6 May with the announcement of John MacBride's execution. Interestingly, the entry for 29 April included the surrender of 'commander-in-chief J. H. Pearce', and the one for 3 May reported that 'Patrick H. Pearse, the "provisional president," was tried by a field court-martial and executed at dawn before a firing squad in Dublin castle.'[26] As John Adams noted long ago, 'Facts are stubborn things' – and some do not become known as they should be until after they have been first reported inaccurately.

Besides the day-to-day summary, the *Post* editorially bolstered its viewpoint in opposition to excessive British retaliation: 'This hasty, ill-considered and unstatesmanlike act of political vengeance is bound to make still more bitter the relations between England and Ireland, and to be a fruitful source of trouble in the years to come.' Referring to 'Pearse and his companions' as 'martyrs and heroes' in the works of Irish history that would be written, the editorial ended with a flourish that minced no words: 'It is one of the worst blunders that even Dublin castle has ever committed, and that is saying much.'[27]

That Sunday 7 May, also provided a second straight Sabbath to organise meetings and religious services for Irish Americans to react to and to learn more about the Rising and its aftershocks. At a meeting arranged by 'the Boston Clan-na-Gael', there was much talk of 'Ireland's martyrology', the *Boston Globe* told its readers the next day.[28] The *New York Times* also covered the same gathering in its 8 May edition, quoting Devoy as telling the 800 people in attendance, 'It is only a question of transportation that prevents 200,000 trained Irishmen here from going over to help.'[29] In New York on that Sunday, a priest at All Saints Church compared Pearse to Washington, according to a two-paragraph brief ('Prayers for rebel dead') below the item focusing on Devoy.[30] Such events – and they proliferated during the days and weeks that followed – received substantial journalistic attention, deepening not only the knowledge of what had happened but also the animosity being directed at the British by the American Irish.

On 12 May, the date when the last two executions took place, several American newspapers published the identical dispatch with a London dateline. Probably distributed by the wire service Associated Press, the story appeared under this sharply phrased headline in the *Chicago Tribune*:

Ireland Seethes with Anger Over British Killings

Though the headlines varied in emphasis, the first-paragraph lead did not

> The most dangerous factor in Ireland's situation, which had been recognized since the brief rising flashed in the pan, was that the punishment of the rebels would cause a reaction of sympathy among the warm hearted and emotional people. This threatening danger appears to be fast materializing.[31]

Those 47 words summarise what was happening in many quarters of Ireland – and also vicariously within Irish-American communities. Individual points stand out and deserve underscoring: 'most dangerous factor', 'brief rising', 'punishment of the rebels', 'reaction of sympathy', 'warm hearted and emotional people', and, finally, 'threatened danger … fast materializing'. It is instructive to compare the thrust of that report to the observations of an Associated Press correspondent in a dispatch that ran in the *Washington Post* ten days earlier, on 2 May. After the journalist watched more than a hundred captured rebels being marched to Richmond Jail on 30 April, he observed: 'The soldiers escorting them were Irish regulars who had fought all through the uprising and were even more bitter against their rebellious fellow countrymen than the troops brought over from England. This feeling seems to be shared by most of the population in Dublin.'[32] Other dispatches at the time mentioned cheering for the British troops and indignation directed at those involved in the revolt.

However, as the days and coverage proceeded, the number and prolonged nature of the executions contributed to a change in public thinking on both sides of the Atlantic. The dreamers and fanatics of the early days became heroes and martyrs as the victims of the firing squads and the number of those arrested mounted. After the executions of Seán Mac Diarmada and James Connolly on 12 May – unfortunately, Connolly's demise had been erroneously reported with considerable fanfare on both 30 April and 4 May – the journalistic spotlight shifted back to Roger Casement: his incarceration, his trial (complete with representation of an American lawyer on his legal team), his appeal, and ultimately his hanging on 3 August, which was not only front-page news but also worthy of 'Extra Editions'. All of the Casement coverage, including the multiple efforts to involve congress and President Wilson in seeking a reprieve, kept the Rising at the centre of Irish-American (and, more generally, American) attention for over three months. Tellingly, from the first bulletins of Casement's arrest until he was put to death, his psychological state received amateur analysis by ink-stained examiners from afar. On page one of the *New York Times* on 25 April, the same paragraph that praised his 'brilliant career' labelled his attempt to land arms 'a madcap enterprise' that gave credence to the opinion that 'he is mentally unbalanced'.[33] Articles continued to explore doubts about Sir Roger's sanity to the point that on 4 June the *Washington Post* published a mock conversation under the headline: 'Madmen make history: Sir Roger Casement would have been immortal if he had succeeded'. One of the fictional speakers recognized close-to-home parallels in Casement's actions. 'If America had not had at all times a sufficient supply of madmen on hand,' he states, 'it would not have become America. It is all very simple.'[34]

Though relatively brief in duration and complicated by Casement's capture and manoeuvrings, the Rising and its aftermath as covered by the American press kept the Irish question, especially the causes of independence and republicanism, as a subject on the public mind in the United States. During the 19-day period (25 April–13 May), front-page stories appeared in the *New York Times* 17 days, the *Boston Globe* 16, the *Washington Post* 13, the *Chicago Tribune* and the *World* (in New York) 11. Even after Casement's hanging, major articles appeared in the public prints with remarkable regularity. After 3 August, for instance, the *New York Times Sunday Magazine* published 'The plight of Home Rule' on 6 August, 'Roger Casement, martyr' on 13 August, 'Irish girl rebel tells of Dublin fighting' (by Joyce Kilmer) on 20 August, 'American sentiment and American apathy' on 24 September, 'Irish leaders fall out over Home Rule fiasco' on 8 October, and 'Bernard Shaw's solution of Ireland's troubles' on 26 November. Serious monthly periodicals also contributed to Americans' understanding of what had happened in Ireland. The *Atlantic Monthly* in 1916 offered in-depth assessments with Henry W. Nevinson's 'Sir Roger Casement and Sinn Féin' (August), Nora Connolly's 'Easter' (November), and Henry W. Massingham's 'Ireland, 1916 – and beyond' (December).

Books, too, appeared before 1916 came to an end. The US edition of *The Insurrection in Ireland* by James Stephens came out as did Thomas MacDonagh's critical study, *Literature in Ireland*. The New York publisher Devin-Adair brought out a 427-page book, *The Irish Rebellion of 1916 and Its Martyrs: Erin's Tragic Easter*.[35] The work of eight authors and edited by Maurice Joy, this volume presents historical background, the report of the Royal Commission, and profiles of the principal participants with an audience beyond Ireland very much in mind. Similar to what we now know as an instant book about a contemporary event, *The Irish Rebellion of 1916 and Its Martyrs* reflects the thinking that in certain American quarters the Rising and everything it represented deserved more lasting attention than the treatment in newspapers or other periodicals. A political situation of continuing significance could be taking shape, both in Ireland and in the United States, and it warranted comprehensive examination. To show this greater depth of interest, the 30 November edition of *The Dial* included a review essay ('Ireland, 1916') by noted critic Van Wyck Brooks in which he evaluated five books about the Rising and other Irish political or literary subjects.[36]

As the press censor in Dublin acknowledged in early June with his formal directive, Americans were being fully and freely informed about Ireland and what was happening there in 1916 by many different print sources. The extensive press coverage provided Americans with a running account of what was happening in Ireland and, just as importantly, with reportage of the US response to the Rising, the executions, and the more encompassing Irish question. For many readers, a more refined understanding and a spirit of sympathy resulted. In *Public Opinion*, published in 1922 and one of the first intellectually rigorous inquiries of journalism, Walter Lippmann observed:

> Popular history is a happy hunting ground of time confusions. To the average Englishman, for example, the behavior of Cromwell, the corruption of the Act of Union, the Famine of 1847 are wrongs suffered by people long dead and done by actors long dead with whom no living person, Irish or English, has any real connection. But in the mind of a patriotic Irishman these same events are almost contemporary. His memory is like one of those historical paintings, where Virgil and Dante sit side by side conversing.[37]

Here and throughout his book, Lippmann explains that journalistic consequences can be unpredictably variable and that people need to be discriminating in assessing the welter of information to which they are exposed to and that they consume. Near the end of *Public Opinion*, he formulates a distinction of wider relevance but pertinent to considering the coverage of 1916:

The hypothesis, which seems to me the most fertile, is that news and truth are not the same thing, and must be clearly distinguished. The function of news is to signalize an event, the function of truth is to bring to light the hidden facts, to set them into relation with each other, and make a picture of reality on which men can act.[38]

The bifocal coverage from Easter Week onwards engaged the citizenry's interest and provoked more sustained consideration of the broader struggle for Irish independence. Journalistic challenges – lack of access to events, incorrect information, transmission difficulties, governmental censorship, and all the rest – presented themselves on a daily basis, particularly in late April and early May; however, a reliable, fact-based depiction of a complex situation emerged as time passed and more information became known. Incrementally, day-by-day, even story-by-story, American journalism brought into sharper focus a picture of reality on which men and women could act in contributing to the shaping of modern Ireland.

# CHAPTER NINETEEN

# TIMELY AND SUBSTANTIAL RELIEF
## NEW YORK'S CARDINAL JOHN FARLEY AND THE 1916 EASTER RISING

## *Kate Feighery*

Despite the American Catholic church's decidedly mixed reaction to the Easter Rising, Irish Americans across New York City rallied in overwhelming support of the Irish bid to establish a republic. Cardinal John Farley, head of the New York Catholic church, reacted particularly cautiously, as expected given his traditional hesitance to weigh in on politics and the American position as a neutral nation in the ongoing European conflict. As it was clear that the Rising could not have taken place without Irish-American support, Farley was put in the delicate situation of balancing the feelings of his parishioners against the official stand of the Catholic church, with its precarious position in the American political and social spheres. A lack of support for the cause of Irish freedom risked alienating a large portion of his flock; however, the church had strived for a position of respectability in American society, which was threatened by charges of anti-Americanism from a mainstream society sympathetic to Britain. Farley in particular had worked hard to prove to the American populace that New York's Catholics had a strong loyalty to the United States, and had given up their ties to their homelands.

Farley toed the official line of the American church by focusing his personal and parochial response on relief for those suffering in Ireland without involving himself or his church in any actions that could be construed as support for the rebellion. Ultimately, Cardinal John Farley left a complicated legacy in respect to his reaction to the Rising and its aftermath by carefully reconciling his own heritage and the sentiments of his flock with his larger goal of integrating the New York Catholic church fully into American culture.

John Farley was Irish-born, a native of Newtown Hamilton, Co. Armagh.[1] He emigrated to New York in 1864, where he enrolled in the seminary at St John's, Fordham.[2] He was later sent to the North American College in Rome, where he was ordained in 1870.[3] From his early years in the priesthood, Farley had a reputation as an extremely careful man, once described as a 'well-intentioned prelate whose ambition and lack of moral fibre would make him an uncertain ally in a crisis'.[4] His two most notable traits were a 'love of peace and an almost excessive caution'.[5] Even after his appointment as archbishop of New York in 1902, a position that centred him in a place of power, he actively avoided city and national politics, to the point that he was known to have never voted.[6] Farley maintained close ties with friends and family in Ireland throughout his life, and connected his Irish heritage to his Catholic faith. In an oft-given St Patrick's Day speech, he acknowledged the debt owed to Ireland for the spread of Catholicism:

> For three hundred years Ireland struggled with the power of England for independence … How faithfully she clung to that heritage of faith when all else was lost … The robbers of her independence would despoil her of her faith. Everything that the cruelty of wicked men could invent was tried, to make her children forswear the religion of their fathers, the faith of Saint Patrick. They burned her Churches, overthrew her monasteries and covered the land … But did Ireland prove false to her God? Never. You yourselves, Irish Catholics and your children, are here to-day the living witnesses to this imparalled resistance … Hitherto this perseverance of the Irish nation has resulted in the spread of the faith over continents where it might never been planned or have vanquished and died as it has in many a land.[7]

However, Farley was also extremely devoted to his adopted country, and it was remembered that 'to America and the American constitution … he was unflinchingly loyal'.[8] As the head of a diocese with a large Irish population, he constantly weighted his loyalty to his adopted country over his home, an allegiance seen most clearly after the events of 1916.

It is clear that during the first decade of the twentieth century, the majority of Irish-American Catholics supported John Redmond's Home Rule movement. The American church hierarchy worried that some radical Irish groups 'held little regard for the interests of the Church',[9] but some, like Cardinal Farley, actively supported the Home Rule movement. Despite his otherwise reticent nature when it came to politics, Farley often 'expressed the hope that Ireland will have home rule in his lifetime'.[10] After his last visit to Ireland in 1912, he told a meeting of the New York Gaelic Society, 'I shall never set foot in Ireland again until our native country has home rule.'[11] Farley believed it offered the best path forward,[12] assured by friends in Ireland that their fellow citizens believed the bill 'marks a milestone in the progress of our nation and ensures for us recognition by the other nations of the earth'.[13] Redmond believed that Farley's support, and with it that of the larger church, was vital, and encouraged him as a 'countrym[a]n in America ... anxious to see peace and liberty given to Ireland' to 'rally to our assistance at what is, perhaps, the most crucial movement in the fortunes of Ireland during the last half-century'.[14] Farley continued to support Home Rule until his death in 1918.[15] This would place him in the minority, as sentiments changed significantly in the United States beginning in 1914 but most especially after the 1916 executions.

The previous chapter in this volume has demonstrated how feelings about the Rising in Ireland and the United States in the immediate days following, were mixed, with most believing it to be a setback for Irish freedom.[16] The church hierarchy in both Ireland and the United States was initially firmly against the Rising[17] and New York's diocesan newspaper, *The Catholic News*, called the events of Easter Week a 'misguided and unfortunate affair'.[18] With the American government firmly opposed to the Rising[19] many in the Irish-American Catholic community feared that the actions would damage the reputations of Catholics.[20] Some even went so far as to issue public pledges of loyalty to President Wilson and the American position.[21]

Cardinal James Gibbons of Baltimore as the head of the American Catholic church was disparaging of those who supported the Rising and Farley in New York openly spoke out about his disapproval of the role the American nationalist group Friends of Irish Freedom (FOIF) had in encouraging rebellion.[22] After the FOIF was founded in March 1916[23] it attempted to sway Farley's support, writing 'We [are] an organization of loyal American citizens, who seek to aid Ireland ... to win her centuries-long struggle for the divine rights of "life, liberty and the pursuit of happiness."'[24] Despite these comparisons with the American struggle for freedom from Britain, Farley was careful to distance himself from the group. When his office received letters complaining about the group, Farley's secretary responded, 'He [Farley] ... has never given his approval to this society. He does not approve of it, and thinks that to encourage it would simply be fomenting rebellion in Ireland.'[25]

It was only after the executions of the Irish rebel leaders by the British that public opinion started to change, both in Ireland and in the United States[26] and by its 6 May issue *The Catholic News* was describing the rising as 'the logical outcome of England's misgovernment and trickery of Ireland'.[27] It went on:

> England denies Ireland justice, and when patriotic Irishmen seek to obtain their rights in the only way that has been effective the world over, England goes back to her brutal methods ... England by this atrocious crime has made it impossible for genuine Irishmen to regard her as anything but the enemy of their race, bent, it would seem, on depopulating Ireland and decimating a warm-hearted and generous people that have suffered persecution at her hands for seven centuries.[28]

Although Cardinal Gibbons encouraged his fellow prelates to remain neutral, in case support could be interpreted as anti-American,[29] he recognised that public opinion was changing rapidly and warned the British ambassador of the danger of 'manufacturing martyrs' to the Irish cause.[30] By this point, however, it was too late, and the tide of public opinion had turned.[31] A meeting of the United Irish Societies and Clan na Gael on 30 April included 'resolutions advocating American opposition to British aggression and a unified push for Irish independence'.[32] By Sunday 7 May 1916, priests were offering prayers for the repose of the souls of the executed in Catholic churches throughout New York City, and the following Sunday 14 May, saw a mass protest against the executions at Carnegie Hall, which attracted over 8,000 people, including two diocesan priests who spoke at the event.[33] On 30 May, Memorial Day, the Ancient Order of Hibernians organised a requiem mass at All Saints Church in Harlem for 'the repose of the souls of the fifteen Irish patriots who were put to death ... for having taken part in the recent endeavor to free Ireland from the tyranny of British rule'.[34]

To the naturally cautious Farley, support for Ireland was not a clear-cut issue. Part of his reluctance stemmed from worry that association with the more radical elements of Irish nationalism would destroy the prestige of the priesthood. As a fellow priest, writing from Ireland, told him in May 1916, 'The rising has been quashed ... and untold misery and disgrace to our country is the result ... the people are crying out indignantly against the action of their priests leading them to war. The result I greatly fear will be a deadly blow to the prestige and influence of the clergy hereafter.'[35] Farley, who had spent much of his career working to improve the reputation of Catholics in New York, feared a similar situation, especially considering the number of complaints his office received. One writer warned that 'politicians in Washington are watching' the actions of the church to ensure that Farley prevented 'any public expression which could be construed as a condemnation of President Wilson and his Administration'.[36]

Other complains were about specific actions by priests: Father Francis Duffy, at Our Saviour on Park Avenue, was flying an Irish flag at half-mast over the church 'as a protest against the unequal treatment that England metes out to Irish rebels, north and south'.[37] Farley, following the lead of Cardinal Gibbons, believed the New York Catholic church should be first and foremost loyal to the American position, first of neutrality, and then, once the United States entered the war, on the side of the Allies. Farley 'kept the Church officially neutral by refraining from any public comments, by enjoining his priests to silence, and by impartially sponsoring relief drives for the war sufferers in both camps'.[38] There was also a concern that if the United States stepped in to the war on the British side, anti-British activities could be construed as treason.[39] Therefore, Farley took every opportunity to affirm New York Catholic commitment to the United States, as he believed that 'Catholic loyalty in the present crisis will also pay us good dividends in the future.'[40] He saw charges of anti-Americanism as especially damaging considering the work the church had done to establish itself as a legitimate institution in Protestant-dominated American society.[41] When the United States finally entered the war, Farley wrote a call to arms to be read in all churches of the archdiocese:

> [W]ith loyalest hearts, and sturdiest arms place all that we have, and all that we are, at our Country's service … We will render to her what our Catholic faith, and our Catholic teaching sanctions, nay sanctifies. No demand on our American manhood or American citizenship will go unanswered, or will not find us true Americans, true children of our Church, that was never found wanting in any crisis of American history … our path of duty lies clear before us.[42]

He was also quick to refute allegations about the lack of Catholic patriotism by pointing out that:

> Every branch of the service is filled with Catholics and it is the testimony of all who are qualified to judge that their patriotism, their efficiency, their orderly and soldierly conduct are of the highest type. There is not a division, there is scarcely a regiment that has not a large percentage of Catholic troops.[43]

Also of concern to Farley was German support for the Irish cause, which he worried could be construed by anti-Catholics as American Catholic support for Germany, and, even more damaging, as anti-American. Although the United States was still technically a neutral nation, the Wilson administration was increasingly leaning towards support for the Allied cause as the war went on.[44] Germany's active support for the Rising led to dissension in New York's Irish-American community, with some remaining hesitant to appear to support the German cause,[45] while others felt more sympathetic.[46] New York's *Catholic News* played on these sympathies, comparing Germany's support to France's help during the American Revolution, telling its readers, 'We all honor France for what she did to secure independence for our country, and doubtless Irishmen will feel well disposed to Germany for her attempt to aid their rising.'[47] Contributing to these friendly feelings was the support German Americans showed for the Irish Relief Fund, which was organised in May 1916 'to relieve the families of the Irish who were killed, wounded, or taken captive during or after the Easter rising of 1916'.[48] R. Bryan Willits's chapter in this volume has provided helpful background as to how German Americans could play a role in, for example, planning the October 1916 Irish Bazaar.[49] It was reported that 'the purpose of the German societies … [was] to raise more money for the Irish bazaar to transmit to the destitute of Ireland than the Irish raise for themselves.'[50]

Cardinal Farley was aware that the association of Ireland with Germany and the active participation of German Americans in pro-Irish activities in New York City could be interpreted as anti-American, and, in fact, some Irish Americans who publicly stated support for the German cause were the targets of charges of anti-Americanism.[51] In light of President Wilson's rhetoric against 'hyphenated Americans' Farley saw the need to prove to detractors that the church was staunchly American, while not alienating one of the major ethnic groups in the archdiocese. In 1915, while the official policy of the United States was still neutrality, Farley personally donated $1,000 to the German Relief Fund,[52] and also held a collection in the churches for the same.[53] As time went on, however, Farley became more cautious about associating New York Catholics with Germany. The last straw seemed to be the Irish Bazaar, when it was ultimately 'reported that the three Roman Catholic Cardinals in the United States would have nothing to do with the bazaar if it was permitted to be used as an instrument for the furtherance of German propaganda in the United States'.[54] Farley ultimately found that the easiest way to balance his desire to stay loyal to the United States with his fear that he would estrange large portions of his flock from the church[55] was to focus his response to the Irish situation on relief for those suffering, rather than support for the rebels themselves. In this way, he was able to send much needed support to his homeland, while still maintaining the official American position, neutrality. It also allowed him to acknowledge the impact British actions were having on Ireland, while still avoiding offering a direct opinion on the situation.[56]

His biggest effort was a collection taken in all the Catholic parishes in the archdiocese of New York for the benefit of the Irish Relief Fund. Farley, along with Cardinals

Gibbons and O'Connell (Boston), served as honorary presidents of the fund.[57] The fund appealed to these prelates because the organisers 'went to great pains to portray the Fund as non-political and to stress the purely humanitarian nature of their objective'.[58] On 2 July 1916, a letter from the cardinal was read in all the churches in the archdiocese:

> The unfortunate and tragic events that have recently occurred in Ireland have brought about, with other consequences, a condition of unspeakable want and distress. The punishment which England meted out so mercilessly, by execution, imprisonment, or deportation, to hundreds, if not thousands, of fathers, husbands, and sons, has fallen with extreme severity and dire misery, on countless women and children and many of the aged of unhappy Erin. Christian charity imposes on us all, irrespective of race, but especially on those of Irish blood, the urgent duty of extending timely and substantial relief to the innocent victims of Ireland's latest affliction. We, therefore, order that a collection for the Irish relief fund be taken up at all the churches of the diocese, at all the Masses, on Sunday, July 9.[59]

The *New York Times* reported that 'the response [to the collection] was unusually generous.'[60] The collection itself ultimately raised about $18,000 for the Irish Relief Fund. Although much less than the October Bazaar's $45,000,[61] it was especially notable considering the average annual total of all Sunday collections in the archdiocese was only about $10,000.[62] The average contribution from an individual parish was about $250. While it was not required for a parish to participate, most did, with some of the largest donations, unsurprisingly, coming from heavily Irish parishes, such as All Saints in Harlem, which raised about $350.[63] German national parishes also contributed generously, raising, on average, about $140 each for the collection, with one of the largest contributions in the entire archdiocese, $500, coming from the German church of St Mary Magdalen on East 17th Street.[64]

Although the collection was Farley's largest effort, he also supported relief work in other ways. He served as patron of a memorial concert by Victor Herbert for the Irish martyrs held on 27 May, with the proceeds to go to the suffering women and children.[65] The famous Irish tenor John McCormack gave a benefit concert on 23 May, also under the patronage of Cardinal Farley, and McCormack specifically requested that the cardinal act as custodian of the funds that were raised.[66]

Farley held himself very carefully to the relief line. He was asked to step in on behalf of American-born Éamon de Valera as it was hoped 'a word from the Cardinal would mean much and would prove an incentive to the Irish Societies, the Senators and the State Department to do all they could for us'.[67] Despite the American connection, Farley hesitated to act, as he did not believe 'these sentences will be pushed after the trouble has blown over'.[68] He was hyper-vigilant that the money raised from his collection would be going purely for relief, and not to the rebels, and was worried his intervention would make people question this.[69] However, other Irish Americans did not feel Farley's hesitation, and the federal government heard from many Irish-American constituents, asking them to step in to stop the executions.[70] The American government had no real response, with President Wilson telling his secretary, 'It would be inexcusable for me to touch this … It would involve serious international embarrassment.'[71]

Despite Farley's request that his priests follow his lead and 'refrain from any criticism of England's methods in dealing with the rebellion',[72] some felt a more direct response was warranted and actively supported Irish freedom. Among the most active priests were Fr James Power (All Saints); Fr Henry Brann (St Agnes); Fr William Livingston (St Gabriel); Rev. John Dooley (Corpus Christi); Fr Patrick O'Leary (Annunciation); Fr Timothy Shanley (St Benedict the Moor); and the Carmelite Fr Peter Magennis (Our Lady of the Scapular).[73] For most of these priests the events of April 1916 were not their first engagement with the Irish cause. Many became active in the Friends of Irish Freedom (FOIF), particularly Fr Power, who was instrumental in organising the first FOIF group in Manhattan, the Inisfall Branch, which met at his parish hall.[74] This was the first of five New York City FOIF branches that used Catholic churches as meeting spaces by the end of 1916.[75] In the days following the Rising, these priests turned out for a nationalist meeting held on 6 May 1916,[76] and on the following day, Sunday 7 May, Fr Power, from the pulpit in All Saints, 'compared Pearse with Washington and said the only difference between the two patriots was that one succeeded while the other failed'.[77]

As the United States officially entered the war in Europe, and concerns over foreigners grew, Cardinal Farley continued to receive complaints about the activities of some of his priests who continued to support Ireland's quest for freedom from the British Empire. From Corpus Christi Church in Morningside Heights, a parishioner wrote in to complain that

> Father [John] Dooley would better attend to the duties of his parish, and the proper office of a real Catholic Priest, instead of giving expression at every opportunity to his political hatreds and animosities, not only towards everything 'British,' but also towards people who do not agree with his flamboyant and unpriestly conduct.[78]

Farley continued to be fearful that charges of anti-Americanism would be raised against Catholics. When a letter addressed the actions of Fr Power at All Saints in Harlem, who, it was said, encouraged portraits of President Wilson in the school to be turned to face the wall, and that distributed literature about Sinn Féin at the church doors after Sunday masses, Farley warned him, 'this is no time to permit in or about the Church, or any institution controlled by it, anything to which the United States Government could take exception.'[79] Corresponding with Fr Dooley, whose church was not flying an American flag, Farley cautioned, 'I deduce that you have permitted your private opinions regarding England to become known in utterances either in the pulpit or in some other way in Church gatherings. I call your attention to the fact that this is a very imprudent course to follow in the present dangerous state of public excitement.'[80] The original letter informing the cardinal of this situation included a threat: 'Even if the pastor Rev. J. H. Dooley hates England he must remember that this is in America. Let the flag fly. From Corpus Christi Church, the only church in the city without one. If something isn't done about this matter soon, we will have to notify the United States Government about it.'[81]

Despite his own Irish heritage, Farley's ultimate goal, until his death in 1918, was to protect his church. This essentially boiled down to avoiding the Irish question entirely and staunchly supporting a pro-American perspective, a position echoed two years later in a letter to prominent businessman Festus Wade: 'If we touch [the Irish question] we shall only create additional trouble ... This is not a religious question; to make it a religious issue seems to be a political expedient ... It has been the aim of the Church in this country to keep out of politics.'[82] To Farley, protecting the New York Catholic church meant proving to its detractors that it was a resoundingly American institution, and that, despite the large number of immigrants among his flock, they would ultimately do what was best for their adopted country.

# CHAPTER TWENTY

# THE AMERICAN CATHOLIC PRESS AND THE EASTER RISING

## Thomas J. Rowland

From the onset of European hostilities in the summer of 1914, the maintenance of American neutrality had proven a serious challenge to the American Catholic press. This was particularly the case in the many papers and periodicals with a distinctive Irish-American flavour. While ethnic, cultural, and religious prejudices vied for the sympathies of all Americans, the American Catholic press steadfastly clung to the government's position of unequivocal neutrality and admonished the Wilson administration for any departure from that stance. The outbreak and subsequent suppression of the Easter Rising in Ireland in the spring of 1916, however, tested the mettle and capacity of Irish-American Catholics to adhere to established policy.

Representing scores of diocesan news organs, the American Catholic press had emerged at the turn of the century as both a reflector and moulder of its community's attitudes, aspirations, and biases. Circulation had risen dramatically in the years leading up to the First World War. Because these papers reported on a wide range of political, social, and religious events, they provided a telling and panoramic view of the divisive issues affecting the community.[1] No issues were more turbulent, yet more germane, to the Irish-American community than the progress of Irish Home Rule and the maintenance of American neutrality.

For a variety of reasons, Irish America rallied strongly in defence of the administration's declaration of neutrality in 1914. Ardent supporters of Irish nationalism, particularly Clan na Gael, though supportive of German war aims as a means of liberating Ireland, laboured passionately to hold the government accountable to its pledge. They doubled their efforts in times when they perceived that American favour was veering towards the Allies. Although others were outspoken in their preference for the Allies, the vast majority of Irish Americans cooled their ardour for Irish nationalism and insisted on neutrality as a way of taming the potentially inflammatory ethnic allegiances of American Catholicism. Such restraint also had the benefit of trumpeting Catholic patriotism and loyalty at the same time. The parameters of this struggle remained relatively fixed through numerous crises and permutations in public opinion leading up to April 1916. Then, the issues of Irish liberation and American neutrality emerged in such a convulsive way as to undermine the fragile balance that had been respected by most in the Irish-American community. The Easter Rising served as both the catharsis and catalyst in reshaping the definition of the status quo.[2]

As news of the rebellion seeped into the United States, it was initially greeted with general disbelief and dismay by the Irish-American Catholic community. In the days before reports of Sir John Maxwell's handiwork in crushing the Rising were revealed, the Irish-American community was incredulous that such a foolhardy enterprise had taken place. John D. Crimmins, former president of the American Irish Historical Society, glibly proclaimed that 'Sir Roger is crazy.' P. T. Barry, Chicago's representative of Redmond's Nationalist Party, sombrely predicted that the rebellion 'is bound to fail'. An emergency session of the New York Council of the United Irish League of America resolved that the insurrection was no more than an 'insane attempt at rebellion', and expressed continued support for Redmond's Home Rule movement.

Other prominent Irish Americans lamented the outbreak of rebellion, not only because it was ludicrous, but because it jeopardised the cause of Home Rule which Redmond and John Dillon were diligently pressing forward in the British parliament. Francis Hackett of the *New Republic* was one of the many Irish Americans disenchanted with the uprising. Claiming that there was 'no chance of material victory', Hackett judged the rebellion as not only imprudent but 'wild and futile' as well. Joseph C. Walsh, editor of *Ireland*, deplored the uprising as a repudiation of the vast sentiments of the Irish people, particularly their civil and religious leaders.[3]

Such moderate and conservative sentiments were repeated in the Catholic press by Irish-American editors. William A. McKearney of the *Catholic Universe* in Cleveland endorsed *Life* magazine's version of the rebellion as a 'crazy outbreak, timed to the hour of England's peril, dangerous, hapless, and pitiable', and added his own opinion that, while some may call the victims 'martyrs or fools … we must acknowledge that their activities have injured rather than helped the cause of a free Ireland'.[4] William A. Hughes in Detroit declared that the 'affair was clumsily managed, started at an inopportune hour and encouraged by men who kept well without the sniper's bullets'. Blaming the Rising on 'over-zealous youths and men, harangued by curb stone agitators', he feared that it would be perceived as 'malice and treason'.[5] One observer bemoaned the Rising as 'all other judicious friends of Ireland have already done'. He expressed a prevailing fear in Irish-American circles that the rash actions of 'a handful of disloyal Irishmen in Dublin' would offset 'the thousands of patriotic Irish soldiers who are doing and dying in the ranks of the Allies'.[6]

Mainstream Irish-American Catholic disenchantment was not reserved entirely for those who responded to the call to arms on Easter Monday. There was a large measure of disgust and contempt left over for those Irish Americans perceived as having encouraged the rebellion. For its duplicity and lacklustre support of the rebellion, the German government was also heavily criticised. Leading the wave of criticism of the role ardent Irish Americans played in fomenting the crisis in Ireland was the dean of the American Catholic prelature, Cardinal James Gibbons. Upon hearing of the outbreak of fighting, Gibbons reportedly confided to the British ambassador, Sir Cecil Spring-Rice, that 'all respectable Irish men condemned [the] revolt in unqualified terms', but feared that if the British did not manage the aftershocks of rebellion carefully, there would be the 'danger of "manufacturing martyrs" for American use'.[7] As Kate Feighery's chapter in this volume showed, in New York Cardinal John Farley immediately condemned the role the Friends of Irish Freedom had played in stirring up rebellious action in Ireland, indicating that he had disapproved of this society from its inception.[8]

While most of the Catholic editors supportive of Sinn Féin's programme initially appeared to offer muted sympathy for Ireland's plight, they also expressed disapproval of the rebellion itself.[9] Most Irish-American editors quickly endorsed John Redmond's indictment of those Irish Americans who encouraged young Irishmen 'into this insane and antipatriotic movement while they have remained in the safe remoteness of American cities'.[10]

From the editorials of the *Catholic Messenger* in Davenport, Iowa, came the most stinging attack upon Irish Americans who encouraged the Rising. The first reaction was that the 'ill-advised propaganda' of Clan na Gael leaders in the United States 'has resulted in the slaughter of their incredulous dupes in Ireland'.[11] When it became known that the United States government intended to investigate whether the Clan's activities were in violation of neutrality, the *Catholic Messenger* applauded this news.[12]

Fr Peter Gannon in Omaha colourfully represented many Catholic editors' feelings when he favourably compared the role of those who died in the uprising to that of the Clan na Gael.

> They certainly stand on a higher plane in public estimation than the contemptible blowhards of New York and other American cities who urged them on ... [these] fools and fakirs can be proud of their work. True Irishmen, loyal to the principle of rational liberty ... have nothing but contempt for men who urge others to enter in a campaign of armed insurrection while they themselves are careful to keep three thousand miles between them and the scene of the conflict.[13]

Thomas O'Flanagan of the Hartford diocese was equally vehement in his denunciation of certain New York clerics for their adoption of revolutionary rhetoric. Noting unanimous disapproval of the rebellion in Irish religious circles, O'Flanagan inveighed against the 'wisdom of a few New York priests' who deemed that their opinions of what was best for Ireland 'may outweigh that of the hierarchy and priesthood of Ireland'.[14]

The Germans did not escape the derision of Catholic editors either. For both their feeble support of the rebellion, which all but assured its failure, and their transparent display of opportunism, they were highly censured. Humphrey Desmond caustically employed biblical metaphor when he claimed that 'Casement was vomited up by a submarine much as the whale disgorged Jonah.' Later, he laconically observed that while the Irish were renowned for their bravery and the Germans for their efficiency, 'the recent German invasion of Ireland and the ensuing Dublin uprising are not the best proofs of either proposition.'[15]

Moderate and conservative Irish Americans also were quick to dispel any notions that Germany was Ireland's friend. P. T. Barry insisted that the Irish people were not in league with the Germans and had 'long ago cast their lot on the side of the Allies and are fighting for them'. Desmond concurred with Barry's assessment, noting that the 'only real rising that day ... were the masses of Irish who went about their usual daily work'. In Hartford, O'Flanagan railed against those who thought 'Germany cares a whole lot for Ireland.' Once Germany's purposes were achieved, 'she would fling Ireland sheer into the jaws of the British lion.'[16]

If John Devoy and others in the Clan na Gael were dismayed by the hostile reception that news of the Rising received in Irish-American and Catholic circles, they were delighted by the revulsion which greeted reports of General Maxwell's bloody dispatching of the rebel leadership. For the first time in the course of the war all segments of the Irish-American Catholic community were unified in their denunciation of British brutality. However, moderate and conservative Irish-American Catholics remained detached from the Clan's agenda, particularly the idea of supporting the Irish-German coalition. While some moderates were weaned from the Home Rule cause, there remained a good measure of support for it in many Irish-American quarters, most notably the American Catholic church. The Dublin executions revived anti-British agitation which had become somewhat muted in the months following German transgressions on the high seas. Similarly, they stimulated Clan na Gael fortunes, and the organisation intensified its efforts to assail the government's pro-Allied policies.

It is hardly surprising that the entire Irish-American community was incensed by the execution of the rebel leaders. American opinion in general reflected shock and disgust with the extent of British savagery in meting out punishment to the Irish. The *Literary Digest*'s survey of American editors pointed to near-unanimity in condemning the executions and cited the *Washington Post*'s terse verdict of British action as 'stupid and vengeful'.[17] British reprisals even horrified some of the nation's leading Anglophiles. In a letter to the *New York Evening Post*, the novelist William Dean Howells remarked, 'In giving way to her vengeance, England has roused the moral sense of mankind against her … she has left us who loved her cause in the war against despotism without another word to say for her.'[18]

British justice might not have rendered all of her American friends speechless, but it did edge popular opinion back towards adherence to strict neutrality. Having earlier believed that Americans sympathised with Britain's wartime plight in Ireland, Walter Lippmann, editor of the *New Republic*, declared, 'The Dublin executions have done more to drive Americans back to isolation than any other event since the war began.' In his frequent reports to the British Foreign Office, Spring-Rice could find little in American opinion to suggest that sentiment towards Britain was anything but hostile and contrary. The British ambassador's German counterpart, von Bernstorff, was finally able to report optimistic news to his superiors, noting that American opinion was 'more favorable owing to the influence of the Irish executions'.[19]

To a great extent, the Catholic press reflected the same ambivalence and tensions expressed in secular circles. Irish-American Catholic editors who had previously voiced support for the overthrow of British rule in Ireland by any means now brandished their pens in defence of the martyred rebels. Fr Thomas V. Shannon of Chicago's *New World* spurned England's posturing as the 'champion and defender of the liberties of smaller nations'. Pointing to the 'historic brutality' of England in South Africa, India, and

Ireland, he compared her to the proverbial leopard which 'does not change its spots'.[20] The *Catholic News* of New York concluded that England had made it 'impossible for genuine Irishmen to regard her as anything but the enemy of their race'.[21] This same paper dramatised this sentiment by describing in gory detail how the noted pacifist Francis Sheehy Skeffington was actually assisting a wounded British officer when he was arrested and murdered. The accompanying editorial contemptuously dismissed the circulating opinion that 'England isn't as brutal as in years gone by,' by retorting, 'England is the same old ruthless England.'[22] In Indiana, Joseph P. O'Mahoney not only condemned the executions, but also assailed moderate Irish Americans for their timidity in defending Ireland. Labelling some men of Irish blood as 'Tories who would have probably endorsed Benedict Arnold', he clarified that they were a 'very small element' who did not represent the views of 'any living Irish society in the nation'.[23]

It is hardly surprising that radical Irish-American editors unleashed a barrage of criticism against the British government for the bloody suppression of the Rising. However, Irish-American Catholic editors who had previously written of the Irish situation in temperate tones now swelled the chorus of condemnation. Fr Richard Tierney, SJ, of *America* concluded that the history of England and Ireland reiterated one ageless theme: 'a narrative of savagery and blood, met by intrepid patriotism and unswerving fidelity to the teachings of Jesus Christ.'[24] In Brooklyn, Fr John L. Whelan sadly reflected that since the uprising had been quickly and almost effortlessly suppressed, there had been no need for such vengeance. Characterising British policy as the 'astoundingly stupid ... work of weak men', he predicted that this action would accord Britain the 'alienation of the sympathies of many men and women all over the world'.[25]

Boston's Cardinal William O'Connell was dramatically radicalised by the British execution of Irishmen. In fact, O'Connell's disassociation from Home Rule and his subsequent endorsement of a free and completely autonomous Ireland can be traced to the executions, and he used the Boston *Pilot* to express his outrage. In a departure from its usually restrained reporting of international news, the 3 June edition printed a collection of articles from both the secular and religious press condemning British atrocities, headlined: 'England arraigned at the bar of humanity'.[26] O'Connell's venom was not reserved for the British only; his paper also assailed those 'English subsidized papers' which presented the uprising as the work of malcontents. In particular, he attacked the *Boston Transcript*, as 'so faithful to the Union Jack ... the Koran of the brahmins'.[27]

With moderate and conservative Irish-American Catholic editors turning their attention to the executions, the ranks of Irish America were massed against the British. Fr Peter Gannon observed that while the rebellion failed to garner the support of Irish

America, the 'cruel infliction of the death penalty … has exerted a feeling of horror everywhere … and there will henceforth be little sympathy for the cause of England among Irishmen in America'.[28] In Philadelphia, Edward Spillane argued that since the rebel leaders had laid down their arms 'to spare further effusion of blood', they should not have been 'butchered by court-martial process'.[29] William Hughes was equally dismayed by this 'latest British, brutish murder', and warned Britain that such action would 'rally every Irishman worthy of the name around the holy cause' for which the rebel leaders had lost their lives.[30]

Fr John Burke, CSP, of the *Catholic World*, the one Irish-American Catholic editor with decided sympathy for the Allies, delivered one of the most stinging rebukes of British policy. Britain's treatment of the rebels was 'atrocious', and her use of courts-martial to execute them was reminiscent of the draconian methods of Lord Castlereagh: 'Whenever the English Government has to deal with Ireland, it shows a pitiful, blundering sense of misunderstanding and oftentimes of injustice which shocks the world.'[31]

Irish-American enmity for Britain was exacerbated later in the summer when Casement was hanged for treason. The Catholic press, which during the summer made little mention of his trial, assailed the British for this deed. The Boston *Pilot* proclaimed that 'another martyr has been added to the long roll of the Irish patriotic dead.' Answering its own question, 'Why Do Irishmen Hate England?' the paper offered that 'once again has England answered the question and answered it in the only way she knows – by the sword.'[32] Thomas Shannon suggested that the 'execution of Sir Roger Casement was logical and stupid', adding that 'it might prove to be the sorriest day's work that England ever did.'[33] Richard Tierney, SJ, of *America*, an inveterate Anglophobe, eulogised Casement by declaring that he 'loved his ideal, and spoke devotion in love's highest terms, and sweetest tone, sacrifice'.[34] Even William Hughes, who frequently assaulted the Clan na Gael and other avid nationalists for their support of Germany, did not spare British feelings. Likening the British government to 'bull hounds', who 'lap their jowls in clean Irish blood', he presented Casement as the apotheosis of Christian martyrdom in his 'suffering the modern crucifixion on a British gibbet'.[35]

It is misleading to conclude from such vituperation over the executions that solidarity among Irish-American Catholics extended into other related issues. Ardent Irish-American nationalists and those in the Catholic press sympathetic to the liberation of Ireland applauded the setback to Home Rule caused by recent events in Ireland. However, the executions did not destroy interest in Home Rule among moderates and conservatives in the Catholic press. Fred Sharon in Iowa reflected that had England enacted Home Rule at the outset of the war, the Rising would have been averted.[36] In Texas, William Campbell noted that, despite the harsh measures undertaken by the British, Redmond's cautious course remained the 'one hope and security of a free future for poor Ireland'.[37] In Cincinnati Dr Thomas P. Hart echoed Campbell's sentiment that the quick enactment of Home Rule would be a judicious decision. Claiming that the British government 'is in a bad odor over all the world', he indicated that the establishment of Home Rule would restore her 'in the good graces of the world at large'.[38] Reflecting several Catholic editors' hopes that there might be a silver lining to the pervasive despair instilled by the uprising and deaths was Thomas O'Flanagan's observation: 'If the present European struggle does not prove to England that she needs Ireland and that both countries are to place their highest hopes in mutual friendship and good will, then she is blind indeed.'[39]

Despite widespread condemnation of British methods in quelling the uprising, mainstream Irish-American Catholics continued to shun the Clan na Gael and other ardent Irish-American nationalists. Moderate and conservative Irish-American Catholics in both secular and religious sectors remained resilient, even resolute, in their endorsement of Home Rule. Their shared distaste for British brutality with other avid nationalists was purely circumstantial and did not signal any departure from positions they held at the outbreak of the war. They continued to profess a strict neutrality with respect to war-ravaged Europe, and they adamantly refused to be pulled into a pro-German orbit.

The reaction of the American Catholic church, particularly its Irish-American leadership, to events in Ireland and Europe paralleled that of the overall community in its varying expressions of ambivalence, apathy, and division. It remains difficult to determine precisely where most rank-and-file Irish-American Catholics stood on the issues generated by the failed Dublin rebellion. Other than O'Connell's sharp denunciation of the Dublin executions, the powerful hierarchy refused to be drawn into any debate over the affair and clearly encouraged their faithful to do the same. Given the authoritarian structure of church discipline with its strong accent on absolute obedience, few priests strayed from the advice tendered by their appointed superiors. The few outspoken clerics, such as Peter Yorke of San Francisco, Timothy Dempsey of St Louis, and the small coterie of priests in the archdiocese of New York who supported the overthrow of British rule, frequently ran afoul of their local ordinaries. Though these clerics appeared to be popular with their parishioners, their voices were muted by the appeals of most clerics for moderation and restraint.[40]

Obedience to hierarchical directives remained the cornerstone of the most popular Irish-American Catholic fraternal organisation, the Knights of Columbus. Despite their distinct Irish identification, the Knights maintained a monumental silence throughout the spring and summer of 1916, eschewing commentary on Irish or European affairs in favour of local and parochial concerns.[41] That the Knights were sometimes the target of Devoy's *Gaelic American* and other Irish-American firebrands for their absolute and unquestioning loyalty to conventional forms of civil authority suggests that they were not to be counted among those fomenting rebellion in Ireland.[42]

Rather than become embroiled in the politics of the Irish question, the institutional church in the United States sought to alleviate the suffering resulting from the ill-fated Rising. Kate Feighery's chapter in this volume outlined the New York response. It is worth noting that in San Francisco, Archbishop Edward J. Hanna actually presided over meetings of the Irish Relief Crusade, which raised over $10,000 in its first week's effort.[43] In other dioceses fairs and bazaars contributed substantially to the growing amounts of cash available for relief distribution.[44] By the end of July 1916, church-sponsored fundraising efforts had netted over $100,000 for Irish relief.[45]

The church hierarchy also refused to issue any political opinions or to forge any partisan attachments over the Irish issue in the spring and summer of 1916. Clearly, partisan expressions would have undermined the neutrality it had long endeavoured to maintain. Moreover, such favouritism might smack of foreign allegiance at a time of heightened anxiety over the issue of hyphenated Americanism. Rather than explicitly condemn the cause of Ireland's misery, or confront the conflicting forces involved, the American Catholic church opted to palliate the suffering caused by conflict and change. In the case of the Irish question, the hierarchy shunned political considerations and directed church efforts to relief.[46] The church also kept these fundraising efforts strictly separate from those conducted by Irish-American societies and organisations. In particular, the church avoided any connection with the Clan na Gael or its offshoot, the Friends of Irish Freedom. Evidently the institutional church's relief efforts received far greater support among Irish-American Catholics than those of secular or fraternal organisations. In Syracuse, for instance, the Friends of Irish Freedom managed to raise a mere $600 while Bishop John Grimes produced $10,000 with minimal effort on his part.[47]

The American Catholic press, much of which was controlled by Irish Americans, reflected the same ambivalence and political diversity over the Irish issue in the summer of 1916. Certain papers such as the *Freeman's Journal*, *Indiana Catholic*, and *The Monitor* hardly needed the provocation of the executions to adopt strident attitudes towards the violent overthrow of British rule in Ireland. These papers had, from the outbreak of the war in 1914, made their pro-German and anti-British feelings patently clear. Only the Boston *Pilot* seemed to accept a more aggressive nationalism as a result of the British suppression of the Irish rebellion.[48] In the months following the Rising until the United States' entry into war, the majority of the American Catholic press continued to toe the hierarchical line by adhering to a strict and impartial attitude towards the Irish issue and how it affected sympathies towards the European belligerents.[49]

Britain's long-standing political and religious oppression of Ireland, highlighted by the executions, made it nearly impossible for Irish-American Catholic editors to avoid criticising her in the summer of 1916. All the same, an aversion to the Germans and Irish-American agitators tended to mute this criticism and reinforce neutral attitudes. Most Irish-American Catholic editors viewed the executions that summer as a political blunder on England's part that made it difficult to accept her avowed altruism in the First World War.[50] Others, like Humphrey Desmond, though outraged by British brutality, continued to hold the Clan na Gael and Sinn Féin factions primarily responsible for the rebellion and the deprivation which followed.[51] This ambivalence over the Irish issue was best demonstrated in William Hughes's exasperated claim, that while the 'moral indignation of the world' might have been aroused by British barbarism, 'we say this not by way of venting anti-British speen [sic], but as a true friend of England who would save her from herself'.[52]

No other event during the extended period of American neutrality raised the anxiety levels of Irish America as Easter Week 1916 and its bloody suppression by the British. Given the nature of the provocation, and the overall negative reaction to it by the American public, Irish-American Catholics might well have indulged in relentless attacks on the British. There were, however, no substantive attitudinal shifts in the Irish question once the initial expressions of shock and outrage were exhausted. As a distinct minority in the Irish-American community, ardent nationalists were no more successful in winning converts to their position than at any other time during the war. This stark reality was not lost on Devoy, who was forced to draw credit from the sale of his own brother's estate in order to provide a legal defence for Casement.[53]

Devoy was also well aware that the nationalist cause languished for want of support by the American Catholic church, and he regretted that the hierarchy had not been won over to his standard. While acknowledging that Cardinal O'Connell was the first to adopt the nationalist position in early 1918, well after the United States' entry into the war, Devoy recalled that it was not until the Irish Convention of February 1919, that the church rallied behind the movement. Then, Devoy noted, 'Cardinal Gibbons, who had up to then opposed the advanced movement ... with twenty-eight bishops

... gave his blessing to the movement.' His frustration with Gibbons actually spilled over into his editorials in *The Gaelic American*. He once censured the cardinal for his continued friendliness towards John Redmond and for his involvement in various international movements to the exclusion of Irish liberation.[54]

The contention that the majority of Irish Americans were patently anti-British, and that they generally expressed 'hopes for a German victory' is difficult to maintain. Nor is it correct that both John Redmond's pledge to recruit Irish soldiers for the British Empire and the bloody suppression of the Rising served as death blows to the Home Rule cause in Irish America.[55] Numerous Irish-American Catholic editors continued to promote Home Rule as the only rational and peaceful alternative for ending Ireland's misery. Their views were underscored by the restraint they exercised in dealing with the British in the spring and summer of 1916. Indeed, they clearly believed Irish-American agitators in collusion with German opportunists had instigated the trouble, and that they had done so in contradiction to the wishes of Irishmen. They pinned blame for the rebellion and its bloody reprisals squarely on the shoulders of the radicals and encouraged their readers to have nothing to do with them. While remaining sympathetic to Irish issues, many Irish-American Catholic editors supported the hierarchical preoccupation with promoting Irish Americans as loyal, patriotic Americans.[56]

In the end, then, it was 'New World' concerns rather than 'Old World' memories that framed the Irish-American Catholic response to 1916. Irish-American Catholics were forced to reconcile long-standing animosity for British and Protestant rule in Ireland with the emerging geopolitical realities in their adopted homeland. It was becoming clearer that should the United States go to war, she would do so as an ally of Great Britain. Their interests as Americans and Catholics prevailed over their sincere longings for a liberated Ireland. Under the leadership of Americanists such as Gibbons, the Catholic church in the United States had long been guiding its faithful along political and social paths compatible with American norms and culture. The Catholic press in the United States was a willing and energetic ally in this cause. When Woodrow Wilson called for the support of the American people in the war against the Central Powers, he could count on the Irish-American Catholic community. Despite the fresh memory of British cruelty, William McKearney of Cleveland's *Catholic Universe* spoke for many Irish-American journalists in declaring:

> We have great allies, and we must stand or fall with them. There can be no such thing as 'hoping the United States wins, but that England loses.' People in this country do not love England. We have sound reasons for not loving her. But now we are fighting the same fight and must win.[57]

# CHAPTER TWENTY-ONE

# AN AMERICAN IN DUBLIN
## JOHN KILGALLON'S RISING

*Marion R. Casey & Ed Shevlin*

The battle for Irish independence in the spring of 1916 thrust a young man from New York, John A. Kilgallon, the son of immigrants from Co. Mayo, into the international spotlight. He was not the only foreigner to serve in the Easter Rising as a combatant,[1] but newly available sources reveal the contours of his life before and after that seminal event.[2] Well may we reflect on the motivations that found him in Ireland in that historic year, in the trust of a high profile nationalist whose rhetoric foreshadowed violence, and yet also consider him as a survivor for whom the memory of his week in Dublin's General Post Office remained indelible.

Kilgallon's father, Luke, was born in Coogue in 1860 and his mother, Nora Walsh, hailed from nearby Knock.[3] They were among the 400,000 men and women from western Ireland who left between 1881 and 1890 under threat of recurring famine, as bad weather led to crop failures, arrears in rent, and a rise in evictions.[4] A blacksmith by trade, Luke Kilgallon moved to New York in 1881, Nora followed four years later, and by 1900 the couple was settled in the seaside resort of Far Rockaway at the edge of New York City's limits.[5] There, together with their son, John Aloysius Kilgallon (b. 1891), they ran a business with seven employees, including two blacksmiths, a horse-shoer, a stableman, a bookkeeper, a cook, a waitress and laundress.[6] His household in 1910 was more modest but now included Nora's brother Stephan (whom Luke also employed as a blacksmith) and nephew Michael, with one servant girl.[7] In 1912 Nora's niece, Agnes Cosgrove, a native Irish speaker, joined the family.[8] Over time, Luke translated the blacksmith shop into a 'prosperous auto repair and gas station', 'patented a device to put tires onto rims', and invested profitably in real estate.[9] Division 5 of the Ancient Order of Hibernians as well as the St Patrick's Society of the borough of Queens counted Luke Kilgallon among their members.[10] John thus grew up in very comfortable circumstances, surrounded by an extended family with connections to the wider New York Irish community.

As Maura Anand's chapter on Padraig Pearse in this volume has so carefully explored, in February of 1914 the Irish educator visited the United States for a well-publicised speaking tour. In the past such tours had yielded great dividends for Irish causes; Pearse's immediate goal on this trip was to raise funds for his school, St Enda's. At some point, possibly when he was speaking at one of several Brooklyn venues, Luke and/or John Kilgallon crossed paths with Pearse. 'I have got another Irish-American for next term,' he wrote in July 1914. 'His name is Kilgallon and his father owns real estate at Far Rockaway. He is quite a young man and will rank as a University resident.'[11]

The enrolment of 23-year-old John Kilgallon at St Enda's is consistent with an advertisement Pearse ran in the *Irish American Weekly* on 25 April 1914, soliciting parents to set up interviews for potential applicants.[12] Tuition money from the United States would help the financially unsound institution move towards solvency while the presence of young Americans at St Enda's could broaden the school's appeal and its mission of legitimising Irish culture, language, and political aspirations. But, during his many public appearances in the United States, Pearse also anticipated more dramatic changes in Ireland in the near future. 'I cannot speak for the Irish Volunteers; I am not authorized to say when they will use their arms or where or how,' Pearse said on 1 March, at the Long Island Clan na Gael's annual Emmet commemoration at Brooklyn's Academy of Music.

> I can speak only for myself; and it is strictly a personal perception I am recording, but a perception that to me is very clear, when I say that before this generation has passed the Volunteers will draw the sword of Ireland … I do not know how nationhood is achieved except by armed men; I do not know how nationhood is guarded except by armed men.[13]

Whether or not the Kilgallons were inspired by such rhetoric is unknown. Perhaps it was simply John's desire to be a college man that found him enrolling for the autumn term at St Enda's in 1914.[14] But there was another reason.[15]

Automobiles, which were still a novelty in the United States and affordable only for wealthy customers, were the family's source of income by this time. Far Rockaway, with its large private residences, was a lucrative place to have a garage to service the needs of area chauffeurs. In the summer of 1912, John Kilgallon – then 21 – had succumbed to the temptation of a new seven-passenger vehicle in his garage and, without the permission of its owner, took it for a late night ride. Ten young people leaving the local Imperial Hotel crowded into the car for a cruise; their return journey ended in tragedy when the car struck a motor buggy on a curve, swerved at high speed, hit a stone, flipped over and landed upside down. Four were seriously injured and the rest, including Kilgallon and the Far Rockaway police chief's son, quickly left the scene. The owner of the car claimed it was grand larceny but what brought this escapade to court in January 1915 was that a young woman was paralysed from the neck down because of the accident.[16] According to the *Brooklyn Daily Eagle*, 'she was carried into the court room by her father' in order to testify in a lawsuit seeking $50,000 in damages.[17] The outcome of the proceedings was reported a week later:

> One of the largest judgments that have been awarded to a plaintiff in the Queens County Supreme Court for personal injuries in many years was returned this morning, when the jury in the case of Cecelia Welstead against John A. Kilgallon, which has been on trial before Justice Scudder, handed him a sealed verdict, giving Miss Welstead $20,000.[18]

Twenty thousand dollars in 1915 would be valued at nearly half a million dollars a century after the trial. Pearse's recruiting efforts the previous year coincided with the preliminary proceedings of this court case and, when the verdict was delivered, John A. Kilgallon was 3,000 miles away, far from the social stigma he had, no doubt, been living with since the accident.

For better or worse, John Kilgallon's destiny was now aligned with that of Padraig Pearse, a man who 'did not accept that the system pertaining in early twentieth century Ireland could be considered educative in terms of the liberal humanist tradition. Rather, it was anti-educational. There was, he argued, "no education system in Ireland" rather, "the simulacrum of an education system."'[19] By the time Kilgallon arrived, St Edna's was based at the Hermitage in Rathfarnham. There, Pearse sought to protect the minds of his pupils from the influences of a society in which 'Englishness' had become normative: 'The notion of a school as a place apart was central to his thinking and in choosing The Hermitage he purposely sought to place St. Enda's in a physically remote location. The concept of freedom as applied to curriculum and methodology [informed] his thinking.'[20]

To round matters out, Pearse placed the English language under a de facto ban at St Enda's. Desmond Ryan, a member of Kilgallon's cohort at the school, remembered:

> His method of making Irish the official language was the simple expedient of speaking it until sheer force of repetition made the new language familiar. 'Cearde?' he would ask with bewilderment the newcomer who addressed him in English, to enjoy with huge secret amusement, a few months later, that dumb new-comer flourishing with great self-assurance the vocabulary and favourite phrases of his instructor.[21]

Kilgallon thus found himself in a unique situation in which he was expected to converse in Irish to the extent that he could.[22] In addition, there was a strict schedule and a code of honour that had at its core the virtue of honesty. Regular religious services were held at St Enda's where attendance was mandatory, and the students were daily participants in drill, a contemporary substitute for physical education with a military gloss. A letter from Eugene Cronin to his aunt in New York noted that 'We are learning how to drill here, how to use a rifle and practicing skirmishing.'[23]

As a member of Pearse's Own, Kilgallon was one of 12 graduates of St Enda's or students still boarding there who formed the Rathfarnham E Company of the Irish Volunteers.[24] Fellow student Michael Cremen relates how, 'with a view towards preventing the arrest of P. H. Pearse, it was a common occurrence for some of the Volunteers, usually the students of St. Enda's, to escort him from the tramway terminus to St. Enda's.'[25] Pearse, by then recognised as a rising star by the Irish Republican Brotherhood and a gifted public speaker, was selected, as we know, to deliver the oration after an elaborate procession to Jeremiah O'Donovan Rossa's graveside in Glasnevin Cemetery in the summer of 1915.[26] It is difficult to imagine that Kilgallon would not have heard Pearse's stirring words connecting past and present patriots; there certainly were many young Volunteers like him in Pearse's entourage that day.

Whether Kilgallon's family understood the nature of events taking place in Ireland is unknown. Nora Kilgallon was relieved that her son seemed to be thriving at St Enda's; however, the financial strain brought about by their obligation to Cecelia Welstead is suggested by a letter she wrote to Pearse on 12 November 1915:

> Mr. Pearse Dear Sir:
>
> Just a note to say I received your kind letter and also your bill for which I now enclose Post Office Orders.
>
> I do hope that you will excuse the delay, it was neglect on my part. I was also pleased to see by your note that John is doing so well.[27]

'This is his last school chance,' Mrs Kilgallon concluded, indicating that his parents placed any social or political concerns on the back burner. As a woman born and raised in Ireland, she was unlikely to question a celebrity schoolmaster about developments there and how they might relate to her son, particularly when remitting tuition arrears. She may have been unaware of the practical patriotism that was an important part of Pearse's curriculum. The students 'assisted Mr. Slattery, the chemistry teacher, in making explosives' and Pearse gave Frank Burke his 'lovely long Lee-Enfield ... some months before' the Rising, which he kept at the head of his bed: 'It was, to me, a lovely weapon and perfectly new and I took great pride in keeping it well-oiled and free from rust.'[28]

As 1916 dawned in Dublin, the atmosphere grew more intense day by day. The students were issued weapons and military training was increased in frequency, which included armed route marches on Sundays.[29] Nora Kilgallon hinted of more financial difficulty when she wrote to Pearse again on 4 April 1916:

> Dear Mr. Pearse,
>     I am enclosing your PO order. I am ashamed to have delayed it so long. I hope it has not inconvenienced you in any way. We were held over for a month or six weeks from getting some money that was coming to us, Therefore I had to delay your order begging to be excused. Mr. Pearse I hope John is getting along well this time and hope he will be able to come back this year as he has done much to advance himself.

The monetary worries alluded to arose from the Welstead judgment that was still 'unsatisfied' two years later. Nevertheless, Mrs Kilgallon wanted 'to have him home now it is safe to travel'.[30] Soon after this, things took a dramatic turn in Dublin. Pearse closed the school and only the boarders remained as sentries and munitions workers after 8 April. He advised the students to 'go to confession and make [their] peace with God' before the Easter maneuvers.[31] If he indeed read Mrs Kilgallon's letter, he may have given the young American the option of returning to New York before the Rising. However, in the context of the honour code and given the camaraderie that existed between the young men, it is not surprising that Kilgallon remained in Ireland. On Holy Saturday afternoon, he took what is now a famous photograph of his comrades in 'full kit' in St Enda's quadrangle.[32]

Eamonn Bulfin picks up the next part of Kilgallon's story:

> On Easter Monday morning I received a fresh mobilisation order, signed by P.H. Pearse ... I was instructed to mobilise the Rathfarnham Company and proceed to Liberty Hall ... I started to get the Company together. The despatch riders succeeded in getting together as many as they could reach. We mobilised and paraded outside

the Church at Rathfarnham. The full strength of the Company was about thirty-five. About twenty men paraded outside the Church. These included the three officers, Mick Boland, Liam Clarke and myself. The following men were also present: the two McGinleys, the two Sweeneys, Frank Burke, Fintan Murphy, Joyce, Slattery, Kilgannon [*sic*] and Kiely ... We boarded a tram at Rathfarnham. When we arrived at the corner of Dame Street and George's Street, the tram stopped and did not go any further ... We heard shots; I think they came from the Castle.[33]

Michael Cremen remembered, 'We met no opposition and the Company reached Liberty Hall without incident. On our arrival there it was learned that Pearse and his officers had gone to the GPO. The Company then marched in a body to the GPO.'[34]

As E Company drew nearer Sackville (O'Connell) Street, they encountered a rapidly escalating situation and had to scramble to avoid the Lancers. Bulfin recalled:

About ten yards down Princes Street, there was a small window, about four feet from the ground, on the side of the Post Office. I broke the window with my rifle and incidentally broke my rifle ... We got into the sorting room, but there was no one there and the door leading into the main hall was locked. I went over to the door – I had an automatic pistol – and I blew the lock on the door and went into the main hall ... We reported to Commandant Pearse, and we were ordered to take up a position on the roof.[35]

The young men from Rathfarnham entered a scene at the GPO the like of which they had never seen before. Desmond Ryan, 2nd Lieutenant, describes the excitement of one Volunteer:

'Holy gee!' cries John A. Kilgallon in his American accent to two bewildered postal officials: 'This ain't no half-arsed revolution! This is the business. Thousands of troops and siege guns outside. The whole country is ablaze. Twenty transports are coming in when the submarines have sunk the rest of the warships. We have our own mint. Light your pipes with Treasury notes and fling all but the gold away. When we do things, we do things.'[36]

Kilgallon's high-spirited manner – full of the enthusiasm common to men his age and with a fair measure of braggadocio – no doubt contributed to the esprit de corps of E Company. His good-natured optimism may well have quelled any fears among the Volunteers as they prepared themselves for the assaults that would be launched against them. As the battle at the GPO progressed, 1st Lieutenant Eamonn Bulfin had very practical concerns on his mind:

We got no sleep on Monday night ... On Tuesday, we were still in our position on the roof. Everything was intensified ... We had our bombs on top of the Post Office, and these fireworks were shooting up in the sky. We were very nervous. We got no sleep on Tuesday night. Sometime early on Wednesday morning, I think Connolly came up to inspect us and we were relieved then on Wednesday evening.[37]

On the GPO rooftop on Tuesday night, Ryan noted conditions:

General preparations to resist siege and, if need be – make a last stand. Rain falls and drenches us to the skins. We get waterproofs. News of Pearse from the gent. in the fur coat (the Yank): 'He's in good form.' No sleep. Hunger a past and dead sensation. Night.[38]

The 'Yank', of course, was John Kilgallon who was apparently being used 'as a discreet messenger by Padraig Pearse, while his absences were masquerading as escapades'.[39]

Lt Bulfin would later describe Kilgallon as the week of fighting drew to a close:

The first gun fire was either Thursday night or Friday. I think there was one gun hidden up beyond the Post Office, at the Y.M.C.A. ... We were informed that the floor above us was made of ferro concrete and that there was absolutely no danger of the floor coming down. I think it must have been Friday. One of the pictures that stands out in my mind is seeing Kilgannon [sic] running round on the roof trying to stop fires. At first, the hoses were working perfectly but, after a while, apparently the water was cut off or the mains failed. There was no water at all.[40]

These uncontrollable conditions factored into the decision to leave the GPO that was taken by the leadership of the Irish forces on Friday. Crossing Henry Street into Henry Place and Moore Lane, the St Enda's contingent went to work:

Myself, Desmond Ryan, Kilgannon [sic] and all of the St. Enda's boys proceeded to break the divisions between the houses for about half the length of the street. The walls were quite thin, and there was no bother breaking them. We reached as far as Price's or O'Hanlon's which was a fish shop. I remember the smells there. We spent Friday night barricading all the houses that we occupied by throwing down all the furniture from the rooms – clearing all the rooms – down the stairways into the bottom halls, blocking up the doorways. One shell hit a house which we evacuated, down at the lower part of Moore Street, and flattened it out absolutely. It went down like a house of cards. We had to evacuate the civilians from the houses, of course – under great pressure too. Some were actually trying to get across the street. We did not get as far as the junction at Sackville Place. We got up quite near the barricade ... as far as I remember. Nothing happened on Saturday until we heard rumors of surrender.[41]

On Saturday afternoon they laid down their arms between the Gresham Hotel and the Parnell Monument on O'Connell Street. They were herded together onto a patch of grass at the Rotunda Gardens and on Sunday morning were marched off to Richmond Barracks.[42]

With the situation in Dublin chaotic, the lack of reliable reporting led to wild speculation as to the disposition of the Irish forces involved in the fighting. In New York, Kilgallon's parents feared that he had been killed in the fighting; according to a story in the *Brooklyn Daily Eagle*, his last letter to them dated 16 April arrived on 29 April and 'predicted that trouble was imminent.' He

> cautioned them not to be alarmed, no matter what they heard, as he would be all right. Since then no word has come, and although Mr. Kilgallon has cabled to friends in Dublin, he has received no reply, nor has the State Department received any reply from Ambassador Page to its inquiry as to Kilgallon's whereabouts. That Pearse was attached to Kilgallon is evidenced by a letter he wrote to Mrs. Kilgallon dated Rathfarnham, March 16, 1915. In it he said: 'John is working very satisfactorily and has made good progress in the reading and writing of French and Spanish, as well as in English literature, commercial arithmetic, some Irish and some law. I ought to add that he is very popular among masters and boys and that he makes himself agreeable in every way.'[43]

The writer and diplomat Shane Leslie was reached for a comment by the *Eagle*:

> It is six years ago that Pearse told me that he one day intended to lead the boys of St. Enda's School into rebellion. I can only look back on the school with an agony of grief. I can see the kilted boys sporting on the grounds, drawn from Irish families all over the world – Pearse instilling the old laws of chivalry, kindness to animals and fervent idealism into the boys in the purest of Irish.[44]

Only a minority of *Brooklyn Daily Eagle* readers were likely to know who Pearse was, while others would be able to connect the name Kilgallon with the record court settlement in 1915 as both the *New York Times* and *New York Tribune* did.[45] Further coverage in the *Eagle* on 24 May, despite inaccuracies, indicated that the young man was in custody, rather than dead.

> It is alleged by British authorities that John J. Kilgallon [*sic*] of Far Rockaway, NY, a 17-year-old [*sic*] student at St. Enda's College, Dublin, who was arrested on the day that the revolution started [*sic*], was caught with others in the act of bearing arms during the revolt. The time of Kilgallon's trial, and the exact charges were not revealed. He is now a prisoner at a detention camp in Stafford, England. The first known of Kilgallon's case was on May 10, when his parents, who are at Far Rockaway made

inquiries. Since then the American Embassy has been very active trying to get at the facts. According to friends of Kilgallon, he had no part in the revolt [sic] but was one of a party of St. Enda's Cadets which was sent out on Easter Monday for a practice march [sic] which ended at Liberty Hall, the fighting started about the time the boys reached there.[46]

Other American newspapers reported that the cadets 'were lured into Liberty Hall, unaware of the coming trouble, and ... unable to get away from the revolutionists' or were 'kept in ignorance of the purpose for which they were being trained' at St Enda's. Even though the *Christian Science Monitor* acknowledged in June that Kilgallon fully knew 'about the plans', as late as August his friends were still asserting 'that Pearse's influence over the boys under his tutelage led many of them to join the rebels'.[47]

The backstory to this hapless teenage non-combatant interpretation is the diplomatic negotiations underway on behalf of a number of American citizens arrested for participation in the Rising. The State Department cabled the US Consul in Dublin about Kilgallon on 5 May.[48] News of Diarmuid Lynch's reprieve from execution on 22 May was coupled with that of Kilgallon's internment, spurring Luke Kilgallon to interest Senator James A. O'Gorman in John's situation in early June to keep up the pressure for his release, especially since he had been moved from Dublin to Stafford.[49] The elder Kilgallon also wrote to the US ambassador to Great Britain, Walter Hines Page, to say that John had sent a letter to his parents before the Rising in which he indicated 'his anxiety to return to the United States'. Page thought this might be helpful information to disprove the charges against him, but nothing came of it.[50] Kilgallon became one of the 1,800 men rounded up in the aftermath of the rebellion who were interned in Frongoch, Wales, for the duration of the war under the Defence of the Realm Act.[51]

Late that year the Kilgallons received word that their son would be released, followed by an unexpected but no doubt very welcome Christmas present in the form of a poem by him which they shared with *Brooklyn Daily Eagle* readers:

### John Kilgallon Free
Under a spreading chestnut tree
The Village Blacksmith Stands;
The smith a mighty man is he,
With strong and sinewy hands.

Yet worried Luke Kilgallon felt,
And mourned since Easter Day;

His son a fine uprising Celt,
Was far from Rockaway.

For John had been at school with Pearse
That Dublin patriot grim;
And, when Pearse led his outbreak fierce,
The Lion seized on him.

Since then, poor John, locked up in Wales,
And even wails suppressed,
Had shared the fare of British jails –
Not quite a merry jest.

'A Merry Christmas, I am free,'
Flashed 'neath the ocean-foam-
The smith, a jolly man is he,
His John is coming home.[52]

When Luke Kilgallon heard of his son's release, he sent a letter to the American ambassador to express the gratitude of Nora and himself. Page replied,

> I have received the letter which you were so good as to address to me on the 12th ultimo, relative to the release from detention of your son, and I assure you that I am very pleased that he has finally been set at liberty. I understand that your son is still in Dublin, where I have sent him the money which you entrusted to the Consul General and self on his behalf. I venture to suggest that it might be well if he used a portion of this to pay his return passage to the United States as I cannot but feel that after his experience of last year he would be better off with you and his mother than in Ireland, where martial law is still in force.[53]

The odyssey of young John Kilgallon – five foot ten with fair hair and blue eyes – seemed to be drawing to a close. On 4 January 1917, Britain initiated deportation proceedings and the American Embassy in London issued him an emergency passport on 20 February.[54] Meanwhile, on 19 February the local Brooklyn paper published a long-delayed letter from him that had been smuggled out of Frongoch by Anita Bulfin, the sister of his best friend at St Enda's, and posted from Buenos Aires to his father, Luke. In it we get a glimpse of the fortitude of the Irish prisoners:

> I suppose you have been wondering why I have not written in such a long time and now that I have the opportunity I will tell you. The military wanted to take some of our fellows who were liable for military service, but when they called our names

and numbers we refused to answer. To punish us we were isolated and denied all privileges such as receiving parcels, writing letters, seeing newspapers, using tobacco, or having a canteen to buy extra food.

The authorities said that they would release some of us if we would sign a form promising not to take arms against His Majesty's forces and give bonds to that effect. You know there are none of us here who could do that without betraying the cause we fought for, so I suppose we will have to stay. But it is worth it after all for if we signed these forms they would say that they were justified in shooting our leaders as we were only dupes who did not know what we were fighting for. But they will never get us to do that, if they keep us here until we rot.

It would be well if you wrote the Ambassador [Page] asking him to visit me here and to look into the condition of the camp as he has permission to do so from the British Government. I wrote him some time ago but never got a reply, so I don't think that he is working as he lets on to be for American citizens. He certainly appears to be more interested in English affairs than affairs of the United States.

You asked me what I do in camp – well I am or was a hut leader up to the time of this last row, following which all the hut leaders except me, were court martialed and are now awaiting sentence. The charge was refusing to answer to name or number, influencing the men to do likewise and refusing to identify our fellow prisoners for the military or in other words to act the spy. They picked out the wrong fellow for me. He was discharged and they are looking for me yet.

Well, keep up your heart and if you don't hear from me for some time, you may rest assured that I am in the best of health and spirits. Don't worry about me in any circumstances.[55]

He arrived back in the United States on 17 April via the *St Paul* from Liverpool.[56]

What then? Less than two months later, describing himself as 'gentleman of leisure', Kilgallon registered for the draft. On his application, under previous military experience, he entered three years as a captain in the infantry of the Irish Republican Army.[57] He was posted to Pensacola and Key West in Florida as an aviation machinist for the navy, serving from December 1917 to December 1918,[58] and was honoured for this service by Far Rockaway's Maris Stella Council of the Knights of Columbus.[59] He tried his hand at selling stocks and bonds for a while but mainly managed the family's automobile garage at 1016 Beach 19th Street in Far Rockaway with the help of his cousin, Agnes Cosgrove.[60] He became a trustee of the Rockaway Post of the Catholic War Veterans in 1936,[61] and in the summer of 1941 applied to the Irish government for a 1916 medal. 'Surely, some of those who fought in the G.P.O. in 1916 must still remember me,' Kilgallon was moved to write when it had not arrived by 1950.[62]

Some of the men who were with him in Stafford and Frongoch did stay in touch. Kilgallon called to see Seán Nunan at the Consulate General offices in New York in 1947.[63] Major General Joseph Sweeney, another St Enda's man who was on the roof of the GPO, stayed with him in Far Rockaway in the summers of 1960 and 1968.[64] They, as well as Frank Burke, James Ryan, who had been the chief medical officer in the GPO, and John ('Jack') Plunkett, Joseph Plunkett's brother, all supported him when, on the advice of friends in New York, he applied for a Military Service Pension on 12 May 1952.[65] He was 61 at the time. Sweeney remembered that Kilgallon 'took part in the Whit Sunday [23 May 1915] Volunteer excursion to Limerick where we were attacked by British organized sympathizers'. According to Plunkett, it was Kilgallon who pulled Eamonn Bulfin to safety through the GPO window.[66] In early 1953, he was recognised at the rank of Grade E (for privates and non-commissioned officers, thus corroborating his 1917 US draft application) and granted an annual pension of £23,15 for four and three-quarters years of service, the equivalent of $63.10 at the time.[67] In June 1953 he returned to Dublin with Agnes Cosgrove to sign the pension paperwork in person.[68] On 25 June they met another 1916 veteran, President Sean T. O'Kelly.[69] Surely they went to the GPO too.

Were one to have speculated in 1912 what the future might hold for the young man who crashed a stolen car while joyriding and critically injured a young woman, it is not likely that it would place him at the side of Padraig Pearse four years later. As fate would have it, Kilgallon rose to the challenges of life at St Enda's. He won the respect not only of his peers but also that of his superiors. His personal growth, as overseen by Pearse and the Irish Volunteers, was profound and his combat experiences in the crucible of the action at the GPO in 1916 remained meaningful to him for the rest of his rather quiet life in Far Rockaway, New York.[70]

This was still not enough for the weight of Irish bureaucracy. Eamon Martin had to enquire about Kilgallon's 1916 medal that still had not been issued in August 1960 – 21 years after his application – as well as to why his pension checks had stopped coming. 'I am neither dead nor missing,' Kilgallon wrote to the Department of Defence and finally got their attention; the medal was authorised in November of that year.[71] But in June 1966, now age 75, he again had to plead, 'I have not received the pension in a few years. What happened?'[72] It was restored, then suspended again in 1968, and he had to ask Sweeney to look into it once more. Not insignificantly, Kilgallon was one of only ten percent of applicants who had been awarded the military pension before 1957 and he was also one of the fortunate few with friends in high places who could intercede like this 'against what must have seemed like a cold, harsh bureaucracy'.[73]

In February 1972 Major General Sweeney informed the Department of Defence that 'my old friend John Kilgallon' had died on 30 January.[74] In March, the Republic of Ireland kept the outstanding balance of his pension that was due to his sole survivor, Agnes Cosgrove, for Irish income tax.[75] £7,55, or $18.90, was John A. Kilgallon's final contribution to Easter 1916.

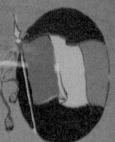

# IRISH
## RELIEF FUND
# BAZAAR

FOR THE BENEFIT
OF THE FAMILIES OF IRISH MARTYRS AND PRISONERS

## MADISON SQUARE GARDEN
## OCTOBER 14 to 22, 1916

1 PM to 11 PM

ADMISSION TO BAZAAR AND THE BIGGEST
SHOW NEW YORK HAS EVER SEEN 50¢

THE EXECUTION OF JAMES CONNOLLY

3254NG

Schutte

# CHAPTER TWENTY-TWO

# JAMES CONNOLLY'S 'GOOD END'
## THE IRISH RELIEF FUND BAZAAR POSTER

## Daphne Dyer Wolf

A life-long socialist, labour organiser, and self-made intellectual, James Connolly has been remembered on both sides of the Atlantic primarily for his dramatic death in front of a British firing squad. While Connolly the executed martyr provided a potent image in the quest for Irish independence, what was lost to popular imagination was Connolly the voracious reader and writer, Connolly the loving father, and Connolly the pugnacious labour agitator who cared deeply about the poor. This chapter suggests that it was in New York City that James Connolly's death was first publicly extricated from his life, and that this was accomplished through the mechanics of American advertising.

When he lived in the United States from 1902 to 1910, Connolly started a newspaper called *The Harp* to convince his hyphenated countrymen and women that Irish independence from Great Britain was worthless without the economic restructuring of socialism.[1] In May 1908, it ran this plea to Irish workers in the United States:

> The enemy of our race is private property … In Ireland it was fundamentally private property in land that was the original and abiding cause of all our woes; in America it is again private property in land and in machinery that recreates in the United States the division of classes into slavers and enslaved … rally around the only banner that symbolises hope for you in America as in Ireland – the banner of Socialism.

For the most part, Irish America was not listening. Along with other Irish Americans, including his friends Patrick L. Quinlan and Elizabeth Gurley Flynn, Connolly formed the Irish Socialist Federation in New York in 1907, whose mouthpiece was *The Harp*, but its membership was so small it was nearly invisible.[2] William Bourke Cockran proclaimed, 'There have been German Socialists and French Anarchists, but I thank God the Irish have never been anything but Democrats and Christians.'[3] Yet Connolly was undeterred, writing articles for *The Harp*, setting type, and paying the bills himself. Flynn remembered that it was 'a pathetic sight to see him standing, poorly clad, at the door of Cooper Union or some other east side hall, selling his little paper. None of the prosperous professional Irish, who shouted their admiration for him after his death, lent him a helping hand at that time.'[4]

Six months after the Easter Rising, the New York committee of the national Irish Relief Fund produced a giant bazaar in the city's Madison Square Garden to raise money for the families of those killed or imprisoned during the fighting. To publicise it, the committee chose a brightly coloured poster showing the visibly wounded Connolly propped up in a chair facing a firing squad. This poster was designed to be displayed on subway platforms before the bazaar, and also to decorate the Garden after it opened on 14 October 1916.[5]

Suddenly, the little-known labour agitator became a useful archetype for some lawyers, businessmen, and politicians, who would never have paused to listen to him in life. By interrogating the bazaar poster, this chapter shows that Connolly's American apotheosis as a founding father of the Irish nation, the moment when he joined the 'great succession of Tone, Emmet, Mitchel, and Davitt',[6] happened in a place where he had been consistently ignored in life, and where his death rapidly became more important than his life. How and why did this happen?

The most obvious reason it happened is because he died. And because he died in a such a spectacularly brutal yet romantic way, killed in a battle he never expected to win by a foe with no premonition of what had been loosed upon the world. A study of representations of the 'Manchester Martyrs' in Ireland in the nineteenth century proposes that 'politics, for most people, most of the time, consists of a "series of pictures in the mind" placed there by newspapers, conversations, songs, magazines, pictures, poems and other agencies.'[7] Connolly's death provided such a visceral mental picture, and the Irish Relief Fund Bazaar poster placed that image in the public's mind in a way that superseded any textual account. Its effect was so incendiary that Ward and Gow, a firm hired to plaster it on subway platforms, began tearing the posters down again almost as soon as they went up, claiming they were too morbid for public view.

The bazaar committee fought them in court, accusing the firm and the subways of capitulating to British pressure.[8]

Even without sufficient evidence to gauge the full sweep of the poster's influence, there is ample reason to use it to examine the reception of the Rising in the United States. The allegiances and motivations of those who organised the bazaar and who, presumably, approved the poster's design can add to our understanding of issues that concerned Irish America, particularly debates over neutrality and pro-German alliances. Above all, the poster provides graphic testimony of the process by which the James Connolly who sold *The Harp* on street corners was substituted in the popular imagination of Irish America with the James Connolly who was shot.

Fundraising bazaars to support those oppressed by the fighting in Europe were common in big cities before the United States entered the First World War, and all sides were represented. In New York there was a Central Powers bazaar and an Allied bazaar, a Jewish War Sufferers bazaar, a Belgian bazaar, and at least two German bazaars. Historian Ross Wilson calls the rapid succession of these fundraisers a 'process of competitive and political suffering'. Establishing a connection to the victims of the fighting abroad was, according to Wilson, a source of 'valuable political capital' to local power brokers as the country wrestled with neutrality and inched closer to war.[9] Like the others, the Irish Relief Fund Bazaar was designed to raise funds through musical acts, sideshow performers, booths selling a variety of products, and special 'nights' that would draw on support from other ethnic groups. There was a carnival atmosphere about them all, despite the serious focus of their fundraising.[10]

It is very probable that this poster is the first visual depiction of Connolly's execution, certainly the first to be plastered on subway platforms in a world capital like New York. Indeed, there have been few representations of his death at any time since, even on wall murals. Robert Ballagh's 1991 graphic for 'Reclaim the Spirit of Easter 1916', which has been reproduced on building walls, depicts Connolly alive with rifle in hand.[11] The few fine-art paintings that refer to the Rising have tended to approach the topic in a more muted or oblique fashion, such as the contemporary work of Jack B. Yeats or Seán Keating, or Micky Donnelly's more recent *Connolly's Hat with Lilies* (1987).[12] In the years after the formation of the Free State, art produced in Ireland about the Rising consisted mainly of formal portraits, statues, and monuments, designed to provide 'positive, inspirational images of historical figures, exemplars to be commemorated and emulated by the nation'.[13]

None of these strategies appear in the bazaar poster, which unlike the artwork created in the Free State, was designed to be thrown away when its job was done.

It is not subtle like Yeats's painting *On Drumcliffe Strand* (1918), nor does it deal in the nationalist symbolism of works like Oliver Sheppard's statue of *The Death of Cúchulainn* in the Dublin's General Post Office.[14] Rather, the Connolly poster reflects common advertising practices in New York City,[15] and must be considered primarily in the context of wartime proselytising. Just like the recruiting posters common then in Ireland and the rest of Europe (and soon in the United States), the Connolly poster provided an emotional jolt that urged viewers to immediate action.

French historian Max Gallo notes that the First World War was the first war fought by conscripts from all levels of society and not mainly by volunteers or paid mercenaries. Therefore, in recruiting posters across Europe 'the appeal was presented in terms of defending one's family rather than one's country … These non-professional soldiers had to be given a personal, immediate reason for fighting.'[16] While the Connolly poster mimics the intent and style of those posters, it does so in some puzzling ways. European war posters often pictured the mightiness of the war machine, using images of heavy artillery, U-boats, or anti-aircraft fire, frequently with a figure pointing from the battlefield towards the brave home front.[17] Instead of picturing a defiant Connolly on the ramparts of Dublin's GPO, the bazaar poster presents him in his last moment of defeat, before his executioners. Also, the soldiers facing him are wearing a costume that resembles a British army uniform of the time, but features smart red jackets, yellow-striped blue trousers, and bright yellow puttees instead of khaki. Together with the lead soldier's curling moustache, they invoke a vaudeville ensemble more than a firing squad.[18]

The images at the top – a forlorn mother and child on one side, and the rebellion's tricolour flag on the right – ably link love of homestead and country. Yet below that, Kilmainham Gaol's high walls have fallen away to reveal a green meadow leading to that most enduring of Irish scenes, a group of rural cottages. On closer inspection, we see the roofs of these cottages are caved in, and a red substance is leeching from them, creating a trail of what must be blood back again to Connolly. By evoking images of eviction and ruin, the artist directly links the struggle over land tenure in Ireland (which had always received strong support from Irish Americans) to the bloodshed of the Easter Rising. Yet in doing so, this recruiting poster is asking potential enlistees to defend a homeland that has already been destroyed.

Who decided that this image should be the public face of the bazaar, and why? The difficulties it presents – the circus colours, the connections to land issues, and the depiction of defeat – may indicate an overriding intent of some kind, or only the use of a haphazard soup of random motifs. There is no trace, within the bazaar committee, of a chain of command that suggested or approved the format. It is quite possible that not a great deal of thought was put into the design at all, and yet ... a poster that becomes the object of a court battle cannot be easily dismissed. If its design was important enough to prompt one party to halt its distribution, and another to fight so it could be seen, it merits examination.

Did the poster matter because it pictured James Connolly? Did mainstream Irish America, let alone the rest of the country, have any idea who James Connolly was? When news of the Rising first arrived, there were few details presented in the press about his life, and a great deal of confusion about his death. He was apparently so unfamiliar to general audiences that a *New York Times* columnist had to point out that the executed man in Dublin was not James B. Connolly, a writer of popular novels.[19] Although he was shot on 12 May, Connolly's 'death' was announced in American papers as early as 30 April, and he was variously reported to have died in a fire in the GPO, or to have been shot in the Tower of London.[20]

Where Connolly was known in the United States at all, he was known as a socialist and labour organiser, not primarily as an Irish republican, and his activities often ran counter to the purposes of established Irish-American groups. Beginning in 1902, he had travelled across the United States for the Socialist Labour Party, which first brought him to the United States to recruit Irish-American membership.[21] In that capacity, he was not successful, possibly because he was not afraid to indict 'Irish skinners of Irish labor'.[22] Later he made speaking tours for the Socialist Party of America, and campaigned for its presidential candidate, Eugene Debs, in 1908, eschewing any affiliation with the Democrats, the party favoured by Irish Americans.[23] He joined the Industrial Workers of the World (IWW) when it was founded in 1905.[24] The IWW, with its belief in worker solidarity across all trades, put Connolly at odds with mainstream labour unions in the United States, like the American Federation of Labor (AFL), which encouraged craft-specific unionism.[25] Those unions, and their leadership, had high quotients of Irish-American membership.

In small towns and industrial centres, often in the west, where he had once been welcomed in other labour circles, newspapers were more likely to champion his life's work and his local connections than they were in New York.[26] *The New Review*, a socialist publication, actually printed an excerpt of his writing after his death in which Connolly demanded Irish sovereignty, but not without the liberation of 'the bondslaves of those who by force or by fraud have managed to possess themselves of property'.[27] There were scattered American protests before and after his execution. In Tulsa, Oklahoma, an Irish-American club wired President Woodrow Wilson requesting his help to spare

Connolly's life. Representatives of 250,000 union workers in Chicago 'pledged themselves to fight for the life of James Connolly, Irish labor leader', and cabled London to demand a pardon.[28] Years later, the son of a Pennsylvania union leader recalled 'angry demonstrations in the mining areas' when news arrived that Connolly had been shot.[29]

Within a week, the gruesome details of his death began to supersede the sparse information about his life. Headlines announced: 'Wounded "General" unable to stand, put to death' and 'Shooting of wounded man stirs horror even in England'.[30] The Irish-American press followed suit. On 20 May, *The Gaelic American* included Connolly as one of the 'Sixteen Martyrs', and identified him in a photo caption as the commandant who was shot while wounded, but provided no details about his life and work. In another reference he became a generic victim: 'The butchery of wounded men who could not stand and had to be propped up to face the firing squad has shocked even the decenter men among the Unionists.' The *Kentucky Irish-American* used the news of his death to hammer Wilson, contrasting the president's support of Armenians, Russian Jews, and Belgians to his lack of protest at 'the action of his English friends in carrying the man Connolly from a hospital and bracing him against the wall to be shot'.[31]

It must have been apparent to the bazaar organisers in New York that details of his execution had ricocheted across the country. That committee operated under the umbrella of the national Irish Relief Fund established in May 1916 with three Roman Catholic cardinals as honorary presidents. At least four members of the national committee, banker Thomas Hughes Kelly, Daniel F. Cohalan, and attorneys George J. Gillespie and Jeremiah A. O'Leary, were on the New York bazaar committee, whose president was Jeremiah's brother, John J., another lawyer. In addition, there was also the German-American Irish bazaar co-committee based in the same building at 43rd Street and Broadway, under the direction of Alphonse G. Koeble, president of the United German Societies of New York.[32] This committee provided so much guidance, inspiration, and organisational skills to the Irish-American bazaar committee that the non-Irish press questioned who was actually in charge.[33]

The O'Leary brothers, whose names were often connected to the bazaar in the press, could have been responsible for the poster's design and message, though it is unlikely either of them had any interest in Connolly's economic ideas.[34] John, however, leaped to the defence of the poster when it was defaced and torn down, and immediately filed an injunction preventing any further desecration. It was he who accused the subway and advertisers of being pawns of J. P. Morgan, which as 'the official agents of England in this country … control the Interborough, which in turn controls Ward and Gow, hence the action against the posters'.[35]

His brother Jeremiah was notoriously anti-British and pro-German as was mentioned in an earlier chapter in this volume. Jeremiah's telegram to Wilson during the presidential campaign of 1916 questioning Wilson's alliance with Great Britain, and Wilson's curt and dismissive reply, became journalistic fodder.[36] Jeremiah was president of an anti-British group, the American Truth Society, and had appeared in the German-American publication *The Fatherland*.[37] If the O'Leary brothers were responsible for the poster, they may have chosen Connolly's death, not for his sake, but rather because the execution of a wounded man made the British look so bad.

Some Irish committee members were not at all comfortable with the implications for American politics in the collaboration with the German-American bazaar committee. Among those who welcomed the cooperation was John, who declared the bazaar 'would be the foundation of the Confederation of the German and Irish people in America'.[38] More reluctant was George J. Gillespie, who appeared to stammer when told that prominent German Americans had been named honorary presidents of the bazaar, claiming it was the first time he had heard of it. 'I would like to see not only Germans,' he said, 'but Frenchmen, Italians, in fact everyone, just so they are good Americans, interested in the bazaar.'[39] The fission continued at a rally on 1 October held to energise support for the bazaar. Alarmed by a series of anti-Wilson speeches delivered there to great applause, John Devoy (whose *Gaelic American* was a strong bazaar supporter) rose to protest the inclusion of 'politics' in a 'philanthropic enterprise to help our suffering people in Ireland'.[40] After the *Times* referred to a report that the three American cardinals would not sanction the bazaar if it was used for German propaganda, the bazaar committee quickly countered with a statement that 'the Cardinals had not been asked to give their official approval.'[41]

The press took keen note of disparities between Irish and German participation in the bazaar. The *New York Sun* reported on October 18, 'Projectors of the bazaar express disappointment because the Irish have not come forward more generally to help … it is a fact that the German contingent is giving more help by far.' Many Irish organisations were reported to be supporting the bazaar, including Cumann na mBan, the Friends of Irish Freedom, the Gaelic League, the Ancient Order of Hibernians, and the United Irish-American Societies of New York.[42] Yet the *Times* proclaimed, 'Germans capture the Irish bazaar', and *The Sun* observed during the bazaar that 'prominent Irish politicians are conspicuous by their absence at Madison Square Garden this week.'[43]

Irish art, industry, and handicrafts were on display at the bazaar, including the *Fenian Ram*, Irish-born John P. Holland's nineteenth-century submarine, which was resurrected from the mud after 34 years and transported from New Haven with great fanfare and considerable expense to the Garden, two days after opening night.[44] The appearance of the *Ram* seems to have been a deliberate attempt to associate Irish ingenuity with German submarine warfare, although no direct mention was made of it in bazaar publicity (nor of the 1915 German attack on the British ocean liner *Lusitania* just off the Irish coast). Still, Irish committee members were reported to have wrangled with the German Americans, insisting that a statue of Irish patriot Robert Emmet appear in the main entrance of the Garden instead of a German submarine.[45]

Many other German contributions were available at the bazaar, including booths selling images of Kaiser Wilhelm and German military heroes, a wood-and-cloth model of a U-boat, and a display of 16-inch German shells.[46] At one German-American booth, women sold pairs of dolls as 'playmates': an Irish peasant girl with a German soldier, and a German peasant girl with an Irish Volunteer.[47] One of the star attractions was opera singer Mme Johanna Gadski, the wife of Col Hans Tauscher, the agent in the United States for the armament-producing Krupp family.[48] *The Sun* wondered if all this was 'wholly agreeable to the old-fashioned St. Patrick's Day Irish who think their bazaar would be more successful if the German influence were lacking'.[49]

If the German and Irish committees could not agree about a display in the main lobby of the bazaar, one wonders what combination of their membership conceived the Connolly poster and chose an artist to carry out that design. Because the poster is signed with the Teutonic-sounding name 'Schutte' it might be tempting to speculate that it was designed in Germany. However, the creator was almost certainly Mitchell A. Schutte, an up-and-coming poster artist in New York City, who was born in Grand Rapids, Michigan, in 1890 to a Dutch-born father and a German-born mother.[50] Schutte created at least one recruiting poster for the United States army,[51] and was the art director of a Western-style show called 'The Stampede' at Sheepshead Bay Raceway in Brooklyn, New York, in August 1916.[52] In 1917 he joined US army, Company F, 25th Engineers, composed of artists, scenic designers, architects, and costume designers, who created camouflage effects for the military to 'Fool the Fritzies' during the war.[53] That he was chosen to design the Connolly poster seems more calculated by proximity and good advertising practices than by any political or cultural motive. Still, someone suggested Connolly's execution to Schutte.

One more possibility remains in the search for the poster's provenance. Connolly's daughter, Nora, arrived in the United States on 1 August 1916, having sailed from England under a false identity.[54] She spoke at the same rally on 1 October where Devoy protested the anti-Wilson tirades of speakers like Jeremiah A. O'Leary, and she opened the bazaar itself by raising the American flag and the Irish Republic's tricolour on the roof of Madison Square Garden.[55] Described as 'a timid little thing in deep mourning',[56] Nora was actually intrepid and quite plucky, as she demonstrated by her secret mission for her father to the United States in 1915, her activities during the Rising, and her well-reasoned defence of the behaviour of the Easter rebels that was printed in the *New York Times*.[57]

She remained in the United States for almost two years, spending time in Boston where she met her future husband, Seamus O'Brien, at an Irish Relief Fund dance. She worked with Irish republican groups and socialist organisations during that time, as she did for the rest of her life in Ireland.[58] Alongside her sobbing mother just before her father was executed, Nora heard him say, 'Hasn't it been a full life, Lillie? And isn't this a good end?'[59] Nora was well known to the Irish Relief Fund Bazaar committee and other Irish-American leaders, and she may have had enough influence to insist that her father's 'good end' be made central to the bazaar's message. If so, she could not have foreseen how his death would soon overshadow his achievements as a thinker and writer, nor his life's work among the poor and powerless. At that point in 1916, she must have assumed that they could never be separated.

# The Suffragist

VOL. V, NO. 68

FIVE CENTS

OFFICIAL WEEKLY ORGAN OF
THE NATIONAL WOMAN'S PARTY

SATURDAY, MAY 12, 1917

Drawn by Nina E. Allender

"Distant Birds Have Bonny Feathers"

# CHAPTER TWENTY-THREE

# THE OTHER NARRATIVE OF 'SISTERHOOD' IN 1916
## IRISH AND IRISH-AMERICAN SUFFRAGISTS

### Patricia Keefe Durso

*Our American Suffragist exchanges show that the ... United States are
moving in earnest ... While Europe rattles back to barbarism, America is fast
realising true democracy. Let Irish men and women cast the barbarism behind
them, and keep their eyes fixed on America as their exemplar.*
'American progress', *Irish Citizen*, 27 February 1915[1]

*The strong feeling in Congress for Irish freedom is creditable to the principles
of democracy the war has led Congress to formulate and is good omen of the
definite support Congress will give democracy for women when the federal
amendment is brought up for passage.*
'Irish freedom', *Suffragist*, 19 May 1917[2]

When 'sisterhood' is mentioned in connection with Ireland in 1916, the story that
comes to mind is typically that of the women who participated in the Easter Rising
– most famously, women like Constance Markievicz, who was second in command at
St Stephen's Green, or women like Elizabeth O'Farrell, who walked through what
was essentially a combat zone to deliver the surrender note to the British. But there

was another sisterhood that was equally significant in 1916, and that is the sisterhood of Irish and Irish-American suffragists and their shared passion and fight for the vote. Some elements of this commitment to Irish nationalism and suffragism were drawn out in the chapter on Dr Gertrude B. Kelly in this volume but, as this chapter shows, Kelly was only one of a number of individuals who simultaneously challenged the status quo with regard to Ireland and women.

The story of Irish suffragists was for many years, like that of the women of the Rising, 'Eire-brush[ed]' out of history.[3] As Louise Ryan points out, the Irish suffrage movement long suffered from significant 'neglect by academic historians'.[4] But in the past few decades, feminists and historians have built on the work of scholars such as Rosemary Cullen Owens and Cliona Murphy and begun to explore the narrative of the Irish suffrage movement in more depth.[5]

Understandably, the initial wave of studies of the Irish suffrage movement focused on documenting the fight for suffrage in Ireland, and when there is discussion of any international connections, the emphasis is typically on the relationship between the Irish and British suffrage movements. Discussion of the American connection to the Irish movement has been limited and often overlooked entirely. While Ryan's invaluable selection of topics and excerpts from the *Irish Citizen* from its beginning in 1912 to its final issues in 1920 does not include any articles, editorials, or correspondence relating to American suffrage, Murphy's work demonstrates that 'strong contacts with the American movement were critically important' to the Irish movement in various ways: the contacts gave the Irish movement encouragement and support and 'helped to counteract the many accusations, more often than not coming from nationalist quarters, that the Irish suffrage movement was merely another branch of the British movement.'[6]

But the connections that Murphy and others have noted do not focus on (and often do not even include) *Irish*-American suffragists, and although their numbers were relatively scarce, their contributions were significant. Hasia Diner notes that in the nineteenth century the 'number of Irish [American] women who involved themselves in the women's suffrage movement amounted to a virtual handful',[7] and by the early twentieth century, that number had increased, but not dramatically. While the scarcity of Irish-American suffragists may be attributable, in part, to the Catholic church's opposition to women's suffrage (despite the fact that the suffrage movement eventually won some converts among priests),[8] it is primarily due to the fact that the majority of suffragists were middle- to upper-class Protestant women who the Irish perceived as anti-Irish, anti-Catholic, and 'out of tune with their own cultural values'.[9] These claims, as James R. Barrett notes, 'had some cause: nineteenth-century suffrage literature had depicted Irish Politicians and voters as a major obstacle and featured Irish jokes and caricatures'.[10] In addition, many Irish-American women (and men) were 'put off by the suffragists' anti-temperance sloganeering.'[11] Still, there were some among them who worked for women's suffrage by the early twentieth century, particularly working-class women who 'increasingly represented the suffrage movement's main link to ethnic working-class communities',[12] such as Agnes Nestor, Mary Kenney O'Sullivan, Leonora O'Reilly, Margaret Foley, Elizabeth Gurley Flynn, and Margaret Hinchey. Others, such as Anne Martin and Lucy Burns (who came out of middle- to upper-class backgrounds) were financially able to dedicate themselves first and foremost to the suffrage cause, and both became leaders in the movement.

The sisterhood that emerges between the Irish suffragists and their counterparts in Irish America in the years around 1916 is best illustrated by two key organisations and the women who led them: The Irish Women's Franchise League (IWFL), led primarily by Hanna Sheehy Skeffington, and the Congressional Union (CU) – which later became the National Woman's Party (NWP) – co-founded and co-led by Lucy Burns, a Brooklyn-born Irish American. These organisations published the *Irish Citizen* (in Ireland) and *The Suffragist* (in the United States), which testify to numerous points at which both suffrage movements intersected and helped to shape and support each other.

Although the suffrage movements in Ireland and the United States had begun in the mid-1800s,[13] by the early 1900s they still had not achieved their main goal: the right to vote for all women, without restrictions.[14] In the years immediately preceding and following 1916, all that changed – the movements on both sides of the Atlantic gained steam, largely as a result of two factors: a new generation of younger, university-educated women in both countries who broke away from long-established suffrage organisations to form new bodies that employed militant strategies; and national and international events, particularly the Rising and the First World War.

In Ireland, the establishment of the IWFL in 1908 was a game-changer. Although it was formed by two couples, James and Margaret Cousins and Hanna and Francis Sheehy Skeffington, it was the Sheehy Skeffingtons who had, by far, the greatest impact on the IWFL and the Irish suffrage movement.[15] With an anti-suffragist father who was active in the Irish Republican Brotherhood (and later an Irish Nationalist MP) and a pro-suffrage uncle (Eugene Sheehy) who was known as the 'Land League priest', Hanna Sheehy Skeffington was schooled in both the republican and women's struggles from an early age. Her 'personal credo', as Margaret Ward has suggested, was 'based on a desire to secure the emancipation of women in tandem with national freedom'.[16] Her husband Francis was an ardent supporter of women's rights (he was reportedly wearing a 'Votes for Women' badge when she met him as a student in Dublin), and together they worked to secure 'Home rule for Irish women as well as Irish men.' The IWFL, militant and 'impatient for change',[17] reflected their shared commitment to equality. The *Irish Citizen* newspaper, edited primarily by Francis Sheehy Skeffington,[18] was a vehicle dedicated to promoting that equality, as stated in its motto: 'For Men and Women Equally, the Rights of Citizenship; From Men and Women Equally, The Duties of Citizenship'. It clearly saw the route to equality, however, as one paved by women's suffrage, as is illustrated in a political cartoon on the 20 March 1915 cover that shows the 'Modern St. Patrick' wearing a 'Votes for Women' ribbon and beckoning the sunlight of women's emancipation behind him while banishing various 'snakes' of women's 'slavery' at his feet. The IWFL believed in the power of civil disobedience and the use of militant tactics to banish those snakes once and for all from Ireland. Unlike older Irish suffrage organisations that confined themselves to 'lady-like' tactics, the IWFL 'flouted social conventions about the acceptable behavior of women', with strategies that ranged from 'addressing crowds on the backs of lorries to picketing public meetings and heckling politicians.'[19]

Although the *Irish Citizen* was 'clearly a mouthpiece' for the IWFL,[20] it is notable that it was also explicitly committed to publishing diverse viewpoints. As the editors stated in an early issue: 'Our columns are open, and will continue to be open, to every relevant criticism of suffragist policy or methods ... Such discussion and frank interchange of opinion we believe to be a valuable educative force ... and we shall set a good example in this direction by giving space to relevant criticism of our own editorial attitude.'[21] This invitation to debate and openness to diverse opinions made the *Irish Citizen* a provocative and vibrant publication that was read both at home and abroad, including in the United States.

Like the IWFL, the Congressional Union (CU), which ultimately became the National Woman's Party (NWP), was also a game-changer. The CU/NWP[22] was co-founded in the United States by Lucy Burns and Alice Paul after they split with the long-established National American Woman Suffrage Association (NAWSA). At what the *New York Times* called 'one of the most important suffrage meetings held in New York' in 1915, the CU – which Burns and Paul had headed since 1913, first as a committee of NAWSA and then as an independent organisation – became a 'new national organization' that promised to take 'from the old national organization [NAWSA] much of its young blood and enthusiastic, radical workers'.[23] The NAWSA had for some time disapproved of the CU's more militant tactics, as well as their insistence on pushing for a federal amendment for women's suffrage (the Susan B. Anthony Amendment) rather than working to pass suffrage on a state-by-state basis, as the NAWSA had long been doing. But at the meeting in New York, Lucy Burns (speaking as vice chairman of the CU) 'repudiated' the NAWSA and 'advised all of its members to cease their membership' and support of the NAWSA 'as long as it continued to favor the Shafroth-Palmer amendment' – an amendment that would make 'State as well as Federal action necessary' in order for women to get the right to vote.[24]

The IWFL clearly admired the CU/NWP. As reported in the *Irish Citizen* in 1915 (in an article reprinted from the *New York Call*), the CU was the 'radical body, the coming power', its 'battle-cry' was: 'Give up working for woman suffrage State by State! Throw all your energy into working for the Susan B. Anthony federal amendment!'[25] The parallel with Ireland did not go unnoticed – at least by the *Irish Citizen*, which pointed out that the 'States Rights doctrine' in the United States, 'like the "must-be-left-to-the-Irish-Parliament" argument here, is merely a cloak to veil fundamental opposition to Woman's Suffrage and fear of the women's vote'.[26]

The CU/NWP shared the IWFL's commitment to militancy and a belief in the power of civil disobedience; they picketed, heckled, rallied, lobbied, and marched. *The Suffragist* included articles, notes, and news, as well as excerpts from other suffrage publications, including, on a regular basis, quotes and notes from the *Irish Citizen*. Its editors included Burns, who took over the job in the spring of 1915 and continued for almost two years, during which *The Suffragist* '"got its stride" … and had an influence far beyond the number of copies printed'.[27] Although Burns's 'activities as speech maker and prison leader make up a vital portion of her service to the Woman's Party, as well as her notoriety, there was virtually no task that [she] did not perform'; during her years with the CU/NWP she acted as '[c]hief organizer, lobby head, newspaper editor, suffrage educator and teacher, orator, architect of the banner campaign' and 'rallying force and symbol'.[28] Burns reportedly spent more time in jail than any other American suffragist[29] and, like many other suffragists at home and abroad (including Hanna Sheehy Skeffington), she waged hunger strikes in prison in an effort to gain recognition as a political prisoner. In 1917, Burns was nominated by the CU/NWP to run for a vacated New York seat in congress, but her arrest and imprisonment for picketing the White House appears to have gotten in the way of any possible run for office. In an interview later in her life, Alice Paul herself – who has received a far larger share of the credit in historical and feminist studies for the work accomplished by the CU/NWP – described Burns as 'a thousand times more valiant than I'.[30]

Lucy Burns was born in Brooklyn, New York on 28 July 1879, to Anna Early Burns and Edward Burns. Her grandparents on her mother's side were both born in Ireland (while her paternal grandfather was born in Scotland and paternal grandmother in Canada).[31] She was one of eight children, fourth in a family of five girls and three boys; her father was a vice president and director of the American Exchange National Bank[32] and the family lived in the upscale neighbourhood of Brooklyn Heights.[33] Lucy attended Packer Collegiate Institute in Brooklyn and then Vassar College, graduating in 1902, and taught English for two years at Erasmus High School in Brooklyn before moving on to graduate study at Yale and Columbia, and then abroad in Berlin, Bonn, and Oxford. It was during her time in Britain, beginning in 1909, that she became impassioned about women's suffrage; the issue became the 'one subject in the world' for her and set her on a path of militant suffragism and dedication to the cause, bringing a 'fierceness and resoluteness to the American woman suffrage movement that was rarely equaled'.[34] As Burns stated in a 1913 interview in the *Brooklyn Daily Eagle*, 'I have always been a suffragist at heart.'[35]

While the CU/NWP became a 'surrogate family' for many suffragists, '[f]or Lucy Burns it was not. Brooklyn was home, family and church.'[36] Numerous sources emphasise Burns's devout Catholicism and commitment to family.[37] Her family was 'a source of great strength' and largely supported the suffragist cause; at least one brother became a 'convert to woman suffrage' and all of her four sisters contributed financially to the national suffrage organisation, with her sisters Janet and Helen contributing their time and energy as well (Janet was 'Joan d'Arc astride a horse in several New York suffrage parades and became press chairman for the Congressional Union branch there,' and Helen 'at one time or another held positions of secretary, treasurer and registration chairman for the New York CU and participated in deputations to congressmen').[38] By mid-1919 – after the Nineteenth Amendment was passed but before ratification and final victory[39] – Burns had permanently 'returned to the Brooklyn from whence she had come and of which she was so much a part'.[40] By that time, Burns had dedicated a full decade of her life to the suffrage movement, a decade during which she had also borne the loss of both parents (her mother died in 1912 and her father in 1914). What Burns wrote about Susan B. Anthony in a 1915 article in *The Suffragist* is equally true of Burns herself: 'If she devoted her life with singular consistency to the one purpose of enfranchising American women, it was because she had the great strength to press her rich gifts into the service of the cause she thought deeper than all others.'[41] After returning to Brooklyn, Burns was offered a job teaching English at Bay Ridge High School, but turned it down;[42] she devoted the remainder of her life to family, caring for her nieces and nephews (her youngest sister died in childbirth). She died in Brooklyn in 1966.[43]

Burns's 'Irishness' is frequently cited in historical accounts of the period. Her 'Irish wit' 'injected levity in difficult situations', and with 'a mass of red hair piled high on her head, she was an arresting figure at hundreds of open air meetings across the country'.[44] *The Story of the Woman's Party*, published in 1921 and written by sister suffragist Inez Haynes Irwin praised her 'intellectuality of a high order' and her 'winning Irishness', 'which supplement[ed] that Intellectuality with grace and charm'.[45] Burns also received high praise for her speeches and editorials in *The Suffragist*.[46] In a speech at the NAWSA convention in 1913, Burns emphasised the responsibility of the party in power, a main tenet of the CU/NWP's campaign. '[T]hose who hold power are responsible to the country,' she stated, for 'the use of it … for what they do and for what they do not do … [I]t is unthinkable that a national Government which represents women … should ignore the issue of their right to political freedom.'[47] Her editorials in *The Suffragist* also testify to the strength and power of her rhetoric, and she frequently reminded her audience of the need to take action: 'It is in our power to end our political enslavement,' she wrote in 1917, '[t]he day of our freedom depends upon ourselves.'[48]

While historical and feminist accounts do not provide an explicit analysis of the relevance of Burns's Irish-American (or Catholic) identity to her suffrage work, it is clear that her Irish appearance and 'charm' won people over and, perhaps, made her 'intellectuality' – which sounds like it could have been intimidating – more approachable. It has also been suggested that her Irishness gave her a 'taste for the sort of romantic adventure' that being a suffrage 'fighter' entailed.[49] And it is impossible not to associate Burns's 'more bitter sense of injustice' with her Irish heritage. While Alice Paul was described by a sister suffragist as a 'moral egalitarian' with an 'acute sense of justice', Burns was described as a woman who was 'passionately idealistic' and 'bitterly resented inaction and unfairness'.[50] This is clear from her editorials in *The Suffragist*, where she wrote in 1916, for example, that '[i]f politicians hate to see women politically divided on sex lines, they must remove sex injustices from politics.'[51] Burns's 'acute sense of injustice' is also evident in her speeches and articles; in her article on Susan B. Anthony, Burns wrote:

> She lived her life in the spirit of a warrior, battling for the mental liberty of women. She was on guard not only against political foes, but against the inherited subservience of women … She felt profoundly the humiliation of disenfranchisement, and spoke with amazing boldness against the tyranny of laws to which she had never given her consent.[52]

Although Burns is often cited as 'the only nationally prominent suffrage leader of Irish-Catholic ancestry',[53] at least one other CU/NWP leader was Irish American: Anne 'O'Hara' Martin.[54] Born in Nevada, her father, William O'Hara Martin, was of Irish descent and was a member of the Nevada senate. A graduate of Nevada State University and a student at the Chase School of Art in New York City (founded in 1896 by the artist William Merritt Chase, and renamed Parsons School of Design in 1941), Martin served on the executive committee of the CU, and in early 1916 became the first chairman of the newly established NWP. After the Rising, Martin was invited to join the Committee of One Hundred on Ireland, 'a nonpartisan committee of representative Americans' formed by the *Nation* to 'designate a select commission to sit at Washington or elsewhere for impartial investigation of reported atrocities in Ireland.'[55] This committee – which grew to be more than 100 – elected an executive group, the American Commission on Ireland, to 'improve the relations between the United States, Great Britain, and Ireland' and 'to obtain facts as to what is actually happening on Irish soil' in order to 'present an actual picture of the crisis to the American people, so that ... constructive suggestions may arise as to a way out'.[56]

Martin, Burns, and Sheehy Skeffington worked in their early years with the long-established British Women's Social and Political Union (WSPU), serving what has been described as an 'apprenticeship'.[57] In addition to exposure to suffrage tactics, their work with the WSPU also provided many suffragists with their first experience of being arrested and imprisoned. But after Britain entered the war in August 1914, and as the drive for Irish independence intensified, the IWFL clearly sought to distance themselves from the WSPU (though cracks in the relationship between the IWFL and the WSPU were beginning to show as early as 1912);[58] turning their gaze away from Britain, they turned towards the United States for support, encouragement, and inspiration instead. The connections that resulted – forged between 1912 and 1915 – would prove to be the foundation for a 'sisterhood' that would strengthen the suffragist movements in both Ireland and the United States and ultimately provide both movements with significant political leverage in the aftermath of the Rising.

The *Irish Citizen* was a powerful 'medium of exchange'[59] through which the IWFL deepened their connection with the American movement, particularly after Britain entered the war and the IWFL took a pronounced anti-war stance (objecting to war in general and to a war that was not Ireland's in particular). As a December 1914 article entitled 'Advancing America' stated:

> We in Ireland, situated as we are between Europe and America, ought to keep our eyes fixed on the great Western Republic ... We should try to follow its movements, and

to derive from it inspiration for the work before us – the emancipation of women in Ireland, that this country, instead of lagging behind with militarist Europe, may take its place with America, in the van of civilization.[60]

A significant number of articles about American suffrage appeared in the *Irish Citizen* in 1914, testifying to the drive on the part of the IWFL to separate from England and align themselves with the United States, itself a former British colony, as Hanna Sheehy Skeffington would later remind Americans in a lecture tour of the United States. Articles such as 'How the vote was won in Illinois', 'Women displace southern Pacific', 'American view', 'Woman's suffrage in America: an Irish woman's impression', 'American affairs', 'Advancing America', and a four-part series on 'An American priest on votes for Women'[61] demonstrated that IWFL suffragists 'closely followed developments in the United States',[62] and particularly focused on victories there in an effort to share strategies, encourage optimism, and counter accusations of anti-suffragists. The *Irish Citizen* also published notes, 'press cuttings', and 'brieflets' with American suffrage news.

Likewise, *The Suffragist* published numerous articles about suffrage in Ireland, largely focusing on the work of the IWFL, and included frequent excerpts and news from the *Irish Citizen*, testifying to their shared philosophies, methods, and strategies, foremost among them an unwavering demand for 'suffrage first'.

Despite the publication of dissenting viewpoints, it was clear that the IWFL and the editor of the *Irish Citizen* (Francis Sheehy Skeffington) believed in 'suffrage first', refusing to 'subordinate the women's campaign for the vote to the parliamentary campaign for Irish home rule'.[63] Article after article emphasised that any Home Rule Bill must include a provision for Irish women's suffrage.[64] After the outbreak of the First World War, the IWFL firmly maintained their 'suffrage first' stance, despite frequent criticism and debate (which appeared even within the *Irish Citizen*'s own pages, in keeping with its commitment to 'frank interchange of opinion'). In a 13 June 1914, article, a contributor to the *Irish Citizen* declared, '"Suffrage first" is a great and fundamental programme indispensable to our welfare as a people' and should be 'our first requirement', clearly echoing the IWFL's position.[65] While this stance was criticised by many – including older Irish suffrage organisations – it was applauded by the CU/NWP in the United States. In November 1914, *The Suffragist* praised the IWFL as one of only two organisations that 'stand out conspicuously from the fifty or more leagues of Suffragists [in Great Britain]' in their firm hold 'on the demand for "suffrage first"'.[66]

Well before the United States entered the First World War in April 1917, talk of preparedness and strong feelings of patriotism put pressure on American suffragists to put aside the fight for the vote and focus on their country. The CU/NWP announced their refusal by proclaiming their organisation to be the 'Woman's Party for "Suffrage First"', a position that was reinforced through numerous articles and editorials in the pages of *The Suffragist*[67] and that resulted in a great deal of criticism. 'The sense of proportion of the federal suffragists', declared the *New York Times* on 30 November 1915, 'is all askew' – 'just as Congress is about to meet, and the vital matter of national preparedness, grave international questions, inescapable questions of revenue and commerce are to be discussed,' the CU insists that there is 'no more important issue than the enfranchisement of women'.[68] The CU promptly responded to the *Times* in the 4 December 1915 issue of *The Suffragist*, re-asserting that 'no other questions should be dealt with by Congress until women are justly represented in Congress and can help to solve these questions … the more important the question is, the more urgent it is that women should be enfranchised.'[69] This argument echoed and reinforced the position that the IWFL consistently put forth in Ireland: 'Without the vote', the *Irish Citizen* argued, women 'can do nothing effective; with it they can drive home the moral of this war in such a manner as to make war in future impossible'.[70]

The IWFL's demand for 'suffrage first' was strongly and visibly articulated in a poster Francis Sheehy Skeffington made and prominently displayed outside the Sheehy Skeffington home when Britain entered the war in August 1914. The poster read: 'Votes for Women Now – Damn Your War!'[71] It did not go unnoticed. In 1915, he was imprisoned for speaking out against the war, and when he was temporarily released due to 'weakened health' (the result of a hunger strike), he escaped to the United States for a lengthy visit to New York City rather than return to prison to serve out his sentence.[72]

During his time in New York, Sheehy Skeffington 'avidly watched what was going on in the American suffrage scene' and 'met and addressed a number of suffragists'.[73] He quickly sent articles to the *Irish Citizen* on what he did, what he read, who he spoke to, and what his overall impressions were of the movement on that side of the Atlantic. He monitored numerous New York newspapers, including pro-suffrage papers like the *New York American* and the *New York Tribune*, as well as that 'press-leader of the anti-suffragists', the *New York Times*.[74] In all, the *Irish Citizen* published 13 articles about American suffrage written by Sheehy Skeffington during his 1915 visit.[75] He wrote about the state campaigns in New Jersey, New York, Massachusetts, and Pennsylvania, with a focus on New York, recognising its leading role on the suffragist stage: 'Enormous importance is attached to New York,' he wrote: 'It is hardly too much to say that upon its decision hangs the whole question of future suffragist tactics.'[76] But in the early 1900s, '[m]ost machine politicians' followed the same line on suffrage as the church and many Irish-American men – that is, they were opposed.[77] So when women's suffrage failed to pass in each of those state referenda, Sheehy Skeffington blamed (as did many others) the special interests of corrupt political machines (often associated, as he noted, with the Irish, and particularly evident in the New York and New Jersey elections).[78] Like his wife, Hanna, he recognised the CU/NWP, led by Burns and Paul, as the 'more advanced of the two bodies of suffragists in the United States' and praised their focus on a federal amendment.[79] He attended numerous suffragist parades and rallies in New York and marvelled at the way in which suffragists appealed to '[a]ll sections of New York's polyglot population', noting that 'Ireland was not forgotten': in one of many parades he attended, a green and gold banner bore the words, 'eirannaigh bean cuimhnigh osainn an Samhain so 1915' and bands played 'The Wearing of the Green'.[80] He gave lectures, including one to the New York Cumman na mBan, which (as the *Irish Citizen* reported) was at the Hotel McAlpin on Tuesday 14 September 1915 with 'Dr. Gertrude Kelly presiding',[81] and many other 'American-Irishmen and women' in attendance, including Marguerite Moore (an Irish-born speaker on social issues, including suffrage, labour, and land reform);[82] Maud Malone (an Irish-born New York librarian and 'intrepid suffragist, socialist, and labor activist' best known, perhaps, for heckling President Wilson about suffrage at a meeting in Brooklyn in 1912);[83] and Leonora O'Reilly (the daughter of Irish immigrants and founding member of the New York branch of the Women's Trade Union League and the Wage Earners' Suffrage League).[84] As the *Irish Citizen* article reported, Moore gave an 'eloquent speech' at the event, winding up by 'declaring, amid enthusiasm, "The Irish women will win freedom for themselves!"'[85]

Francis Sheehy Skeffington's articles from the States increasingly called attention to the Irish-American connection, with a particular focus on New Yorkers working for women's suffrage. In a description of the 23 October 1915 suffrage parade in New York City, for example, he stated that the 'biggest and most impressive group' (teachers) was 'headed by an Irish woman, Miss Katherine Devereux Blake'; 'another Irish woman, Miss Leonora O'Reilly', headed the Women's Trade Union League section; and an 'Irish banner' flew with those from other nations in the International Woman Suffrage Alliance section.[86] His final article from the States, 'American notes', aimed to show that 'the Irish Americans are doing their share towards the emancipation of American woman' (though he was careful to point out that '[t]hey are not by any means unanimous about it'). His observations emphasise that Irish-Americans in many lines of work (e.g., labour leaders, politicians, police officers, and teachers) supported the suffrage cause.[87]

Sheehy Skeffington's experience in New York clearly provided him with knowl-edge and insight into the Irish in the United States in general and the American suffrage movement in particular, as well as with new contacts and strategies that he brought back to Ireland. He left the United States in December 1915,[88] and arrived back in Ireland in early 1916. Shortly thereafter, and just weeks before the Rising, *The Suffragist* published a front-page article on 'Suffrage in Ireland', reporting that it was 'proceeding with almost undiminished vigor in spite of the war. The Irish Women's Franchise League has just held its annual meeting [at which surely the Sheehy Skeffingtons were both in attendance] and adopted plans for an extended campaign during 1916.'[89]

The events of Easter 1916, however, tragically changed any plans the IWFL and the Sheehy Skeffingtons, 'both feminists and pacifists', had. Although neither 'took an active part in the Rising', they could not just 'stand by when others needed support'.[90] Hanna (who had been named as one of a 'five-member Civil Provisional Government to be put into effect if the Rising proved successful'), spent the early days of the Rising delivering food to the GPO and messages 'to the various encampments', while Francis organised a 'citizens' militia' to help stop the looting in Dublin.[91] While he was out on patrol, however, he was arrested, brought to Portobello Barracks, held without charge, and killed two days later by firing squad on the orders of a British army captain later deemed insane.[92]

Suffragists 'world-wide' supported Hanna Sheehy Skeffington's 'campaign to force the British government to hold a public enquiry into the murder', and American suffragists were among those who sent donations to keep the *Irish Citizen* in existence 'in tribute to' Francis, 'its murdered editor'.[93] The IWFL stayed strong and continued their fight for women's suffrage after Francis's death. On 2 December 1916, *The Suffragist* published a front-page note announcing that the 'Irish Citizen Continues Publication'; although it had been 'suspended since the tragic death of its editor', it would 'be published hereafter as a monthly'.[94] That same article also notes that 'the *Citizen* speaks of the necessity for making it clear that woman suffrage must enter into any new scheme that purposes [sic] to deal with the government of Ireland.' Clearly, the IWFL's commitment to 'suffrage first' was unwavering, even after the Rising and Francis Sheehy Skeffington's death. As Hanna Sheehy Skeffington stated: '[i]t would be a poor tribute to my husband if grief were to break my spirit.'[95]

In late 1916, Hanna Sheehy Skeffington left Ireland for an extended lecture tour in the United States.[96] The tour was arranged through the relatively new organisation, Friends of Irish Freedom. Her first major lecture was at Carnegie Hall in New York

City on 6 January 1917.[97] A 'digest' of her American lectures, 'British militarism as I have known it', was banned in both Britain and Ireland until the end of the war,[98] as it included a discussion of the Rising and the murder of her husband and others. She drew clear parallels between the respective quests for independence in Ireland and the United States, comparing the leaders of the Rising to the leaders of the Revolutionary War,[99] and she called upon her audiences to support not only Irish independence and freedom from Britain, but women's equality, reminding them that the leaders of the Rising gave 'equal citizenship to women' in their Proclamation.[100] During her time in the United States, Sheehy Skeffington 'made and renewed many lasting friendships … with other politically active and courageous women', including Alice Paul of the NWP, Elizabeth Gurley Flynn, Dr Gertrude B. Kelly, and Jane Addams.[101] Before leaving the United States, Sheehy Skeffington met with President Wilson to deliver a petition from the Irishwomen's Council of Cumann na mBan that asked the American government 'to call for political independence for Ireland' – for an Irish Republic that 'would give women full recognition'.[102]

Sheehy Skeffington recognised the Easter Rising as a 'seminal moment in the long campaign for women's citizenship, the point in time where republicanism and feminism connected'.[103] And indeed, it had a significant impact on the suffrage movements in both Ireland and the United States – a point that has not been sufficiently acknowledged, if at all, in historical or feminist studies. This is most visible in the rhetoric and activities of the IWFL and the CU/NWP, and in large part attributable to the sense of sisterhood that was forged between them prior to the Rising.

While the emphasis in Sheehy Skeffington's lectures was on independence for Ireland, Irish suffragists were determined 'that whatever type of new Ireland would emerge [after the Rising] Irish women would be a part of it'.[104] On 22 July 1916 – soon after the Rising and while the *Irish Citizen*'s regular publication was suspended following Francis Sheehy Skeffington's murder – *The Suffragist* ran a front-page article entitled 'Irish women urge suffrage in Home Rule government'.[105] It reported that the IWFL passed a resolution stating, in part: '[N]o reform of Irish Government can be considered acceptable or permanent by Irish suffragists which does not include votes for Irish women on the same terms as Irish men.'[106] Clearly, even during those months when the *Irish Citizen* suspended publication,[107] the CU/NWP monitored the Irish suffrage movement closely, ensuring that the IWFL's words and actions would be heard by the international suffrage movement and mainstream press. (It is notable that these and other articles about the IWFL and suffrage in Ireland were largely published in *The Suffragist* during Lucy Burns's tenure as editor.)[108]

The Irish question also played a significant role in the *American* suffrage movement after the Rising. While the IWFL used their contacts with American suffragists to put 'pressure on both Irish and British politicians to include a women's suffrage amendment in the Irish Home Rule Bill',[109] American suffragists used the issue of Home Rule and the question of Irish independence to put pressure on American politicians to pass a federal amendment for women's suffrage in the United States. A 15 July 1916 *Suffragist* piece about the upcoming presidential election, for example, included the following excerpt from *Everywoman*: 'Gentlemen: We are ashamed of you! You are playing with us as England played with Home Rule. Does it pay? We are willing to love, honor and to trust you; but self-respect demands reciprocity.'[110] In this analogy, American women are figured as Ireland (the colonised, the powerless, the victim), and American politicians are figured as England (the coloniser, the powerful, the aggressor). The CU/NWP also used the issue of Irish independence as political leverage in their fight for the vote, as demonstrated by a political cartoon on the 12 May 1917 cover of *The Suffragist*, which showed a congressman asking England to 'free Ireland' while ignoring the plea of an American woman, calling attention to the irony of congressional support for Irish independence abroad but denial of women's equality at home.[111] Using the issues of Home Rule and Irish independence to frame their fight for the vote helped the CU/NWP emphasise that women's suffrage was, at heart, about democracy, freedom, and justice. It also helped them connect their fight for the vote to the considerable 'ground swell' of Irish-American 'emotional support for [Irish] independence' after the Rising.[112]

'Irish organizers' in the American suffrage movement (most notably those who worked for the NAWSA, such as Margaret Hinchey and Margaret Foley – dubbed 'Maggie and Maggie' by the *New York Times*)[113] also invoked the Rising and Irish-American sentiment to appeal to Irish-American voters. In a letter to the editor of the New York-based *Gaelic American* newspaper before the 1917 New York suffrage referendum, for example, Hinchey wrote

> On Nov. 6, all the Irish voters of New York City will be given an opportunity to vote on the woman suffrage amendment ... I call upon all Irishmen true to their race and to themselves to champion woman suffrage. Let them remember that a year ago in Ireland the new Constitution drawn up by Connolly, McDermott and other Irish patriots contained a clause that granted the ballot to Irish women.[114]

In addition to influencing the rhetoric and tenor of the American suffrage campaign, the Rising also provided new ammunition for their lobbying efforts. During a stay in Washington, DC, Hanna Sheehy Skeffington was impressed by the CU/NWP's lobbying, stating in a letter in the *Irish Citizen* that she ran into 'lobbyists of the National Woman's Party' in the 'corridors of Congress or Senate' on a 'daily and hourly' basis.[115] During her time in DC lobbying 'on the Irish question',[116] she also met with prominent suffragists, including Lucy Burns (who was one of her American correspondents)[117] after a suffrage debate in the House. As Margaret Ward has noted – and as is evident from numerous articles in the *Irish Citizen* on 'suffrage first' and the American movement (discussed above) – Burns's CU/NWP was the women's organisation 'with which Hanna felt most in sympathy',[118] and she clearly admired their unrelenting lobbying and militant picketing tactics. The CU/NWP carefully 'kept track of how Congressmen voted on different measures and wherever it was possible, they linked it up with Suffrage'.[119] After the Rising, there was no congressional 'measure' that could be linked to suffrage more powerfully or productively than the Irish question. Inez Haynes Irwin notes that when the 'Irish Mission visited Congress, and two hundred and fifty voted for the freedom of Ireland, [suffragists] lobbied these Congressmen to vote for the freedom of women'.[120] And when 'one hundred and thirty-two members of the House of Representatives … cabled Premier Lloyd-George' in 1917 to ask 'that he further a quick settlement of the Irish question by giving Ireland home rule', the NWP conducted an intense lobbying effort (led by Irish-American Anne Martin) to make congressmen see the 'inconsistency' of supporting Home Rule while opposing women's suffrage.[121]

It has been argued that the relationship between Irish and American suffragists ultimately 'became strained during the war'[122] when Sheehy Skeffington accused American suffragists of putting the struggle for suffrage aside, but this claim is only partly true. While the relationship between the IWFL and the NAWSA did, in fact, become strained, the relationship between the IWFL and the CU/NWP was actually strengthened. Sheehy Skeffington accused NAWSA leaders of 'turn[ing] their backs on suffrage and preach[ing] to their followers the urgent need of winning the war above all else'. While the NAWSA 'put suffrage on the shelf', Sheehy Skeffington significantly pointed out that the CU/NWP did not:

> A comfortable and decent burial was ready for the suffrage corpse, and the interment would have taken place duly but for the militant section, known as the National Woman's Party, headed by Alice Paul (a Quaker) and Lucy Burns (an Irishwoman). These women were not content to bury suffrage 'till the war was over,' but, on the contrary, showed a most insistent desire to have it 'right now.'[123]

Despite objections from the NAWSA (published in the *Irish Citizen*),[124] Sheehy Skeffington stood her ground, emphasising that her conclusion was drawn from personal observation and interaction with suffrage organisations and individuals in the United States (e.g., during her visit to Washington, DC). In fact, in her reply to the NAWSA's objections (also published in the *Irish Citizen*), she intensified her rhetoric, stating that the NAWSA and its leaders had 'become conservative and fossilized', and had not 'enter[ed] the movement for the Federal Amendment until the younger and more progressive movement [the CU/NWP] had practically compelled it to do so'. Furthermore, she suggested that objectors to her statements should become better informed about the difference between militant and constitutional suffragists by reading the *'Suffragist*, the weekly organ of the militants'.[125] While Sheehy Skeffington also praised four other American newspapers,[126] *The Suffragist* – edited by Lucy Burns – was first and foremost among her recommendations. Sheehy Skeffington knew that *The Suffragist* demonstrated a strong interest in, and understanding of, the Irish suffrage movement. In terms of their militant tactics and their unwavering demand for 'suffrage first', the women of the IWFL and CU/NWP clearly connected, understood each other, and stayed informed about the status and progress of each other's movements.

In 1989, Cliona Murphy observed that the 'relationship between the Irish and American women reinforced a feeling of sisterhood, and helped the Irish [suffragists] formulate their own distinct identity'.[127] Now – decades later, with much more documented about the work of both Irish and American suffragists – it is clear that this 'feeling of sisterhood' is particularly evident in the connections between the IWFL, led by Hanna Sheehy Skeffington, and the CU/NWP, co-led by Lucy Burns, that 'fiery red-headed Irish Catholic'[128] suffragist from Brooklyn. And it is nowhere more visible than in New York City, as the birthplace of Irish-American suffrage leaders such as Burns, as the destination of visiting Irish suffragists such as Francis and Hanna Sheehy Skeffington, as the home of thousands of Irish-American immigrants[129] like Maggie Hinchey, and as a central stage in the suffrage movement.[130] These suffragists shared not only 'Irish blood', but a passion for equality and a strong sense of injustice.

As this chapter has shown, the fight for women's suffrage was intensified by the First World War, the Rising, and the issues of Home Rule and Irish independence. These events could have put a halt to the women's suffrage movements in Ireland and the United States. But the IWFL and CU/NWP passionately insisted on 'suffrage first' and then – after the Rising – harnessed the surge of American support for Ireland and used it to drive home their fight for the vote. Indeed, it could be argued that credit for the women's suffrage victories in both countries (which came in 1918 in Ireland and

1920 in the United States)[131] is in large part attributable to the 'sisterhood' of these Irish and Irish-American suffragists and their organisations, forged in the years prior to 1916 and reinforced in the aftermath of the Rising.

*This chapter is based in part on a presentation at 'The Other 1916 Conference' at the Institute for Art, Design, and Technology (IADT) in Dún Laoghaire, Ireland, 3 June 2016. I would like to thank the organisers of the conference, Caitriona Kirby, Jenny McDonnell, and Maria Parsons, as well as the other panellists and conference attendees, for a fascinating and thought-provoking exchange on 'other' narratives of 1916.*

# CHAPTER TWENTY-FOUR

# THE EASTER RISING AND NEW YORK'S ANTICOLONIAL NATIONALISTS

## *David Brundage*

There is a growing body of research focused on the impact of the Easter Rising on anticolonial movements beyond Ireland and the Irish diaspora. Though the process of decolonisation in Asia, Africa, and the Caribbean only hit full stride in the years after the Second World War, it has long been recognised that the First World War and its immediate aftermath gave an important boost to anticolonial nationalist efforts in these places, prefiguring developments that would come to fruition a quarter of a century later. While some historians have emphasised the influence of Woodrow Wilson's ideas in this period, however, the pages that follow take a different approach, positing the significance of the Easter Rising and the subsequent Irish revolution (as these were understood by both Irish and non-Irish political activists) in the long struggle to win independence for a variety of what came to be called Third World nations.[1]

The presidency of Woodrow Wilson (1913–21) casts a long shadow over our understanding of international history in this era. Although most contemporary scholars are sceptical of the depth of the twenty-eighth president's commitment to making the 'world safe for democracy', arguing instead that his main goal was the creation of stable multilateral international institutions, the influential recent work of Erez Manela has pointed to some of the unintended consequences of Wilson's lofty rhetoric in the closing months of the war. 'For colonized, marginalized, and stateless peoples from all over the world – Chinese and Koreans, Arabs and Jews, Armenians and Kurds, and many others', Manela writes, the American president was often imagined as 'an icon of their aspirations and a potential champion of their cause, a dominant figure in the world arena committed, he had himself declared, to the principle of self-determination for all peoples'. Despite their disappointment at the results of the spring 1919 Paris Peace Conference, Wilson's incapacity following a stroke in the fall of that year, and his replacement (for some of them) by Lenin and the Bolshevik Revolution as the main inspiration for their anticolonial efforts, the heady period from the autumn of 1918 to the spring of 1919 that Manela calls 'the Wilsonian moment' helped shape the eventual course of Third World decolonisation.[2]

This is a stimulating, complex, and generally persuasive analysis. But for some of those seeking to voice the aspirations of what they called 'subject nationalities' in this period, it was neither Wilson's United States nor Lenin's Russia, but another nation, Ireland, that did the most to stir their hopes and imaginations. This was so for a number of reasons. The Irish revolution that began with the 1916 Easter Rising provided an extremely potent example of the ability of a handful of militants to challenge a great empire; of a revolutionary dynamic that could sweep aside compromises and halfway measures (such as Home Rule) almost overnight; and of the deeply inspiring will-ingness of dedicated rebels to sacrifice their own lives for the sake of a larger cause. For those anticolonial activists who resided in the United States in the years from 1916 to 1921, there was yet another factor at work: in linking their struggles to that of Ireland, they were fastening onto the national cause with by far the most favourable American publicity and popular enthusiasm. Finally, as the Irish revolution unfolded, some Irish-American nationalists, seeking to build an ever-stronger movement in its support, began reaching out to activists from other national groups and in so doing intensified the attraction of the Irish model.

For many such activists the meeting ground was New York City. From the days of the United Irishmen, exiled to the United States following their defeat in the bloody 1798 rebellion, the city had been a focal point for all varieties of Irish nationalism. Daniel O'Connell's constitutional movement to repeal the Act of Union had built considerable strength there, but so too had the physical-force Fenian Brotherhood; the 1878 New Departure that for a time linked physical force and constitutional national-ists in a powerful transatlantic movement seeking both Home Rule and far-reaching social reform had been hammered out in New York as well. The city was, as the noted historian of the Irish in the United States, Dennis Clark, once put it, 'the overseas capital of Irish nationalist agitation and mobilization'.[3]

But as an increasingly cosmopolitan urban magnet that attracted immigrants, political exiles, university students, and visiting nationalist leaders from many different parts of the world, New York was also what the literary scholar Mary Louise Pratt has called a 'contact zone'. Like London and Paris in the interwar period, the American metropolis was 'a space in which peoples geographically and historically separated [came] into contact with each other'. The following pages will explore the implications of this perspective, with particular attention to the growth and interaction of three important anticolonial movements of the First World War era: Irish nationalism, the Indian independence movement, and pan-Africanism. All three were examples of what some social scientists have called 'long-distance' or 'diaspora' nationalism, the phenomenon of nationalist activity and enthusiasm among far-flung groups of emigrants, exiles, or refugees. Irish, Indian, and African-American nationalism, of course, also had support in other sections of the United States in these years, but New York's central importance to all three makes the city worthy of intensive focus.[4]

As the twentieth century opened, decades of substantial Irish emigration had led to a situation in which nearly as many Irish people lived outside of Ireland as within its borders. No city illustrated the increasing importance of the Irish diaspora better than New York. Over 250,000 Irish-born people resided in the metropolis in 1900, making it (after Dublin and Belfast) the largest centre of Irish population in the world. But a focus on the Irish-born actually understates the Irish character of the city, for by 1900 the real demographic weight lay with the second- and increasingly even third-generation American-born Irish. Irish immigrants and Irish Americans were still overwhelmingly working class, with particularly strong representation in New York's important trade and transportation sectors, but the Irish were also heavily represented in the skilled trades and in municipal employment. Many by this time were small business owners, operating neighbourhood stores and saloons, while several very wealthy Irish Americans, like the lawyer John Quinn and the construction magnate John D. Crimmins, had found a secure place within New York's increasingly cohesive urban elite.[5]

As earlier chapters in this volume have demonstrated, although the republicans of Clan na Gael (the American successor to the Fenians) maintained a presence in New York, Irish nationalism in the early years of the twentieth century was dominated by the United Irish League of America (UILA). However, this balance of forces changed dramatically with the outbreak of war in Europe and Redmond's decision to support the British war effort. The postponement of Home Rule inadvertently transformed the Irish nationalist movement in the United States. Overall, the developments of 1914 served to undermine support for the UILA and were accompanied by a sharp rise in Irish-American interest in revolutionary nationalism. The shift was marked by the March 1916 birth of a new organisation, the Friends of Irish Freedom (FOIF), as Michael Doorley has examined in his chapter in this volume. In the wake of the Rising the following month and the subsequent execution of its leaders and of the internationally renowned Sir Roger Casement in August, and the onset of the Irish War of Independence in 1919, American support for Irish revolutionary nationalism expanded dramatically. The FOIF claimed nearly 300,000 members by 1919, and its later rival, the American Association for the Recognition of the Irish Republic (AARIR), founded by Éamon de Valera during his 18-month organising campaign in the United States, had 700,000 members and had raised over ten million dollars for the proclaimed Irish Republic by 1921. Both organisations had significant strength in New York, while smaller (and sometimes more radical) Irish organisations could be found there as well. The Irish Progressive League (IPL), which was active from the autumn of 1917 until its merger with the AARIR in November 1920, for example, brought together anti-war liberals, left-wing progressives, women suffragists, and socialists in its campaign for Irish independence.[6] Dr Gertrude B. Kelly provides an illustrative example of the outlook of the IPL.

Far smaller than the Irish-American population, there were nonetheless more than 60,000 African Americans living in New York at the beginning of the twentieth century, representing about two percent of the total population. After the collapse of the Harlem real estate market in 1905, landlords in this section of upper Manhattan began lowering rents, drawing African Americans to this previously white area for the first time. By 1914, Harlem alone counted over 50,000 black residents. During the war years, New York's black population grew rapidly, drawn not only from the American South but also from the English-speaking islands of the Caribbean. With most black New Yorkers experiencing segregated housing and racial discrimination that restricted them to the lowest paying, often menial, jobs, there was an accumulation of grievances in the city that made it a natural locale for various forms of political activism and protest. The National Association for the Advancement of Colored People (NAACP), founded in 1909, was headquartered in New York, and it was there that the prominent African-American scholar and activist, W. E. B. Du Bois, edited *The Crisis*, which served not only as the NAACP's official monthly organ but also as an important journal of thought and culture, publishing, for example, many of the poets, playwrights, and prose writers of what would be called the Harlem Renaissance.[7]

Pan-Africanism, the doctrine holding that the peoples of Africa and its diaspora had interests in common — and in opposition to the European colonial powers that controlled much of the continent and the black Caribbean – was, for the first years of the twentieth century, the preserve of a relatively small group of intellectuals. Du Bois was an important figure in its development and its origins are sometimes dated to the Pan-African Congress meetings in London that he attended in July 1900. With the emigration of Marcus Garvey from his native Jamaica to New York in March 1916, however, the situation changed substantially. The pan-Africanist Universal Negro Improvement Association (UNIA), which Garvey had founded in Jamaica in 1914, was from this point on headquartered in Harlem. Over the next few years, the UNIA grew rapidly, partly because of Garvey's talents as a charismatic orator and forceful writer (using his weekly newspaper, *The Negro World*, as his forum) and partly from the activism of African-American soldiers returning from the war to find a sharp resurgence of white racism. By the early 1920s, the UNIA had chapters in 30 American cities, 65,000–75,000 dues-paying members, and African-American supporters that some historians estimate to number in the millions. Though Du Bois regarded Garvey with suspicion and hostility, even he had to concede the power of a movement that could bring thousands of people onto the streets of Harlem or into large venues like Madison Square Garden for meetings, demonstrations, or parades.[8]

In comparison to the size of the Irish or African-American communities in the metropolis, South Asian New York was extremely small. Although groups of Indian merchants could be found in the city as early as the eighteenth century, substantial migration from the Indian subcontinent to North America began only in the early twentieth century and was then composed largely of Punjabi Sikh agricultural and lumber workers, who settled primarily in the states of the West Coast and in British Columbia. Among these migrants, whose total number never exceeded 10,000 before the First World War, was an even smaller group of business people, students, intellectuals, and professionals, who gravitated towards western cities like San Francisco and Seattle. Some also made their way to New York, where as early as 1906 a small but growing number of Indian university students could be found.[9]

Despite these small numbers, North America became the base for a vibrant diasporic wing of Indian nationalism in these years. On the West Coast, a revolutionary organisation called the Ghadar Party emerged in 1913, shaped in equal measures by opposition to British rule at home and to the often violent expressions of anti-Asian racism in the United States. But New York was an important centre for radical anti-colonial activism as well. Summarising his interactions with other Indian activists in America during the First World War, the Punjabi nationalist Lajpat Rai observed that 'most of them were extremists, only a few moderates'. Like Clan na Gael, which served as an American conduit for secret wartime contacts between the German government and the Dublin rebels who were planning what would become the Easter Rising, many Indian nationalists in New York and other cities were also, as Rai noted disapprovingly, 'in alliance with Germany and were being supplied with money by German government agents'. However, a more public and moderate direction within the movement began to emerge with the arrival of Rai himself.[10]

Born in humble circumstances in Punjab in 1865, Rai was a lawyer and, beginning in 1907, a leader of the militant, but nonviolent, Swadeshi movement against British rule in the province. In April 1914, he left India on a political organising trip to Britain that he anticipated would last 'no more than six months'. The outbreak of war, however, changed his plans. Fearing arrest if he returned to India, he instead sailed for New York, where he arrived in November. Except for a six-month trip to Japan he would reside in the city for the next five years. In January 1918 Rai founded the Indian Home Rule League of America. The goal of the New York-based organisation was to make the Indian question an international one and, in particular, to reach out to potentially sympathetic Americans. To further this goal, the group began publishing what soon became an influential monthly magazine, *Young India*. British consular officials and intelligence agents watched these developments with increasing concern, worried especially about the possible links that might develop between Indian nationalists and New York's growing contingent of Irish republicans.[11]

However, the historian must ask: how real was this threat? And how real was the parallel threat of Irish republicans making common cause with the UNIA, which appears to have been of even greater concern to the US Justice Department's General Intelligence Division, whose young leader, J. Edgar Hoover, regarded Marcus Garvey as 'the foremost radical among his race' and a serious danger to the American social order? In the case of Garvey and the UNIA, it seems clear, the contacts and influences were highly significant. As Robert A. Hill has shown, the example provided by Irish nationalism played a central role in shaping Garvey's entire political outlook. His first encounter with Irish nationalism had come in 1910, when he became the assistant secretary of the National Club of Jamaica. S. A. G. Cox, the National Club's founder, had absorbed the political programme of Sinn Féin while studying law in London; he chose the name *Our Own* (a very rough translation of 'Sinn Féin') for the club's newspaper. More important was Garvey's own experience in London, where he lived from 1912 to 1914, the years of the Home Rule crisis when the Irish question was in the news almost continuously.[12]

But it was the Rising and the subsequent development of the Irish revolutionary struggle that had the biggest impact on Garvey's political thinking. He found the willingness of the Rising's leaders to give up their lives for the sake of a larger cause to be worthy of both admiration and emulation. In his dedication of Liberty Hall, the UNIA's new headquarters on 138th Street in Harlem, on 27 July 1919, Garvey proclaimed that 'the time had come for the Negro race to offer up its martyrs upon the altar of liberty even as the Irish had given a long list from [United Irishman] Robert Emmet to Roger Casement.' Even the name 'Liberty Hall' reflected Garvey's appreciation for this sacrifice, for he had named it after Liberty Hall, Dublin, one of the sites from which the Easter Rising had been launched. In a speech at Carnegie Hall the following month, Garvey returned to this theme: 'From the time when Robert Emmett [sic], when he lost his head, to the time of Roger Casement, Ireland has been fighting, agitating and offering up her sons as martyrs'. As such men 'bled and died for Ireland, so we who are leading [the] Universal Negro Improvement Association, are prepared at any time to free Africa and free the negroes of the world'.[13]

Despite the deep currents of anti-black racism that ran through the history of the Irish in the United States, among some New York Irish republicans – and particularly the liberals, socialists, and feminists of the Irish Progressive League – there was reciprocal enthusiasm. 'The UNIA', proclaimed the IPL's Helen Golden, after meeting with some of the organisation's leaders in 1920, 'has inaugurated a history making movement' whose goal of 'eliminating all race prejudice' deserved the support of all Irish republicans. W. E. B. Du Bois, it should be noted, was considerably less enthusiastic than Garvey with Ireland's 1916 turn to rebellion. Though he lamented Casement's execution in an editorial in *The Crisis*, his purpose was less to praise Casement's heroic sacrifice than to condemn what he regarded as Britain's political misstep in executing him: 'Someone has blundered,' Du Bois pointedly observed. But while careful to note the long history of Irish-American racism, he now expressed the hope that 'all this is past', and that Irish and African-American anticolonial activists could make common cause. By October 1920, Du Bois was taking an active stand in support of Irish independence, joining a distinguished group of politicians and social reformers on the so-called Committee of One Hundred, organised by New York's Irish nationalist leader, Dr William Maloney, to 'place the Irish case before the tribunal of the civilized world'.[14]

As was the case with pan-Africanists, there was also considerable variation in the response of Indian nationalists in the United States to the 1916 Irish rebellion. Not surprisingly, the revolutionary wing of the Indian independence movement embraced the Rising with genuine enthusiasm. In May 1916, San Francisco's *Ghadar* newspaper hailed the leaders of rebellion, comparing them to Robert Emmet (as had Garvey) and opining that in Ireland 'the blood of martyrs is not wasted' for 'every drop was as seed sown which has produced many harvests'. In August 1917, the paper again lauded the courage and self-sacrifice that characterised the Rising: 'Oh Irish, you kept your sword on high and did not show the white feather.'[15]

The more moderate Lajpat Rai, who opposed insurrectionists among his fellow Indian nationalists, was similarly unenthusiastic about their Irish counterparts. In the first year of his New York sojourn, he felt more akin to the UILA and he soon developed a friendly relationship with John Quinn, an influential supporter of Irish Home Rule. But pragmatically appreciating the rising tide of popular support for Irish republicanism in the city, and throughout the nation, he developed cooperative relationships with Irish and Irish-American republicans as well. A key event in this turn was Rai's role in helping to found a new body called the Friends of Freedom for India in the autumn of 1919. Though formally led by Robert Morss Lovett, a University of Chicago professor, the principal organiser of the group was its 27-year-old general secretary, a feminist and militant anticolonial activist named Agnes Smedley, who had ties to more revolutionary figures among Indian nationalists in the United States. The association's national council boasted a number of eminent Americans, including Columbia University anthropologist Franz Boas and social reformer Upton Sinclair. Nonetheless it was New York's Irish republicans who provided the most vigorous American support for the new organisation. Frank P. Walsh, the well-known labour lawyer who had served as part of an Irish-American delegation to the Paris Peace Conference – styling itself the American Commission on Irish Independence – and who would go on to play an important role in the AARIR and as Éamon de Valera's main American legal advisor, became a vice president of the Friends of Freedom for India, while the (similarly named) Friends of Irish Freedom provided a good deal of moral and financial support.[16]

Contact and mutual support between diverse groups of anticolonial activists took the form of other new organisations as well, associations that sought to put forward what might be termed a broad 'anticolonial front'. The first of such associations was a body called the League of Small and Subject Nationalities, led by Frederic C. Howe, a well-known progressive reformer and Woodrow Wilson's commissioner of immigration. Howe established the league in May 1917 as 'a permanent congress of the small, subject and oppressed nationalities of the world', which he hoped would 'assert the right of each nationality to direct representation at the peace conference following this war [and] present the case of these nationalities to the world'. The objectives of the league reflected Howe's view that American entry into the war could only be justified – and he was, in fact, a war supporter – if Wilson's idealistic wartime rhetoric was taken at face value and made the basis for a sweeping transformation of the world's balance of power, and he argued forcefully for 'the right of self-government as an indispensable condition for world peace'. Though sympathetic to the Irish cause, Howe came from a small town in Pennsylvania that he once described as 'a comfortable little world, Republican in politics, careful in conduct, Methodist in religion'. He was not an Irish nationalist nor did he privilege the Irish case for independence in his overall political outlook.[17]

Nonetheless, the post-1916 Irish question had an important (and sometimes disruptive) effect on the new organisation almost immediately and continued to shape it for its entire existence. At its first large public meeting in October 1917 fallout from the Rising – or more specifically the presence of the Irish republican and feminist Hanna Sheehy Skeffington as the only speaker representing Ireland – nearly tore the infant organisation apart. Sheehy Skeffington was one of the most famous of the Irish republican émigrés working to generate American public support for independence after 1916. Her presence – in conjunction with the *absence* of representatives from such pro-Ally 'small and subject' nations as Armenia, Belgium, or Poland – led no fewer than eight other speakers to back out of their commitments at the last minute. 'Mrs. Sheehy-Skeffington is the sole representative of Ireland,' the eight noted in an angry statement released to the press. 'Does she represent the Irish people or only the pro-German wing of the Sinn Fein?' The league weathered this initial storm, and as the war came to an end in November 1918 it boasted representatives from no fewer that 22 national groups, ranging from Poland, Denmark, and Ireland (now represented by New York's well-known Irish-American nationalist leader Dr Gertrude B. Kelly) to Korea, India, and the Transvaal. 'Hebrews' were represented by Columbia University's Dr Samuel Joseph and the Zionist activist Bernard G. Richards, while W. E. B. Du Bois spoke for Africa.[18]

The Irish question erupted again the following month, however, when a British Labour Party representative named P. W. Wilson, who had been invited to speak at the league's second public meeting on 14 December 1918, made what a correspondent for *Young India* characterised as 'certain remarks against Ireland which were resented by the audience'. Wilson 'assumed an attitude of hostility toward the league and toward Ireland', and as a result his speech was interrupted by boos and hisses. Though Lajpat Rai responded directly to Wilson in a speech of his own that followed, the Irish question and the voicing of what the *New York Times* called 'attacks on England' by Indian nationalists and Irish republicans again proved disruptive.[19]

Frederic Howe himself attended the Paris Peace Conference as a consultant on the Mediterranean, but the failure of the talks to take up anything resembling global self-determination led to his disillusionment with prospects for decolonisation, and he moved on to other reform issues. Absent his leadership, the League of Small and Subject Nationalities was dead by November 1919. Taking up the same project, however, was a new organisation, the League of Oppressed Peoples, which held its inaugural public meeting the same month at New York's Lexington Theatre, with representatives of Ireland, India, and Korea in attendance. This time, however, it was not a small-town American reformer, but a leading New York Irish-American republican nationalist who was the dominant figure: a lawyer and political activist by the name of Dudley Field Malone. With an executive committee that included Lajpat Rai, the group began reaching out to notable figures involved in anticolonial activities. At Malone's behest, for example, the organisation's secretary contacted Du Bois, who agreed to participate, as did some of the others who had been involved in the earlier association.[20]

Unlike Howe's organisation, however, Irish nationalists figured prominently at every stage in the development of this new one. In fact, the original idea for the League of Oppressed Peoples apparently came from Frank P. Walsh, with financial support from yet another anticolonial activist, Sa'd Zaghlul, who had led the Egyptian delegation to the Paris Peace Conference. Walsh later told Dr William Maloney that Zaghlul had approached him at the Paris talks and asked him to serve as 'Egyptian Counsel' in the United States, a role similar to that he would later play for Ireland's Éamon de Valera. An arrangement worked out by Seán T. O'Kelly and George Gavan Duffy (who were also in Paris, representing the proclaimed Irish Republic) provided Walsh with $90,000 in expenses and fees. Once back in New York, according to Maloney, Walsh used some of this money to pay journalists to 'throw open their columns to Egyptian affairs' and some of it to pay the expenses of his old friend and political ally, the former governor of Missouri, Joseph W. Folk, to present the Egyptian case before the Senate Committee on Foreign Relations. But Walsh used $2,000 of the Egyptian money to found the League of Oppressed Peoples. The Friends of Irish Freedom supplemented the Egyptian funds with a pledge of $2,500.[21]

Though actively involved in numerous reform activities in these years – work with the National Civil Liberties Bureau, the forerunner of the American Civil Liberties Union, to take just one example – Walsh continued to play an important role in the League of Oppressed Peoples, serving as one of its vice presidents through the end of 1920. Other Irish and Irish-American nationalists, especially those on the left of the political spectrum, also gravitated to the organisation. John Fitzpatrick, the long-time president of the Chicago Federation of Labor, served as an officer of the league and Peter Golden, a leader of the Irish Progressive League, worked to distribute its informational materials to potentially sympathetic New York newspapers such as the *Jewish Daily Forward* and the socialist *New York Call*. Meanwhile, three of the Irish Republic's envoys in New York, Harry Boland, Liam Mellows, and Patrick McCartan, served as the official representatives of 'Ireland' on the central committee of the organisation. Such individuals (along with the poet and IPL activist Padraic Colum) were seen by a worried US Army Intelligence agent as 'focusing a large radical Irish element' upon the association.[22]

In the end, however, the most important individual in the league was Dudley Field Malone. Born to a prosperous Irish-American family on Manhattan's West Side in 1882, Malone attended St Francis Xavier's College (where he majored in French) and received a law degree from Fordham University in 1905. By the second decade of the century he was active in anti-Tammany Democratic reform circles, drawing positive attention from then-New Jersey governor Woodrow Wilson. In return for Malone's tireless work in his 1912 election campaign, Wilson appointed him to the important position of collector of the port of New York. But Malone resigned his post in the summer of 1917, in a dramatic protest of the administration's failure to endorse women's suffrage and its arrest of militant suffragists picketing in Washington. This principled action drew much criticism and cost Malone some old friends, but it gained him a host of new ones, including the suffragist leader Carrie Chapman Catt, who called it 'the noblest act that any man ever did on behalf of our cause'. Frederic Howe, who would resign his own position as US immigration commissioner in September 1919 to protest Wilson's deportation of alien radicals, described Malone as 'a magnetic personality in any group', noting that 'he was gifted with extraordinary ability as a public speaker, a richly endowed personality, and a generosity that went out to causes only less whole-heartedly than it went out to personal friends.'[23]

Not surprisingly, one of Malone's main 'causes' was post-1916 Irish republicanism. Though he does not seem to have been active in either the FOIF or the AARIR, he did accompany Éamon de Valera on part of his American tour, speaking alongside the Irish leader at a large rally in Detroit in the summer of 1920, for example. But Malone's main efforts in this period were focused on the forging of links of mutual support and cooperation between Irish activists and those representing other nationalities. It was Malone, for example, who arranged the September 1920 meeting between the IPL's Helen Golden and representatives of the Universal Negro Improvement Association, and when he spoke at the UNIA's Harlem Liberty Hall headquarters that month on the subject of 'Irish Freedom', he was, according to Marcus Garvey, the first white person to do so. Malone was not only a vice president of Lajpat Rai's Friends of Freedom for

India but also developed what he called an 'abiding friendship' with Rai, 'the most modest but most inspiring patriot I have ever known'. It was direct personal inter-actions like these – efforts to link 'peoples geographically and historically separated' in the concentrated metropolitan 'contact zone' that was First World War-era New York – that made Malone the natural leader of an organisation that aspired to speak not only for Ireland, India, or the African diaspora, but for those it called 'oppressed peoples' generally.[24]

More research is required to determine precisely what happened to such linkages after the end of the Irish War of Independence. The conflict over the Anglo-Irish Treaty and the subsequent Irish Civil War focused the attention of many Irish-American nationalists on this bitter internecine struggle, while many others simply drifted away from the movement altogether. The federal government's concerted offensive against the UNIA (culminating in Marcus Garvey's arrest, conviction, and eventual imprisonment for mail fraud) drastically weakened the forces of pan-Africanism by the mid-1920s, though Du Bois continued to take part in international pan-African conferences through the rest of the decade. In the Indian independence movement, the growing dominance of Gandhian nonviolence made the Irish model a significantly less attractive one over time, though recent scholars have explored various Irish-Indian contacts that persisted into the 1940s. The League of Oppressed Peoples itself both shrank and changed dramatically over the course of the 1920s, turning sharply away from the Irish revolution as a source of guidance and inspiration. In 1927 its remnants merged with the League against Imperialism, a front organisation funded and directed by the Moscow-dominated Communist International.[25]

In drawing attention to the impact of the Easter Rising on New York's antico-lonial activists, this chapter has neglected a related and perhaps equally important theme: direct influences and interactions between Indian and African-American political activists themselves. Such influences were clearly at work. Hubert Harrison, the St Croix-born African-American intellectual sometimes described as 'the father of Harlem radicalism', drew not only on Ireland but on India as well in his 1917 campaign for black electoral representation; anyone who sought 'to lead the Negro race', Harrison argued, had to 'follow the path of the Swadesha [sic] movement of India', as well as 'the Sinn Fein movement of Ireland'. Marcus Garvey, for all his admiration of the heroism and sacrifice of the Easter Rising rebels, was also influenced by the tactics of the more moderate Friends of Freedom for India. And Lajpat Rai developed a close friendship not only with Dudley Field Malone but with W. E. B. Du Bois, whom he got to know while making a study of race relations in the United States.

Nonetheless, in the era of the First World War and its aftermath, the Easter Rising and the Irish struggle for independence more generally served to focus the attention of a range of anticolonial nationalists in New York and opened up hitherto unimagined opportunities for contact, cooperation, and mutual support.[26]

# NOTES

## INTRODUCTION

1 Shane Leslie, *The Irish Issue in Its American Aspect* (London: T. Fisher Unwin Ltd, 1917, 177.

2 J. J. Lee, Glucksman Ireland House NYU to mark America and Ireland's 1916 Easter Rising (July 2015), YouTube video, available at: youtube.com/watch?v=EpZDXOXoqxI.

3 *Ireland*, 8 January 1916, available at: babel.hathitrust.org/cgi/pt?id=umn.31951000750823 q;view=1up;seq=14.

4 Ibid.

5 Ibid.

6 The history of the UILA and the origins of *Ireland* are explored more fully by Francis M. Carroll, 'The collapse of Home Rule and United Irish League of America, 1910–18: the centre did not hold', in this volume.

7 Clan na Gael had most recently come together in 1900 under the leadership of John Devoy, Daniel F. Cohalan, and Joseph McGarrity, with a commitment to the goal of an independent republican Ireland and proclaimed that 'the only policy which it believes will attain that object is physical force'. See David Brundage, *Irish Nationalists in America: The Politics of Exile* (New York: Oxford University Press, 2016), 138.

8 *Ireland*, 4 March 1916.

9 Andrew J. Wilson, *Irish America and the Ulster Conflict 1968–1995* (Belfast: Catholic University of America Press, 1995), 4.

10 Ronald H. Bayor and Timothy J. Meagher, eds, *The New York Irish* (Baltimore: Johns Hopkins University Press, 1996), 3.

11 Ibid.

12 Ibid.

13 If we know there were 196,372 New Yorkers (Manhattan, Annexed District, and Brooklyn) of Irish stock as late as 1890 then we must assume that there were no less than 100,000 in 1910. (Irish stock: offspring of an Irish mother, that is, born in Ireland or elsewhere of an Irish mother.) See Ibid., 558–9.

14 Lawrence J. McCaffrey, 'Forging forward and looking back', in Bayor and Meagher, eds, *The New York Irish*, 216.

15 David Brundage, '"In times of peace, prepare for war": key themes in the social thought of New York's Irish nationalists, 1890–1916', in Bayor and Meagher, eds, *The New York Irish*, 322.

16 J. J. Lee, *1916: The Irish Rebellion*, television series, episode one: 'Awakening'.

17 Brundage, *Irish Nationalists in America*, 139.

18 Quoted in Alan Ward, *Ireland and Anglo-American Relations* (London: The London School of Economics and Political Science, 1969), 70.

19 Mona Harrington, 'Loyalties: dual and divided', in Michael Walzer, Edward T. Kantowicz, John Higham, and Mona Harrington, eds, *The Politics of Ethnicity* (Cambridge: Harvard University Press, 1980), 94.

20 Michael Goebel, *Anti-Imperial Metropolis: Interwar Paris and the Seeds of Third World Nationalism* (Cambridge: Cambridge University Press, 2015), 13.

21 Ibid.

22 Timothy J. Meagher, *The Columbia Guide to Irish American History* (New York: Columbia University Press, 2005), 198

23 J. J. Lee, *Ireland, 1912–1985: Politics and Society* (Cambridge: Cambridge University Press, 1990), 29.

24 Alan O'Day, 'Irish diaspora politics in perspective: the United Irish Leagues of Great Britain and America, 1900–14', in Donald Mac Raild, ed., *The Great Famine and Beyond* (Dublin: Irish Academic Press, 2000), 234.

25 Brundage, *Irish Nationalists in America*, 139.

26 Alan O'Day, 'Irish nationalism and Anglo-American relations in the later nineteenth and early twentieth centuries', in Fred M. Leventhal and Roland Quinault, eds, *Anglo-American Attitudes: From Revolution to Partnership* (London: The London School of Economics and Political Science, 1969), 179.

27 Robert Schmuhl, *Ireland's Exiled Children: America and the Easter Rising* (Oxford: Oxford University Press, 2016), 4.

28 Harrington, 'Loyalties: dual and divided', in Walzer, Kantowicz, Higham and Harrington, eds, *The Politics of Ethnicity*, 93–4.

29 *Ireland*, 8 January 1916.

30 Ibid.

31 Ibid.

32 Ibid.

33 J. J. Lee, *Sunday Times*, February 2016.

34 Leslie, *The Irish Issue in Its American Aspect*, 180.

35 *Ireland*, 19 February 2016.

36 Ibid.

37 Ibid., 4 March 1916.

38 Ibid.

39 Ibid.

40 Fearghal McGarry, *The Rising: Ireland, Easter 1916* (Oxford: Oxford University Press, 2010), 95.

41 Brundage, *Irish Nationalists in America*.

42 Dennis J. Clark, *Irish Blood: Northern Ireland and the American Conscience* (Port Washington, NY: Kennikat Press, 1977), 4.

43 Ibid.

44 Ruth Dudley Edwards, cited in Robert Schmuhl, 'An American tale', *Irish Independent*, 6 February 2016.

45 For example, Tom Clarke sold *The Gaelic American* in Dublin and she mentions being sent newspapers from Ireland in the aftermath of the outbreak of war in 1914. See Sydney Gifford-Czira (John Brennan), *The Years Flew By* (Dublin: Gifford & Craven, 1974), 70, 79.

46 He also spoke in Baltimore, Buffalo, and Chicago while he was in the United States in 1914.

47 See Lucy McDiarmid, 'Casement, New York, and the Easter Rising', in this volume.

48 Ibid.

49 Rogers Brubaker, *Ethnicity without Groups* (Cambridge: Harvard University Press, 2006), 166.

50 For an overview on the lockout see Padraig Yeates, 'The Dublin 1913 lockout', *History Ireland* 9:2 (2001).

51 Brundage, *Irish Nationalists in America*, 150.

52 *Ireland*, 18 March 1916.

53 *Ireland*, 4 March 1916.

54 See R. Bryan Willits, 'The stereopticon: German and Irish propaganda of deed and word and the 1916 Easter Rising', in this volume.

55 See Úna Ní Bhroiméil, 'An American opinion: John Quinn and the Easter Rising', in this volume.

56 *New York Times*, 4 July 1914.

57 Brundage, *Irish Nationalists in America*, 134.

58 McCaffrey, 'Forging ahead and looking back', in Bayor and Meagher, eds, *The New York Irish*, 223–7.

59 The *Irish World* was founded by Patrick Ford, who turned over its operations to his sons Robert and Augustine in 1911 two years before his death. See James P. Rodechko, *Patrick Ford and His Search for America: A Case Study of Irish-American Journalism, 1870–1913* (New York: Arno Press, 1976).

60 Reinhard Doerries, *Prelude to the Easter Rising: Sir Roger Casement in Imperial Germany* (New York: Routledge, 2000), 83.

61 Terry Golway, 'Journalism, Irish-American', in Michael Glazier, ed., *The Encyclopedia of the Irish in America* (Notre Dame: University of Notre Dame Press, 1999), 485–6; O'Day,

'Irish diaspora politics in perspective', in MacRaild, ed., *The Great Famine and Beyond*, 229.

62 O'Day, 'Irish nationalism and Anglo-American relations in the later nineteenth and early twentieth centuries', in Leventhal and Quinault, eds, *Anglo-American Attitudes*, 177.

63 Schmuhl, *Ireland's Exiled Children*.

64 See Patricia Keefe Durso, 'The other narrative of 'sisterhood' in 1916: Irish and Irish-American suffragists', in this volume.

65 See David Brundage, 'The Easter Rising and New York's anticolonial nationalists', in this volume.

66 *Ireland*, 6 May 1916.

67 Ibid.

68 *Ireland*, 13 May 1916.

69 Ibid.

70 Ibid.

71 Leslie, *The Irish Issue in Its American Aspect*, 177.

72 See Brundage, 'The Easter Rising and New York's anticolonial nationalists'.

73 Leslie, *The Irish Issue in Its American Aspect*, 189–90.

74 See Carroll, 'The collapse of Home Rule and United Irish League of America, 1910–18'.

## 1. JOHN DEVOY AND THE EASTER RISING

1 John Devoy, *Recollections of an Irish Rebel* (New York: Charles Young, 1929), 458.

2 *Documents Relative to the Sinn Féin Movement* (London: HMSO, 1921), 9.

3 Terry Golway, *Irish Rebel: John Devoy and America's Fight for Ireland's Freedom* (New York: St Martin's Griffin, 1998), 145.

4 *The Gaelic American*, 17 January 1925.

5 Golway, *Irish Rebel*, 79, 208.

6 Ibid., 217–19.

7 *The Gaelic American*, 21 August 1915.

8 For background see Gillian O'Brien, '"A diabolical murder": Clan na Gael, Chicago and the murder of Dr Cronin', *History Ireland* 23:3 (2015): 32–5.

9 Golway, *Irish Rebel*, 80.

10 Ibid., 142, 182.

11 *New York Herald*, 25 October 1878.

12 Ibid.

13 Golway, *Irish Rebel*, 104–14.

14 Eric Foner, 'Class, ethnicity and radicalism in the gilded age: the Land League and Irish America', *Marxist Perspectives* 1:2 (1978); John Devoy, *Land of Eire* (New York: Patterson and Neilson, 1882), 64.

15 Approximately worth $12,000,000 in 2015. See Samuel H. Williamson, 'Seven ways to compute the relative value of a US dollar amount, 1774 to present', MeasuringWorth.com, 2016.

16 Robert Kee, *The Laurel and the Ivy* (London: Hamish Hamilton, 1993), 218.

17 Golway, *Irish Rebel*, 162.

18 Ibid., 176–81.

19 MS 9,919, John Devoy Papers, National Library of Ireland (NLI).

20 Ibid.

21 Golway, *Irish Rebel*, 178.

22 MS 9,919, John Devoy Papers, NLI.

23 Golway, *Irish Rebel*, 182.

24 *The Gaelic American*, 23 February 1911. The arbitration treaty eventually passed the senate, but only after a series of amendments that rendered it ineffective, at least in the view of supporters. See *New York Times*, 8 March 1912.

25 *The Gaelic American*, 4 February 1911.

26 Golway, *Irish Rebel*, 199.

27 Devoy, *Recollections*, 403.

28 Ibid.

29 Ibid.

30 MS 18,157, John Devoy Papers, NLI.

31 Golway, *Irish Rebel*, 207.

32 William O'Brien and Desmond Ryan, eds, *Devoy's Post Bag 1871–1928*, volume 2 (Dublin: C. J. Fallon, 1953), 484.

33 Golway, *Irish Rebel*, 458.

34 See Devoy, *Recollections*, 458–60; Sean Cronin, *The McGarrity Papers* (Tralee: Anvil Books, 1972), 60; *Documents Relative to the Sinn Féin Movement*, 9–10.

35 Devoy, *Recollections*, 460.

36 O'Brien and Ryan, eds, *Devoy's Post Bag*, 485–7.

37 Devoy, *Recollections*, 463.

38 Ibid., 449.

39 Ibid., 457.

40 Ibid., 463.

41 Ibid., 465.

42 *The Gaelic American*, 6 May 1916.

43 Ibid.

44 *The Times*, 1 October 1928.


## 2. THE COLLAPSE OF HOME RULE AND THE UNITED IRISH LEAGUE OF AMERICA, 1910–18: THE CENTRE DID NOT HOLD

1 The history of the Home Rule movement and John Redmond have been the subjects of revived interest, a selection of recent studies are, Ronan Fanning, *Fatal Path: British Government and Irish Revolution, 1910–1922* (London: Faber and Faber, 2013); Alvin

Jackson, *Home Rule: An Irish History, 1800–2000* (London: Weidenfeld & Nicolson, 2003); Jeremy Smith, *The Tories and Ireland, 1910–1914* (Dublin: Irish Academic Press, 2000); James McConnel, *The Irish Parliamentary Party and the Third Home Rule Crisis* (Dublin: Four Courts Press, 2013); Gabriel Doherty, ed., *The Home Rule Crisis, 1912–14* (Cork: Mercier Press, 2014); Paul Bew, *John Redmond* (Dundalk: Historical Association of Ireland, 1996); Joseph P. Finnan, *John Redmond and Irish Unity, 1912–1918* (Syracuse: Syracuse University Press, 2004); and Dermot Meleady, *John Redmond: The National Leader* (Dublin: Merrion Press, 2014). For a good discussion of the historiography of the fate of Home Rule, see Euginio Biagini, 'The Third Home Rule Bill in British history', in Doherty, ed., *The Home Rule Crisis*, 412–42.

2 On the United Irish League see Philip Bull, 'The formation of the United Irish League, 1898–1900: the dynamics of Irish agrarian agitation', *Irish Historical Studies* 33:132 (2003): 404–23.

3 Roughly $2,500,000 today. See Samuel H. Williamson, 'Seven ways to compute the relative value of a US dollar amount, 1774 to present', MeasuringWorth.com, 2016.

4 See T. St John Gaffney to John Redmond, 7 January 1902, Redmond Papers, National Library of Ireland (NLI).

5 F. M. Carroll, *American Opinion and the Irish Question, 1910–1923* (New York: St Martin's Press, 1978), 7–8; Alan J. Ward, *Ireland and Anglo-American Relations, 1899–1921* (London: Weidenfeld & Nicolson, 1969), 14–15.

6 Michael J. Ryan to John Redmond, 27 February 1910, Redmond Papers, NLI.

7 Finnan, *John Redmond and Irish Unity*, 156–7; Carroll, *American Opinion and the Irish Question*, 15–17; Ward, *Ireland and Anglo-American Relations*, 15–19.

8 Patrick Egan to John Redmond, 1 March 1910, Redmond Papers, NLI; Theodore Roosevelt to Robert John Wynne, 11 April 1910, in E. E. Morison, ed., *The Letters of Theodore Roosevelt*, volume 7 (Cambridge: Harvard University Press, 1954), 68–9.

9 James A. O'Gorman et al. to John Redmond, 12 April 1912, Redmond Papers, NIL; William Bourke Cockran to John Redmond, 13 April 1912, Box 18, William Bourke Cockran Papers, New York Public Library (NYPL).

10 Patrick Ford to Theodore Roosevelt, 23 January 1913, Series I, Box 239, Roosevelt Papers, Library of Congress; *New York Times*, 11 May 1912.

11 Martin J. Keogh to John Redmond, 27 May 1912, Redmond Papers, NLI; Carroll, *American Opinion and the Irish Question*, 20–2.

12 For background to the Irish Volunteers see Joseph E. A. Connell Jr, 'Founding the Irish Volunteers', *History Ireland* 6 (2013), available at: historyireland.com/18th-19th-century-history/founding-irish-volunteers/.

13 William Bourke Cockran to Moreton Frewen, 25 March 1914, Box 16, William Bourke Cockran Papers, NYPL.

14 B. L. Reid, *The Man from New York: John Quinn and His Friends* (New York: Oxford University Press, 1968), 185–6.

15 John Quinn to John Purroy Mitchel, 31 July 1914, Box 7, Mitchel Papers, Library of Congress; Carroll, *American Opinion and the Irish Question*, 23–5.

16 See Robert Ford, circular letter, 28 July 1914, Box E–J, John Devoy Papers, NLI.

17 *Irish World*, 1 August 1914; *The Gaelic American*, 1 August 1914.

18 Denis Gwynn, *The Life of John Redmond* (London: George G. Harrap & Co. Ltd., 1932), 356–7.

19 *Irish World*, 26 September 1914.

20 Ibid., 10, 14 October 1914.

21 Patrick Egan to John Redmond, 20 October 1914, and P. T. Barry to John Redmond, 31 October 1914, Redmond Papers, NLI.

22 Gwynn, *The Life of John Redmond*, 417.

23 Ibid. Ryan's pro-German views are often attributed to his German-American wife, but he took a very public stand in supporting Germany and also associating with Clan and Friends of Irish Freedom events.

24 Ibid., 416–19.

25 Patrick Egan to John Redmond, 12 October 1914, Redmond Papers, NLI.

26 William Dillon to William Bourke Cockran, 26 October 1914, Box 18, William Bourke Cockran Papers, NYPL.

27 John G. Coyle to John Redmond, 18 December 1914, and Michael J. Ryan to Stephen McFarland, 9 March 1915, Redmond Papers, NLI.

28 Michael J. Jordan to John Redmond, 31 December 1914, Redmond Papers, NLI.

29 Michael J. Jordan to John Redmond, 25 February 1915, Redmond Papers, NLI.

30 Patrick Egan to Michael J. Jordan, 27 February 1915, Redmond Papers, NLI.

31 Stephen McFarland et al. to Michael J. Ryan, 6 March 1915, Michael J. Ryan to Stephen McFarland, 9 March 1915, Stephen McFarland to John Redmond, and R. J. Waddell to Michael J. Jordan, 12 March 1915, Redmond Papers, NLI.

32 Michael Jordan to John Redmond, 9 April 1815, Redmond Papers, NLI; Ward, *Ireland and Anglo-American Relations*, 80.

33 For a detailed study of the emergence of the republican nationalist movement in the United States, see Michael Doorley, *Irish-American Diaspora Nationalism: The Friends of Irish Freedom, 1916–1935* (Dublin: Four Courts Press, 2005), passim.

34 Patrick Egan to John Redmond, 20 October 1914, Patrick Egan to T. J. Hanna, 12 December 1914, and Michael J. Jordan to John Redmond, 31 December 1914, Redmond Papers, NLI.

35 Patrick Egan to T. J. Hanna, 7 May 1915, Redmond Papers, NLI.

36 John Redmond to Daniel Boyle, 13 October 1915, Box 18, William Bourke Cockran Papers, NYPL.

37 Shane Leslie to John Redmond, 9 March 1917, Redmond Papers, NLI; Thomas R. Greene, 'Shane Leslie and *Ireland* (1916–1917): "England's little Irish organ in New York"', *Éire-Ireland* 22:4 (winter 1987), 72–92.

38 Cited in Finnan, *John Redmond and Irish Unity*, 180; Shane Leslie, *The Irish Issue in Its American Aspect* (London: T. Fisher Unwin, Ltd, 1917), 181–3.

39 *Irish World*, 26 April 1916.

40 *Christian Science Monitor*, 2–3 May 1916.

41 *Chicago Tribune*, 26 April 1916.

42 Stephen McFarland to John Redmond, 4 May 1916, Redmond Papers, NLI.

43 Michael J. Ryan to John Redmond, 15 May 1916, Redmond Papers, NLI.

44 Shane Leslie to John Redmond, May 16, 1916, Redmond Papers, NLI.

45 Memorandum on Irish America, by J. Joyce Broderick, 19 January 1917, FO 371/3071, The National Archives, Kew.

46 Shane Leslie to John Redmond, 16 May 1916, Redmond Papers, NLI.

47 See Carroll, *American Opinion and the Irish Question*, 90–102.

48 Shane Leslie to John Redmond, 15 May 1917, Redmond Papers, NLI.

49 John Redmond to Michael J. Ryan, 1 May 1917, and John Redmond, circular letter, 2 May 1917, Redmond Papers, NLI.

50 Michael J. Jordan to John Redmond, 7 May 1917, Redmond Papers, NLI. Leslie, who claimed the friendship of Joseph Tumulty, Wilson's secretary, may have had some insight into the White House. See Shane Leslie, *Long Shadows* (London: John Murray, 1966), 177.

51 Shane Leslie to John Redmond, 6 May 1917, Redmond Papers, NLI.

52 Transcript of Irish deputation, 4 May 1917, John Quinn Papers, NLI; Carroll, *American Public Opinion and the Irish Question*, 95–6; Catherine Shannon, *Arthur J. Balfour and Ireland, 1874–1922* (Washington, DC: Catholic University of America Press, 1988), 228–32. The deputation was made up of John Quinn, Mayor John F. Fitzgerald, Lawrence Godkin, Col Robert Temple Emmet, Judge Morgan J. O'Brien, John J. Wynne, SJ, and Monsignor Sigourney Fay. Balfour reported the gist of the meeting to Cabinet.

53 H. Fyfe, *T. P. O'Connor* (London: George Allen & Unwin, 1934), 266–7.

54 T. P. O'Connor to John Dillon, cited in Finnan, *John Redmond and Irish Unity*, 179.

55 Roughly $1,350,000 today. See Samuel H. Williamson, 'Seven ways to compute the relative value of a US dollar amount, 1774 to present', MeasuringWorth.com, 2016.

56 Fyfe, *T. P. O'Connor*, 217.

57 Richard Hazleton to John Redmond, 5 December 1917, Redmond Papers, NLI; Richard Hazleton to Shane Leslie, 26 September 1917, Box 18, William Bourke Cockran Papers, NYPL.

58 Leslie, *Long Shadows*, 192.

59 Ironically, Michael J. Ryan, its president, was active in the Irish Race Convention in 1919 under the auspices of the Friends of Irish Freedom, and became one of the American commissioners on Irish independence.

60 For a discussion of how the ideology of the World War and the creation of new states in its aftermath changed the language of self-government and national identity, see Biagini, 'The Third Home Rule Bill in British history', in Doherty, ed., *The Home Rule Crisis*, 435–42.

## 3. TOM CLARKE'S NEW YORK: A REFUGE (1880) AND A HOME (1899–1907)

1 Michael T. Foy, *Tom Clarke: The True Leader of the Easter Rising* (Dublin: The History Press, 2014), 7–8.

2 James Reidy, 'Thomas J. Clarke', in *The Irish Rebellion of 1916 and Its Martyrs* (New York: The Devin-Adair Company, 1916), 394–6; and John Daly Clarke, 'US consular application, 1921', Ancestry.com.

3 Louis Le Roux, *Tom Clarke and the Irish Freedom Movement* (Dublin: Talbot Press, 1936), 8; Foy, *Tom Clarke*, 8, 23.

4 Le Roux, *Tom Clarke*, 8–9.

5 Ibid., 9.

6 Ibid., 10.

7 Kathleen Clarke to Michael Whelan, 5 June 1966, File 1598, Local Studies Collection, Leitrim County Library.

8 Ciarán Ó Gríofa, 'John Daly the Fenian mayor of Limerick', in David Lee, ed., *Remembering Limerick: Historical Essays Celebrating the 800th Anniversary of Limerick's First Charter Produced in 1197* (Limerick: Limerick Civic Trust, 1997), 198.

9 Statement of William Kelly Sr, Papers of Father Louis O'Kane, O'Fiaich Library and Archive, Armagh (OFLA).

10 Ibid.

11 Ibid.

12 *Belfast Morning News*, 18 August 1880.

13 Ibid.

14 Statement of William Kelly Sr, OFLA.

15 Ibid.

16 Louis Le Roux, *Tom Clarke*, 18.

17 Statement of William Kelly Sr, OFLA.

18 Ibid.

19 Louis Le Roux, *Tom Clarke*, 24.

20 Ibid., 24–5.

21 Oldbaileyon-line.org.

22 Le Roux, *Tom Clarke*, 31.

23 Ibid., 31, 33.

24 Ibid.

25 Ibid., 35.

26 *Southern Star*, 8 October 1898. I am grateful to Pat Bermingham for this reference.

27 *Tyrone Courier*, 27 October 1898.

28 Box 2, Folder 51, Daly Papers, University of Limerick Archives (ULA).

29 Ibid.

30 Statement, 26 May 1899, John Redmond to Tom Clarke, 26 May 1899, and John Dillon to Tom Clarke, 29 May 1899, ACC 6410, Box 3, Thomas Clarke Papers, National Library of Ireland (NLI).

31 Helen Litton, ed., *Kathleen Clarke: Revolutionary Woman, an Autobiography* (Dublin: O'Brien Press, 1991), 22.

32 Auction accession lot 371, 2006, Daly Papers, ULA.

33 Gríofa, 'John Daly, the Fenian mayor of Limerick', in Lee, ed., *Remembering Limerick*, 199.

34 Ibid.

35 Le Roux, *Tom Clarke*, 56.

36 Litton, ed., *Kathleen Clarke*, 24–5.

37 Ibid., 25.

38 Ibid.

39 Sean McGarry, Witness Statement 368, Bureau of Military History, National Archives of Ireland.

40 Kathleen Daly to Tom Clarke, 24 August 1899, and Tom Clarke to Kathleen Daly, 15 September 1899, ACC 6410, Box 1, I.i.3, Thomas Clarke Papers, NLI.

41 Le Roux, *Tom Clarke*, 58.

42 Tom Clarke to Kathleen Daly, 28 November 1899, ACC 6410, Box 1, I.ii.1, Thomas Clarke Papers, NLI.

43 Despite the fact that he had been forced to leave Ireland, his friends continued to seek employment for him and in August 1900 the Amnesty Association put his name forward for the post of superintendent of the Dublin abattoirs. He returned to Dublin but he was once again to be disappointed. See Tom Clarke to Kathleen Daly, 5 November 1899, ACC 6410, Box 3, V. vi, Box 1, I.ii.1, Thomas Clarke Papers, NLI; Le Roux, *Tom Clarke*, 58–9.

44 The term 'Friends' was a code used by members of Clan na Gael when communicating amongst themselves.

45 Tom Clarke to Kathleen Daly, 12 May 1900, ACC 6410, Box 3, V. vi, Box 1, I.ii.1, Thomas Clarke Papers, NLI; John T. Ridge, 'Irish County Societies in New York, 1880–1914', in Ronald H. Bayor and Timothy J. Meagher, eds, *The New York Irish* (Baltimore and London: John Hopkins University Press, 1996), 299.

46 Tom Clarke to Kathleen Daly, 11 November 1899, ACC 6410, Box 1, I.ii.1, Thomas Clarke Papers, NLI.

47 Le Roux, *Tom Clarke*, 60.

48 John Daly Clarke, 'US consular application, 1921', Ancestry.com.

49 Litton, ed., *Kathleen Clarke*, 30.

50 *The Clansman, Souvenir of the Celtic and Emmet Clubs, Irish Picnic and Games*, 17 June 1905.

51 Tom Clarke to Kathleen Clarke, 4 August 1905, ACC 6410, Box 1, I.ii.6, Thomas Clarke Papers, NLI.

52 Le Roux, *Tom Clarke*, 67–8.

53 Ibid., 62.

54 Ibid., 63.

55 Ibid., 68–9.

56 Ibid., 71.

57 Ibid., 72.

58 Litton, ed., *Kathleen Clarke*, 33; Kathleen Clarke to Tom Clarke, 4 October 1905, ACC 6410, Box 1, I.i.12, Thomas Clarke Papers, NLI.

59 Tom Clarke's certificate of American citizenship, 2 November 1905, EW 375, National Museum of Ireland (NMI).

60 Litton, ed., *Kathleen Clarke*, 33.

61 Ibid.

62 Ibid., 35.

63 *The Gaelic American*, 1 June 1907.

64 Marnie Hay, *Bulmer Hobson and the Nationalist Movement in Twentieth-Century Ireland* (Manchester: Manchester University Press, 2009), 67–71; Le Roux, *Tom Clarke*, 80.

65 Precis of police reports, December 1907, Colonial Office Papers (CO) 904/117, National Archives, Kew (ENA).

66 Tom Clarke to James Reidy, 28 December 1907, EW 2086, NMI.

67 Ibid.

68 Kathleen Clarke to P. T. Madden, 5 June 1961, MS 31,696, P. T. Madden Papers, NLI.

69 Kathleen Clarke to Tom Clarke, 6 January 1908, ACC 6410, Box 1, I.i.14, Thomas Clarke Papers, NLI.

70 Kathleen Clarke to Tom Clarke, 8 May 1908, Box 1, I.i.18, Thomas Clarke Papers, NLI.

71 Tom Clarke to Kathleen Clarke, 31 March 1908, Box 1, I.ii.12, Thomas Clarke Papers, NLI.

72 Tom Clarke to James Reidy, 16 April 1909, Box 2, Folder 47 (7), Daly Papers, ULA.

73 Tom Clarke to John Daly, 18 June 1911, Box 2, Folder 47 (4), Daly Papers, ULA.

74 Tom Clarke to John Daly, 28 June 1907, Box 2, Folder 47 (2), Daly Paper, ULA.

75 Ibid.

76 Tom Clarke to Jim Bermingham, 28 January 1900, MS 26,761, Fred Allan Papers, NLI.

77 Tom Clarke to James Reidy, 3 January 1909, Box 2, Folder 47 (4), Daly Papers, ULA.

78 CO 904/12, October 1910, ENA. The importance of the financial backing provided to Irish republicans by their American counterparts cannot be overstated. In June 1907, Joe McGarrity sent a cheque for £10 to Bulmer Hobson to help him settle the affairs of the Dungannon Clubs journal, the *Republic*. See Joe McGarrity to Bulmer Hobson, 26 June 1907, 17612, Joseph McGarrity Papers, NLI. Similarly, in October 1908, Pat McCartan informed McGarrity that the *Peasant* was 'on its last legs for want of capital' claiming that its demise 'would be regarded as a great triumph for clericalism'. Within a month, Bulmer Hobson had received £100 to 'keep the *Peasant* afloat'. See Pat McCartan to Joe McGarrity, 31 October 1908 and 21 November 1908, 17612 (2), Joseph McGarrity Papers, NLI. In addition, ad hoc subscriptions regularly made their way across the Atlantic. Hence, George Doris, a resident of Philadelphia, but 'formerly a prominent IRB man in Cookstown, County Tyrone', sent £1 to the IRB in January 1914. See CO 904/120, 23 January 1914, ENA.

79 CO 904/13, July and August 1911, ENA.

80 Marie Veronica Tarpey, *The Role of Joseph McGarrity in the Struggle for Irish Independence* (New York: Arno Press, 1976), 72.

81 CO 904/13, August 1911, ENA.

82 CO 904/119, August 1911, ENA.

83 CO 904/13, September and October 1911, ENA.

84 William O'Brien and Desmond Ryan, eds, *Devoy's Post Bag 1871–1928*, volume 2 (Dublin: C. J. Fallon, 1953), 410–12.

85 Ibid. Clarke's excitement at the Bodenstown attendance is all the more understandable given that eight years earlier the same occasion had drawn a crowd of only 80 people. The authorities regarded this as being representative of the 'failure of treasonable or revolutionary demonstrations in Ireland at the present day'. See CO 904/117, July 1905, ENA.

86 Sean Cronin, *The McGarrity Papers* (Tralee: Anvil Books, 1992), 37–8.

87 O'Brien and Ryan, eds, *Devoy's Post Bag*, 444–6.

88 MS 17,609 (9), Joseph McGarrity Papers, NLI.

89 MS 18,137 (4), John Devoy Papers, NLI.

90 MS 31,653, Denis McCullough Papers, NLI.

91 Seán McConville, *Irish Political Prisoners, 1848–1922: Theatres of War* (London: Routledge, 2005), 414.

## 4. THE BOLD FENIAN WIFE: MARY JANE O'DONOVAN ROSSA

1 Baptism, 1845, Church Records of Baptism, Marriage and Burial, Department of Arts, Heritage and the Gaeltacht, Dublin, available at: churchrecords.irishgenealogy.ie/churchrecords/details/fad50c0029145.

2 Academic award presented to Mary Jane Irwin, 1861, MS 22,917, Papers Collected by Sean O'Luing, National Library of Ireland (NLI); Rossa family Bible, Rossa Family Private Collection, Patricia R. Byrne Residence, Milford, CT.

3 Mary Jane O'Donovan Rossa, 'Rossa's death described by Mrs Rossa', *The Gaelic American*, 11 September 1915.

4 Jeremiah O'Donovan Rossa, *Irish Rebels in English Prisons: A Record of Prison Life* (New York: Sadlier, 1878); 'Prison life', *Irish American Weekly*, 3 January 1874.

5 Jeremiah O'Donovan Rossa, *Rossa's Recollections, 1838 to 1898: Memoirs of an Irish Revolutionary* (Guilford, CT: Lyons Press, 2004).

6 'Selection of O'Donovan Rossa by Tipperary', *Irish Times*, 11 February 1870; 'Gen. Sigel's indorsement of O'Donovan Rossa', *New York Times*, 6 November 1871.

7 'Appeal to the women of Ireland', *The Irishman*, 29 June 1867.

8 John Devoy, *Recollections of an Irish Rebel* (Shannon: Irish University Press, 1969), 113.

9 Sylke Lehne, 'Fenianism – a male business?: a case study of Mary Jane O'Donovan Rossa (1845–1916)' (Master's thesis, St Patrick's College, 1995), 26.

10 'News of the city-Chicago republican', *Daily Inter Ocean*, 2 March 1869.

11 'News of the city-nugget of gold', *Daily Inter Ocean*, 1 February 1869.

12 'Mrs O'Donovan Rossa's readings', *Providence Evening Press*, 14 September 1868; 'Mrs O'Donovan Rossa: announcement', *Daily Eastern Argus*, 2 October 1868; 'Mrs O'Donovan Rossa Ohio and Illinois', *Irish American Weekly*, 15 May 1869; 'Mrs O'Donovan Rossa in Peoria', *Irish American Weekly*, 6 March 1869; 'Mrs O'Donovan Rossa in Canada', *Frank Leslie's Illustrated Newspaper*, 23 October 1869; 'Mrs O'Donovan Rossa in Brookline', *Irish American Weekly*, 5 September 1868; 'Mrs O'Donovan Rossa in Augusta', *Daily Inter Ocean*, 26 April 1869; 'Mrs O'Donovan Rossa', *Leavenworth Bulletin*, 9 March 1869; 'Mrs O'Donovan Rossa', *Hartford Daily Courant*, 25 November 1868.

13 Mary Jane O'Donovan Rossa, scrapbook from 1868–70, Rossa Family Private Collection, Patricia R. Byrne Residence, Milford, CT.

14 W. S. Neidhardt, *Fenianism in North America* (University Park: Pennsylvania State University, 1975), 111.

15 Maxwell Irwin to Mary Jane O'Donovan Rossa, 27 February 1868, 014/05/02/22, Fenian Brotherhood and O'Donovan Rossa Personal Papers, American Catholic History Research Centre and University Archives (ACUA), Washington, DC.

16 John Devoy, 'Widow of O'Donovan Rossa dies suddenly', *The Gaelic American*, 26 August 1916.

17 Mary Jane O'Donovan Rossa, a notebook containing poems and sketches, 1870, MS 412, O'Donovan Rossa Papers, NLI.

18 'Irish lyrical poems: a volume of poems, by Mrs J. O'Donovan (Rossa)', *Irish American Weekly*, 23 November 1867.

19 Mary Jane O'Donovan Rossa, a notebook containing poems and sketches, 1870, MS 412, O'Donovan Rossa Papers, NLI.

20 Elsie M. Wilbor, ed., *Werner's Directory of Elocutionists, Readers, Lecturers and other Public Instructors and Entertainers* (New York: Edgar S. Werner, 1887), 272.

21 Joseph Edwin Frobisher to Mrs O'Donovan Rossa, 14 October 1868, 014/05/02/26, Fenian Brotherhood and O'Donovan Rossa Personal Papers, ACUA.

22 'Readings from the Irish and American poets', *The Sun*, 17 June 1868.

23 'Readings from the poets', *Irish American Weekly*, 27 June 1868.

24 'Irish Republican Convention', *Daily Inter Ocean*, 7 July 1869.

25 'The Irish in New York', *The Nation*, 25 July 1868.

26 Ibid.

27 'A wife worth having', *Cleveland Daily Leader*, 7 November 1870.

28 'Departure of the Fenian prisoners for America', *Manchester Evening News*, 9 January 1871.

29 David Brundage, '"In time of peace, prepare for war": key themes in the social thought of New York's Irish nationalists, 1890–1916', in Ronald H. Bayor and Timothy J. Meagher, eds, *The New York Irish* (Baltimore and London: Johns Hopkins University Press, 1996), 331.

30 'Mr O'Donovan Rossa; Mr Preston; Baltimore', *Alexandria Gazette*, 18 March 1871.

31 'A plea for a Fenian', *Brooklyn Daily Eagle*, 17 January 1870; 'The Fenians, visit of the exiles to President Grant', *New York Times*, 23 February 1871.

32 Rossa family Bible, Rossa Family Private Collection, Patricia R. Byrne Residence, Milford, CT.

33 'The university law school', *Irish American Weekly*, 26 May 1877; Denis O'Donovan Rossa to Mary Jane O'Donovan Rossa, 5 July 1876, 014/05/03, Fenian Brotherhood and O'Donovan Rossa Personal Papers, ACUA.

34 'Irish-American obituary', *Irish American Weekly*, 5 January 1878.

35 Jeremiah O'Donovan Rossa to John Devoy, 4 December 1871, MS 18,009/11/2, John Devoy Papers, NLI.

36 Jeremiah O'Donovan Rossa to John Devoy, 30 March 1874, MS 18,009/11/5, John Devoy Papers, NLI.

37 Pamphlet from Northern Hotel, 014/05/11b, Fenian Brotherhood and O'Donovan Rossa Personal Papers, ACUA.

38 Jeremiah O'Donovan Rossa, ledger from the O'Donovan Rossa Hotel, 1875, 014/5/11/1, Fenian Brotherhood and O'Donovan Rossa Personal Papers, ACUA.

39 Patrick Ford, 'Skirmishing fund', *Irish World*, 4 March 1876.

40 Jeremiah O'Donovan Rossa, 'The skirmishing fund', *Irish World*, 25 March 1876.

41 John Devoy, 'O'Donovan Rossa, some light let in on a dark and dirty subject', *Irish Nation*, 2 September 1882.

42 John O'Leary, 'O'Donovan Rossa's skirmishing fund', *Irish American Weekly*, 22 April 1876.

43 Margaret O'Donovan Rossa, *My Father and Mother Were Irish* (New York: Devin-Adair 1939), 18.

44 Devoy, 'Widow of O'Donovan Rossa dies suddenly'.

45 'O'Donovan Rossa the Irish nationalist gives up his hotel want of patronage the cause', *New York Herald*, 10 August 1877.

46 'O'Donovan Rossa, a midnight riot in Toronto', *New York Evening Express*, 19 March 1878.

47 William O'Brien and Desmond Ryan, eds, *Devoy's Post Bag 1871–1928*, volume 1 (Dublin: C. J. Fallon, 1948), 316.

48 'Personal – Mrs O'Donovan Rossa and family', *Irish American Weekly*, 7 September 1878.

49 'Mrs O'Donovan Rossa', *Irish American Weekly*, 7 December 1878.

50 O'Brien and Ryan, eds, *Devoy's Post Bag*, 353.

51 Rossa family Bible, Rossa Family Private Collection, Patricia R. Byrne Residence, Milford, CT; 'Death certificate, Amelia M. O'Donovan Rossa, Philadelphia, Pennsylvania, Death Certificates Index, 1803–1915', Ancestry.com.

52 'Summary of news', *Kildare Observer*, 12 March 1881.

53 Jeremiah O'Donovan Rossa to Mary Jane O'Donovan Rossa from New York Hospital, 2 February 1885, MS 10,974 (iii), O'Donovan Rossa Papers, NLI.

54 'O'Donovan Rossa's assailant; Mrs Dudley to be confined in an asylum in England', *New York Times*, 3 March 1891.

55 1880 United States census, Philadelphia, Pennsylvania, National Archives and Records Administration, Washington, DC, Familysearch.org.

56 Rossa family Bible, Rossa Family Private Collection, Patricia R. Byrne Residence, Milford, CT.

57 'Mortuary notice, James Maxwell O'Donovan Rossa', *New York Herald*, 23 November 1893.

58 Mary Jane O'Donovan Rossa to Jeremiah O'Donovan Rossa, 6 August 1894, MS 10,974 (iii), O'Donovan Rossa Papers, NLI.

59 'Passing events', *Irish World*, 21 July 1894.

60 'Ejected from the chamber', *Boston Herald*, 9 May 1895.

61 'Alas! Poor O'Donovan (Rossa)', *New York Times*, 17 August 1894.

62 'Maud Gonne's lecture', *Brooklyn Daily Eagle*, 3 February 1900.

63 Mary Jane O'Donovan Rossa to Mariana Wright Chapman, 10 May 1896, RG5/260, Series 1, Box 1, 2ALsS, Mariana Wright Chapman Family Papers, Friends Historical Library at Swarthmore College, Swarthmore, PA.

64 'Rossa, Cork County Council', *Syracuse Journal*, 21 September 1906; 'O'Donovan Rossa, greeting in his native town', *Southern Star*, 26 November 1904.

65 Publisher of Anvil Books Limited to Sean O'Luing, 12 February 1970, MS UR 076989, Sean O'Luing Papers, NLI.

66 Mary Jane O'Donovan Rossa to Margaret O'Donovan Rossa, 28 February 1906, Williams Rossa Cole Private Collection, Williams Rossa Cole Residence, Brooklyn, NY.

67 'Mrs O'Donovan Rossa ill', *Irish American Weekly*, 14 April 1906.

68 O'Donovan Rossa, *My Father and Mother Were Irish*, 154.

69 'Coler gives Rossa inspectorship', *Alton Evening Telegraph*, 22 November 1906.

70 Thomas Addis Emmet to Jeremiah O'Donovan Rossa, 5 January 1907, MS 10,974 (i), O'Donovan Rossa Papers, NLI; Thomas Addis Emmet to Mrs O'Donovan Rossa, 28 June 1913, MS 8,648/2, O'Donovan Rossa Papers, NLI.

71 Post Office Department, discontinuance of *United Irishman* on 31 December 1910, 29 June 1912, MS 22,917, Papers Collected by Sean O'Luing, NLI.

72 Mary Jane O'Donovan Rossa to John Devoy, 26 December 1912, MS 18,009/12/2, John Devoy Papers, NLI.

73 Mary Jane O'Donovan Rossa to John Devoy, 24 February 1913, MS 18,009/11/1, John Devoy Papers, NLI.

74 Mary Jane O'Donovan Rossa to John Devoy, 16 September 1913, MS 18,009/14/7, John Devoy Papers, NLI.

75 Mary Jane O'Donovan Rossa to John Devoy, 20 December 1913, MS 18,009/17/5, John Devoy Papers, NLI.

76 Mary Jane O'Donovan Rossa to John Devoy, 30 November 1913, MS 18,009/16/6, John Devoy Papers, NLI.

77 'O'Donovan Rossa, patriot, dies at 83', *New York Times*, 30 June 1915.

78 Jeremiah O'Donovan Testimonial Committee, fund raising letter, 28 August 1890, MS 18,090/19/6, John Devoy Papers, NLI.

79 'The remains of T. B. McManus', *New York Times*, 21 November 1861.

80 Mary Jane O'Donovan Rossa to Tom Clarke, 1 July 1915, MS 18,009/25, John Devoy Papers, NLI.

81 Mary Jane O'Donovan Rossa, 'A memorable nationalist demonstration', *The Gaelic American*, 25 December 1915.

82 Ibid.

83 Mary Jane O'Donovan Rossa, 'The old spirit revived in Ireland', *The Gaelic American*, 6 November 1915.

84 Mary Jane O'Donovan Rossa to John Devoy, 9 February 1916, MS 18,009/24/2, John Devoy Papers, NLI.

85 Mary Jane O'Donovan Rossa to Margaret O'Donovan Rossa, 27 July 1916, Williams Rossa Cole Private Collection, Williams Rossa Cole Residence, Brooklyn, NY.

86 Eileen O'Donovan Rossa to John Devoy, 22 March 1916, MS 18,009/10/5, John Devoy Papers, NLI.

87 Mary Jane O'Donovan Rossa to John Devoy, 6 April 1916, MS 18,009/24/6, John Devoy Papers, NLI.

88 'Four Irish rebel leaders executed', *New York Times*, 4 May 1916; Mary Jane O'Donovan Rossa to Margaret O'Donovan Rossa, 4 May 1916, Williams Rossa Cole Private Collection, Williams Rossa Cole Residence, Brooklyn, NY.

89 'Irish pay tribute to Dublin rebels', *New York Times*, 15 May 1916.

90 Mary Jane O'Donovan Rossa to Ellen Regan Jolly, 26 June 1916, Rossa Family Private Collection, Patricia Byrne Residence, Milford, CT.

91 Mary Jane O'Donovan Rossa to Margaret O'Donovan Rossa, 27 July 1916, Williams Rossa Cole Private Collection, Williams Rossa Cole Residence, Brooklyn, NY.

92 Mary Jane O'Donovan Rossa to John Devoy, 11 July 1916, MS 18,009/24/7, John Devoy Papers, NLI.

93 Mary Jane O'Donovan Rossa, 'Countess Markievicz', *The Gaelic American*, 15 July 1916.

94 Mary Jane O'Donovan Rossa, scrapbook of poetry, August 1916, Private Collection of Kathleen Gelson McEachern, Rindge, NH; O'Donovan Rossa, 'Countess Markievicz'.

95 Devoy, 'Widow of O'Donovan Rossa dies suddenly'.

## 5. DR GERTRUDE B. KELLY AND THE FOUNDING OF NEW YORK'S CUMANN NA MBAN

1 *Liberty*, 18 September 1886: 5 on *The Libertarian Labyrinth*, available at: library.libertarian-labyrinth.org/items/show/2788. Dr Kelly was responding to the fallout from the Haymarket Riots. For more, see Wendy McElroy, *Individualist Feminism of the Nineteenth Century: Collected Writings and Biographical Profiles* (Jefferson, NC: McFarland & Company Inc., Publishers, 2001), 167–8.

2 'Heredity is revealed in the eyes of the cat.' This proverb basically takes up the argument of nature versus nurture.

3 Bruce Nelson contends that Dr Kelly may have been involved in a 'Boston marriage' (two women who lived together as companions who were financially independent of men)

but this aspect of her personal life seems to require further examination in order to be conclusive. See Bruce Nelson, *Irish Nationalists and the Making of the Irish Race*, (Princeton: Princeton University Press, 2012). Dr Kelly's US federal census returns would seem to demonstrate that she lived in the same address as a Mary Walsh in 1910, 1920, and 1930. For example, '1910 United States federal census', Ancestry.com. Mary Walsh is also listed as being her long-time companion in all obituaries but she is reported as Mary 'Dutton' at Dr Kelly's 1929 testimonial dinner. She is listed as 'Mary Walsh' in all of the census returns. See *New York Herald Tribune*, 18 April 1929; *New York Times*, 17 February 1934; *New York Herald Tribune*, 17 February 1934.

4  *New York Times*, 4 July 1914.

5  Joe Doyle, 'Striking for Ireland on the New York docks', in Ronald H. Bayor and Timothy J. Meagher, eds, *The New York Irish* (Baltimore: The Johns Hopkins University Press, 1996), 359.

6  'Ballyneale; County of Tipperary; Diocese of Waterford and Lismore. Baptisms, Jan. 1862 to May 1862', *Catholic Parish Registers at the NLI*, available at: registers.nli.ie/; *New York Times*, 17 February 1934. Slater's 1856 *Directory of Ireland* lists a 'John' (presumably an entry that should have listed 'Jeremiah') and 'Catherine Kelly' as schoolmaster and schoolmistress in Carrick-on-Suir's Poor Law Union. See: igp-web.com/tipperary/slaters/slaters3.htm. Carrick-on-Suir is in Co. Tipperary but it is very close to Counties Waterford and Kilkenny. An article on Gertrude's brother John Forrest Kelly claims him as a Tipperaryman. See *Kilkenny People*, 6 August 1938. For a general overview of Kelly see: fenian graves.net/Kelly,%20Dr.%20Gertrude/Dr.%20Kelly%20obio.htm.

7  The 1900 US federal census entry states that Gertrude arrived in the United States in 1873; *New York Times*, 17 February 1934; *New York Herald Tribune*, 17 February 1934.

8  *Cork Weekly Examiner*, 11 March 1939; *Kilkenny People*, 6 August 1938.

9  Newspaper reports spell his name 'Jeremiah' but in census records, Mr Kelly wrote it as 'Jermiah'. See, for example, US federal census 1880 and 1910; *New York Herald Tribune*, 17 February 1934. Jermiah became principal for the Training School for Teachers of the State of New Jersey, a position he held for over 30 years. See *Cork Weekly Examiner*, 11 March 1939.

10  1910 Census US federal census; *Munster Express*, 18 November 1922.

11  Michael E. Chapman, '"How to smash the British Empire': John Forrest Kelly's *Irish World* and the boycott of 1920–1', *Éire-Ireland* 43 (2008): 220. It is worth noting here that the 'Jeremiah F. Kelly' who is listed as part of the welcoming deputation for Michael Davitt to New York in June 1882 is Gertrude's father. See *New York Tribune*, 18 June 1882.

12  See Chapman, '"How to smash the British Empire': John Forrest Kelly's *Irish World* and the boycott of 1920–1', 201, note 4. See also *New York Herald Tribune*, 17 February 1934.

13  US federal census 1880. In this census entry she is listed as 'Bride' but she starts appearing as 'Gertrude B. Kelly' soon thereafter in various sources. For example, she is listed as 'Gertrude B. Kelly', secretary of the Newark Liberal League in *Liberty* 3:25, 6 March 1886: 8.

14  Janis M. Ely, *A Greater Ireland: The Land League and Transatlantic Nationalism in Gilded Age America* (Madison: University of Wisconsin Press, 2015), 116.

15  Ibid.

16  *Irish World*, 25 September 1880.

17  *New York Herald Tribune*, 17 February 1934; Regina Morantz-Sanchez, 'Emily Blackwell', in *American National Biography* (New York: Oxford University Press, 2010). Also Regina Markell Morantz-Sanchez, *Sympathy and Science: Women Physicians in American Medicine* (New York: Oxford University Press, 1985), 72–4; for a contemporary history of this institution, see *New York Tribune*, 24 December 1898.

18  *New York Tribune*, 24 December 1898; *New York Herald Tribune*, 17 February 1934.

19  At the close of the nineteenth century, female physicians numbered between four and five percent of the profession in the United States and this proportion would hold for approximately six decades. See Morantz-Sanchez, *Sympathy and Science*, 49.

20  *New York Times*, 17 February 1934; *New York Herald Tribune*, 17 February 1934.

21  Ibid.

22  It is worth stressing that Dr Kelly dedicated herself to this for her entire career through social activism and her practice of accessible medicine: 'She assists at the most difficult operations, is called into service every day, but without taking a fee advises and helps all the poor sick working girls who came her way.' See *Brooklyn Life*, 30 September 1905. Not only did she not take a fee for her consultations, but she was widely known to have 'slipped $5 under the plate' of needy patients and did things like draw attention to the plight of women forced into prostitution. See *New York Times*, 17 February 1934; *Liberty*, 12 September 1885: 5 on *The Libertarian Labyrinth*, available at: library.libertarian-labyrinth.org/items/show/2766.

23  McElroy, *Individualist Feminism of the Nineteenth Century*, 164; John Forrest Kelly also wrote for *Liberty*.

24  McElroy, *Individualist Feminism of the Nineteenth Century*, 166. Ireland featured in the columns of *Liberty* and it is clear that Dr Kelly did keep track of Henry's Appleton's musing. See her letter, as published in *Liberty*, where she writes as secretary of the Newark Liberal League, *Liberty* 8:3, 6 March 1886: 8.

25  McElroy, *Individualist Feminism of the Nineteenth Century*, 166.

26  Niall Whelehan, *The Dynamiters: Irish Nationalism and Political Violence in the Wider World, 1867–1900* (Cambridge: Cambridge University Press, 2012), 247.

27  Doyle, 'Striking for Ireland on the New York docks', in Bayor and Meagher, eds, *The New York Irish*, 363. For Henry George, Patrick Ford, and Ireland see Ely, *A Greater Ireland*, 129–32; James P. Rodechko, 'Irish World Land League', in Michael F. Funchion, ed., *Irish American Voluntary Organizations* (Westport, Connecticut: Greenwood Press, 1983), 212–8.

28  *New York Times*, 16 March 1914.

29  Francis Carroll, *American Opinion and the Irish Question 1910–1923* (New York: St Martin's Press, 1978), 23.

30  *Irish American Weekly*, 18 March 1914.

31  Ibid.; *New York Times*, 16 March 1914.

32  Ibid.

33 *Irish American Weekly*, 28 March 1914.

34 Chapman, "'How to smash the British Empire': John Forrest Kelly's *Irish World* and the boycott of 1920–1', 221, note 4.

35 James Lunney and Linde Lunney, 'John Forrest Kelly', in James McGuire and James Quinn, eds, *Dictionary of Irish Biography* (Cambridge: Cambridge University Press, 2009).

36 Carroll, *American Opinion*, 48. It is of note that the Irish Parliamentary Party was seen to have had a 'tempestuous relationship' with Irish women's struggle for suffrage. See Cliona Murphy, *The Women's Suffrage Movement and Irish Society in the Early Twentieth Century* (Philadelphia: Temple University Press, 1989), chapter 7.

37 *New York Times*, 4 July 1914.

38 Ibid. and *Butte Independent*, 4 April 1914.

39 *New York Times*, 4 July 1914.

40 This is most amply demonstrated by her appeal, which forms the opening epigraph of this chapter.

41 Marie Veronica Tarpey, *The Role of Joseph McGarrity in the Struggle for Irish Independence* (New York: Arno Press, 1976), 61–2.

42 Clan na Gael leader Joseph McGarrity cabled the leader of the Irish Volunteers, Eoin MacNeill, with the following after the Howth gun-running interception and the Bachelor's Walk incident: 'Irish America will with rage. American people horrified. The blood of these martyrs not shed in vain. Retribution will be swift and sure from the Irish race throughout the world.' Quoting *The Gaelic American*, 1 August 1914, in Tarpey, *The Role of Joseph McGarrity in the Struggle for Irish Independenec*, 66–7.

43 Ruth Dudley Edwards, *Patrick Pearse: The Triumph of Failure*, 1977 (Dublin: Poolbeg Press, 1990), 189.

44 *The Gaelic American*, 3 October 1914.

45 Ibid.

46 Gertrude B. Kelly to William Bourke Cockran, 2 October 1914, Box 4, Folder 3, William Bourke Cockran Papers, New York Public Library.

47 Margaret Ward, *Unmanageable Revolutionaries: Women and Irish Nationalism* (East Haven, Connecticut: Pluto Press, 1989), 92.

48 Cal McCarthy, *Cumann na mBan and the Irish Revolution* (Cork: The Collins Press, 2007), 17.

49 Sydney Gifford-Czira (John Brennan), *The Years Flew By* (Dublin: Gifford & Craven, 1974), 72–6. On the Gifford family see Anne Clare, *Unlikely Rebels: The Gifford Girls and the Fight for Freedom* (Cork: Mercier Press, 2011). Grace and Muriel Gifford were left widows after the 1916 Rising on the executions of Joseph Plunkett and Thomas MacDonagh.

50 Gifford-Czira, *The Years Flew By*.

51 Ibid., 75.

52 *New York Times*, 4 July 1914.

53 McCarthy, *Cumann na mBan and the Irish Revolution*, 13, 16.

54 *The Gaelic American*, 7 December 1914. Dr Kelly was not actually mentioned in this initial announcement but her personal address was listed as the contact in the newspaper column

carrying it. She never seemed to completely exclude men: 'All interested, men and women, are cordially invited.'

55 Ibid., 19 December 1914.

56 *Washington Post*, 15 December 1914. According to Sydney Gifford the Ladies Auxiliary of the Ancient Order of Hibernians provided valuable workers in founding the first branches of Cumann na mBan in Manhattan and later Brooklyn. See Gifford-Czira, *The Years Flew By*, 76–7.

57 Margaret Moore is interchangeably referred to as 'Marguerite' Moore in contemporary references. For biographical information on her see Mrs Marguerite Moore entry in Frances E. Willard and Mary A. Livermore, eds, *American Women: Fifteen Hundred Biographies with over 1,400 Portraits*, volume 2 (New York: Mast, Crowell & Kirkpatrick, 1897), 517.

58 *The Gaelic American*, 19 December 1914.

59 Ibid.

60 Ibid. Note 'Dr Meyers talk embarrassed many of the members', *Washington Post*, 15 December 1914. Curiously, the *New York Tribune* also had the same editorial comment. See *New York Tribune*, 15 December 1914.

61 *The Gaelic American*, 19 December 1914.

62 *New York Tribune*, 15 December 1914.

63 Catherine M. Burns, 'Kathleen O'Brennan and American identity in the transatlantic Irish republican movement', in David T. Gleeson, ed., *The Irish in the Atlantic World* (Columbia: University of South Carolina Press, 2010), 181.

64 Mary C. Kelly, *The Shamrock and the Lily: The New York Irish and the Creation of a Trans-atlantic Identity, 1845–1921* (New York: Peter Lang, 2005), 63.

65 David Brundage, '"In time of peace, prepare for war": key themes in the social thought of New York's Irish nationalists, 1890–1916', in Bayor and Meagher, eds, *The New York Irish*, 322.

66 Ward, *Unmanageable Revolutionaries*, 39.

67 For example, *Irish American Weekly*, 15 February 1908, 13 February 1909, 21 June 1913, and 3 August 1912.

68 Úna Ní Bhroiméil, *Building Irish Identity in America, 1870–1915: The Gaelic Revival* (Dublin: Four Courts Press, 2003).

69 For background on Fianna na hÉireann see Joseph E. A. Connell Jr, 'Countdown to 2016: Fianna na hÉireann/Na Fianna Éireann', *History Ireland* 20:6 (2012): 66.

70 For a short intervention on this see fiannaeireannhistory.wordpress.com/2014/03/11/fianna-league-of-america/.

71 Ibid. Another good example of transatlantic networks is provided by Joseph McGarrity. While on honeymoon in Ireland in 1911 he undertook the underwriting of certain costs of Fianna na hÉireann for Countess Markievicz. See Tarpey, *The Role of Joseph McGarrity in the Struggle for Irish Independenec*, 72–3.

72 John Devoy, *Recollections of an Irish Rebel*, 1929 (Shannon: Irish University Press, 1969), 446.

73 Ibid., 447.

74 Ibid.

75 Ibid.

76 For example, regarding Cumann na mBan, Devoy is reported to have advised: 'Keep your girl away from those women. They don't know what they are talking about.' See Florence Montieth Lynch, *The Mystery Man of Banna Strand* (New York: Vantage Press, 1959), 77.

77 *The Gaelic American*, 3 October 1914.

78 Devoy, *Recollections*, 449.

79 Ibid., 393.

80 Sydney Gifford lamented her ability to organise more effectively: 'The chief source of trouble was the underground influence of Devoy and his immediate friends. Their followers were afraid to commit themselves to any line of action until the heads had pronounced their opinion. Devoy and his followers regarded themselves as the émigré government of Ireland. They were even not over-scrupulous in denouncing as spies anyone who did not fall in with their wishes and who showed any inclination to align themselves with the policy prescribed from Ireland.' See Gifford-Czira, *The Years Flew By*, 77.

81 Rose McDermott was the sister of Seán Mac Diarmada. See: irishtimes.com/news/politics/five-sisters-of-executed-1916-leader-se%C3%A1n-mac-diarmada-received-pensions-1.1949967.

82 Kelly, *The Shamrock and the Lily*, 65.

83 Mary Jane O'Donovan Rossa to John Devoy, n.d. (autumn 1915), in William O'Brien and Desmond Ryan, eds, *Devoy's Post Bag 1871–1928*, volume 2 (Dublin: C. J. Fallon, 1953), 482–4.

84 Ibid., 483.

85 George A. Schilling, 'Our voting women: will they make good?', *Life and Labor* 11 (1921): 56.

86 *Liberty*, 12 March 1887: 8, on *The Libertarian Labyrinth*, available at: library.libertarian-labyrinth.org/items/show/2796.

87 *Brooklyn Daily Eagle*, 21 February 1934.

88 A scholar who has worked on a related topic contends that all Kelly family papers were destroyed because of John Forrest Kelly's 'anti-Catholic anarchism'. Private email message to author, 3 April 2015.

89 Devoy, *Recollections*, 442, 448.

90 *Southern Star*, 23 October 1915.

91 Minute book entries, 9 April 1916, 110–11, Box 2, Volume of Meeting Minutes, 1909–18, Gaelic Society of New York Records, AIA.025, Archives of Irish America, Tamiment Library and Robert F. Wagner Labor Archives, New York University.

92 *The Gaelic American*, 12 February 1916.

93 McElroy, *Individualist Feminism of the Nineteenth Century*, 164.

94 *The Gaelic American*, 27 May 1916.

95 Ibid., 3 June 1916.

96 For insights on the Irish Progressive League see C. Desmond Greaves, *Liam Mellows and the Irish Revolution* (Belfast: An Ghórta Gafa, 2005), 149–65. On the earlier point about the role of individuals organisationally connecting Ireland and the United States: 'Hanna Sheehy Skeffington provided the link with the Socialist Party of Ireland', ibid., 149.

97 Doyle, 'Striking for Ireland on the New York docks', in Bayor and Meagher, eds, *The New York Irish*, 357–73.

98 *New York Times*, 17 February 1934.

99 *Irish Press*, 8 March 1934. She probably met Pearse at a Gaelic League gathering on 12 April 1914, when he delivered a talk, 'Some aspects of Irish literature', which 'included representatives from almost every Gaelic society from Greater New York', *Irish American Weekly*, 18 April 1914.

100 Jeremiah A. O'Leary, *My Trial and Political Experiences* (New York: Jefferson Publishing Company, 1881), 188, 221, 407.

101 Greaves, *Liam Mellows*, 206.

102 Elizabeth Gurley Flynn, *The Rebel Girl: An Autobiography* (New York: International Publishers, 1994), 269; Greaves, *Liam Mellows*, 216; Nelson, *Irish Nationalists and the Making of the Irish Race*, 225–6.

103 Marie Equi's mother was Irish. See Gurley Flynn, *The Rebel Girl*, 270.

104 *Brooklyn Eagle*, 3 May 1921.

105 Cormac K. H. O'Malley and Anne Dolan, *'No Surrender Here': The Civil War Papers of Ernie O'Malley 1922–1924* (Dublin: The Lilliput Press, 2007), 340.

106 *New York Times*, 10 January 1923.

107 Peter and Helen Golden were close associates of Dr Kelly, especially in the Irish Progressive League. See Francis M. Carroll, 'Irish Progressive League', in Funchion, ed., *Irish American Voluntary Organizations*, 206–10. In 2006, Dr Marion R. Casey and Elizabeth Bedell interviewed the daughter of Peter and Helen Golden, Eithne Merriam Golden Sax, for NYU's Archives of Irish America. Eithne and her twin sister had been delivered by Dr Kelly in 1919. See nyu.edu/library/bobst/research/aia/.

108 W. E. B. Du Bois, 1868–1963; Letter from W. E. B. Du Bois to The Gertrude B. Kelley [*sic*] Testimonial Dinner Committee, 11 April 1929, MS 312, W. E. B. Du Bois Papers, Special Collections and University Archives, University of Massachusetts Amherst Libraries, available at: credo.library.umass.edu/view/full/mums312-b049-i252; *New York Herald Tribune*, 18 April 1929.

109 Nelson, quoting Frank P. Walsh, *Irish Nationalists and the Making of the Irish Race*, 224.

110 Doyle, 'Striking for Ireland on the New York docks', in Bayor and Meagher, eds, *The New York Irish*, 363. Tracking the entirety of Kelly's activities would demand almost a discrete study of itself. In addition to the organisations explicitly mentioned in this chapter, she was also a member of the Women's Peace Party, the American Pickets for the Enforcement of America's War Aims, and the Women's International League, see Burns, 'Kathleen O'Brennan and American identity in the transatlantic Irish republican movement', in Gleeson, ed., *The Irish in the Atlantic World*, 181–2.

111 *Brooklyn Daily Eagle*, 21 February 1934.

112 *New York Times*, 17 May 1936.

113 Kelly had assisted people like Father O'Flanagan, Dr Douglas Hyde, Nellie O'Brien, the early Abbey Players, Padraic Colum, Éamon de Valera, Constance Markievicz, 'And she liked the rebels best of all'. See *Irish Press*, 8 March 1934.

114 Micheline Sheehy Skeffington's foreword in Joanne Mooney Eichacker, *Irish Women in America: Lecture Tours 1916–1925* (Dublin: Irish Academic Press, 2002), xiv.

115 *Irish Press*, 8 March 1934.

116 There are prominent examples of activists who were not born in Ireland, during this period, but these were the exception rather the norm: e.g. Judge Daniel F. Cohalan, Jeremiah A. O'Leary. Consider those profiled in this volume: Kelly, Devoy, McGarrity, the Colums, Bourke Cockran, Farley, O'Donovan Rossa, who were all born in Ireland.

117 McElroy, *Individualist Feminism of the Nineteenth Century*, 166.

118 Nelson, *Irish Nationalists and the Making of the Irish Race*, 225.

119 Ibid.

120 *Irish Press*, 8 March 1934.

121 Ely, *A Greater Ireland*, 114.

## 6. CASEMENT, NEW YORK, AND THE EASTER RISING

1 MS 1689, Roger Casement Papers, National Library of Ireland (NLI).

2 Joseph Roth, *The Hotel Years*, Michael Hoffman, trans. (New York: New Directions, 2015), 158.

3 15 October 1914, MS 36,199/4, Roger Casement Papers, NLI.

4 13 October 1914, MS 36,202/3, Roger Casement Papers, NLI.

5 Although some of Casement's letters are written on the stationery of the *Prince* George Hotel, an elegant building on Fifth Avenue and 28th Street, there is no evidence that Casement every stayed there. It is possible that he was looking for the *St* George Hotel at the time and helped himself to the stationery.

6 Box 2/33, Maloney Collection of Irish Historical Papers, New York Public Library.

7 For a more detailed discussion of 'Casement's homosexual discourse', see Lucy McDiarmid, *The Irish Art of Controversy* (Dublin: The Lilliput Press, 2005), 173–81. I use the term 'gay' in this essay because such usage has become standard in scholarship on sexuality, as in, for instance, the title and text of George Chauncey's excellent book *Gay New York: Gender, Urban Culture, and the Making of the Gay Male World 1890–1940* (New York: Basic Books, 1995).

8 Reinhard R. Doerries, *Prelude to the Easter Rising: Sir Roger Casement in Imperial Germany* (London and New York: Frank Cass, 2000), 43.

9 Jeffrey Dudgeon, *Roger Casement: The Black Diaries, with a Study of His Background, Sexuality and Irish Political Life* (Belfast: Belfast Press, 2002), 429.

10 Doerries, *Prelude to the Easter Rising*, 192–203.

11 Ibid. Also see ibid., 29, note 64: 'The plan to dispatch Casement to Ireland together with the Irish Brigade appears to have originated in Department IIIb [of the Deputy German Staff]. Whether at this time Devoy clearly perceived that Casement wanted to prevent the rising remains somewhat uncertain.' Doerries also cites Devoy in *The Gaelic American*, 4 October 1924: 2: 'Knowing that ... Casement would surely endeavor to get them [IRB] to alter their plans ... I asked the German Government to request him to remain in Germany to look after Irish interests.'

12 'seedy', 14 June 1914, MS 36,202/3, Roger Casement Papers, NLI.

13 John Devoy, *Recollections of an Irish Rebel* (Dublin: Irish University Press, 1969), 412.

14 Redmond, as quoted in Séamas Ó Síocháin, *Roger Casement: Imperialist, Rebel, Revolutionary* (Dublin: The Lilliput Press, 2007), 378.

15 Casement's 21 July letter to Devoy, in William O'Brien and Desmond Ryan, eds, *Devoy's Post Bag 1871–1928* (Dublin: C. J. Fallon, 1953), 462.

16 Bulmer Hobson, Witness Statement (WS) 50, Bureau of Military History (BMH), National Archives of Ireland (NAI).

17 Patrick McCartan, WS 916, BMH, NAI.

18 Helen Litton, *Thomas Clarke* (Dublin: O'Brien Press, 2014), 117.

19 For more details about this matter, see O'Brien and Ryan, eds, *Devoy's Post Bag*, 456. Hobson was reappointed, but for reasons relating to the war, 'no further articles by Hobson appeared'. For Devoy's term 'surrender', see Devoy, *Recollections of an Irish Rebel*, 409. For more discussion of Casement's attitude at this time, see Sean O'Kelly, WS 1765, BMH, NAI.

20 O'Brien and Ryan, eds, *Devoy's Post Bag*, 461–3.

21 Devoy, *Recollections*, 413.

22 Because Casement was staying at Joseph McGarrity's house in Philadelphia on the day the guns were landed at Howth, another chapter in this volume, 'The man in Philadelphia: Joseph McGarrity and 1914', also covers this important episode.

23 Patrick McCartan, WS 766, BMH, NAI.

24 Another shipment of arms bought at the same time was transported in the *Kelpie*, skippered by Conor O'Brien and delivered at Kilcoole, Wicklow, on Monday 27 July. For more details, see F. X. Martin, ed., *The Howth Gun-Running and the Kilcoole Gun-Running 1914* (Kildare: Irish Academic Press, 2014).

25 Patrick McCartan, WS 766, BMH, NAI. McCartan also writes, 'The Howth gun-running had set him up with the Clan na Gael. They believed – and I believe, that that was so – that Casement was chiefly responsible for the Howth gun-running. I understand that it was he who made contact with Childers and arranged for the services of his yacht and it was he who was able to interest Mrs. Green in the project. Though the details in Ireland may have been dealt with by someone else, I believe it was Casement who made these arrangements.'

26 Ibid.

27 F. X. Martin, 'The McCartan documents, 1916', *Clogher Record* 6:1 (1966): 13.

28 For Casement's account see 'The man in Philadelphia: Joseph McGarrity and 1914', in this volume.

29  As quoted in Ó Síocháin, *Roger Casement*, letter 27 July 1914, 383.

30  Statistics about the number of injured differ. S. J. Connolly (2002) says 38 injured; Padriag Yeates (2011) says 85 injured (of whom 30 were seriously wounded).

31  Sean Cronin, 'Casement in America', *Irish Times*, 11 April 1966.

32  Ó Síocháin, *Roger Casement*, 384.

33  Mary Colum, *Life and the Dream* (New York: Doubleday, 1947), 218.

34  Ibid., 218–19.

35  William M. Murphy, *Prodigal Father: The Life of John Butler Yeats (1839–1922)* (Syracuse: Syracuse University Press, 1978), 424.

36  As quoted in Ó Síocháin, *Roger Casement*, 386

37  As quoted in ibid., 385.

38  Casement to Alice Stopford Green, 15 August 1914, as quoted in Doerries, *Prelude to the Easter Rising*, 47.

39  Ibid. See also 11 August letter to Gertrude Bannister, MS 36,202/3, Roger Casement Papers, NLI.

40  Casement to Gertrude Bannister, 11 August 1914, MS 36,202/3, Roger Casement Papers, NLI.

41  Ó Síocháin, *Roger Casement*, 593, note 18.

42  Dudgeon, *Roger Casement*, 499.

43  Ó Síocháin, *Roger Casement*, 337.

44  Ibid., 354.

45  Ibid., 366. See also ibid. on Casement's 1912 trip to Germany with his friend Dick Morten and also his encounters with the German journalist Oskar Schweriner, 337, 372–3.

46  Bulmer Hobson, WS 85, BMI, NAI.

47  Doerries, *Prelude to the Easter Rising*, 46.

48  Ó Síocháin, *Roger Casement*, 387; Doerries, *Prelude to the Easter Rising*, 2.

49  Devoy, *Recollections*, 403.

50  Ibid., 403.

51  Ó Síocháin, *Roger Casement*, 388–9.

52  Devoy, *Recollections*, 405.

53  Ibid., 406.

54  Ibid., 404.

55  Roger Casement, *Ireland, Germany and the Freedom of the Seas: A Possible Outcome of the War of 1914* (New York and Philadelphia: Irish Press Bureau, September 1914); and *The Crime against Europe* (Berlin: The Continental Times, 1915). As quoted in Ó Síocháin, *Roger Casement*, 389, 595.

56  Roger Casement, 'Ireland and the Empire: Sir Roger Casement's views', *Irish Independent*, 5 October 1914.

57  Unsigned editorial, *Irish Independent*, 5 October 1914.

58  'German diary', MS 1,689, Roger Casement Papers, NLI.

59  MS 36,199/4, 15 October 1914, Roger Casement Papers, NLI.

60 MS 36,202/3, 2 December 1914, Roger Casement Papers, NLI.

61 Doerries, *Prelude to the Easter Rising*, 48.

62 Devoy, *Recollections*, 417.

63 Cronin, 'Casement in America'.

64 Patrick McCartan, WS 766, BMI, NAI.

65 Devoy, *Recollections*, 417.

66 Ibid.

67 Chauncey, *Gay New York*, 162.

68 Marcia Biederman, 'Journey to an overlooked past', *New York Times*, 11 June 2000, available at: nytimes.com/2000/06/11/nyregion/journey-to-an-overlooked-past.html.

69 'Captain Steven Rogers: a history through art', Archivefourown.org, available at: archiveofourown.org/works/5181992/chapters/11940113.

70 See, for instance, 'Times Square: a gay history', *New York City: A Gay History*, 8 August 1997, available at: huzbears.com/nychistory/ts.html#L7.

71 Chauncey, *Gay New York*, 162, 191, 301–3, 309, 314, 353, 416, 420, etc. The bar at the Astor Hotel (45th Street and Seventh Avenue) 'had been a gay meeting place since 1910' (see 'Times Square: a gay history'), and 42nd Street and Eigth Avenue had been 'as far back as the 1920s a center for male hustlers'. See '8th Avenue, West 42nd Street', *42nd Street: A New York Songline*, available at: nysonglines.com/8av.htm#42st.

72 'German diary', MS 1,689, Roger Casement Papers, NLI.

73 See B. L. Reid, *The Lives of Roger Casement* (New Haven: Yale University Press, 1976), 16, 196.

74 Jana Verhoeven, *Max O'Rell and the Transnational Debate over Manners and Morals in Late 19th Century France, Britain and the United States* (Cambridge: Cambridge Scholars Press, 2012), 40.

75 Chauncey, *Gay New York*, 184–5.

76 Ibid., 375.

77 Dudgeon, *Roger Casement*, 437–8.

78 Ibid., 438.

79 For the only available extended analysis of the Casement-Christensen relationship, see ibid., chapter 15.

80 Ibid., 437.

81 '[W]ithout Adler the homosexual aspect of Casement's life and the Black Diaries might never have surfaced, for it was the Norwegian who first opened that closet door to London officials'. See ibid., 432.

82 Ibid., 439.

83 Ibid.

84 Ó Síocháin, *Roger Casement*, 393–4.

85 Devoy, *Recollections*, 418.

86 Dudgeon, *Roger Casement*, 402.

87 For the use of the name 'Mary', see Doerries, *Prelude to the Easter Rising*, 49; for the use of the name 'Bridget', see Cronin, 'Casement in America'.

88 Ó Síocháin, *Roger Casement*, 392.

89 Cronin, 'Casement in America'.

90 Ó Síocháin, *Roger Casement*, 397.

91 Bernard Reilly, WS 349, BMH, NAI.

92 Devoy, *Recollections*, 419. Devoy cautiously notes, 'I cannot vouch for the truth of this story, nor of any other told by Christensen, but give it for what it may be worth.'

93 The last two sentences of this paragraph as well as some sentences in the following two paragraphs are taken from McDiarmid, *The Irish Art of Controversy*, 180. The code identifying Casement's project changed also: sometimes it was Catholic, and he himself a priest, as when he wrote to McGarrity on 23 Septmber 1914: 'Things look fairly good regarding the establishment of the mission which we all discussed … The Fathers here think that Father Rogers should go to Roma, as he can do most there … Many good Catholics here would object to the project if it were made public, as it would be misunderstood.' See Doerries, *Prelude to the Easter Rising*, 49. And sometimes it was Protestant, as in a fake 'letter' to a 'sister' from an 'American' girl, in which the letter-writer purported to be one of a group of people making changes to 'the *Book of Common Prayer*'. In that letter (actually a diary or record of events disguised as a letter) Christensen's gender was changed also: describing the quick disguise required when the ship was boarded by the British officers, Casement wrote, 'that dear Norwegian girl helped and stowed all the old Hairpins away' (i.e., Christensen helped Casement shave quickly and get rid of the razors). See MS 13,082/4, Roger Casement Papers, NLI.

94 Dudgeon, *Roger Casement*, 464.

95 MS 13,600 (copy), Roger Casement Papers, NLI, as quoted in Ó Síocháin, *Roger Casement*, 440, note 4, 609.

96 Robert Monteith, *Casement's Last Adventure* (Dublin: Moynihan, 1953; revised edition), 153.

## 7. THE MAN IN PHILADELPHIA: JOSEPH MCGARRITY AND 1914

1 Joseph McGarrity, 'Twenty years ago in America', *An Camán*, 31 March 1934, Metro Edition.

2 Photostat notes by Joseph McGarrity about Roger Casement after his departure to Germany, MS 17,428/6, Joseph McGarrity Papers, National Library of Ireland (NLI).

3 Diary of Joseph McGarrity, 9–12, MS 17,551/4, Joseph McGarrity Papers, NLI, available at: catalogue.nli.ie/Record/vtls000583241; Terry Golway, *Irish Rebel: John Devoy and America's Fight for Ireland's Freedom* (Newbridge: Irish Academic Press, 2015), 194; Marie Veronica Tarpey, *The Role of Joseph McGarrity in the Struggle for Irish Independence* (New York: Arno Press, 1976), 76. Tarpey, based on an account from Bulmer Hobson, contends that Pearse was unaware of Hobson's attempt to 'interest the German ambassador in Washington in the national movement in Ireland'. See Tarpey, *The Role of Joseph McGarrity in the Struggle for Irish Independence*, 76.

4 There is scope to extend the focus to Dr Patrick McCartan's visit to McGarrity in the late summer. While it is mentioned briefly in the chapter, it does merit more sustained examination. There is much less written on McCartan and overall he is long overdue a full-scale biography. His friendship with McGarrity is pivotal and probably has been underestimated. See F. X. Martin, 'The McCartan documents, 1916', *Clogher Record* 6:1 (1966): 5–65, available at: jstor.org/stable/27695579; and 'Extracts from the papers of the late Dr Patrick MacCartan: part two', *Clogher Record* 5:2 (1964): 190.

5 For a biography of John Devoy see Terry Golway, *Irish Rebel*. Where relevant, Golway maps out the interrelations between Devoy and the younger man, including when their relationship soured. It is worth noting that McGarrity goes unmentioned in Devoy's book of recollections, written after the break with McGarrity. See John Devoy, *Recollections of an Irish Rebel* (New York: Charles Young, 1929).

6 F. X. Martin, ed., *Leaders and Men of the Easter Rising: Dublin 1916* (Ithaca, NY: Cornell University Press, 1967).

7 Tarpey, *The Role of Joseph McGarrity in the Struggle for Irish Independence*, preface.

8 Ibid. and Sean Cronin, *The McGarrity Papers: Revelations of the Irish Revolutionary Movement in Ireland and America 1900–1940* (Tralee: Anvil Books, 1972).

9 Helene Anne Spicer, *The McGarrity Chronicles* (draft, 1995), in the McGarrity Collection, Villanova Digital Library, hereafter Villanova, available at: digital.lbrary.villanova.edu/item/vudl% 3A132311.

10 Francis M. Carroll, 'Joseph McGarrity', in James McGuire and James Quinn, eds, *Dictionary of Irish Biography* (Cambridge: Cambridge University Press, 2009); Patrick J. Blessing, 'Joseph McGarrity', in Michael Glazier, ed., *The Encyclopedia of the Irish in America* (Notre Dame: University of Notre Dame Press, 1999).

11 Tarpey, *The Role of Joseph McGarrity in the Struggle for Irish Independence*, 5.

12 Joseph McGarrity, 'Memoirs of Joseph McGarrity', 1939, available at: library.villanova. edu/Find/Record/vudl:137850.

13 Tarpey, *The Role of Joseph McGarrity in the Struggle for Irish Independence*, chapter 11; Carroll, 'Joseph McGarrity', in McGuire and Quinn, eds, *Dictionary of Irish Biography*.

14 McGarrity, 'Memoirs of Joseph McGarrity'; Spicer, *The McGarrity Chronicles*, 3, 4.

15 McGarrity, 'Memoirs of Joseph McGarrity'.

16 Spicer, *The McGarrity Chronicles*, 9, 23, 41. According to this source, McGarrity's wife, Kathryn/Catherine Hynes, was born in Philadelphia in 1886. They married on 11 June 1911, and honeymooned in Ireland. He became a naturalised citizen in 1897. See digital. library.villanova.edu/Item/vudl:144029.

17 Tarpey, *The Role of Joseph McGarrity in the Struggle for Irish Independence*, 73. He was more than just a 'wine merchant' and had extensive dealing in whiskey in particular. See digital. library.villanova.edu/Item/vudl:142014; and NLI's collection of letters regarding the liquor, for example a letter from GeorgeMcKnight available at: catalogue.nli.ie/Record/vtls000616695.

18 Carroll, 'Joseph McGarrity', in McGuire and Quinn, eds, *Dictionary of Irish Biography*.

19 Marnie Hay, *Bulmer Hobson and the Nationalist Movement in Twentieth-Century Ireland* (Manchester and New York: Manchester University Press; distributed in the USA by Palgrave Macmillan, 2009), 104. See also primary documents available at catalogue.nli.ie/Record/vtls000548768 and catalogue.nli.ie/Record/vtls000548749.

20 Hay, *Bulmer Hobson and the Nationalist Movement in Twentieth-Century Ireland*, 70.

21 MS 18,000–157, John Devoy Papers, NLI.

22 Hay, *Bulmer Hobson and the Nationalist Movement in Twentieth-Century Ireland*, 82.

23 Tarpey, *The Role of Joesph McGarrity in the Struggle for Irish Independence*, 72.

24 Letter from Hobson to Devoy, 11 October 1913, MS 18,006/7/4, John Devoy Papers, NLI.

25 Michael Foy, *Tom Clarke: The True Leader of the Easter Rising* (Dublin: The History Press, 2014), 111.

26 William O'Brien and Desmond Ryan, eds, *Devoy's Post Bag 1871–1928*, volume 2 (Dublin: C. J. Fallon, 1953), 413.

27 Ben Novick, 'The arming of Ireland: gunrunning and the Great War 1914–16', in Adrian Gregory and Senia Pašeta, eds, *Ireland and the Great War: A War to Unite Us All?* (Manchester and New York: Manchester University Press; distributed in the USA by Palgrave Macmillan, 2002), 96.

28 McGarrity, 'Twenty years ago in America'.

29 Hay, *Bulmer Hobson and the Nationalist Movement in Twentieth-Century Ireland*, 114.

30 Joseph McGarrity, memoranda, minutes, and notes, 1914–16, 1919, MssCol 1854, Box 8, Folder 3, Maloney Collection of Irish Historical Papers, New York Public Library.

31 Ruan O'Donnell, *America and the 1916 Rising* (New York: Friends of Sinn Féin New York, 2015), 11.

32 MS 17633/6, Joseph McGarrity Papers, NLI. Soon after his execution in 1916, McGarrity penned a poem about his friend Pearse. It was carried in a Philadelphia newspaper. See *Clan-Na-Gael Journal*, 25 June 1916.

33 Golway, *Irish Rebel*, 164

34 Padraic Pearse and Séamas Ó Buachalla, *The Letters of P. H. Pearse* (Atlantic Highlands, NJ: Humanities Press, 1980), 299.

35 McGarrity, 'Twenty years ago in America'.

36 Ibid.

37 For a short overview of the Curragh Mutiny see *History Ireland* 1:22 (2014), available at: historyireland.com/volume-22/countdown-2016-curragh-mutiny/.

38 McGarrity, 'Twenty years ago in America'.

39 Ibid.

40 Pearse and Ó Buachalla, *The Letters of P. H. Pearse*, 302, letter 360, 1 April 1914.

41 Ibid., 314.

42 Letter, 28 April 1914, MS 18,007/26/1, John Devoy Papers, NLI.

43 Pearse and Ó Buachalla, *The Letters of P. H. Pearse*, 305, letter 363, 13 April 1914.

44 NLI online exhibit, 'The 1916 Rising: personalities and perspectives', 13–15; Letter, 16 March 1914, MS 17,476/2/1, Joseph McGarrity Papers, NLI.

45  Pearse and Ó Buachalla, *The Letters of P. H. Pearse*, xvi.

46  McGarrity, 'Twenty years Ago in America'.

47  Hay, *Bulmer Hobson and the Nationalist Movement in Twentieth-Century Ireland*, 115.

48  Ticket to 23 March event, available at: catalogue.nli.ie/Record/vtls000516210; and for the records of what was said see 'Report of addresses by P. H. Pearse, Bulmer Hobson and others, Philadelphia, March 1914; relating to conditions in Ireland, the Irish Volunteers, Home Rule', 1914, 1–26, MS 17,634, Joseph McGarrity Papers, NLI.

49  Pearse and Ó Buachalla, *The Letters of P. H. Pearse*, 314, letter 371, 19 June 1914.

50  Patrick Maume, 'Bulmer Hobson', in Lawrence William White, James Quinn, and David Rooney, eds, *1916 Portraits and Lives* (Dublin: Royal Irish Academy, 2015), 129.

51  O'Brien and Ryan, eds, *Devoy's Post Bag*, 462.

52  Diary of Joseph McGarrity, MS 17,551/4, Joseph McGarrity Papers, NLI, available at: catalogue.nli.ie/Record/vtls000583241.

53  Constitution of the Irish National Volunteer Fund Committee of America adopted 12 July 1914, Villanova, available at: digital.library.villanova.edu/Item/vudl:138667?viewer =legacy#.

54  Letter from Eoin MacNeill to Joseph McGarrity, 1 July 1914, Villanova, available at: digital.library.villanova.edu/Item/vudl%3A138687.

55  Diary of Joseph McGarrity, MS 17,551/4, Joseph McGarrity Papers, NLI, available at: catalogue.nli.ie/Record/vtls000583241; O'Donnell, *America and the 1916 Rising*, 14.

56  Hay, *Bulmer Hobson and the Nationalist Movement in Twentieth-Century Ireland*, 114–15; Desmond Ryan, *The Rising: The Complete Story of Easter Week* (Dublin: Golden Eagle Books Ltd, 1966), 21; Angus Mitchell, *Roger Casement* (Dublin: O'Brien Press, 2013), 207; Entry in diary of Joseph McGarrity, 21 July 1914, MS 17,551/4, Joseph McGarrity Papers, NLI.

57  O'Donnell, *America and the 1916 Rising*, 15.

58  Roger Casement, *Sir Roger Casement's Diaries: His Mission to Germany and the Findlay Affair*, Charles E. Curry, ed. (Munich: Arche Publishing Co., 1922), 27–8; Diary of Joseph McGarrity, 16, MS 17,551/4, Joseph McGarrity Papers, NLI, available at: catalogue.nli.ie/ Record/vtls000583241.

59  Séamas Ó Síocháin, *Roger Casement: Imperialist, Rebel, Revolutionary* (Dublin: The Lilliput Press, 2008), 382; B. L. Reid, *The Lives of Roger Casement* (New Haven: Yale University Press, 1976), 198.

60  Casement to Mrs Hynes, 10 August 1914, MS 17,428/1, Joseph McGarrity Papers, NLI.

61  Ibid.; Memo about the departure of Sir Roger Casement, MS 17,428/11, 17 October 1914, Joseph McGarrity Papers, NLI.

62  Reid, *The Lives of Roger Casement*, 293; McGarrity to Casement, in Reinhard Doerries, *Prelude to the Easter Rising: Sir Roger Casement in Imperial Germany* (New York: Routledge, 2000), 159. McGarrity was also sure to tell Casement in late 1915 that both his children said nightly prayers on his behalf.

63  Reid, *The Lives of Roger Casement*, 227. Casement to Meyer, November 12, 1914.

64  Meyer to Casement, 24 November 1914, in Doerries, *Prelude*, 65.

65 Matthew Erin Plowman, 'Irish republicans and the Indo-German conspiracy of World War I', *New Hibernia Review* 7:3 (2003): 90; Mitchell, *Roger Casement*, 256.

66 Captain Rudolf Nadolny, Department IIIb, Deputy General Staff, to Foreign Office, 24 January 1915, in Doerries, *Prelude*, 81–2. The message reads in part: 'For military Attaché. People suitable for German sabotage in the United States and Canada to be named by the following persons: 1) Joseph McGarrity [*sic*], 5412 Springfield, Philadelphia, PA., 2) John P. Keating, Maryland Avenue, Chicago, 3) Jeremia [*sic*] O'Leary, Par row [*sic*], New York.'

67 Doerries, *Prelude*, 11; Count Johann Heinrich von Bernstorff to Foreign Office via German Legation in Stockholm, 14 December 1914, in ibid., 69; Father Nicholson to McGarrity, 2 April 1929, MS 17,534/1/9, Joseph McGarrity Papers, NLI. McGarrity and Father Nicholson remained in constant contact for most of the remainder of McGarrity's life.

68 McGarrity to prisoner identified only as 'Barry', undated, MS 17,428/7, Joseph McGarrity Papers, NLI.

69 'Extracts from the papers of the late Dr Patrick MacCartan: part two', *Clogher Record* 5:2 (1964): 190.

70 Ibid.,189.

71 Cronin, *The McGarrity Papers*, 29–30.

72 O'Donnell, *America and the 1916 Rising*, 35.

73 'Extracts from the papers of the late Dr Patrick MacCartan: part two', 191.

74 For more on this see both the chapters by Lucy McDiarmid and R. Bryan Willits in this volume. See also Gerard MacAtasney, *Tom Clarke Life Liberty Revolution* (Sallins: Merrion, 2013), 270.

75 Cronin, *The McGarrity Papers*, 33.

76 O'Donnell, *America and the 1916 Rising*, 5.

77 Ibid., 14.

78 Foy, *Tom Clarke*, 121.

79 Pearse and Ó Buachalla, *The Letters of P. H. Pearse*, 297; Brian Crowley, *Patrick Pearse: A Life in Pictures* (Cork: Mercier Press, 2013), 120.

80 Martin, ed., *Leaders and Men of the Easter Rising*, xi.

81 Dennis Clark, *The Irish in Philadelphia: Ten Generations of Urban Experience* (Philadelphia: Temple University Press, 1981), 149.

82 Cronin, *The McGarrity Papers*, 39; O'Brien and Ryan, eds, *Devoy's Post Bag*, 354. Dillon was one of Devoy's close friends and associates and he spent 14 years in prison for his part in an attempt to blow up the Welland Canal during the Boer War.

83 *Clan-Na-Gael Journal*, 21 November 1914, Villanova. See Emmet O'Connor's chapter in this volume for more on Larkin in the United States in this period.

84 *Clan-Na-Gael Journal*, 21 November 1914.

85 Michael Doorley, *Irish-American Diaspora Nationalism: The Friends of Irish Freedom, 1916–1935* (Dublin and Portland, OR: Four Courts Press, 2005), 28.

86 Dennis Clark, *Erin's Heirs: Irish Bonds of Community* (Lexington, KY: University Press of Kentucky, 1991), 153.

87 Marie V. Tarpey, 'Joseph McGarrity, fighter for Irish freedom', *Studia Hibernica* 11 (1971): 178. The McGarritys had nine children.

88 Notebook entry, 16 August 1914, MS 17,552/1, Joseph McGarrity Papers, NLI.

89 Letter from Keating to Devoy, December 1914, MS 18,006/23/6, John Devoy Papers, NLI. The irony is that Keating himself would be dead within the year as he lost a battle against illness on 24 June 1915. See *The Gaelic American*, 3 July 1915.

90 Tarpey, 'Joseph McGarrity, fighter for Irish freedom', 179.

91 'To My Orange Countrymen', Joseph McGarrity Collection, Villanova, available at: digital. library.villanova.edu/Item/vudl:136005.

92 Tarpey, *The Role of Joseph McGarrity in the Struggle for Irish Independence*, 87–90.

93 See Carroll, 'Joseph McGarrity', in McGuire and Quinn, eds, *Dictionary of Irish Biography*.

94 Ibid.

95 Ironically McGarrity had played a pivotal role in saving de Valera from execution in 1916. See Tarpey, *The Role of Joseph McGarrity in the Struggle for Irish Independence*, 93–4.

## 8. 'ST. ENDA'S IS NOW ONLY PART OF A BIGGER THING …': PADRAIG PEARSE'S AMERICAN INTERLUDE

1 Papers of William Patrick Ryan, IE UCDA LA 11/94, University College Dublin (UCD).

2 Patrick Pearse, MS 40,454/1/8, Patrick Pearse's Correspondence, National Library of Ireland (NLI).

3 Brian Crowley, *Patrick Pearse: A Life in Pictures* (Cork: Mercier Press, 2013), 121.

4 Joost Augusteijn, *Patrick Pearse: The Making of a Revolutionary* (New York: Palgrave Macmillan, 2010), 242.

5 NLI online exhibit, 'The 1916 Rising: personalities and perspectives'.

6 Elaine Sisson, *Pearse's Patriots: St Enda's and the Cult of Boyhood* (Cork: Cork University Press, 2004), 39.

7 Brendan Walsh, *Boy Republic: Patrick Pearse and Radical Education* (Dublin: The History Press, 2013), 96.

8 Ibid., 229.

9 Padraic Pearse and Séamas Ó Buachalla, *The Letters of P. H. Pearse* (Atlantic Highlands, NJ: Humanities Press, 1980), 157, letter 168, 10 May 1910; Eoin MacNeill's sons, the MP Stephen Gwynn's son, W. P. Ryan's son, and Colonel Maurice Moore's son all attended St Enda's.

10 Ibid., 444. Thomas MacDonagh was a poet, teacher, and revolutionary. He taught at St Enda's from its inception in 1908. He was executed in 1916.

11 Ibid., 155, letter 168, 10 May 1910.

12 Sisson, *Pearse's Patriots*, 5.

13 Samuel Levenson, *Maud Gonne* (New York: Reader's Digest Press; distributed by Crowell, 1976), 290.

14 *Irish American Weekly*, 6 May 1911; Martin J. Keogh was the treasurer of the Eastern Gaelic League of America in 1911. Pearse had long enjoyed the patronage of the Irish abroad, an example being that of William Bulfin, editor of *The Southern Cross* in Buenos Aires, Argentina, whose son Eamonn was one of the first pupils at St Enda's. See Pearse and Ó Buachalla, *The Letters of P. H. Pearse*, 144

15 Pearse and Ó Buachalla, *The Letters of P. H. Pearse*, 478, letter 443, 2 May 1910.

16 Ibid., 168, letter 181, 26 June 1910.

17 Sisson, *Pearse's Patriots*, 154.

18 William O'Brien and Desmond Ryan, eds, *Devoy's Post Bag 1871–1928*, volume 2 (Dublin: C. J. Fallon, 1953), 412.

19 Papers of William Patrick Ryan, IE UCDA LA 11/94, UCD.

20 Ruth Dudley Edwards, *Patrick Pearse: The Triumph of Failure* (London: Gollancz, 1977), 188.

21 Pearse and Ó Buachalla, *The Letters of P. H. Pearse*, 309, letter 367, 27 April 1914.

22 Pearse, MS 40,454/1/723, Patrick Pearse's Correspondence, NLI.

23 *An Claidheamh Soluis* translates as the 'Sword of Light'.

24 Sisson, *Pearse's Patriots*; Augusteijn, *Patrick Pearse*; Edwards, *Patrick Pearse*. The Hermitage was linked with the United Irishmen, with the Emmet Rising, and with 1848, and Pearse found this historic link extremely appealing. Emmet and his love, Sarah Curran, reportedly used to walk the grounds. Pearse wanted an impressive building on a par with Clongowes Wood College and Castleknock College, both prestigious boys' schools.

25 Augusteijn, *Patrick Pearse*, 226.

26 Padraic Pearse, *The Coming Revolution: The Political Writings and Speeches of Patrick Pearse* (Cork: Mercier Press, 2012), 51.

27 Cumann na Saoirse translates as the 'Freedom Association'; *An Barr Buadh* translates as the 'Trumpet of Victory'.

28 J. J. Lee, 'Patrick Pearse', in James McGuire and James Quinn, eds, *Dictionary of Irish Biography* (Cambridge: Cambridge University Press, 2009).

29 Pearse, *The Coming Revolution*, 79.

30 Patrick Maume, '1916 portraits and lives', in Lawrence William White, James Quinn, and David Rooney, eds, *1916 Portraits and Lives* (Dublin: Royal Irish Academy, 2015), 131.

31 J. J. Lee, 'Patrick Pearse', in White, Quinn, and Rooney, eds, *1916 Portraits and Lives*.

32 Ibid.

33 Michael Doorley, *Irish-American Diaspora Nationalism: The Friends of Irish Freedom, 1915–1935* (Dublin and Portland, OR: Four Courts Press, 2005), 15. Doorley states that under Devoy's leadership the Clan effectively replaced the Fenians to become the most durable revolutionary organisation in Irish-American history. Its constitution declared as its object the complete independence of Ireland and the establishment of an Irish Republic, to be achieved by physical-force means.

34 Janet Egleson Dunleavy and Gareth W. Dunleavy, *Douglas Hyde: A Maker of Modern Ireland* (Berkeley: University of California Press, 1991), chapter 13.

35 Augusteijn, *Patrick Pearse*, 248. Quinn had grown tired of being asked for financial help from representatives of various Irish causes.

36 MS 18,000–157, John Devoy Papers, NLI. Hobson had a history of interceding with Devoy on behalf of politically involved individuals leaving Ireland for New York, an example being a letter dated 10 August 1909, introducing a Mr and Mrs Moloney, who had a connection with the Sinn Féin executive and who were seeking a new beginning in New York. In that same letter Hobson praised Devoy for some recent articles on the Fenians that he had enjoyed reading and stated that Devoy was the only man who could speak with such authority on the subject. This speaks to the extent of the expatriate Devoy's influence in Ireland and his long reach impacting the nationalist cause from the distant shores of the United States.

37 Ibid.

38 Ibid.

39 Joseph McGarrity, born in Co. Tyrone, was a key figure in Clan na Gael in Philadelphia. A prominent businessman, he was to spend his life working for the cause of Irish freedom. He was a close associate of Devoy and Cohalan. See Sean Cronin, *The McGarrity Papers: Revelations of the Irish Revolutionary Movement in Ireland and America 1900–1940* (Tralee: Anvil Books, 1972).

40 Crowley, *Patrick Pearse*, 122.

41 MS 18,000–157, John Devoy Papers, NLI.

42 *The Gaelic American*, 14 February 1914, Falvey-Villanova, available at: digital.library.edu/item/vudl:331165.

43 Edwards, *Patrick Pearse*, 186.

44 Papers of William Patrick Ryan, IE UCDA LA 11/94, UCD.

45 Pearse and Ó Buachalla, *The Letters of P. H. Pearse*, 299. When in New York Pearse stayed with Miss McKenna at 517 West 144th Street.

46 Ibid., 299, letter 355, 17 February 1914.

47 MS 162, Papers of Patrick Pearse (1879–1916) and His Family (1886–1953), Manuscript and Archives Research Library, Trinity College Library (TCD). This letter from Peter Conroy of Boston to Pearse is an example of the extent of the fundraising for various Irish causes and charities within Irish America. Conroy advises Pearse that he would try to divert funds to St Enda's although he was currently involved in collecting for Novitiate House, Drumgriffin, Co. Galway.

48 B. L. Reid, *The Man from New York: John Quinn and His Friends* (New York: Oxford University Press, 1969), 212.

49 Eileen McGough, *Diarmuid Lynch: A Forgotten Irish Patriot* (Cork: Mercier Press, 2013), 36.

50 *The Gaelic American*, 14 February 1914.

51 O'Brien and Ryan, eds, *Devoy's Post Bag*, 425.

52 *Irish World*, 25 April 1914.

53 *The Gaelic American*, 7 March 1914, Falvey-Villanova, available at: digital.library.villanova.edu/Item/vudl:331195.

54 Francis M. Carroll, *American Opinion and the Irish Question, 1910–23: A Study in Opinion and Policy* (Dublin and New York: Gill and Macmillan, and St Martin's Press, 1978), 23.

55  Ibid., 24.

56  Edwards, *Patrick Pearse*, 189.

57  Doorley, *Irish-American Diaspora Nationalism*, 32.

58  'Nationality: P. H. Pearse and the soul of the nation', *Irish American Weekly*, 18 April 1914.

59  Ibid.

60  Ibid.

61  Ibid.

62  For more detailed information on individual highlights of Pearse's itinerary please see Ruan O'Donnell, *Patrick Pearse* (Dublin: O'Brien Press, 2016).

63  *The Gaelic American*, 7 March 1914.

64  Pearse, *The Coming Revolution*, 66.

65  Pearse and Ó Buachalla, *The Letters of P. H. Pearse*, 299, letter 356, 2 March 1914.

66  Edwards, *Patrick Pearse*, 191.

67  *The Gaelic American*, 7 March 1914.

68  Marie Veronica Tarpey, *The Role of Joseph McGarrity in the Struggle for Irish Independence* (New York: Arno Press, 1976), 76.

69  Pearse, *The Coming Revolution*, 68.

70  Angus Mitchell, 'Robert Emmet and 1916', *History Ireland* 3 (autumn 2003): 4, available at: historyireland.com/20th-century-contemporary-history/robert-emmet-and-1916/.

71  *The Gaelic American*, 7 March 1914.

72  Joseph McGarrity, 'Twenty years ago in America', *An Camán*, 31 March 1934, Metro Edition. This event was held in the auditorium of the Parkway Building. Unfortunately, due to an error in stenography that night, Pearse's eloquent speech was not preserved.

73  Ibid.

74  Pearse stayed at the McGarrity home at 5412 Springfield Avenue while in Philadelphia. After his return to Ireland, Pearse wrote to McGarrity in June 1914 inviting the family to visit him in Ireland. In a jocular fashion Pearse mentioned that he would love to see one of the McGarrity automobiles coming up the Pearse driveway. See Pearse and Ó Buachalla, *The Letters of P. H. Pearse*, 315, letter 371, 19 June 1914. On Pearse's death, McGarrity was moved to write a poetic elegy for him. See Joseph McGarrity Papers, Villanova Digital Library.

75  Pearse and Ó Buachalla, *The Letters of P. H. Pearse*, 303, letter 361, 9 April 1914.

76  Ibid., 303, editorial comment.

77  'St Enda's Field Day programme', 19 April 1914, Pearse Museum.

78  Pearse and Ó Buachalla, *The Letters of P .H. Pearse*, 308 letter 366, 27 April 1914. Pearse thanks Major Nolan, Colonel Crowley, and Captains Guinan, Meenan, and Collins for their aid during the scuffle.

79  Pearse returned to Philadelphia, this time accompanied by Devoy, for a banquet on 26 April, where he again lectured and raised additional funds. He returned to New York for some final speaking engagements, one held by the American Irish Society of Brooklyn at 529 Vanderbilt Avenue, Brooklyn, on 3 May, and another, on the eve of his departure, at the Harlem Gaelic Society at 11 East 125th Street.

80 *The Gaelic American*, 9 May 1914.

81 Ibid., 21 March 1914.

82 Pearse and Ó Buachalla, *The Letters of P. H. Pearse*, 304, letter 361, 9 April 1914.

83 Ibid., 312.

84 Roughly $97,300 today. See Samuel H. Williamson, 'Seven ways to compute the relative value of a US dollar amount, 1774 to present', MeasuringWorth.com, 2016.

85 *The Gaelic American*, 16 May 1914.

86 Roughly $243,000 today. See Samuel H. Williamson, 'Seven ways to compute the relative value of a US dollar amount, 1774 to present', MeasuringWorth.com, 2016; David Brundage, '"In time of peace, prepare for war": key themes in the social thought of New York's Irish nationalists, 1890–1916', in Ronald H. Bayor and Timothy J. Meagher, eds, *The New York Irish* (Baltimore and London: Johns Hopkins University Press, 1996), 330.

87 *The Gaelic American*, 9 May 1914.

88 'St Enda's Field Day programme'.

89 David M. Emmons, 'Fr Michael Hannan: an Irish republican in Butte', *American Journal of Irish Studies* 12 (2015): 77–116.

90 MS 8,265, Papers of Patrick Pearse (1879–1916) and His Family (1886–1953), Manuscript and Archives Research Library, TCD.

91 Roughly $79,700 today. See Samuel H. Williamson, 'Seven ways to compute the relative value of a US dollar amount, 1774 to present', MeasuringWorth.com, 2016.

92 Ruan O'Donnell, *America and the 1916 Rising* (New York: Friends of Sinn Féin New York, 2015), 35.

93 Pearse and Ó Buachalla, *The Letters of P. H. Pearse*, 304.

94 Marion R. Casey and Ed Shevlin shed fascinating light on Kilgallon's experiences in Ireland in 1916 in a later chapter in this volume. See Marion R. Casey and Ed Shevlin, 'An American in Dublin: John Kilgallon's Rising'.

95 Pearse and Ó Buachalla, *The Letters of P. H. Pearse*, 315.

96 Ibid., 311, letter 369, 12 May 1914.

97 Ibid., 305, letter 362, 13 April 1914.

98 Pearse, MS 40,454/1/4, Patrick Pearse's Correspondence, NLI.

99 *The Gaelic American*, 7 March 1914.

100 Reid, *The Man from New York*, 233.

101 Box 4, Folder 2, n.d., William Bourke Cockran Papers, New York Public Library.

102 O'Donnell, *America and the 1916 Rising*, 12.

103 Augusteijn, *Patrick Pearse*; Edwards, *Patrick Pearse*; Sisson, *Pearse's Patriots*; Seán Farrell Moran, *Patrick Pearse and the Politics of Redemption: The Mind of the Easter Rising, 1916* (Washington, DC: Catholic University of America Press, 1994).

104 J. J. Lee, '1916 portraits and lives: Patrick Pearse', in White, Quinn, and Rooney, eds, *1916 Portraits and Lives*, 245.

105 Charles Callan Tansill, *America and the Fight for Irish Freedom, 1866–1922* (New York: Devin-Adair, 1957), letter of 6 May 1914, Pearse to Cohalan.

106 Edwards, *Patrick Pearse*, 197.

107 Augusteijn, *Patrick Pearse*, 248.

108 Ibid., 262.

109 Pearse and Ó Buachalla, *The Letters of P. H. Pearse*, 329, letter 379, 26 September 1914.

110 Papers of William Patrick Ryan, IE UCDA LA 11/94, UCD.

111 Pearse, *The Coming Revolution*, 112.

112 O'Brien and Ryan, eds, *Devoy's Post Bag*, 436.

## 9. 'BIG JIM' LARKIN, THE UNITED STATES AND THE EASTER RISING

1 Written by James Plunkett, a former official in Larkin's union, the play *The Risen People*, first staged in 1958, about the 1913 lockout, was chosen as the motif of the Irish Congress of Trade Unions' centenary celebrations in 1994. More influential again was Plunkett's fiction, above all *Strumpet City* (London: Hutchinson, 1969), about Dublin before and during the lockout. *Strumpet City* became the *Uncle Tom's Cabin* of Irish labour.

2 For the most recent biography, see Emmet O'Connor, *Big Jim Larkin: Hero or Wrecker?* (Dublin: UCD Press, 2015).

3 Dermot Keogh, *The Rise of the Irish Working Class: The Dublin Trade Union Movement and Labour Leadership, 1890–1914* (Belfast: Appletree Press, 1982), 139.

4 *Irish Worker*, 4 January 1913.

5 See, for example, Emmet Larkin, *James Larkin: Irish Labour Leader, 1876–1947* (London: Routledge, 1965), 182–3.

6 The definitive history of the lockout is Padraig Yeates, *Lockout: Dublin 1913* (Dublin: Gill and Macmillan, 2000).

7 Donal Nevin, 'The Irish Citizen Army, 1913–16', in Donal Nevin, ed., *James Larkin: Lion of the Fold* (Dublin: Gill and Macmillan, 1998), 257– 65.

8 *Irish Worker*, 28 March 1914.

9 Nevin, 'The Irish Citizen Army, 1913–16', in Nevin, ed., *James Larkin*, 260; Fred Bower, *Rolling Stonemason: An Autobiography* (London: Jonathon Cape, 1936), 182.

10 O'Connor, *Big Jim Larkin*, 158–9.

11 File 233B, CO 904/206/4, James Larkin, 1914–15, National Archives of the United Kingdom (NAUK), London.

12 C. Desmond Greaves, *Seán O'Casey: Politics and Art* (London: Lawrence and Wishart, 1979), 148; Christopher Murray, *Seán O'Casey: Writer at Work, a Biography* (Dublin: Gill and Macmillan, 2004), 92; ITGWU, *The Attempt to Smash the Irish Transport and General Workers' Union* (Dublin: ITGWU, 1924), xiii, 165; *Irish Worker*, 24 October 1914.

13 File 233B, CO 904/206/4, James Larkin, 1914–15, NAUK.

14 *The Gaelic American*, 7 July 1923.

15 'The Larkin affidavit', in Nevin, ed., *James Larkin*, 298–312.

16 Quoted in Jerome aan de Wiel, *The Irish Factor, 1988–1919: Ireland's Strategic and Diplomatic Importance for Foreign Powers* (Dublin: Irish Academic Press, 2009), 255.

17 See, for example, the *Belvidere Daily Republican*, 28 November 1914; *New York American*, 7 December 1914; *Brooklyn Times*, 7 December 1914; and *New York Sun*, 18 December 1914.

18 Larkin, *James Larkin*, 199.

19 Cabinet papers, 'Intrigues between Sinn Fein leaders and the German government', CAB/24/117, NAUK.

20 File 233B, CO 904/206/4, James Larkin, 1914–15, NAUK.

21 'The Larkin affidavit', in Nevin, ed., *James Larkin*, 301–2.

22 Larkin, *James Larkin*, 201.

23 *Northwest Worker*, 12 August 1915.

24 *Santa Cruz Evening News*, 17 July 1915.

25 Larkin, *James Larkin*, 193.

26 'The Larkin affidavit', in Nevin, ed., *James Larkin*, 298–312; 15674(1), Part 1, William O'Brien Papers, National Library of Ireland (NLI); de Wiel, *The Irish Factor, 1888–1919*, 184, 186; File 233A, CO 904/206/4, James Larkin, 1915–19, NAUK.

27 'The Larkin affidavit', in Nevin, ed., *James Larkin*, 298–312; Larkin's claim is challenged by Frank Robbins, later a bitter opponent in the Irish trade union movement, in Frank Robbins, *Under the Starry Plough: Recollections of the Irish Citizen Army* (Dublin: Academy Press, 1977), 164. German sources on the subject are not extant.

28 'The Larkin affidavit', in Nevin, ed., *James Larkin*, 298–312; 15676(2), Part 1, William O'Brien Papers, NLI; 33718/A(8).

29 *Workers' Republic*, 7 August 1915.

30 Larkin, *James Larkin*, 206–7, 209.

31 Ibid., 210–11.

32 ITGWU, *The Attempt to Smash*, xxx–xxi; Larkin, *James Larkin*, 211.

33 See *Washington Post*, 29 April 1916; *Harrisburg Telegraph*, 29 April 1916; *Boston Post*, 30 April 1916; *Winnipeg Tribune*, 22 May 1916; *Brooklyn Daily Eagle*, 23 June 1917.

34 *New York Times*, 30 April 1916; *Atlanta Constitution*, 30 April 1916.

35 *Irish Worker*, 21 November 1931.

36 See, for example, minutes of the Anglo-American secretariat, 20 February 1928, 495/72/34–1/28, Russian State Archive for Social and Political History (RGASPI), Moscow; Bertram Wolfe, *Strange Communists I Have Known* (London: George Allen and Unwin, 1966), 64–5; Robbins, *Under the Starry Plough*, 164; and Harry Wicks, *Keeping My Head: The Memoirs of a British Bolshevik* (London: Socialist Platform, 1992), 122.

37 *Belvidere Daily Republican*, 22 May 1916; *Greensboro Daily News*, 22 May 1916; Larkin, *James Larkin*, 211–13; Donal Nevin, 'Solidarity for ever', in Nevin, ed., *James Larkin*, 275.

38 Cited in David M. Emmons, *The Butte Irish: Class and Ethnicity in an American Mining Town, 1875–1925* (Chicago: Illini Books, 1990), 358–9.

39 15679(15), William O'Brien Papers, NLI.

40 Richard Hudelson, 'Jack Carney and the *Truth* in Duluth', *Saothar* 19 (1994): 129–39.

41 15679(15), William O'Brien Papers, NLI.

42 Terry Golway, *Irish Rebel: John Devoy and America's Fight for Ireland's Freedom* (New York: St Martin's, 1999), 223.

43 References to the Bureau of Investigation, from 1935 the Federal Bureau of Investigation, are from the Federal Bureau of Investigation file, James Larkin, 62–312, Section 1. The file is not paginated; Larkin, *James Larkin*, 214.

44 Captain Henry Landau, *The Enemy within: The Inside Story of German Sabotage in America* (New York: G. P. Putnam's Sons, 1937), 77–80.

45 'The Larkin affidavit', in Nevin, ed., *James Larkin*, 216.

46 Ibid., 307–12.

47 O'Connor, *Big Jim Larkin*, 218–20; William O'Brien, *Forth the Banners Go: Reminiscences of William O'Brien as Told to Edward MacLyaght, D. Litt* (Dublin: Three Candles, 1969), 77–81; ITGWU, *The Attempt to Smash*, 147; *Irish Independent*, 16 May, 12 June 1923; *The Gaelic American*, 7 July 1923.

48 O'Brien, *Forth the Banners Go*, 77–81; 15679(23), William O'Brien Papers, NLI.

49 Alan J. M. Noonan, '"Real patriots would scorn to recognise the likes of you': Larkin and Irish-America', in David Convery, ed., *Locked Out: A Century of Irish Working Class Life* (Dublin: Irish Academic Press, 2013), 72.

50 O'Connor, *Big Jim Larkin*, 215–302, passim.

## 10. JUDGE COHALAN AND AMERICAN INVOLVEMENT IN THE EASTER RISING

1 'Death of Judge Cohalan', *Irish Press*, 14 November 1946. This obituary also noted Cohalan's 'obstruction' of de Valera's work in 1919–20. No biography has ever been published on Cohalan. In 1967 Sidney Brown completed a valuable MA thesis (unpublished) on Cohalan that drew on then living members of the Cohalan family such as his son Monsignor Florence Cohalan. See Sidney Albert Brown, 'Daniel Florence Cohalan, 1865–1946: a study of an Irish-American leader' (Master's thesis, University of Maryland, 1967). See also, Michael Doorley, 'Judge Daniel Cohalan: a nationalist crusader against British influence in American life', *New Hibernia Review* 19:2 (summer 2015): 113–29.

2 'Obituary of Timothy Cohalan', *New York Times*, 9 December 1909 and *The Gaelic American*, 18 December 1909. Family information also supplied by Peter Fox Cohalan who has compiled an extensive family history of the Cohalan family. Peter Fox Cohalan is a grandnephew of Daniel Cohalan and is himself a retired State Supreme Court judge. Occupations from the 1860 New York State census, Wallkill, Orange County.

3 'Daniel F. Cohalan, ex-justice, dies', *New York Times*, 13 November 1946. Charles Murphy had emerged as the boss of Tammany Hall, the Democratic Party's political machine in New York in 1902. For more on the politics behind Cohalan's appointment see *New York Times*, 19 May 1911. See also Golway's book on Tammany politics in this era: Terry Golway, *Machine Made: Tammany Hall and the Creation of Modern American Politics* (New York: Liveright, 2014).

4 This correspondence is available at the American Irish Historical Society (AIHS), New York, where Cohalan's papers are stored. William Borah (1865–1940), was a Republican

senator for Idaho for 33 years and was well known for his isolationist views; James Reed (1861–1944), was Democratic senator for Missouri from 1911 to 1929 and like Cohalan opposed the League of Nations; Bainbridge Colby (1869–1950) was secretary of state from 1920 to 1921 during the last year of Wilson's administration; Frank Walsh (1864–1939) was a labour lawyer and chairman of the American Commission on Irish Independence.

5 Brown, 'Daniel Florence Cohalan, 1865–1946', 1–2; *The Gaelic American*, 18 December 1909. According to *The Gaelic American*, Timothy was old enough to remember the horrors of the Irish Famine, which he blamed on British policy in Ireland.

6 *The Gaelic American*, 18 December 1909; Ibid., 1 July 1911.

7 The Clan sent sums amounting to between £600 and £1,000 to the IRB each year. See Leon O' Broin, *Revolutionary Underground: The Story of the Irish Republican Brotherhood, 1858–1924* (Dublin: Gill and Macmillan, 1976), 140. For more on the relationship between the Clan and Ireland see Francis Carroll, 'America and the 1916 Rising', in Gabriel Doherty and Dermot Keogh, eds, *1916: The Long Revolution* (Cork: Mercier press, 2007), 121–40; and Michael Doorley, *Irish-American Diaspora Nationalism: The Friends of Irish Freedom, 1916–1935* (Dublin: Four Courts Press, 2005), 15–16.

8 Cohalan's speech at Hoffman House, August 1900, Box 2, fl 27, Cohalan Papers, AIHS. See also Brown, 'Daniel Florence Cohalan, 1865–1946', 7–9.

9 *National Hibernian Digest*, April/May 1948. James Reidy, who was a prominent member of the Clan in the early twentieth century, sent a copy of this biographical sketch of Daniel Cohalan to Frank Robbins on 24 April 1949, MS 18,011/8/1, John Devoy Papers, National Library of Ireland (NLI). Frank Robbins had been a member of James Connolly's Citizen Army and had taken part in the 1916 Rising. Robbins had later spoken in New York at meetings hosted by the Clan where he met Cohalan. In a later account of his experiences in New York, Robbins had nothing but praise for Cohalan's assistance. See Frank Robbins, *Under the Starry Plough: Recollections of the Irish Citizen Army* (Dublin: Academy Press, 1977), 161, 189–90.

10 Bradford Perkins has pointed to an alignment of diplomatic, political, military, and economic interests, between the United States and Britain in the period 1895–1915. See Bradford Perkins, *The Great Rapprochement: England and the United States, 1895–1914* (New York: Scribner, 1968), 296–314. For a contemporary account of the Irish question in Anglo-American relations, see David Sim, *A Union Forever: The Irish Question and US Foreign Relations in the Victorian Age* (New York: Cornell University Press, 2013).

11 See Francis Carroll on Clan efforts to defeat the Anglo-American Arbitration Treaty that came before the senate in 1911–1912. The senate amended the treaty to such a degree that President Taft refused to sign it. Francis Carroll, *American Opinion and the Irish Question, 1910–1923* (Dublin: Gill and Macmillan, 1978), 28. The Clan worked closely with German-American groups in this battle. See letter from James Reidy to John Devoy regarding the activity of the German American alliance and the relationship between the Irish and German groups in general in the United States, 27 January 1912, MS 18,011/8/3, John Devoy Papers, NLI. See also speech by Daniel Cohalan condemning the Anglo-American

Arbitration Treaty and British attempts to forge an Anglo-American alliance, made at the Irish Race Convention in March 1916 and reported in full by *The Gaelic American*, 11 March 1916.

12 Daniel Cohalan, *Democracy or Imperialism: Which?* (New York: Friends of Irish Freedom, 1925). Other pamphlets which indicate Cohalan's American isolationism include: Daniel Cohalan, *The Menace of Foreign Entanglements: Let Us Awaken before It Is Too Late!* (New York: Friends of Irish Freedom, 1923); D. Cohalan, *Political Isolation Is Independence, World Court a Danger to Our Liberty* (New York: Friends of Irish Freedom, 1923). Copies of Cohalan's pamphlets and speeches are available in the AIHS. In his writings and speeches, Cohalan was critical of what he perceived as a growing 'Anglo-Saxonism in American foreign policy'. For a contemporary study of this issue see Paul A. Kramer, 'Empires, exceptions, and Anglo-Saxons: race and rule between the British and United States empires, 1880–1910', *Journal of American History* 88:4 (2002): 1315–35.

13 Monsignor John O'Leary, unlike most of his clerical colleagues, remained a strong supporter of Charles Stewart Parnell after the Parnellite split. He was also, for a time, the chairman of the board of the *Southern Star* newspaper which often included accounts of Cohalan's visits to West Cork. See for instance, *Southern Star*, 11 July 1914 which wished Cohalan a pleasant stay in the area.

14 *The Gaelic American*, 1 July 1911; *New York Times*, 19 May 1911; *Irish Press*, 14 November 1946. Tragically, Hanna died giving birth to the couple's eighth child in June 1911. The child christened Gerard also died. Hanna's funeral was covered extensively in *The Gaelic American*, 1 July 1911, and in the *Southern Star*, 11 July 1914. Cohalan later married Hanna's sister Madge in 1915.

15 Forrest Davis, 'Tammany's war lords: Dan Cohalan, New York and Skibbereen, split attention of Yankee squire of Erin', *New York World-Telegram*, 21 August 1931. Davis was writing a series of articles on prominent figures in the Tammany Hall political machine.

16 Inspector General's monthly report for August 1906, Box 10, Crime Branch Special, Inspector General's County Inspections, National Archives of Ireland.

17 James Reidy to Frank Robbins, 24 April 1924, MS 18,011/8/1, John Devoy Papers, NLI. Cohalan's chairmanship of the Clan is also noted in the British government publication, *Documents Relative to the Sinn Féin Movement* (London: HMSO, 1921), xxix, 13, 429. This report includes extracts from a number of Cohalan's speeches which highlights Cohalan's importance in British eyes.

18 Tom Clarke to Major McBride, 18 June 1901, quoted in Gerard MacAtasney, *Tom Clarke Life Liberty Revolution* (Sallins: Merrion, 2013), 256–7. In his letter, Clarke spells MacBride's name as McBride. As the New York District Organizer or DO1, Cohalan issued strident directives warning Clan members to have nothing to do with constitutional nationalism. See circular signed by Daniel F. Cohalan, District Officer, District One, Clan na Gael, New York, 26 October 1901, Box 2, Cohalan Papers, AIHS.

19 Devoy to Joseph McGarrity, 16 April 1913, Box 1, fl 2, Maloney Collection of Irish Historical Papers (MCIHP), Maloney Papers, New York Public Library (NYPL).

20 *National Hibernian Digest*, April/May 1948; MS 18,075, John Devoy Papers, NLI.

21 James Reidy to Frank Robbins, 24 April 1949, MS 18,011/8/1, John Devoy Papers, NLI.

22 This is evident in Devoy's correspondence with Cohalan in the John Devoy Papers, MS 15,416, NLI.

23 John Devoy, 'The story of the Clan na Gael', *The Gaelic American*, 6 June 1925. As Golway points out, Devoy used the offices of *The Gaelic American* for his duties as leader of the Clan na Gael. See Terry Golway, *Irish Rebel: John Devoy and America's Fight for Ireland's Freedom* (New York: St Martin's Press, 1998), 183–4.

24 A copy of a 'Gaelic American Publishing Company' share certificate, with Cohalan listed as president, is contained in the John Devoy Papers, MS 18,075, NLI.

25 MS 17,660, Joseph McGarrity Papers, NLI. See also Michael Doorley, 'The *Gaelic American* and the shaping of Irish-American opinion', in Wendy Everham, ed., *Probing the Past: Festschrift in Honor of Leo Schelbert* (New York: Peter Lang, 2015), 63–72.

26 Doorley, 'The *Gaelic American* and the shaping of Irish-American opinion', in Everham, ed., *Probing the Past*, 69–71.

27 J. Quinn, 'Tom Clarke', in Lawrence William White, James Quinn, and David Rooney, eds, *1916 Portraits and Lives* (Dublin: Royal Irish Academy, 2015), 72–9.

28 *Irish Press*, 14 November 1946. Cohalan was active in Irish politics on other fronts during this same visit. The front page of the *Irish Independent* includes a photograph of Cohalan addressing a crowd in Skibbereen, Co. Cork, in support of recruitment to the Irish Volunteers. See 'The movement's progress', *Irish Independent*, 15 July 1914.

29 Devoy to Cohalan, 29 November 1911, MS 15,416 (1), Cohalan Papers, NLI.

30 Lynch subsequently became national secretary of the Friends of Irish Freedom. See Doorley, *Irish-American Diaspora Nationalism*, 78. For more on Cohalan's close friendship with Lynch see Eileen McGough, *Diarmuid Lynch: A Forgotten Irish Patriot* (Cork: Mericer Press, 2013), 22–3. McGough, drawing on a private collection of Lynch papers, highlights Lynch's role in Irish and Irish-American nationalist activities during the revolutionary period.

31 J. J. Lee, 'Patrick Pearse', in White, Quinn, and Rooney, eds, *1916 Portraits and Lives*, 249.

32 Davis, 'Tammany's war lords: Dan Cohalan'. George William Russell (1867–1935), was an Irish writer, poet, and nationalist who wrote under the pseudonym 'AE'; Denis Tilden Lynch wrote a biography of Tammany boss William Tweed (1823–1878) in 1927 entitled *'Boss' Tweed: The Story of a Grim Generation* (New York: Boni and Liveright, 1927). Tweed had earned notoriety for greed and corruption during his tenure as Tammany boss from 1866 to 1871.

33 For more on Cohalan's friendship with Quinn see Benjamin Lawrence Reid, *The Man from New York: John Quinn and His Friends* (Oxford: Oxford University Press, 1968).

34 Úna Ní Bhroiméil, *Building Irish Identity in America, 1890–1915: The Gaelic Revival* (Dublin: Four Courts Press, 2003), 119, 121, 127; Doorley, 'Judge Daniel Cohalan: a nationalist crusader', 34.

35 Pearse to Cohalan, 6 May 1914, the full text of this letter and two other letters from Pearse to Cohalan relating to St Enda's, dated 28 December 1914, and 15 October 1915, is reproduced

in full in the appendix of Charles Tansill, *America and the Fight for Irish Freedom 1866–1922* (New York: Devin-Adair, 1957), 444–5. Tansill dedicated his book to both Cohalan and Devoy. Eileen McGough points out, in her biography of Diarmuid Lynch, that within the extensive gardens of Cohalan's house in Glandore, there is a 'Pearse Walk' in memory of Pearse who stayed there as a guest of Cohalan. See McGough, *Diarmuid Lynch*, 22. Pearse's visit is confirmed in James Coombes's short work on the history of Glandore. See James Coombes, *Utopia in Glandore* (Cork: Butlerstown, 1970), 41.

36 *New York Times*, 31 July 1903.

37 Ibid.

38 John L. Gannon to Devoy, 4 November 1905, MS 18,005/14/10, John Devoy Papers, NLI. Gannon was a wealthy businessman and a leading member of the Clan in Providence, Rhode Island. Responding to Cohalan's calls, he made several large donations to *The Gaelic American* including one for $2,000. See Gannon to Devoy, 27 November 1905, MS 18,005/14/11, John Devoy Papers, NLI.

39 Note by Joe McGarrity, 5 October 1914, McGarrity File, Box 2, MCIHP, NYPL.

40 Casement to Cohalan, 8 October 1914, MS 22,463, Cohalan Papers, NLI.

41 Note by Joe McGarrity, 10 October 1914, McGarrity File, Box 2, MCIHP, NYPL.

42 *New York Times*, 9 May 1915.

43 Reinhard R. Doerries, *Prelude to the Easter Rising: Sir Roger Casement in Imperial Germany* (London: Frank Cass Publishers, 2000), 6. Doerries, a German academic, drew on little-used German records on the Irish rebellion, located in the German Foreign Office archive in Bonn.

44 Sean Cronin, *The McGarrity Papers: Revelations of the Irish Revolutionary Movement in Ireland and America, 1900–1940* (Tralee: Anvil Books, 1972), 53.

45 Cited in Doerries, *Prelude to the Easter Rising*, 8.

46 Casement to Cohalan, 12 November 1914, MS 22,463, Cohalan Papers, NLI.

47 Minutes of Executive Meeting, MS 18,017/20, John Devoy Papers, NLI.

48 *The Gaelic American*, 11 March 1916.

49 John Devoy, *Recollections of an Irish Rebel* (New York: Chase D. Young, 1929), 450.

50 *The Gaelic American*, 11 March 1916.

51 Ibid.

52 Doorley, *Irish-American Diaspora Nationalism*, 38.

53 Devoy to Cohalan, 29 November 1911, MS 15,416(1), Cohalan Papers, NLI. This objective was set out in the convention committee's 'Call for a convention', 9 February 1916. For a full transcript of this 'call' see Doorley, *Irish-American Diaspora Nationalism*, appendix 1, 177.

54 M. L. Saunders, 'Wellington House and British propaganda during the First World War', *Historical Journal* 18:1 (March 1975): 119, 130–1. This type of propaganda was more subtle than that used by Germany and targeted America's elite with material that did not on the surface appear as propaganda. For a definition of this so-called 'gray propaganda' see Nicholas J. Cull et al., 'Gray propaganda', in *Propaganda and Mass Persuasion: A Historical Encyclopedia, 1500 to the Present* (Santa Barbara, CA: ABC-CLIO, 2003), 152.

55 *The Gaelic American*, 11 March 1916.

56 William O'Brien and Desmond Ryan, eds, *Devoy's Post Bag 1871–1928*, volume 2 (Dublin: C. J. Fallon, 1958), 485.

57 Memorandum by McGarrity on 1916, MS 17,550, Joseph McGarrity Papers, NLI.

58 Sir Roger Casement for Justice Cohalan, 51 Chambers Street, New York, undated but probably November 1914, quoted in Doerries, *Prelude to the Easter Rising*, 57. This message, sent to Cohalan's legal office in Manhattan, also asked for the dispatch of a priest to minister to the small number of recruits in Casement's so-called Irish Brigade. Casement's relationship with his German hosts soon deteriorated given his failure to raise a substantial Irish brigade and the German refusal to send troops to aid any Irish Rising.

59 The full transcript of Cohalan's message was later incorporated into the British parliamentary White Paper in 1921. See *Documents Relative to the Sinn Féin Movement*, 13.

60 *New York Times*, 23 September 1917. See also article entitled 'Defend Cohalan and Devoy: Friends of Irish Freedom declare they are persecuted', *New York Times*, 12 October 1917. In this article the John P. Holland branch of the FOIF declare their faith in Cohalan and Devoy and condemn 'sinister attacks' on Cohalan as the work of British agents.

61 In a statement issued to *The Gaelic American* and other New York newspapers, Cohalan compared the release of this document to the forged Pigott letters that British authorities had unsuccessfully used to try to incriminate Irish leader Charles Stewart Parnell. See *The Gaelic American*, 29 September 1917.

62 McGarrity to Casement, McGarrity File, Box 1, MCIHP, NYPL. See also 17427, Joseph McGarrity Papers, NLI. The reference to the landing of German troops by airship in Cohalan's message may have been Cohalan's own innovation. Cohalan was an admirer of the latest technology. In 1923 Cohalan accompanied Irish Free State President William T. Cosgrave on an election tour of Ireland in a small aircraft. This was the first use of planes in an Irish election campaign. See *Irish Times*, 20 August 1923.

63 Carroll, 'America and the 1916 Rising', in Doherty and Keogh, eds, *1916 the Long Revolution*, 136.

64 Memorandum by McGarrity on 1916, MS 17,550, Joseph McGarrity Papers, NLI. Sean Cronin claims that this message was sent directly to Cohalan. See Cronin, *McGarrity Papers*, 62. Donald de Cogan argues that the coded message was sent first to Devoy. See D. Cogan, 'Ireland, telecommunications and international politics', *History Ireland* 1:2 (summer 1993).

65 *New York Times*, 1 May 1916. The British army had suffered defeats at the hands of the Turks in Gallipoli in 1915 and Kut in 1916. Japan, for its own strategic reasons, chose to ally itself with Britain in the First World War but had its own long-term imperial ambitions in Asia.

66 Sir Cecil Spring-Rice to the Foreign Office, 10 May 1916 and 26 May 1916, FO 95.776, Public Record Office, London. Spring-Rice urged that Casement's life be spared though this advice was ignored. See B. L. Reid, *The Lives of Roger Casement* (New Haven: Yale University Press, 1976), 389.

67 Diarmuid Lynch, *History of the FOIF*, MS 32,597, Lynch ts, NLI. Lynch completed a draft history of the FOIF in the 1930s but never developed this into a publication. Since Lynch served as national secretary of the FOIF for many years, the typescript is a valuable source on the membership and the history of the FOIF. It is strongly pro-Cohalan in tone.

68 Albert Shaw, ed., *The Messages and Papers of Woodrow Wilson*, volume 1 (New York: Review of Reviewers Corporation, 1924), 151. In a letter to Devoy, which was published in *The Gaelic American*, Hanna Sheehy Skeffington expressed alarm at hostile American media reaction to her lecture tour, which denounced her as a 'traitor' for spreading pernicious doctrines about 'our ally' Britain. See *The Gaelic American*, 23 June 1917.

69 Doorley, *Irish-American Diaspora Nationalism*, 57–5. For a discussion of the impact of these appeals on congress, and for more on the politics surrounding the Irish Relief Fund, see Carroll, *American Opinion and the Irish Question*, 74–81. John D. Moore, national secretary of the FOIF, was also secretary of the Irish Relief Fund.

70 *New York Times*, 6 April 1917.

71 *Brooklyn Tablet*, 21 April 1917. For more on the ethnic defensiveness of Irish America during the Great War see: Thomas J. Rowland, 'Irish-American Catholics and the quest for respectability in the coming of the Great War, 1900–1917', *Journal of American Ethnic History* 15:2 (winter, 1996): 3–29.

72 Mellows's speech to the convention, quoted in Desmond Greaves, *Liam Mellows and the Irish Revolution* (London: Lawrence & Wishart, 2005; second edition), 158–9.

73 Doorley, *Irish American Diaspora Nationalism*, 188.

## 11. VICTOR HERBERT, NATIONALISM, AND MUSICAL EXPRESSION

1 Quoted in Neil Gould, *Victor Herbert: A Theatrical Life* (Bronx, NY: Fordham University Press, 2008), 440–1, citing Harvard University Theatre Collection.

2 Quoted in Edward N. Waters, 'Victor Herbert: romantic idealist', *Western Pennsylvania Historical Magazine* 50:2 (April 1967): 131.

3 For example, the work of Thomas M. Brown, Michael Gordon, Eric Foner, Kerby Miller, James S. Donnelly Jr, and Francis M. Carroll, *American Opinion and the Irish Question, 1910–1923* (Dublin: Gill and Macmillan, 1978), 2–13.

4 'Victor Herbert', *Irish American Weekly*, 25 September 1909; Joseph Kaye, *Victor Herbert: The Biography of America's Greatest Romantic Composer* (New York: G. Howard Watt, 1931); Claire Lee Purdy, *Victor Herbert: American Music Master* (New York: Julian Messner, 1944); Edward N. Waters, *Victor Herbert: A Life in Music* (New York: The Macmillan Company, 1955); 'Herbert, Victor', in Oscar Thompson, ed., *The International Cyclopedia of Music and Musicians* (New York: Dodd, Mead and Company, 1958), 784; Isaac Goldberg, *Tin Pan Alley: A Chronicle of American Popular Music* (New York: Frederick Ungar, 1930, 1961), 178–96; Gould, *Victor Herbert*; William H. A. Williams, 'Victor August Herbert', in James Patrick Byrne and Philip Coleman, eds, *Ireland and the Americas: Culture, Politics,*

*and History*, volume 2 (Santa Barbara: ABC-CLIO, 2008), 411–13; Patrick M. Geoghegan, 'Victor Herbert', in James McGuire and James Quinn, eds, *Dictionary of Irish Biography* (Cambridge: Cambridge University Press, 2009); Aaron C. Keebaugh, 'Irish music and Home Rule politics, 1800–1922' (Ph.D. thesis, University of Florida, 2011), 139–53, 192–228; Steven Ledbetter and Orly Leah Krasner, 'Herbert, Victor', in Charles Hiroshi Garrett, ed., *Grove Dictionary of American Music*, volume 4 (New York: Oxford University Press, 2013), 134–8. For Irving Caesar's recollection, see Michael Whorf, *American Popular Song Lyricists: Oral Histories, 1920s–1960s* (North Carolina: McFarland & Company, 2012), 38–9.

5 Gould, *Victor Herbert* includes a Herbert-Lover family tree, with a paternal line back to the barrister Richard Townsend Herbert (1754–1832); this is incorrect (see note 93 below).

6 Waters, *Victor Herbert*, 3–4; Kaye, 21; Gould, 6, citing an interview with Herbert in *Broadway Magazine* (March 1915). 'My father was German,' Herbert once explained to reporters, by which he presumably meant Dr. Carl Schmid, his mother's second husband and the father of Herbert's half-brother Willi. *Boston Daily Globe*, April 16, 1916.

7 Gould, *Victor Herbert*, 6; 'Victor Herbert discusses art, drama, music', *Christian Science Monitor*, 4 December 1915. Herbert seems to have told this story to several journalists; Gould, *Victor Herbert*, cites Stanley Olmstead, 'The boy who played cello', *New York Morning Telegraph*, 13 December 1914.

8 Waters, *Victor Herbert*, 2–25.

9 Naturalization petitions of the US District Court, 1820–1930, and Circuit Court, 1820–1911, for the Western District of Pennsylvania, 2 October–25 November 1902, M1537, Roll 098, National Archives and Records Administration, Washington, DC.

10 Edward Waters concluded meaninglessly, 'His continuous loyalty to this organization [Friendly Sons of St Patrick] was both curious and touching; it revealed a quest for emotional satisfaction which could be found only in a society inspired by the political misery and legendary wealth of a famed land.' See Waters, *Victor Herbert*, 469; Kaye, *Victor Herbert*, 241; Purdy, *Victor Herbert*, 153.

11 To hear a selection of his works, see 'The Musical Worlds of Victor Herbert', Concert, Library of Congress, 3 December 2012, available at: youtube.com/watch?v=jnFC-uAEIow4. It includes two of his Irish pieces: 'Barney O'Flynn' from *Babes in Toyland* (1903) at 1:28:56–1:32:55 and 'Thine Alone' from *Eileen* (1916) at 1:36:52–1:42:30. The finding aid to the Victor Herbert Collection, Music Division, Library of Congress is available at: lcweb2.loc.gov/service/music/eadxmlmusic/eadpdfmusic/2012/mu012013.pdf.

12 Marion R. Casey, 'Victor Herbert: an Irishman and the New York Philharmonic', *New York Irish History* 2 (1987): 8–9.

13 Herbert's contract with Edison, for example, gave him an advisory role in the selection of compositions and artists to be recorded. See Waters, *Victor Herbert*, 347.

14 Ledbetter and Krasner, 'Herbert, Victor', in Garrett, ed., *Grove Dictionary of American Music*.

15 See, for example, *New York Telegraph*, 30 January 1904; *Musical America*, 16 December, 1916: 21; *Brooklyn Daily Eagle*, 21 January 1917.

16 *Christian Science Monitor*, 13 February 1917. The music critic James Gibbons Huneker recalled Herbert explaining why his harmonies were Irish. See Gould, *Victor Herbert*, 22, quoting from James G. Huneker, *Steeplejack II* (New York: Scribner's, 1922).

17 Waters, *Victor Herbert*, 66; Casey, 'Victor Herbert', 9. *Irish Rhapsody* was not published until 1910. For a musicological perspective, see programme notes for the Philharmonic Society of New York by W. H. Humiston, 16 December 1917, and Lawrence Gilman, 29 November 1924, New York Philharmonic Archives.

18 *New York Tribune*, 16 April 1911.

19 *Irish American Weekly*, 13 January 1912; Waters, *Victor Herbert*, 410–11.

20 Nielsen and Herbert both adored their Irish mothers. Sara Kilroy, who emigrated to Boston from Donegal when she was two, taught her daughter, Alice, to sing *sean-nós*, and is said to have been an ardent Irish nationalist. See Dall Wilson, *Alice Nielsen and the Gayety of Nations* (Raleigh, NC: lulu.com, 2010), 16–17, 133; *Irish American Weekly*, 30 March, 6 April 1912.

21 *Irish American Weekly*, 29 March 1913.

22 Programme, Irish Day, St Louis Exposition, *St Louis Republic*, 21 September 1896; programme, Hudson-Fulton Celebration Irish Concert, Carnegie Hall, 26 September 1909, *Journal of the American Irish Historical Society* 9 (1910): 136; programme, Friendly Sons of St Patrick, 17 March 1911, available at: friendlysonsnyc.com/index.cfm?fl=1911; programme, Carnegie Hall, 23 March 1913, Victor Herbert Papers, Library of Congress.

23 Richard Murphy and Lawrence Mannion, *History of the Society of the Friendly Sons of St Patrick in the City of New York* (NY: By the Society, 1962), 415; Waters, *Victor Herbert*, 316; Gould, *Victor Herbert*, 434. Herbert was also a member of the Irish Musical Society, est. 1886. See Gould, *Victor Herbert*, 435; *Brooklyn Eagle*, 14 August 1921: 29.

24 *Brooklyn Eagle*, 27 January 1915; *Irish American Weekly*, 9 May 1914; Murphy and Mannion, *History of the Society of the Friendly Sons of St Patrick in the City of New York*, 411, 426; *New York Times*, 28 February 1925; Terry Golway, *Irish Rebel: John Devoy and America's Fight for Ireland's Freedom* (New York: St Martin's Press, 1988), 6.

25 Waters, *Victor Herbert*, 470. For how Mitchel represented something other than he was trying to portray, see John F. McClymer, 'Of "Mornin' Glories" and "Fine Old Oaks": John Purroy Mitchel, Al Smith, and reform as an expression of Irish-American aspiration', in Ronald H. Bayor and Timothy J. Meagher, eds, *The New York Irish* (Baltimore: Johns Hopkins University Press, 1996), 374–94.

26 *The Gaelic American*, 27 March 1915. Herbert again conducted 'The Hail of the Friendly Sons' and 'New Ireland' at this event.

27 Kaye, *Victor Herbert*, 244, implies, without any evidence, that Herbert was seen 'as having a slower mind' by such 'Irish intellectuals'. Purdy, *Victor Herbert*, 152, concludes Herbert 'was not much of a "politician"'.

28 John Devoy, *Recollections of an Irish Rebel* (New York: Charles P. Young Co., 1929), 453.

29 Ibid., 455–6.

30  *Kentucky Irish American*, 11 March 1916. Judge Cohalan and John Devoy, the acerbic editor of *The Gaelic American*, conceived the idea for this 1916 Irish Race Convention as a means of establishing a front organisation for the secretive Clan that could lobby the American people directly. See Michael Doorley, *Irish-American Diaspora Nationalism: The Friends of Irish Freedom, 1916–1935* (Dublin: Four Courts Press, 2005), 36–8.

31  *Anaconda Standard*, 5 March 1916: 1; *Idaho Statesman*, 6 March 1916; *Kentucky Irish American*, 11 March 1916; Waters, *Victor Herbert*, 480–1.

32  Devoy, *Recollections*, 449, 457; *Anaconda Standard*, 6 March 1916: 7.

33  *The Gaelic American*, 11 March 1916.

34  Waters, *Victor Herbert*, 481; Kaye, *Victor Herbert*, 242–4, claims this was written by Judge Cohalan; Gould, *Victor Herbert*, 436–7, mistakenly associates this with the Irish Relief Fund Bazaar in October 1916. Another example of Herbert's political thinking, chiefly concerned with John Redmond, appeared on the front page of the *Kentucky Irish American* the week of the Rising, 29 April 1916.

35  Kaye, *Victor Herbert*, 243. The use of the word *ráiméis* indicates a familiarity with the Irish language; it is not implausible that Herbert picked up a bit of Irish from the Gaelic Society, given his fluency in other languages. None of his biographers mention this.

36  *Boston Daily Globe*, 16 April 1916.

37  Advertisement, *New York Times*, 22 June 1916; *Herbert v. Shanley Co.*, 242 US 591 (1917); Waters, *Victor Herbert*, 434–7, 447–55; Leo J. Shanley, 'The Shanleys of Broadway', *New York Irish History* 5 (1990–1): 19. In January 1917, not only was Herbert victorious in a landmark decision, but Tom Shanley was so enraged at the amount of royalties he owed that he destroyed all the Herbert sheet music and recordings in his home.

38  *Boston Daily Globe*, 25 April 1916; Waters, *Victor Herbert*, 474–7. *The Princess Pat* was in Clarksburg, West Virginia, on 10 April and by Christmas it was in Bryan, Texas. See *Bryan Daily Eagle and Pilot*, 22 December 1916. The *Daily Telegram*, 6 April 1916, said, 'it is of the highest class and the first Victor Herbert opera to be seen in West Virginia.'

39  He had done this once before with 'Barney O'Flynn' in *Babes in Toyland* (1903).

40  Victor Light Opera Company, *Gems from the Princess Pat* (Victor 35517), recorded in Camden, New Jersey, 3 December 1915, available at: loc.gov/jukebox/recordings/detail/id/4197/. Columbia released another version the following month, *Discography of American Historical Recordings*, 'Columbia matrix 46352. Two laughing Irish eyes / Eleanor Painter', available at: adp.library.ucsb.edu/index.php/matrix/detail/2000023638/46352-Two_laughing_Irish _eyes. More than 250,000 low-priced Victrolas were being sold in the United States at the time. Sales prices and production numbers are on the Victor-Victrola page, available at: victor-victrola.com/History%20of%20the%20Victor%20Phonograph.htm. See also Thomas J. Rowland, 'Irish-American Catholics and the quest for respectability in the coming of the Great War, 1900–1917', *Journal of American Ethnic History* 15:2 (winter 1996): 3–31.

41  Wayne D. Shirley, 'A bugle call to arms for national defense!: Victor Herbert and his score for *The Fall of a Nation*', *The Quarterly Journal of the Library of Congress* 40:1 (winter 1983): 28, 33, 41; Waters, *Victor Herbert*, 485. There is a claim that this was attempted earlier by

the Kalem Film Company. See Herbert Reynolds, 'Aural gratification with Kalem Films: a case history of music, lectures and sound effects, 1907–1917', *Film History* 12:4 (2000): 417–42.

42 *New York Times*, 14 May 1916.

43 Gould, *Victor Herbert*, 463–4.

44 *The Fall of a Nation* was advertised as 'positively the greatest spectacle ever filmed in Ten Massive Reels', with 'Thrilling, Startling, Realistic Effects' from a cast of thousands (people as well as horses). See, for example, *Durant Weekly News*, 1 September 1916.

45 Shirley, 'A bugle call to arms for national defense!', 30, 34, 38–40, 47.

46 Gould, *Victor Herbert*, 465–71; Waters, *Victor Herbert*, 486–7; Anthony Slide, *American Racist: The Life and Films of Thomas Dixon* (Kentucky: University of Kentucky Press, 2004), 102.

47 *New York Times*, 7 June 1916; *New York Tribune*, 7 June 1916; *Musical America*, 17 June 1916; Waters, *Victor Herbert*, 490–1. *The Plain Dealer*, 18 June 1916, concluded, 'the preposterous handling of the [film's] theme neutralizes its thrills.'

48 *Musical America*, 13 May 1916; Purdy, *Victor Herbert*, 216–18; Slide, *American Racist*, 94. At the same time, Herbert was involved in the Carnegie Hall tribute to the 'Dublin Rebels' on 14 May 1916.

49 'Help for the Irish', *New-Yorker Staats-Zeitung*, 25 May 1916.

50 *New York Tribune*, 19 April 1916; *New York Times*, 29 June 1916.

51 *New York Times*, 28 May 1916; *Musical America*, 27 May 1916: 28; ibid., 3 June 1916: 36; ibid., 10 June 1916: 8.

52 *The Sun*, 28 May 1916; John Quinn to Maude Gonne, 29 July 1916, MssCol 2513, John Quinn Papers, New York Public Library.

53 Gould, *Victor Herbert*, 234; Kuno Francke, 'The duty of German Americans', *The New Republic*, 13 May 1916: 42–3. Waters, *Victor Herbert*, 479, says Victor Herbert 'reaped considerable criticism for his actions' during 1916 and 'found himself completely repudiated in England'.

54 It was initially announced in May 1916 but arrangements with the producers quickly fell through and it was midsummer before Herbert could move forward: 'I may not be able to start real work until after the first of August – but then – with *both feet!*' See Victor Herbert to Harold Sanford, 20 July 1916 (emphasis in the original), Box 187, Folder 17, Victor Herbert Papers, Library of Congress; *Musical America*, 13 May 1916: 32 and *Evening World*, 13 May 1916; premature and misleading announcements were not atypical in the theatrical business according to Waters, *Victor Herbert*, 401.

55 Waters, *Victor Herbert*, 418.

56 Thomas S. Hischak, 'Tin Pan Alley', in Garrett, ed., *Grove Dictionary of American Music*, volume 8, 214–16; Goldberg, *Tin Pan Alley*, 213.

57 Michael J. Budds, 'Olcott, Chauncey', in Garrett, ed., *Grove Dictionary of American Music*, volume 6, 195. Olcott was preceded in Irish roles by the popular actor-singers Andrew Mack and William J. Scanlan.

58 A third strand is what we now call Irish traditional music and has a different history in the United States vis-à-vis nationalism. See Rebecca S. Miller, 'Irish traditional and popular

music in New York City: identity and social change, 1930–1975', in Bayor and Meagher, eds, *The New York Irish*, 481–507 and Mick Moloney, 'Irish-American popular music', in J. J. Lee and Marion R. Casey, eds, *Making the Irish American: History and Heritage of the Irish in the United States* (New York: New York University Press, 2006), 391–8.

59 Rowland, 'Irish-American Catholics and the quest of respectability in the coming of the Great War, 1900–1917', and Colleen McDannell, 'True men as we need them: Catholicism and the Irish American male', *American Studies* 27:2 (1986).

60 Joseph I. C. Clarke, 'The Irish share in the Hudson-Fulton celebration', *Journal of the American Irish Historical Society* 9 (1910): 135. This is part of a long description (113–52) of the 1909 civic events in New York City that included an Irish concert conducted by Victor Herbert. Clarke writes that organising the programme 'involved some sacrifice on [Herbert's] part but he gladly made it, and the success of the result must certainly have compensated him.' For details on the concert, see 130, 133–7.

61 Ellen Marie Peck, 'Caldwell, Donnelly and Young: women writing in the American musical theatre', in Paul Fryer, ed., *Women in the Arts in the Belle Epoque: Essays on Influential Artists* (Jefferson: McFarland, 2012), 154–5. Each of these plays had less than 35 performances; for details refer to the Internet Broadway Database, available at: ibdb.com/.

62 Henry Blossom and Victor Herbert, *Eileen* (New York: Witmark & Sons, 1917); Waters, *Victor Herbert*, 498–501.

63 Alexander Woollcott in the *New York Times*, 25 March 1917, quoted in Waters, *Victor Herbert*, 501–2. The *Boston Daily Globe*, 16 January 1917, called it 'rather conventional in its fidelity to the stage tales of Irish patriotism that have been standard since the days of Boucicault'. See also *Musical America*, 24 March 1917: 49; *The Theatre* 25 (1917): 278. The *Brooklyn Eagle*, 21 March 1917, was kinder, calling it 'old fashioned … thank the Lord for that!' Whatever John Devoy actually thought of its artistic merit, he understood the propaganda value and pointed to positive reviews in *The Sun* and the *Herald*, ignoring the *Times*. *The Gaelic American*, 24 March 1917, declared that *Eileen* 'pulsates with a passionate devotion to Ireland and breathes the deathless spirit of Irish nationhood'.

64 Goldberg, *Tin Pan Alley*, 195.

65 *New York Times*, 20, 25 March 1917; *New York Tribune*, 20 March 1917; *Musical America*, 24 March 1917.

66 Purdy, *Victor Herbert*, 216; Goldberg, *Tin Pan Alley*, 184.

67 Waters, *Victor Herbert*, 498. Herbert followed this uilleann pipe sequence with a choral rendition of 'Ave Maria'. Both appear to be intentional acknowledgments of the 'real' Irish Catholic world that was invisible on the New York stage. See 'Opening Act III', *Eileen*, conducted by David Brophy with the Orchestra of Ireland (New York: New World Records, 2012), Disc 2, Track 2. On Hennessy, see advertisements he placed in the *Irish Advocate* in 1906.

68 *Brooklyn Daily Eagle*, 21 March 1917. The reviewer for *The Theatre* (May 1917) called her 'colorless' and the *New York Tribune*, 20 March 1917, said she was 'timid' and knew 'little of acting'.

69 *Musical America*, 24 March 1917; *Brooklyn Daily Eagle*, 23 August 1921; Joseph I. C. Clarke, *My Life and Memories* (New York: Dodd, Mead and Company, 1925), 69–70. Breen too

was the author of *Thirty Years of New York Politics Up to Date* (1889) and was buried from the Convent of the Sacred Heart in Manhattan (see also note 84).

70 *Brooklyn Life*, 8 November 1913; *Musical America*, 24 March 1917: 49; *Musical Courier*, 29 March 1917; *New York Tribune*, 20 March, 10 July 1917; *New York Times*, 23 August 1921. Their son, William Clarke Jr died on the Western Front during the Second World War, *New York Times*, 24 January 1945.

71 *The Gaelic American*, 24 March 1916.

72 Fanny Schmid, 'The author of 'Rory O'More': recollections of Samuel Lover, by his daughter', *Century Magazine* 53:4 (February 1897); Samuel Lover, *The Songs of Ireland* (New York: Dick & Fitzgerald, 1860); William H. A. Williams, *'Twas Only an Irishman's Dream: The Image of Ireland and the Irish in American Popular Song Lyrics, 1800–1920* (Champaign: University of Illinois Press, 1996), 30, 67; Gould, *Victor Herbert*, 5.

73 James Jeffrey Roche, ed., *The Collected Works of Samuel Lover, Vol. 1: Rory O'More* (Boston: Little, Brown and Co., 1903); *The O'Kalem Collection: 1910-1915* (Irish Film Institute & BIFF Productions, 2011); Gary W. Harner, 'The Kalem Company, travel and on-location filming: the forging of an identity', *Film History* 10:2 (1988): 188–207.

74 Bayle Bernard, *The Life of Samuel Lover, RHA* (London: Henry S. King & Co., 1874), 4, 7–8; Kaye, *Victor Herbert*, 9; Purdy, *Victor Herbert*, 39–40. Neither Waters, *Victor Herbert*, nor Gould, *Victor Herbert*, mentions this.

75 At the Irish Race Convention in March 1916, the oratory acknowledged the rebellions of 1798 and 1803 ('Who fears to speak of '98?' and 'Emmet's speech from the dock', respectively). As one reviewer wrote, 'Pity the poor librettist who has to sit down and concoct a book out of the hackneyed ingredients of the Irish Rebellion of a hundred years ago! … The result is … a threadbare, clumsy, naïve plot that carries you nowhere and creaks badly at every turn.' See *The Theatre* 25 (1917): 278.

76 *New York Tribune*, 23, 29 February 1904; *New York Times*, 29 February 1904; *The Gaelic American*, 7 March 1914; Marianne Elliott, *Robert Emmet: The Making of a Legend* (London: Profile Books Ltd, 2003), 197.

77 Herbert used the same phrase when he opened the Carnegie Hall tribute on 14 May 1916. See *New York Times*, 15 May 1916. Waters, *Victor Herbert*, 481–3, calls Herbert 'the best known if not the wisest Irish leader in America' and considers the Bazaar 'the climax of Herbert's flirtation with political Irish nationalism'. Madame Gadski sang Irish songs at this fundraising event too.

78 Gould, *Victor Herbert*, 439.

79 *Boston Daily Globe*, 16, 18 January 1917.

80 Ibid., 20 January 1917. Since Herbert was never in Ireland, his understanding of the Irish people was based on his Irish American circles in the United States, especially in New York City.

81 Ibid.; Waters, *Victor Herbert*, 497; Gould, *Victor Herbert*, 439; liner notes to *Eileen*, conducted by Brophy with the Orchestra of Ireland, 16.

82 'Taking a stand on being Irish', *Plain Dealer*, 8 December 1916.

83 *Musical America*, 30 December 1916, 5 August 1917; *Christian Science Monitor*, 13 February 1917; Waters, *Victor Herbert*, 499.

84 According to Gould, *Victor Herbert*, 442–3, Cohalan had reservations about *Eileen's* national tour. See also the *New York Times*, 20 October 1930, 15 August 1933, and the *Reading Times*, 16 August 1933, which, in announcing that Aileen Cohalan was entering a convent and that her brother Patrick was becoming a Jesuit, appear to be repeating a family story. There is no other documentation and none of Herbert's biographers seem to have been aware of this claim. While not discounting it entirely, in light of the casting of Grace Breen, other influences seem more probable. Mother Aileen Cohalan, RSCJ, went on to be the director of the Pius X School of Liturgical Music at Manhattanville College, then taught for six years in Ireland (where the old Cohalan house in Glandore, Co. Cork, was a convent for her order, the Sacred Heart Sisters), before being appointed a lecturer in music at the Newtown College of the Sacred Heart (later merged with Boston College). See *885*: 1 (1 October 1959), available at: newspapers.bc.edu; 'Comings and goings in West Cork', *Irish Times*, 30 March 2000; Jeffrey Wills, *The Catholics of Harvard Square* (Baltimore: Saint Bede's Publications, 1993), 189.

85 W. H. Grattan Flood, 'Eibhlin a Ruin', *The Irish Monthly* 50:586 (April 1922): 171–5; Gerald Griffin, 'Eibhlín a Rúin', in M. J. Barry, ed., *The Songs of Ireland* (Dublin: James Duffy, 1845), 154–6; Thomas Davis, 'Eibhlin a Ruin', in *The Poems of Thomas Davis: Now First Collected* (Dublin: James Duffy, 1857), 39–40. These versions are said to have been the inspiration for an operatic libretto by John Millington Synge sometime around 1893. See Axel Klein, 'Celtic legends in Irish opera, 1900–1930', *Proceedings of the Harvard Celtic Colloquium* 24/25 (2004/2005): 46.

86 'This was an often well-intentioned but in practice rather manipulative attempt to control their music and their culture.' See Jürgen Kloss, 'How "Robin Adair" came to Germany' and 'Herder's cuckoo's egg: some notes about the term "Volkslied"', *Just Another Tune: Songs & Their History*, available at: justanothertune.com/html/raig.html.

87 Arrangements were made by Silcher (1834) and Erk (1845). See Jürgen Kloss, 'Friedrich Silcher and Ludwig Erk', *Just Another Tune: Songs & Their History*, available at: justanothertune .com/html/raig.html.

88 Kloss, 'Herder's cuckoo's egg'.

89 Waters, *Victor Herbert*, 4; Jürgen Kloss, '"Treu und herzinniglich, Robin Adair": a British tune In Germany', *Just Another Tune: Songs & Their History*, available at: justanothertune. com/html/raig.html. See also Veronica ní Chinnéide, 'The sources of Moore's Melodies', *Journal of the Royal Society of Antiquaries of Ireland* 89 (1959): 118; Klein, 'Celtic legends in Irish opera', 46; Gould, *Victor Herbert*, 6.

90 The programme for this concert was announced in the *St Louis Republic*, 21 September 1896. Both titles are frequently found in the pages of *Musical America*. On music for *The Colleen Bawn* see Reynolds, 'Aural gratification with Kalem Films', 429.

91 Axel Klein, 'Stage-Irish, or the national in Irish opera, 1780–1925', *Opera Quarterly* 21 (2005): 27–67 and especially on Charles Villiers Stanford's *Shamus O'Brien* (1895), 46–8. Herbert most likely knew about the Irish-language opera *Muirgheis* (1903) published

in New York by Breitkopf and Härtel in 1910, before the tragic death of its composer, Thomas O'Brien Butler on the *Lusitania*. See Klein, 'Celtic legends in Irish opera', 44–6.

92 Herbert's great friend, the Irish tenor John McCormack, recorded 'Eibhlin a Ruin' twice during this period, first in 1909 and then in 1912.

93 Herbert's genealogy seems to have been intentionally obfuscated by his mother, who encouraged his identification with Ireland. Although she wrote to him in 1904 that his paternal forebears, including his father, were 'all gifted and distinguished men and thorough Irishmen', there is no evidence that the composer ever knew the truth, now revealed by digitised resources. Victor Herbert was conceived extramaritally, born most probably on the Channel island of Guernsey, and baptised in Freibourg, Germany, the son of Fanny Lover and August Herbert, about whom nothing is known at present. At the time Lover was married to Frederick Muspratt (father of her first two children), who divorced her over Victor in 1861. Their fathers, Samuel Lover and the chemical industrialist James Muspratt, were life-long friends. See 'James Muspratt', *Dictionary of National Biography* 39 (1894): 433; Peter Reed, *Entrepreneurial Ventures in Chemistry: The Muspratts of Liverpool, 1793–1934* (London: Routledge, 2016), 84, 90–1, 93–4, 102; 'Baden, Germany, Lutheran baptisms, marriages, and burials, 1502–1985', 272–3, Ancestry.com; 'Census of England, 1861 [Hampshire/Southampton St Mary/District 23], No. 103', 20, Ancestry.com; 'Court for divorce and matrimonial causes, Nov. 23', *The Times* of London, 25 November 1861: 9.

94 *New York Times*, 25 March 1917; Gould, *Victor Herbert*, 439–41. *Eileen* for the stage was ultimately the victim of the First World War and a disastrous fire in Dayton, Ohio that destroyed its sets, costumes, and orchestral parts. See Waters, *Victor Herbert*, 503–4.

95 Daniel C. Cohalan Papers, American Irish Historical Society, quoted in Gould, *Victor Herbert*, 441–3. There is no discussion of *Eileen* in Kaye, *Victor Herbert*.

96 *Irish American Weekly*, 6 April 1907, 1 February 1908. Herbert's biographers seem to be unaware of this arrangement.

97 Ibid., 29 May 1909; *New Zealand Truth*, 18 November 1916; 'Old Ireland Shall Be Free', Frances G. Spencer Collection of American Popular Sheet Music, Baylor University, available at: digitalcollections.baylor.edu/cdm/ref/collection/fa-spnc/id/9249, recorded on *Collected Songs of Victor Herbert* (Anthology of American Music, 2012), available at: youtube.com/watch?v=-TZtsjbSKbM. It was introduced to Americans by William Ludwig (the pseudonym for William Ledwidge), a Dublin-born baritone famous for his interpretation of Wagner who made several tours of the United States late in his career.

98 *New York Tribune*, 24 January 1915. McCormack also recorded 'It's a Long Way to Tipperary' on the Victor label in November 1914, a month before Irish republicans in Ireland and the United States began to protest its adoption by British troops at the front. See Joost Augusteijn, *The Irish Revolution, 1913–1923* (Basingstoke: Palgrave Macmillan, 2002), 44. 'Tipperary' had long been an Irish cue for Tin Pan Alley; McCormack's version appears to have divorced it from association with either the Alley or the army in American popular culture until the war and Irish objections escalated.

99 For example, Gordon Johnstone and Samuel S. Krams, 'I Had a Dream that Ireland Was Free among the Nations of the Earth' (New York: Waterson Berlin & Snyder Co.,1917),

and Robert S. Vaughan and W. Carroll, 'Oh God, Set Old Ireland Free' (Brooklyn: Will Carroll Co., 1917).

100 *Musical America*, 24 March 1917: 49. On 4 May 1916 – the day the British executed Willie Pearse, Joseph Plunkett, Edward Daly, and Michael O'Hanrahan – Victor Herbert led school children in singing another new anthem, 'Orange, White and Blue', composed for the Holland Society to protest the preferment of New York's British history over that of the Dutch in the great seal of the city. See *New York Tribune*, 5 May 1916.

101 Liner notes to *Eileen*, conducted by Brophy with the Orchestra of Ireland.

102 *Musical America*, 24 March 1917: 49.

103 Florence Monteith Lynch, *Mystery Man at Banna Strand* (New York: Vantage Press, 1959), 78. I have been unable to find out anything else about Fr O'Reilly. St Gabriel's was a large Irish parish on Manhattan's East Side.

104 'The Soldier's Song', words by Peadar Ó Cearnaigh, music by Pádraig Ó hAonaigh, arranged by Cathal Mac Dubhghaill (Dublin: Whelan & Son, 1916),16902-SM, Irish Traditional Music Archives, available at: itma.ie/digitallibrary/book/soldiers-song; Joseph E. A. Connell Jr, 'A Soldier's Song/Amhrán na bhFiann', *History Ireland* (March/April 2013): 66.

105 Paul Hurley, 'An Irishman's diary', *Irish Times*, 10 September 2007; *Catalog of Copyright Entries: Musical Compositions*, part 3, volume 12, issue 1 (Washington, DC: United States Government Printing Office, 1917), 816. According to Joseph Connell, Herbert signed over royalties to Kearney and Heaney.

106 *San Francisco Chronicle*, 2 March 1917; *The Gaelic American*, 7 April 1917; *Seattle Daily Times*, 14 May 1917.

107 *The Gaelic American*, 14 April 1917. Herbert was noted for his ability to galvanise audiences, see recollection by Peggy Woods in Waters, *Victor Herbert*, 568.

108 *New York Times*, 9 April 1917; *New York Tribune*, 9 April 1917. There was no official American national anthem at this time but most Irish-American events preferred 'The Star-Spangled Banner'. Herbert and John McCormack were interviewed about their anthem preferences by *Musical America*, 9 June 1917.

109 *The Gaelic American*, 28 April 1917.

110 *San Diego Union*, 22 November 1919; *Springfield Republican*, 8 February 1920; *San Francisco Chronicle*, 18 March 1920; *Times-Picayune*, 26 February 1921; *Boston Herald*, 12 March 1921. The version on the Emerson label can be heard at 02:47 online in the 78rpms and Cylinder Recordings Collection, Internet Archive, available at: archive.org/details/SoldiersOfErin. *Talking Machine World*, 15 August 1919: 176; *Charleston Evening Post*, 26 September 1919; *Plain Dealer*, 28 November 1920: 63.

111 Herbert's score for 'Soldiers of Erin' is in the Library of Congress and is available at: loc. gov/exhibits/musical-worlds-of-victor-herbert/exhibition-items.html#obj34. Three piano versions of 'Soldiers of Erin' – which include this quote in an editor's note – are part of the Irish Sheet Music Archives, Ward Music Archives, Milwaukee, WI (IF SL 02–476, IF SL 01–460, IF SM 01–843), available at: irishsheetmusicarchives.com/BrowseCollection. htm?F1_keywordFilter=soldier%27s%20of%20erin.

112 *Irish American Weekly*, 9 May 1914; advertisement, *Washington Post*, 13 May 1914; programme, *The John Barry Memorial*, 1906, Joseph McGarrity Books, Villanova University.

113 *New York Times*, 19 April 1914. By December 1915, Herbert was blending music and politics in statements to the press. See *Christian Science Monitor*, 4 December 1915.

114 *New York Times*, 25 March 1917; *New York Tribune*, 20 March 1917.

115 Reginald De Koven, 'Nationalism in music', *North American Review* 189:640 (March 1909): 389, 394, 396; Barbara L. Tischler, 'One hundred percent Americanism and music in Boston during World War I', *American Music* 4:2 (summer 1986): 166, 168; J. E. Vacha, 'When Wagner was verboten: the campaign against German music in World War I', *New York History* 64:2 (April 1983): 175, 187; Joseph Horowitz, 'Henry Krehbiel: German American, music critic', *The Journal of the Gilded Age and Progressive Era* 8:2 (April 2009), 183, 185.

116 Gould, *Victor Herbert*, 434.

117 Waters, *Victor Herbert*, 369.

118 Ibid., 372–9, quote from 379; Kaye, *Victor Herbert*, 192–202; Gould, *Victor Herbert*, 408–18.

119 *Dramatic Mirror*, 31 March 1917, quoted in Waters, *Victor Herbert*, 503.

120 *Musical America*, 17 February 1917; *Wisconsin State Journal*, 14 February 1917.

121 Gould, *Victor Herbert*, 434; Purdy, *Victor Herbert*, 216–7.

122 Waters, *Victor Herbert*, 509; Purdy, *Victor Herbert*, 217.

123 Gould, *Victor Herbert*, 434. In May 1918 Herbert was succeeded as president of the Friends of Irish Freedom by the Carmelite Fr Peter Magennis. See *Boston Daily Globe*, 20 May 1918.

124 Giollamuire Ó Murchú, *Jerome Connor, Irish-American Sculptor 1874–1943* (Dublin: The National Gallery of Ireland, 1993), 36–37, 75. The quote is excerpted from Emmet's famous 'speech from the dock' (19 September 1803) prior to his execution. The statue was later replaced by an elephant and put into storage until 1966 when, to mark the fiftieth anniversary of the Easter Rising, it was relocated to Massachusetts Avenue NW and 24th Street, in Washington, DC.

## 12. THE STEREOPTICON: GERMAN AND IRISH PROPAGANDA OF DEED AND WORD AND THE 1916 EASTER RISING

1 Robert Schmuhl, 'Peering through the fog: American newspapers and the Easter Rising', *Irish Communications Review* 22 (2010): 37–8. See 25 April 1916 editions of: *San Francisco Chronicle*; *Chicago Tribune*; *Chicago Examiner*; *New York Times*; *Atlanta Constitution*; *New York Tribune*; *New York Evening World*; *Evening Star*; *New York Press*; *Washington Post*; and *Boston Daily Globe* etc.

2 Carl Wittke, *The German Language Press in America* (Lexington: University of Kentucky Press, 1957), 243–4; J. R. Arndt and May E. Olson, *German-American Newspapers and Periodicals, 1732–1955* (New York: Johnson Reprint Corporation, 1965; second edition), 399–400; La Vern J. Rippley, *The German-Americans* (Boston: Twayne Publishers, 1976), 163–6.

3 The so-called 'Findlay affair' was Casement's campaign of exposing the efforts of Mansfeldt de Cardonnel Findlay, the British minister at Christiania, to apprehend Casement through Casement's valet, Eivind Adler Christensen.

4 Reinhard R. Doerries, *Prelude to the Easter Rising: Sir Roger Casement in Imperial Germany* (London: Frank Cass, 2000), 12–13; von Papen to Foreign Office, 9 August 1914, quoted in ibid., 46; Reinhard R. Doerries, *Imperial Challenge: Ambassador Count Bernstorff and German-American Relations, 1908–1917*, Christa D. Shannon, trans. (Chapel Hill: University of North Carolina Press, 1983), 160–1; Séamas Ó Síocháin, *Roger Casement: Imperialist, Rebel, Revolutionary* (Dublin: The Lilliput Press, 2008), 436.

5 The frequency of front-page coverage declined after 23 May, but coverage of the Rising and related events remained on the front and inside pages long thereafter.

6 Rippley, *The German-Americans*, 181; Niel M. Johnson, *George Sylvester Viereck: German-American Propagandist* (Urbana: University of Illinois Press, 1972), 8–9; Subcommittee of the Committee on the Judiciary, *National German-American Alliance: Hearings Before the Subcommittee of the Committee on the Judiciary: A Bill to Repeal the Act Entitled 'An Act to Incorporate the National German-American Alliance,' Approved February 25, 1907*, 65th Cong., 2d sess., S. 3529, 23 February–13 April 1918 (Washington, DC: Government Printing Office, 1918), 697–8. The Deutsch-Amerikanischer Nationalbund (National German-American Alliance in English) became the largest ethnic organisation ever in the history of the United States, and by 1914 claimed chapters in 40 states and boasted a membership of two million.

7 *Philadelphia North American*, 24 January 1907, quoted in Subcommittee of the Committee on the Judiciary, *National German-American Alliance*, 647; *Boston Globe*, 25 January 1907, quoted in ibid., 646–7; Carl Wittke, *The Irish in America* (Baton Rouge: Louisiana State University Press, 1956), 274–6; Doerries, *Imperial Challenge*, 72–3; Reinhard R. Doerries, *Iren und Deutsche in der Neuen Welt* (Stuttgart: Franz Steiner, 1986), 11–12.

8 *San Francisco Chronicle*, 26 December 1899; *New York Times*, 5 March 1900; *New York Tribune*, 3 March 1902; Ibid., 6 September 1902.

9 Michael Doorley, 'The Friends of Irish Freedom: a case study', *History Ireland* 16:2 (March/April 2008): 24; Francis M. Carroll, *American Opinion and the Irish Question 1910–23* (New York: St Martin's Press, 1978), 28–9; John E. Noyes, 'William Howard Taft and the Taft arbitration treaties', *Villanova Law Review* 56 (2011): 545. Acting on the same rationale years before, John Devoy and Daniel Cohalan were active in protesting an arbitration treaty in 1897 similar to those later proposed under the Taft administration.

10 21 February 1911 editions of *New York Daily Tribune*, and *New York Times*; *The Gaelic American*, 13 June 1925; *Columbia Spectator*, 14 February 1902. Subcommittee of the Committee on the Judiciary, *Brewing and Liquor Interests and German Propaganda: A Resolution Authorizing and Directing the Committee on the Judiciary to Call for Certain Evidence and Documents Relating to Charges Made against the United States Brewers' Association and Allied Interests and to Submit a Report of Their Investigation to the Senate*, 65th Cong., 2d and 3d sess., S. Res. 307, volume 2 (Washington, DC: Government Printing Office, 1919), 1,973; Emil Witte, *Revelations of a German Attaché: Ten Years of German American Diplomacy* (New York: George H. Doran

Company, 1916), 145. Von Skal was a fin de siècle editor of the *NYSZ* and worked with Herman Ridder in the early twentieth century.

11 Terry Golway, *Irish Rebel: John Devoy and America's Fight for Ireland's Freedom* (New York: St Martin's Press, 1998), 187.

12 Carroll, *American Opinion*, 28–9.

13 David Brundage, '"In time of peace, prepare for war": key themes in the social thought of New York's Irish nationalists, 1890–1916', in Ronald H. Bayor and Timothy J. Meagher, eds, *The New York Irish* (Baltimore: Johns Hopkins University Press, 1996), 331–4; Michael Doorley, *Irish American Diaspora Nationalism: The Friends of Irish Freedom, 1916–1935* (Dublin: Four Courts Press, 2005), 34–5.

14 Jeremiah A. O'Leary, *My Political Trial and Experiences* (New York: Jefferson Publishing Co., 1919), 11; Ross J. Wilson, *New York and the First World War* (Burlington: Ashgate Publishing Company, 2014), 74. The ATS was established in New York in January, 1912.

15 O'Leary, *Political Trial and Experiences*, 3–7.

16 Ibid., 9; *Clan na Gael Emmet Anniversary Magazine: Academy of Music Philadelphia, Thursday Evening, March 9th, 1916* (Philadelphia: Bradley Brothers, 1916), 6–7.

17 *Clan na Gael Emmet Anniversary Magazine*, 6–7. This Clan na Gael magazine was replete with advertisements for German businesses and for a Central Powers benefit bazaar under the auspices of the United German War Relief Organization.

18 Wilson, *New York and the First World War*, 127–9.

19 Ibid., 74, 127–9; O'Leary, *Political Trial and Experiences*, 39; Subcommittee of the Committee on the Judiciary, *Brewing and Liquor Interests and German Propaganda*, volume 2, 1,411, 1,543, 2,696.

20 Doerries, *Imperial Challenge*, 5–8. Von Bernstorff served as the imperial ambassador to the United States from late 1908 until President Woodrow Wilson severed diplomatic ties with the Germans on 3 February 1917.

21 Denis Gwynn, *Traitor or Patriot: The Life and Death of Roger Casement* (New York: Jonathan Cape and Harrison Smith, 1931), 214–17; Carroll, *American Opinion*, 29; Frederick C. Luebke, *Bonds of Loyalty: German Americans and World War One* (DeKalb: Northern Illinois University Press, 1974), 127–8; Subcommittee of the Committee on the Judiciary, *Brewing and Liquor Interests and German Propaganda*, volume 1, xv; Doerries, *Imperial Challenge*, 41. The new service was originally set up under Drs Bernhard Dernburg, Carl Alexander Fuehr, and Heinrich Albert, the commercial attaché to the ambassador, et. al.

22 Carl Wittke, *German-Americans and the World War* (Columbus: Ohio State Archaeological and Historical Society, 1936), 24; Doerries, *Imperial Challenge*, 41, 68–9; Subcommittee of the Committee on the Judiciary, *Brewing and Liquor Interests and German Propaganda*, volume 2, 1,396, 1,686; ibid., volume 1, xv. Von Skal, von Bernstorff, Karl Boy-Ed, the navel attaché, Franz von Papen, the military attaché, and Wolf von Igel, von Papen's secretary, were all in some capacity involved in the operations of the information service, making it difficult to ascertain where the line between the embassy and the information service was drawn, if it was even demarcated at all.

23 Wittke, *German-Americans*, 24; Doerries, *Imperial Challenge*, 41, 68–9.

24 Carl W. Ackerman, *Germany: The Next Republic?* (New York: Grosset and Dunlap, 1917), 86, 89–90; John Price Jones and Paul Merrick Hollister, *The German Secret Service in America 1914–1918* (Boston: Small, Maynard and Company, 1918), 43–59, 236; Subcommittee of the Committee on the Judiciary, *Brewing and Liquor Interests and German Propaganda*, volume 2, 1,768, 2,627.

25 Wittke, *German-Americans*, 8–12, 24–6; Wittke, *German Language Press*, 238; Doerries, *Imperial Challenge*, 44, 51–2, 262, note 27; letter from Dr Charles Hexamer quoted in *The Fatherland*, 11 November 1914; *The Fatherland*, 6 September 1914; Subcommittee of the Committee on the Judiciary, *Brewing and Liquor Interests and German Propaganda*, volume 2, 1,388–9, 2,693–5, 2,699; Viereck to Dr Albert, 27 April 1915, quoted in ibid., 1,423–4; ibid., volume 1, xviii.

26 John Devoy, *Recollections of an Irish Rebel* (New York: Charles Young, 1929), 446; Subcommittee of the Committee on the Judiciary, *Brewing and Liquor Interests and German Propaganda*, volume 2, 1,369.

27 Subcommittee of the Committee on the Judiciary, *Brewing and Liquor Interests and German Propaganda*, volume 2, 1,397, 1,542–3.

28 Ibid., 1,396–8; *The Fatherland*, 12 May 1915; Sean Cronin, *The McGarrity Papers: Revelations of the Irish Revolutionary Movement in Ireland and America, 1900–1940* (Tralee: Anvil Books, 1972), 53.

29 Subcommittee of the Committee on the Judiciary, *Brewing and Liquor Interests and German Propaganda*, volume 2, 1,396.

30 James K. McGuire, *The King, The Kaiser, and Irish Freedom* (New York: The Devin Adair Company, 1915), 256.

31 James K. McGuire, *What Could Germany Do for Ireland?* (New York: Wolfe Tone Company, 1916); see 27 October, 3, 10 November 1915, 8 March, 5, 26 April 1916 issues of *The Fatherland*.

32 Arndt and Olson, *German-American Newspapers*, 399; Wittke, *German Language Press*, 243–4. By 1918 the *NYSZ*'s circulation was down to 114,564, and by 1920 dropped again to 58,500. The estimates for circulation of German-language papers vary. Wittke, though careful to state that the Ayers data upon which he relies could be inaccurate, claims that there were at least 50 German-language dailies in the war years with as many as 950,000 readers by 1917.

33 Jones and Hollister, *German Secret Service*, 203–31; Subcommittee of the Committee on the Judiciary, *Brewing and Liquor Interests and German Propaganda*, volume 2, 2,773–6; Doerries, *Imperial Challenge*, 51; Henry Landau, *The Enemy within: The inside Story of German Sabotage in America* (New York: G. P. Putnam and Sons, 1937), 101. The investor was Adolf Pavenstedt.

34 Doerries, *Imperial Challenge*, 50–1; Kenneth T. Jackson, ed., *The Encyclopedia of New York City* (New Haven: Yale University Press, 2010; second edition), 640; *Irish American Weekly*, 23 May 1914. The *NYSZ* had a large readership base in the New York German population; largely

concentrated in Yorkville on Manhattan's Upper East Side. There were 278,114 German-born living in the cities of New York and Brooklyn according to the 1910 federal census. Irish lived in Yorkville too, but it was the Yorkville Casino, a popular venue for large events, that regularly drew Irish from all over the city to this German neighbourhood. For example, Padraig Pearse held a fundraiser for St Enda's at the Yorkville Casino on 30 May 1914.

35 *New York Times*, 20 August 1906; Witte, *Revelations of a German Attaché*, 35, 254; Subcommittee of the Committee on the Judiciary, *Brewing and Liquor Interests and German Propaganda*, volume 2, 1,569–71; Doerries, *Imperial Challenge*, 52; Arndt and Olson, *German-American Newspapers*, 399–400. The *NYSZ* also had particularly good relations with the German government that predated the war. Ridder had been privately received by the Kaiser, and maintained a regular correspondence with von Papen and Boy-Ed, who frequently provided commentary and suggestions for the paper's content. Ridder's pro-German leanings were clear to both Pavenstedt and von Bernstorff, but the influential paper was brought even closer to the official German line when von Bernstorff installed Reginald Schroeder, a close confidant of the embassy, as a manager of the paper. Schroeder was also the Washington correspondent for the *NYSZ* for a time, and took over as editor from 1919–20. Herman Ridder continued to steer the content of the *NYSZ* until his death in 1915, which was thereafter directed by his sons.

36 *Program for the Mass Meeting of the Friends of Peace at Madison Square Garden, New York, June 24, 1915* (New York: Robert P. Sachs, 1915); Wittke, *German-Americans*, 63. Viereck, Ridder, and Frederick Franklin Schrader, a German-American journalist and co-founder of *The Fatherland*, were all prominent members of the ATS.

37 *New York Times*, 2 November 1914.

38 *The Fatherland*, 23 February 1916.

39 *Vital Issue*, 2 January 1915; Subcommittee of the Committee on the Judiciary, *National German-American Alliance*, 259; Count Johann Heinrich von Bernstorff, *My Three Years in America* (London: Skeffington and Son Ltd, 1920), 31; Luebke, *Bonds of Loyalty*, 127. Dernburg did not originally come to America with von Bernstorff in 1914 to run the GIS, but rather, to fundraise for the German Red Cross. The money raised for this organisation was sent to von Bernstorff, who allegedly forwarded it to Germany.

40 See 31 August, 6 September, 11 November issues of *The Fatherland*.

41 *NYSZ*, 27 April 1916.

42 *Documents Relative to the Sinn Féin Movement* (London: HMSO, 1921), 2; *The Fatherland*, 3 November 1915; General Friedrich von Bernhardi, *Germany and the Next War*, Allen H. Powles, trans. (New York: Longmans, Green, and Co., 1914), 78, 100; Gustavus Ohlinger, *Their True Faith and Allegiance* (New York: Macmillan Company, 1916), 63–4. Casement's essay, 'Ireland, Germany and the next war' was sent to Germany in 1912 where it elicited responses in the German press, and was referenced by General von Bernhardi. Casement's, 'Ireland Germany and the freedom of the seas' also appeared in September 1914 in an issue of *The Gaelic American*, with excerpts also published in the 23 September 1914 issue of *The Fatherland*.

43 For a list of Casement's publications in English and German, see James Carty, *Bibliography of Irish History: 1912–1921* (Dublin: Department of Education Stationary Office, 1936), 38–9.

44 *Vital Issue*, 20 February 1915; note by McGarrity, 10 October 1914, quoted in Doerries, *Prelude*, 50; Kuno Meyer to Roger Casement quoted in ibid., 65; Seán McConville, *Irish Political Prisoners, 1848–1922: Theatres of War* (London: Routledge, 2003), 554.

45 *Documents Relative to the Sinn Féin Movement*, 2; *Chicago Daily Tribune*, 25 April 1916; Devoy, *Recollections*, 416; John Quinn to T. W. H. Rolleston, 8 February 1915, quoted in Doerries, *Prelude*, 48; McConville, *Irish Political Prisoners*, 557. It remains uncertain if Casement was intent on going to Germany to court military support at this stage, though Devoy and one of Casement's New York hosts, John Quinn, were certain that he meant to go there even before the war. Devoy also told Casement's sister that the idea to go to Germany was Casement's alone, and that nobody encouraged or asked him to go on the mission.

46 Sir Roger Casement, *The Crime against Ireland: And How the War May Right It* (New York, 1914), 1–6.

47 Devoy, *Recollections*, 408; Casement to William Bourke Cockran, 27 July 1914, quoted in Doerries, *Prelude*, 44.

48 Eoin MacNeill to Casement, 7 July 1914, quoted in Doerries, *Prelude*, 43; Casement to Devoy, 31 July 1914, quoted in William O'Brien and Desmond Ryan, eds, *Devoy's Post Bag*, volume 2 (Dublin: C. J. Fallon, 1953), 464–5; Devoy, *Recollections*, 418.

49 Devoy, *Recollections*, 403–4. Von Skal, von Papen, von Igel, and Dernburg were all present according to Devoy's account.

50 Ibid., 403–6, 431; von Bernstorff, *Three Years in America*, 30, 32. The veracity of Devoy's account must be questioned since von Bernstorff was not in the United States when Devoy claimed the meeting took place. There was a meeting with von Bernstorff and the Clan after von Bernstorff's return to the United States, and while Devoy's mistake might have simply been a matter of advanced age or confusion over dates, it is also in keeping with his tendency to depict the primacy of his leadership and to diminish Casement's role in the Rising.

51 Von Papen to Foreign Office, 9 August 1914, quoted in Doerries, *Prelude*, 46.

52 Roger Casement, 'Open letter to the Irish people', quoted in Gwynn, *Traitor or Patriot*, 250–2. This letter was published in the United States and in the *Irish Independent* on 5 October 1914.

53 'Official statement of the German imperial government concerning its position on Ireland', quoted in Doerries, *Prelude*, 60–1; *Documents Relative to the Sinn Féin Movement*, 4.

54 Gwynn, *Traitor or Patriot*, 254–5; *Documents Relative to the Sinn Féin Movement*, 2.

55 Casement to McGarrity, 11 November 1914, quoted in Doerries, *Prelude*, 59; Meyer to Casement, 27 November 1914, quoted in ibid., 65.

56 Kuno Meyer, 'Message to the Irish people', speech at the celebration of the anniversary of the Manchester Martyrs by the Clan na Gael of Long Island at the Academy of Music, Brooklyn, New York, Sunday 6 December 1914.

57 *Washington Post*, 15 December 1914; *New York Tribune*, 15 December 1914; *Manchester Guardian*, 17 December 1914; *New York Times*, 18 December 1914; *New York Tribune*, 18

December 1914; *Boston Daily Globe*, 19 December 1914; *Hartford Currant*, 19 December 1914; *New York Tribune*, 21 December 1914; *Irish Times*, 24 December 1914; *New York Times*, 25 December 1914; *Irish Times*, 26 December 1914; *New York Times*, 28 December 1914; *Weekly Irish Times*, 2 January 1915.

58 *Vital Issue*, 9 January 1915.

59 See also handwritten text by Casement quoted in Doerries, *Prelude*, 60, note 1.

60 *NYSZ*, 25 April 1916.

61 *New York Evening World*, 25 April 1916; Stephen Ferguson, *GPO Staff in 1916: Business as Usual* (Cork: Mercier Press, 2012), 58. All private and press telegrams from Ireland were also to be held as of 25 April.

62 Donard de Coogan, 'Ireland, telecommunications and international politics 1866–1922', *History Ireland* 1:2 (1993): 34–8; Jones and Hollister, *German Secret Service*, 305; Cronin, *McGarrity Papers*, 62; A. Cotton, 'Kerry's place in the general plan, 1916', in Brian Ó Conchubhair, ed., *Kerry's Fighting Story 1916–1921: Told by the Men Who Made It* (Cork: Mercier Press, 2009), 95; P. J. Cahill, 'There was no blunder', in ibid., 135; *Documents Relative to the Sinn Féin Movement*, 11; Devoy to von Bernstorff, 16 February 1916 quoted in Doerries, *Prelude*, 182; memorandum by McGarrity on 1916, MS 17,550, Joseph McGarrity Papers, National Library of Ireland. Accounts from those involved in the Kerry uprising in addition to telegrams sent by Devoy that went by way of von Bernstorff to the German Foreign Office on 16 February and 15 March 1916, reveal that plans to utilise wireless stations on Ireland's west coast existed before the Rising took place. The recipient of the message still remains unclear, however, as reports that differ from de Coogan's are in the *Chicago Tribune* on 26 April 1916, which claim O'Leary received the cable, who is quoted as saying that he believed it arrived because 'some Irish cable operator on the Kerry coast slipped by the censor and sent it to friends here'. This supports de Coogan's assertions of the cable's origin, but not its recipient. Jones and Hollister, *German Secret Service*, similarly claimed that O'Leary received the cable on Easter Monday before the censors prevented the news from reaching America. Cronin, *McGarrity Papers*, though he fails to verify his source, also claims that such a message went through, but in his account it was received from Valencia Island on 22 April, and forwarded from Cohalan to McGarrity that same evening. His source was almost certainly a memorandum on the Rising written by McGarrity in which he makes the same claim.

63 De Coogan, 'Telecommunications', 34–8.

64 Robert Schmuhl, *Ireland's Exiled Children: America and the Easter Rising* (Oxford: Oxford University Press, 2016), 31–3.

65 *NYSZ*, 3 May 1916.

66 Ibid., 30 April 1916.

67 Ibid., 29, 30 April 1916.

68 Ibid., 28 April 1916; Neil R. Storey, *Zeppelin Blitz: The German Air Raids on Great Britain During the First World War* (Gloucestershire: The History Press, 2015), 171, 325; *Documents Relative to the Sinn Féin Movement*, 13; Captain Karl Spindler, *The Mystery of the Casement*

*Ship* (Berlin: Kribe-Verlag, 1931), 20, 264–56. Concurrent with the Rising in Dublin, the German naval and air forces had in fact executed a coordinated attack on the east coast of England. This was allegedly done in order to create a diversion for Captain Spindler, the captain of the *Aud*, thereby abetting him in breaking through the British naval blockade so that he might unload the *Aud*'s cargo of arms and explosives in Ireland. Spindler's account later corroborated the story in the *NYSZ* by claiming that before the *Aud* ever set sail, it was decided that a 'simultaneous naval demonstration on the east coast of England was to create a favorable opportunity for the landing of the arms, by diverting attention from the west coast of Ireland'. Though he does not say who told him, Spindler was probably made aware of the support mission by Admiral Scheer, the commander of the Hochseeflotte, who spoke with Spindler just before he set sail for Ireland. If such attacks on the English coast were indeed a part of the large-scale plan as Spindler and the *NYSZ* suggested, then appraisals downplaying the amount of support the German's were willing to give to the Irish cause must be reconsidered in light of the propagandistic, material, naval, and air support that the Germans offered the rebels.

69 Doerries, *Prelude*, 214; Spindler, *Casement Ship*, 236, 257–65; Admiral Scheer, *Germany's High Seas Fleet in the World War with a Portrait of 28 Plans* (London: Cassell and Company Ltd, 1920), 123; Patrick Beesly, *Room 40: British Naval Intelligence 1914–1918* (London: Hamish Hamilton, 1982), 147–8.

70 *NYSZ*, 28 April 1916; *New York Times*, 28 April 1916; ibid., 11 January 1921; *Documents Relative to the Sinn Féin Movement*, 13. *The New York Times* also reported that Casement 'expected the Germans to start with fleet operations, Zeppelin raids, and all other means possible to keep Britain so engaged that the Irish revolt could be put through to a successful end. In fact, there is no doubt in the minds of the officials here that the German attack on Lowestoft was part of the whole plot engineered by Sir Roger and that the riots breaking out in Dublin are another phase of it.'

71 *NYSZ*, 4 May 1916. In this case, the call was specifically made for German Americans to give money and support to a Red Cross committee under the auspices of the Dublin Club of New York.

72 15, 27 May 1916 editions of *NYSZ*.

73 *The Fatherland*, 16 August 1916.

74 Ibid.

75 *Documents Relative to the Sinn Féin Movement*, 28; *New York Times*, 11 January 1921. T. St John Gaffney was the American consul general at Munich who was, amongst other reasons, recalled during the war for allegedly neglecting the English under his care in Munich and for allowing meetings of the Munich-based pro-German 'Truth Society' to take place at the consulate.

76 Christopher M. Andrew, *Defend the Realm: The Authorized History of MI5* (New York: Alfred A. Knopf, 2009), 90.

77 Franz von Papen, foreword to Robert Monteith, *Casement's Last Adventure* (Dublin: Michael F. Moynihan Publishing Company, 1953), ix–xii.

78 Spindler, *Casement Ship*, 278.

79 McConville, *Irish Political Prisoners*, 557.

80 *Daily Boston Globe*, 13 April 1931; *Chicago Daily Tribune*, 19 April 1931; *Los Angeles Times*, 5 May 1931.

81 Gavin Wilk, *Transatlantic Defiance: The Militant Irish Republican Movement in America, 1923–1945* (Manchester: Manchester University Press, 2014), 82–3.

82 John de Courcy Ireland, 'Remembering Raimond Weisbach', *Irish Sword* 16 (summer 1986): 221; *Irish Times*, 7, 15 April 1966, 31 July 1970, 16 May 1980. Weisbach also remembered Casement fondly, even 50 years after their encounter.

## 13. AN AMERICAN OPINION: JOHN QUINN AND THE EASTER RISING

1 B. L. Reid, *The Man from New York: John Quinn and His Friends* (New York: Oxford University Press, 1968), 3–6. Quinn was actually born in Tiffin, Ohio, but the family moved to Fostoria when he was an infant. His parents were both born in Ireland, his father in Co. Limerick and his mother in Co. Cork.

2 See: nypl.org/sites/default/files/archivalcollections/pdf/quinn.pdf.

3 Liz Stanley terms this body of writing an epistolarium. See Liz Stanley, 'The epistolarium: on theorizing letters and correspondences', *Auto/Biography* 12 (2004): 201–35.

4 Ibid., 207.

5 R. F. Foster, *Vivid Faces: The Revolutionary Generation in Ireland 1890–1923* (London: Penguin Random House, 2015), xx.

6 Stanley, 'The epistolarium', 212.

7 Reid, *The Man from New York*, 8–10.

8 R. F. Foster, *W. B. Yeats: A life; Vol. 1, The Apprentice Mage: 1865–1914* (Oxford: Oxford University Press, 1997), 302–6, 308–15; Úna Ní Bhroiméil, *Building Irish Identity in America: The Gaelic Revival, 1870–1915* (Dublin: Four Courts Press, 2003), 62–70, 73–88; Reid, *The Man from New York*, 16–20, 40–3.

9 See for example John Quinn to Martin J. Keogh, 22 January 1913, John Quinn Memorial Collection, New York Public Library (NYPL). All letters are taken from this collection unless otherwise cited. Keogh, a judge of the New York Supreme Court and the treasurer of the Gaelic League in America, had asked Quinn to send him a list of wealthy Irish Catholics in New York who might subscribe to the Irish Christian Brothers in New York. See Martin J. Keogh to John Quinn, 12 July 1912.

10 John Quinn to Gordon Craig, 16 February 1915. Edward Gordon Craig was an English theatre director, actor, and stage designer then living in Italy.

11 See for example John Quinn to Martin J. Keogh, 16 November 1912; P. H. Pearse to John Quinn, 6 May 1914; John Quinn to Mary Colum, 4 September 1917.

12 John Quinn to Martin J. Keogh, 16 November 1912.

13 Colm Tóibín, *Lady Gregory's Toothbrush* (London: Picador, 2003); see for example *The Gaelic American*, 2, 9, 11 December 1911, 20 January 1912.

14 John Quinn to Daniel F. Cohalan, 3 February 1913; John Quinn to Martin J. Keogh, 29 November 1912; John Quinn to James Byrne, 7 October 1911.

15 John Quinn to Martin J. Keogh, 24 January 1913; John Quinn to James Byrne, 7 October 1911: 'It is a mere absurdity for a man like Yeats or a lady like Lady Gregory to discuss questions of art with Patrick Ford or John Devoy. The only way to treat patriots of this sort is to ignore them utterly. What they want is to be noticed and their letters replied to. The ordinary Irishman, whether in Ireland or in America, has about as much notion of art, as for example Martin Littleton has, or some other ex-resident of Tennessee or Texas.'

16 John Quinn to Mrs James Byrne, 13 November 1911. Quinn also made a similar comment about modern art and the Armory Show in New York in 1913. See John Quinn to Maurice Leon, 21 February 1913.

17 See John Quinn to Victor J. Dowling, 23 November 1911, discussing the writing of an article for the *New York World* about the Irish in New York.

18 Some of them lived upstate such as Keogh. Cohalan and Quinn were close in the early decades of the twentieth century but his association with Devoy cut him off from Quinn, although they did correspond until 1919 at least.

19 John Quinn to Mrs James Byrne, 15 March 1911. James Byrne was the Harvard Corporation's first Roman Catholic member. See: thecrimson.com/article/1926/10/13/byrne-abandons-post-as-member-of/.

20 Lawrence Godkin was a Protestant and Quinn himself was not a practicing Catholic. David Brundage suggests in fact that he was anti-clerical. See David Brundage, '"In time of peace, prepare for war": key themes in the social thought of New York's Irish nationalists, 1890–1916', in Ronald H. Bayor and Timothy J. Meagher, eds, *The New York Irish* (Baltimore: Johns Hopkins University Press, 1996), 332.

21 John Quinn to George Russell (AE), 15 May 1912.

22 See Quinn's description of this group in comparison to the 'irreconcilables' in the memorandum 'In the Matter of Sir Roger Casement', Folder 490, Foster Murphy Collection, NYPL.

23 They fit in some ways with what Foster has termed a 'generation' although they were bound more by professional association by age. See Foster, *Vivid Faces*, 6.

24 See for example Ruth Dudley Edwards, *Patrick Pearse: The Triumph of Failure* (Dublin: Poolbeg, 1990), 184; Joost Augusteijn, *Patrick Pearse: The Making of a Revolutionary* (Basingstoke: Palgrave Macmillan, 2010), 248; Bernadette Whelan, *United States Foreign Policy and Ireland: From Empire to Independence, 1913–29* (Dublin: Four Courts Press, 2006), 66, 133–4; F. M. Carroll, *American Opinion and the Irish Question, 1910–23: A Study in Opinion and Policy* (Dublin and New York: Gill and Macmillan and St Martin's Press, 1978), 64, 94.

25 John Quinn to Martin J. Keogh, 15 January 1911.

26 John Quinn to George Russell (AE), 15 May 1912.

27 Úna Ní Bhroiméil, 'Political cartoons as visual opinion discourse: the rise and fall of John Redmond in the *Irish World*', in Karen Steele and Michael DeNie, eds, *Ireland*

*and the New Journalism* (Basingstoke: Palgrave Macmillan, 2014), 119–141; Patrick Ford edited the *Irish World* until his death in September 1913 when the editorship passed to his son Robert.

28 John Quinn to Martin J. Keogh, 7 July 1914.

29 Ibid.

30 John Quinn to Lady Gregory, 19 March 1914; see for example John Quinn to Edward Flynn, 13 January 1915.

31 John Quinn to Ernest Boyd, 13 August 1914.

32 Carroll, *American Opinion*, 32; Angus Mitchell, *Casement* (London: Haus Publishing, 2003), 92–3.

33 Even after the establishment of the Irish Free State Quinn held this position. He wrote to Shane Leslie in March 1923, stating that 'I am for the Free state as it holds the only chance of Ulster coming in.' See John Quinn to Shane Leslie, 2 March 1923.

34 See for example John Quinn to Edward Flynn, 31 January 1913.

35 Quinn refused even to buy German art, stating that it was 'too beery'. See John Quinn to Charles Shannon, 18 November 1912. Until April 1917, the Irish and Germans met regularly to show common cause with each other within the United States and these meetings were reported widely in the New York newspapers. During March 1915, for example, *The Gaelic American* carried drawings of prominent German generals on the front page of each of its editions.

36 Quinn was approached to serve as chairman of the East of the Democratic National Convention in 1908 and declined but served on the National Advisory Committee instead. See Reid, *The Man from New York*, 64. See for example John Quinn to Charles Shannon, 8 June 1915: 'Mr Wilson, the president of the country for the time being, is a theorist, a mere essayist. He won't fight. Bryan, the Secretary of State, is a windbag. He has about as much sense as a Methodist parson and talks and thinks like one. He has been for years one of the peace spouters; a fifth rate man in a big place and a tragic misfit'; in a letter to George Russell (AE), 13 January 1916, Quinn called the president 'Herr Wilson'.

37 See John Quinn to Andre Dunoyer de Segonzac, 22 November 1919; John Quinn to Walter Pach, 12 September 1919.

38 John Quinn to Andre Dunoyer de Segonzac, 20 September 1917.

39 John Quinn to Kuno Meyer, 11 December 1914.

40 Maurice Leon to John Quinn, 23 November 1914, 24 August 1916. Quinn did not break with Meyer until Meyer reacted badly to Quinn's attitude to Germany in his defence of Casement in 1916.

41 Reid, *The Man from New York*, 187–9.

42 John Quinn to James Byrne, 21 October 1914.

43 John Quinn to Douglas Hyde, 6 April 1916.

44 John Quinn to Charles Shannon, 8 June 1915.

45 Maurice Leon to John Quinn, 13 September 1917, 24 July 1919.

46 Quinn's opposition to Germany was epitomised in his efforts to have the Trading with the Enemy Act passed in 1917 that restricted US trade with Germany. See John Quinn to Cecil Spring-Rice, 13 September 1917.

47 John Quinn to Joseph Conrad, 11 May 1916.

48 John Quinn to James Huneker, 1 May 1916.

49 He had met Pearse, Connolly, and Plunkett. George Russell (AE) pointed out to Quinn on 13 January 1919, that he could not possibly know the state of Ireland unless he was on the ground.

50 John Quinn to Lawrence Godkin, 25 July 1916: 'The pity of it is, in the face of Asquith's duplicity and Lloyd George's trickery, that there wasn't more patience among the Volunteers, that they didn't wait and wait until succeeding chapters of Tory duplicity had been written. Then they would have had the whole of Nationalist Ireland back of them. In politics no less than in business patience is often greater than genius.'

51 Reid, *The Man from New York*, 232.

52 John Quinn to Mrs Roosevelt, 15 August 1917. Quinn sent her a book of Pearse's poems translated into English and wrote, 'Although Pearse raised a storm, he was a gentle man … However much one may differ from his political beliefs, one must admire his ideality, his undaunted spirit, and the purity of the motives that always moved him.'

53 John Quinn to Douglas Hyde, 2 January 1917.

54 It also caused him to condemn Redmond yet again for not making an effort to stop the executions. See for example John Quinn to Lawrence Godkin, 18 May 1916.

55 John Quinn to Lady Gregory, 9 June 1916.

56 Ibid.

57 Ibid. Quinn was after all only ten years older than the 36-year-old Pearse. Tom Clarke, whom Quinn never mentions in his letters, was 58.

58 John Quinn to Charles Burlingham, 21 June 1916.

59 There are no letters to Keogh or to Hyde or to Russell about the Rising in the collection. That might have been expected although he stated to Maud Gonne in July that people seemed to be afraid to write to him about the Rising. See John Quinn to Maud Gonne, 29 July 1916.

60 Reid, *The Man from New York*, 233.

61 'In the matter of Sir Roger Casement', 9, Folder 490, Foster Murphy Collection, NYPL. Quinn referred to the suggestion in some papers that he 'was abnormal or addicted to abnormal practices' but 'having him in my house for some weeks I am positively convinced that there was nothing of that sort in his make-up. I believe that his life personally was one of absolute purity.' As F. M. Carroll has pointed out, there were many appeals to President Wilson from Irish Americans, from congressmen, and from Senator James A. Martine. Cardinal Gibbons and some groups of African Americans petitioned the British government. Interestingly, Senator Henry Cabot Lodge advised Sir Edward Grey that England's enemies hoped Casement would be executed while her friends hoped he would be spared. This echoes Quinn's memorandum. See Carroll, *American Opinion*, 69–78.

62 'In the matter of Sir Roger Casement', 18–20, Folder 490, Foster Murphy Collection, NYPL.

63 'Roger Casement, martyr: some notes for a chapter of history by a friend whose guest he was when the war broke out', *New York Times*, 13 August 1916; John Quinn to Cecil Spring-Rice, 15 August 1916.

64 John Quinn to Maud Gonne, 29 July 1916. See also John Quinn to Daniel J. Cohalan, 13 May 1916, for the stipulations he mentions.

65 *The Irish Home Rule Convention: Thoughts for a Convention by George W. Russell (AE), a Defence of the Convention by the Right Honorable Sir Horace Plunkett, an American Opinion by John Quinn* (New York: The Macmillan Company, 1917); John Quinn to George Russell (AE), 30 May 1917; John Quinn to Theodore Roosevelt, 1 May 1917; Whelan, *United States Foreign Policy and Ireland*, 133–4; Theodore Roosevelt to John Quinn, 20 July 1917. Quinn wrote to Russell that Devoy accused him in *The Gaelic American* of 'crawling before Balfour' and 'running in and out of the British Embassy in Washington'. See John Quinn to George Russell (AE), 18 September 1917.

66 John Quinn to James Byrne, 9 May 1917.

67 Martin J. Keogh's, James Byrne's, and Roosevelt's sons all fought in the First World War.

68 John Quinn to George Russell (AE), 6 August 1917.

69 John Quinn to Theodore Roosevelt, 1 May 1917: 'I am going down to Washington on Friday of this week as one of the deputation, or rather I have organized this deputation to see Balfour. It will consist of Father John F. Wynne S.J. and Father Sigourney Fay representing Catholic Irishmen, Colonel Robert Temple Emmet and Lawrence Godkin representing Protestant Irishmen, and Morgan J. O'Brien and myself representing American neutral Irishmen but nationalists. This is a great chance for England to make a generous settlement.'

70 John Quinn to James Byrne, 23 June 1917.

71 John Quinn to Shane Leslie, 6 September 1917: 'your article will certainly give the impression that Cohalan, Devoy, Maguire and company represent Irish-American opinion, which they most emphatically do not.'

72 Brundage suggests that Quinn became isolated because of 'his extreme identification with English civilization'. See Brundage, 'In time of peace', in Bayor and Meagher, eds, *The New York Irish*, 327.

73 R. F. Foster's term for those whose lives and minds he explores in the period 1890–1923 in Ireland in the book, *Vivid Faces*, xv–xxiii.

74 John Quinn to Gordon Craig, 25 March 1915; John Quinn to Jacob Epstein, 28 April 1913.

75 Quinn had begun his working life in Washington, DC, as the private secretary to the secretary of the treasury in President Harrison's cabinet, Charles W. Foster. See Reid, *The Man from New York*, 5–6. In 1913 he campaigned successfully before House committees for the removal of the tariff on imported original works of art. He would campaign again in 1918 and in 1922 for the removal of the tariff on modern art. See John Quinn to Paul Rosenberg, 8 May 1922; John Quinn to James Huneker, 26 August 1918.

## 14. 'BURSTS OF IMPASSIONED ELOQUENCE': WILLIAM BOURKE COCKRAN, AMERICAN INTERVENTION, AND THE EASTER RISING

1  'The Havana tragedy', *New York Times*, 4 December 1871.

2  Ibid.

3  Ibid.

4  'Editorial article 4', *Irish Times and Daily Advertiser*, 1 December 1871; 'Superb stock of Christmas presents', ibid., 21 December 1871.

5  'The massacre in Havannah', *The Times*, 30 December 1871.

6  'The Havana tragedy'.

7  Ibid.

8  Ibid.

9  Ibid.

10  'Formally declared', *The Times*, 26 April 1898.

11  'The Havana tragedy'.

12  Graham A. Cosmas, *An Army for Empire: The United States Army in the Spanish-American War* (College Station: A & M University Press, 1998), chapters 3–4.

13  'Back to the land, or Irish Zionism', *Weekly Irish Times*, 5 September 1903.

14  'US first, Cockran urges', *New York Times*, 7 February 1916.

15  'COCKRAN, William Bourke: biographical information', *Bibliographical Dictionary of the United States Congress*, available at: bioguide.congress.gov/scripts/biodisplay.pl?index=C000575. No less than four presidential invitations to dine at the White House remain in the Bourke Cockran collection, including Presidents Grover Cleveland, Howard Taft, and Theodore Roosevelt.

16  'Addresses and speeches 1886–1923', May 1914, Box 27, Folder 2, William Bourke Cockran Papers, New York Public Library (NYPL).

17  David Brundage, '"In time of peace, prepare for war": key themes in the social thought of New York's Irish-American nationalists, 1900–1916', in Ronald H. Bayor and Timothy J. Meagher, eds, *The New York Irish* (Baltimore: Johns Hopkins University Press, 1996), 321–7.

18  '"Plea for peace," subject of Speaker, Hon. W. Bourke Cockran', *Boston Daily Globe*, 17 October 1915. Eventually, he would fully support the United States' entry into the First World War. By 1919, in a speech in Rochester, Bourke Cockran exclaimed, 'Now this country has drawn the sword to extend over the whole world the justice which Abraham Lincoln enthroned throughout the United States … That for which we fought triumphantly in the United States we must now fight decisively, triumphantly throughout the whole world.' See 'America in arms', Box 28, Folder 6, William Bourke Cockran Papers, NYPL. See also John French, 'Irish-American identity, memory, and Americanism during the eras of the Civil War and First World War' (Ph.D. thesis, Marquette University, 2009).

19  'Correspondence, 1916 Jan 22–Oct 31', Box 22, Folder 26, 247, William Bourke Cockran Papers, NYPL.

20  Devoy, Redmond, Casement, Quinn, de Valera and others were his long-time intimates. See 'Correspondence', Box 1–5, William Bourke Cockran Papers, NYPL. 'Mr Redmond's New

Home Rule', *Irish Times*, 14 October 1910, reports that, 'The real sinews of war, however, which keep the Parliamentary party in funds are subscribed by a mere handful of wealthy and responsible Irish Americans; men such as John D. Crimmins, Judge Martin Keogh, W. Bourke Cockran' and others. Also, that 'Everyone knows that the Irish-American Nationalists who are the main financial supporters of the Redmondite party in Parliament.'

21 J. O. Baylen, '"What Mr Redmond thought": an unpublished interview with John Redmond, Dec. 1906', *Irish Historical Studies* 19:74 (1974).

22 'Bourke Cockran pleads for Cuba', *New York Tribune*, 28 November 1896.

23 Year: 1910, census place: North Hempstead, Nassau, New York, roll: T624_995, page: 21B, enumeration district: 1128, FHL microfilm: 1375008; Greg McKevitt, 'Winston Churchill: the Irishman who taught him gift of the gab: BBC News', BBC News, available at: bbc.com/news/uk-northern-ireland-31024736.

24 McKevitt, 'Winston Churchill'.

25 James McGurrin, *Bourke Cockran: A Free Lance in American Politic* (New York: Charles Scribner's Sons, 1948), 7.

26 Greg McKevitt, 'Winston Churchill'.

27 McGurrin, *Bourke Cockran*, 11.

28 Ibid., 228.

29 Arriving the same year as the infamous Orange Riot of 1871, Bourke Cockran would have quickly become aware of the duelling identities many nineteenth-century Irish immigrants wrestled with in New York.

30 McGurrin, *Bourke Cockran*, 19.

31 Ibid., 21. Bourke Cockran sought out the help and advice from one Edward Martin, a distant relative and childhood friend of Bourke Cockran's father.

32 Ibid., 22.

33 James McGurrin, president of the American Historical Society from 1933 to 1963 and Bourke Cockran biographer, writes that Bourke Cockran's perfect fluency in French, sans accent, endeared him to the clergy of St Teresa's as well as several French consular officials. Both regularly sought him out for social calls and even professional advice as well. See McGurrin, *Bourke Cockran*, 26.

34 'Personal and miscellaneous', invitations, Box 40, Folder 2, William Bourke Cockran Papers, NYPL. In a life that would become replete with illustrious achievements, there is no doubt that Bourke Cockran regarded his newfound citizenship as a personal milestone. No less than seven officially requested copies of that Citizenship Certificate can be found within his collection of personal papers.

35 McGurrin, *Bourke Cockran*, 33.

36 Ibid., 89. Both James McGurrin and Richard B. Morris write that John Kelly, chief of Tammany Hall at the time, soon realised Bourke Cockran's danger as an adversary and potential value as an ally, and invited him into the Tammany fold by 1883. Tammany's good graces bore fruit quickly and that same year Bourke Cockran became the private counsel to the New York County Sheriff.

37  Hearing the New York delegates jeered and dismissed for their stand against Cleveland, Bourke Cockran gave a booming speech, demanded the right for all voices to be heard and weighed equally, and even threatened to lead his New York colleagues out of the convention in protest. It was later reported that the sheer forcefulness and power of Bourke Cockran's address brought the entire convention to order. Now the national Democratic Party had gotten a glimpse of his potential.

38  McGurrin, *Bourke Cockran*, 104.

39  Ibid., 105, 184–6. If Bourke Cockran's potency as an orator of immense political value was best illustrated at the 1884 Democratic National Convention, it was his address at Madison Square Garden in 1896, the historic 'Sound money' speech that demonstrated undeniably the independence and mobility of his political mind. Considered to be 'the peak of his oratorical efforts', Bourke Cockran famously came out against (his own) Democratic Party nominee, William Jennings Bryan, and his Free Silver campaign, the most controversial issue of the election. See McGurrin, *Bourke Cockran*, chapter 10.

40  'COCKRAN, William Bourke | US House of Representatives: History, Art & Archives', available at: history.house.gov/People/Detail/11169?ret=True.

41  'Personal and miscellaneous', sketch of William Bourke Cockran by Richard B. Morris, Box 40, Folder 4, 256–7, William Bourke Cockran Papers, NYPL.

42  Paul Rouse says Bourke Cockran spoke at the Irish Race Convention in New York in March 1916, but that cannot be corroborated in the newspaper reports. See Paul Rouse, 'Cockran, William Bourke', in James McGuire and James Quinn, eds, *Dictionary of Irish Biography* (Cambridge: Cambridge University Press, 2009), available at: dib.cambridge .org/viewReadPage.do?articleId=a1785. The scores of boxes of speeches, notes, and correspondence are at once an unruly amalgamation of American and European politics with fervent Irish nationalism and classic ideals of American representative government at its core. It could be said that the tangled mess of Irish and American patriotism is the perfect analogy for the personal and political life of William Bourke Cockran himself.

43  William Bourke Cockran, *In the Name of Liberty*, Robert McElroy, ed. (New York: G. P. Putnam's Sons, Knickerbocker Press, 1925), ix.

44  Brundage, 'In time of peace', in Bayor and Meagher, eds, *The New York Irish*, 322.

45  'Sir Wilfrid Laurier and Home Rule', *The Times*, 13 October 1910; 'Mr Bourke Cockran and Home Rule', *Irish Times*, 18 November 1910. It is reported that 'Mr. Cockran is an old friend of Mr. Dillon, and was one of the largest subscribers to the Redmond Fund in America last year.' Bourke Cockran was, as early as 1891, also one of the original members of the short-lived Irish Nationalist Federation of America (INFA). See Bayor and Meagher, eds, *The New York Irish*, 325.

46  See McGurrin, *Bourke Cockran*, 226.

47  'Sudden death of Mr Bourke Cockran', *The Times*, 2 March 1923. The Bourke Cockran collection at NYPL is replete with letters from Redmond spanning the years 1898–1915. Many are labelled 'Confidential' and 'Private'. While most are straightforward requests for funds, one handwritten letter from Redmond on 2 September 1904 writes of the Land

Bill, 'This great achievement was only rendered possible by the fact that the Irish National Party received substantial assistance during the past 3 years from Irish sympathizers in America.' Another telegram, one sentence only, from April 1912 reads: 'Please cable me as many expressions [of] approval [of] Home Rule Bill from prominent American Irishmen as possible.' Cockran evidently wasted no time in complying with the request. He replied the same day with a telegram of his own: 'Hearty Congratulations to you and the Irish Party on marvelous success, and to [the] Irish people on splendid prospect afforded by Home Rule Bill.' Below were the names of 15 'prominent American Irishmen' including Martin Keogh, James O'Gorman, and Bourke Cockran himself.

48 'Congestion in Ireland', *Weekly Irish Times*, 21 July 1906. Bourke Cockran's business dealings with Sir Horace Plunkett, father of executed Rising leader Joseph Plunkett, were widely reported. While not executed until August 1916, Roger Casement, in particular, met with Cockran on many occasions and maintained a regular correspondence regarding Irish affairs with the New York congressman. Within the Cockran Papers at the NYPL can be found one opened envelope addressed to William Bourke Cockran from Casement, stamped at 12.30 a.m. from 15 May 1916.

49 'Calls Irish revolt justifiable', *New York Times*, 15 May 1916.

50 'Irish as allies of Germans', ibid. Rochester, NY, branch of the Friends of Irish Liberty declared their 'quasi-affiliation' with the German-American alliance.

51 McGurrin, *Bourke Cockran*, 236.

52 '3,500 cheer Irish rebels, hoot British', *New York Tribune*, 15 May 1916.

53 'Speech at meeting at Carnegie Hall', New York City, to protest against the continued executions of the Irish prisoners of war, 14 May 1916, 'Addresses and speeches', May–June 1916, Box 28, Folder 2, William Bourke Cockran Papers, NYPL.

54 Ibid.

55 Ibid.

56 Ibid.

57 'Mr Redmond's new Home Rule', *Irish Times*, 14 October 1910.

58 'Death threat upon Irish massmeeters; police act', *Chicago Daily Tribune*, 3 June 1916. The article went on to report that 'the police fear a serious clash between Irish and British sympathizers.'

59 'Irish here to rally dead republic: 100 baskets piled with money to save widows of the 16 martyrs', *New York Tribune*, 11 June 1916. Bourke Cockran co-led a fundraising speech at Madison Square Garden on 10 June 1916 for the widows and orphans of the executed Rising leaders; the meeting was said to have raised '100 baskets of money' totalling $35,000. One thousand dollars was given by 'German friends of the families of the heroic [Irish] dead'.

60 Bourke Cockran maintained a close relationship with the Churchill clan, with both Jennie and her son, until the end of his life. In fact, Bourke Cockran was arguably a surrogate father figure to Winston Churchill from 1896 onward, keeping up a voluminous correspondence together over the years and hosting Winston for extended visits at the Bourke Cockran estate in Manhattan. This life-long mentorship of young Winston was acknowledged as late as 1953. See McKevitt, 'Winston Churchill'.

61 Michael McMenamin and Curt J. Zoller, *Becoming Winston Churchill: The Untold Story of Young Winston and His American Mentor* (Oxford: Greenwood World Publishing, 2007), chapter 2.

62 'Speech at meeting at Carnegie Hall', 'Addresses and speeches', May–June 1916, Box 28, Folder 2, William Bourke Cockran Papers, NYPL.

63 Ibid.

64 Ibid.

65 'Big Cuban meeting in New York', *Chicago Daily Tribune*, 28 November 1896, reports Bourke Cockran calling for American action on behalf of the memory of the executed Cuban students from 1871. Bourke Cockran reportedly says, 'It is time this government should speak out and have the courage of its conviction. I hope it does, and it will not be to annex Cuba, but to liberate it.'

66 'Speech at meeting at Carnegie Hall', 'Addresses and speeches', May–June 1916, Box 28, Folder 2, William Bourke Cockran Papers, NYPL.

67 'Appeals for the Irish Relief Fund', *Boston Daily Globe*, 26 June 1916, subtitled 'Suggests United States should act as it did in Cuba'.

68 'Speech made at Boston, Mass. asking American intervention in Ireland, June 25th 1916', 'Addresses and Speeches', May–June 1916, Box 28, Folder 2, William Bourke Cockran Papers, NYPL.

69 Ibid.

70 Ibid.

71 Arthur S. Link, *Woodrow Wilson and the Progressive Era, 1910–1917* (New York: Harper & Row, 1963), 252.

72 Immediately following the executions of the Easter Rising leaders, according to Augustine Birrell, chief secretary of Ireland until May 1916, the British government had been 'very anxious … that news should not reach the neutral countries, and particularly our friends in America'. They were, however, also quite concerned with what many in England perceived as a growing alliance between Irish- and German- American 'extremists'. See 'Scanty news from Ireland' and 'American comment', *The Times*, 29 April 1916; Ruan O'Donnell, *America and the 1916 Easter Rising* (New York: Friends of Sinn Féin, 2015), 45.

73 'Speech made at Boston', 'Addresses and Speeches', May–June 1916, Box 28, Folder 2, William Bourke Cockran Papers, NYPL.

74 *Monthly Catalogue United States Public Documents*, July 1915–June 1916 (1916): 749

75 Ibid., 781.

76 'House Resolution 150', Congressional Record, 15 July 1921, 67th Congress, Session 1. The following year, April 1922, an ageing Bourke Cockran applied for an updated passport to travel to Europe including the Irish Free State on official business. He listed the countries in which he anticipated spending time: France, Belgium, Holland, Italy, Switzerland, Germany, Austria, Hungary, Czechoslovakia, Gibraltar, Spain, Algeria, Morocco, Portugal, and, written last and by his own hand, 'Irish Free State'. See 'Special passport applications, 1914–1925', Box 4208, Volume 21, Military, Civilian, Federal Employees and Dependents, National Archives and Records Administration, Washington, DC.

77 'Personal and miscellaneous papers', obituaries, Box 41, Folder 4, William Bourke Cockran Papers, NYPL. Bourke Cockran died, just one day after his sixty-ninth birthday, having made a speech to congress the previous afternoon. He was also remembered as 'the leading Roman Catholic layman' and 'the strongest and most influential supporter of the Home Rule cause in the United States'. See 'Sudden death of Mr Bourke Cockran', *The Times*, 2 March 1923. See also Antonia Leslie, 'Antonia Leslie: great Scott! Was Gatsby Irish?', *Irish Independent*, 6 February 2013; Luke Henderson, 'Moves to have memorial to famous Sligo-born orator', *Sligo Weekender*, 7 May 2015.

## 15. THE HAND OF FRIENDSHIP: PROTESTANTS, IRISH AMERICANS, AND 1916-ERA NATIONALISM

1 Lady Wilde, 'The American Irish' (Dublin: William McGee, 1877), 40, microfiche PR8833. G724x1988, O'Neill Library, Boston College.

2 Shane Leslie, 'Robert Emmet, failure and hero', *Ireland*, 4 March 1916: 7.

3 Amanda Sebestyen, ed., *Prison Letters of Countess Markievicz*, 1934 (London: Virago Press, 1986), 144.

4 'Divided loyalties: Protestant nationalism in Ireland: the 1916 diary of Dorothy Stopford Price, 2015', available at: dh.tcd.ie/pricediary/historical-context/divided-loyalties-history -of-anglo-irishprotestant-activism/. R. F. Foster discusses Protestant activists in *Vivid Faces: The Revolutionary Generation in Ireland 1890–1923* (London: Penguin Books, 2015). Several, including Markievicz and Casement prior to his hanging, converted to Catholicism.

5 As Rankin Sherling stated: 'It is hard to overstate the seeming ubiquity of Irish Protestants and their descendants in the pantheon of American achievement. They can, and should, be studied, faulty U.S. census material or no. Not to include them in the historiography along with their Catholic brethren is to rob Irish Americans, Catholic and Protestant, of much of their heritage.' See Rankin Sherling, 'Irish Protestants and Irish-Protestant Americans, 1870–1940', in Elliott Robert Barkan, ed., *Immigrants in American History: Arrival, Adaptation, and Integration*, volume 1 (Santa Barbara, CA, Denver, CO, and Oxford: ABC Clio, 2013): 427–37, 435.

6 David Fitzpatrick noted that 'even at its height, the "Ascendancy" was utterly unrepresentative of Irish Protestants.' See David Fitzpatrick, *Descendancy: Irish Protestant Histories since 1795* (Cambridge: Cambridge University Press, 2014), 3–7.

7 James E. Doan, 'Ulster Presbyterian immigration to America', in Mervyn Busteed, Frank Neal, and Jonathan Tonge, eds, *Irish Protestant Identities* (Manchester and New York: Manchester University Press, 2008): 187–99.

8 See Donald Akenson, *Small Differences: Irish Catholics and Irish Protestants, 1815–1922* (Montreal: McGill-Queen's University Press, 1988); and Michael P. Carroll, 'How the Irish became Protestant in America', *Religion and American Culture: A Journal of Interpretation* 16:1 (winter 2006): 25–54, available at: jstor.org/stable/10.1525/rac.2006.16.1.25.

9 William H. Mulligan Jr addresses the need for further study of Protestants in 'How the Irish became American: reflections on the history of the Irish in the United States', in Diane Sabenacio Nititham and Rebecca Boyd, eds, *Heritage, Diaspora and the Consumption of Culture: Movements in Irish Landscapes* (Surrey and Burlington, VT: Ashgate Publishing, 2014), 93–111. See also Donald Akenson, 'The historiography of the Irish in the United States of America', in Patrick O'Sullivan, ed., *The Irish in the New Communities*, volume 2, *The Irish World Wide: History, Heritage, Identity* (Lesicester: Leicester University Press, 1992), 99–127, 99.

10 Lindsey J. Flewelling, 'Ulster unionism and America, 1880–1920' (Ph.D. thesis, University of Edinburgh, 2012), 13; Patrick O'Sullivan, introduction, in O'Sullivan, ed., *The Irish in the New Communities*, 11; Carroll, 'How the Irish became Protestant', 31; William Jenkins, 'Ulster transplanted: Irish Protestants, everyday life and constructions of identity in late Victorian Toronto', in Nititham and Boyd, eds, *Heritage, Diaspora*, 200–20.

11 Timothy J. Meagher, *The Columbia Guide to Irish American History* (New York: Columbia University Press, 2005), 27.

12 Emmet converted to Catholicism in mid-life.

13 Isaac Butt, *The Irish People and the Irish Land, etc.* (Dublin: J. Falconer, 1867), 239, quoted by Thomas Addis Emmet, *Ireland under English Rule, or a Plea for the Plaintiff*, volume 2 (New York and London: G. P. Putnam's Sons and The Knickerbocker Press, 1903), 84, available at: archive.org/stream/irelandundereng1o2emme#page/n7/mode/2up.

14 Thomas Addis Emmet, *Incidents of My Life: Professional, Literary, Social, with Services in the Cause of Ireland* (New York and London: G. P. Putnam's Sons and The Knickerbocker Press, 1911), 427, available at: babel.hathitrust.org/cgi/pt?id=mdp.39015033176937;view=1up;seq=25; Patrick Maume, 'Nationalism', in S. J. Connolly, ed., *The Oxford Companion to Irish History* (Oxford and New York: Oxford University Press, 1998), 380.

15 See references in Mary C. Kelly, *The Shamrock and the Lily: The New York Irish and the Creation of a Transatlantic Identity, 1845–1921* (New York: Peter Lang Publishing, 2005).

16 Catherine B. Shannon, *'With Good Will Doing Service': The Charitable Irish Society of Boston (1737–1857)* (Westfield, MA: Institute for Massachusetts Studies, 2015), 17.

17 Appendix C, 'Organizations pertinent to the history of Protestant Irish America', in Michael F. Funchion, *Irish American Voluntary Organizations* (Westport, CT: Greenwood Press, 1983), 301.

18 Wilde, 'The American Irish'. Speranza referenced a trio of Protestants: MP Henry Grattan and lawyers Charles Kendal Bushe and William Conyngham Plunket, 1st Baron Plunkett.

19 James Quinn, *John Mitchel* (Dublin: UCD Press, 2008), xi–xix. See discussion of Mitchel in Mary C. Kelly, *Ireland's Great Famine in Irish American History: Enshrining a Fateful Memory* (Lanham, MD: Rowman & Littlefield, 2014).

20 'John Mitchel centenary', *The Gaelic American*, 18 December 1915: 2.

21 Henry Osborne, 'Belfast man from Armagh appeals to the Irish in America to stand by the principles of Tone, Emmet and Mitchel', *The Gaelic American*, 31 January 1914: 2.

22 'Patrick Pearse's eulogy of Theobald Wolfe Tone', *The Gaelic American*, 22 May 1914: 3.

23 Kevin Whelan, 'Robert Emmet: between history and memory', *History Ireland* 11:3, Robert Emmet Bicentenary (autumn 2003): 50–4.

24 'Ready for New York Emmet celebration', *The Gaelic American*, 7 March 1914: 5.

25 Patrick Pearse, 'Robert Emmet: an address delivered at an Emmet commemoration in New York on March 9th, 1914', pamphlet published by Kilmainham Jail Historical Museum, 1975, AIA 047, Pamphlets, Box 2, Archives of Irish America, Tamiment Library, New York University.

26 *Clan-na-Gael Emmet Anniversary Magazine*, Academy of Music, Philadelphia, Wednesday 4 March 1914; Joseph McGarrity Collection, Villanova, available at: digital.library.villanova.edu/Item/vudl:136005.

27 'Robert Holmes, brother-in-law of Robert Emmet', *The Gaelic American*, 31 January 1914: 3; Whelan, 'Robert Emmet', 54

28 'FOIF branches-membership fees ledger, 1916–17', Box 24, Folder 1, Friends of Irish Freedom Papers, American Irish Historical Society, New York.

29 'Sir Roger Casement's work for Ireland', *The Gaelic American*, 6 February 1915: 2.

30 Mulligan offers updated insights in 'How the Irish became American', in Nititham and Boyd, eds, *Heritage, Diaspora*, 93–111.

31 Wilde, 'The American Irish', 39.

32 'Why I am a nationalist', *The Irish American Weekly*, 21 February 1914: 8, American Irish Historical Society holdings.

33 Flewelling, 'Ulster unionism', 59–60.

34 Dorothy Macardle, *The Irish Republic: A Documented Chronicle of the Anglo-Irish Conflict and the Partitioning of Ireland, with a Detailed Account of the Period 1916–1923*, 1937 (New York: Farrar, Straus and Giroux, 1965), 69.

35 Alden Jamison, 'Irish Americans: the Irish question and American diplomacy, 1895–1921' (Ph.D. thesis, Harvard University, 1942), 24.

36 'A prospering Ireland, the epistles of Shebna the Scribe', *Church of Ireland Gazette*, 20 January 1911: 52. 'Shebna' was the nom de plume of Reverend William Shaw Kerr (1897–1960), bishop of Down and Dromore, available at Church of Ireland website, esearch. informa.ie/Exe/ZyNET.exe?ZyAction=ZyActionr&Client=7094_RCB%20Library%20 Archive&User=ANONYMOUS&Password=ANONYMOUS.

37 Siobhan Jones, 'The "Irish Protestant" under the editorship of Lindsay Crawford, 1901–6', *Saothar* 30 (2005): 85–96, available at: jstor.org/stable/23199801; Peter Murray, 'Lindsay Crawford's "impossible demand"?: the southern Irish dimension of the Independent Orange project', 5, Working Paper Series, Department of Sociology, NUI Maynooth, February 2002, available at: maynoothuniversity.ie/social-sciences-institute/ working-papers.

38 See Léon Ó Broin, *Protestant Nationalists in Revolutionary Ireland: The Stopford Connection* (Totowa, NJ: Barnes and Noble, 1985), and Foster's references in *Vivid Faces*.

39 Stopford Green to Crawford, 30 May 1906, letters from correspondents, number 4, second page, MS 11,415, Letters and Papers of Robert Lindsay Crawford, National Library of Ireland.

40 Crawford expanded his profile through the Protestant Friends of Ireland organisation in New York in 1919. See his 'The problem of Ulster', reprinted from *The Statesman* for the

Protestant Friends of Ireland, New York, 1920, available at: digital.library.villanova.edu/ Item/vudl%3A138924.

41 'Impressions of Easter Week', *Church of Ireland Gazette*, 28 April–5 May 1916: 325.

42 John Bernard, Church of Ireland archbishop of Dublin, 'The lesson and the need', *Church of Ireland Gazette*, 12 May 1916: 343.

43 John Redmond and T. P. O'Connor, 'Irish optimistic on St Patrick's Day', in 'Greetings to America, declare Home Rule is near', *New York Times*, 17 March 1911: 4.

44 'Mr Redmond's mission', ibid., 14 September 1912: 12.

45 'Irish here demand volunteers arm: fund committee cables', ibid., 6 July 1914: 14.

46 Jamison, 'Irish Americans', 158, 181–3, 446.

47 *The Catholic Church in the United States of America: Undertaken to Celebrate the Golden Jubilee of His Holiness, Pope Pius X* (New York: Catholic Editing Company, 1914), 308, available at: books.google.com/books?id=KL4YAAAAYAAJ; Frederick Franklin Schrader, *Handbook: Political, Statistical and Sociological, for German Americans and All Other Americans Who Have Not Forgotten the History and Traditions of Their Country, and Who Believe in the Principles of Washington, Jefferson and Lincoln* (New York: published by the author, 1916), 86, available at: books.google.com/books?id=L50-AAAAYAAJ.

48 Jamison, 'Irish Americans', 465–7, quotation 465.

49 'Justice Goff's keynote speech', *The Gaelic American*, 11 March 1916: 2.

50 *The Gaelic American*, 18 March 1916: front page.

51 John Quinn, 'Roger Casement: martyr – some notes for a chapter of history by a friend whose guest he was when the war broke out', *New York Times*, 13 August 1916: SM1. The front page of *The Gaelic American*, 6 May 1916, featured a signed image of Markievicz captioned 'Countess Constance de Markievicz'.

52 Smaller organisations such as the Scotch Irish Society in Tennessee, 1889–1901 strove to cultivate ancestral ties to Ulster. See Flewelling, 'Ulster unionism', 99, 116, 119–20.

53 'Imperial necessities', *Church of Ireland Gazette*, 16 June 1916: 415–16.


## 16. THE IRISH-LANGUAGE COMMUNITY IN NEW YORK ON THE EVE OF THE EASTER RISING

1 'Supplement to *The Gael*, December 1900', *An Gaodhal* 19:12 (December 1900).

2 Timothy G. McMahon, *Grand Opportunity: The Gaelic Revival and Irish Society, 1893–1910* (Syracuse: Syracuse University Press, 2008), 9–12.

3 'Father O'Growney in America', *Irisleabhar na Gaedhilge* 5:10 (1 January 1895): 159. For instances of 'The Star-Spangled Banner' sung in Irish at New York revivalist society meetings and concerts, see *New York Times*, 30 October 1898, 16 April 1906, 16 April 1911; *New York Tribune*, 8 April 1912. See also Úna Ní Bhroiméil, *Building Irish Identity in America, 1870–1915* (Dublin: Four Courts Press, 2003), 53; Philip O'Leary, *The Prose Literature of the Gaelic Revival, 1881–1921* (University Park: Pennsylvania State University Press, 1994), 357.

4 Francis M. Carroll, *American Opinion and the Irish Question, 1910–1923* (Dublin: Gill and Macmillan, 1978), 10.

5 Kenneth E. Nilsen, 'The Irish language in New York, 1850–1900', in Ronald H. Bayor and Timothy J. Meagher, eds, *The New York Irish* (Baltimore: The Johns Hopkins University Press, 1996), 252–74; Stiofán Ó hAnnracháin, ed., *Go Meiriceá Siar: Na Gaeil agus Meiriceá, Cnuasach Aistí* (Baile Átha Cliath: An Clóchomhar Tta, 1979); Jeffrey L. Kallen, 'Language and ethnic identity: the Irish language in the United States', in Liam Mac Mathúna and David Singleton, eds, *Language across Cultures* (Dublin: Irish Association for Applied Linguistics, 1984), 101 12; William Mahon, *Thomas Griffin (1829 96) of Corca Dhuibhne and the Irish Community of Lawrence, Massachusetts* (Aberystwyth: Aberystwyth University Press, 2007).

6 All summary statistics offered here are derived from the IPUMS-USA one percent microdata samples for the 1910 and 1920 United States censuses. See Steven Ruggles, Katie Genadek, Ronald Goeken, Josiah Grover, and Matthew Sobek, *Integrated Public Use Microdata Series: Version 6.0*, machine-readable database (Minneapolis: University of Minnesota, 2015).

7 The Bronx was created as a separate county by the time of the 1920 census. To maintain consistency from 1910 to 1920, it is included here as a part of New York County for both years.

8 The IPUMS one percent sample for 1910 yields over 200 occupations for Irish-born individuals. These were coded into three main categories such that occupations done in industrial factories, performed using mass-produced techniques, exclusively reliant on manual labour, or that had a high likelihood of mass unionisation were considered working and labouring class individuals. Well-paid supervisory positions, high-skill professional positions, occupations reliant on advanced education, or others indicative of solid and even upper-middle-class status were encoded as middle class. The remainder, a large variety of semi-skilled, skilled, artisanal, clerical white collar, consumer-oriented, and small-scale production occupations were encoded as lower middle class.

9 Ní Bhroiméil, *Building Irish Identity*, 37–44.

10 Minute book entries, 11 November 1914, 78, 2 May 1915, 98, Box 2, Volume of Meeting Minutes, 1909–18, Gaelic Society of New York Records, AIA.025, Archives of Irish America, Tamiment Library and Robert F. Wagner Labor Archives, New York University (hereafter cited as GSNY).

11 Minute book entries, 3 June 1899, 178, Box 2, Volume of Meeting Minutes, 1894–9, GSNY; *Irish World*, 13 June 1903; *New York Tribune*, 11 April 1915; Nilsen, 'Irish Language in New York', in Bayor and Meagher, eds, *The New York Irish*, 268–9.

12 Minute book entries, 3 June 1899, 178, Box 2, Volume of Meeting Minutes, 1894–9, GSNY.

13 Ní Bhroiméil, *Building Irish Identity*, 55, 89, 93–7.

14 Ibid., 97–8.

15 *The Gaelic American*, 25 March 1916.

16 Ní Bhroiméil, *Building Irish Identity*, 97–8; Michael Doorley, 'Judge Daniel Cohalan: a

nationalist crusader against British influence in American life', *New Hibernia Review* 19:2 (summer 2015): 118–19.

17 Senia Pašeta, *Before the Revolution: Nationalism, Social Change, and Ireland's Catholic Elite, 1879–1922* (Cork: Cork University Press, 1999), 1, 45–9. See also R. F. Foster, *Vivid Faces: The Revolutionary Generation in Ireland 1890–1923* (London: Allen Lane, 2014); Patrick Maume, 'Charles Dawson and the public sphere in late Victorian and Edwardian Dublin', *Éire-Ireland* 50:3/4 (autumn/winter 2015): 113–32, and *The Long Gestation: Irish Nationalist Life, 1891 1918* (New York: St Martin's Press, 1999); Fergal McCluskey, 'Fenians, Ribbonmen, and popular ideology's role in nationalist politics: East Tyrone, 1906 9', *Irish Historical Studies* 37:145 (May 2010): 61 82; Michael Wheatley, *Nationalism and the Irish Party: Provincial Ireland, 1910 1916* (Oxford: Oxford University Press, 2010).

18 Nilsen, 'Irish Language in New York', in Bayor and Meagher, eds, *The New York Irish*, 261–71; Fionnuala Uí Fhlannagáin, *Mícheál Ó Lócháin agus An Gaodhal* (Baile Átha Cliath: An Clóchomhar Tta, 1990), 22–36, 64–77.

19 Douglas Hyde (An Craoibhín Aoibhinn), *Mo Thurus go hAmerice nó Imeasg na nGaedheal ins an Oileán Úr* (Baile Átha Cliath: Oifig Díolta Foillseacháin Rialtais, 1937), 16.

20 *Irish American Weekly*, 15 June 1912.

21 *New York Times*, 7 April 1912; *Irish American Weekly*, 1 February 1913.

22 *Irish American Weekly*, 1 February 1913; Axel Klein, 'Celtic legends in Irish opera, 1900–1930', *Proceedings of the Harvard Celtic Colloquium* 24/25 (2004/2005): 44–7; Sean Beecher, *An Ghaeilge in Cork City: An Historical Perspective to 1894* (Cork: Goldy Angel Press, 1993), 49–50; Liam Ó Dochartaigh, 'Nótaí ar ghluaiseacht na Gaeilge i Meiriceá, 1872–1891', in Ó hAnnracháin, ed., *Go Meiriceá Siar*, 73–84; Liam Mac Cóil, *An Chláirseach agus an Choróin: Seacht gCeolsiansa Stanford* (Indreabhán: Leabhar Breac, 2010), 194–5; Ní Bhroiméil, *Building Irish Identity*, 40 1; Máire Ní Mhurchú, Diarmuid Breathnach, and Fiontar DCU, Ainm.ie (Dublin City University and Cló Iar-Chonnacht, 2011), s.v. 'Patterson, Annie (1868–1934)', available at: ainm.ie/Bio.aspx?ID=288, and 'Butler, Thomas O'Brien (1861–1915)', available at: ainm.ie/Bio.aspx?ID=239. Hereafter cited as Ainm.ie.

23 *The Sun*, 18 January 1914.

24 *Irish American Weekly*, 25 May 1912.

25 Minute book entries, 7 May 1916, 113, Box 2, Volume of Meeting Minutes, 1909–18, GSNY.

26 Ní Bhroiméil, *Building Irish Identity*, 57; Carroll, *American Opinion*, 30.

27 *The Gaelic American*, 4 March 1916; Ainm.ie, s.v. 'Chevasse, Claude (1886–1971)', available at: ainm.ie/Bio.aspx?ID=242.

28 See, for example, Meyer's 1916 contention of the authenticity of war letters purporting to describe an Irish man's resistance to Casement's recruiting in Germany that were published in the *New York Times*, 8 September 1916.

29 Carroll, *American Opinion*, 37–43.

30 Minute book entries, 3 January 1915, 82–4, 7 May 1916, 113, Box 2, Volume of Meeting Minutes, 1909–18, GSNY. For McAuliffe, see *Irish American Weekly*, 25 January 1913.

31 *The Gaelic American*, 12 February 1916; *New York Times*, 2 March 1916.

32 Minute book entries, 27 February 1916, 107, 5 March 1916, 108, Box 2, Volume of Meeting Minutes, 1909–18, GSNY; Carroll, *American Opinion*, 52.

33 Minute book entries, 9 April 1916, 110–11, Box 2, Volume of Meeting Minutes, 1909–18, GSNY.

34 *The Gaelic American*, 6 May 1916; *New York Times*, 1 May 1916; Carroll, *American Opinion*, 66.

35 Carroll, *American Opinion*, 63; Eileen McGough, *Diarmuid Lynch: A Forgotten Irish Patriot* (Cork: Mercier Press, 2013), 12–28; Marie Coleman, 'Lynch, Diarmuid', in James McGuire and James Quinn, eds, *Dictionary of Irish Biography* (Cambridge: Cambridge University Press, 2009); *Irish Advocate*, 18 November 1950.

36 *The Gaelic American*, 20 May 1916; minute book entries, 7 May 1916, 112–19, Box 2, Volume of Meeting Minutes, 1909–18, GSNY.

37 *Irish World*, 3 June 1916; minute book entries, 24 May 1916, 120, 9 August 1916, 126, 5 November 1916, 129, Box 2, Volume of Meeting Minutes, 1909–18, GSNY.

## 17. THE IRISH COUNTY ASSOCIATIONS IN NEW YORK AND THE EASTER RISING

1 Kevin Kenny, 'American-Irish nationalism', in J. J. Lee and Marion R. Casey, eds, *Making the Irish American: History and Heritage of the Irish in the United States* (New York: New York University Press, 2006), 293–5; David Brundage, '"In time of peace prepare for war": key themes in the social thought of New York's Irish nationalists, 1890–1916', in Ronald H. Bayor and Timothy J. Meagher, eds, *The New York Irish* (Baltimore: Johns Hopkins University Press, 1996), 325–34.

2 Lawrence J. McCaffrey, 'Forging ahead and looking back', in Bayor and Meagher, eds, *The New York Irish*, 223–7. A fourth newspaper, the *Irish American Weekly*, existed until 1914.

3 Miriam Nyhan, 'Oral history: county societies in Irish New York', *American Journal of Irish Studies* 12 (2015), 159–69.

4 John T. Ridge, 'Irish county societies in New York, 1880–1914', in Bayor and Meagher, eds, *The New York Irish*, 275–300.

5 Marion R. Casey and Miriam Nyhan, 'The fifth province: county societies in Irish America', *Glucksman Ireland House NYU*, 28 August 2016, available at: nyu.edu/as/irelandhouse/fifthprovince/women.php.

6 *Irish Advocate*, April 1917; *Freeman's Journal*, 26 September 1916.

7 *Irish American*, 3 February 1917.

8 Francis M. Carroll, 'America and Irish political independence, 1910–1933', in P. J. Drudy, ed., *The Irish in America: Emigration, Assimilation and Impact* (Cambridge: Cambridge University Press, 1985), 271–4; Kerby A. Miller, *Emigrants and Exiles: Ireland and the Irish Exodus to North America* (New York: Oxford University Press, 1985), 541–2.

9 *Irish Advocate*, 8 October 1910.

10 Ibid., 26 March 1904.

11 Ibid., 4 May 1912.

12 *Anglo-Celt*, 2 May 1914; *Freeman's Journal*, 31 July 1914.

13 Brundage, 'In time of peace', in Bayor and Meagher, eds, *The New York Irish*, 333–4.

14 The volume of emigration from Ireland to the United States was cut in half by the First World War, dropping from 339,065 in the decade 1901–10 to 146,181 between 1911–20. See Table 1 in Patrick Blessing, 'Irish in America', in Michael Glazier, ed., *The Encyclopedia of the Irish in America* (Notre Dame: University of Notre Dame Press, 1999), 454.

15 *Irish Advocate*, 1 August 1914; ibid., 16 October 1914. Ulster, it should be noted, had historically sent smaller numbers to New York, gravitating towards Philadelphia and vicinity instead.

16 These conclusions are based on my research on the three main Irish-American newspapers published in New York in 1916. Details by specific county have been published by the United Irish Counties Association, *The 1916 Easter Rising: New York and beyond* (New York: The United Irish Counties Association of New York, Inc., 2016).

17 *Irish Advocate*, 6 May 1916. The economic power of $1,000 in 1916 is the equivalent of $346,000 in 2014. See Samuel H. Williamson, 'Seven ways to compute the relative value of a US dollar amount, 1774 to present', MeasuringWorth.com, 2016.

18 *Irish American Weekly*, 8 August 1914.

19 *Irish Advocate*, 15 July 1922.

20 *Kerryman*, 14 March 1936.

21 Ibid., 12 March 1927; *Irish Advocate*, 6 May 1916. Dan McCarthy's brother, Tom, served under Austin Stack, the Kerry IRB leader in 1916, in securing arms for the rebellion. Dan McCarthy was a close friend of Stack's from Gaelic football days in Ireland.

22 *Irish Advocate*, 10 June 1916.

23 James Quinn, 'Clarke, Thomas James ("Tom")', in James McGuire and James Quinn, eds, *Dictionary of Irish Biography* (Cambridge: Cambridge University Press, 2012).

24 James McElroy, *Red Bricks and Green Bushes: The Story of the County Tyrone Society* (New York: County Tyrone Society of New York, *c.* 1955), 60–1.

25 *Irish Advocate*, 21 October 1916.

26 *The Gaelic American*, 5 August 1916.

27 *Remember Limerick* (New York: Limerick Men's B. & S. Association, 1974), 11.

28 *Irish Advocate*, 20 May 1916.

29 Ibid.

30 Ibid., 27 May 1916.

31 Ibid., 20 May 1916.

32 Ibid., 26 August 1916.

33 Ibid., 27 May 1916.

34 Ibid., 6 May 1916.

35 *The Gaelic American*, 9 September 1916; *Irish Advocate*, 14 December 1916; *Irish World*, 24 March 1917.

36 *Irish Advocate*, 3 June 1916.

37 Ibid., 14 October 1916. See also internet site IrishMedals.org, Louth Volunteers. This Dundalk branch of the AOH was a militant Hibernian faction affiliated with the American AOH and had been founded by Major Edward McCrystal, a leader in New York of the private military organisation Irish Volunteers, the Ancient Order of Hibernians, and the semi-secret nationalist society Clan na Gael, who had gone to Dundalk ten years before to organise Hibernians who wanted to be separate from the larger, but Redmondite, Board of Erin AOH. The Irish Volunteer unit which included Coburn, and probably Finn, used the Dundalk Knights of Hibernia Hall (the American affiliated AOH) to drill and train.

38 They both reconnected with the Louth football team in New York. Later Coburn returned to Dundalk in 1919 where he eventually found employment as a rate collector. Coburn was an anti-Treaty Irish republican, even though his brother was a prominent Redmondite and later served as a Fine Gael TD in the Irish Dáil for more than 30 years. See *Anglo-Celt*, 11 March 193; *Irish Press*, 19 September 1967. Although Finn was identified as Jim Finn in the *Irish Advocate*, no listing of a 1916 veteran of that name appears on the list of New York residents in Ireland's Bureau of Military History archives list of 1916 veterans. There is a Patrick Finn, however, one of at least six veterans of the Dundalk Battalion of the Irish Volunteers, included in the list.

39 *Irish Advocate*, 10 June 1916.

40 *Irish American*, 15 April 1916.

41 *Freeman's Journal*, 25 September 1916.

42 *Irish Advocate*, 13 May 1916.

43 Cork Men's P. & B. minutes, 18 May 1916, Archives of Irish America, New York University; *Freeman's Journal*, 25 September 1916.

44 *Irish Advocate*, 6 May 1916.

45 Ibid., 3 March 1951.

## 18. BIFOCALISM OF US PRESS COVERAGE: THE EASTER RISING AND IRISH AMERICA

1 'Revolt on in Ireland,' *Washington Post*, 25 April 1916.

2 'Revolt in Dublin, rumor', *Chicago Tribune*, 25 April 1916.

3 For an explanation of John Devoy's role in the Easter Rising and his involvement in the republican cause, see Robert Schmuhl, *Ireland's Exiled Children: America and the Easter Rising* (New York: Oxford University Press, 2016), 15–43.

4 'Dublin is still cut off', *New York Times*, 28 April 1916.

5 *N. W. Ayer & Son's American Newspaper Annual and Directory* (Philadelphia: N. W. Ayer & Son, 1916), 11.

6 'Newspapers: by the numbers', The State of the News Media 2013, The Pew Research Center's Project for Excellence in Journalism.

7  'Irish advices here say revolt has spread', *New York Times*, 26 April 1916; 'Irish societies call Sir Roger Patriot; has followed example of Washington in seeking freedom', *Washington Post*, 26 April 1916.

8  See Conor Cruise O'Brien, 'The embers of Easter', *The Irish Times*, 7 April 1966.

9  'Press censorship records 1916–1919', Box 3, Folder 128, National Archives of Ireland, Dublin.

10  'How the Irish press is gagged', *The Gaelic American*, 8 July 1916.

11  'One Clancy quells an Irish uprising', *New York Times*, 29 April 1916.

12  'Ireland's sudden revolt', *New York Times Sunday Magazine*, 30 April 1916.

13  Ibid., 2.

14  'How England deals with high treason', *Washington Post*, 30 April 1916, 'Editorial and society', 1.

15  Padraic Colum, 'Asserts Irish rebellion grew out of fundamental conflict of England and Emerald Isle', *Washington Post*, 30 April 1916.

16  Walter Green, 'Irish uprising was in the air', *Boston Globe*, 30 April 1916.

17  'Sir Roger Casement's astounding career', ibid.

18  'Crazy over Irish turmoil', *New York Times*, 30 April 1916.

19  'Irish cheer Germany and Lusitania horror', *Los Angeles Times*, 1 May 1916.

20  'Irishmen uphold revolt in Dublin', *New York Times*, 1 May 1916.

21  'Revolt put down, Redmond cables', ibid.

22  'The Irish uprising', editorial, *Washington Post*, 2 May 1916.

23  'The Irish revolt', editorial, *Chicago Tribune*, 2 May 1916.

24  'Call executed men martyrs to cause', *New York Times*, 4 May 1916.

25  Joyce Kilmer, 'Poets marched in the van of Irish revolt', *New York Times Sunday Magazine*, 7 May 1916. For a discussion of Kilmer's prose and poetry in response to the Rising, see Schmuhl, *Ireland's Exiled Children*, 45–73.

26  'Events of Dublin uprising chronicled day by day as battle raged in Irish capital', *Washington Post*, 7 May 1916.

27  'Irish executions', editorial, ibid.

28  'Praise Irish, score England', *Boston Globe*, 8 May 1916

29  'Says next revolt will win', *New York Times*, 8 May 1916.

30  'Prayers for rebel dead', ibid.

31  'Ireland seethes with anger over British killings', *Chicago Tribune*, 12 May 1916.

32  'Dublin rebels quit; city now is quiet', *Washington Post*, 2 May 1916.

33  'Sink German ship off Irish coast, catch Casement', *New York Times*, 25 April 1916.

34  'Madmen make history', *Washington Post*, 4 June 1916.

35  Maurice Joy, ed., *The Irish Rebellion of 1916 and Its Martyrs: Erin's Tragic Easter* (New York: Devin-Adair Company, 1916).

36  See Van Wyck Brooks, 'Ireland, 1916', *The Dial* 61:730 (1881): 458–60.

37  Walter Lippmann, *Public Opinion* (New York: Harcourt, Brace, 1922), 144.

38  Ibid., 358.

## 19. TIMELY AND SUBSTANTIAL RELIEF: NEW YORK'S CARDINAL JOHN FARLEY AND THE 1916 EASTER RISING

1 Rev. John C. Reville, SJ, 'John Cardinal Farley', *Historical Records and Studies* (1919): 142; James Dominick Hackett, *Bishops of the United States of Irish Birth or Descent* (New York: American Irish Historical Society, 1936), 51– 2.

2 Reville, 'John Cardinal Farley', 142–3.

3 Ibid., 143–4.

4 Thomas J. Shelley, 'John Cardinal Farley and modernism in New York', *Church History* 61:3 (1992): 360.

5 Msgr Florence Cohalan, *A Popular History of the Archdiocese of New York* (Yonkers: United States Catholic Historical Society, 1999; second edition), 212.

6 Ibid., 233.

7 'Lecture delivered by Cardinal Farley on March 17, 1881, St Mary's Church, Wappinger's Falls; March 17, 1884, St Patrick's, Mott Street; March 17, 1889, St Gabriel's', Box I–37, Folder 2, Collection 005, John Cardinal Farley Collection, Archives of the Archdiocese of New York (AANY), Yonkers, NY.

8 Reville, 'John Cardinal Farley', 145.

9 Letter, James McFaul, bishop of Trenton, to Archbishop Farley, 20 September 1909, Box I–12, Folder Mc, Collection 005, AANY.

10 'Farley waits for Irish Home Rule', *New York Times*, 17 February 1912.

11 Ibid.

12 Francis Carroll, 'America and the 1916 Rising', in Gabriel Doherty and Dermot Keogh, eds, *1916: The Long Revolution* (Cork: Mercier press, 2007), 123, 126; Michael Doorley, 'The Friends of Irish Freedom: a case study', *History Ireland* 16:2 (March/April 2008), 16.

13 Letter, Rev. D. O'Connor to Cardinal Farley, 20 September 1914, Box I–17, Folder 1914 O–Q, Collection 005, AANY.

14 Letter, Cardinal Farley from John Redmond, 2 May 1917, Box I–23, Folder R, Collection 005, AANY.

15 Carroll, 'America and the 1916 Rising', 123, 126.

16 Thomas J. Rowland, 'The American Catholic press and the Easter rebellion', *The Catholic Historical Review* 18:1 (January 1995): 70; Carroll, 'America and the 1916 Rising', 137.

17 Charles Callan Tansill, *America and the Fight for Irish Freedom, 1866–1922* (New York: Devin-Adair, 1957), 201–2.

18 'The Irish revolution', *The Catholic News*, 6 May 1916: 4.

19 Tansill, *America and the Fight for Irish Freedom*, 201–2.

20 Rowland, 'The American Catholic press and the Easter rebellion', 70.

21 William J. Leary Jr, 'Woodrow Wilson, Irish Americans, and the election of 1916', *The Journal of American History* 54:1 (June 1967): 59.

22 Rowland, 'The American Catholic press and the Easter rebellion', 72.

23 William J. Carr, *The Irish Carmelites of New York City and the Fight for Irish Independence, 1916–1919* (Middletown, NY: The Vestigium Press, St Albert's Jr Seminary, 1973), 11; Tansill, *America and the Fight for Irish Freedom*, 189.

24 Letter, Msgr Carroll from Michael J. Twomey, 1 June 1918, Box I–25, Folder 1918, Rev Peter Magennis, Collection 005, AANY.

25 Letter, to Rev Bernard Kevenhoorster, 10 June 1916, Box I–26, Folder 1916–17 H–L, Collection 005, AANY.

26 Leary, 'Woodrow Wilson, Irish Americans, and the election of 1916', 59; Rowland, 'The American Catholic press and the Easter rebellion', 70.

27 'The Irish revolution'.

28 Ibid.

29 John Tracy Ellis, *The Life of James Cardinal Gibbons, Archbishop of Baltimore 1834–1921*, volume 2 (Milwaukee: Bruce Publishing Co., 1952), 227.

30 Doorley, 'The Friends of Irish Freedom', 80; Thomas J. Rowland, 'Irish-American Catholics and the quest for respectability in the coming of the Great War, 1900–1917', *Journal of American Ethnic History* 15:2 (winter 1996): 17.

31 Alan J. Ward, 'America and the Irish problem, 1899–1921', in Lawrence J. McCaffrey, ed., *Irish Nationalism and the American Contribution* (New York: Arno Press, 1976), 78.

32 Nicholas M. Wolf, 'The Irish-language community in New York on the eve of the Easter Rising', in this volume.

33 Carr, *The Irish Carmelites of New York City*, 22.

34 'Mass for Irish martyrs', *The Catholic News*, 27 May 1916.

35 Letter, Rev. D. O'Connor to Cardinal Farley, 15 May 1916, Box I–21, Folder 1916 O, Collection 005, AANY.

36 Letter, Msgr William T. Russell to Cardinal Farley, 22 August 1916, Box I–21, Folder 1916 R, Collection 005, AANY.

37 'Father Duffy half-masts flag for the Irish dead', *The Gaelic American*, 13 May 1916.

38 John Patrick Buckley, 'The New York Irish: their view of American foreign policy, 1914–1921' (Ph.D. thesis, New York University, 1974), 54.

39 Tansill, *America and the Fight for Irish Freedom*, 220.

40 Letter, Cardinal Farley to Most Rev John Bonzano, 21 May 1917, Box I–26, Folder 1916–17 A–C, Collection 005, AANY.

41 Ellis, *The Life of James Cardinal Gibbons*, 227; Thomas N. Brown, *Irish-American Nationalism, 1870–1890* (Westport, CT: Greenwood Press, 1980), 56; Doorley, 'The Friends of Irish Freedom', 44; Timothy J. Meagher, 'Another new departure?: the American Catholic church, Irish nationalism, and the revolution, 1914 to 1921' (presentation, Independent Sprit: America and the 1916 Easter Rising, New York, NY, 21–22 April 2016).

42 Circular letter, 12 April 1917, Box I–36, Folder 8, Collection 005, AANY.

43 'Cardinal praises Catholics in war', *New York Times*, 28 February 1918.

44 Tansill, *America and the Fight for Irish Freedom*, 220.

45 Buckley, 'The New York Irish', 36.

46 Carroll, 'America and the 1916 Rising', 133.

47 *The Catholic News*, 6 May 1916: 4.

48 Lina D. Miller, *The New York Charities Directory: A Reference Book of Social Service in or Available for Greater New York* (New York: Charity Organization Society, 1918; twenty-seventh edition).

49 'Great Bazaar for Irish Relief Fund', *The Catholic News*, 7 October 1916.

50 'Irish Relief Fund Bazaar features', ibid., 14 October 1916.

51 Doorley, 'The Friends of Irish Freedom', 93.

52 Letter, John Hasslocker from Cardinal Farley, 11 January 1915, Box I–26, Folder 1915 H–K, Collection 005, AANY.

53 Letter, Cardinal Farley to John B. Hasslocker, 11 January 1915, Box I–26, Folder 1915 H–K, Collection 005, AANY.

54 'Germans capture the Irish Bazaar', *New York Times*, 4 October 1916.

55 Brown, *Irish-American Nationalism*, 35.

56 Rowland, 'The American Catholic press and the Easter rebellion', 79.

57 Miller, *The New York Charities Directory*.

58 Doorley, 'The Friends of Irish Freedom', 88.

59 'Cardinal aids Irish Fund', *The Catholic News*, 18 July 1916.

60 'Aid for Irish sufferers', *New York Times*, 10 July 1916.

61 'Irish Relief Fund Bazaar nets $45,000', *The Catholic News*, 25 November 1916.

62 Parish annual financial reports, Archdiocese of New York, 1916, Collection 021.002, Parish Financial Reports, AANY.

63 All Saints annual financial report, Archdiocese of New York, 1916, Collection 021.002, Parish Financial Reports, AANY.

64 Parish annual financial reports, Archdiocese of New York, 1916, Collection 021.002, Parish Financial Reports, AANY; St Mary Magdalen annual financial report, Archdiocese of New York, 1916, Collection 021.002, Parish Financial Reports, AANY.

65 'Memorial concert for Irish martyrs' families', *The Gaelic American*, 27 May 1916.

66 Editorial, *The Catholic News*, 13 May 1916: 3.

67 Letter, Francis Fischer, CSSR, to Msgr Thomas Carroll, 8 July 1916, Box I–20, Folder 1916 E–F, Collection 005, AANY.

68 Letter, Msgr Thomas Carroll to Rev Francis Fischer, CSSR, 11 July 1916, Box I–20, Folder 1916 E–F, Collection 005, AANY.

69 Ibid.

70 Tansill, *America and the Fight for Irish Freedom*, 218.

71 Sean Cronin, *Washington's Irish Policy 1916–1986: Independence, Partition, Neutrality* (Dublin: Anvil Books, 1987), 13.

72 'Aid for Irish sufferers', *New York Times*, 10 July 1916.

73 Carr, *The Irish Carmelites of New York City*, 11–12, 21.

74 Ibid., 14.

75 Ibid., 26.

76 'Pledge support to Ireland's fighting men', *The Gaelic American*, 6 May 1916.

77 'Prayers for Irish martyrs', ibid., 20 May 1916.

78 Letter, Cardinal Hayes from 'Alumnus', 1 December 1920, Box O–9, Folder 1920 Do, Collection 006, Patrick Cardinal Hayes Collection, AANY.

79 Letter, Msgr James W. Power from Cardinal Farley, 4 May 1918, Box I–25, Folder 1918 P–Q, Collection 005, AANY.

80 Letter, Rev John H. Dooley from Cardinal Farley, 4 May 1918, Box I–24, Folder 1918 D–E, Collection 005, AANY.

81 Letter, to Cardinal Farley, n.d., Box I–24, Folder 1918 D–E, Collection 005, AANY.

82 Letter, Festus J. Wade from Cardinal Farley, 8 May 1918, Box I–25, Folder W–Z, Collection 005, AANY.

## 20. THE AMERICAN CATHOLIC PRESS AND THE EASTER RISING

1 Research for this chapter included a review of over 20 diocesan newspapers and Catholic periodicals. Research focused on the English-speaking press, nearly all of which was controlled by Irish Americans. It should be noted that in several American cities Catholic papers were edited and managed by German Americans. For insight into the increase in both circulation and influence of the Catholic press by the First World War, see Donna Merwick, *Boston Priests: A Study of Social and Intellectual Change* (Cambridge, MS: Harvard University Press, 1973), 189, and Aaron I. Abell, *American Catholicism and Social Action: A Search for Social Justice, 1865–1950* (Garden City, NY: Hanover House, 1960), 289.

2 For a useful discussion on the tensions and divisions affecting the Irish-American community during the First World War, see Thomas Brown, *Irish American Nationalism* (Philadelphia: J. B. Lippincott Company, 1966); Edward Cuddy, *Irish-Americans and National Isolationism, 1914–1917* (New York: Arno Press, 1976); F. M. Carroll, *American Opinion and the Irish Question, 1910–1923* (New York: St Martin's Press, 1978).

3 John Quinn to Joseph Conrad, 1 May 1916, John Quinn Papers, New York Public Library (NYPL); Crimmins quoted in *New York Times*, 25 April 1916; ibid., 29 April 1916; quoted in *New York Times Magazine*, 30 April 1916; *New Republic*, 6, 13 May 1916; Walsh quoted in *New York Times Magazine*, 30 April 1916.

4 *Catholic Universe*, 2 June 1916.

5 *Michigan Catholic*, 4 May 1916.

6 *Southern Messenger*, 16 May 1916.

7 Quoted in Carroll, *American Opinion and the Irish Question*, 64.

8 Quoted in Patrick J. Buckley, 'The New York Irish: their view of American foreign policy, 1914–1921' (Ph.D. thesis, New York University, 1974), 30.

9 *The Freeman's Journal, Catholic News, Boston Pilot*, and *The Monitor* all questioned the wisdom of the uprising. Of all those editors in this survey who generally supported strong measures on behalf of Irish freedom, only Joseph P. O'Mahoney in Indianapolis gave unqualified support for the Easter uprising from the start. See *Indiana Catholic*, 5 May 1916.

10 *Strong Words from Mr Redmond: Treason to the Home Rule Cause* (London: J. Causton, 1916), 5.

11 *Catholic Messenger*, 27 April 1916.

12 Ibid., 4 May 1916.

13 *True Voice*, 5 May 1916.

14 *Catholic Transcript*, 4 May 1916.

15 *Catholic Citizen*, 6 May 1916.

16 Barry quoted in *New York Times*, 27 April 1916; *Catholic Citizen*, 16 May 1916; *Catholic Transcript*, 27 April 1916.

17 *Literary Digest* 52 (6 May 1916): 1,263–5, 1,355.

18 Quoted in Arthur S. Link, *Campaigns for Progressivism and Peace* (Princeton: Princeton University Press, 1965), 13.

19 *New Republic* 7 (29 July 1916): 321–2; Sir Cecil Spring-Rice to Lord Grey, 10, 19, 30 May 1916, in Stephen A. Gwynn, ed., *The Letters and Friendships of Sir Cecil Spring-Rice*, volume 2 (London: Constable, 1929),327, 331, 334; Johann von Bernstorff, *My Three Years in America* (London: Skeffington & Son, Ltd, 1930), 264.

20 *New World*, 19 May 1916.

21 *Catholic News*, 6 May 1916.

22 Ibid, 20 May 1916.

23 *Indiana Catholic*, 5 May 1916.

24 *America*, 29 May 1916.

25 Brooklyn *Tablet*, 20 May 1916.

26 *Boston Pilot*, 3 June 1916.

27 Ibid, 1 July 1916.

28 *True Voice*, 12 May 1916.

29 *Standard and Times*, 20 May 1916.

30 *Michigan Catholic*, 25 May 1916.

31 *Catholic World* 103 (June 1916): 430–1.

32 *Boston Pilot*, 12 August 1916.

33 *New World*, 11 August 1916.

34 *America*, 12 August 1916.

35 *Michigan Catholic*, 10 August 1916.

36 *Catholic Messenger*, 1 June 1916.

37 *Southern Messenger*, 3 June 1916.

38 *Catholic Telegraph*, 8 June 1916.

39 *Catholic Transcript*, 11 May 1916.

40 John C. Crighton, *Missouri and the World War, 1914–1917* (Columbia, MO: University of Missouri, 1947), 98. See also, *New York Times*, 10 July 1916.

41 Of the four Catholic papers (*Boston Pilot*, Brooklyn *Tablet*, *Catholic Messenger*, and *Indiana Catholic*) which regularly printed summaries of the Knights of Columbus meetings, none revealed any comments or opinions regarding the Dublin uprising or its suppression except to mention relief efforts underway. An examination of the two institutional histories of the Knights of Columbus does not uncover any involvement in the issue. See

Maurice Francis Egan and John B. Kennedy, *The Knights of Columbus in Peace and War*, 2 volumes (New Haven: Knights of Columbus, 1920), and Christopher J. Kauffman, *Faith and Fraternalism: The History of the Knights of Columbus, 1882–1982* (New York: Harper & Row, 1992; revised edition).

42 *The Gaelic American*, 23 October 1915.

43 *The Monitor*, 17 June 1916.

44 *Michigan Catholic*, 24 August 1916; *Pittsburgh Catholic*, 18 January 1917.

45 Carroll, *American Opinion and the Irish Question*, 79

46 While both Farley and Gibbons refused to condemn British actions, they quickly assumed leading roles in the Irish Relief Fund effort. Farley accepted the position of honorary chairman while Gibbons joined him later as honorary president. See *New York Times*, 18, 28 May 1916.

47 John A. Beadles, 'The Syracuse Irish, 1812–1928: immigration, Catholics, socio economic status, politics and Irish nationalism' (Ph.D. thesis, Syracuse University, 1974), 274.

48 In an editorial on Casement's death, the paper concluded that 'England by their deaths has justified the growing sentiment that the sword is the only answer to the sword.' See *Boston Pilot*, 12 August 1916.

49 *Catholic Transcript*, 12 October 1916; *Baltimore Catholic Review*, 10 February, 10 March 1917; *Pittsburgh Catholic*, 22 March 1917; *Freeman's Journal*, 24 February 1917; *Catholic Telegraph*, 23 February 1917.

50 *Catholic Messenger*, 10 August 1916.

51 *Catholic Citizen*, 2 June, 30 September 1916.

52 *Michigan Catholic*, 3 August 1916.

53 John Devoy, *Recollections of an Irish Rebel* (New York: Charles Young, 1929), 496. For the depressed financial condition of the Clan na Gael on the eve of the Easter rebellion, see Michael J. Jennings to Joseph McGarrity, 24 February 1916, Joseph McGarrity Papers, NYPL.

54 Devoy, *Recollections*, 126–7; *The Gaelic American*, 1 April 1916.

55 Arthur S. Link, *Wilson: The Struggle for Neutrality, 1914–1915* (Princeton: Princeton University Press, 1960), 22; Cuddy, *Irish-Americans and National Isolationism*, 44–7; Edward Cuddy, 'Irish-American propagandists and neutrality, 1914–1917', *Mid America* 49 (June 1967): 259.

56 *Catholic Transcript*, 12 October 1916; *Catholic Messenger*, 8 February 1917; Brooklyn *Tablet*, 10 February 1917; Baltimore *Catholic Review*, 10 February, 10 March 1917; *Catholic Telegraph*, 8 March 1917; *Pittsburgh Catholic*, 22 March 1917.

57 *Catholic Universe*, 20 April 1917. While mainstream Irish-American Catholic opinion reflected conservative views on the Irish question, it did not spare the Wilson administration criticism for some of its other policies. The American Catholic press was very critical of Wilson's anti-hyphenate campaign, his Mexican policies, and his overt violations of the neutrality pledge. See Brooklyn *Tablet*, 1 July 1916; T. J. Walsh to George Cardinal Mundelein, 13 September 1916, T. J. Walsh Papers, Library of Congress; *Catholic Universe*, 3 November 1916; Denver *Catholic Register*, 11 January 1917.

## 21. AN AMERICAN IN DUBLIN: JOHN KILGALLON'S RISING

1 For example, see Damien Shiels, 'Nordic rebels: the Swede and Finn who fought in the GPO, 1916', TheJournal.ie, 29 December 2013, available at: thejournal.ie/readme /ordic-rebels-%E2%80%93-the-swede-and-finn-who-fought-in-the-gpo-1916-1230007 -Dec2013/; and Andy Pollak, 'An Irishman's diary on Argentina's link to 1916: Eamon Bulfin and the Tricolour', *Irish Times*, 12 May 2015, available at: irishtimes.com/opinion /an-irishman-s-diary-on-argentina-s-link-to-1916-1.2208410.

2 John Kilgallon's name is frequently misspelled; sometimes his middle initial is incorrectly given as J., sometimes his last name is spelled Kilgallen or Kilgannon.

3 *Registration of American Citizens at the US Consul Offices in Dublin, Cork and Belfast* (US National Archives, Record Group 84), excerpts reproduced by Ireland Genealogy Projects Archives, 'General Ireland, miscellaneous: Irish gleanings 1907–1928', available at: igp-web.com/IGPArchives/ire/countrywide/xmisc/gleanings.txt .

4 Kerby A. Miller, *Emigrants and Exiles: Ireland and the Irish Exodus to North America* (New York: Oxford University Press, 1985), 399–401; Noel McLachlan, 'Davitt, Michael', in James McGuire and James Quinn, eds, *Dictionary of Irish Biography* (Cambridge: Cambridge University Press, 2009).

5 Nora Walsh emigrated in 1885. In 1910 the Kilgallons lived in Queens Ward 5, New York, '1910 United States federal census', Ancestry.com.

6 Luke Kilgallon, Greenwood Court, Far Rockaway, New York, '1900 US federal census', Ancestry.com.

7 Luke Kilgallon, '1910 US federal census', Ancestry.com.

8 Agnes Cosgrove, '1920 US federal census', Ancestry.com.

9 Gregory Dehler, 'My tenuous genealogical connection to the 1916 Easter Rising', *The Dynamo and the Virgin: A Blog Dedicated to the Study of the Gilded Age, Progressive Era, and History of the Environment*, 20 April 1914, available at: gregshistoryblog.blogspot. com/2014/04/my-tenuous-genealogical-connection-to.html. The tire tool patent claim is unverified at this time; Dehler is related to Kilgallon through Agnes Cosgrove's mother.

10 *Brooklyn Daily Eagle*, 12 August 1910, 18 March 1913.

11 Padraic Pearse and Séamas Ó Buachalla, *The Letters of P. H. Pearse* (Buckinghamshire: Colin Smythe L, 1980), 316, letter 372.

12 *Irish American Weekly*, 25 April 1914.

13 *Brooklyn Daily Eagle*, 27 February, 2 March 1914; *The Gaelic American*, 7 March 1914: 7; Angus Mitchell, 'Robert Emmet and 1916', *History Ireland* 11:3 (autumn 2003).

14 When John Kilgallon registered with the US Consulate in Dublin in August 1914, he stated he was a 'student at St. Andrews College' and was in Ireland with his mother for 'touring', but a month later he was enrolled at St Enda's. See *Registration of American Citizens at the US Consul Offices in Dublin, Cork and Belfast*.

15 'To release Kilgallon', *New York Times*, 18 May 1916; 'Think Kilgallon will be freed from prison', *New York Tribune*, 18 May 1916.

16 *Brooklyn Daily Eagle*, 20 August 1912.

17 She had to have her fifth and sixth vertebrae removed following the accident. See 'Carry girl into court to testify', ibid., 9 January 1915.

18 'Girl auto victim gets $20,000 verdict crippled for life when Rockaway man's car sped into wagon', ibid., 11 January 1915. Kilgallon's attorney was John J. Halpin. See *New York Times*, 18 May 1916.

19 Brendan Walsh, *The Pedagogy of Protest: The Educational Thought and Work of Patrick H. Pearse* (Bern: Peter Lang, 2007), 89.

20 Brendan Walsh, *Boy Republic: Patrick Pearse and Radical Education* (Dublin: The History Press, 2013), 175.

21 Desmond Ryan, *The Man Called Pearse* (Dublin: Maunsel and Company, Ltd, 1919), 18.

22 Perhaps he had basic Irish already, learned from his Mayo-born mother and her niece. Agnes Cosgrove reported her native tongue as 'Celtic' on the 1920 United States census. In a 1960 letter to Ireland's Department of Defence, Kilgallon began 'A chara' and ended with 'Mise, le meas'. See John A. Kilgallon to the Irish Minster of Defence, W34E9684, Military Service Pension Collection (MSPC), Military Archives, Department of Defence, Republic of Ireland.

23 'The insurgent Con Colbert taught drill in St. Enda's while Tom Clarke gave instruction in code signaling.' See Walsh, *The Pedagogy of Protest*, 278.

24 *Brooklyn Daily Eagle*, 9 May 1916; Charles Donnelly, Witness Statement (WS) 824, Bureau of Military History (BMH), National Archives of Ireland (NAI), available at: bureauofmilitaryhistory.ie/index.html. The honour guard for Pearse at Glasnevin was A Company: Sean Whelan, WS 1294, BMH, NAI; Feargus de Burca (Frank Burke), WS 694, BMH, NAI.

25 Michael Cremen, WS 563, BMH, NAI.

26 J. J. Lee, 'Pearse, Patrick Henry', in McGuire and Quinn, eds, *Dictionary of Irish Biography*.

27 Nora Kilgallon to Patrick Pearse, 12 November 1915, MS 8,265, Papers of Patrick Pearse, Trinity College Dublin.

28 Walsh, *The Pedagogy of Protest*, 278; Frank Burke, WS 694, BMH, NAI; Fearghal McGarry, *The Rising Ireland: Easter 1916* (Oxford: Oxford University Press, 2011), 64.

29 Frank Burke, WS 694, BMH, NAI.

30 Nora Kilgallon to Patrick Pearse, 6 April 1916, MS 8,265, Papers of Patrick Pearse, Trinity College Dublin. The $20,000 verdict handed down by Justice Scudder combined with legal fees, and the replacement or repair of the involved automobile, was a heavy financial burden. See *Brooklyn Daily Eagle*, 11 January 1915; *New York Times*, 18 May 1916.

31 Frank Burke, WS 694, BMH, NAI.

32 Ibid.; Dehler, 'My tenuous genealogical connection to the 1916 Easter Rising'; Office of Public Works, 'A group of ex-pupils in Irish Volunteer uniforms at St Enda's on Easter Sunday, 1916', Pearse Museum, available at: pearsemuseum.ie/gallery/#jp-carousel-39; Eddie Bohan, 'John "The Yank" Kilgallon', 1916EasterRisingCoachTour.Blogspot.ie, 18 March 2015, available at: 1916easterrisingcoachtour.blogspot.com/2015/03/john-yank-kilgallon.html.

33 Eamonn Bulfin, WS 497, BMH, NAI.

34 Michael Cremen, WS 563, BMH, NAI.

35 Eamonn Bulfin, WS 497, BMH, NAI; Michael Cremen, BMH, NAI; Stephen Ferguson, *Business as Usual: GPO Staff in 1916* (Cork: Mercier Press, 2012), 42–6.

36  Desmond Ryan, WS 724, BMH, NAI.

37  Eamonn Bulfin, WS 497, BMH, NAI.

38  Desmond Ryan, *Remembering Sion: A Chronicle of Storm and Quiet* (Dublin: Arthur Barker, 1934), 204–5.

39  John Plunkett to Defence, 22 October 1952, WMSP34REF62860, MSPC, Military Archives, Department of Defence. It is not clear whether the fur coat was Kilgallon's own or a costume appropriated from the nearby Wax Works in Henry Street. See Seamus Ua Caomhanaigh, WS 889, BMH, NAI.

40  Eamonn Bulfin, WS 497, BMH, NAI.

41  Ibid.

42  Ibid.

43  'Kilgallon's family fear he was killed in Dublin', *Brooklyn Daily Eagle*, 9 May 1916; *New York Times*, 11, 18 May 1916; *New York Tribune*, 18, 23, 25 May 1916; *Washington Post*, 23, 25 May 1916.

44  *Brooklyn Daily Eagle*, 9 May 1916.

45  'To release Kilgallon'; 'Think Kilgallon will be freed from prison'.

46  'John J. Kilgallon, an armed rebel, Britain alleges', *Brooklyn Daily Eagle*, 24 May 1916.

47  *New York Tribune*, 18 May 1916; *Washington Post*, 19 May 1916; *Los Angeles Times*, 25 May 1916; *Christian Science Monitor*, 6 June 1916; *Washington Post*, 22 August 1916.

48  Bernadette Whelan, *United States Foreign Policy and Ireland: From Empire to Independence, 1913–1929* (Dublin: Four Courts Press, 2006), 105.

49  'Wilson's plea saves Lynch … Long Island man spared', *New York Tribune*, 23 May 1916; *New York Times*, 7 June 1916; 'To intern Kilgallon, Far Rockaway boy may be held until war ends', *Brooklyn Daily Eagle*, 7 June 1916; ibid., 8 June 1916; *Washington Post*, 11 June 1916.

50  'Working for Kilgallon', *New York Times*, 4 August 1916; 'Kilgallon is set free', ibid., 26 December 1916; Series III, Box 27, Folders 369–70, Frank Lyon Polk Papers, Yale University.

51  Graham Clifford, 'Frongoch: university of the revolution', *Irish Independent*, 21 February 2016, available at: independent.ie/irish-news/1916/after-the-rising/frongoch-university-of-the-revolution-34466342.html.

52  'Kilgallon is set free'; 'British free Kilgallon, Rockaway youth held for part in Sinn Fein rebellion', *Brooklyn Daily Eagle*, 26 December 1916; 'John Kilgallon free', ibid., 28 December 1916.

53  'Rockaway youth, rebel in Ireland, writes home from prison camp', *Brooklyn Daily Eagle*, 19 February 1917; Whelan, *United States Foreign Policy and Ireland*, 107, note 11.

54  John Kilgallon, No. 8328, emergency passport application, 20 February 1917, US Passport Applications, 1795–1925, Ancestry.com.

55  *Brooklyn Daily Eagle*, 19 February 1917. This account is corroborated by Seamus Ua Caomhanaigh, WS 889, BMH, NAI.

56  John A. Kilgallon, 'New York, passenger lists, 1820–1957', Ancestry.com.

57  John A. Kilgallon, No. 179, Registrar's Report 31–9–181A, 'US, World War I draft registration cards, 1917–1918', Ancestry.com.

58 John A. Kilgallon, Service No. 102–48–42, 'WWI navy cards', New York (State) Adjutant General's Office, 'Abstracts of World War I military service, 1917–1919', Series B0808, New York State Archives, Albany, New York, Ancestry.com.

59 *Brooklyn Daily Eagle*, 14 November 1919; Maurice Francis Egan and John B. Kennedy, *The Knights of Columbus in Peace and War*, volume 2 (New Haven, CT: Knights of Columbus, 1920), 235.

60 John A. Kilgallon, '1920 US federal census', Ancestry.com; John A. Kilgallon, U0891, 'WWII draft registration, US, World War II draft registration cards, 1942', Ancestry.com.

61 *Brooklyn Daily Eagle*, 1 February 1936.

62 John A. Kilgallon to Defence, 15 December 1950, W34E9684, MSPC, Military Archives, Department of Defence.

63 Seán Nunan to J. O'Connor, 27 November 1952, MSP34REF62860, MSPC, Military Archives, Department of Defence; Michael Kennedy, 'Nunan, Seán', in McGuire and Quinn, eds, *Dictionary of Irish Biography*.

64 Joseph Sweeney to Defence, 27 October 1952, W34E9684, MSPC, Military Archives, Department of Defence; Joseph Sweeney to Defence, 24 July 1968, W34E9684, MSPC, Military Archives, Department of Defence; Tom Feeney, 'Sweeney, Joseph Aloysius', in McGuire and Quinn, eds, *Dictionary of Irish Biography*; 'Sweeney Clan: notable Sweeneys: Major General Joseph A. Sweeney', available at: cgim.org/sweeneyclan/misc/32.html.

65 Frank Burke to Defence, 22 October 1952, W34E9684, MSPC, Military Archives, Department of Defence; Desmond Ryan to Defence, 23 October 1952, W34E9684, MSPC, Military Archives, Department of Defence; Patrick Maume, 'Ryan, James', in McGuire and Quinn, eds, *Dictionary of Irish Biography*; John (Jack) Plunkett, WS 865, BMH, NAI. Sam O'Reilly was one of those New York friends; his pension was awarded in 1943 (Defence, MSPC W34E8529). He used to visit 'Jack' Kilgallon in Far Rockaway in later years, personal communication with Geraldine O'Reilly Johnson, 24 April 2016. See also John Garvey, 'Sam O'Reilly', in *Easter Rising Commemorative Book* (New York: United Irish Counties Association, 2016), 69–70; and Mike McCormack, 'Padraig Pearse remembered', *The Irish Echo*, 3 May 2016, available at: irishecho.com/2016/05/padraic-pearse-remembered/.

66 Joseph Sweeney to Defence, 27 October 1952, W34E9684, MSPC, Military Archives, Department of Defence; John Plunkett to Defence, 22 October 1952, WMSP34REF62860, MSPC, Military Archives, Department of Defence.

67 Because it was retroactive to December 1949, Kilgallon's first payment was eventually a lump sum of approximately $228 in 1953. On what Grade E signified see Patrick Brennan, 'Origin, scope and content of the collection', in Caitriona Crowe, ed., *Guide to the Military Service (1916–1923) Pensions Collection* (Dublin: Óglaigh na hÉireann, 2012), 23.

68 Kilgallon was in Dublin on 22 June 1953, and stayed at the Central Hotel, W34E9684, MSPC, Military Archives, Department of Defence. They travelled on the SS *United States*, departing New York on 8 May 1953 and returning on 21 July 1953. See 'New York, passenger lists, 1820–1957', Ancestry.com.

69 'Social and personal', *Irish Times*, 26 June 1953: 7. Sean T. O'Kelly was in and out of the GPO during Easter Week. See Clair Wills, *Dublin 1916: The Siege of the GPO* (Cambridge: Harvard University Press, 2009), 41, 137, 178.

70 'My mother who had known John described him as a very quiet, almost meek man. She could not believe he would have participated in such a violent event.' See Dehler, 'My tenuous genealogical connection to the 1916 Easter Rising'.

71 John A. Kilgallon to Defence, 10 August 1960, W34E9684, MSPC, Military Archives, Department of Defence; 1916 medal authorisation, Defence, 11 November 1960, W34E9684, MSPC, Military Archives, Department of Defence; Eamon Murphy, 'Martin, Eamon', in McGuire and Quinn, eds, *Dictionary of Irish Biography*.

72 John A. Kilgallon to Defence, 15 June 1966, W34E9684, MSPC, Military Archives, Department of Defence. Apparently he had not cashed a 1961 check while he was in the hospital, so Defence stopped payment. See John A. Kilgallon to Defence, 30 July 1966, W34E9684, MSPC, Military Archives, Department of Defence.

73 Diarmaid Ferriter, '"Always in danger of finding myself with nothing at all': the Military Service Pension and the battle for material survival, 1925–1955', in Crowe, ed., *Guide to the Military Service (1916–1923) Pensions Collection*, 130, 132.

74 Joseph Sweeney to Defence, 21 February 1972, W34E9684, MSPC, Military Archives, Department of Defence.

75 Joseph Sweeney to Defence, 24 July 1968, W34E9684, MSPC, Military Archives, Department of Defence; Defence to Agnes Cosgrove, 16 March 1972, W34E9684, MSPC, Military Archives, Department of Defence.

## 22. JAMES CONNOLLY'S 'GOOD END': THE IRISH RELIEF FUND BAZAAR POSTER

1 Details on Connolly's life in the United States can be found in Carl Reeve and Ann Barton Reeve, *James Connolly and the United States: The Road to the 1916 Irish Rebellion* (Atlantic Highlands, NJ: Humanities Press, 1978). Other biographies include: C. Desmond Greaves, *The Life and Times of James Connolly* (New York: International Publishers, 1961), and Donal Nevin, *James Connolly: 'A Full Life'* (Dublin: Gill and Macmillan, 2005). For commentary on his intellectual life, see David Howell, *A Lost Left: Three Studies in Socialism and Nationalism* (Chicago: University of Chicago Press, 1986); Gregory Dobbins, 'Whenever green is red: James Connolly and postcolonial theory', *Nepantla: Views from the South* 1:3 (2000): 605–48; and David Lloyd, 'Why read Connolly?', *Interventions: International Journal of Postcolonial Studies* 10:1 (25 June 2008): 116–23.

2 Elizabeth Gurley Flynn, *The Rebel Girl: An Autobiography, My First Life (1906–1926)* (New York: International Publishers, 1955), 74–5.

3 *New York Times*, 5 November 1905.

4 Flynn, *The Rebel Girl*, 76.

5 *New York Tribune*, 15 October 1916.

6  Patrick L. Quinlan, 'James Connolly: Irish republican leader and international socialist', *The New Age* 10:492 (26 January 1922): 7.

7  Gary Owens, 'Constructing the Martyrs: the Manchester executions and the nationalist imagination', in Lawrence W. McBride, ed., *Images, Icons and the Irish Nationalist Imagination* (Dublin: Four Courts Press, 1999), 18. Owens quotes Murray Edelman, *The Symbolic Uses of Politics* (Urbana: University of Illinois Press, 1964), 5.

8  *New York Times*, 14 October 1916.

9  Ross Wilson, *New York and First World War: Shaping an American City* (Farnham, Surrey: Ashgate Publishing Ltd, 2014), 102.

10  *The Gaelic American* reported on 4 November 1916, that the bazaar had earned 'at least' $40,000.

11  Sighle Breathnach-Lynch, *Ireland's Art Ireland's History: Representing Ireland 1845 to Present* (Omaha, NE: Creighton University Press, 2007), 246; 'Marches and murals, linking 1916 and the present', *Ireland in Schools*, available at: iisresource.org/Documents/0A3_Marches_Murals_1916_Present.pdf.

12  Fiona Barber, *Art in Ireland since 1910* (London: Reakton Books, 2013), 33, 212.

13  Sighle Breathnach-Lynch, 'The Easter Rising 1916: constructing a canon in art and artefacts', *History Ireland* 5:1 (spring 1997): 38; see also Breathnach-Lynch, *Ireland's Art Ireland's History*, 135–57, 183–249.

14  Barber, *Art in Ireland since 1910*, 33; Breathnach-Lynch, 'The Easter Rising', 37.

15  An associate of Ward and Gow wrote that 'small posters displayed on the station platforms everywhere throughout the routes of the subway and elevated systems afford an ideal opportunity for repeat impressions upon the eyes and minds of millions of New York City's active industrious people.' See W. J. Lockwood, 'Small posters in New York City', *Advertising and Selling* (26 July 1919): 10.

16  Max Gallo, *The Poster in History*, with essays by Carlo Arturo Quintavalle and Charles Flowers (New York and London: W. W. Norton and Co., 2001), 190.

17  Ibid., 185–203.

18  There is even some resemblance to the 'Mulligan Guards' of nineteenth-century New York showmen Edward Harrigan and Tony Hart. See Mick Moloney, 'Harrigan, Hart, and Braham: Irish America and the birth of the American musical', in John P. Harrington, ed., *Irish Theater in America* (Syracuse: Syracuse University Press, 2009), 5–14.

19  *New York Times*, 4 June 1916.

20  *San Francisco Chronicle*, 30 April, 22 May 1916; *Hartford Courant*, 30 April 1916; *New York Tribune*, 4 May 1916.

21  Reeve and Reeve, *James Connolly and the United States*, 27; Greaves, *The Life and Times of James Connolly*, 112.

22  *Daily People*, 15 September 1902.

23  Nevin, *James Connolly*, 281.

24  Ibid., 250.

25  Ibid., 252.

26 *Hartford Courant*, 30 April, 13 May 1916; *San Francisco Chronicle*, 29 April, 22 May 1916; *Anaconda Standard*, 4 May 1916; *Fergus County Democrat*, 4 May 1916.

27 James Connolly, 'Erin's hope', *The New Review: A Critical Survey of International Socialism* 4:6 (June 1916): 192.

28 *The Day Book*, 12 May 1916; *The West Virginian*, 11 May 1916; *Columbus Ledger*, 11 May 1916; *San Francisco Chronicle*, 22 May 1916.

29 Pat Toohy (*sic*) in a letter to Ann and Carl Reeve, 13 October 1977, TAM.317, Box 1, Folder 8, Carl Reeve Papers, The Tamiment Library and Robert F. Wagner Labor Archives, Bobst Library, New York University.

30 *Washington Post*, 13 May 1916.

31 *Kentucky Irish-American*, 20 May 1916.

32 'Statement of amounts advanced in behalf of the Irish Relief Fund by John Devoy', MS 18,157 (21), John Devoy Papers, Manuscript Collection, National Library of Ireland; *New York Times*, 18, 2, May 1916.

33 *New York Times*, 4, 15 October 1916; *New York Tribune*, 15 October 1916.

34 Jeremiah would announce in later years, 'I am not a Socialist'. He also served as an attorney for a union trying to bar aliens from subway construction jobs in New York, a project that Connolly, who often worked with immigrants from southern and eastern Europe, would have abhorred. See *New York Tribune*, 25 March 1919, 4 July 1918.

35 *New York Times*, 14 October 1916.

36 Ibid., 30 September 1916; *New York Sun*, 2, 19 October 1916; *Atlanta Constitution*, 30 September 1916; *Boston Daily Globe*, 30 September 1916; *Washington Post*, 30 September 1916.

37 *The Fatherland* 3:13 (3 November 1915): cover, 259.

38 *New York Times*, 4 October 1916.

39 Ibid.

40 Ibid.

41 *New York Sun*, 2 October 1916.

42 *New York Times*, 22 September 1916; *The Gaelic American*, 7 October 1916.

43 *New York Times*, 4 October 1916; *New York Sun*, 18 October 1916.

44 *New York Tribune*, 17 October 1916; *The Gaelic American*, 21 October 1916.

45 *New York Sun*, 15 October 1916.

46 *New York Times*, 15 October 1916.

47 *The Gaelic American*, 7 October 1916.

48 *New York Times*, 15 October 1916.

49 *New York Sun*, 15 October 1916.

50 *Grand Rapids Press*, 1 August 1916; Bernardus Schutte, '1900 United States federal census', Ancestry.com.

51 'Join the engineers and make American history, first replacement regiment of engineers // Schutte', POS–WWI–US, no. 6 (C size), Library of Congress Prints and Photographs Division.

52 *Grand Rapids Press*, 1 August 1916; *New York Clipper*, 15 July 1916; *New York Times*, 1 August 1916.

53 *Grand Rapids Press*, 11 November 1917; Mitchell A. Schutte, 'New York, abstracts of World War I military service, 1917–1919', Ancestry.com.

54 Nora Connolly, *The Irish Rebellion of 1916: The Unbroken Tradition* (New York: Boni and Liveright Inc., 1918), 193.

55 *New York Tribune*, 2 October 1916; *The Gaelic American*, 21 October 1916.

56 *New York Tribune*, 15 October 1916.

57 Nora Connolly O'Brien, *A Rebel Father* (Dublin: Four Masters, 1975), 209–21; Mrs Nora Connolly O'Brien, Witness Statement 286, Bureau of Military History, National Archives of Ireland, 15–23, available at: bureauofmilitaryhistory.ie/reels/bmh/BMH.WS0286.pdf; *New York Times*, 30 August 1916.

58 *New York Tribune*, 12 July 1918; *Boston Daily Globe*, 8, 25 February 1916; Eileen O'Brien, 'Nora Connolly O'Brien', *Irish Times*, 24 April 1976: 5; *New York Tribune*, 25 October 1917; *New York Times*, 5 November 1917.

59 Connolly O'Brien, *A Rebel Father*, 321.

## 23. THE OTHER NARRATIVE OF 'SISTERHOOD' IN 1916: IRISH AND IRISH-AMERICAN SUFFRAGISTS

1 'American progress', *Irish Citizen*, 27 February 1915: 314. I am grateful to Iris Bedford and the staff at the Department of Early Printed Books at Trinity College Dublin for providing me with access to the original copies of the *Irish Citizen* in their collection (copies which belonged to Hanna Sheehy Skeffington and were given to the library by A. D. Sheehy Skeffington in memory of Hanna's son Owen Sheehy Skeffington).

2 I would like to thank Kathleen Stein Smith, Paul Dunphy, Deborah Daniele, and the rest of the Giovatto Library staff at Fairleigh Dickinson University for their assistance procuring numerous resources for this study, particularly issues of *The Suffragist*.

3 Sadhbh Walshe, 'The sisterhood of the Easter Rising', *New York Times*, 16 March 2016.

4 Louise Ryan, *Irish Feminism and the Vote: An Anthology of the* Irish Citizen *Newspaper 1912–1920* (Dublin: Follens, 1996), 5.

5 It was not until Rosemary Cullen Owens's *Smashing Times: A History of Irish Women's Suffrage Movement, 1889–1922* (Dublin: Attic Press, 1984), and then Cliona Murphy's more comprehensive study, *The Women's Suffrage Movement and Irish Society in the Early Twentieth Century* (Philadelphia: Temple University Press, 1989), that the Irish suffrage movement received serious historical and critical attention. Prior to these studies, if the Irish movement was mentioned at all, it was 'in passing' and referenced as either 'a shadow of the British [suffragist] movement' or a 'weak extension of the Irish Nationalist movement'. See Murphy, *The Women's Suffrage Movement*, 1. More recent studies of the Irish

suffrage movement include biographies of key figures, overviews of the movement as a whole, histories of specific suffrage organisations, and anthologies of critical essays.

6 Cliona Murphy briefly discusses the connection between Irish and American suffragists in *The Woman's Suffrage Movement* and discusses it in more detail in '"The tune of the stars and stripes": the American influence on the Irish suffrage movement', in Maria Luddy and Cliona Murphy, eds, *Women Surviving: Studies in Irish Women's History in the Nineteenth and Twentieth Centuries* (Dublin: Poolbeg, 1990), 181–2. Surprisingly, there have been few studies – if any – since Murphy's 1989 article that have explored the Irish and American suffrage connection in any depth.

7 Hasia Diner, *Erin's Daughters in America: Irish Immigrant Women in the Nineteenth Century* (Baltimore, MD: Johns Hopkins University Press, 1983), 151.

8 In 1871, the editor of the Catholic newspaper *The Pilot* ranted against suffrage as an 'unjust, unreasonable, unspiritual abnormality' (Maureen Dezell, *Irish America: Coming into Clover* (New York: Doubleday, 2000), 98), and in 1894 the *Irish World* ran a full article on Cardinal Gibbons's opposition to woman suffrage 'for the sake of Womanhood', emphasising Gibbons's argument that '[t]he proper sphere of women is in the home, and the more influence she gains in public life the more she will lose in private life.' See 'Woman suffrage', *Irish World*, 13 October 1894. By the early twentieth century, the cause of women's suffrage had won some converts in the church. For example, see Diner, *Erin's Daughters*, 184, note 3; also see the *Irish Citizen*'s four-part series on 'An American priest on votes for women', 19, 26 December 1914, 2, 9 January 1915.

9 Diner, *Erin's Daughters*, 147.

10 James R. Barrett, *The Irish Way: Becoming American in the Multiethnic City* (New York: Penguin Press, 2012; Kindle version), 217.

11 Sally Barr Ebest, 'Irish American women: forgotten first-wave feminists', *Journal of Feminist Scholarship* (autumn 2012): 60. Maureen Dezell also points out that some of feminism's 'founding mothers', including suffragist Susan B. Anthony, 'were active in the temperance movement, a reform effort disdained by many and particularly noxious to the Irish, who were so frequently the targets of nineteenth-century nativist Protestant social reform.' See Dezell, *Irish America*, 99.

12 Barrett, *The Irish Way*, 217.

13 The suffragist movement in the United States effectively began with the Women's Rights Convention in Seneca Falls, New York in 1848; the movement in Ireland began in the 1870s, most notably with the formation of the Irish Women's Suffrage and Local Government Association in 1876. Selected texts that provide a history of the Irish suffrage movement include: Cullen Owens, *Smashing Times* and Murphy, *The Women's Suffrage Movement*. For a concise overview of the Irish movement, see the introduction to Ryan's *Irish Feminism and the Vote*. Selected texts that provide a history of the American suffrage movement include: Ida Husted Harper, ed., *The History of Woman Suffrage Volume VI, 1900–1920* (New York: National American Woman Suffrage Association, 1922); Aileen S. Kraditor, *The Ideas of the Woman Suffrage Movement: 1890–1920* (New York: W. W. Norton, 1981;

original publication by Columbia University Press, 1965); Mari J. and Paul Buhle, eds, *The Concise History of Woman Suffrage: Selections from the Classic Work of Stanton, Anthony, Gage, and Harper* (Chicago: University of Illinois Press, 1978); Marjorie Spruill Wheeler, ed., *One Woman, One Vote: Rediscovering the Woman Suffrage Movement* (Troutdale, OR: NewSage Press, 1995); Linda G. Ford, *Iron-Jawed Angels: The Suffrage Militancy of the National Woman's Party, 1912–1920* (Lanham, MD: University Press of America, 1991); and Christine A. Lunardini, *From Equal Suffrage to Equal Rights: Alice Paul and the National Woman's Party, 1910–1928* (New York: New York University Press, 1986).

14 In Ireland at this time, women could vote in municipal elections. In the United States, women could vote in some western states (as of 1910, for example, women in Wyoming, Colorado, Utah, Idaho, and Washington could vote).

15 As many have noted, Hannah Sheehy and Francis Skeffington combined their last names when they got married as a statement of their shared commitment to equality of the sexes.

16 Margaret Ward, 'The political career of Hanna Sheehy Skeffington: challenging feminism and republicanism', Hanna's House online, 1.

17 Ryan, *Irish Feminism*, 8.

18 In its early years, the *Irish Citizen* was edited by both Francis Sheehy Skeffington and James Cousins, but after Cousins left Ireland in 1913, Sheehy Skeffington became the sole editor.

19 Ryan, *Irish Feminism*, 8.

20 Murphy, 'The tune', in Luddy and Murphy, eds, *Women Surviving*, 183.

21 'On criticism', *Irish Citizen*, 18 October 1913.

22 As Ford notes in *Iron-Jawed Angels*, 45, the CU originally began as a NAWSA committee in 1913, headed by Burns and Paul. Working in 1914 as the 'independent Congressional Union,' they upped the intensity of their power politics by utilizing a British-style, national "party responsibility" policy, to the shocked dismay of NAWSA'. In 1916, the CU formed the Woman's Party 'as leverage to open the political system to women' (45). At the CU Convention in 1917, the CU and Woman's Party merged to become the National Woman's Party. See Ford, *Iron-Jawed Angels*, 131. Although their relationship and history are some-what complicated, the leadership, membership, philosophy, tactics, and goals of the CU and NWP overlapped substantially even before they officially merged. For the sake of consistency and clarity, I will refer to the Congressional Union and the National Woman's Party as the CU/NWP throughout this chapter.

23 'Women organize new suffrage move', *New York Times*, 1 April 1915: 24.

24 Ibid. Mainstream publications in New York such as the *New York Times*, *The Sun*, the *New York Tribune*, *New York Daily People*, and even the *Brooklyn Daily Eagle* frequently reported suffrage news – including news of the CU/NWP – with demonstrated interest. In at least one article, the *New York Daily People* quoted from CU/NWP's newspaper, *The Suffragist*. See 'The vote on creating suffrage committee', 26 January 1915. The New York *Irish American* also reported limited (but generally anti-) suffrage news. See, for example,

'Sins against suffrage', 9 May 1914; 'Authors favor suffrage', 9 May 1909; 'Dublin suffragettes – amusing incidents – four of them put in zoo', 17 August 1912.

25 'Militants versus constitutionalists in America', *Irish Citizen*, 3 July 1915. Reprinted in the *Irish Citizen* from the *New York Call* as an 'excellent summary of the divergencies of opinion and method between two branches of the woman suffrage movement in the United States', 50.

26 'Asquithianism in America', *Irish Citizen*, 23 January 1915: 277.

27 Sidney Bland, '"Never quite as committed as we'd like": the suffrage militancy of Lucy Burns', *The Journal of Long Island History* 17:2 (1981): 14. Prior to Burns's tenure as editor of *The Suffragist*, it was edited by Rheta Childe Dorr.

28 Ibid., 4.

29 Christine A. Lunardini, *From Equal Suffrage to Equal Rights: Alice Paul and the National Woman's Party, 1910–1928* (New York: New York University Press, 1986), 9. Burns's experiences in jail with other suffragists were well-publicised in both suffrage papers and the mainstream press. For example see 'Lucy Burns was made fast to bars, she says: story of indignities smuggled from workhouse to suffrage headquarters', *The Sun*, 17 November 1917: 1; 'Suffragists to obtain writ: Occoquan prisoners to obtain habeas corpus proceedings', *New York Times*, 18 November 1917.

30 Amelia R. Fry, 'Conversations with Alice Paul: woman suffrage and the Equal Rights Amendment', Suffragists Oral History Project (Regents University of California, 1976), 48.

31 Identification of Burns's ancestry is based on a review of census records; see, for example, US Census Bureau, thirteenth census of the United States, 1910, Brooklyn Ward 22, Kings, New York, Roll T624_971, Page 4A, Enumeration District 0569, FHL microfilm 1374984, National Archives and Records Administration, Washington, DC. Lucy Burns's mother is referred to as 'Anna' in her obituary (*New York Times*, 11 October 1912: 11), but as 'Annie' and 'Ann' in census records; I will refer to her as 'Anna' here. All that is known of Anna's parents is that their last name was 'Early' (e.g., see death notice for 'Anna Early Burns' in the *Brooklyn Daily Eagle*, 11 October 1912: 24) and they were born in Ireland (as documented by census records); genealogical research conducted to date has not been able to determine more specifics. At this time, there is no book-length biography of Lucy Burns and existing articles about her do not provide any more specifics about her Irish ancestry. Ford, in *Iron-Jawed Angels*, refers to Sidney Bland as Burns's biographer and J. D. Zahniser and Amelia R. Fry refer to Bland's article as the 'best source of information about her'. See J. D. Zahniser and Amelia R. Fry, *Alice Paul: Claiming Power* (New York: Oxford University Press, 2014). While Bland's article, 'Never quite as committed', 4–23, is informative, it does not provide insight into Burns's heritage other than identifying her as an 'Irish Catholic from Brooklyn' (and he erroneously identifies her father, Edward Burns, as Irish, although census records indicate that he is Scottish and Canadian).

32 As reported in Edward Burns's obituary, *Brooklyn Eagle*, 18 May 1914: 1.

33 Bland identifies Pierrepont Street in Brooklyn as the childhood home of Lucy and the Burns family ('Never quite as committed', 5), but the Pierrepont Street address was actually

the home – in later years – of Lucy's brother Robert Burns and his wife. See obituary of Robert Burns, *New York Times*, 21 August 1964. Numerous newspaper articles of the time, along with census records, show that the Burns family lived at 46 Sterling Place and then in 1900 purchased a home at 904 President Street. For example see *Brooklyn Daily Eagle* articles on 18 November 1913, 18 May 1914 and *Brooklyn Life* articles on 21 April 1900, 14 June 1902.

34 Bland, 'Never quite as committed', 7, 19.

35 The *Brooklyn Daily Eagle* published numerous articles on Burns and suffrage. Examples include: 'Brooklyn women in suffrage march', 4 May 1912 (Lucy's sisters Helen and Anna are among those listed as marchers); 'Lucy Burns addresses women voters', 18 August 1913: 22; 'Suffrage news', 30 July 1913: 18 (includes a picture of Burns); 'Miss Burns awaits arrest for writing on capital walks', 18 November 1913 (includes a picture of 'Miss Lucy Burns', 'Brooklyn Suffragist'); 'Woman's Party plans meeting in interest of Woman suffrage', 28 May 1917: 18.

36 Bland, 'Never quite as committed', 20.

37 For example, Ford writes that '[t]he Catholic Lucy Burns had a very close and devoted relationship with her family. She would on numerous occasions return home to see to their concerns during a suffrage campaign'. See *Iron-Jawed Angels*, 25. Sidney Bland, quoting from an interview with Alice Paul on 8 May 1969, says that Burns 'was so devoted to her Irish Catholic family that she was "never committed quite as much as we'd like"'. See 'Techniques of persuasion: the National Woman's Party and suffrage, 1913–1919' (Ph.D. thesis, George Washington University, 1972), 180. And in an oral history in the 1970s, Alice Paul stated that Burns was 'a very devout Catholic'; although she did not keep in touch with Burns after their work together in the suffrage movement, she said 'I think she devoted herself entirely to her family and her church'. See Fry, 'Conversations with Alice Paul', 257.

38 Bland, 'Never quite as committed', 16.

39 The Nineteenth Amendment, which gave all women in the United States the right to vote, was passed by congress on 4 June 1919 and ratified on 18 August 1920.

40 Bland, 'Never quite as committed', 4.

41 Lucy Burns, 'Susan B. Anthony', *Suffragist*, 13 February 1915: 5.

42 Bland, 'Never quite as committed', 19.

43 Burns died on 22 December 1966 and is buried at Holy Cross Cemetery in Brooklyn.

44 Barbara Sicherman and Carol Hurd Green, eds, *Notable American Women: The Modern Period: A Biographical Dictionary*, volume 4 (Cambridge: Belknap Press of Harvard University Press, 1980), 125.

45 Inez Haynes Irwin, *The Story of the Woman's Party* (New York: Harcourt, Brace and Company, 1921), Project Gutenburg, 17.

46 See, for example, ibid.

47 Bland, 'Never quite as committed', 10.

48 'How long must women wait?', *Suffragist*, 17 February 1917: 6.

49 Ford, *Iron-Jawed Angels*, 25.

50 Ibid., 48.

51 'Putting suffrage first', *Suffragist*, 26 August 1916.

52 Burns, 'Susan B. Anthony', 6.

53 Kraditor, *The Ideas of the Woman Suffrage Movement*, 280. It should be noted, however, that Kraditor's study relegates Burns to one footnote and one appendix entry.

54 Other Irish-American suffragists, such as Margaret Foley, Margaret Hinchey, and Catherine Flanagan, also made significant contributions to the cause as 'workers' and 'organizers'. Their work was primarily for the NAWSA, although Catherine Flanagan eventually left that organisation to work with the CU/NWP.

55 Invitation to prospective members of the Committee of One Hundred, *America* 23 (2 October 1920): 555. Martin's membership on the Committee of One Hundred on Ireland was reported by the New York *Nation* 111 (13 October 1920): 397.

56 'The Irish committee at work', New York *Nation* 111 (10 November 1920): 530–1. Jane Addams was among those selected to serve on the American Commission on Ireland.

57 Maria Luddy, 'Separate but equal', *Irish Times*, 17 October 2012, available at: irishtimes.com/culture/heritage/century/century-women-and-the-vote/separate-but-equal-1.553482.

58 In July 1912, for example, Prime Minister Asquith visited Dublin and was scheduled to speak with John Redmond at the Royal Theatre. Both Asquith and Redmond had blocked any effort for women's suffrage, and Asquith had refused to meet with any suffrage groups during his visit. In response, the IWFL decided to give Asquith a peaceful, though vocal, 'suffragists' welcome' (Leah Levenson and Jerry H. Natterstad, *Hanna Sheehy-Skeffington: Irish Feminist* (Syracuse: Syracuse University Press, 1986), 40), but three English suffragists in Dublin planned a more violent 'welcome', which involved throwing a hatchet at Asquith and Redmond as they travelled in an open carriage and attempting to set a fire in the Royal Theatre. See Rosemary Cullen Owens, *A Social History of Women in Ireland, 1870–1970* (Dublin: Gill and Macmillan, 2005). After these incidents, the IWFL 'immediately denied all knowledge of the presence of English suffragettes in Dublin', and stated that they 'had no association with their English counterparts beyond unity of demand'.

59 In *Women, Press, and Politics during the Irish Revival* (Syracuse: Syracuse University Press, 2007; Kindle edition), Karen Steele notes that Irish women used the press as a 'medium of exchange' within Ireland, but newspapers such as the *Irish Citizen*, circulated internationally, also functioned as a 'medium of exchange' with women in other countries.

60 'Advancing America', *Irish Citizen*, 12 December 1914: 236–7.

61 Publication dates of articles referenced: 'How the vote was won in Illinois', 10 January 1914; 'Women displace Southern Pacific', 10 January 1914; 'American view', 4 July 1914; 'Woman's suffrage in America: an Irish woman's impression', 13 August 1914; 'American affairs', 14 November 1914; 'Advancing America', 12 December 1914; 'An American priest on votes for women', parts I, II, III, and IV, 19, 26 December 1914, 2, 9 January 1915.

62 Murphy, 'The tune', in Luddy and Murphy, eds, *Women Surviving*, 184.

63 Ward, 'The political career of Hanna Sheehy Skeffington', 2.

64 See, for example: 'Votes and Home Rule', 11 April 1914; 'Suffragists and Home Rule', 23 May 1914; 'Amending Home Rule', 13 June 1914; 'Home Rule and suffrage', 15 August 1914; and 'Home Rule in September: suffrage when?', 17 July 1915.

65 E. A. Browning, 'Suffrage first', *Irish Citizen*, 13 June 1914: 29.

66 Alice Park, 'Suffrage in England', *Suffragist*, 14 November 1914: 7. Park, the founder of the Women's International League for Peace and Freedom, praises the *Irish Citizen* newspaper and Hanna Sheehy Skeffington in particular.

67 The drawing on the cover of the 8 April 1916 issue of *The Suffragist*, for example, clearly identifies the NWP as the 'Woman's Party for "Suffrage First"', as do numerous articles on 'Suffrage First'. In a 'Suffrage First' article in the 25 March 1916 issue, *The Suffragist* proclaimed that '"Suffrage first" is good democracy, and still better tactics.' Yet another 'Suffrage First' article, 17 June 1916, quoted an 'eloquent speech' at an NWP convention, which called for 'votes for women right away!': 'Have women no part in world issues? ... To believe that we have no part in the determination of national events is to believe that women are not human beings.'

68 'The wrong time', *New York Times*, 30 November 1915: 12.

69 'Suffrage first', *Suffragist*, 4 December 1915: 7.

70 'Votes for women now!', *Irish Citizen*, 15 August 1914: 100. In 'The duty of suffragists' (published alongside 'Votes for women now!'), Hanna Sheehy Skeffington rails against those who ask women to put down their suffrage banners to 'help the men' by knitting, nursing, and feeding, and she sends a 'reply to all those who would enlist our services – Suffrage First!': 'The suffragist who turns aside from the cause of Votes for Women at this hour,' she warns, 'is helping to put back the clock.' See *Irish Citizen*, 15 August 1914: 100–1).

71 Margaret Ward, '"Rolling up the map of suffrage": Irish suffrage and the First World War', in Louise Ryan and Margaret Ward, eds, *Irish Women and the Vote: Becoming Citizens* (Dublin: Irish Academic Press, 2007), 141.

72 Ryan, *Irish Feminism*, 11. The *Irish Citizen* of 26 June 1915, reprinted an article from *Votes for Women* (the suffrage paper of the WSPU) which noted that an editorial from 'this week's "Nation"' stated that Francis Sheehy Skeffington was '[c]harged under Section 27 of the Defence of the Realm Act, with making "statements likely to be prejudicial in recruiting"' in a speech in Dublin and was 'sentenced, not merely to six months' hard labour, but to a further six months ... unless he found bail'. He was '[r]efused treatment as a political prisoner', so 'he adopted the hunger-strike, and as we go to press we hear that he has been released "owing to his health being impaired from the effects" of this strike', 45.

73 Murphy, *The Women's Suffrage Movement*, 71.

74 F. Sheehy Skeffington, 'Suffrage in America', *Irish Citizen*, 11 September 1915: 90.

75 During his 1915 visit to the United States, Francis Sheehy Skeffington published numerous articles on American suffrage in the *Irish Citizen*: 'Suffrage in the air', 28 August 1915: 82; 'Suffrage in America', 11 September 1915: 90; 'American politics and woman suffrage', 18 September 1915: 96; 'American notes', 25 September 1915: 104; 'American notes', 2 October 1915; 'The Hearst newspapers and the women's movement',

9 October 1915: 120; 'Suffrage at the theatre', 16 October 1915: 128; 'American notes', 23 October 1915: 136; 'American notes', 6 November 1915: 152; 'American notes', 13 November 1915: 160; 'The American "defeats"', 20 November 1915: 168; and 'American notes', 27 November 1915: 176.

76 Sheehy Skeffington, 'Suffrage in America'.

77 Barrett, *The Irish Way*, 217.

78 See Sheehy Skeffington's indictment of American political machines in 'American notes', 6 November 1915: 152 and in 'The American "defeats"', 168.

79 Sheehy Skeffington, 'American notes', 2 October 1915.

80 Sheehy Skeffington, 'American notes', 25 September 1915: 104.

81 As Sally Barr Ebest notes in *The Banshees: A Literary History of Irish American Women Writers* (Syracuse: Syracuse University Press, 2013; Kindle edition), Dr Gertrude Kelly was an 'Irish-born feminist' who 'issued a call for "women of Irish blood" to organize an American chapter of Cumann na mBan (Irish Women's Council) to collect funds for Irish volunteers'. Barr Ebest also notes that Kelly was among a group of women, including Hanna Sheehy Skeffington, who participated in a strike against British ships at Chelsea Pier in 1920.

82 Francis Elizabeth Willard and Mary Ashton Rice Livermore, eds, *American Women: Fifteen Hundred Biographies with Over 1,400 Portraits*, volume 2 (New York: Mast, Crowell, and Kirkpatrick, 1897), 517.

83 Mary Walton, *A Woman's Crusade: Alice Paul and the Battle for the Ballot* (New York: Palgrave Macmillan, 2010), 46.

84 Jane Bernard-Powers, 'O'Reilly, Leonora', American National Biography Online.

85 'American militants', *Irish Citizen*, 2 October 1915.

86 Sheehy Skeffington, 'American notes', 13 November 1915: 160.

87 Irish Americans he mentions in this article include 'an ex-Lieutenant-Governor of Kansas, named Morgan' and 'a legal officer in New York City, named O'Leary' (neither of whom in Sheehy Skeffington's estimation 'did much credit to Irish oratory'); a labour leader, Frank P. Walsh, who was 'born in America of Irish parents'; Leonora O'Reilly, who is 'Irish of the second generation and looks forward to the day when she can visit the land of her parents' birth and help to ameliorate the condition of its women'; Mr Edmond McKenna, of the 'Masses' staff; and 'Miss K.D. Blake, head of the Woman Teachers' organisation for suffrage'. See Sheehy Skeffington, 'American notes', 27 November 1915: 176.

88 As reported on the front page of the 11 December 1915 *Irish Citizen*, Francis Sheehy Skeffington sailed on the *St Louis* from New York on 11 December 1915.

89 'Suffrage in Ireland', *Suffragist*, 15 April 1916.

90 Joanne Mooney Eichacker, *Irish Republican Women in America: Lecture Tours, 1916–1925* (Dublin: Irish Academic Press, 2003), 14.

91 Ibid.

92 As reported in the *New York Times*, 11 June 1916, the 'court-martial which tried Captain Bowen-Colthurst on the charge of shooting F. Sheehy Skeffington, editor of The Irish

Citizen, and two others, during the recent rebellion in Ireland, has found him guilty, but insane, at the time of the shooting'. See 'Capt. Colthurst guilty', 12. Hanna Sheehy Skeffington gives her account of the court martial in *British Militarism as I Have Known It* (New York: The Donnelly Press, 1917), 26–7. Also see 'Court martial finds Capt Bowen-Colthurst "guilty but insane"', *Century Ireland*, 12 June 1916 and Leah Levenson, *With Wooden Sword: A Portrait of Francis Sheehy-Skeffington* (Lebanon, HW: UPNE/ Northeastern University Press, 1983), 235.

93 Ward, 'Rolling up the map of suffrage', in Ryan and Ward, eds, *Irish Women and the Vote*, 150. In the archived copies of the *Irish Citizen* at Trinity College Dublin, a flyer for the '*Irish Citizen* Fund' appears bound between the July and September 1916 issues; this flyer explains that the money will be used to 'clear off existing liabilities' and continue the *Irish Citizen*.

94 '"Irish Citizen" continues publication', *Suffragist*, 2 December 1916. In its December 1916 article about the *Irish Citizen* resuming publication, *The Suffragist* seems to suggest that the paper had just recently resumed, but there was actually a 'Memorial Number' of the *Irish Citizen* issued in July 1916, as well as issues in September and October of 1916. There were obviously delays in the mail between Ireland and America during the war and the ongoing fight for Irish independence (these mail delays are, in fact, noted in the *Irish Citizen* as early as 12 December 1914, and the delays surely got worse after the Rising).

95 Sheehy Skeffington, *British Militarism As I Have Known It*, 30.

96 A good friend of her late husband who lived in New York City, J. F. Byrne, convinced Hanna to make the trip, despite the fact that she had to sneak into the United States under another name because the British government would not give her a passport.

97 Levenson and Natterstad, *Hanna Sheehy-Skeffington*, 101.

98 Sharon Ouditt, *Women Writers of the First World War: An Annotated Bibliography* (New York: Routledge, 2000), 81. *British Militarism as I Have Known It* was first published in New York by Donnelly Press in 1917 and reprinted by The Kerryman Limited in 1946. It should be noted that while the published digest of Sheehy Skeffington's lectures from her 1917–18 American tour is titled *British Militarism as I Have Known It*, the advertised title of her lectures actually changed to 'What does Ireland want?' after the United States entered the war and Sheehy Skeffington intensified her call for US recognition of the Irish Republic. See Eichacker, *Irish Republican Women in America*, 59. Sheehy Skeffington also published another pamphlet, *Impressions of Sinn Fein in America* (Dublin: Davis Publishing Company, 1919), based on her 1917–18 tour in the United States.

99 Sheehy Skeffington, *British Militarism As I Have Known It*, 26.

100 Ibid., 30. The Proclamation of the Provisional Government of the Irish Republic positioned women as equals not only in its direct address to 'Irishmen and Irishwomen', but also in its call for the 'allegiance of every Irishman and Irishwoman' and for a government representative of 'the whole people of Ireland and elected by the suffrages of all her men and women'.

101 Eichacker, *Irish Republican Women in America*, 59, also see 47.

102 The meeting with Wilson occurred on 11 January 1918; Sheehy Skeffington was part of a delegation of 38 women. See Levenson and Natterstad, *Hanna Sheehy-Skeffington*, 106; Eichacker, *Irish Republican Women*, 81.

103 Ward, 'The political career of Hanna Sheehy Skeffington', 12.

104 Murphy, *The Women's Suffrage Movement*, 46.

105 Attention by American suffragists to the connection between Home Rule and Irish women's suffrage was certainly evident before 1916. As David Brundage notes, one of the 'central demands' in the landmark May 1912 suffragist demonstration in New York City 'was the extension of the vote to Irish women in the [new] Home Rule bill introduced that year'. See *Irish Nationalists in America: The Politics of Exile, 1798–1998* (Oxford: Oxford University Press, 2016), 138. The parade and the American demand in support of Irish women's suffrage were reported in the *Irish Citizen* newspaper in May 1912. 'We trust,' they wrote, that the 'Irish Party [and Mr Redmond] will not be blind to the significance of the action of the American women and will learn in time the moral danger of a position which claims Home Rule for the Irish men and denies it to Irish women'. See Murphy, *The Women's Suffrage Movement*, 176. Murphy points out that during an earlier visit to the United States, Redmond was 'told by Irish [American] women there that they could not provide him with funds unless the Irish Party at Westminster would press forward on votes for women' and '[l]etters appeared periodically in suffrage journals reminding Redmond that votes for Irish women was certainly not another domestic issue but caused grave concern across the Atlantic'. See *The Women's Suffrage Movement*, 175. *The Suffragist* also closely monitored the question of Irish women's suffrage and Home Rule. See for example 'Suffrage in Ireland', 20 June 1914: 2; 'Votes for Irish women', 12 December 1914: 2.

106 'Irish women urge suffrage in Home Rule government', *Suffragist*, 22 July 1916: 3.

107 Regular publication by the *Irish Citizen* was suspended in June, July, and August 1916 (although there was a July issue, it was a 'Memorial Number' devoted entirely to testimonies, letters, and articles about the late Francis Sheehy Skeffington).

108 As noted earlier, Burns took over as editor in the spring of 1915 and continued for almost two years.

109 Murphy, 'The tune', in Luddy and Murphy, eds, *Women Surviving*, 184.

110 'Heartnote of today is woman suffrage', *Suffragist*, 15 July 1916: 9. The excerpt with the Home Rule analogy is reprinted in *The Suffragist* from *Everywoman* (a California publication).

111 In this cartoon on the 12 May 1917 cover of *The Suffragist*, a member of the US congress is shown shouting over the ocean to England through a megaphone: 'Say why don't you free Ireland?' In the meantime, an 'American woman' (identified as such in the writing on her hem) stands behind him, about to tap him on the shoulder, asking 'What about me?', while an Englishman ('J. Bull') on the other side is yelling to the congressman, 'Look behind you!' 'J. Bull' stands for John Bull, the British equivalent of Uncle Sam. John Bull was used as a personification of Great Britain during the nineteenth century and into the early twentieth; popularised by cartoons in the British magazine *Punch*, he was 'portrayed

as an honest, solid, farmer figure, often in a Union Jack waistcoat, and accompanied by a bulldog'. See 'John Bull and Uncle Sam: four centuries of British-American relations', Library of Congress, available at: loc.gov/exhibits/british/britintr.html.

112 As Chris McNickle notes in 'When New York was Irish, and after', in Ronald H. Bayor and Timothy J. Meagher, eds, *The New York Irish* (Baltimore: Johns Hopkins University Press, 1996), 350, 'before the First World War most Irish Americans were content with proposals for home rule, and few spent much time actively working toward the cause of Irish freedom,' but 'the attitude of the majority of Irish Americans began to change after the Easter Rebellion executions. The harshness of the English response to the uprising shocked them and created a ground swell of emotional support for independence.'

113 'Maggie and Maggie to shake for votes: Miss Foley of Boston and Miss Hinchey of New York to put Irish vim into campaign', *New York Times*, 8 September 1915. While Irish-American suffragist leaders such as Burns and Martin organised marches and parades and lobbied congress, other Irish-American suffragists worked – sometimes literally – in the 'trenches'. As Tara McCarthy notes, workers like Foley and Hinchey were sent to the Bowery, piers, and subway tunnels to appeal to workers. See 'Woman suffrage and Irish nationalism: ethnic appeals and alliances in America', *Women's History Review* (2014): 188–203. Unlike the middle- and upper-class Irish-American women who worked at leadership levels in the CU/NWP (e.g., Burns and Martin), suffragists such as Hinchey and Foley were cast in stereotypical Irish terms, both by the local and national press and the green and shamrock-decorated literature that they distributed. This was particularly true of Hinchey, who immigrated to New York from Limerick in 1897 and spoke with a pronounced brogue. Speaking to workers in the subway in 1915, for example, Hinchey called upon immigrant- and class-solidarity in her campaign for women's suffrage: 'Hinchey displayed her Irish union card and asked, "Brothers, are ye going to give us the vote in November?" "Sure, we are," came the reply.' See Barrett, *The Irish Way*.

114 Margaret Hinchey, 'Votes for women: appeal to Irish citizens to support the woman suffrage amendment', *The Gaelic American*, 27 October 1917: 3.

115 Correspondence, 'H. S. S. reply to M. Sheepshanks of the NAWSA', the *Irish Citizen*, December 1918. Sheehy Skeffington pointedly notes that while she ran into NWP workers lobbying on a regular basis, she 'never once encountered one of Mrs. Catt's followers [i.e., members of the NAWSA] in the corridors of Congress or Senate'.

116 Ibid.

117 Murphy, 'The tune', in Luddy and Murphy, eds, *Women Surviving*, 186.

118 Margaret Ward, *Hanna Sheehy Skeffington: A Life* (Cork: Attic/Cork University Press, 1997), 199.

119 Haynes Irwin, *Story of the Woman's Party*, 322.

120 Ibid.

121 'Congressmen who urge Irish Home Rule lobbied', *Suffragist*, 12 May 1917: 9.

122 Murphy, 'The tune', in Luddy and Murphy, eds, *Women Surviving*, 198.

123 Hannah Sheehy Skeffington, 'How the pickets won the vote', *Irish Citizen*, October 1918: 626–7.

124 See correspondence in the December 1918 and January 1919 *Irish Citizen*.

125 Correspondence, 'H. S. S. response to M. Sheepshanks of the NAWSA', *Irish Citizen*, December 1918: 637. When Ida Husted Harper (of the NAWSA) wrote to object to the accusation that they had put suffrage 'on the shelf', Sheehy Skeffington (in a reply published in the *Irish Citizen*) called attention to Harper's lack of knowledge about the Irish movement: 'Miss Harper,' she wrote, 'does not seem to be aware of the plot to exclude Irishwomen from the recent franchise' and what is more insulting, she 'confuses the British and Irish militants (quite distinct bodies)'.

126 Sheehy Skeffington also recommended reading the *Maryland Suffragist News*, the *Liberator*, the *New Republic*, and the *New York Call*.

127 Murphy, 'The tune', in Luddy and Murphy, eds, *Women Surviving*, 199.

128 Lynn Wenzel and Carol J. Binkowski, *More than Petticoats: Remarkable New Jersey Women* (Guilford, CT: TwoDot/Globe Pequot Press, 2003), 114. Burns appears in a chapter on Alice Paul.

129 As Lawrence J. McCaffrey notes, in 1870 'more than 200,000 Irish immigrants (21.4% of the city's population) lived in Manhattan, and 73,985 (18.7%) resided in Brooklyn; in 1890, 196,372 in Brooklyn and 399,348 in New York had Irish immigrant mothers.' See 'Looking forward and looking back', in Bayor and Meagher, eds, *The New York Irish*, 216.

130 New York City became the site of the first suffrage parade in the United States when a group of 23 women 'marched up Broadway … to a meeting hall on East 23rd Street' in 1908, and two years later the city was home to the 'first sizable suffrage parade' on 21 May 1910, where '[m]ore than 400 women marched and many more rode in automobiles'. See 'Tactics and techniques of the National Woman's Party suffrage campaign', American Memory Project, Library of Congress, available at: loc.gov/collections/static/women-of-protest/images/tactics. pdf. Increasingly larger suffrage parades followed in New York City on a regular basis in the years that followed, with participants growing to 20,000 and beyond.

131 In 1918, women in the United Kingdom – including Ireland – won the right to vote in all elections, but there were restrictions: only women over 30 with property and/or a university degree could vote. With the establishment of the Irish Free State in 1922, women were given full voting rights, without restrictions. In the United States, the ratification of the Nineteenth Amendment in 1920 gave all women the right to vote (though women in some states had won the vote earlier during the state-by-state campaigns).

## 24. THE EASTER RISING AND NEW YORK'S ANTICOLONIAL NATIONALISTS

1 For an incisive discussion of some of the themes of this emerging body of research, see Fearghal McGarry, '"A land beyond the wave": transnational perspectives on Easter 1916', in Niall Whelehan, ed., *Transnational Perspectives on Modern Irish History* (New York:

Routledge, 2015), 165–88. Important book-length studies of Irish nationalism's impact on other anticolonial movements include Kate O'Malley, *Ireland, India and Empire: Indo-Irish Radical Connections, 1919–64* (Manchester: Manchester University Press, 2008); Michael Silvestri, *Ireland and India: Nationalism, Empire and Memory* (Basingstoke: Palgrave Macmillan, 2009); and Bruce Nelson, *Irish Nationalists and the Making of the Irish Race* (Princeton, NJ: Princeton University Press, 2012).

2 Erez Manela, *The Wilsonian Moment: Self-Determination and the International Origins of Anticolonial Nationalism* (New York: Oxford University Press, 2007), 4. For an emphasis on the centrality of the Bolshevik Revolution to the decolonisation struggles that followed, see E. J. Hobsbawm, *The Age of Extremes: A History of the World, 1914–1991* (New York: Pantheon, 1994).

3 Dennis Clark, *Hibernia America: The Irish and Regional Cultures* (Westport, CT: Greenwood Press, 1986), 58. For the long history of Irish nationalism in New York, as well as in other US locales, see David Brundage, *Irish Nationalists in America: The Politics of Exile, 1798–1998* (New York: Oxford University Press, 2016).

4 Mary Louise Pratt, *Imperial Eyes: Travel Writing and Transculturation* (London: Routledge, 1992), 6. For recent studies of interwar London and Paris that have influenced my approach to anticolonial activism in New York, see Marc Matera, *Black London: The Imperial Metropolis and Decolonization in the Twentieth Century* (Berkeley, CA: University of California Press, 2015); and Michael Goebel, *Anti-Imperial Metropolis: Interwar Paris and the Seeds of Third World Nationalism* (New York: Cambridge University Press, 2015). For brief but influential discussions of diaspora nationalism, see Benedict Anderson, *The Spectre of Comparisons: Nationalism, Southeast Asia, and the World* (London: Verso, 1998), 58–74; and Stéphane Dufoix, *Diasporas* (Berkeley, CA: University of California Press, 2008), 92–7.

5 McGarry, 'The land beyond the wave', in Whelehan, ed., *Transnational Perspectives on Modern Irish History*, 167; Sven Beckert, *The Moneyed Metropolis: New York City and the Consolidation of the American Bourgeoisie, 1850–1896* (New York: Cambridge University Press, 2001), 166–7. For a good overview of Irish New York in this period, see Chris McNickle, 'When New York was Irish, and after', in Ronald H. Bayor and Timothy J. Meagher, eds, *The New York Irish* (Baltimore: Johns Hopkins University Press, 1996), 337–56.

6 The most thorough treatment of Irish-American nationalism in these years remains Francis M. Carroll, *American Opinion and the Irish Question, 1910–23: A Study in Opinion and Policy* (New York: St Martin's, 1978), but for the FOIF, see also Michael Doorley, *Irish-American Diaspora Nationalism: The Friends of Irish Freedom, 1916–1935* (Dublin: Four Courts, 2005), 21–137.

7 The standard work is Gilbert Osofsky, *Harlem: The Making of a Ghetto: Negro New York, 1890–1930* (New York: Harper & Row, 1971), but for an important recent study, see Shannon King, *Whose Harlem Is This, Anyway?: Community Politics and Grassroots Activism during the New Negro Era* (New York: New York University Press, 2015).

8 David Levering Lewis, *W. E. B. Du Bois*, 2 volumes (New York: Henry Holt, 1993–2000), 1: 248–51, 2: 61–3. For a recent survey of UNIA's global significance in this era, see Adam

Ewing, *The Age of Garvey: How a Jamaican Activist Created a Mass Movement and Changed Global Black Politics* (Princeton, NJ: Princeton University Press, 2014).

9 Seema Sohi, *Echoes of Mutiny: Race, Surveillance, and Indian Anticolonialism in North America* (New York: Oxford University Press, 2014), 35; Joan M. Jensen, *Passage from India: Asian Indian Immigrants in North America* (New Haven, CT: Yale University Press, 1988), 24–41.

10 Lala Lajpat Rai, *The Story of My Life: An Unknown Fragment*, 1928 (New Delhi: Gitanjali Prakashan, 1978), 70; Sohi, *Echoes of Mutiny*, 45–67. See also Maia Ramnath, *Haj to Utopia: How the Ghadar Movement Charted Global Radicalism and Attempted to Overthrow the British Empire* (Berkeley, CA: University of California Press, 2011).

11 Rai, *The Story of My Life*, 20, 69; Sohi, *Echoes of Mutiny*, 68–76.

12 Hoover quoted in Kenneth O'Reilly, *Racial Matters: The FBI's Secret File on Black America, 1960–1972* (New York: Free Press, 1989), 13. For the influence of Irish nationalism on Garvey, see Robert A. Hill, 'General introduction', in Robert A. Hill, ed., *The Marcus Garvey and Universal Negro Improvement Association Papers*, 10 volumes (Berkeley, CA: University of California Press, 1983–2006), 1: lxx–viii.

13 Hill, ed., *The Marcus Garvey Papers*, 1: 472, 506–7, 2: 649; 4: 259.

14 Helen Golden to Welsh, 19 September 1920, Peter Golden Papers, National Library of Ireland; 'Sir Roger Casement, patriot, martyr', *The Crisis*, September 1916: 215–16; Lewis, *W. E. B. Du Bois*, 1: 516. Maloney is quoted in Carroll, *American Opinion and the Irish Question*, 163–4.

15 Quoted in Silvestri, *Ireland and India*, 27.

16 Manela, *The Wilsonian Moment*, 171–2; Ruth Price, *The Lives of Agnes Smedley* (New York: Oxford University Press, 2005), 77–8; 'Report of Friends of Freedom for India, August 12, 1919', and Tarak Nath Das to Diarmuid Lynch, 16 December 1921, both in Daniel Cohalan Papers, American Irish Historical Society, New York. See also Doorley, *Irish-American Diaspora Nationalism*, 59, 155.

17 'Small nations leagued together', *The Survey*, 5 May 1917: 120; Frederic C. Howe, *Confessions of a Reformer*, 1925 (Chicago: Quadrangle, 1967), 9–10. It should be noted, however, that on his father's side Howe was descended from eighteenth-century Scotch-Irish immigrants, whom he sarcastically described as 'Scotch Presbyterians who went over to Ireland and took the land away from the Irish and gave their Scotch brand of religion in exchange'.

18 *New York Times*, 29 October 1917; Marion A. Smith to Frank Walsh, 7 December 1918, Frank Walsh Collection, New York Public Library (NYPL); *American Jewish Chronicle*, 13 April 1917: 761; 'Bernard G. Richards, veteran Zionist, honored on his 75th birthday', *Jewish Telegraphic Agency*, 26 March 1952. The controversy that swirled around Sheehy Skeffington during her time in the United States is a central theme of Joanne Mooney Eichacker, *Irish Republican Women in America: Lecture Tours, 1916–1925* (Dublin: Irish Academic Press, 2003), 58–91. See also Margaret Ward, *Hanna Sheehy Skeffington: A Life* (Cork: Attic/Cork University Press, 1997), 184–210.

19 'The Small and Subject Nations League and the *New York Times*', *Young India*, January 1919: 23; *New York Times*, 20 December 1918.

20 'A new league', *Young India*, November 1919: 248; Arthur Upham Pope to W. E. B. Du Bois, 10 November 1919, W. E. B. Du Bois Papers, Special Collections and University Archives, University of Massachusetts Amherst Libraries.

21 W. J. M. A. Maloney, untitled typescript, 30 December 1921, W. J. M. A. Maloney Collection, NYPL; Dudley Field Malone to Frank Walsh, 8 October 1919, Walsh Collection, NYPL. Folk's connection with the Egyptian nationalists, and his subsequent litigation over funds he felt they owed him, is discussed briefly in Manela, *The Wilsonian Moment*, 153–5.

22 Spofford to Frank Walsh, 21 September 1919, Peter Golden to Frank Walsh, 3 October 1919, Walsh Collection, NYPL; US Military Intelligence, memorandum on League of Oppressed Peoples, *c.* June 1920, quoted in David Fitzpatrick, *Harry Boland's Irish Revolution* (Cork: Cork University Press, 2003), 370.

23 Carrie Chapman Catt to Malone, 15 September 1917, quoted in Dudley Field Malone, *'Unaccustomed as I Am—': Miscellaneous Speeches* (New York: Little and Ives, 1929), 50; Howe, *Confessions of a Reformer*, 249.

24 Katherine O'Doherty, *Assignment: America; De Valera's Mission to the United States* (New York: De Tanko, 1957), 101; Hill, ed., *The Marcus Garvey Papers*, 3: 12–14, 87–8; Malone, *'Unaccustomed as I Am—'*, 176, 178; Silvestri, *Ireland and India*, 28; Pratt, *Imperial Eyes*, 6. Malone was also an early supporter of the NAACP.

25 Brundage, *Irish Nationalists in America*, 167–9; O'Reilly, *Racial Matters*, 14; O'Malley, *Ireland, India and Empire*, 3, 156–78. For the League against Imperialism, see E. H. Carr, *The Twilight of the Comintern, 1930–1935* (London: Macmillan, 1982), 385, 420; and Ward, *Hanna Sheehy Skeffington*, 295–6.

26 Jeffrey B. Perry, ed., *A Hubert Harrison Reader* (Middletown, CT: Wesleyan University Press, 2001), 139.

# INDEX